ST/ESA/STAT/SER.X/32

Department of Economic and Social Affairs
Statistics Division

National Accounts Statistics: Analysis of Main Aggregates, 2002-2003

United Nations New York, 2004

The Department of Economic and Social Affairs of the United Nations Secretariat is a vital interface between global policies in the economic, social and environmental spheres and national action. The Department works in three main interlinked areas: (i) it compiles, generates and analyses a wide range of economic, social and environmental data and information on which Member States of the United Nations draw to review common problems and to take stock of policy options; (ii) it facilitates the negotiations of Member States in many intergovernmental bodies on joint courses of action to address ongoing or emerging global challenges; and (iii) it advises interested Governments on the ways and means of translating policy frameworks developed in United Nations conferences and summits into programmes at the country level and, through technical assistance, helps build national capacities.

NOTE

Symbols of United Nations documents are composed of capital letters combined with figures. The first 14 editions of this publication were issued without series symbols.

ST/ESA/STAT/SER.X/32

UNITED NATIONS PUBLICATION
Sales No. E.04.XVII.12

ISBN 92-1-161476-7

Enquiries should be directed to:
SALES SECTION
UNITED NATIONS
NEW YORK, NY 10017

CONTENTS

C. GROWTH RATES OF MAIN NATIONAL ACCOUNTING AGGREGATES AT CONSTANT PRICES OF 1990

D. IMPLICIT PRICE DEFLATORS OF GROSS DOMESTIC PRODUCT: INDIVIDUAL COUNTRIES OR AREAS (INDEX NUMBERS 1990=100)

I. Introduction

This is the thirty-fourth issue of the United Nations publication, *National Accounts Statistics: Analysis of Main Aggregates (AMA).* It is presented as part of a series that also includes the annual principal publication containing detailed national accounts information, *National Accounts Statistics: Main Aggregates and Detailed Tables (MADT)*[i].

The last publication of AMA was prepared and published in 2003 by the Statistics Division of the Department of Economic and Social Affairs of the United Nations Secretariat with the assistance and cooperation of national statistical services. It is issued in accordance with the recommendation of the Statistical Commission at its first session[ii] that the Statistics Division of the United Nations should publish regularly the most recent available data on national accounts for as many countries and areas as possible.

The current publication presents, in the form of analytical tables, a summary of the principal national accounting aggregates based on official detailed national accounts data for more than 200 countries and areas of the world. The basic data was extracted from MADT and supplemented by estimates prepared by the Statistics Division of the United Nations when official data are not available.

SCOPE OF PUBLICATION

The present volume consists of two parts: *Introduction (I) and Analytical Tables (II).*

General information on the methods of data collection, estimation and derivation of analytical measures, the conversion factors used in converting national currency into United States dollars, conceptual references, country nomenclature, fiscal year references and regional groupings are included in the Introduction. Information on analytical measures is further elaborated in a separate section in part II, Analytical Tables, prior to the presentation of the tables.

The tables include analysis of data on gross domestic product (GDP) by different structural components. In general, data presented in the tables are based on GDP definitions as given in the 1993 System of National Accounts (SNA).

The types of analysis presented are classified into four major categories:

(a) Analysis of the level of total and per capita gross domestic product (Tables 1A and 1B);

(b) Analysis of economic structures expressed in terms of percentage shares of gross domestic product by type of expenditure and kind of economic activity (Tables 2 and 3);

(c) Analysis of economic development expressed in terms of the real growth of gross domestic product and its components by type of expenditure and kind of economic activity (Tables 4, 5 and 6); and,

(d) Analysis of price development expressed in terms of implicit price deflators of gross domestic product (Table 7).

The analytical presentations are based on a homogeneous data series that were made smooth and consistent from original individual country data series. The use of such homogeneous data series as the basis for the analysis presented in this volume serves to facilitate cross-table analysis concerning one or more countries and/or regions.

Users interested in making alternative analysis across countries may subscribe to the electronic output of the entire AMA data with the relevant specifications. All such requests should be addressed to the Director of the UN Statistics Division.

COLLECTION OF DATA

The present AMA database includes GDP estimates by type of expenditure and kind of economic activity expressed in current prices and constant prices of 1990 for some or all of the years 1970 to 2003 for total GDP. These

---

[i] United Nations publication, ST/ESA/STAT/SER.X.

[ii] Official Records of the Economic and Social Council, 1947, Supplement No. 6 (E/264), chap. VIII, para. 42.

were compiled from country replies to the regular national accounts questionnaire of the Statistics Division of the United Nations as well as from estimates prepared by its staff members so to adjust data inconsistencies and fill data gaps. The questionnaire is sent annually to the national statistical offices of all UN member states and areas of the world. Data submitted with the questionnaire are generally supplemented, for the purpose of the Analysis of Main Aggregates, by reliable information obtained from other national and international sources. The recipients of the questionnaire are requested to indicate where the scope and coverage of the country estimates differ, for conceptual or statistical reasons, from the definitions and classifications recommended in the 1993 SNA.

ESTIMATION OF DATA

The methodology employed to arrive at the basic data for computation of global and regional aggregates, growth rates and index numbers is as follows: official data of countries as reported in MADT are supplemented by estimates prepared by the Statistics Division of the United Nations, based on official and unofficial data and proxy economic indicators derived from national and international sources. For a majority of countries, both the official statistics and proxy indicators may be based on different series due to multiple data configurations and/or characteristics. Before merging these into one data file, all inconsistencies in series and coverage are smoothed out by linking the multiple series into one homogeneous set of data from which the analytical measures are derived.

The current price series are converted into a common unit of currency the United States dollars by applying the corresponding exchange rates. (For a more detailed explanation, reference is made to the general notes to Tables 1A and 1B)

The constant price series, principally based on officially reported data from member states and supplemented by estimates prepared by the Statistics Division of the United Nations, are presented in index numbers on country basis for each item and year and re-based to 1990. The indices are then applied to the corresponding 1990 current dollar values per country and item, which serve as weights, and extrapolated by individual growth rates in order to arrive at the regional and world totals for each year. (For a more detailed explanation in the calculation of growth rates and index numbers, reference is made to the general notes for Tables 4, 5, 6 and 7, respectively.)

In preparing estimates to supplement the official data, the sequence or priority of data sources sought is as follows: national publications, internet websites of national statistics offices, central banks or relevant government ministries, economic surveys and estimates prepared by the regional economic commissions of the United Nations; estimates and indicators available from other international organizations such as the International Monetary Fund (IMF), the World Bank and other international institutions, studies prepared by experts under the United Nations technical cooperation programmes; economic reports and studies by regional development banks; For countries that are members of regional affiliate organizations and specialized groups, such as the Organization of Petroleum Exporting Countries (OPEC), the Commonwealth of Independent States (CIS), etc., the information available from these organizations are given priority over non-United Nations sources.

DATA CONVERSION TO UNITED STATES DOLLARS

In converting estimates expressed in national currency units into United States dollars, the prevailing annual average of market exchange rates as reported by the IMF has been used. For countries that are non-members of the IMF, the conversion rate used is usually the annual average of United Nations operational rates of exchange.

It should be noted that the international comparability of data expressed in United States dollars between countries may not be entirely scientific because the exchange rates applied may, in practice, only be used for the conversion of a limited number of external transactions and may not be relevant for the much larger portion of GDP covering domestic transactions.

Alternative methods of making international comparisons have been developed in recent years. One is the Purchasing Power Parities (PPPs) which have been developed as part of the International Comparison Project (ICP); another one is the World Bank Atlas method of conversion based on the average of the exchange rates of the current year and the two immediately preceding years that have been adjusted for differences in inflation rates between individual countries and the average of G-5 countries (Germany, France, Japan, the United Kingdom, and the United States); and, the Statistics Division of the United Nations has developed the Price Adjusted Rates of Exchange (PARE)[iv] which, like the Atlas method is designed to adjust exchange rates that do not adequately reflect relative movements of domestic and international inflation.

NOMENCLATURE

Designations for country or areas, which have changed in recent years, are as follows:

Hong Kong Special Administrative Region (SAR), China - Pursuant to a Joint Declaration signed on 19 December 1994, the United Kingdom re-stored Hong Kong to the People's Republic of China with effect from 1 July 1997; the People's Republic of China resumed the exercise of sovereignty over the territory with effect from that date.

The data for Hong Kong SAR is shown separately from that of the People's Republic of China.

Macao Special Administrative Region (SAR), China - Pursuant to a Joint Declaration signed on April 13, 1987, the Portugal re-stored Macao to the People's Republic of China with effect from 20 December 1999; the People's Republic of China resumed the exercise of sovereignty over the territory with effect from that date.

The data for Macao SAR is shown separately from that of the People's Republic of China.

Czech Republic, Slovakia - Data for Czech Republic and Slovakia are shown separately under the appropriate country name. For period prior to 1 January 1993, data for the former Czechoslovakia are shown under the country name Czechoslovakia (Former)

Yugoslavia (Former) – Following the adoption and the promulgation of the Constitutional Charter of Serbia and Montenegro by the Assembly of the Federal Republic of Yugoslavia on 4 February 2003, the name of the State of the Federal Republic of Yugoslavia was changed to Serbia and Montenegro. All data for former Yugoslavia prior to 1 January 1992 refer to the Socialist Federal Republic of Yugoslavia that was then composed of six republics. After that date, when available, data for the republics, Bosnia and Herzegovina, Croatia, Slovenia, The Former Yugoslav Republic of Macedonia, and Serbia and Montenegro are shown separately.

USSR (Former) - In 1991, the Union of Soviet Socialist Republics formally dissolved into fifteen independent republics (Armenia, Azerbaijan, Belarus, Georgia, Kazakhstan, Kyrgyzstan, Latvia, Lithuania, Republic of Moldova, Russian Federation, Tajikistan, Turkmenistan, Ukraine and Uzbekistan). When available, data are shown for the individual republics. All data for the former USSR are shown under the country name USSR (Former)

Ethiopia, Eritrea - Data for Ethiopia and Eritrea are shown separately under the appropriate country name. For the period prior to 1993, data for the former Ethiopia are shown under the country name Ethiopia (Former).

Germany – On October 1990, the Federal Republic of Germany and the German Democratic Republic united to form one sovereign State under the designation Germany. Official data from Germany for the period 1970—1990 is the combined data of the former Federal Republic of Germany and the former German Democratic Republic.

Yemen - In May 1990, Yemen and Democratic Yemen united to form a single State. Since that date they have been represented as one country with the name "Yemen".

Standard country or area designations and classification of geographical regions for statistical use are posted on the United Nations website. Interested users could refer to the following web-link for further details:

http://unstats.un.org/unsd/methods/m49/m49.htm

[iv] Reference could be made to the latest Report of the Committee on Contribution in the United Nations General Assembly Official Records.

COUNTRY COVERAGE AND GROUPINGS

There are two types of alternative country groupings or aggregations of country data applied in the tables: by geographical region and by grouping based on economic categories, i.e. developed, developing and transition economies. The tables on the level of GDP and growth rates by GDP components (Tables 1A, 1B and 4 through 6) include aggregations of country data by geographical region and economic categories while the tables on percentage distribution of GDP as well as implicit price deflators (Tables 2, 3 and 7), present country data only according to geographical regions. Where individual country data are presented, they are generally listed by region and, within the regions, in alphabetical order.

The designations "developed" and "developing" economies used in some tables are intended for statistical convenience and do not necessarily express a judgement about the stage reached by a particular country or area in the development process.

The geographical coverage for the world, regional and economic development groupings used in the analyses is as follows:

WORLD
Total of developed, developing and transition economies.

DEVELOPED ECONOMIES
Northern America, Europe (excluding Transition Economies in Europe), Japan, Australia and New Zealand

DEVELOPING ECONOMIES
Africa, Americas excluding Canada and the United States in Northern America, Caribbean, Central America, South America, Asia excluding Japan and Transition Economies in Asia, and Oceania excluding Australia and New Zealand.

TRANSITION ECONOMIES
Commonwealth of Independent Countries
Armenia, Azerbaijan, Belarus, Georgia, Kazakhstan, Kyrgyzstan, Republic of Moldova, Russian Federation, Tajikistan, Turkmenistan, Ukraine and Uzbekistan.

Other Europe
Albania, Bosnia and Herzegovina, Bulgaria, Croatia, Czech Republic, Estonia, Hungary, Latvia, Lithuania, Poland, Romania, Serbia and Montenegro, Slovakia, Slovenia, The Former Yugoslav Republic of Macedonia.

REGIONAL CLASSIFICATION[v]

AFRICA - comprised of Eastern Africa, Middle Africa, Northern Africa, Southern Africa and Western Africa.

Eastern Africa - Burundi, Comoros, Djibouti, Eritrea, Ethiopia, Kenya, Madagascar, Malawi, Mauritius, Mozambique, Reunion, Rwanda, Seychelles, Somalia, Uganda, United Republic of Tanzania, Zambia, Zimbabwe
Middle Africa - Angola, Cameroon, Central African Republic, Chad, Congo, Democratic Republic of the Congo, Equatorial Guinea, Gabon, Sao Tome and Principe
Northern Africa - Algeria, Egypt, Libyan Arab Jamahiriya, Morocco, Sudan, Tunisia
Southern Africa - Botswana, Lesotho, Namibia, South Africa, Swaziland
Western Africa - Benin, Burkina Faso, Cape Verde, Cote d'Ivoire, Gambia, Ghana, Guinea, Guinea-Bissau, Liberia, Mali, Mauritania, Niger, Nigeria, Senegal, Sierra Leone, Togo.

AMERICAS - comprised of Caribbean, Central America, South America and Northern America.

Caribbean - Anguilla, Antigua and Barbuda, Aruba, Bahamas, Barbados, British Virgin Islands, Cayman Islands, Cuba, Dominica, Dominican Republic, Grenada, Guadeloupe, Haiti, Jamaica, Martinique, Montserrat, Netherlands Antilles, Puerto Rico, Saint Kitts and Nevis, Saint Lucia, Saint Vincent and the Grenadines, Trinidad and Tobago, Turks and Caicos Islands.

---

[v] Not all countries or territories are included in the regional classification, as the Statistics Division of the United Nations may not have the access to reliable data sources or viable estimation methods to prepare data for all countries or areas.

Central America - Belize, Costa Rica, El Salvador, Guatemala, Honduras, Mexico, Nicaragua, Panama
South America - Argentina, Bolivia, Brazil, Chile, Colombia, Ecuador, French Guiana, Guyana, Paraguay, Peru, Suriname, Uruguay, Venezuela
Northern America - Bermuda, Canada, and United States of America.

ASIA - comprised of Eastern Asia, South-central Asia, South-eastern Asia and Western Asia.

Eastern Asia - China, Hong Kong Special Administrative Region of China, Macao Special Administrative Region of China, Democratic People's Republic of Korea, Japan, Mongolia, Republic of Korea.
South-central Asia - Afghanistan, Bangladesh, Bhutan, India, Iran (Islamic Republic of) Kazakhstan*, Kyrgyzstan*, Maldives, Nepal, Pakistan, Sri Lanka, Tajikistan*, Turkmenistan*, Uzbekistan*,
South-eastern Asia - Brunei Darussalam, Cambodia, Indonesia, Lao People's Democratic Republic, Malaysia, Myanmar, Philippines, Singapore, Thailand, Timor-Leste, Viet Nam.
Western Asia – Armenia*, Azerbaijan*, Bahrain, Cyprus, Georgia*, Iraq, Israel, Jordan, Kuwait, Lebanon, Oman, Qatar, Saudi Arabia, Syrian Arab Republic, Turkey, United Arab Emirates, Yemen.

EUROPE - comprised of Eastern Europe, Northern Europe, Southern Europe and Western Europe.

Eastern Europe – Belarus*, Bulgaria, Czech Republic**, Hungary, Poland, Republic of Moldova*, Romania, Russian Federation*, Slovakia**, Ukraine*,
Northern Europe –Denmark, Estonia*, Finland, Iceland, Ireland, Latvia*, Lithuania*, Norway, Sweden, United Kingdom of Great Britain and Northern Ireland.
Southern Europe - Albania, Andorra, Bosnia and Herzegovina, Croatia, Greece, Holy See, Italy, Malta, Portugal, San Marino, Serbia and Montenegro, Slovenia, Spain, The former Yugoslav Republic of Macedonia.

Western Europe - Austria, Belgium, France, Germany, Liechtenstein, Luxembourg, Monaco, Netherlands and Switzerland.

OCEANIA - comprised of Australia and New Zealand, Melanesia, Micronesia, and Polynesia.

Australia and New Zealand – Australia, New Zealand.
Melanesia - Fiji, New Caledonia, Papua New Guinea, Solomon Islands, Vanuatu
Micronesia –Kiribati, Marshall Islands, Micronesia (Federated States of), Nauru, Palau.
Polynesia –Cook Islands, French Polynesia, Samoa, Tonga, Tuvalu.

CONCEPTUAL REFERENCES

The concepts used in the statistical tables in the present volume are the same as those used in Main Aggregates and Detailed Tables. They generally conform to the recommendations in the revised System of National Accounts 1993.

INTERNATIONAL COMPARABILITY OF NATIONAL ACCOUNTS DATA

Every effort has been made to present the estimates of the various countries or areas in a form designed to facilitate international comparability. To this end, some important differences in concept, scope, coverage and classification have been described in respective footnotes for individual countries.

The data contained in the tables relate to the calendar year against which they are shown unless otherwise indicated as the following:

(a) Year beginning 1 July – Australia, Bangladesh, Cameroon, Egypt, Gambia, Pakistan, Puerto Rico, Saudi Arabia, Sierra Leone, Sudan and United Republic of Tanzania.

(b) Year beginning 1 April – Bermuda, India, Myanmar (except 1970-1974, which are ending 30 September), New Zealand and Nigeria.

* Since 1990
** Since 1980

(c) Year Beginning 21 March – Afghanistan and Iran (Islamic Republic of)

(d) Year ending 30 June – Botswana, Swaziland and Tonga.

(e) Year ending 7 July – Ethiopia

(f) Year ending 15 July – Nepal

(g) Year ending 30 September – Haiti

EXPLANATION OF SYMBOLS

The following symbols have been employed:

Data not available	...
Category not applicable	..
Data in units	(u)
Data in thousands	(t)

Decimals and percentages in tables may not add up to totals due to rounding.

GENERAL DISCLAIMER

The designations employed and the presentation of material in this publication do not imply the expression of any opinion whatsoever on the part of the United Nations Secretariat concerning the legal status of any country, territory, or area or of its authorities, or concerning the delimitation of its frontiers or boundaries.

All data presented in this publication are prepared from the most recent available data by July 2004. In general, figures for the most recent years are to be regarded as provisional and subject to further revision. For more up-to-date information, interested users should login at: http://www.un.org/Depts/unsd/nataccts/.

II. Analytical Tables

A. Estimates of Main National Accounting Aggregates at Current Prices

Description of Analysis in Table 1A and Table 1B

A. Level of total and per capita gross domestic product.

Table 1A and Table 1B present estimates of total and per capita gross domestic product (GDP) expressed in current United States dollars. The tables are intended to facilitate international comparisons of levels of income generated in production. Countries within regions, country groupings into developed, developing and transition economies as well as global aggregations are shown in rows. The columns list total and per capita GDP in terms of United States dollars for the selected ten years 1970, 1980, 1990 and 1997 through 2003.

Official data and estimates of total and per capita GDP have been converted to United States dollars using prevailing exchange rates. As a rule, the exchange rates used for conversion of national currency data into US dollars are the average market exchange rates (MERs) as published by the International Monetary Fund in the *International Financial Statistics.* These are averages based on the market rates communicated to the IMF by the monetary authority of each member country or end-of-month quotations in the market of the country. MERs generally consist of three types of rates: a) market rates, determined largely by market forces; b) official rates, determined by government authorities; and c) principal rates, for countries maintaining multiple exchange rates arrangements. The preference is always market rates; only when a free market rate is not available is use made of other rates.

For a few countries for which no International Monetary Fund conversion rates were available, the conversion rates used are the average of United Nations operational rates of exchange which were established for accounting purposes and which are applied in official transactions of the United Nations with those countries. These rates are based on official, commercial and/or tourist rates of exchange.

In a number of countries for some or all of the years, the use of MERs for conversion to US dollars may generate distortions in income levels due to a variety of reasons. For some, the use of official rates of exchange reflects government policies that fix conversion factors at unrealistic levels, thus resulting in estimates of GDP in US dollars that are not consonant with the true economic picture. Others suffer from inordinate growth in domestic inflation that movements in exchange rates cannot keep pace with.

The GDP estimates and exchange rate conversions have been prepared in response to numerous requests for statistics of this nature. However, it should be noted that there are practical constraints in the use of MERs for conversion purposes, particularly in the case of countries with multiple exchange rates, those coping with inordinate levels of inflation or experiencing misalignments caused by market distortions, the use of which may result in excessive fluctuations in the dollar income levels of a number of countries. Caution is therefore urged when making inter-country comparisons of incomes as expressed in US dollars over time. The comparability over time may be distorted due to excessive fluctuations in exchange rates and domestic inflation movements. In those instances, the present volume uses price-adjusted rates of exchange (PARE) for selected countries and years for which conversion to US dollars led to large distortions in the dollar levels of per capita GDP when using MERs: including Afghanistan, Democratic People Republic of the Congo, Iraq, Nigeria, Suriname, Syrian Arab Republic, and Vietnam.

For inter-country comparisons over time, it would be more appropriate to use the growth rate information based on constant price data, presented in Table 4 of the present volume, which are more indicative of inter-country and intra-grouping comparisons of development trends of total GDP.

Table 1.A. Estimates of Gross Domestic Product in US Dollars at Current Prices by Major Area, Region and Country

Major area, region and country	(Millions of Dollars)									
	1970	1980	1990	1997	1998	1999	2000	2001	2002	2003
WORLD	**3 253 300**	**11 933 000**	**22 742 800**	**29 916 200**	**29 731 200**	**30 767 200**	**31 535 500**	**31 204 000**	**32 400 700**	**36 211 700**
DEVELOPED ECONOMIES	**2 185 800**	**7 993 700**	**16 955 600**	**22 382 300**	**22 677 400**	**23 793 400**	**23 998 100**	**23 684 200**	**24 675 800**	**27 685 500**
DEVELOPING ECONOMIES	**582 500**	**2 762 900**	**3 927 600**	**6 602 300**	**6 229 000**	**6 252 300**	**6 765 100**	**6 652 400**	**6 744 300**	**7 339 000**
TRANSITION ECONOMIES	**485 000**	**1 176 400**	**1 859 700**	**931 600**	**824 900**	**721 500**	**772 200**	**867 300**	**980 600**	**1 187 200**
AFRICA	**83 400**	**466 100**	**528 900**	**607 300**	**597 100**	**564 200**	**577 200**	**557 800**	**553 200**	**645 200**
Eastern Africa	*15 300*	*68 800*	*58 000*	*70 400*	*69 400*	*67 700*	*68 700*	*72 100*	*74 800*	*78 500*
Burundi	250	950	1 150	980	900	810	710	660	630	590
Comoros	20	140	250	190	200	200	180	200	220	280
Djibouti	70	300	460	490	500	540	550	570	590	620
Eritrea	...	...	...	740	780	750	750	920	1 050	1 260
Ethiopia	...	...	...	6 180	6 310	6 160	6 020	6 050	5 950	6 440
Ethiopia (Former)	1 780	4 110	8 130	...	...	...	...	...	...	...
Kenya	1 700	7 090	8 530	10 610	11 470	10 550	10 450	11 240	12 310	14 200
Madagascar	900	3 260	3 080	3 550	3 740	3 720	3 880	4 570	4 440	5 540
Malawi	320	1 240	1 750	2 590	1 750	1 790	1 740	1 710	2 020	1 910
Mauritius	190	1 150	2 590	4 180	4 150	4 270	4 550	4 530	4 720	5 610
Mozambique	2 770	4 320	2 650	3 380	3 870	3 980	3 680	3 440	3 490	4 200
Reunion	360	2 000	5 210	6 930	7 170	7 180	6 510	6 740	8 080	11 050
Rwanda	240	1 280	2 570	1 870	2 010	1 870	1 730	1 650	1 650	1 550
Seychelles	20	150	370	560	610	620	600	580	700	710
Somalia	340	2 750	990	1 480	1 930	2 020	2 050	1 310	1 220	1 540
Uganda	1 890	24 950	3 650	6 590	6 320	6 000	5 740	5 760	6 020	6 250
United Republic Of Tanzania	1 340	5 140	3 780	7 680	8 380	8 640	9 090	9 450	9 700	10 020
Zambia	1 660	4 640	4 080	3 910	3 240	3 130	3 240	3 640	3 700	4 310
Zimbabwe	1 510	5 350	8 770	8 500	6 050	5 490	7 200	9 060	8 300	2 460
Middle Africa	*7 400*	*37 500*	*45 200*	*33 500*	*32 200*	*31 500*	*35 100*	*34 100*	*37 900*	*44 600*
Angola	2 860	5 380	10 290	7 650	6 510	6 150	9 130	8 940	9 800	9 870
Cameroon	1 320	9 680	14 310	9 200	9 740	9 760	9 270	8 970	10 090	12 860
Central African Republic	150	710	1 300	930	980	990	910	910	990	1 260
Chad	410	920	1 540	1 540	1 700	1 490	1 300	1 480	1 730	2 490
Congo	260	1 710	2 800	2 320	1 950	2 350	3 220	2 790	3 010	3 910
Democratic Republic of the Congo	1 870	14 720	9 350	5 950	6 220	5 330	4 960	4 910	5 530	5 670
Equatorial Guinea	200	60	160	550	450	760	1 250	1 720	2 150	2 920
Gabon	340	4 280	5 430	5 340	4 670	4 610	5 020	4 330	4 560	5 520
Sao Tome and Principe	20	50	60	40	40	50	50	50	50	60
Northern Africa	*23 300*	*139 100*	*233 000*	*232 500*	*236 600*	*245 000*	*256 100*	*246 400*	*238 200*	*247 100*
Algeria	5 170	42 350	61 890	48 180	47 840	48 640	54 460	54 930	56 220	65 170
Egypt	6 830	24 500	71 060	84 810	90 790	100 170	103 310	96 070	92 230	76 400
Libyan Arab Jamahiriya	3 990	35 720	28 290	37 080	32 370	30 480	33 960	28 420	19 130	20 210
Morocco	3 960	18 820	25 820	33 410	35 820	35 250	33 340	33 900	36 090	44 700
Sudan	1 930	8 990	33 640	10 110	9 920	9 700	11 550	13 070	13 520	15 440
Tunisia	1 440	8 740	12 310	18 900	19 810	20 800	19 440	19 970	21 020	25 180
Southern Africa	*19 000*	*86 400*	*119 400*	*159 800*	*144 100*	*141 400*	*138 700*	*124 400*	*116 100*	*174 400*
Botswana	100	1 070	3 520	4 860	4 770	4 650	4 970	5 030	5 060	7 110
Lesotho	70	380	620	1 020	890	910	860	750	690	1 070
Namibia	510	2 020	2 340	3 640	3 400	3 390	3 460	3 160	2 880	4 590
South Africa	18 260	82 350	112 010	148 810	133 660	131 070	128 020	114 230	106 340	159 890
Swaziland	110	590	870	1 440	1 350	1 380	1 390	1 270	1 170	1 780
Western Africa	*18 200*	*134 300*	*73 300*	*111 000*	*114 800*	*78 600*	*78 600*	*80 800*	*86 100*	*100 600*
Benin	290	1 360	1 840	2 160	2 330	2 390	2 250	2 370	2 720	3 510
Burkina Faso	400	1 710	2 860	2 290	2 490	2 470	2 190	2 480	2 870	3 820
Cape Verde	60	140	310	510	540	580	540	560	630	820
Cote d'Ivoire	1 490	10 180	11 890	11 720	12 640	12 560	10 680	10 740	11 720	14 740
Gambia	50	240	330	390	420	430	420	390	360	320
Ghana	2 210	15 580	6 230	6 880	7 470	7 490	4 980	5 300	6 150	7 410
Guinea	720	1 940	2 820	3 780	3 590	3 460	3 060	2 990	3 210	3 600
Guinea-Bissau	90	240	230	280	210	240	220	250	250	310
Liberia	280	820	380	290	360	440	540	530	560	610
Mali	140	1 420	2 510	2 440	2 700	2 710	2 440	2 630	3 150	3 870
Mauritania	200	830	1 020	1 070	980	960	900	960	970	1 100
Niger	400	2 540	2 510	1 860	2 080	2 020	1 800	1 910	2 130	2 720
Nigeria	10 330	92 080	32 420	70 660	72 290	35 950	42 250	42 750	43 890	48 420
Senegal	870	2 990	5 700	4 380	4 650	4 750	4 370	4 610	5 040	6 480
Sierra Leone	410	1 100	630	850	670	670	640	970	990	980
Togo	260	1 130	1 570	1 500	1 420	1 410	1 330	1 330	1 480	1 850

Table 1.A. Estimates of Gross Domestic Product in US Dollars at Current Prices by Major Area, Region and Country

Major area, region and country	(Millions of Dollars)									
	1970	1980	1990	1997	1998	1999	2000	2001	2002	2003
AMERICAS	**1 317 200**	**3 970 900**	**7 485 300**	**10 986 200**	**11 441 400**	**11 756 100**	**12 567 500**	**12 759 500**	**12 918 500**	**13 545 700**
NORTHERN AMERICA	**1 110 900**	**3 037 700**	**6 327 000**	**8 887 000**	**9 330 200**	**9 867 300**	**10 479 300**	**10 728 000**	**11 111 700**	**11 715 300**
Bermuda	260	920	2 000	2 890	3 050	3 270	3 400	3 600	3 720	4 240
Canada	85 110	265 270	574 200	627 600	606 920	651 200	713 790	704 710	724 840	853 830
United States	1 025 500	2 771 500	5 750 800	8 256 500	8 720 200	9 212 800	9 762 100	10 019 700	10 383 100	10 857 200
LATIN AMERICA AND THE CARIBBEAN	**206 300**	**933 200**	**1 158 300**	**2 099 200**	**2 111 200**	**1 888 800**	**2 088 200**	**2 031 500**	**1 806 800**	**1 830 500**
Caribbean	*17 300*	*54 800*	*89 900*	*135 300*	*143 200*	*151 800*	*164 900*	*171 500*	*178 800*	*182 700*
Anguilla	...	10	50	90	90	100	110	110	110	120
Antigua and Barbuda	50	110	330	510	550	570	590	610	630	660
Aruba	380	640	1 080	1 530	1 670	1 720	1 860	1 890	1 900	2 000
Bahamas	500	1 440	3 050	3 450	3 670	4 010	4 310	4 310	4 430	4 540
Barbados	190	870	1 720	2 210	2 370	2 480	2 590	2 550	2 570	2 670
British Virgin Islands	20	40	240	510	590	660	690	780	870	970
Cayman Islands	20	130	710	1 170	1 240	1 280	1 360	1 440	1 520	1 620
Cuba	5 190	13 070	19 640	22 950	23 900	25 500	27 630	28 810	29 240	31 220
Dominica	30	60	170	250	260	270	270	260	250	260
Dominican Republic	1 780	7 960	9 140	19 180	20 180	22 130	25 090	27 500	27 490	21 060
Grenada	30	70	200	270	300	320	350	340	340	340
Guadeloupe	240	1 390	2 790	4 450	4 700	4 650	4 290	4 460	5 020	6 380
Haiti	330	1 380	2 610	3 100	3 520	3 920	3 510	3 320	3 000	2 500
Jamaica	1 410	2 700	4 270	7 290	7 480	7 530	7 710	7 780	8 100	7 430
Martinique	290	1 440	3 550	4 380	4 620	4 570	4 110	4 160	4 560	5 690
Montserrat	10	20	70	40	40	40	30	30	40	40
Netherlands Antilles	300	960	2 020	2 810	2 760	2 690	2 770	2 840	2 860	2 930
Puerto Rico	5 650	15 960	32 290	54 090	57 840	61 040	67 900	69 660	74 990	80 730
Saint Kitts and Nevis	20	50	160	270	290	300	330	340	360	370
Saint Lucia	40	110	420	580	630	660	680	650	670	690
Saint Vincent and the Grenadines	20	60	200	290	320	330	340	350	360	380
Trinidad and Tobago	820	6 240	5 070	5 740	6 040	6 810	8 170	9 100	9 310	9 910
Turks and Caicos Islands	10	30	90	150	170	180	200	210	220	220
Central America	*46 400*	*234 000*	*295 300*	*460 000*	*484 900*	*546 200*	*649 400*	*695 800*	*712 500*	*694 100*
Belize	50	190	410	620	630	690	760	790	820	860
Costa Rica	1 250	6 140	7 250	12 830	14 090	15 800	15 950	16 390	16 820	17 480
El Salvador	1 030	3 570	5 330	11 130	12 000	12 460	13 130	13 800	14 280	15 000
Guatemala	1 900	7 880	7 650	17 800	19 010	17 950	18 900	20 560	22 800	24 240
Honduras	690	2 570	3 050	4 720	5 260	5 420	5 900	6 270	6 430	6 800
Mexico	39 610	207 660	262 710	400 870	421 010	480 490	580 760	623 890	637 040	615 050
Nicaragua	860	2 410	3 600	3 380	3 570	3 740	3 950	4 010	4 000	4 100
Panama	1 000	3 540	5 310	8 660	9 340	9 640	10 020	10 080	10 280	10 610
South America	*142 600*	*644 500*	*773 100*	*1 503 900*	*1 483 100*	*1 190 900*	*1 274 000*	*1 164 200*	*915 500*	*953 600*
Argentina	31 030	206 840	141 350	293 010	299 100	283 660	284 350	268 830	102 040	129 710
Bolivia	1 010	5 020	4 870	7 930	8 500	8 290	8 390	8 020	7 800	7 740
Brazil	67 090	245 940	438 260	807 750	787 740	536 630	601 730	508 430	460 840	481 870
Chile	9 290	29 480	33 510	82 810	79 370	73 000	74 860	68 260	66 420	71 490
Colombia	8 550	39 590	47 740	106 670	98 510	86 300	83 770	81 720	81 120	77 120
Ecuador	1 760	12 350	11 250	23 640	23 260	16 670	15 930	21 020	24 570	27 410
French Guiana	50	290	1 200	1 500	1 520	1 490	1 320	1 310	1 410	1 730
Guyana	270	590	400	750	720	690	710	710	740	770
Paraguay	590	4 450	5 260	9 610	8 600	7 740	7 720	6 850	5 590	5 890
Peru	6 230	17 800	31 140	59 030	56 640	51 420	53 090	53 660	56 430	60 790
Suriname	280	890	1 150	780	940	760	780	660	820	980
Uruguay	2 300	9 640	8 370	21 700	22 370	20 910	20 090	18 560	12 280	11 180
Venezuela	14 130	71 580	48 600	88 700	95 850	103 310	121 260	126 200	95 420	76 950
ASIA	**497 600**	**2 430 700**	**5 484 900**	**8 252 500**	**7 502 900**	**8 301 300**	**8 897 000**	**8 272 500**	**8 416 900**	**9 229 300**
Eastern Asia	*320 900*	*1 522 100*	*3 948 100*	*6 180 400*	*5 659 900*	*6 332 900*	*6 798 400*	*6 224 200*	*6 192 700*	*6 720 800*
China	91 500	301 590	383 010	898 220	946 310	991 360	1 080 410	1 159 030	1 266 050	1 409 850
Democratic People's Rep. of Korea	2 860	8 670	16 800	10 320	10 270	10 280	10 610	11 020	11 110	11 210
Hong Kong SAR of China	3 860	28 930	75 930	173 670	165 250	160 640	165 360	162 840	161 530	159 450
Japan	206 810	1 075 220	3 053 140	4 323 060	3 946 210	4 469 580	4 763 830	4 175 590	3 987 510	4 317 130
Macao SAR of China	180	1 030	3 260	7 010	6 500	6 130	6 200	6 200	6 750	7 890
Mongolia	1 240	3 010	3 140	1 070	990	910	950	1 020	1 120	1 200
Republic of Korea	8 780	62 210	252 620	476 490	317 080	406 070	461 520	427 230	476 690	527 510

Table 1.A. Estimates of Gross Domestic Product in US Dollars at Current Prices by Major Area, Region and Country

Major area, region and country	(Millions of Dollars) 1970	1980	1990	1997	1998	1999	2000	2001	2002	2003
South Central Asia	*96 800*	*332 300*	*656 100*	*705 200*	*707 200*	*736 400*	*747 600*	*768 000*	*840 000*	*951 200*
Afghanistan	1 400	3 440	5 410	4 180	4 390	3 850	2 170	2 090	3 240	3 990
Bangladesh	10 330	19 750	31 830	45 610	46 840	48 300	48 630	48 630	51 910	56 470
Bhutan	50	140	280	390	400	440	480	520	570	680
India	60 990	183 320	324 250	419 280	421 960	449 870	468 230	486 590	508 030	591 460
Iran (Islamic Republic of)	9 960	91 300	90 370	106 710	104 410	108 880	102 930	109 980	136 850	143 270
Kazakhstan	...	...	71 880	22 170	22 140	16 870	18 290	22 150	24 640	27 550
Kyrgyzstan	...	...	12 850	1 770	1 640	1 250	1 370	1 530	1 610	1 910
Maldives	20	50	220	510	540	590	620	620	640	720
Nepal	970	1 950	3 520	4 840	4 560	5 010	5 340	5 470	5 410	5 860
Pakistan	10 700	28 230	47 240	65 440	65 380	63 580	63 680	60 180	67 280	76 530
Sri Lanka	2 400	4 160	7 990	15 210	15 800	15 700	16 280	15 620	16 410	17 400
Tajikistan	...	...	110	920	1 320	1 090	870	1 070	1 220	1 550
Turkmenistan	...	...	11 410	2 680	2 860	3 860	4 930	6 510	12 270	14 980
Uzbekistan	...	...	48 690	15 530	14 990	17 080	13 760	7 050	9 900	8 820
South-Eastern Asia	*38 100*	*191 500*	*355 000*	*708 800*	*490 100*	*572 800*	*613 000*	*594 500*	*660 800*	*731 500*
Brunei Darussalam	180	4 930	3 590	5 140	3 900	4 220	4 320	4 150	4 280	4 630
Cambodia	2 680	2 100	1 730	3 320	3 030	3 310	3 370	3 410	3 680	3 930
Indonesia	8 920	72 480	114 430	215 750	95 450	140 000	150 200	141 260	172 910	207 530
Lao People's Democratic Republic	300	850	870	1 750	1 290	1 450	1 730	1 750	1 830	2 040
Malaysia	3 460	24 490	44 020	100 170	72 180	79 150	90 040	88 050	94 990	103 250
Myanmar	2 840	5 850	17 100	26 090	27 450	35 590	41 680	50 370	55 750	58 070
Philippines	6 690	32 450	44 310	82 340	65 170	76 160	75 910	72 040	77 950	80 420
Singapore	1 900	11 720	36 900	95 390	81 910	81 380	91 480	84 870	86 970	90 140
Thailand	7 130	32 350	85 360	150 890	111 860	122 630	122 570	115 310	126 650	142 830
Timor-Leste	...	...	180	380	390	270	320	390	380	340
Vietnam	3 990	4 250	6 470	27 610	27 460	28 680	31 350	32 940	35 360	38 300
Western Asia	*41 800*	*384 800*	*525 800*	*658 100*	*645 700*	*659 200*	*738 100*	*685 700*	*723 400*	*825 700*
Armenia	...	...	15 110	1 640	1 890	1 850	1 910	2 120	2 370	2 770
Azerbaijan	...	...	22 010	3 960	4 450	4 580	5 270	5 710	6 240	7 140
Bahrain	250	3 290	4 290	6 350	6 180	6 620	7 970	7 930	8 420	9 080
Cyprus	550	2 150	5 580	8 500	9 060	9 240	8 820	9 120	10 090	12 860
Georgia	...	...	22 470	3 510	3 610	2 800	3 040	3 210	3 400	3 950
Iraq	3 520	42 440	38 360	12 900	14 830	16 020	17 780	20 450	19 120	14 950
Israel	6 010	23 500	57 240	108 230	108 130	108 570	120 350	117 790	108 400	116 450
Jordan	590	4 010	4 020	7 320	7 960	8 130	8 480	8 950	9 340	9 860
Kuwait	2 870	28 690	18 470	29 870	25 120	29 190	35 830	32 790	35 330	34 390
Lebanon	1 490	4 070	2 810	14 290	16 170	16 460	16 460	16 790	17 460	18 350
Oman	270	6 330	11 690	15 840	14 090	15 710	19 870	19 950	20 310	21 060
Qatar	300	7 840	7 360	11 300	10 260	12 390	17 760	17 740	17 880	21 160
Saudi Arabia	5 090	147 570	104 670	164 990	145 970	161 170	188 690	186 490	188 330	207 320
Syrian Arab Republic	1 790	13 060	14 000	23 850	25 470	24 570	24 710	25 550	26 370	26 650
Turkey	17 910	68 790	150 680	189 880	200 310	184 860	199 260	145 570	183 120	243 780
United Arab Emirates	660	29 630	33 780	48 750	45 900	49 780	53 310	57 040	58 170	66 270
Yemen	...	...	13 260	6 880	6 250	7 270	8 530	8 540	9 070	9 690
Yemen Arab Republic (Former)	280	2 780	...	...	...	...	...	...	...	...
Yemen Democratic (Former)	210	670	...	...	...	...	...	...	...	...
EUROPE	**1 303 900**	**4 869 500**	**8 878 400**	**9 571 400**	**9 749 600**	**9 669 700**	**9 041 500**	**9 182 100**	**10 031 900**	**12 177 600**
Eastern Europe	*469 100*	*1 104 200*	*1 512 200*	*791 000*	*681 300*	*578 800*	*639 000*	*729 400*	*816 300*	*989 600*
Belarus	...	...	60 060	14 100	15 220	12 160	10 420	12 350	14 590	17 500
Bulgaria	11 200	19 990	20 730	10 360	12 740	12 960	12 600	13 600	15 560	20 000
Czech Republic	...	34 730	37 720	57 300	61 600	59 500	55 600	61 080	73 570	90 420
Czechoslovakia (Former)	14 500	...	...	...	...	...	...	...	...	...
Hungary	6 200	24 740	36 110	45 720	47 050	48 040	46 680	51 830	64 930	82 810
Poland	20 180	55 030	61 420	150 010	165 890	161 480	164 150	183 390	189 000	206 620
Republic of Moldova	...	...	19 040	1 930	1 700	1 170	1 290	1 480	1 660	1 960
Romania	14 330	26 930	38 240	35 290	42 120	35 590	37 030	40 170	45 750	56 950
Russian Federation	...	...	967 270	404 940	270 950	195 910	259 720	306 620	345 610	433 490
Slovakia	...	14 450	16 310	21 200	22 180	20 410	20 290	20 880	24 190	32 520
Ukraine	...	...	255 260	50 150	41 880	31 580	31 260	38 010	41 480	47 290
USSR (Former)	402 710	928 350	...	...	...	...	...	...	...	...
Northern Europe	*203 300*	*874 400*	*1 720 500*	*2 130 900*	*2 240 400*	*2 299 200*	*2 250 800*	*2 235 900*	*2 459 000*	*2 895 600*
Denmark	16 290	68 450	133 360	169 030	172 430	173 120	158 450	159 230	172 930	211 850
Estonia	...	...	11 980	4 610	5 220	5 200	5 150	5 600	6 500	8 250
Finland	11 150	52 280	136 970	122 580	129 410	127 830	119 910	121 010	131 490	161 770
Iceland	520	3 360	6 230	7 250	8 020	8 420	8 430	7 650	8 500	10 520
Ireland	4 220	20 860	47 300	80 140	86 960	95 470	94 750	102 680	121 730	153 730
Latvia	...	...	18 750	5 630	6 090	6 650	7 170	7 660	8 400	10 280

Table 1.A. Estimates of Gross Domestic Product in US Dollars at Current Prices by Major Area, Region and Country

Major area, region and country	(Millions of Dollars) 1970	1980	1990	1997	1998	1999	2000	2001	2002	2003
Lithuania	...	...	20 140	9 630	10 890	10 650	11 170	11 870	13 800	17 920
Norway	12 750	63 650	116 110	157 120	150 050	158 100	166 910	169 780	190 480	221 580
Sweden	34 780	129 700	240 150	247 320	248 040	251 320	239 570	219 420	240 580	301 130
United Kingdom	123 640	536 130	989 560	1 327 600	1 423 320	1 462 430	1 439 280	1 430 980	1 564 610	1 798 540
Southern Europe	*181 500*	*822 500*	*1 863 800*	*2 029 600*	*2 092 700*	*2 099 800*	*1 922 000*	*1 972 700*	*2 173 900*	*2 723 700*
Albania	1 300	2 220	2 170	2 240	2 820	3 550	3 840	4 260	4 830	6 060
Andorra	20	200	680	910	950	970	910	960	1 110	1 450
Bosnia and Herzegovina	...	...	13 110	3 780	4 230	4 690	4 440	4 670	5 420	6 710
Croatia	...	...	24 780	20 290	21 630	19 910	18 430	19 860	22 420	28 330
Greece	11 280	48 820	84 070	121 340	121 960	125 630	113 460	117 250	133 030	172 220
Holy See		10	10	20	20	20	10	10	20	20
Italy	107 700	448 830	1 102 440	1 166 800	1 196 660	1 180 440	1 074 760	1 091 840	1 184 270	1 465 830
Malta	230	1 130	2 310	3 340	3 510	3 650	3 560	3 630	3 860	4 650
Portugal	7 360	29 860	71 470	106 370	112 390	115 090	106 460	110 110	121 670	147 350
San Marino	70	290	710	750	810	850	780	790	860	1 060
Serbia and Montenegro	...	...	30 200	19 310	15 580	17 840	11 010	11 700	15 570	19 400
Slovenia	...	...	17 380	19 190	20 600	21 120	18 960	19 530	21 960	27 440
Spain	38 960	221 220	509 970	561 550	588 020	602 390	561 760	584 590	655 220	838 620
TFYR Macedonia	...	...	4 470	3 720	3 580	3 670	3 590	3 440	3 710	4 570
Yugoslavia (Former)	14 550	69 960	...	...	...	...	...	...	...	...
Western Europe	*450 000*	*2 068 300*	*3 781 900*	*4 619 900*	*4 735 100*	*4 691 900*	*4 229 700*	*4 244 100*	*4 582 600*	*5 568 700*
Austria	14 920	79 470	161 690	205 750	211 900	209 950	190 410	190 160	205 480	253 120
Belgium	25 650	121 790	197 170	244 890	250 320	251 130	228 300	227 110	244 700	301 880
France	147 000	682 080	1 215 890	1 406 120	1 451 950	1 443 710	1 308 400	1 320 420	1 436 940	1 757 550
Germany	203 710	893 320	1 671 310	2 110 970	2 144 480	2 107 970	1 870 280	1 855 640	1 986 160	2 403 070
Liechtenstein	70	430	960	1 130	1 170	1 160	1 090	1 130	1 240	1 460
Luxembourg	1 260	5 220	11 080	17 470	18 900	19 960	19 590	19 680	21 080	26 000
Monaco	70	340	640	780	810	810	740	750	820	1 010
Netherlands	35 390	178 150	294 760	376 900	393 470	398 530	370 640	384 000	418 470	512 880
Switzerland	21 920	107 470	228 410	255 890	262 100	258 640	240 270	245 240	267 740	311 740
OCEANIA	**51 200**	**195 800**	**365 400**	**498 800**	**440 300**	**475 900**	**452 300**	**432 100**	**480 200**	**613 900**
Australia & New Zealand	*49 400*	*188 700*	*354 200*	*483 100*	*426 400*	*462 200*	*439 700*	*420 200*	*467 300*	*598 300*
Australia	42 870	165 830	310 590	416 530	371 850	405 580	388 040	368 760	408 980	523 350
New Zealand	6 550	22 850	43 620	66 610	54 570	56 660	51 690	51 390	58 360	74 990
Melanesia	*1 400*	*5 500*	*7 500*	*11 000*	*9 100*	*8 900*	*8 300*	*7 700*	*8 300*	*9 900*
Fiji	220	1 200	1 340	2 120	1 590	1 860	1 650	1 670	1 860	2 320
New Caledonia	380	1 180	2 530	3 290	3 160	3 050	2 680	2 540	3 110	3 830
Papua New Guinea	770	2 820	3 290	4 910	3 790	3 420	3 420	2 900	2 810	3 290
Solomon Islands	30	140	210	410	360	380	340	330	270	270
Vanuatu	30	110	150	250	230	230	220	210	200	240
Micronesia	*100*	*200*	*400*	*500*	*500*	*500*	*500*	*500*	*600*	*600*
Kiribati	10	30	30	50	50	50	50	50	50	70
Marshall Islands	10	20	70	90	100	100	100	100	110	110
Micronesia (Federated States of)	20	80	150	210	210	220	230	240	240	250
Nauru	10	40	50	40	30	30	30	30	40	50
Palau	10	20	70	110	120	110	120	120	120	130
Polynesia	*300*	*1 500*	*3 300*	*4 200*	*4 200*	*4 200*	*3 800*	*3 800*	*4 100*	*5 000*
Cook Islands	10	20	60	90	80	80	80	90	100	130
French Polynesia	210	1 260	2 930	3 700	3 750	3 700	3 300	3 290	3 550	4 380
Samoa	60	150	200	240	220	230	240	240	260	320
Tonga	10	50	110	160	150	150	140	130	140	170
Tuvalu	...	...	10	10	10	10	10	10	20	20

Table 1.B. Estimates of Per Capita Gross Domestic Product in US Dollars by Major Area, Region and Country

(Dollars)

Major area, region and country	1970	1980	1990	1997	1998	1999	2000	2001	2002	2003
WORLD	**880**	**2 690**	**4 320**	**5 130**	**5 030**	**5 140**	**5 200**	**5 080**	**5 210**	**5 750**
DEVELOPED ECONOMIES	**3 110**	**10 570**	**21 110**	**26 610**	**26 810**	**27 970**	**28 050**	**27 530**	**28 530**	**31 850**
DEVELOPING ECONOMIES	**220**	**840**	**970**	**1 440**	**1 340**	**1 320**	**1 410**	**1 360**	**1 360**	**1 460**
TRANSITION ECONOMIES	**1 370**	**3 060**	**4 510**	**2 260**	**2 000**	**1 750**	**1 880**	**2 120**	**2 400**	**2 910**
AFRICA	**230**	**990**	**850**	**820**	**790**	**730**	**730**	**690**	**670**	**760**
Eastern Africa	*140*	*480*	*300*	*300*	*290*	*280*	*270*	*280*	*280*	*290*
Burundi	70	230	205	160	147	131	113	104	95	86
Comoros	71	350	475	300	296	298	262	274	300	369
Djibouti	421	922	866	813	795	828	830	842	855	886
Eritrea	...	...	...	221	224	210	203	239	264	305
Ethiopia	...	...	...	102	101	96	92	90	86	91
Ethiopia (Former)	58	109	161	...	...	...	...	...	...	...
Kenya	149	433	362	369	390	352	342	362	390	444
Madagascar	129	361	258	242	248	240	243	278	262	318
Malawi	71	200	185	247	162	162	153	147	170	158
Mauritius	232	1 186	2 449	3 638	3 571	3 634	3 840	3 779	3 902	4 594
Mozambique	295	357	197	201	226	227	206	189	189	222
Reunion	787	3 949	8 627	10 075	10 253	10 102	9 014	9 188	10 849	14 614
Rwanda	63	249	380	317	306	260	224	205	199	185
Seychelles	379	2 311	5 200	7 354	7 868	7 983	7 603	7 335	8 704	8 814
Somalia	95	425	139	191	239	241	235	144	129	155
Uganda	200	2 002	210	307	286	263	244	238	241	242
United Republic Of Tanzania	97	273	145	236	251	253	261	266	267	271
Zambia	392	776	497	398	322	306	311	344	346	398
Zimbabwe	292	741	838	700	490	439	570	710	647	190
Middle Africa	*180*	*700*	*640*	*380*	*360*	*350*	*380*	*360*	*390*	*440*
Angola	513	764	1 102	668	555	511	737	700	743	725
Cameroon	199	1 105	1 227	652	673	660	613	582	641	803
Central African Republic	80	307	441	265	273	270	244	242	261	325
Chad	111	204	264	215	230	195	166	183	208	290
Congo	197	946	1 122	740	601	703	934	787	830	1 050
Democratic Republic of the Congo	91	527	250	129	133	112	102	99	108	107
Equatorial Guinea	669	257	461	1 310	1 037	1 707	2 746	3 680	4 463	5 915
Gabon	633	6 156	5 695	4 559	3 883	3 748	3 995	3 379	3 490	4 155
Sao Tome and Principe	290	497	497	318	288	323	311	312	345	364
Northern Africa	*270*	*1 250*	*1 630*	*1 420*	*1 420*	*1 440*	*1 480*	*1 400*	*1 320*	*1 350*
Algeria	376	2 260	2 474	1 670	1 633	1 634	1 801	1 787	1 798	2 049
Egypt	194	558	1 274	1 325	1 392	1 507	1 524	1 390	1 308	1 062
Libyan Arab Jamahiriya	2 010	11 739	6 570	7 508	6 428	5 935	6 484	5 322	3 514	3 640
Morocco	258	971	1 051	1 205	1 271	1 231	1 145	1 146	1 200	1 463
Sudan	133	464	1 350	344	330	315	367	406	411	459
Tunisia	281	1 352	1 501	2 056	2 129	2 210	2 043	2 075	2 160	2 561
Southern Africa	*740*	*2 620*	*2 840*	*3 300*	*2 930*	*2 840*	*2 750*	*2 440*	*2 260*	*3 380*
Botswana	139	1 084	2 600	2 987	2 868	2 743	2 881	2 872	2 857	3 983
Lesotho	71	297	394	592	508	515	483	419	386	594
Namibia	631	1 986	1 661	2 078	1 886	1 829	1 826	1 639	1 469	2 307
South Africa	806	2 826	3 040	3 515	3 112	3 012	2 910	2 572	2 376	3 551
Swaziland	246	990	1 028	1 460	1 340	1 341	1 330	1 204	1 090	1 653
Western Africa	*190*	*1 050*	*430*	*530*	*540*	*360*	*350*	*350*	*360*	*410*
Benin	109	394	397	374	395	394	362	371	415	521
Burkina Faso	73	250	320	210	221	213	184	202	228	294
Cape Verde	240	492	882	1 238	1 289	1 368	1 241	1 259	1 387	1 765
Cote d'Ivoire	271	1 207	951	782	828	808	675	667	716	886
Gambia	99	367	356	330	339	339	321	289	257	224
Ghana	257	1 411	408	375	398	391	254	265	300	354
Guinea	184	414	460	492	457	434	377	362	384	424
Guinea-Bissau	160	298	230	221	160	182	164	174	173	208
Liberia	200	438	180	121	139	160	184	172	173	181
Mali	25	202	277	223	240	235	205	214	249	298
Mauritania	162	515	503	441	394	375	340	353	345	381
Niger	97	454	328	192	207	195	167	171	184	227
Nigeria	215	1 431	377	669	665	322	368	363	363	390
Senegal	209	540	776	500	520	518	466	479	511	641
Sierra Leone	156	340	157	205	160	156	144	212	207	197
Togo	131	449	455	363	331	319	291	284	308	377

Table 1.B. Estimates of Per Capita Gross Domestic Product in US Dollars by Major Area, Region and Country

Major area, region and country	(Dollars)									
	1970	1980	1990	1997	1998	1999	2000	2001	2002	2003
AMERICAS	**2 550**	**6 430**	**10 330**	**13 690**	**14 060**	**14 250**	**15 030**	**15 060**	**15 060**	**15 590**
NORTHERN AMERICA	**4 790**	**11 870**	**22 320**	**29 050**	**30 170**	**31 570**	**33 180**	**33 620**	**34 470**	**35 980**
Bermuda	4 462	13 545	26 901	36 904	38 743	41 247	42 533	44 753	45 909	51 991
Canada	3 919	10 820	20 729	20 956	20 076	21 347	23 198	22 715	23 179	27 097
United States	4 881	11 976	22 489	29 923	31 261	32 672	34 253	34 788	35 676	36 924
LATIN AMERICA AND THE CARIBBEAN	**720**	**2 580**	**2 620**	**4 230**	**4 180**	**3 690**	**4 010**	**3 850**	**3 370**	**3 370**
Caribbean	*700*	*1 880*	*2 660*	*3 710*	*3 880*	*4 080*	*4 390*	*4 520*	*4 680*	*4 740*
Anguilla	425	1 236	6 058	8 320	8 691	9 380	9 481	9 416	9 573	9 854
Antigua and Barbuda	747	1 742	5 299	7 392	7 790	8 091	8 282	8 461	8 689	9 036
Aruba	6 764	10 698	16 399	18 041	18 950	19 017	19 922	19 762	19 473	20 100
Bahamas	2 952	6 844	11 935	11 816	12 405	13 374	14 217	14 041	14 277	14 462
Barbados	776	3 474	6 689	8 338	8 937	9 314	9 688	9 486	9 556	9 867
British Virgin Islands	1 583	3 703	13 956	26 933	30 789	33 891	34 849	38 530	42 365	46 549
Cayman Islands	1 778	7 669	27 464	35 288	35 952	35 990	36 912	37 891	38 928	40 025
Cuba	609	1 347	1 848	2 073	2 150	2 285	2 467	2 563	2 594	2 762
Dominica	393	795	2 322	3 210	3 374	3 459	3 484	3 379	3 235	3 279
Dominican Republic	403	1 398	1 295	2 412	2 496	2 692	3 003	3 241	3 191	2 408
Grenada	323	837	2 345	3 321	3 656	3 962	4 307	4 189	4 252	4 262
Guadeloupe	748	4 242	7 145	10 693	11 172	10 947	10 030	10 323	11 507	14 518
Haiti	73	254	378	403	452	496	439	410	365	300
Jamaica	754	1 265	1 803	2 899	2 950	2 945	2 988	2 990	3 083	2 802
Martinique	885	4 427	9 848	11 573	12 125	11 914	10 664	10 723	11 677	14 504
Montserrat	568	2 059	6 252	5 257	6 015	7 268	8 916	10 184	11 459	10 690
Netherlands Antilles	1 916	5 546	10 769	13 376	13 017	12 611	12 862	13 061	13 044	13 261
Puerto Rico	2 079	4 992	9 152	14 461	15 356	16 099	17 794	18 150	19 432	20 812
Saint Kitts and Nevis	358	1 084	3 893	6 343	6 686	7 165	7 797	8 200	8 524	8 927
Saint Lucia	395	1 003	3 166	4 057	4 370	4 572	4 639	4 406	4 515	4 611
Saint Vincent and the Grenadines	204	589	1 800	2 539	2 728	2 822	2 850	2 924	3 031	3 137
Trinidad and Tobago	847	5 765	4 171	4 504	4 725	5 302	6 340	7 031	7 174	7 607
Turks and Caicos Islands	1 807	4 126	7 669	8 924	9 667	10 222	10 938	10 854	10 817	10 914
Central America	*690*	*2 600*	*2 650*	*3 590*	*3 720*	*4 110*	*4 800*	*5 060*	*5 090*	*4 880*
Belize	376	1 354	2 183	2 744	2 740	2 932	3 152	3 212	3 271	3 363
Costa Rica	687	2 616	2 359	3 510	3 760	4 113	4 059	4 085	4 108	4 189
El Salvador	286	778	1 043	1 889	2 001	2 041	2 114	2 187	2 227	2 302
Guatemala	363	1 155	874	1 690	1 756	1 614	1 655	1 753	1 895	1 963
Honduras	267	719	626	791	859	862	914	947	948	980
Mexico	783	3 073	3 157	4 252	4 393	4 933	5 870	6 211	6 248	5 945
Nicaragua	404	827	941	722	742	757	779	771	750	750
Panama	666	1 818	2 204	3 114	3 294	3 331	3 396	3 352	3 355	3 400
South America	*740*	*2 660*	*2 610*	*4 530*	*4 400*	*3 480*	*3 670*	*3 300*	*2 560*	*2 630*
Argentina	1 295	7 363	4 346	8 210	8 273	7 747	7 670	7 163	2 687	3 375
Bolivia	240	937	730	1 014	1 064	1 017	1 009	946	902	878
Brazil	699	2 022	2 945	4 893	4 708	3 165	3 503	2 922	2 615	2 700
Chile	978	2 645	2 558	5 661	5 353	4 858	4 917	4 427	4 254	4 523
Colombia	379	1 392	1 365	2 668	2 421	2 084	1 989	1 908	1 864	1 744
Ecuador	295	1 551	1 096	1 999	1 934	1 364	1 283	1 666	1 918	2 108
French Guiana	1 076	4 225	10 299	10 086	9 854	9 341	8 011	7 737	8 108	9 705
Guyana	378	777	542	1 001	954	919	939	935	975	1 010
Paraguay	253	1 429	1 248	1 892	1 650	1 450	1 412	1 222	975	1 001
Peru	472	1 028	1 432	2 392	2 255	2 014	2 046	2 035	2 108	2 238
Suriname	758	2 507	2 860	1 872	2 252	1 795	1 838	1 539	1 900	2 240
Uruguay	818	3 307	2 694	6 644	6 796	6 305	6 011	5 514	3 620	3 274
Venezuela	1 318	4 743	2 492	3 883	4 110	4 341	4 995	5 098	3 783	2 994
ASIA	**240**	**940**	**1 730**	**2 340**	**2 100**	**2 290**	**2 420**	**2 220**	**2 230**	**2 420**
Eastern Asia	*330*	*1 290*	*2 920*	*4 280*	*3 880*	*4 310*	*4 590*	*4 170*	*4 120*	*4 440*
China	112	307	337	736	768	798	862	918	995	1 100
Democratic People's Rep. of Korea	199	504	842	474	468	465	476	492	493	494
Hong Kong SAR of China	978	5 743	13 311	26 973	25 147	23 989	24 292	23 596	23 140	22 618
Japan	1 982	9 205	24 714	34 269	31 203	35 258	37 500	32 809	31 280	33 819
Macao SAR of China	690	4 084	8 767	16 385	14 926	13 837	13 778	13 616	14 677	17 007
Mongolia	991	1 809	1 415	440	404	366	379	402	437	462
Republic of Korea	275	1 632	5 893	10 400	6 867	8 730	9 854	9 063	10 050	11 059

Table 1.B. Estimates of Per Capita Gross Domestic Product in US Dollars by Major Area, Region and Country

Major area, region and country	(Dollars) 1970	1980	1990	1997	1998	1999	2000	2001	2002	2003
South Central Asia	*130*	*350*	*540*	*500*	*490*	*500*	*500*	*510*	*550*	*610*
Afghanistan	110	227	392	206	214	184	101	95	141	167
Bangladesh	156	232	291	353	355	358	352	345	361	385
Bhutan	44	106	168	208	203	222	234	243	261	303
India	110	266	383	434	429	450	460	471	484	555
Iran (Islamic Republic of)	346	2 321	1 594	1 665	1 609	1 658	1 549	1 635	2 010	2 079
Kazakhstan	...	...	4 276	1 369	1 385	1 068	1 170	1 426	1 593	1 785
Kyrgyzstan	...	...	2 925	377	344	258	278	306	317	372
Maldives	129	298	1 000	1 912	1 972	2 087	2 146	2 084	2 070	2 260
Nepal	80	131	189	220	203	218	227	228	220	233
Pakistan	173	350	426	496	483	457	446	411	449	498
Sri Lanka	195	286	475	840	864	851	876	833	868	913
Tajikistan	...	...	21	157	221	180	143	174	197	249
Turkmenistan	...	...	3 111	610	638	845	1 062	1 380	2 559	3 078
Uzbekistan	...	...	2 374	656	622	697	552	278	385	338
South-Eastern Asia	*130*	*540*	*810*	*1 430*	*970*	*1 120*	*1 180*	*1 130*	*1 230*	*1 350*
Brunei Darussalam	1 375	25 534	13 972	16 534	12 261	12 923	12 922	12 135	12 229	12 919
Cambodia	386	317	178	273	243	258	256	253	266	278
Indonesia	74	483	628	1 063	464	671	710	659	796	944
Lao People's Democratic Republic	111	265	209	355	255	282	328	325	331	361
Malaysia	319	1 779	2 467	4 674	3 286	3 519	3 915	3 748	3 964	4 227
Myanmar	106	174	422	573	594	759	877	1 045	1 141	1 174
Philippines	183	675	725	1 154	895	1 026	1 003	934	992	1 005
Singapore	914	4 853	12 234	25 793	21 495	20 771	22 775	20 676	20 790	21 195
Thailand	197	698	1 569	2 554	1 874	2 033	2 012	1 873	2 036	2 273
Timor-Leste	...	...	244	487	523	378	457	542	512	434
Vietnam	93	80	98	368	361	372	401	416	441	471
Western Asia	*570*	*3 880*	*3 490*	*3 710*	*3 560*	*3 560*	*3 900*	*3 550*	*3 670*	*4 110*
Armenia	...	...	4 261	508	595	587	614	686	770	905
Azerbaijan	...	...	3 061	498	554	566	646	694	752	853
Bahrain	1 138	9 487	8 763	10 171	9 627	10 032	11 775	11 436	11 872	12 542
Cyprus	893	3 525	8 198	11 157	11 777	11 906	11 259	11 552	12 678	16 038
Georgia	...	...	4 115	660	681	529	578	614	656	770
Iraq	376	3 274	2 212	603	674	709	766	857	780	594
Israel	2 076	6 243	12 682	19 168	18 707	18 369	19 920	19 080	17 194	18 101
Jordan	366	1 803	1 235	1 595	1 679	1 663	1 684	1 726	1 753	1 803
Kuwait	3 860	20 867	8 619	16 332	12 759	13 791	15 947	13 935	14 460	13 641
Lebanon	603	1 526	1 037	4 333	4 811	4 814	4 733	4 747	4 856	5 023
Oman	364	5 327	6 332	6 633	5 726	6 201	7 615	7 423	7 337	7 389
Qatar	2 711	34 191	15 747	20 693	18 373	21 739	30 558	29 998	29 752	34 685
Saudi Arabia	887	15 365	6 323	8 191	7 019	7 507	8 520	8 169	8 007	8 561
Syrian Arab Republic	280	1 458	1 100	1 552	1 616	1 520	1 492	1 506	1 517	1 497
Turkey	495	1 491	2 616	2 913	3 025	2 749	2 918	2 101	2 604	3 418
United Arab Emirates	2 954	29 182	16 603	18 469	16 991	18 029	18 906	19 816	19 806	22 130
Yemen	...	...	1 110	422	371	418	474	458	469	484
Yemen Arab Republic (Former)	57	437	...	...	...	...	...	...	...	...
Yemen Democratic (Former)	138	359	...	...	...	...	...	...	...	...
EUROPE	**1 850**	**6 490**	**12 310**	**13 150**	**13 390**	**13 280**	**12 420**	**12 630**	**13 800**	**16 770**
Eastern Europe	*1 430*	*3 080*	*4 870*	*2 570*	*2 220*	*1 890*	*2 100*	*2 410*	*2 710*	*3 300*
Belarus	...	...	5 850	1 385	1 502	1 206	1 038	1 237	1 468	1 768
Bulgaria	1 319	2 256	2 377	1 251	1 549	1 587	1 556	1 693	1 954	2 533
Czech Republic	...	3 378	3 660	5 557	5 982	5 786	5 415	5 955	7 180	8 834
Czechoslovakia (Former)	1 012	...	...	...	...	...	...	...	...	...
Hungary	600	2 311	3 484	4 509	4 659	4 778	4 662	5 200	6 543	8 384
Poland	618	1 547	1 612	3 880	4 289	4 175	4 245	4 745	4 893	5 355
Republic of Moldova	...	...	4 363	447	395	273	301	346	389	459
Romania	708	1 213	1 648	1 564	1 869	1 581	1 647	1 790	2 044	2 550
Russian Federation	...	...	6 523	2 748	1 845	1 339	1 784	2 116	2 399	3 026
Slovakia	...	2 904	3 103	3 940	4 118	3 788	3 764	3 871	4 481	6 019
Ukraine	...	...	4 919	985	829	630	629	771	848	975
USSR (Former)	1 659	3 498	...	...	...	...	...	...	...	...
Northern Europe	*2 560*	*10 730*	*18 810*	*22 890*	*24 000*	*24 560*	*23 980*	*23 760*	*26 070*	*30 620*
Denmark	3 304	13 362	25 946	32 088	32 615	32 633	29 772	29 833	32 314	39 497
Estonia	...	...	7 561	3 280	3 751	3 767	3 767	4 141	4 860	6 232
Finland	2 420	10 938	27 468	23 841	25 105	24 744	23 161	23 327	25 299	31 069
Iceland	2 563	14 719	24 432	26 509	29 001	30 146	29 848	26 846	29 576	36 328
Ireland	1 428	6 134	13 458	21 753	23 327	25 301	24 808	26 564	31 126	38 864
Latvia	...	...	6 911	2 312	2 524	2 778	3 022	3 260	3 608	4 453

Table 1.B. Estimates of Per Capita Gross Domestic Product in US Dollars by Major Area, Region and Country

Major area, region and country	(Dollars) 1970	1980	1990	1997	1998	1999	2000	2001	2002	2003
Lithuania	...	...	5 385	2 731	3 094	3 033	3 192	3 408	3 984	5 203
Norway	3 289	15 578	27 374	35 658	33 880	35 519	37 317	37 783	42 200	48 881
Sweden	4 324	15 607	28 059	27 918	27 999	28 378	27 050	24 764	27 131	33 925
United Kingdom	2 255	9 655	17 434	22 852	24 415	25 001	24 524	24 303	26 488	30 355
Southern Europe	*1 400*	*5 850*	*13 040*	*14 050*	*14 440*	*14 440*	*13 180*	*13 510*	*14 870*	*18 610*
Albania	607	831	660	713	905	1 140	1 232	1 365	1 538	1 915
Andorra	1 153	5 893	12 975	13 947	14 541	14 835	13 785	14 302	15 990	20 424
Bosnia and Herzegovina	...	...	3 042	1 073	1 148	1 219	1 117	1 149	1 314	1 613
Croatia	...	...	5 117	4 602	4 891	4 486	4 145	4 468	5 052	6 398
Greece	1 283	5 063	8 275	11 400	11 350	11 595	10 406	10 710	12 127	15 690
Holy See	2 001	7 953	19 437	20 307	20 810	20 519	18 680	18 982	20 602	25 527
Italy	2 001	7 953	19 437	20 307	20 810	20 519	18 680	18 982	20 602	25 527
Malta	752	3 501	6 420	8 713	9 103	9 426	9 136	9 274	9 824	11 790
Portugal	848	3 058	7 220	10 687	11 268	11 514	10 629	10 975	12 108	14 645
San Marino	3 615	13 490	30 687	29 194	30 917	32 282	29 039	29 174	31 320	38 397
Serbia and Montenegro	...	...	2 973	1 824	1 472	1 688	1 043	1 109	1 478	1 843
Slovenia	...	...	9 063	9 612	10 325	10 603	9 531	9 824	11 058	13 831
Spain	1 153	5 893	12 975	13 947	14 541	14 835	13 785	14 302	15 990	20 424
TFYR Macedonia	...	...	2 342	1 872	1 790	1 826	1 772	1 689	1 815	2 225
Yugoslavia (Former)	668	2 902	...	...	...	...	...	...	...	...
Western Europe	*2 720*	*12 130*	*21 480*	*25 350*	*25 920*	*25 630*	*23 050*	*23 070*	*24 850*	*30 120*
Austria	1 998	10 527	20 920	25 420	26 163	25 921	23 503	23 460	25 333	31 187
Belgium	2 656	12 353	19 782	24 038	24 520	24 549	22 271	22 108	23 767	29 257
France	2 895	12 659	21 431	23 993	24 683	24 449	22 065	22 168	24 009	29 222
Germany	2 606	11 411	21 041	25 722	26 102	25 638	22 730	22 534	24 100	29 137
Liechtenstein	3 543	17 007	33 422	35 725	36 556	36 063	33 498	34 190	37 334	43 486
Luxembourg	3 727	14 341	29 346	41 871	44 662	46 515	45 001	44 590	47 129	57 379
Monaco	2 895	12 659	21 431	23 993	24 683	24 449	22 065	22 168	24 009	29 222
Netherlands	2 714	12 590	19 714	24 096	25 017	25 203	23 314	24 026	26 046	31 759
Switzerland	3 543	17 007	33 423	35 725	36 556	36 063	33 498	34 190	37 334	43 486
OCEANIA	**2 650**	**8 640**	**13 820**	**16 900**	**14 710**	**15 690**	**14 710**	**13 880**	**15 230**	**19 240**
Australia & New Zealand	*3 220*	*10 670*	*17 490*	*21 760*	*18 990*	*20 360*	*19 170*	*18 140*	*19 980*	*25 350*
Australia	3 420	11 382	18 391	22 491	19 846	21 404	20 260	19 056	20 926	26 525
New Zealand	2 322	7 342	12 980	18 077	14 674	15 104	13 662	13 470	15 177	19 350
Melanesia	*420*	*1 250*	*1 370*	*1 680*	*1 370*	*1 310*	*1 190*	*1 070*	*1 130*	*1 330*
Fiji	424	1 898	1 848	2 693	1 995	2 312	2 031	2 035	2 241	2 761
New Caledonia	3 592	8 285	14 786	16 289	15 298	14 486	12 455	11 552	13 868	16 751
Papua New Guinea	302	871	799	992	747	656	641	531	504	577
Solomon Islands	199	627	653	1 026	872	897	774	743	591	568
Vanuatu	404	968	1 023	1 398	1 240	1 192	1 123	1 062	976	1 140
Micronesia	*480*	*1 030*	*1 550*	*1 890*	*1 860*	*1 900*	*1 920*	*1 950*	*2 000*	*2 120*
Kiribati	293	482	396	613	565	650	574	554	617	781
Marshall Islands	345	763	1 546	1 878	1 914	1 921	1 910	1 967	2 021	2 108
Micronesia (Federated States of)	390	1 059	1 572	1 958	1 952	2 029	2 138	2 215	2 216	2 281
Nauru	2 008	4 798	5 428	3 290	2 773	2 837	2 698	2 500	2 759	3 465
Palau	1 208	1 869	4 400	6 301	6 383	6 037	6 150	6 234	6 194	6 174
Polynesia	*790*	*3 490*	*6 870*	*8 120*	*8 040*	*7 890*	*7 040*	*6 940*	*7 430*	*9 060*
Cook Islands	523	1 207	3 193	4 581	4 060	4 393	4 413	4 666	5 583	7 332
French Polynesia	1 917	8 341	14 995	16 666	16 614	16 127	14 132	13 881	14 767	17 918
Samoa	414	997	1 255	1 451	1 316	1 353	1 363	1 399	1 496	1 807
Tonga	124	548	1 157	1 654	1 471	1 485	1 421	1 270	1 317	1 626
Tuvalu	185	607	1 079	1 414	1 394	1 469	1 409	1 378	1 845	2 285

B. Percentage Distribution of Main National Accounting Aggregates at Current Prices: Individual Countries or Areas

Description of Analysis in Tables 2 and 3

B. Economic structure expressed in terms of percentage shares of gross domestic product.

The tables included in this section of the publication disaggregate GDP at current market prices into component parts and express these as percentage shares that outline the different economic structures existing in countries. The years of coverage vary: for countries that have officially reported complete data, percentage shares are listed for the years 1970, 1975, 1980, 1985, 1990, and 1995 through 2003; while, for those countries with very limited data and for which estimates have been made by the Statistics Division of United Nations in order to supplement the official data, percentage shares are only shown for selected years.

GDP estimates according to type of expenditure are shown in Table 2 and by kind of economic activity in Table 3. Differences in the concepts and coverage in classifications used are indicated in the footnotes. Both tables are designed to provide an overview of the structure of the economic system expressed in current prices.

GDP estimates of the countries are expressed in millions of the national currency as indicated in the first column of both tables. For tabulation purposes, the values of the GDP estimates of some countries prior to a high inflation period might be qualified with unit (u) or thousand (t) to reflect the measurement in a single unit or thousand of units of national currency.

Table 2 features the distribution of GDP based on expenditure components. It shows what portion of income is spent by the household sector or by the government on consumption, what is spent on investment, and what revenues are obtained from exports after deducting the expenditures on imports.

It is noted that in some instances the shares for changes in inventories should be used with caution as countries may also include such items in statistical errors. This problem is apparent in the inordinately high shares of changes in inventories as a percentage of GDP for many consecutive years.

Table 3 presents the shares of the components of GDP by kind of economic activity: agriculture; total industrial activity consisting of mining, manufacturing and utilities; manufacturing (as a separate activity); construction; wholesale and retail trade, restaurants and hotels; transport, storage and communication; and other activities which include financial and community services, producers of government services and other producers.

As in the preceding table, the distributive shares of GDP are presented, this time originating from each industry component based on the classification by tabulation category of the International Standard Industrial Classification of all Economic Activities[iii]. This table reflects the economic structure of production in the country. For example, it identifies the value-added shares from different sources of production, e.g., oil, gas and other minerals. It also illustrates that many developing countries heavily depend on income mainly originating in agriculture, while relatively more developed countries generate a much larger portion of income in the industrial and services sectors.

Note that the breakdown in shares of GDP at current market prices by type of expenditure in Table 2 might not add-up to 100 per cent due to statistical discrepancies. The breakdown by kind of economic activity in Table 3 might not add-up to 100 percent due to one or a combination of the following treatments: (i) taxes on production and imports, (ii) Financial Intermediation Services Indirectly Measured (FISIM), and (iii) statistical discrepancies.

[iii] Statistical Papers, Series M, No. 4, Rev. 3 (United Nations publication, Sales No. E.90.XVII.11)

Table 2. Gross Domestic Product by Type of Expenditure: Individual Countries or Areas

Major area, region and country	Year	Gross Domestic Product (at current prices) Million	Household final consumption expenditure 1	General government final consumption expenditure 2	Gross fixed capital formation 3	Changes in inventories 4	Exports of goods and services 5	Imports of goods and services 6
			Percentage Distribution					
AFRICA								
Algeria (Dinars)	1970	25509	59	13	31	3	22	27
	1975	61574	51	13	39	6	34	43
	1980	162507	43	14	34	5	34	30
	1985	291597	48	16	32	1	24	20
	1990	554388	57	16	26	3	23	25
	1995	2004995	56	17	27	5	27	31
	1996	2570030	52	16	25	0	30	23
	1997	2780170	51	17	23	0	30	21
	1998	2810122	55	18	26	2	23	23
	1999	3238198	52	17	24	2	28	23
	2000	4098816	42	14	21	2	42	21
	2001	4241803	44	15	23	4	37	22
	2002	4479695	44	15	25	6	36	26
	2003	5044000	42	14	25	6	38	25
Angola (Kwanzas)	1970	82 (u)	67	15	13	...	28	23
	1975	80 (u)	52	21	8	...	48	29
	1980	161 (u)	48	21	9	...	52	30
	1985	205 (u)	47	31	17	1	33	29
	1990	308 (u)	29	45	11	1	39	24
	1995	14	50	34	18	7	69	78
	2000	91666	30	18	23	...	93	68
	2002	426428	39	21	23	...	77	67
Benin (CFA Francs)	1970	81809	78	13	15	...	28	35
	1975	132742	85	12	20	...	27	49
	1980	288239	90	9	20	...	24	46
	1985	469778	80	13	13	2	33	41
	1990	502300	80	13	13	1	20	28
	1995	1005882	79	10	19	2	29	39
	2000	1605500	76	9	19	1	27	31
	2003	2040300	81	8	20	1	22	31
Botswana [1] (Pula)	1970	70	68	19	34	3	24	58
	1975	263	53	17	24	13	41	56
	1980	832	46	19	31	4	49	59
	1985	2146	36	22	21	0	61	48
	1990	6552	30	24	33	6	56	50
	1995	12262	33	29	26	0	50	39
	1996	14204	31	28	26	-2	52	37
	1997	17740	28	27	24	2	56	38
	1998	20163	29	27	26	4	57	44
	1999	21524	31	31	29	8	47	46
	2000	25363	29	30	27	-8	60	39
	2001	29353	28	32	23	-7	56	33
	2002	32000	27	32	26	-2	48	35
Burkina Faso (CFA Francs)	1970	109936	93	8	8	2	9	20
	1975	168467	82	17	21	4	13	38
	1980	360929	85	17	24	2	16	45
	1985	622711	85	15	20	6	10	31
	1990	778376	80	15	22	1	11	29
	1995	1106300	81	17	25	-0	14	30
	2000	1560600	77	15	28	-0	11	30
	2002	2003800	73	17	26	-1	10	24
Burundi (Francs)	1970	21476	87	10	4	1	11	11
	1975	32671	91	12	9	-2	8	19
	1980	85607	82	16	13	1	9	20
	1985	141347	77	16	14	0	10	18
	1990	196656	83	19	16	-1	8	26
	1995	250448	90	11	12	...	17	30
	2000	512231	95	9	10	...	10	24
	2003	638392	92	10	10	...	10	23

Table 2. Gross Domestic Product by Type of Expenditure: Individual Countries or Areas

Major area, region and country	Year	Gross Domestic Product (at current prices) Million	Household final consumption expenditure 1	General government final consumption expenditure 2	Gross fixed capital formation 3	Changes in inventories 4	Exports of goods and services 5	Imports of goods and services 6
			Percentage Distribution					
Cameroon	1970	365638	81	14	15	2	22	37
(CFA Francs)	1975	747890	82	13	17	0	19	33
	1980	2044294	76	10	23	2	18	33
	1985	4672835	70	13	23	0	18	27
	1990	3896040	77	11	15	-0	18	21
	1995	4465080	68	12	13	-0	24	18
	1996	4793080	68	12	13	-0	25	17
	1997	5370580	70	12	13	0	24	19
	1998	5744000	71	12	14	-0	24	20
	1999	6008400	64	9	17	...	22	17
	2000	6602500	61	9	15	...	27	15
	2001	6577194	65	9	16	...	25	16
	2002	7031810	65	9	16	...	24	15
	2003	7473689	64	9	15	...	24	15
Cape Verde	1970	1844	83	13	43	-0	9	49
(Escudos)	1975	3009	119	18	43	-4	6	87
	1980	5715	93	15	39	3	17	67
	1985	12625	88	24	47	-2	23	79
	1990	21573	89	19	41	3	17	69
	1995	37705	86	23	39	2	17	66
	1996	41476	110	20	16	1	19	62
	1997	47158	103	20	18	1	22	63
	1998	52867	100	18	23	1	19	60
	1999	60400	107	20	22	1	19	66
	2000	64700	95	25	32	0	18	70
	2001	69000	105	19	29	1	18	70
	2002	73780	96	21	19	0	22	58
	2003	79889	97	19	19	0	22	58
Central African Republic	1970	41341	72	20	18	...	32	42
(CFA Francs)	1975	86470	88	17	14	...	21	40
	1980	149718	94	15	7	0	25	41
	1985	337755	79	15	12	3	22	32
	1990	353000	88	14	11	...	17	30
	1995	531738	84	13	13	...	14	24
	2000	646020	92	4	10	...	13	16
	2003	730710	89	4	9	...	13	15
Chad	1970	114202	85	11	10	1	23	30
(CFA Francs)	1975	187481	90	9	17	1	17	34
	1980	193869	86	10	16	1	22	35
	1985	412267	92	17	12	-1	16	36
	1990	419083	96	21	11	-1	18	46
	1995	720000	87	16	11	-1	23	37
	2000	928000	91	18	16	2	18	45
	2003	1449832	81	16	35	3	18	53
Comoros	1970	5424	83	18	24	1	18	42
(Comoro Francs)	1975	12832	99	17	22	1	11	46
	1980	28628	75	28	23	6	11	43
	1985	51700	73	28	28	4	17	50
	1990	68074	80	26	12	8	12	37
	1995	80343	80	21	18	3	17	39
	2000	98694	82	18	16	...	21	38
	2002	117180	82	20	17	1	20	40
Congo	1970	72453	62	21	26	4	30	42
(CFA Francs)	1975	146458	58	24	25	3	38	48
	1980	360397	41	18	33	3	56	51
	1985	970850	41	16	29	2	57	45
	1990	762000	51	19	17	-1	49	34
	1995	1056200	47	17	13	0	48	26
	2000	2292500	33	10	19	2	80	44
	2003	2271591	38	15	24	1	78	56

Table 2. Gross Domestic Product by Type of Expenditure: Individual Countries or Areas

Major area, region and country	Year	Gross Domestic Product (at current prices) Million	Household final consumption expenditure 1	General government final consumption expenditure 2	Gross fixed capital formation 3	Changes in inventories 4	Exports of goods and services 5	Imports of goods and services 6
			Percentage Distribution					
Cote d'Ivoire	1970	414862	59	16	20	2	37	34
(CFA Francs)	1975	834545	62	17	22	0	38	39
	1980	2149886	65	17	24	2	36	44
	1985	3134800	59	14	12	1	47	32
	1990	3238000	69	21	8	-2	29	25
	1995	5543000	64	17	12	2	37	32
	1996	6209810	65	16	14	-3	41	33
	1997	6841856	63	15	14	-0	43	35
	1998	7457508	65	14	14	1	41	35
	1999	7734000	63	15	15	-1	40	31
	2000	7605000	67	16	12	-1	40	34
	2001	7869500	67	14	10	1	40	29
	2002	8166900	65	16	10	-1	42	32
Democratic Republic of the Congo	1970	0.003 (u)	44	28	22	4	44	43
(Congo Francs)	1975	0.006 (u)	63	24	29	3	27	46
	1980	0.14 (u)	61	16	20	5	36	37
	1985	1.2 (u)	48	12	22	8	72	61
	1990	22.4 (u)	55	18	22	...	59	55
	1995	396	80	5	9	...	29	24
	2000	297066	82	8	10	1	7	7
	2003	2298000	...	...	...	...	0	0
Djibouti	1970	14155	65	21	14	...	53	54
(Djibouti Francs)	1975	27847	66	24	16	...	46	54
	1980	53527	64	34	13	1	39	51
	1985	62303	70	44	24	...	51	89
	1990	81203	67	34	27	-0	81	109
	1995	90572	63	35	19	-0	39	56
	1996	88233	65	34	19	-1	40	57
	1997	87289	59	35	21	0	42	58
	1998	88461	67	29	23	0	43	63
	1999	95275	79	26	9	...	47	61
	2000	98267	80	25	13	...	45	63
	2001	101932	80	25	10	...	45	60
	2002	105274	73	28	15	0	44	61
	2003	110606	76	27	14	0	45	61
Egypt [2]	1970	2971	68	24	11	2	13	18
(Egyptian Pounds)	1975	5247	59	26	24	9	18	36
	1980	17149	65	17	30	1	31	43
	1985	40820	73	17	32	2	20	32
	1990	110143	76	10	22	-1	28	36
	1995	229400	77	10	16	1	21	27
	1996	265900	68	10	18	-0	19	25
	1997	287400	69	10	20	0	16	26
	1998	307600	68	10	19	1	15	23
	1999	340100	68	10	18	1	16	23
	2000	358700	68	10	17	1	17	22
	2001	381700	68	10	16	0	18	23
	2002	415000	73	13	16	1	22	24
Equatorial Guinea	1970	13780	71	35	19	...	32	58
(CFA Francs)	1975	12306	71	35	19	...	32	57
	1980	11908	73	36	19	...	31	60
	1985	38067	80	16	12	-5	27	31
	1990	44349	80	40	17	...	32	70
	1995	81600	56	16	76	...	55	104
	2000	891900	19	7	38	...	95	58
	2003	1698890	16	6	20	...	86	36
Eritrea	1995	3726	90	46	28	...	24	88
(Nafka)	2000	6200	75	54	36	...	16	80
	2002	9031	79	48	38	...	19	83
Ethiopia	1995	33885	82	11	16	...	14	24
(Birr)	1996	37938	82	11	19	...	13	26
	1997	41465	79	11	19	-2	16	23

Table 2. Gross Domestic Product by Type of Expenditure: Individual Countries or Areas

Major area, region and country	Year	Gross Domestic Product (at current prices) Million	Household final consumption expenditure 1	General government final consumption expenditure 2	Gross fixed capital formation 3	Changes in inventories 4	Exports of goods and services 5	Imports of goods and services 6
			Percentage Distribution					
	1998	44896	78	14	19	-1	16	26
	1999	48949	81	16	21	-3	15	30
	2000	49459	79	23	13	-1	16	31
	2001	51180	81	18	17	-1	15	31
	2002	50982	77	20	18	...	15	28
	2003	55346	77	20	18	...	15	30
Gabon.. (CFA Francs)	1970	93100	40	19	28	2	48	37
	1975	462441	24	12	56	7	50	48
	1980	904500	26	13	28	...	65	32
	1985	1645800	30	19	37	...	57	43
	1990	1477400	50	13	21	0	46	31
	1995	2475200	42	14	22	1	59	37
	2000	3576883	36	9	21	...	66	33
	2003	3208524	42	10	23	...	60	34
Gambia [3].. (Dalasis)	1970	97	58	27	35	...	32	44
	1975	278	71	13	30	...	28	52
	1980	412	84	21	47	...	23	71
	1985	1073	73	15	16	...	44	47
	1990	2627	82	14	18	...	43	58
	1995	3508	88	11	20	...	45	64
	2000	5389	84	13	17	...	48	62
	2003	8790	83	13	18	-0	51	65
Ghana [4]... (Cedis)	1970	2259	74	13	12	2	23	24
	1975	5283	73	13	12	1	19	18
	1980	42854	84	11	6	-0	8	9
	1985	343048	83	9	10	0	10	12
	1990	2031700	85	11	12	0	15	24
	1995	7752600	76	12	21	-1	24	33
	1996	11339200	76	12	21	1	25	35
	1997	14113400	80	10	23	1	24	38
	1998	17296000	78	10	22	1	27	38
	1999	20002100	79	10	23	1	24	37
	2000	27153000	76	11	25	1	36	50
	2001	38014000	73	11	24	2	39	51
	2002	48789123	82	12	22	1	44	61
	2003	64337885	82	12	21	1	44	61
Guinea.. (French Francs)	1970	17742	73	11	16	...	29	29
	1975	25991	73	11	16	...	29	29
	1980	36837	73	11	16	...	29	29
	1985	61031	73	11	16	...	29	29
	1990	1860450	70	12	18	...	31	31
	1995	3696760	78	7	21	...	19	25
	2000	5351500	79	4	21	1	0	0
	2002	6350000	76	7	22	0	24	30
Guinea-Bissau... (CFA Francs)	1970	41	77	20	30	...	4	30
	1975	65	82	23	15	...	5	26
	1980	123	73	28	28	...	13	42
	1985	608	95	18	35	...	10	58
	1990	7848	87	10	30	...	10	37
	1995	68045	95	6	8	14	12	35
	2000	159900	95	14	18	...	32	58
	2003	180746	95	13	16	...	28	53
Kenya.. (Kenyan Pounds)	1970	606	61	16	19	5	28	29
	1975	1194	68	18	20	-2	30	35
	1980	2629	61	20	24	6	29	40
	1985	5042	58	17	18	8	25	26
	1990	9777	62	19	21	4	26	31
	1995	23264	69	15	21	0	33	39
	1996	26436	68	16	20	1	33	37
	1997	31168	73	16	18	1	28	35
	1998	34606	74	16	16	1	25	33
	1999	37107	73	17	15	1	26	31

Table 2. Gross Domestic Product by Type of Expenditure: Individual Countries or Areas

Major area, region and country	Year	Gross Domestic Product (at current prices) Million	Household final consumption expenditure 1	General government final consumption expenditure 2	Gross fixed capital formation 3	Changes in inventories 4	Exports of goods and services 5	Imports of goods and services 6
			Percentage Distribution					
	2000	39817	77	17	15	1	27	36
	2001	44136	78	19	14	1	27	38
	2002	48468	72	19	13	0	27	31
Lesotho........	1970	52	119	8	9	-0	11	45
(Loti)	1975	110	164	15	19	-1	14	105
	1980	296	138	24	32	1	23	124
	1985	568	160	23	39	-1	14	141
	1990	1600	132	14	53	-0	17	122
	1995	3384	111	18	61	-1	21	120
	1996	4054	111	16	58	0	24	118
	1997	4720	105	17	55	-1	27	112
	1998	4921	102	21	49	-2	27	107
	1999	5565	91	21	48	1	24	95
	2000	5986	91	20	44	-2	30	92
	2001	6478	93	18	43	-3	39	100
	2002	7323	91	20	36	-1	46	110
Liberia [5]........	1970	277	47	13	22	-2	77	59
(Liberian Dollars)	1975	544	42	12	26	9	66	61
	1980	818	47	20	21	5	67	67
	1985	942	67	13	12	1	45	31
	1990	384	70	13	10	0	34	28
	1995	135	70	13	10	0	36	29
	2000	542	70	13	10	0	33	27
	2002	562	70	13	10	0	33	27
Libyan Arab Jamahiriya........	1970	1426	33	18	17	0	61	28
(Lybian Dinars)	1975	3780	32	28	28	3	54	44
	1980	10575	27	22	23	1	62	35
	1985	8277	38	32	20	0	37	27
	1990	8010	33	26	21	...	50	30
	1995	10679	56	21	12	0	28	22
	2000	17395	46	21	13	0	36	15
	2002	24309	57	17	14	0	48	36
Madagascar [6]........	1970	249400	67	18	16	...	23	24
(Malagasy Francs)	1975	395200	76	15	13	...	19	23
	1980	689800	76	17	23	1	14	31
	1985	1553400	78	13	14	...	14	20
	1990	4601600	86	8	17	...	16	27
	1995	13458000	90	7	11	...	24	31
	2000	26242000	83	9	15	...	31	38
	2003	34270819	83	9	14	...	24	31
Malawi [7]........	1970	267	71	15	23	3	23	35
(Kwacha)	1975	530	69	14	25	9	29	46
	1980	1005	72	19	22	...	25	39
	1985	1929	74	18	13	...	24	30
	1990	4782	92	16	17	...	25	36
	1995	21376	75	19	15	3	34	45
	1996	35359	84	13	10	3	24	33
	1997	42634	88	12	10	2	22	35
	1998	54308	80	12	11	2	33	38
	1999	79060	88	12	12	2	28	43
	2000	103799	85	12	12	1	26	36
	2001	123525	82	14	13	1	28	38
	2002	154564	80	25	9	1	24	41
Mali [8]........	1970	76300	71	11	13	4	19	19
(CFA Francs)	1975	129500	77	10	17	2	17	27
	1980	300600	82	10	16	1	18	30
	1985	520200	84	20	19	-2	19	39
	1990	683300	79	15	20	2	17	34
	1995	1152970	78	14	23	...	21	36
	2000	1739500	75	16	21	...	27	40
	2003	2251625	70	16	21	...	27	34

Table 2. Gross Domestic Product by Type of Expenditure: Individual Countries or Areas

Major area, region and country	Year	Gross Domestic Product (at current prices) Million	Household final consumption expenditure 1	General government final consumption expenditure 2	Gross fixed capital formation 3	Changes in inventories 4	Exports of goods and services 5	Imports of goods and services 6
			Percentage Distribution					
Mauritania (Ouguiyas)	1970	11330	53	16	21	2	42	34
	1975	20595	57	25	34	10	39	64
	1980	38070	74	24	20	6	30	56
	1985	52665	67	22	29	4	59	81
	1990	82350	68	19	18	0	58	60
	1995	137340	60	17	14	0	59	59
	2000	215010	74	20	13	3	42	52
	2002	263017	72	20	14	3	43	51
Mauritius (Rupees)	1970	1067	69	16	14	...	50	48
	1975	3416	55	13	33	...	66	65
	1980	8805	75	15	23	-2	51	61
	1985	16825	66	12	18	5	53	55
	1990	38462	65	13	31	-1	67	74
	1995	70283	64	13	24	2	59	61
	1996	79086	63	13	26	-1	64	64
	1997	88099	62	13	27	3	62	66
	1998	99564	63	13	23	2	66	67
	1999	107444	64	13	28	-1	64	68
	2000	119529	62	13	23	2	62	62
	2001	131835	61	13	22	-1	69	63
	2002	141408	62	13	22	-0	62	59
	2003	156533	62	13	23	1	57	55
Morocco (Dirhams)	1970	20020	73	12	15	4	18	21
	1975	36410	68	16	25	1	23	33
	1980	74090	67	18	22	2	18	27
	1985	129510	65	16	23	4	25	33
	1990	212850	65	15	24	1	25	30
	1995	282467	68	18	21	-1	23	30
	1996	319390	67	17	19	0	22	26
	1997	318342	65	18	21	0	23	27
	1998	344005	64	18	22	0	23	27
	1999	345594	62	19	24	-1	24	29
	2000	354208	64	19	24	-0	26	33
	2001	383185	61	20	22	1	28	31
	2002	397782	60	20	23	-0	29	32
	2003	428013	62	19	23	-0	26	30
Mozambique (Meticais)	1970	79532	95	11	8	2	5	24
	1975	112329	95	11	8	2	5	24
	1980	142600	90	10	9	2	7	23
	1985	268746	95	9	4	-0	2	8
	1990	2515606	102	12	20	-0	6	38
	1995	20678102	99	10	27	4	13	52
	1996	32718600	93	8	20	2	12	36
	1997	39819429	89	9	21	-0	11	31
	1998	46911782	82	10	18	6	10	28
	1999	51913228	78	12	20	17	10	38
	2000	56917388	78	14	51	-17	13	39
	2001	71134761	73	15	22	4	22	35
	2002	82747356	74	20	21	...	24	39
Namibia [9] (Namibia Dollars)	1970	362	60	26	26	1	64	83
	1975	696	59	25	26	1	65	82
	1980	1574	45	19	29	2	75	76
	1985	2735	50	32	16	-4	62	60
	1990	6054	47	31	21	13	52	68
	1995	12706	53	30	22	-0	49	56
	1996	15011	54	30	24	-0	51	59
	1997	16754	57	30	20	1	48	58
	1998	18790	56	30	23	3	46	58
	1999	20681	56	30	23	0	46	57
	2000	23995	56	28	19	1	45	51
	2001	27231	58	28	22	2	44	54
	2002	30364	54	26	20	-1	44	48

Table 2. Gross Domestic Product by Type of Expenditure: Individual Countries or Areas

Major area, region and country	Year	Gross Domestic Product (at current prices) Million	Household final consumption expenditure 1	General government final consumption expenditure 2	Gross fixed capital formation 3	Changes in inventories 4	Exports of goods and services 5	Imports of goods and services 6
			Percentage Distribution					
Niger (CFA Francs)	1970	111000	85	12	7	3	15	22
	1975	180300	77	13	20	3	19	33
	1980	536208	71	10	25	6	24	37
	1985	647100	79	15	14	1	21	30
	1990	682300	74	17	12	1	17	21
	1995	834600	78	16	12	3	20	28
	2000	1280400	82	12	12	1	16	23
	2003	1582752	85	12	10	1	17	25
Nigeria (Naira)	1970	7381	67	11	18	-1	13	10
	1975	22722	62	12	20	-0	24	18
	1980	50346	58	12	20	-1	30	20
	1985	72355	75	10	8	-1	17	9
	1990	260637	60	4	12	0	43	19
	1995	1977737	76	7	16	0	44	44
	2000	4296276	44	20	22	...	51	40
	2002	5292589	52	25	21	...	41	40
Reunion (Euros)	1970	307	71	33	28	-2	14	45
	1975	692	75	34	21	3	6	39
	1980	1288	84	33	21	2	7	47
	1985	2600	85	33	22	-3	6	45
	1990	4326	80	28	29	-0	4	41
	1995	5646	80	28	28	...	4	39
	2000	7070	80	28	28	...	3	39
	2002	8591	80	28	28	...	3	39
Rwanda (Francs)	1970	23768	82	8	9	1	9	11
	1975	58174	80	10	15	2	7	13
	1980	119048	83	7	14	6	11	19
	1985	191487	80	7	17	4	8	15
	1990	212653	84	10	14	...	6	14
	1995	336489	101	9	14	...	6	29
	1996	426175	96	10	14	...	6	27
	1997	563416	95	9	14	...	8	25
	1998	627342	92	9	15	...	6	21
	1999	633299	90	10	18	...	6	23
	2000	681455	90	9	18	...	6	23
	2001	732276	90	10	17	...	9	26
	2002	784000	92	10	18	...	7	25
Sao Tome and Principe (Dobras)	1970	614	64	33	23	...	43	59
	1975	881	78	24	25	...	34	62
	1980	1629	84	34	31	...	25	75
	1985	2319	76	47	34	...	30	86
	1990	8250	80	38	36	...	23	72
	1995	64613	80	28	41	...	24	73
	2000	369500	75	28	43	...	35	82
	2002	491000	80	25	44	...	38	83
Senegal (CFA Francs)	1970	241668	78	13	10	-1	24	26
	1975	409054	76	14	11	-1	33	34
	1980	631400	83	20	13	-2	28	42
	1985	1158200	85	17	11	-2	30	41
	1990	1551500	76	15	13	1	25	30
	1995	2234000	79	12	15	2	32	40
	1996	2380000	79	12	16	2	31	40
	1997	2554300	77	12	16	2	29	36
	1998	2746000	76	12	18	2	30	37
	1999	2925000	74	13	20	1	30	38
	2000	3114000	73	14	17	6	30	40
	2001	3379600	75	16	18	-0	29	38
	2002	3511700	75	15	21	-1	29	37
Seychelles [10] (Rupees)	1970	110	81	14	42	-3	56	90
	1975	292	65	22	37	2	65	90
	1980	942	55	29	37	2	50	72
	1985	1205	58	35	23	...	48	64

Table 2. Gross Domestic Product by Type of Expenditure: Individual Countries or Areas

Major area, region and country	Year	Gross Domestic Product (at current prices) Million	Household final consumption expenditure 1	General government final consumption expenditure 2	Gross fixed capital formation 3	Changes in inventories 4	Exports of goods and services 5	Imports of goods and services 6
			Percentage Distribution					
	1990	1967	52	28	23	2	62	67
	1995	2420	51	28	30	0	-9	...
	1996	2500	42	29	40	-1	-11	...
	1997	2830	50	30	28	4	-11	...
	1998	3201	50	31	34	1	-16	...
	1999	3330	45	28	41	2	-16	...
	2000	3424	39	27	36	0	-3	...
	2001	3419	45	29	36	1	-11	...
	2002	3830	45	29	36	1	-11	...
Sierra Leone [11]	1970	346	77	9	13	2	31	32
(Leones)	1975	573	83	11	13	2	27	37
	1980	1156	91	8	15	1	23	38
	1985	4785	84	7	9	1	10	11
	1990	96133	80	8	9	0	26	24
	1995	657604	82	10	6	-0	31	20
	2000	1330433	86	10	6	0	17	20
	2002	2068668	85	10	6	-0	19	20
Somalia [12]	1970	2436	97	8	7	2	8	19
(Shillings)	1975	4765	97	16	11	3	10	35
	1980	17341	89	14	10	-1	5	17
	1985	87290	90	11	9	3	4	17
	1990	1738800	71	10	23	1	1	6
	1995	6424840	72	8	21	0	0	2
	2000	19641182	72	9	20	0	0	2
	2002	24414329	72	9	20	0	0	2
South Africa	1970	13045	64	13	24	4	21	24
(Rand)	1975	27868	60	14	29	3	27	29
	1980	64141	53	14	26	5	35	27
	1985	128773	56	18	23	-3	31	22
	1990	289816	63	20	19	-2	25	19
	1995	548100	63	18	16	2	23	22
	1996	617954	62	19	16	1	25	23
	1997	685730	63	19	17	0	25	23
	1998	738926	63	19	17	-0	26	25
	1999	800769	63	19	15	0	26	23
	2000	888454	63	19	15	1	29	26
	2001	983450	62	19	15	0	31	27
	2002	1120895	62	19	15	1	33	30
	2003	1209495	61	19	15	1	27	26
Sudan	1970	67	69	21	10	2	16	18
(Dinars)	1975	168	82	14	14	3	11	25
	1980	449	76	13	20	6	10	25
	1985	1703	76	13	20	6	10	25
	1990	15139	76	13	20	6	10	25
	1995	810318	78	6	20	-1	3	7
	1996	1033070	82	7	12	10	8	19
	1997	1592931	90	6	13	6	11	20
	1998	1991613	92	4	18	...	6	20
	1999	2448876	86	5	17	...	8	16
	2000	2969452	75	6	18	...	17	16
	2001	3380555	75	7	18	...	15	15
	2002	3559000	83	6	18	...	11	17
Swaziland [13]	1970	78	65	14	22	3	70	74
(Lilangeni)	1975	216	63	17	19	-1	70	67
	1980	460	96	19	25	5	66	109
	1985	813	103	23	24	2	54	99
	1990	2253	79	18	19	1	73	89
	1995	4949	79	19	19	1	75	93
	1996	5686	84	21	20	1	72	98
	1997	6613	72	25	20	1	76	93
	1998	7449	73	24	22	...	79	99
	1999	8408	74	22	19	...	73	88

Table 2. Gross Domestic Product by Type of Expenditure: Individual Countries or Areas

Major area, region and country	Year	Gross Domestic Product (at current prices) Million	Household final consumption expenditure 1	General government final consumption expenditure 2	Gross fixed capital formation 3	Changes in inventories 4	Exports of goods and services 5	Imports of goods and services 6
			Percentage Distribution					
	2000	9639	75	20	20	...	64	79
	2001	10971	77	18	18	...	70	83
	2002	12287	76	19	20	...	69	83
Togo (CFA Francs)	1970	73171	77	10	13	2	30	31
	1975	128302	75	15	23	6	28	46
	1980	238872	66	15	29	7	38	55
	1985	338200	66	14	23	5	42	51
	1990	427600	70	13	22	0	23	28
	1995	652500	86	12	15	2	36	51
	2000	946100	85	11	21	...	33	49
	2002	1031100	84	11	19	-1	32	45
Tunisia (Dinars)	1970	756	66	17	21	1	22	26
	1975	1741	62	15	26	2	31	36
	1980	3541	62	14	28	1	41	46
	1985	7018	59	17	28	2	32	38
	1990	10816	64	16	24	3	44	51
	1995	17052	63	16	24	1	45	49
	1996	19066	61	16	23	2	42	44
	1997	20898	60	16	25	2	44	46
	1998	22561	61	16	25	2	43	46
	1999	24672	60	16	25	1	43	45
	2000	26651	61	16	26	1	45	48
	2001	28729	61	16	26	2	48	52
	2002	29879	63	16	25	0	45	50
	2003	32447	62	16	25	-0	46	51
Uganda (Shillings)	1970	135	73	10	12	1	22	19
	1975	321	81	14	7	1	8	10
	1980	1851	83	14	2	1	3	6
	1985	26961	74	14	8	0	11	11
	1990	1566257	82	10	15	0	7	18
	1995	5858367	77	12	17	...	11	19
	1996	6409571	80	14	16	...	14	27
	1997	7141605	80	13	16	...	11	20
	1998	7844329	79	13	18	...	11	23
	1999	8723138	81	13	20	...	12	24
	2000	9431690	81	14	20	...	11	24
	2001	10116389	81	15	21	...	12	27
	2002	10825290	78	16	22	...	12	28
United Republic Of Tanzania (Shillings)	1970	9568	68	13	23	3	23	27
	1975	19829	72	16	21	3	17	30
	1980	42118	77	13	20	3	13	26
	1985	112000	76	15	17	2	7	17
	1990	736338	73	10	38	4	14	39
	1995	3020500	84	15	20	0	24	41
	2000	7277800	83	7	17	0	15	23
	2002	9374559	80	6	19	0	17	22
Zambia (Kwacha)	1970	1185	17	41	25	...	58	40
	1975	1837	24	69	24	...	31	48
	1980	3656	21	64	18	...	35	38
	1985	9351	18	66	16	...	29	29
	1990	123487	14	55	31	...	34	34
	1995	2999000	72	15	12	3	36	40
	1996	3951000	76	18	11	2	31	39
	1997	5141000	73	17	13	2	30	35
	1998	6028600	80	16	15	2	27	39
	1999	7479500	88	13	16	2	22	41
	2000	10074600	82	10	17	1	21	31
	2001	13132693	70	13	19	1	27	30
	2002	16260430	69	13	22	1	24	29
	2003	20377051	67	15	25	1	21	28

Table 2. Gross Domestic Product by Type of Expenditure: Individual Countries or Areas

Major area, region and country	Year	Gross Domestic Product (at current prices) Million	Household final consumption expenditure 1	General government final consumption expenditure 2	Gross fixed capital formation 3	Changes in inventories 4	Exports of goods and services 5	Imports of goods and services 6
			Percentage Distribution					
Zimbabwe	1970	1079	66	12	16	3	25	25
(Zimbabwe Dollars)	1975	1998	60	13	23	4	30	31
	1980	3441	63	20	15	3	30	33
	1985	9097	61	20	14	4	22	22
	1990	21494	63	19	18	-1	23	23
	1995	61759	64	18	25	-5	38	41
	1996	85551	63	17	18	1	36	36
	1997	102982	71	16	18	1	37	44
	1998	143364	63	17	21	0	43	45
	1999	210409	69	15	15	1	46	47
	2000	319998	61	24	12	0	29	27
	2001	498598	72	19	8	0	22	21
	2002	457042	67	22	8	0	24	22
NORTHERN AMERICA								
Bermuda	1970	259	66	9	12	-0	51	41
(Bermudian Dollars)	1975	480	68	10	12	-0	52	42
	1980	919	67	10	18	-0	52	45
	1985	1433	64	12	20	-0	47	41
	1990	1997	68	12	17	-0	48	44
	1995	2544	63	12	14	-0	45	36
	1996	2680	62	12	15	-0	47	37
	1997	2889	61	12	16	0	48	38
	1998	3053	60	11	19	1	47	39
	1999	3272	61	11	19	1	47	39
	2000	3397	60	11	19	1	47	39
	2001	3599	60	11	21	1	47	40
	2002	3719	60	11	21	1	47	40
Canada	1970	88933	55	21	22	0	23	20
(Canadian Dollars)	1975	171163	53	22	25	1	23	24
	1980	310160	52	22	24	-0	28	26
	1985	478829	53	22	20	1	28	26
	1990	669967	55	23	22	-0	26	26
	1995	798300	55	22	18	1	38	35
	1996	824041	56	21	18	0	39	35
	1997	868979	56	20	20	1	40	38
	1998	900350	56	20	20	1	42	40
	1999	967511	55	19	20	1	44	40
	2000	1060058	54	19	20	1	46	40
	2001	1091424	55	19	20	-0	44	38
	2002	1137511	55	19	20	0	42	37
United States [14]	1970	1025500	63	18	18	0	6	5
(Dollars)	1975	1617800	64	18	18	-0	9	8
	1980	2771500	64	17	20	-0	10	11
	1985	4174900	65	18	20	1	7	10
	1990	5750800	67	17	17	0	10	11
	1995	7338400	68	15	18	0	11	12
	1996	7751100	68	15	18	0	11	12
	1997	8256500	67	15	19	1	12	13
	1998	8720200	67	14	19	1	11	13
	1999	9212800	68	14	20	1	11	13
	2000	9762100	68	15	20	1	11	15
	2001	10019700	70	15	19	-1	10	14
	2002	10383100	70	16	18	0	10	14
	2003	10857200	70	16	18	-0	10	14
LATIN AMERICA and the CARIBBEAN								
Anguilla	1970	6	50	15	43	...	65	73
(EC Dollars)	1975	12	50	15	43	...	65	73
	1980	24	50	15	43	...	65	73
	1985	52	46	15	44	...	69	72
	1990	147	52	13	41	...	76	80
	1995	202	77	18	29	...	76	100
	1996	214	80	18	29	...	74	102
	1997	240	74	18	25	...	76	94
	1998	255	70	14	35	...	88	107
	1999	280	86	15	44	...	69	115
	2000	288	88	20	44	...	65	116

Table 2. Gross Domestic Product by Type of Expenditure: Individual Countries or Areas

Major area, region and country	Year	Gross Domestic Product (at current prices) Million	Household final consumption expenditure 1	General government final consumption expenditure 2	Gross fixed capital formation 3	Changes in inventories 4	Exports of goods and services 5	Imports of goods and services 6
			Percentage Distribution					
	2001	291	80	20	30	...	69	99
	2002	301	87	20	20	...	63	90
	2003	315	82	18	35	...	71	105
Antigua and Barbuda (EC Dollars)	1970	98	58	18	21	...	66	62
	1975	152	58	18	21	...	66	62
	1980	297	69	19	31	...	67	87
	1985	541	70	18	28	-1	74	94
	1990	902	42	19	37	-3	83	83
	1995	1176	43	22	41	-3	74	83
	2000	1603	30	23	53	-4	61	67
	2003	1781	30	25	52	...	61	69
Argentina (Pesos)	1970	1.2 (u)	65	10	25	...	7	8
	1975	19.2 (u)	58	13	30	...	6	7
	1980	3800 (u)	63	13	26	...	5	8
	1985	5	65	11	18	...	12	6
	1990	68922	68	12	14	...	10	5
	1995	258032	69	13	18	...	10	10
	1996	272150	69	13	18	...	10	11
	1997	292859	69	12	19	...	11	13
	1998	298948	69	12	20	...	10	13
	1999	283522	70	14	18	...	10	12
	2000	284204	69	14	16	...	11	12
	2001	268697	69	14	14	...	11	10
	2002	312580	62	12	12	...	28	13
	2003	376232	63	11	15	...	25	14
Aruba (Aruban Florin)	1970	685	31	4	45	-10	78	44
	1975	888	34	5	41	-7	79	50
	1980	1151	38	7	37	-5	79	55
	1985	1492	42	10	34	-3	80	62
	1990	1934	46	13	31	-1	80	69
	1995	2364	50	20	28	3	85	86
	1996	2470	53	20	26	2	87	89
	1997	2742	50	24	28	2	83	86
	1998	2981	50	22	29	3	80	84
	1999	3087	52	22	27	2	81	84
	2000	3326	50	20	24	1	75	70
	2001	3381	53	23	20	1	72	69
	2002	3403	55	25	20	1	69	71
	2003	3580	56	25	24	1	65	71
Bahamas (Bahamian Dollars)	1970	502	61	9	0	3	32	1
	1975	723	60	9	2	4	39	10
	1980	1438	75	12	15	0	62	57
	1985	2171	51	13	10	8	50	26
	1990	3047	67	14	21	0	56	53
	1995	3069	68	16	23	0	55	59
	1996	3277	67	16	23	0	54	60
	1997	3451	67	17	23	1	54	61
	1998	3670	67	17	23	1	53	62
	1999	4005	67	17	23	1	53	63
	2000	4309	67	18	23	1	52	64
	2001	4307	66	18	23	1	52	65
	2002	4430	67	17	23	1	53	63
Barbados (Barbados Dollars)	1970	370	81	20	25	...	49	75
	1975	812	74	17	19	1	50	60
	1980	1730	62	15	23	2	70	72
	1985	2410	58	19	15	0	68	60
	1990	3440	64	20	19	-0	49	52
	1995	3742	62	20	15	1	58	55
	1996	3995	59	21	16	-1	60	55
	1997	4413	63	21	18	0	55	57
	1998	4747	63	21	18	0	53	55
	1999	4965	65	21	19	1	51	57
	2000	5183	67	21	18	0	50	56
	2001	5093	65	22	16	-0	51	54
	2002	5149	66	23	17	-0	48	53

Table 2. Gross Domestic Product by Type of Expenditure: Individual Countries or Areas

Major area, region and country	Year	Gross Domestic Product (at current prices) Million	Household final consumption expenditure 1	General government final consumption expenditure 2	Gross fixed capital formation 3	Changes in inventories 4	Exports of goods and services 5	Imports of goods and services 6
			Percentage Distribution					
Belize	1970	77	68	14	24	3	70	78
(Belize Dollars)	1975	189	66	11	28	4	51	57
	1980	389	77	15	23	1	35	46
	1985	418	56	21	17	4	60	60
	1990	811	60	14	26	0	60	61
	1995	1173	65	16	23	-1	51	54
	1996	1207	63	16	22	0	51	53
	1997	1231	66	17	22	2	54	61
	1998	1258	67	17	21	3	53	62
	1999	1377	65	17	26	3	51	63
	2000	1514	68	15	31	3	49	67
	2001	1577	68	16	30	...	46	63
	2002	1640	69	16	33	...	46	66
Bolivia	1970	12 (t)	75	8	17	...	25	25
(Bolivianos)	1975	48 (t)	73	10	19	4	25	33
	1980	123 (t)	67	13	15	1	26	20
	1985	2867	63	8	12	5	29	17
	1990	15443	77	12	13	-0	23	24
	1995	32235	76	14	16	-0	23	27
	1996	37537	75	13	16	0	23	27
	1997	41644	75	14	19	1	21	29
	1998	46822	75	14	23	0	20	33
	1999	48156	77	15	19	-0	17	27
	2000	51884	77	15	18	0	18	27
	2001	53010	76	15	15	-0	20	26
	2002	55933	75	15	16	-1	22	27
Brazil	1970	0.1 (u)	61	9	24	2	6	6
(Reais)	1975	0.6 (u)	61	8	29	3	7	10
	1980	4.7 (u)	50	21	29	3	4	6
	1985	448 (u)	70	11	18	-0	13	8
	1990	11	58	17	23	-0	8	6
	1995	646192	60	20	21	2	8	9
	1996	778887	63	18	19	2	7	9
	1997	870743	63	18	20	2	8	10
	1998	914188	62	19	20	1	7	10
	1999	973846	62	19	19	1	10	12
	2000	1101255	61	19	19	2	11	12
	2001	1198736	61	19	19	2	13	14
	2002	1346028	58	20	18	1	15	13
British Virgin Islands	1970	16	69	8	48	13	21	60
(US Dollars)	1975	21	70	8	26	14	40	58
	1980	44	53	10	28	11	62	63
	1985	72	53	14	28	2	89	86
	1990	240	49	14	25	1	95	84
	1995	385	49	14	25	1	95	84
	2000	691	42	11	26	...	108	83
	2002	870	40	11	25	...	106	79
Cayman Islands	1970	16	72	12	24	...	52	64
(Dollars)	1975	45	71	13	23	1	57	65
	1980	110	68	15	25	-1	69	76
	1985	264	63	16	20	0	70	70
	1990	590	63	14	21	-0	64	58
	1995	849	65	15	22	-0	63	59
	2000	1131	67	15	23	-0	65	61
	2002	1270	68	16	23	-0	66	62
Chile	1970	105	67	16	18	-1	15	14
(Pesos)	1975	37891	69	19	21	-7	25	27
	1980	1149700	68	15	19	2	22	27
	1985	2930460	65	14	18	-0	27	24
	1990	10216526	60	10	25	1	33	29
	1995	28593362	61	11	25	1	29	27
	1996	31237289	63	11	26	1	27	29
	1997	34722636	63	11	27	1	27	29
	1998	36534873	64	11	26	1	26	30
	1999	37138542	64	12	21	0	30	27
	2000	40393464	63	12	21	1	32	30
	2001	43343584	63	13	21	1	34	32
	2002	45762505	63	13	21	1	34	32

Table 2. Gross Domestic Product by Type of Expenditure: Individual Countries or Areas

Major area, region and country	Year	Gross Domestic Product (at current prices) Million	Household final consumption expenditure 1	General government final consumption expenditure 2	Gross fixed capital formation 3	Changes in inventories 4	Exports of goods and services 5	Imports of goods and services 6
			Percentage Distribution					
Colombia [15] (Pesos)	1970	157666	70	10	22	2	12	16
	1975	480111	71	10	19	2	15	15
	1980	1871842	68	11	21	2	15	16
	1985	5886995	68	12	22	1	12	13
	1990	23979488	64	11	20	2	19	16
	1995	84439109	66	15	22	3	15	21
	1996	100711389	65	18	22	1	15	21
	1997	121707501	65	20	20	1	15	21
	1998	140483322	66	20	19	1	15	21
	1999	151565005	64	22	13	-0	18	18
	2000	174896258	63	21	13	1	22	19
	2001	187935734	65	20	14	1	21	22
	2002	203141712	65	21	15	...	20	21
Costa Rica (Colones)	1970	8291	87	10	18	-3	24	33
	1975	21352	86	12	20	-4	26	36
	1980	52610	80	15	22	-3	23	35
	1985	251474	73	13	17	1	27	31
	1990	664322	75	15	20	-1	30	39
	1995	2105687	71	14	19	-1	38	40
	1996	2459957	74	13	17	-1	39	43
	1997	2984020	73	13	18	0	41	45
	1998	3625330	69	13	20	0	47	50
	1999	4512763	65	13	18	-1	52	46
	2000	4914498	67	13	18	-1	49	46
	2001	5391466	68	14	18	2	41	44
	2002	6051467	68	15	19	3	42	48
	2003	6969245	67	15	20	0	46	48
Cuba (Cuban Pesos)	1970	5192	54	32	13	2	15	20
	1975	9742	45	27	18	8	27	28
	1980	13075	53	32	19	5	33	38
	1985	19145	52	31	25	3	34	45
	1990	19645	54	31	25	0	30	41
	1995	21737	71	24	8	-1	13	16
	1996	22815	71	24	10	-3	16	18
	1997	22952	72	24	10	-2	16	19
	1998	23901	72	24	10	-2	15	18
	1999	25504	71	23	10	-2	16	19
	2000	27635	69	23	11	-1	16	18
	2001	28806	68	26	9	-1	15	17
	2002	29239	41	35	11	...	31	16
	2003	31216	41	35	11	...	35	18
Dominica (EC Dollars)	1970	55	84	25	27	...	37	73
	1975	73	73	23	24	...	43	63
	1980	160	92	27	46	4	22	93
	1985	266	72	22	28	...	37	60
	1990	452	64	20	40	1	50	75
	1995	592	64	21	32	...	51	67
	1996	638	61	20	29	...	52	62
	1997	662	62	22	31	...	56	71
	1998	701	59	22	27	...	58	66
	1999	723	61	22	28	...	59	67
	2000	732	63	22	27	...	53	67
	2001	713	66	22	25	...	46	63
	2002	685	70	21	22	...	46	59
Dominican Republic [16] (Pesos)	1970	1784	78	9	15	5	29	39
	1975	4323	70	5	21	5	47	44
	1980	7964	78	6	22	4	32	46
	1985	16782	78	6	18	3	49	55
	1990	77911	79	3	19	2	44	47
	1995	209646	79	4	16	3	34	37
	1996	232993	81	5	17	4	18	25
	1997	273559	77	8	20	0	47	52
	1998	308079	77	8	23	0	47	56
	1999	354744	75	8	24	0	46	53
	2000	411783	78	8	24	0	45	55
	2001	466243	76	9	23	0	39	46
	2002	511667	77	10	22	0	38	47
	2003	649274	70	9	23	0	52	54

Table 2. Gross Domestic Product by Type of Expenditure: Individual Countries or Areas

Major area, region and country	Year	Gross Domestic Product (at current prices) Million	Household final consumption expenditure 1	General government final consumption expenditure 2	Gross fixed capital formation 3	Changes in inventories 4	Exports of goods and services 5	Imports of goods and services 6
			Percentage Distribution					
Ecuador (US Dollars)	1970	1762	73	17	16	2	13	19
	1975	4536	62	21	22	4	25	34
	1980	12351	56	21	23	3	24	27
	1985	16797	62	17	15	2	26	22
	1990	11248	67	13	18	-1	31	29
	1995	20196	68	13	19	3	26	28
	1996	21268	66	12	18	2	26	24
	1997	23636	66	12	18	4	26	26
	1998	23255	69	12	20	5	21	28
	1999	16674	66	13	17	-2	32	25
	2000	15934	64	10	20	-0	37	31
	2001	21024	69	10	22	4	27	31
	2002	24572	69	10	24	6	26	35
El Salvador (Colones)	1970	2571	75	11	12	1	25	25
	1975	4478	73	11	23	-1	33	38
	1980	8917	72	14	14	-0	34	33
	1985	14331	81	15	12	-1	22	30
	1990	36487	89	10	14	0	19	31
	1995	83130	87	9	19	1	22	38
	1996	90261	88	9	16	-1	21	34
	1997	97428	87	9	16	-1	26	38
	1998	105074	85	10	17	1	25	37
	1999	109066	86	10	16	0	25	37
	2000	114924	88	10	17	-0	27	42
	2001	120783	89	10	16	0	26	42
	2002	124984	89	10	16	...	27	41
	2003	131219	90	9	16	...	27	43
French Guiana (Euros)	1970	44	81	53	28	1	3	64
	1975	88	79	51	23	-1	2	55
	1980	186	87	53	40	1	8	90
	1985	484	68	42	38	0	54	102
	1990	995	64	35	48	-0	67	114
	1995	1275	59	37	34	2	63	95
	2000	1429	59	37	32	2	62	91
	2002	1495	59	37	31	...	62	90
Grenada (EC Dollars)	1970	60	76	18	2	3	84	89
	1975	107	83	20	7	6	68	89
	1980	202	85	21	26	4	53	89
	1985	311	77	22	31	-2	48	76
	1990	541	65	20	39	3	44	72
	1995	638	67	17	36	...	44	66
	1996	687	69	17	41	...	43	70
	1997	738	70	17	42	...	42	71
	1998	808	72	17	43	...	46	78
	1999	871	57	15	47	...	56	75
	2000	942	59	15	49	...	56	80
	2001	913	68	18	38	...	49	73
	2002	924	68	19	41	...	44	73
	2003	924	65	17	44	...	50	76
Guadeloupe (Euros)	1970	203	91	27	20	1	16	54
	1975	431	87	28	19	-0	13	47
	1980	893	87	32	25	1	8	53
	1985	1494	95	35	22	0	7	59
	1990	2317	93	31	34	1	5	63
	1995	3378	88	30	31	1	5	56
	2000	4662	92	32	33	1	5	59
	2002	5329	94	32	34	...	6	60
Guatemala (Quetzalas)	1970	1904	78	8	13	0	19	18
	1975	3646	79	7	16	0	22	24
	1980	7879	79	8	16	-1	22	25
	1985	11180	83	7	11	1	18	20
	1990	34317	84	7	13	1	20	24
	1995	85157	86	6	15	1	19	25
	1996	95479	87	5	13	-1	18	23
	1997	107943	87	5	15	-1	18	24
	1998	121548	87	6	16	-0	18	26
	1999	132588	86	7	17	-1	19	27

Table 2. Gross Domestic Product by Type of Expenditure: Individual Countries or Areas

Major area, region and country	Year	Gross Domestic Product (at current prices) Million	Household final consumption expenditure 1	General government final consumption expenditure 2	Gross fixed capital formation 3	Changes in inventories 4	Exports of goods and services 5	Imports of goods and services 6
			Percentage Distribution					
	2000	146755	85	8	15	2	20	29
	2001	161581	86	8	15	2	18	29
	2002	178365	88	8	15	3	16	28
Guyana (Dollars Guyana)	1970	536	60	17	21	2	56	57
	1975	1188	47	20	29	4	75	74
	1980	1508	53	29	27	3	69	81
	1985	1964	54	36	21	...	53	63
	1990	15665	61	14	42	...	68	92
	1995	88271	46	16	45	...	122	130
	1996	99038	45	18	44	...	120	126
	1997	106678	45	20	44	...	116	125
	1998	108002	49	21	41	...	113	125
	1999	123665	44	24	38	...	116	121
	2000	130013	50	28	39	...	113	129
	2001	133403	55	23	39	...	113	130
	2002	142019	49	23	40	...	114	126
Haiti (Gourdes)	1970	1656	85	10	10	...	16	21
	1975	3407	84	9	16	...	23	32
	1980	6919	88	11	18	...	31	48
	1985	10047	83	11	17	...	27	38
	1990	13068	82	7	14	...	18	22
	1995	35265	101	7	14	...	11	33
	1996	42744	98	6	15	...	12	31
	1997	51578	96	7	12	...	11	27
	1998	59055	96	6	13	...	13	29
	1999	66425	96	6	13	...	13	28
	2000	74411	100	6	13	...	14	32
	2001	81201	101	6	12	...	11	28
	2002	87712	132	10	21	...	35	101
Honduras (Lempiras)	1970	1382	73	12	19	2	29	35
	1975	2248	78	12	21	-2	30	40
	1980	5132	69	13	25	0	37	44
	1985	7279	74	13	17	0	25	30
	1990	12537	67	13	20	3	37	40
	1995	37507	64	9	24	8	44	48
	1996	47763	64	10	24	7	47	52
	1997	61322	65	9	26	7	46	52
	1998	70438	67	10	28	3	46	54
	1999	77095	69	11	30	5	41	56
	2000	87523	70	12	27	5	42	56
	2001	96981	72	13	25	6	39	55
	2002	105604	73	13	23	6	38	54
	2003	117929	70	12	27	...	41	55
Jamaica (Jamaican Dollars)	1970	1174	61	12	31	0	33	37
	1975	2618	66	18	23	2	35	45
	1980	4805	66	20	14	1	50	53
	1985	11278	72	16	24	2	60	71
	1990	30682	62	14	27	0	52	56
	1995	200027	63	11	29	0	52	62
	1996	237382	62	13	29	0	45	56
	1997	258026	62	15	30	0	40	53
	1998	273429	61	17	27	0	42	52
	1999	294076	61	16	25	0	42	51
	2000	329171	62	16	27	0	44	56
	2001	358036	63	15	30	0	41	56
	2002	392136	63	16	30	...	40	55
Martinique (Euros)	1970	244	87	31	24	-1	10	51
	1975	512	81	34	18	-1	12	44
	1980	930	90	37	21	3	9	59
	1985	1903	87	34	17	-0	12	49
	1990	2945	84	30	27	2	8	50
	1995	3681	84	29	25	1	7	46
	2000	4464	85	29	25	1	8	49
	2003	5045	85	29	25	1	8	52
Mexico [17] (New Pesos)	1970	495	74	7	20	5	8	11
	1975	1226	70	9	21	4	7	11
	1980	4766	63	10	24	6	13	16

Table 2. Gross Domestic Product by Type of Expenditure: Individual Countries or Areas

Major area, region and country	Year	Gross Domestic Product (at current prices) Million	Household final consumption expenditure 1	General government final consumption expenditure 2	Gross fixed capital formation 3	Changes in inventories 4	Exports of goods and services 5	Imports of goods and services 6
			Percentage Distribution					
	1985	50530	63	9	18	5	18	13
	1990	738898	70	8	18	5	19	20
	1995	1837019	67	10	16	4	30	28
	1996	2525575	65	10	18	5	32	30
	1997	3174275	64	10	20	6	30	30
	1998	3846350	67	10	21	3	31	33
	1999	4593685	66	11	21	2	31	32
	2000	5491373	66	11	21	2	31	33
	2001	5828591	69	12	20	1	27	30
	2002	6151219	69	12	19	1	27	29
	2003	6635793	72	10	19	1	34	37
Montserrat	1970	13	107	23	36	4	33	102
(EC Dollars)	1975	25	107	23	36	4	33	102
	1980	66	109	18	33	8	24	92
	1985	100	86	20	33	2	33	73
	1990	181	62	18	72	2	29	81
	1995	162	62	23	33	2	61	81
	1996	132	13	40	37	2	116	109
	1997	110	42	55	49	0	54	100
	1998	101	52	55	66	0	38	111
	1999	96	34	58	63	0	61	116
	2000	94	70	51	47	0	49	116
	2001	94	88	52	42	...	43	125
	2002	103	92	45	51	...	41	129
	2003	101	67	52	54	...	46	119
Netherlands Antilles [18]	1970	575	66	24	18	3	105	115
(Guilders)	1975	916	66	24	18	3	105	115
	1980	1734	63	25	18	3	98	107
	1985	2187	61	29	17	1	70	81
	1990	3619	37	39	27	3	82	86
	1995	4699	59	25	23	0	76	84
	2000	4956	53	23	27	...	69	75
	2002	5113	52	22	29	...	66	73
Nicaragua	1970	2 (u)	69	9	15	1	16	18
(Gold Cordobas)	1975	4 (u)	73	8	21	-1	17	23
	1980	7 (u)	78	17	12	1	14	26
	1985	38 (u)	45	33	19	1	9	14
	1990	507	62	30	19	-0	15	27
	1995	24029	78	15	20	2	19	35
	1996	28009	78	15	22	4	20	39
	1997	31967	79	14	24	7	23	48
	1998	37805	77	14	25	6	23	47
	1999	44198	75	16	33	6	22	55
	2000	50145	75	17	30	4	24	51
	2001	53653	75	18	30	2	23	49
	2002	57051	77	16	28	4	23	49
	2003	61927	77	16	25	7	23	48
Panama	1970	1003	63	15	26	4	82	93
(Balboas)	1975	1820	59	19	30	4	103	121
	1980	3545	58	19	25	6	97	104
	1985	5006	66	21	17	-0	68	72
	1990	5313	57	18	9	8	87	79
	1995	7906	52	15	26	4	101	98
	1996	8151	53	16	25	5	93	92
	1997	8658	54	16	27	5	98	100
	1998	9345	57	16	28	4	90	95
	1999	9637	55	16	30	3	77	81
	2000	10019	57	16	26	2	79	81
	2001	10079	59	15	29	3	79	85
	2002	10277	61	16	27	4	77	85
Paraguay [19]	1970	74921	77	9	15	0	15	16
(Guaranies)	1975	190439	75	6	21	3	13	19
	1980	560459	71	6	27	2	14	20
	1985	1393890	76	6	21	1	22	26
	1990	6474434	77	6	22	1	33	39
	1995	17699000	85	7	23	1	35	51
	2000	26920974	83	10	21	1	20	34
	2002	31976903	86	8	18	1	31	44

Table 2. Gross Domestic Product by Type of Expenditure: Individual Countries or Areas

Major area, region and country	Year	Gross Domestic Product (at current prices) Million	Household final consumption expenditure 1	General government final consumption expenditure 2	Gross fixed capital formation 3	Changes in inventories 4	Exports of goods and services 5	Imports of goods and services 6
			Percentage Distribution					
Peru (New Soles)	1970	241 (u)	72	13	13	...	21	18
	1975	573 (u)	75	13	20	...	13	24
	1980	5143 (u)	62	12	22	...	26	25
	1985	170530 (u)	64	12	20	...	24	17
	1990	5851	72	9	19	-1	14	13
	1995	120858	71	10	24	1	13	18
	1996	136929	72	10	22	0	13	18
	1997	157274	70	10	24	0	14	19
	1998	165949	71	10	24	0	13	19
	1999	173957	70	11	22	-1	15	17
	2000	185281	71	11	20	-0	16	18
	2001	188172	72	11	19	0	16	18
	2002	198437	72	10	18	1	16	17
Puerto Rico (US Dollars)	1970	5647	76	16	28	2	41	63
	1975	8969	84	18	20	2	47	70
	1980	15956	75	16	14	1	68	73
	1985	21969	72	15	11	-0	67	63
	1990	32287	62	14	16	0	78	71
	1995	45341	59	14	17	1	64	57
	1996	48187	60	14	18	1	64	59
	1997	54086	57	13	17	0	67	56
	1998	57841	56	13	20	1	70	62
	1999	61045	57	12	19	1	73	63
	2000	67897	53	11	17	1	78	63
	2001	69664	52	11	17	1	82	66
	2002	74993	50	10	17	1	87	67
Saint Kitts and Nevis (EC Dollars)	1970	34	98	22	15	6	34	73
	1975	74	77	16	10	2	63	69
	1980	129	72	20	38	...	67	97
	1985	211	71	23	28	2	55	79
	1990	430	58	18	55	...	52	83
	1995	623	57	20	46	...	51	75
	1996	663	61	20	46	...	52	79
	1997	742	57	19	44	...	51	71
	1998	775	53	19	43	...	52	67
	1999	823	68	21	36	...	47	72
	2000	888	59	21	50	...	46	75
	2001	929	49	21	54	...	46	69
	2002	963	59	19	47	...	46	71
Saint Lucia (EC Dollars)	1970	79	95	19	26	5	41	82
	1975	129	95	19	26	5	41	82
	1980	305	74	19	44	9	70	115
	1985	441	61	23	18	...	45	53
	1990	1123	70	15	25	...	68	78
	1995	1496	59	17	25	...	69	70
	1996	1543	64	17	25	...	62	68
	1997	1562	65	18	27	...	62	72
	1998	1695	66	18	25	...	61	69
	1999	1786	66	18	27	...	57	69
	2000	1826	62	19	26	...	59	66
	2001	1747	55	22	25	...	55	60
	2002	1804	59	22	22	...	55	59
	2003	1857	57	23	21	...	54	57
Saint Vincent and the Grenadines (EC Dollars)	1970	37	83	23	32	...	53	91
	1975	71	83	23	32	...	53	91
	1980	160	88	23	39	...	56	107
	1985	305	58	20	25	3	73	79
	1990	535	68	21	30	1	66	77
	1995	713	64	20	30	...	52	66
	1996	752	65	20	28	...	53	67
	1997	793	78	19	31	...	50	78
	1998	857	75	18	36	...	49	78
	1999	892	67	19	35	...	53	74
	2000	906	61	19	27	...	53	61
	2001	935	61	20	30	...	50	61
	2002	975	61	21	30	...	49	60

Table 2. Gross Domestic Product by Type of Expenditure: Individual Countries or Areas

Major area, region and country	Year	Gross Domestic Product (at current prices) Million	Household final consumption expenditure 1	General government final consumption expenditure 2	Gross fixed capital formation 3	Changes in inventories 4	Exports of goods and services 5	Imports of goods and services 6
			Percentage Distribution					
Suriname (Guilders)	1970	532	52	25	18	...	54	49
	1975	931	53	21	27	5	62	68
	1980	1590	58	21	22	5	69	74
	1985	1746	55	34	18	-3	37	40
	1990	3170	54	24	18	2	27	27
	1995	250571	15	18	40	7	92	80
	1996	289431	62	15	31	7	67	78
	1997	311191	66	19	26	6	63	71
	1998	377553	77	23	25	...	44	60
	1999	650353	24	7	77	...	56	63
	2000	1032979	19	6	69	...	62	56
	2001	1436483	22	7	68	...	75	72
	2002	1926645	24	7	79	...	49	58
Trinidad and Tobago (Trinidad and Tobago Dollars)	1970	1644	62	13	21	5	46	49
	1975	5300	44	12	20	7	57	42
	1980	14966	47	12	28	3	55	46
	1985	18071	56	23	20	-1	35	34
	1990	21539	55	16	14	0	49	34
	1995	31697	49	16	19	2	54	39
	1996	34587	50	16	23	1	51	41
	1997	35871	58	15	29	1	54	57
	1998	38065	58	14	31	2	48	54
	1999	42889	59	15	21	0	50	44
	2000	51485	54	12	20	0	59	45
	2001	56700	54	13	22	0	53	43
	2002	58200	55	15	23	...	49	42
Turks and Caicos Islands (US Dollars)	1970	10	63	25	37	...	70	95
	1975	16	63	25	37	...	70	95
	1980	31	63	25	37	...	70	95
	1985	56	63	25	37	...	70	95
	1990	94	64	25	37	...	70	96
	1995	122	63	26	37	...	72	98
	1996	134	59	25	31	...	69	84
	1997	147	67	23	38	...	68	96
	1998	166	67	25	41	...	65	98
	1999	182	64	26	41	...	74	106
	2000	202	59	28	33	...	82	103
	2001	208	60	30	35	...	82	106
	2002	215	63	27	38	...	75	102
Uruguay [20] (Pesos)	1970	1	69	16	14	2	13	14
	1975	8	71	14	17	3	17	21
	1980	87	70	13	21	4	16	22
	1985	479	69	14	10	2	27	21
	1990	9784	69	14	11	0	26	20
	1995	122521	73	12	14	2	19	19
	1996	163546	72	13	14	1	20	20
	1997	204926	72	12	14	1	21	21
	1998	234267	72	13	15	1	20	21
	1999	237143	73	13	14	1	18	19
	2000	243027	75	13	13	1	19	21
	2001	247211	74	14	13	1	18	20
	2002	260967	74	13	10	1	22	20
	2003	315446	73	12	10	3	26	23
Venezuela (Bolivares)	1970	62884	53	11	25	11	21	17
	1975	142749	48	11	29	7	30	23
	1980	307262	54	12	28	1	31	23
	1985	464741	61	10	17	1	25	16
	1990	2279261	61	8	14	-4	39	20
	1995	13685686	68	7	16	2	27	22
	1996	29437682	62	5	16	1	37	21
	1997	43343669	64	6	19	2	28	22
	1998	52482466	70	8	19	3	20	21
	1999	62577039	67	8	16	2	22	16
	2000	82450674	62	7	14	3	28	16
	2001	91324773	65	9	16	3	22	17
	2002	110782356	64	8	14	-1	29	17

Table 2. Gross Domestic Product by Type of Expenditure: Individual Countries or Areas

Major area, region and country	Year	Gross Domestic Product (at current prices) Million	Household final consumption expenditure 1	General government final consumption expenditure 2	Gross fixed capital formation 3	Changes in inventories 4	Exports of goods and services 5	Imports of goods and services 6
			Percentage Distribution					
ASIA								
Armenia [21]	1990	50	49	17	44	3	35	46
(Drams)	1995	522256	106	11	16	2	24	62
	1996	661209	100	11	18	2	23	56
	1997	804336	103	11	16	3	20	58
	1998	955385	100	11	16	3	19	53
	1999	987444	96	12	16	2	21	50
	2000	1031338	97	12	18	0	23	51
	2001	1175877	93	11	18	2	25	46
	2002	1356983	89	10	19	2	30	47
Azerbaijan [22]	1990	1466	52	18	20	6	44	39
(Azerbaijan Manats)	1995	10669000	84	13	16	8	32	53
	1996	13663200	87	12	29	-0	25	56
	1997	15791400	73	13	37	-3	29	53
	1998	17203100	79	15	36	-2	23	55
	1999	18875400	74	16	29	-2	28	42
	2000	23590500	63	15	23	-2	40	38
	2001	26578000	60	14	23	-2	42	37
	2002	30312300	58	13	34	-2	43	50
	2003	35053400	57	10	51	-0	40	62
Bahrain [23]	1970	119	64	11	30	-4	95	100
(Dinars)	1975	410	63	12	18	1	103	103
	1980	1241	51	11	22	16	92	102
	1985	1472	48	29	22	5	77	81
	1990	1614	56	24	18	-1	92	90
	1995	2199	53	21	17	-3	82	70
	1996	2294	54	20	12	2	88	76
	1997	2387	54	19	12	5	79	70
	1998	2325	57	21	14	7	65	64
	1999	2489	55	21	14	-6	79	63
	2000	2997	47	18	14	-3	89	64
	2001	2981	47	18	13	-1	82	60
	2002	3165	45	18	17	5	81	67
Bangladesh [24]	1970	75214	83	1	10	0	7	...
(Taka)	1975	145481	90	4	14	0	4	13
	1980	305196	84	4	23	1	6	15
	1985	614824	85	4	17	0	6	13
	1990	1100331	83	4	15	2	7	12
	1995	1663240	81	4	20	...	11	19
	1996	1807013	80	4	21	...	12	18
	1997	2001766	78	5	22	...	13	18
	1998	2196972	78	5	22	...	13	19
	1999	2370856	78	5	23	...	14	19
	2000	2535464	77	5	23	...	15	22
	2001	2714142	78	4	23	...	17	23
	2002	3004850	77	5	23	...	13	19
Bhutan	1970	346	75	25	43	-3	16	56
(Ngultrum)	1975	870	75	25	43	-3	16	56
	1980	1095	68	25	30	1	13	37
	1985	2392	63	23	42	3	15	47
	1990	4983	52	16	37	-1	28	32
	1995	10064	34	24	45	2	37	42
	1996	11808	44	21	43	2	34	43
	1997	14314	50	26	39	-4	33	43
	1998	16337	57	20	38	0	32	47
	1999	19123	53	22	42	1	30	48
	2000	21698	52	20	44	0	30	46
	2001	24317	54	21	49	0	24	45
	2002	27779	53	22	42	-1	30	46
Brunei Darussalam [25]	1970	546	7	17	3	0	90	17
(Brunei Darussalam Dollars)	1975	2770	11	17	5	0	90	23
	1980	10554	7	8	3	0	93	12
	1985	7752	11	9	10	-0	88	19
	1990	6509	11	12	10	-0	106	39
	1995	7394	11	11	9	-0	90	26
	1996	7409	11	12	10	-0	104	32
	1997	7628	11	12	10	-0	106	33

Table 2. Gross Domestic Product by Type of Expenditure: Individual Countries or Areas

Major area, region and country	Year	Gross Domestic Product (at current prices) Million	Household final consumption expenditure 1	General government final consumption expenditure 2	Gross fixed capital formation 3	Changes in inventories 4	Exports of goods and services 5	Imports of goods and services 6
			Percentage Distribution					
	1998	6534	11	11	9	-0	100	31
	1999	7145	11	11	10	-0	98	29
	2000	7441	11	11	10	-0	98	29
	2001	7436	11	11	10	-0	98	29
	2002	7664	11	11	10	-0	98	29
Cambodia (Riels)	1970	10708	93	7	12	-0	2	10
	1975	8830	93	7	12	-0	2	10
	1980	8395	93	7	12	-0	2	10
	1985	16965	93	7	12	-0	2	10
	1990	723653	95	7	9	-0	2	8
	1995	8110680	89	5	13	0	33	44
	1996	8885580	88	6	12	2	27	40
	1997	9778060	87	6	13	1	34	42
	1998	11363640	88	5	12	-1	37	45
	1999	12587090	86	5	14	1	38	46
	2000	12931530	82	6	15	-2	49	51
	2001	13364930	80	6	16	2	51	53
	2002	14397172	78	6	19	-0	55	56
China (Yuan Renminbi)	1970	225270	65	8	23	6	3	3
	1975	299730	62	8	24	7	5	5
	1980	451780	51	15	29	6	6	7
	1985	872944	53	14	30	9	10	14
	1990	1831950	50	12	26	9	18	12
	1995	5847810	46	11	35	6	21	19
	1996	6788460	47	12	34	5	21	19
	1997	7446260	47	12	34	4	23	19
	1998	7834520	47	12	36	3	22	18
	1999	8206750	48	13	36	1	22	19
	2000	8944220	49	13	36	-0	26	23
	2001	9593330	48	14	38	1	26	24
	2002	10479060	46	13	40	0	29	26
Cyprus [26] (Pounds)	1970	229	80	10	24	3	38	47
	1975	260	86	18	20	5	35	56
	1980	760	66	14	34	4	45	63
	1985	1481	63	14	27	3	49	59
	1990	2556	59	17	25	2	52	57
	1995	4007	64	16	19	3	47	50
	1996	4161	65	18	20	2	47	53
	1997	4371	66	19	19	1	47	52
	1998	4694	67	19	19	2	44	51
	1999	5019	66	17	18	1	45	48
	2000	5487	69	16	18	1	46	52
	2001	5865	69	17	17	1	47	52
	2002	6161	69	18	19	1	42	50
	2003	6655	68	19	17	1	39	45
Georgia [27] (Laris)	1990	15 (t)	61	17	24	7	40	46
	1995	3694	76	8	19	5	14	29
	1996	3868	107	8	14	1	13	32
	1997	4555	101	10	15	-1	16	42
	1998	5022	87	11	17	2	16	37
	1999	5669	83	11	22	0	19	38
	2000	6015	89	9	21	1	23	40
	2001	6647	83	10	20	1	25	39
	2002	7455	82	10	20	1	29	41
	2003	8466	74	9	18	1	31	45
Hong Kong SAR of China (Hong Kong Dollars)	1970	23369	63	7	20	1	92	85
	1975	50012	62	7	22	1	82	78
	1980	143976	58	6	33	3	87	89
	1985	275832	59	7	21	1	106	98
	1990	591507	54	7	26	1	131	123
	1995	1096263	58	9	31	4	145	150
	1996	1210925	58	9	31	1	138	140
	1997	1344546	57	8	34	1	129	133
	1998	1279850	57	9	30	-1	125	125
	1999	1246134	56	10	26	-1	130	125
	2000	1288338	55	9	27	1	145	142

Table 2. Gross Domestic Product by Type of Expenditure: Individual Countries or Areas

Major area, region and country	Year	Gross Domestic Product (at current prices) Million	Household final consumption expenditure 1	General government final consumption expenditure 2	Gross fixed capital formation 3	Changes in inventories 4	Exports of goods and services 5	Imports of goods and services 6
			Percentage Distribution					
	2001	1269975	55	10	26	-0	141	137
	2002	1259771	53	10	23	0	151	142
	2003	1241561	55	10	27	-0	165	154
India [28] (Rupees)	1970	457435	82	9	15	3	4	4
	1975	834698	79	10	17	4	6	7
	1980	1441446	78	10	19	2	6	9
	1985	2779213	73	11	21	4	5	8
	1990	5675511	67	12	23	2	7	9
	1995	11880120	64	11	24	2	11	12
	1996	13682080	66	11	23	-1	11	12
	1997	15225470	64	11	22	1	11	12
	1998	17409850	65	12	22	-0	11	13
	1999	19369250	65	13	22	2	12	14
	2000	21042980	65	13	22	1	14	15
	2001	22960490	65	13	22	1	13	14
	2002	24695640	64	13	23	...	15	16
Indonesia (Rupiahs)	1970	3238000	80	9	14	...	13	16
	1975	12643000	69	10	20	...	23	22
	1980	45446000	61	10	21	...	30	22
	1985	96997000	59	11	23	5	22	20
	1990	210866000	57	9	28	2	25	24
	1995	454513000	61	8	28	3	26	28
	1996	532567000	62	8	30	1	26	26
	1997	627695000	61	7	28	3	28	28
	1998	955754000	67	6	25	-9	53	43
	1999	1099730000	73	7	20	-9	36	27
	2000	1264919000	67	7	21	-6	43	32
	2001	1449398000	68	8	21	-4	42	34
	2002	1610012000	72	8	20	-5	35	27
Iran (Islamic Republic of) (Rials)	1970	754383	43	18	36	-3	20	30
	1975	3282929	34	24	42	-13	43	49
	1980	6447256	43	22	33	3	13	24
	1985	15335563	49	16	26	-1	8	12
	1990	35623226	55	12	23	11	15	27
	1995	188969300	46	16	21	10	21	13
	1996	250411700	45	14	26	10	21	15
	1997	296604100	47	13	28	8	17	15
	1998	334740200	54	14	29	5	13	15
	1999	454232900	49	13	27	5	21	14
	2000	589894400	47	14	26	8	22	17
	2001	677792500	47	14	29	8	21	19
	2002	945231400	43	14	27	13	26	23
Iraq (Dinars)	1970	1257	46	22	15	1	35	19
	1975	4090	35	21	26	9	51	41
	1980	15948	23	15	24	7	63	31
	1985	15494	52	29	28	-4	24	29
	1990	23297	50	26	27	-4	18	18
	1995	1940994	75	22	5	-2	2	2
	1996	2379254	78	23	2	-1	5	7
	1997	3269914	76	19	7	-1	10	12
	1998	4570100	75	18	8	-0	12	13
	1999	6809790	75	17	9	-0	13	14
	2000	7398604	74	16	11	-0	15	15
	2001	8878324	74	15	12	-0	16	17
	2002	9903371	75	17	10	...	14	15
Israel (New Shekels)	1970	2	48	39	28	0	22	39
	1975	9	45	45	30	0	25	45
	1980	120	46	38	23	-0	38	47
	1985	31596	50	33	19	0	38	43
	1990	115409	54	28	20	0	31	35
	1995	286428	54	28	24	1	29	37
	1996	333702	54	28	24	1	28	36
	1997	373326	53	28	22	1	29	34
	1998	410914	53	27	21	1	30	33
	1999	449463	53	27	21	1	35	38
	2000	490721	53	26	19	1	38	39
	2001	495390	54	28	18	1	34	37
	2002	513558	55	30	17	0	35	39

Table 2. Gross Domestic Product by Type of Expenditure: Individual Countries or Areas

Major area, region and country	Year	Gross Domestic Product (at current prices) Million	Household final consumption expenditure 1	General government final consumption expenditure 2	Gross fixed capital formation 3	Changes in inventories 4	Exports of goods and services 5	Imports of goods and services 6
			Percentage Distribution					
Japan (Yen)	1970	74450690	48	10	36	4	11	9
	1975	150563261	53	14	33	0	13	13
	1980	243796700	54	13	32	1	13	14
	1985	326815700	54	14	28	1	14	11
	1990	442072300	52	13	32	1	10	9
	1995	498872300	54	15	28	0	9	8
	1996	511946800	54	15	28	1	10	9
	1997	523051100	54	15	28	1	11	10
	1998	516579200	55	16	27	0	11	9
	1999	509115900	55	16	26	-0	10	8
	2000	513376800	54	17	26	-0	11	9
	2001	507455500	55	17	26	-0	10	10
	2002	499986500	56	18	24	-0	11	10
Jordan [29] (Dinars)	1970	212	76	36	13	-1	8	36
	1975	390	83	37	25	2	30	77
	1980	1196	74	27	36	4	39	80
	1985	2020	89	26	19	1	39	74
	1990	2668	74	25	26	6	62	93
	1995	4773	64	23	29	3	51	72
	1996	4982	69	24	29	1	52	77
	1997	5193	70	25	26	-0	49	71
	1998	5646	72	24	21	1	45	64
	1999	5765	74	25	19	...	45	64
	2000	6012	76	24	20	...	47	66
	2001	6343	77	24	19	...	47	67
	2002	6625	77	24	20	...	47	67
Kazakhstan (Tenge)	1990	96	63	12	39	8	8	30
	1995	1014190	70	14	23	0	39	44
	1996	1415750	66	13	17	-1	35	36
	1997	1672142	70	12	16	-1	35	37
	1998	1733264	73	11	16	0	30	35
	1999	2016456	72	12	16	2	42	40
	2000	2599902	61	12	17	1	57	48
	2001	3250593	57	13	24	3	46	48
	2002	3776277	57	12	24	3	47	46
Kuwait (Dinars)	1970	1026	39	14	12	-0	60	24
	1975	3485	22	11	12	1	81	26
	1980	7755	30	11	13	1	78	33
	1985	6450	48	22	20	-1	54	43
	1990	5328	59	39	16	0	45	58
	1995	7925	41	33	14	1	54	43
	1996	9303	44	28	14	1	53	40
	1997	9060	46	27	14	0	54	40
	1998	7656	57	31	19	0	45	53
	1999	8886	51	28	15	0	47	41
	2000	10991	42	23	8	...	59	32
	2001	10057	48	26	9	...	55	37
	2002	10738	50	28	9	...	48	39
Kyrgyzstan (Som)	1990	43	68	25	22	2	29	50
	1995	16145	73	20	20	-2	29	42
	1996	23399	80	19	22	3	31	57
	1997	30686	67	17	12	9	38	46
	1998	34181	87	18	13	3	36	58
	1999	48744	74	19	16	2	42	57
	2000	65358	63	20	18	2	42	48
	2001	73883	62	17	17	1	37	37
	2002	75367	65	19	16	1	40	43
	2003	83421	70	19	16	2	39	42
Lao People's Democratic Republic (Kips)	1970	36	90	8	7	...	3	8
	1975	194	90	8	7	...	3	8
	1980	8481	90	8	7	...	4	8
	1985	84374	90	9	7	...	4	10
	1990	612447	93	12	17	...	18	40
	1995	1430361	80	8	26	...	23	37
	2000	13672336	81	6	25	...	37	48
	2002	18390380	77	6	26	...	35	47

Table 2. Gross Domestic Product by Type of Expenditure: Individual Countries or Areas

Major area, region and country	Year	Gross Domestic Product (at current prices) Million	Household final consumption expenditure 1	General government final consumption expenditure 2	Gross fixed capital formation 3	Changes in inventories 4	Exports of goods and services 5	Imports of goods and services 6
			Percentage Distribution					
Lebanon (Lebanese Pounds)	1970	4866	86	11	19	-1	24	39
	1975	7500	87	6	18	...	19	30
	1980	14000	92	25	54	-38	39	72
	1985	29988	120	59	36	...	15	130
	1990	1954275	90	46	39	...	16	91
	1995	17779000	108	10	36	...	11	65
	2000	24816000	78	31	29	...	63	101
	2002	26324000	78	31	29	...	63	101
Macao SAR of China (Patacas)	1970	1060	80	3	21	0	111	104
	1975	2361	65	4	22	0	110	96
	1980	5250	53	5	22	1	109	89
	1985	10950	45	6	22	3	105	80
	1990	26175	37	9	25	1	97	67
	1995	55333	33	8	29	0	74	46
	1996	55294	36	9	21	1	76	44
	1997	55894	37	10	21	0	76	45
	1998	51902	39	12	19	-0	77	47
	1999	49021	40	14	18	0	80	53
	2000	49742	40	12	12	0	94	59
	2001	49802	40	12	10	0	98	62
	2002	54229	38	12	10	1	100	62
	2003	63289	33	11	13	1	99	58
Malaysia (Ringgit)	1970	10588	60	16	16	3	41	36
	1975	22332	59	18	25	-2	46	45
	1980	53308	51	17	31	-1	58	55
	1985	77470	52	15	30	-2	55	50
	1990	119081	52	14	33	-1	74	72
	1995	222473	48	12	44	0	94	98
	1996	253732	46	11	42	-1	92	90
	1997	281795	45	11	43	-0	93	92
	1998	283243	42	10	27	-0	116	94
	1999	300764	42	11	22	0	121	96
	2000	342157	42	11	26	1	125	105
	2001	334589	45	13	25	-1	116	98
	2002	360960	44	14	23	0	115	97
	2003	392340	43	14	22	-0	115	94
Maldives (Rufiyaa)	1970	74	36	18	32	...	92	77
	1975	152	36	18	32	...	92	77
	1980	356	36	18	32	...	92	77
	1985	596	36	18	32	...	92	77
	1990	2060	36	18	32	...	92	77
	1995	4696	36	17	31	-0	93	77
	1996	5301	35	16	31	...	92	73
	1997	5982	36	18	33	...	91	78
	1998	6357	35	18	30	...	92	76
	1999	6935	35	21	34	...	91	80
	2000	7348	33	23	26	...	89	72
	2001	7651	32	23	28	...	87	70
	2002	8186	30	23	25	...	86	65
Mongolia (Tughriks)	1970	4980	54	24	60	4	29	62
	1975	6530	54	24	60	4	29	62
	1980	8723	54	24	60	4	29	62
	1985	12102	54	25	62	5	31	68
	1990	13514	63	27	41	0	19	40
	1995	554249	63	13	27	5	48	49
	1996	659698	65	14	27	2	40	47
	1997	846344	60	13	25	2	58	52
	1998	833727	66	17	34	2	54	67
	1999	925801	68	17	35	2	59	72
	2000	1018886	72	18	32	5	66	83
	2001	1115640	73	17	32	5	65	82
	2002	1240787	68	17	31	3	60	71
Myanmar [30] (Kyats)	1970	13504	...	92	11	3	4	12
	1975	23477	...	91	7	3	5	6
	1980	38609	...	82	19	3	8	12
	1985	55989	...	88	15	0	5	9
	1990	151941	...	88	15	-1	2	4
	1995	604729	...	87	14	1	1	2

Table 2. Gross Domestic Product by Type of Expenditure: Individual Countries or Areas

Major area, region and country	Year	Gross Domestic Product (at current prices) Million	Household final consumption expenditure 1	General government final consumption expenditure 2	Gross fixed capital formation 3	Changes in inventories 4	Exports of goods and services 5	Imports of goods and services 6
			Percentage Distribution					
	1996	791980	...	89	15	-3	1	1
	1997	1109554	...	88	14	-1	1	1
	1998	1559996	...	89	12	-1	1	1
	1999	2120782	...	88	12	...	0	1
	2000	2663942	...	94	13	...	0	1
	2001	3669602	...	92	13	...	0	1
	2002	5688124	...	80	12	...	0	0
Nepal	1970	9816	86	9	5	1	5	7
(Rupees)	1975	16571	81	8	13	1	9	13
	1980	23351	82	7	16	3	11	19
	1985	46587	77	9	20	2	12	20
	1990	103416	83	9	16	2	11	21
	1995	219175	76	9	22	3	24	35
	1996	248913	77	9	23	5	22	36
	1997	280513	77	9	22	4	26	38
	1998	300845	77	9	22	3	23	34
	1999	342036	77	9	19	1	23	30
	2000	379488	76	9	19	5	23	32
	2001	410287	75	10	19	5	22	31
	2002	421333	78	10	19	5	16	29
	2003	446177	78	10	19	7	15	29
Oman	1970	113	31	8	12	-0	67	19
(Rials)	1975	767	23	21	29	2	65	42
	1980	2185	42	14	20	0	59	36
	1985	3591	41	22	25	0	48	36
	1990	4493	41	27	12	0	47	28
	1995	5307	49	28	15	0	44	36
	1996	5874	48	25	13	0	50	36
	1997	6090	48	23	18	0	50	39
	1998	5416	57	26	24	0	42	49
	1999	6041	50	24	15	0	49	38
	2000	7639	40	21	12	0	59	31
	2001	7670	43	22	13	-0	57	35
	2002	7809	43	23	13	0	57	36
Pakistan	1970	50938	76	10	15	2	8	10
(Rupees)	1975	130741	76	11	20	-0	11	18
	1980	278196	81	10	17	2	13	22
	1985	514532	76	13	17	2	12	20
	1990	1020600	68	14	17	2	17	18
	1995	2120173	73	13	17	2	17	21
	1996	2428312	75	12	16	2	16	21
	1997	2677656	72	11	15	3	16	18
	1998	2938379	76	10	14	2	15	17
	1999	3147167	74	11	14	2	16	18
	2000	3416252	75	10	14	2	18	19
	2001	3726611	75	11	12	2	18	18
	2002	4018112	74	11	15	...	20	20
Philippines	1970	39505	66	9	18	3	22	21
(Pesos)	1975	107953	62	11	25	6	21	27
	1980	243749	63	9	27	2	24	28
	1985	571883	74	8	16	-2	24	22
	1990	1077237	71	10	23	1	28	33
	1995	1905951	74	11	22	0	36	44
	1996	2171922	73	12	23	1	41	49
	1997	2426743	73	13	24	0	49	59
	1998	2665060	74	13	21	-1	52	59
	1999	2976904	73	13	19	-0	51	51
	2000	3354727	70	13	21	-0	55	53
	2001	3673687	70	12	20	1	49	52
	2002	4022694	68	12	19	0	49	49
	2003	4359045	71	13	20	-0	51	53
Qatar	1970	1437	23	21	23	1	63	30
(Riyals)	1975	9707	23	21	23	1	63	30
	1980	28663	16	20	17	0	74	26
	1985	22398	25	35	18	0	51	30
	1990	26792	28	33	17	1	53	32
	1995	29622	32	32	30	5	44	43
	1996	32976	27	33	35	1	44	40

Table 2. Gross Domestic Product by Type of Expenditure: Individual Countries or Areas

Major area, region and country	Year	Gross Domestic Product (at current prices) Million	Household final consumption expenditure 1	General government final consumption expenditure 2	Gross fixed capital formation 3	Changes in inventories 4	Exports of goods and services 5	Imports of goods and services 6
			Percentage Distribution					
	1997	41124	23	30	35	1	48	36
	1998	37330	25	32	31	1	51	40
	1999	45111	21	26	18	1	60	26
	2000	64646	15	20	19	1	67	22
	2001	64579	16	20	23	1	65	24
	2002	65088	16	20	22	1	66	24
Republic of Korea [31] (Wons)	1970	2725185	74	9	26	-0	14	24
	1975	10228062	68	11	27	2	27	36
	1980	37788497	63	12	32	-0	33	41
	1985	81312283	56	10	29	1	33	32
	1990	178796762	51	10	37	0	29	30
	1995	377349800	54	10	37	0	30	32
	1996	418478988	55	10	37	1	30	34
	1997	453276389	55	10	35	-1	35	36
	1998	444366540	54	11	30	-9	50	36
	1999	482744175	55	10	28	-1	42	35
	2000	521959212	56	10	28	-0	45	42
	2001	551557522	58	10	27	-0	42	40
	2002	596381162	59	11	27	-1	40	39
Saudi Arabia [32] (Riyals)	1970	22921	28	17	13	-1	66	23
	1975	164526	15	18	20	0	73	26
	1980	490942	22	17	21	-0	71	30
	1985	313941	51	36	24	-3	36	44
	1990	391993	40	32	19	2	47	39
	1995	478652	40	26	20	1	44	31
	1996	590749	44	25	17	1	40	27
	1997	617902	42	26	18	1	39	26
	1998	546648	46	28	21	2	30	27
	1999	603589	42	26	20	2	35	23
	2000	706657	37	26	17	1	44	25
	2001	698403	37	27	18	1	42	24
	2002	705293	32	26	15	...	52	25
Singapore [33] (Singapore Dollars)	1970	5805	68	12	33	6	-20	...
	1975	13443	60	11	36	4	-11	...
	1980	25091	51	10	41	6	-9	...
	1985	38924	45	14	42	0	-2	...
	1990	66884	46	10	32	4	9	...
	1995	118963	41	9	33	1	16	...
	1996	130035	40	9	38	-2	15	...
	1997	141641	40	9	39	1	13	...
	1998	137085	38	10	38	-5	21	...
	1999	137935	41	10	34	-2	18	...
	2000	157700	41	11	30	2	16	...
	2001	152066	44	13	29	-5	20	...
	2002	155727	43	13	26	-5	24	...
Sri Lanka (Rupees)	1970	14259	71	12	17	3	24	27
	1975	26890	81	10	13	3	27	35
	1980	68809	78	10	33	1	31	53
	1985	158852	74	12	24	0	27	39
	1990	320098	74	13	20	1	30	38
	1995	666956	70	15	26	0	36	45
	1996	776739	68	14	26	1	35	43
	1997	897218	67	14	26	0	36	43
	1998	1018330	66	14	26	0	36	42
	1999	1108845	68	14	26	1	35	43
	2000	1253622	70	14	25	1	39	50
	2001	1396314	70	13	21	2	39	46
	2002	1570260	71	13	21	2	36	43
Syrian Arab Republic (Syrian Pounds)	1970	6848	73	17	13	1	17	21
	1975	20711	63	21	25	4	21	34
	1980	51270	66	23	28	...	18	35
	1985	83225	66	24	24	...	12	25
	1990	268328	69	14	17	...	28	28
	1995	570975	66	13	27	...	31	38
	1996	690857	71	12	24	...	32	38
	1997	745569	69	11	21	...	32	34
	1998	790444	69	11	21	...	31	31
	1999	819092	70	11	19	...	32	32

Table 2. Gross Domestic Product by Type of Expenditure: Individual Countries or Areas

Major area, region and country	Year	Gross Domestic Product (at current prices) Million	Household final consumption expenditure 1	General government final consumption expenditure 2	Gross fixed capital formation 3	Changes in inventories 4	Exports of goods and services 5	Imports of goods and services 6
			Percentage Distribution					
	2000	903944	63	12	17	...	36	29
	2001	954051	60	13	21	...	38	31
	2002	999451	59	13	20	...	40	32
Tajikistan (Somani)	1990	73 (t)	63	7	7	5	57	40
	1995	70	59	11	21	7	112	121
	1996	308	57	9	13	9	73	63
	1997	518	58	11	18	2	82	85
	1998	1025	67	8	13	2	50	57
	1999	1345	70	9	17	1	68	66
	2000	1807	72	9	9	2	85	75
	2001	2529	74	10	9	7	67	69
	2002	3366	73	9	11	7	66	65
Thailand (Baht)	1970	148274	69	11	26	2	15	19
	1975	305149	68	10	25	4	18	23
	1980	662482	65	12	28	1	24	30
	1985	1056496	62	14	27	1	23	26
	1990	2184000	57	9	40	1	34	42
	1995	4186212	53	10	41	1	42	49
	1996	4611041	54	10	41	1	39	46
	1997	4732610	55	10	34	-0	48	47
	1998	4626447	54	11	22	-2	59	43
	1999	4637079	56	11	21	-0	58	46
	2000	4916505	56	11	22	1	67	58
	2001	5123418	57	12	23	1	66	60
	2002	5441070	58	12	23	1	65	57
	2003	5925325	56	11	22	0	63	53
Timor-Leste (Rupiah)	1990	181	93	37	30	...	13	73
	1995	315	93	37	30	...	13	73
	2000	321	93	53	29	...	8	83
	2002	378	95	49	32	...	15	92
Turkey (Liras)	1970	206000	73	9	18	1	4	6
	1975	674000	72	11	20	3	5	11
	1980	5231000	81	8	16	1	5	12
	1985	35095000	71	9	22	0	16	19
	1990	393060170	69	11	23	1	13	18
	1995	7762456069	70	11	24	2	20	24
	1996	14772110189	67	12	25	-1	22	28
	1997	28835883135	68	12	26	-1	25	30
	1998	52224945129	69	13	25	-0	24	28
	1999	77415272308	72	15	22	1	23	27
	2000	124583458275	72	14	22	2	24	32
	2001	178412438500	72	14	18	-1	34	31
	2002	276002987851	67	14	17	5	29	30
Turkmenistan (Manats)	1990	7600	49	23	38	2	58	70
	1995	652044	60	8	23	10	142	145
	1996	7751754	49	7	41	9	106	107
	1997	11108783	68	13	41	8	51	82
	1998	13994739	52	9	34	9	100	103
	1999	20056000	52	9	34	9	100	103
	2000	25648000	52	9	34	9	100	103
	2001	33863000	52	9	34	9	100	103
	2002	63800000	52	9	34	9	100	103
United Arab Emirates (Dirhams)	1970	3160	13	12	20	4	85	34
	1975	39460	16	8	31	...	75	29
	1980	109833	17	11	27	1	78	34
	1985	99416	28	20	25	0	58	31
	1990	124008	39	16	19	1	65	41
	1995	155210	49	17	29	...	67	63
	2000	195779	51	17	27	...	68	62
	2003	243391	48	17	25	...	67	58
Uzbekistan (Sums)	1990	32	60	25	31	1	29	48
	1995	302787	50	22	33	-9	32	29
	1996	559072	54	22	37	-14	34	35
	1997	976830	60	20	34	-15	30	30
	1998	1416157	59	21	30	-9	29	30
	1999	2128660	61	21	27	-10	30	30

Table 2. Gross Domestic Product by Type of Expenditure: Individual Countries or Areas

Major area, region and country	Year	Gross Domestic Product (at current prices) Million	Household final consumption expenditure 1	General government final consumption expenditure 2	Gross fixed capital formation 3	Changes in inventories 4	Exports of goods and services 5	Imports of goods and services 6
			Percentage Distribution					
	2000	3255600	61	19	24	-4	30	30
	2001	4868400	61	18	26	-6	30	30
	2002	7469300	60	20	28	-9	30	30
Vietnam [34]	1970	3989	90	7	12	2	-21	...
(Dong)	1975	4071	90	7	12	2	-21	...
	1980	14031	90	7	11	2	-21	...
	1985	123000	91	6	12	2	-14	...
	1990	41955000	90	8	13	1	-9	...
	1995	228892000	74	8	25	2	-9	...
	1996	272036000	74	8	26	2	-11	...
	1997	313623000	72	8	27	2	-8	...
	1998	361017000	71	8	27	2	-7	...
	1999	399942000	69	7	26	2	-3	...
	2000	444139000	67	6	27	2	-2	...
	2001	485109000	65	6	28	2	-2	...
	2002	540346284	65	6	29	2	-2	...
Yemen	1990	129960	72	17	12	3	14	20
(Rials)	1995	511058	84	14	21	1	22	42
	1996	736385	66	13	21	2	39	41
	1997	888808	64	13	22	3	36	38
	1998	849321	68	15	32	1	28	43
	1999	1132619	68	14	23	1	36	43
	2000	1379812	58	14	18	1	50	41
	2001	1439834	63	15	18	1	41	40
	2002	1592168	64	16	17	1	48	43
EUROPE								
Albania [35]	1970	6480	56	9	33	1	23	23
(Leks)	1975	11462	56	9	33	1	23	23
	1980	15533	56	9	33	1	1	...
	1985	16857	59	9	33	0	-2	...
	1990	16813	73	10	35	-10	-7	...
	1995	229793	47	53	18	...	12	34
	1996	315835	103	10	17	-6	12	35
	1997	333071	103	10	15	-3	10	36
	1998	425356	100	9	14	-0	11	33
	1999	488610	90	9	17	0	15	31
	2000	551281	81	9	20	11	18	39
	2001	611622	86	9	27	...	20	42
	2002	677272	94	11	20	...	19	43
Austria	1970	28184	52	15	25	4	30	29
(Euros)	1975	49196	54	18	26	-1	31	31
	1980	74723	53	18	25	2	36	38
	1985	100772	55	20	22	1	40	40
	1990	133603	54	19	24	1	40	38
	1995	172287	54	20	23	1	37	38
	1996	178045	55	20	23	0	38	39
	1997	182486	56	20	24	1	42	43
	1998	190628	55	20	24	1	43	44
	1999	197064	55	20	24	1	45	46
	2000	206671	55	19	24	0	50	51
	2001	212511	55	19	23	0	53	52
	2002	218333	55	19	22	0	53	51
	2003	224270	55	19	23	0	52	50
Belarus [36]	1990	4	50	25	25	...	50	50
(Belarussian Roubles)	1995	121403	56	21	25	0	50	54
	1996	191839	57	21	21	2	46	50
	1997	366830	55	20	25	2	60	66
	1998	702161	55	20	26	1	59	64
	1999	3026064	57	20	26	-3	59	62
	2000	9133776	55	19	25	0	69	72
	2001	17173230	56	22	23	1	67	70
	2002	26138302	58	21	22	0	64	67
Belgium	1970	31788	51	18	25	2	52	49
(Euros)	1975	57501	53	21	25	-0	53	53
	1980	88287	55	23	23	1	58	61
	1985	121935	57	23	18	-0	72	71

Table 2. Gross Domestic Product by Type of Expenditure: Individual Countries or Areas

Major area, region and country	Year	Gross Domestic Product (at current prices) Million	Household final consumption expenditure 1	General government final consumption expenditure 2	Gross fixed capital formation 3	Changes in inventories 4	Exports of goods and services 5	Imports of goods and services 6
			Percentage Distribution					
	1990	163341	54	20	22	-0	71	69
	1995	202174	53	21	20	0	69	65
	1996	206989	53	22	20	-0	71	67
	1997	217173	53	21	20	-0	75	70
	1998	225244	53	21	21	-0	75	71
	1999	235713	53	21	21	-0	76	71
	2000	247792	53	21	21	0	86	82
	2001	253800	53	22	21	-0	86	83
	2002	260011	53	22	20	-0	84	80
Bosnia and Herzegovina..............................	1990	1	69	20	19	1	48	56
(Convertible Marka)	1995	2860	67	25	17	3	43	55
	1996	4125	51	23	16	4	34	45
	1997	6562	61	28	20	5	41	54
	1998	7439	61	28	20	5	41	54
	1999	8604	61	28	20	5	41	54
	2000	9433	61	28	20	5	41	54
	2001	10217	60	27	19	4	40	53
	2002	11264	89	23	20	...	27	61
	2003	11635	89	23	20	...	28	61
Bulgaria [37]...	1970	13	58	4	37	...	33	39
(Leva)	1975	18	59	6	39	...	33	48
	1980	26	62	6	28	...	33	35
	1985	33	61	8	26	...	33	35
	1990	45	67	7	21	...	33	37
	1995	880	70	15	15	0	45	46
	1996	1761	74	12	14	-5	55	50
	1997	17433	73	13	11	-1	58	54
	1998	22421	67	15	13	4	47	47
	1999	23790	71	17	15	3	45	50
	2000	26753	69	18	16	3	56	61
	2001	29709	69	17	18	2	56	63
	2002	32324	69	18	18	2	53	60
	2003	34655	70	17	19	2	53	62
Croatia..	1990	280	66	24	13	...	78	81
(Kuna)	1995	98382	64	28	16	2	39	49
	1996	107981	61	25	20	1	40	50
	1997	123811	62	24	24	3	41	57
	1998	137604	59	25	23	1	40	49
	1999	141579	58	27	23	-0	41	49
	2000	152519	59	25	22	-2	47	52
	2001	165640	59	22	22	2	48	54
	2002	176429	60	22	25	2	46	55
	2003	189908	61	20	26	...	51	61
Czech Republic [38]..	1980	495654	42	22	23	6	50	45
(Koruny)	1985	565354	43	26	24	0	49	42
	1990	677090	47	25	25	0	42	39
	1995	1493310	48	22	31	2	50	54
	1996	1694342	50	22	31	3	49	55
	1997	1816477	51	22	30	2	52	58
	1998	1988582	50	21	28	1	54	55
	1999	2056925	51	22	27	1	56	57
	2000	2146174	51	22	27	2	65	68
	2001	2323091	51	22	28	2	66	69
	2002	2408433	52	22	26	2	62	64
	2003	2550798	51	22	26	2	62	65
Denmark..	1970	122143	55	21	25	1	27	30
(Kroner)	1975	223381	53	25	22	-0	29	30
	1980	385808	53	27	20	-0	32	33
	1985	634018	51	26	21	1	36	36
	1990	825311	48	26	20	0	36	31
	1995	1009756	50	26	19	1	35	31
	1996	1060887	49	26	19	0	36	31
	1997	1116324	49	25	20	1	36	33
	1998	1155407	50	26	21	1	36	34
	1999	1207749	49	26	20	-0	38	33
	2000	1280784	47	25	21	0	44	38
	2001	1325272	46	26	20	0	45	39
	2002	1365214	47	26	20	0	45	39

Table 2. Gross Domestic Product by Type of Expenditure: Individual Countries or Areas

Major area, region and country	Year	Gross Domestic Product (at current prices) Million	Household final consumption expenditure 1	General government final consumption expenditure 2	Gross fixed capital formation 3	Changes in inventories 4	Exports of goods and services 5	Imports of goods and services 6
			Percentage Distribution					
Estonia [39] (Krooni)	1990	798	64	13	24	6	42	50
	1995	40897	58	26	26	1	72	80
	1996	52423	60	25	27	1	67	79
	1997	64045	59	23	28	3	78	90
	1998	73538	58	23	30	-0	80	90
	1999	76327	58	23	25	-0	77	82
	2000	87379	56	21	25	2	94	98
	2001	97895	55	20	26	2	89	93
	2002	108024	56	20	29	3	84	94
Finland (Euros)	1970	7874	52	15	28	4	24	26
	1975	17770	52	18	33	2	23	29
	1980	32796	51	18	27	3	32	33
	1985	56663	51	21	26	-0	29	28
	1990	88080	48	22	29	0	23	24
	1995	95262	49	23	17	1	37	29
	1996	98634	50	23	17	-0	37	30
	1997	107030	49	22	19	0	39	31
	1998	116311	48	22	19	1	39	30
	1999	119985	48	22	20	-0	38	29
	2000	130145	47	21	20	1	43	34
	2001	135228	48	21	21	0	40	32
	2002	139716	49	22	19	0	39	30
	2003	143333	50	22	18	1	37	30
France (Euros)	1970	124467	55	17	25	3	15	15
	1975	230245	55	20	25	-1	18	18
	1980	439384	55	22	24	1	20	23
	1985	727369	57	24	20	-0	23	24
	1990	1009345	55	22	23	1	21	22
	1995	1181849	55	24	19	0	23	21
	1996	1212178	55	24	18	-0	23	21
	1997	1251163	54	24	18	-0	26	23
	1998	1305852	54	23	18	1	26	23
	1999	1355102	54	23	19	0	26	24
	2000	1420138	54	23	20	1	29	27
	2001	1475584	54	23	20	0	28	26
	2002	1526820	54	24	19	-0	27	25
Germany (Euros)	1970	381209	56	17	28	2	16	18
	1975	580477	59	22	23	-0	19	21
	1980	830212	59	22	25	1	20	25
	1985	1034570	58	21	22	-0	25	27
	1990	1380690	55	20	23	0	25	25
	1995	1801300	55	20	22	0	24	24
	1996	1833700	56	20	22	-0	25	24
	1997	1871600	56	19	21	0	28	27
	1998	1929400	56	19	21	0	29	28
	1999	1978600	57	19	22	0	30	29
	2000	2030000	57	19	22	0	34	33
	2001	2073700	57	19	20	-1	35	33
	2002	2110400	57	19	19	-1	36	32
Greece (Euros)	1970	993	65	11	26	5	10	17
	1975	2305	62	13	24	7	17	23
	1980	6106	65	13	29	-3	24	28
	1985	16646	64	17	22	4	20	27
	1990	39111	71	15	23	0	18	28
	1995	79927	73	15	19	0	18	25
	1996	87851	73	15	19	0	18	26
	1997	97235	72	15	20	0	20	27
	1998	105773	71	15	21	0	20	28
	1999	112686	70	15	23	-0	22	31
	2000	121668	69	16	24	0	26	34
	2001	131026	68	15	24	0	24	31
	2002	141354	67	16	24	0	21	28
	2003	152594	66	15	26	0	20	28
Hungary [40] (Forints)	1970	372184	48	19	36	-3	29	29
	1975	538863	48	19	40	-3	39	43
	1980	804910	49	20	34	-4	37	36
	1985	1153905	50	21	27	-2	40	35
	1990	2282416	48	22	22	3	30	26

Table 2. Gross Domestic Product by Type of Expenditure: Individual Countries or Areas

Major area, region and country	Year	Gross Domestic Product (at current prices) Million	Household final consumption expenditure 1	General government final consumption expenditure 2	Gross fixed capital formation 3	Changes in inventories 4	Exports of goods and services 5	Imports of goods and services 6
			Percentage Distribution					
	1995	5614042	53	24	20	2	44	44
	1996	6893935	51	22	21	4	48	48
	1997	8540669	49	22	22	4	55	54
	1998	10087434	50	22	24	5	63	64
	1999	11393500	51	22	24	5	65	68
	2000	13172293	51	21	24	7	75	79
	2001	14849623	52	21	24	4	74	76
	2002	16743688	53	23	23	2	65	68
Iceland	1970	460	58	13	25	0	44	43
(Kroner)	1975	2148	55	17	33	3	33	41
	1980	16112	55	17	26	2	35	35
	1985	120373	61	18	22	-2	41	41
	1990	362817	58	20	20	-0	34	33
	1995	442256	56	22	16	1	36	33
	1996	474586	57	22	19	0	37	37
	1997	513749	55	22	20	0	37	37
	1998	568885	55	22	25	0	36	40
	1999	609413	57	23	23	0	35	40
	2000	662433	57	24	24	0	35	42
	2001	745188	53	24	22	-0	41	41
	2002	778960	51	26	19	-0	40	38
	2003	806951	53	26	22	-0	35	39
Ireland	1970	2231	69	16	22	2	34	43
(Euros)	1975	5222	64	20	22	0	40	47
	1980	12891	66	21	28	-1	46	60
	1985	24500	59	20	18	1	56	56
	1990	36312	56	16	19	2	57	52
	1995	52641	51	16	17	1	76	65
	1996	58080	51	16	19	1	78	66
	1997	67123	48	15	21	1	80	67
	1998	77543	47	14	22	2	86	75
	1999	89614	46	14	24	0	88	74
	2000	102845	46	14	24	1	97	84
	2001	114743	45	15	23	0	98	83
	2002	129344	43	15	22	0	94	75
Italy	1970	34765	57	16	25	2	16	16
(Euros)	1975	71985	58	17	26	-1	20	20
	1980	198524	58	17	25	3	22	25
	1985	420324	58	19	22	2	22	23
	1990	682153	57	20	21	1	20	20
	1995	923052	58	18	18	1	27	23
	1996	982443	58	18	18	0	26	21
	1997	1026285	58	18	18	1	26	22
	1998	1073019	59	18	18	1	26	23
	1999	1107994	60	18	19	1	26	23
	2000	1166548	60	18	20	0	28	27
	2001	1220147	60	19	20	-0	28	27
	2002	1258349	60	19	20	0	27	26
	2003	1298780	60	19	19	0	25	25
Latvia [41]	1990	62	53	8	23	17	48	49
(Lats)	1995	2329	63	22	15	2	47	50
	1996	2807	68	22	18	0	51	59
	1997	3270	66	19	19	4	51	60
	1998	3592	64	21	27	0	51	65
	1999	3890	63	21	25	2	44	54
	2000	4348	62	20	26	1	46	54
	2001	4813	62	19	27	3	44	56
	2002	5195	63	19	26	2	45	56
Lithuania [42]	1990	134	57	19	28	5	52	61
(Litas)	1995	24781	65	23	22	1	52	63
	1996	31529	65	23	22	-0	53	63
	1997	38520	62	23	23	2	54	65
	1998	43555	61	25	25	2	47	58
	1999	42608	64	23	23	1	40	50
	2000	44698	64	22	19	1	46	52
	2001	47498	64	20	21	0	51	56
	2002	50758	63	20	21	1	54	60

Table 2. Gross Domestic Product by Type of Expenditure: Individual Countries or Areas

Major area, region and country	Year	Gross Domestic Product (at current prices) Million	Household final consumption expenditure 1	General government final consumption expenditure 2	Gross fixed capital formation 3	Changes in inventories 4	Exports of goods and services 5	Imports of goods and services 6
			Percentage Distribution					
Luxembourg	1970	1567	50	12	21	2	94	81
(Euros)	1975	2469	58	18	25	-5	98	94
	1980	3784	59	20	25	-2	93	95
	1985	5842	59	19	16	2	114	110
	1990	9180	51	18	23	2	104	100
	1995	13214	47	18	22	-0	109	97
	1996	13927	47	19	21	0	111	100
	1997	15490	44	18	22	1	119	106
	1998	17006	43	17	23	1	127	112
	1999	18739	41	17	24	1	136	120
	2000	21258	39	16	21	3	151	130
	2001	21987	40	17	23	1	153	136
	2002	22395	41	18	23	-1	146	129
Malta [43]	1970	95	78	19	29	3	50	80
(Maltese Lira)	1975	166	72	18	23	1	83	96
	1980	392	65	16	22	2	91	96
	1985	476	70	18	26	2	73	88
	1990	735	63	18	32	2	85	99
	1995	1146	61	21	32	0	94	107
	1996	1201	64	22	29	-0	87	101
	1997	1288	62	20	25	0	85	94
	1998	1362	62	20	24	-1	88	93
	1999	1456	63	19	23	1	91	96
	2000	1558	64	19	26	2	103	114
	2001	1632	64	20	23	-3	87	92
	2002	1673	65	20	23	-5	86	89
Netherlands	1970	58136	52	20	28	2	44	46
(Euros)	1975	105419	51	24	22	-0	49	46
	1980	160721	52	25	22	0	52	53
	1985	199073	51	24	21	-0	62	58
	1990	243561	49	23	22	1	54	51
	1995	302233	49	24	20	1	57	52
	1996	315059	49	23	21	0	58	52
	1997	333725	49	23	21	0	61	55
	1998	354194	49	23	22	1	61	56
	1999	374070	50	23	23	0	60	56
	2000	402291	49	23	22	0	67	62
	2001	429127	49	23	22	0	65	60
	2002	444649	49	25	21	-0	63	58
Norway	1970	91100	49	16	27	6	37	37
(Kroner)	1975	169896	47	19	34	3	36	42
	1980	314363	44	19	27	1	43	37
	1985	547286	45	18	25	2	43	35
	1990	726799	47	21	21	2	40	34
	1995	937445	47	22	20	3	38	32
	1996	1026924	46	21	20	1	41	32
	1997	1111349	45	20	22	2	41	33
	1998	1132134	47	22	25	2	38	36
	1999	1233039	45	21	22	2	39	32
	2000	1469075	41	19	19	2	47	29
	2001	1526601	41	20	18	2	46	29
	2002	1520728	43	22	17	2	41	27
	2003	1568823	44	22	16	1	41	27
Poland	1970	81	75	23	15	-4	41	53
(Zlotych)	1975	144	68	22	23	-5	39	51
	1980	243	63	20	26	-5	30	36
	1985	1005	57	22	22	0	19	20
	1990	58351	46	21	20	4	28	21
	1995	320882	58	19	18	1	24	22
	1996	403911	61	19	20	1	23	25
	1997	491941	61	18	23	1	24	29
	1998	576519	61	18	24	1	27	32
	1999	640627	62	18	24	1	25	31
	2000	713391	63	18	24	1	28	35
	2001	750786	64	18	21	0	28	32
	2002	771113	65	18	19	-0	30	33

Table 2. Gross Domestic Product by Type of Expenditure: Individual Countries or Areas

Major area, region and country	Year	Gross Domestic Product (at current prices) Million	Household final consumption expenditure 1	General government final consumption expenditure 2	Gross fixed capital formation 3	Changes in inventories 4	Exports of goods and services 5	Imports of goods and services 6
			Percentage Distribution					
Portugal	1970	1056	63	13	24	4	22	27
(Euros)	1975	2240	74	14	27	-8	18	28
	1980	7458	65	13	30	4	24	36
	1985	20923	65	14	23	-1	33	35
	1990	50817	62	16	26	2	33	39
	1995	80827	62	19	23	1	30	36
	1996	86230	62	19	23	1	30	36
	1997	93014	61	19	26	1	30	38
	1998	100962	61	19	27	1	31	40
	1999	108030	61	20	27	1	30	40
	2000	115548	60	21	28	1	32	43
	2001	123054	59	21	27	1	31	41
	2002	129280	59	21	25	1	30	38
	2003	130559	60	21	22	...	31	36
Republic of Moldova	1990	13	61	10	23	7	49	51
(Lei)	1995	6480	56	26	16	9	60	68
	1996	7798	67	26	20	4	55	74
	1997	8917	67	29	20	4	53	74
	1998	9122	75	25	22	4	45	72
	1999	12322	74	15	18	4	52	65
	2000	16020	88	15	15	9	50	77
	2001	19052	86	14	17	7	50	74
	2002	22556	82	20	16	5	52	77
	2003	27297	89	18	17	5	53	84
Romania [44]	1970	227348	52	21	24	5	22	26
(Lei)	1975	384219	48	22	28	7	22	33
	1980	484684	52	13	35	5	22	22
	1985	623460	51	12	30	3	29	20
	1990	857851	65	13	20	10	17	26
	1995	72135548	67	14	21	3	28	33
	1996	108919636	69	13	23	3	28	37
	1997	252925736	74	12	21	-1	29	36
	1998	373798214	75	15	18	-0	23	31
	1999	545730127	73	14	18	-2	28	33
	2000	803773100	69	16	19	1	33	38
	2001	1167242800	68	16	20	2	33	41
	2002	1512256600	66	16	21	2	35	41
Russian Federation	1990	644200	47	21	29	1	18	18
(Roubles)	1995	1428522	50	19	21	5	29	26
	1996	2007825	50	19	20	3	26	22
	1997	2342514	53	21	18	4	25	23
	1998	2629623	56	19	16	-1	31	25
	1999	4823234	52	15	15	0	43	26
	2000	7305646	45	15	17	2	44	24
	2001	8943600	49	16	19	3	37	24
	2002	10834200	50	18	18	2	35	25
	2003	13304700	49	17	18	2	35	23
San Marino	1970	22	46	14	38	4	217	220
(Italian Lire)	1975	46	46	14	38	4	217	220
	1980	128	46	14	38	4	217	220
	1985	271	46	14	38	4	217	220
	1990	439	46	14	38	4	217	220
	1995	595	46	14	38	4	216	219
	2000	843	45	14	39	4	211	214
	2003	939	45	14	39	5	206	209
Serbia and Montenegro [45]	1990	34174	65	21	13	4	11	14
(New Dinars)	1995	43984	67	21	12	5	7	11
	1996	79396	72	22	12	5	16	27
	1997	109352	68	26	12	3	18	27
	1998	148370	70	29	12	-1	23	33
	1999	191099	69	28	13	-0	11	20
	2000	381661	70	29	15	-7	9	17
	2001	771800	70	27	13	0	16	25
	2002	1006900	69	28	13	-1	15	24
Slovakia	1980	206213	50	20	30	5	31	36
(Koruny)	1985	244360	50	20	28	2	31	32
	1990	292800	54	23	30	1	26	34

Table 2. Gross Domestic Product by Type of Expenditure: Individual Countries or Areas

Major area, region and country	Year	Gross Domestic Product (at current prices) Million	Household final consumption expenditure 1	General government final consumption expenditure 2	Gross fixed capital formation 3	Changes in inventories 4	Exports of goods and services 5	Imports of goods and services 6
			Percentage Distribution					
	1995	576502	51	21	25	-0	58	56
	1996	638449	53	22	32	3	54	65
	1997	712679	53	22	34	0	57	66
	1998	781437	54	22	36	-2	60	70
	1999	844108	56	20	30	-2	61	66
	2000	934079	56	20	26	0	71	73
	2001	1009839	57	20	29	1	73	82
	2002	1096384	57	20	27	2	72	79
	2003	1195812	56	20	26	-1	78	80
Slovenia [46] (Tolars)	1990	196762	52	17	19	-2	91	79
	1995	2342142	58	20	20	2	52	54
	1996	2698033	57	20	21	1	53	54
	1997	3065101	56	20	23	1	54	55
	1998	3422378	56	20	24	1	54	55
	1999	3839852	56	19	26	1	50	54
	2000	4222404	55	20	26	1	57	60
	2001	4740122	55	21	24	0	58	59
	2002	5275827	53	21	23	1	58	56
	2003	5683856	54	20	25	1	61	63
Spain (Euros)	1970	16392	62	10	27	1	13	14
	1975	37638	63	11	27	2	13	17
	1980	95334	64	14	23	1	15	17
	1985	175624	62	16	21	0	22	20
	1990	312424	60	17	26	1	16	20
	1995	437787	59	18	22	0	23	23
	1996	464251	59	18	22	0	24	23
	1997	494140	59	18	22	0	27	26
	1998	527975	59	17	23	0	27	27
	1999	565419	59	17	24	0	28	29
	2000	609734	58	18	25	0	30	32
	2001	653289	58	18	25	0	30	32
	2002	696208	58	18	25	0	28	30
	2003	743046	57	18	26	0	28	30
Sweden (Kroner)	1970	179928	50	22	23	4	24	24
	1975	314236	49	25	22	4	27	27
	1980	548581	48	30	21	2	29	31
	1985	899754	48	28	21	1	35	33
	1990	1421418	47	27	23	0	30	29
	1995	1770248	48	27	16	1	39	33
	1996	1815144	48	28	16	0	38	31
	1997	1888231	48	27	16	0	41	34
	1998	1971871	48	27	16	1	43	36
	1999	2076525	48	27	17	0	43	36
	2000	2194967	48	27	18	1	46	40
	2001	2266387	47	27	17	0	46	40
	2002	2342554	47	28	17	0	44	37
	2003	2435019	46	28	16	0	43	37
Switzerland (Swiss Francs)	1970	95863	55	10	29	5	31	33
	1975	148190	58	12	25	-1	30	27
	1980	180095	60	12	25	4	35	38
	1985	237206	59	13	24	1	38	37
	1990	317304	55	14	27	1	36	36
	1995	363329	58	14	21	0	35	31
	1996	365833	58	15	20	0	36	32
	1997	371372	59	14	20	1	40	35
	1998	379989	59	14	20	1	40	36
	1999	388518	59	14	20	-1	42	37
	2000	405772	58	14	21	0	46	41
	2001	413866	58	14	20	1	45	41
	2002	417297	59	14	19	-1	44	37
TFYR Macedonia (Denars)	1990	506	66	19	18	1	26	36
	1995	169521	70	19	17	4	33	43
	1996	176444	72	18	17	3	28	39
	1997	186019	73	20	17	4	37	51
	1998	194979	72	20	17	5	41	56
	1999	209010	69	21	17	3	42	52

Table 2. Gross Domestic Product by Type of Expenditure: Individual Countries or Areas

Major area, region and country	Year	Gross Domestic Product (at current prices) Million	Household final consumption expenditure 1	General government final consumption expenditure 2	Gross fixed capital formation 3	Changes in inventories 4	Exports of goods and services 5	Imports of goods and services 6
			Percentage Distribution					
	2000	236389	74	18	16	5	48	62
	2001	233841	69	25	15	3	42	55
	2002	238890	71	21	16	4	42	55
Ukraine (Hryvnias)	1990	2	53	18	24	6	29	29
	1995	54516	50	21	23	3	47	50
	1996	81519	53	22	21	2	46	48
	1997	93365	54	24	20	2	41	44
	1998	102593	57	22	20	1	42	44
	1999	130442	55	20	19	-2	54	49
	2000	170070	54	19	20	0	62	57
	2001	204190	55	20	20	2	55	54
	2002	220932	54	20	20	-1	56	52
United Kingdom (Pounds Sterling)	1970	51515	59	18	19	1	22	21
	1975	105773	59	22	21	-1	25	27
	1980	230695	58	22	19	-1	27	25
	1985	354952	58	21	18	0	29	28
	1990	557300	61	20	21	-0	24	27
	1995	719176	62	20	16	1	28	29
	1996	763290	62	19	17	0	29	30
	1997	810944	62	18	16	1	29	29
	1998	859436	62	18	18	1	27	28
	1999	903865	63	18	17	1	26	28
	2000	951265	63	19	17	1	28	30
	2001	994037	64	19	17	0	27	30
	2002	1043945	64	20	16	0	26	29
	2003	1101556	63	21	16	0	25	28
OCEANIA								
Australia (Australian Dollars)	1970	38277	56	14	29	2	13	14
	1975	79386	57	19	25	0	14	14
	1980	145643	58	19	27	0	16	18
	1985	248131	58	20	26	0	16	19
	1990	397881	59	19	23	-0	17	17
	1995	502828	60	18	22	-0	20	20
	1996	529886	59	18	22	-0	20	20
	1997	561229	60	18	23	0	20	21
	1998	591917	60	18	23	1	19	21
	1999	628621	60	18	24	0	20	22
	2000	669307	60	18	21	-0	23	23
	2001	712980	60	18	22	0	21	22
	2002	752760	61	18	24	0	20	22
Cook Islands [47] (New Zealand Dollars)	1970	10	80	32	26	...	32	71
	1975	13	108	32	26	...	30	96
	1980	22	120	32	26	...	22	100
	1985	51	119	32	26	...	11	89
	1990	98	115	32	26	...	8	81
	1995	142	85	32	26	...	4	48
	2000	178	86	32	26	...	4	48
	2002	221	86	32	26	...	4	48
Fiji (Fiji Dollars)	1970	192	65	14	18	4	48	52
	1975	562	68	12	18	2	43	44
	1980	984	58	16	25	6	48	52
	1985	1316	64	19	18	1	44	45
	1990	1980	73	17	17	2	62	67
	1995	2799	63	16	13	1	55	58
	2000	3518	62	18	10	1	60	64
	2002	4072	71	16	13	1	58	59
French Polynesia (French Francs)	1970	21468	81	47	23	...	13	63
	1975	45020	67	42	29	1	11	50
	1980	96832	61	50	25	-1	7	43
	1985	226772	53	42	35	0	9	39
	1990	290064	62	40	20	0	9	32
	1995	373136	63	42	17	...	9	28
	2000	426800	63	42	17	...	9	28
	2003	462984	63	42	17	...	9	28

Table 2. Gross Domestic Product by Type of Expenditure: Individual Countries or Areas

Major area, region and country	Year	Gross Domestic Product (at current prices) Million	Household final consumption expenditure 1	General government final consumption expenditure 2	Gross fixed capital formation 3	Changes in inventories 4	Exports of goods and services 5	Imports of goods and services 6
			Percentage Distribution					
Kiribati	1970	13	45	22	8	...	59	33
(Australian Dollars)	1975	42	45	22	8	...	59	33
	1980	25	45	22	8	...	59	33
	1985	30	45	22	8	...	59	33
	1990	36	45	22	8	...	59	33
	1995	62	45	22	8	...	59	33
	2000	83	43	22	8	...	57	32
	2002	98	43	22	8	...	57	32
Marshall Islands	1970	7	57	28	11	...	44	39
(U.S. Dollars)	1975	15	37	18	5	...	68	28
	1980	23	94	59	33	...	23	110
	1985	38	97	53	56	...	20	126
	1990	69	98	50	88	...	11	147
	1995	105	91	54	56	...	13	114
	2000	98	90	54	56	...	12	112
	2002	106	89	53	55	...	12	111
Micronesia (Federated States of)	1970	24	45	22	8	...	59	33
(U.S. Dollars)	1975	56	45	22	8	...	59	33
	1980	77	45	22	8	...	59	33
	1985	102	45	22	8	...	59	33
	1990	151	45	22	8	...	59	33
	1995	215	45	22	8	...	59	33
	2000	229	43	22	8	...	57	32
	2002	240	43	22	8	...	57	32
Nauru	1970	12	45	22	8	...	59	33
(Australian Dollars)	1975	19	45	22	8	...	59	33
	1980	32	45	22	8	...	59	33
	1985	52	45	22	8	...	59	33
	1990	66	45	22	8	...	59	33
	1995	55	45	22	8	...	59	33
	2000	57	45	22	8	...	59	33
	2002	65	45	22	8	...	59	33
New Caledonia [48]	1970	38204	57	28	11	...	44	39
(CFP Francs)	1975	63643	37	18	5	...	68	28
	1980	90847	94	59	33	0	23	110
	1985	139650	97	53	58	-2	20	126
	1990	250427	98	50	93	-5	11	147
	1995	329296	94	51	66	...	14	124
	2000	347303	94	51	66	...	14	124
	2002	393996	94	51	66	...	14	124
New Zealand	1970	5846	61	16	23	2	22	25
(New Zealand Dollars)	1975	11334	60	18	29	-1	23	30
	1980	23464	58	21	20	0	30	31
	1985	46212	58	19	27	-0	30	33
	1990	73113	60	19	20	-0	27	27
	1995	92679	58	18	21	1	29	29
	1996	97239	59	17	21	1	28	28
	1997	100739	59	18	20	1	28	28
	1998	101959	60	18	19	0	30	30
	1999	107068	60	19	20	1	31	32
	2000	113778	59	18	19	1	36	34
	2001	122241	57	18	19	2	36	33
	2002	126195	58	19	20	1	33	32
Palau	1970	14	45	22	8	...	59	33
(U.S. Dollars)	1975	52	45	22	8	...	59	33
	1980	23	45	22	8	...	59	33
	1985	30	45	22	8	...	59	33
	1990	67	45	22	8	...	59	33
	1995	95	45	22	8	...	59	33
	2000	118	43	22	8	...	57	32
	2002	124	43	22	8	...	57	32
Papua New Guinea	1970	689	56	30	37	5	18	49
(Kina)	1975	1185	50	36	13	4	37	38
	1980	1894	55	25	19	3	43	46
	1985	2451	59	25	17	3	45	49
	1990	3138	52	26	23	1	43	45

Table 2. Gross Domestic Product by Type of Expenditure: Individual Countries or Areas

Major area, region and country	Year	Gross Domestic Product (at current prices) Million	Household final consumption expenditure 1	General government final consumption expenditure 2	Gross fixed capital formation 3	Changes in inventories 4	Exports of goods and services 5	Imports of goods and services 6
			Percentage Distribution					
	1995	5888	42	17	20	3	62	43
	2000	9515	75	18	13	2	50	54
	2002	10963	69	18	13	3	49	51
Samoa	1970	43	94	18	39	...	22	73
(Tala)	1975	85	94	18	39	...	22	73
	1980	142	87	18	33	...	25	63
	1985	271	87	18	31	...	28	64
	1990	465	81	19	34	...	31	65
	1995	496	83	22	40	...	27	76
	2000	775	106	29	52	...	24	113
	2002	890	106	29	50	...	24	113
Solomon Islands	1970	29	81	19	19	-5	25	40
(Solomon Islands Dollars)	1975	50	90	19	19	5	24	58
	1980	119	99	21	19	3	51	93
	1985	237	64	28	21	5	51	70
	1990	526	58	31	17	3	47	57
	1995	1242	49	33	18	2	58	59
	2000	1721	48	32	18	1	59	59
	2002	1848	48	32	20	...	59	59
Tonga [49]	1970	10	88	17	21	-0	38	64
(Pa 'anga)	1975	25	89	17	23	5	43	73
	1980	47	93	15	29	1	30	68
	1985	86	100	16	23	3	30	72
	1990	147	94	19	18	0	34	65
	1995	198	107	20	22	...	20	69
	1996	209	107	21	22	1	22	72
	1997	208	100	22	17	1	21	62
	1998	219	108	21	18	1	16	66
	1999	238	97	22	20	1	13	54
	2000	252	97	21	21	1	16	56
	2001	274	102	23	20	1	13	59
	2002	296	101	22	19	1	16	59
Tuvalu	1970	1	57	28	11	...	44	39
(Australian dollars)	1975	2	37	18	5	...	68	28
	1980	4	94	59	33	...	23	110
	1985	5	100	55	58	...	21	126
	1990	12	103	53	93	...	12	147
	1995	16	91	54	56	...	13	114
	2000	25	91	54	56	...	13	114
	2002	36	89	53	55	...	12	111
Vanuatu	1970	3508	55	34	29	...	48	68
(Vatu)	1975	5084	55	34	29	...	48	68
	1980	7746	55	34	29	...	48	68
	1985	12534	57	36	23	6	51	72
	1990	17900	63	28	40	3	46	77
	1995	27255	47	25	30	2	44	54
	1996	28227	50	28	26	2	46	54
	1997	29477	49	26	24	3	47	53
	1998	29545	47	26	25	2	44	52
	1999	29523	47	26	25	2	44	52
	2000	30423	47	26	25	2	44	52
	2001	31153	47	26	25	2	44	52
	2002	28114	48	26	25	2	45	53

Notes for Table 2:

1/ (a) Exports of goods and services
1972-1979
Exports of goods only.

(b) Imports of goods and services
1972-1979
Includes imports of goods plus net imports of services.

2/ Gross Domestic Product
1972-1979
For years 1972-1979 estimates relate to calendar year.

3/ (a) Gross fixed capital formation
1970-1972, 1974-1993
The estimates refer to central government capital formation only.

(b) Exports of goods and services
1970-1993
Includes net travel and tourism income.

(c) Imports of goods and services
1970-1993
Includes net freight and insurance.

4/ (a) Changes in inventories
1970-1996
Cocoa is valued at cost to the Ghana Cocoa Marketing Board. Stocks of other export commodities, including minerals, are valued at export prices.

(b) Gross Domestic Product
1970-1979
Gross domestic product at purchaser's prices.

5/ Changes in inventories
1970-1989
Includes only increase in iron ore stocks. Beginning 1981, it includes increase in iron ore and rubber stocks.

6/ Household final consumption expenditure
1970-1985, 1987-1992
Obtained as a residual.

7/ Household final consumption expenditure
1980-1993
Includes Changes in inventories.

8/ Gross Domestic Product
1972-1979
Discrepancy between components and total.

9/ Household final consumption expenditure
1980-1989
Obtained as a residual.

10/ Exports of goods and services
1994-2002
Exports less imports.

11/ (a) Exports of goods and services
1970-1990
Includes an upward adjustments for the estimated value of diamond smuggled out of the country.

(b) Imports of goods and services
1987-1990
Includes an upward adjustments for the estimated value of diamond smuggled out of the country.

12/ (a) Household final consumption expenditure
1980-1987
Obtained as a residual.

(b) General government final consumption expenditure
1980-1987
Includes the value of technical assistance from abroad.

(c) Gross fixed capital formation
1970-1987
Includes the value of technical assistance from abroad.

(d) Changes in inventories
1970-1987
Includes livestock only.

(e) Exports of goods and services
1970-1987
Exports of goods only.

(f) Imports of goods and services
1970-1987
Refers to imports of goods and non-factor services.

13/ (a) Household final consumption expenditure
1975-1979
As of 1975, the significant increase is due to the sharp increases in salary. Estimates also include errors and omissions.

(b) Exports of goods and services
1970-2001
Estimates are on calendar year basis.

(c) Imports of goods and services
1970-2001
Estimates are on calendar year basis.

14/ Household final consumption expenditure
1970-2002
Includes Final consumption expenditure of NPISH's.

15/ Household final consumption expenditure
1980-1992
Excludes direct purchases abroad by resident households and direct purchases in the domestic market by non-resident households.

16/ Changes in inventories
1970-1991
Includes only increase of stocks of mining, manufacturing, peanuts, raw tobacco and beans.

17/ Household final consumption expenditure
1980-1992
Includes NPISHs final consumption expenditure.

18/ Exports of goods and services
Imports of goods and services
1979-1985
Exports and imports of merchandise are recorded on the basis of the crossing of frontiers. No data are available on the basis of changes in the ownership of the goods. Imports and exports are recorded on a cash basis and the imports and exports of oil refineries are not included in the estimates.

19/ (a) Gross fixed capital formation
1980-1995
Includes communications equipment.

(b) Changes in inventories
1980-1995
Includes livestock only.

20/ (a) Household final consumption expenditure
1980-2003
Includes NPISHs final consumption expenditure.

(b) Changes in inventories
1970-2003
Refers to increase in stocks of wool and livestock in the private sector, and to stocks held by the public sector.

21/ Changes in inventories
1990-2002
Includes Acquisitions less disposal of valuables.

22/ Changes in inventories
1990-2003
Includes Acquisitions less disposal of valuables.

23/ Changes in inventories
1987-1992
Includes net errors and omissions.

24/ (a) Exports of goods and services
1972-1979
Refers to exports of goods and non-factor services.

(b) Imports of goods and services
1972-1979
Refers to imports of goods and non-factor services.

25/ Changes in inventories
1974-1979
Land improvement is not included in Other construction and land improvement, etc..

26/ Gross Domestic Product
2000-2001
Provisional data.

27/ Changes in inventories
1995-2003
Includes Acquisitions less disposal of valuables.

28/ (a) Household final consumption expenditure
1990-1993
Refers to expenditure in the domestic market only.

(b) Gross fixed capital formation
1990-1993
Calculated based on type of asset.

29/ General government final consumption expenditure
Gross fixed capital formation
1970-1979,1987-2001
Government final consumption expenditure includes pension payments less employees' pension contributions. Some non-capital development expenditure of the central government is included in fixed capital formation.

30/ Gross Domestic Product
1970-1974
Estimates refer to year ending 30 September.

31/ Changes in inventories
1970-2002
Includes Acquisitions less disposal of valuables.

32/ Gross Domestic Product
2000-2001
Provisional data.

33/ Exports of goods and services
1971-2002
Exports less imports.

34/ Exports of goods and services
1970-2002
Exports less imports.

35/ Exports of goods and services
1980-1990
Exports less imports.

36/ Changes in inventories
1994-2002
Includes Acquisitions less disposal of valuables.

37/ (a) Household final consumption expenditure
1979-1990
Includes the consumption of goods and services of resident and non-resident units in the country, without adjustments for purchases abroad and net gifts in kind received from abroad.

(b) General government final consumption expenditure
1979-1990
Government consumption expenditure on collective goods.

(c) Changes in inventories
1979-2002
Includes Acquisitions less disposal of valuables.

38/ (a) General government final consumption expenditure
1987-1990
Includes consumption expenditure of the private non-profit institutions serving households.

(b) Changes in inventories
1985-1990
Includes Acquisitions less disposal of valuables.

39/ Changes in inventories
1987-2002
Includes Acquisitions less disposal of valuables.

40/ (a) Household final consumption expenditure
1988-1991
Includes total final consumption expenditure in domestic market of households. Consumption from own-account production is evaluated at basic prices. The wage-like part of the business travel cost (i.e. per diem) is treated as private consumption expenditure.

(b) General government final consumption expenditure
1988-1991
Includes health, social and cultural expenditure of enterprises and final consumption expenditure of non-profit institutions.

(c) Changes in inventories
1988-1991
Includes gains or losses arising from fluctuations in prices.

(d) Exports of goods and services
1988-1991
Does not include direct purchases in the domestic market by non-resident households.

(e) Imports of goods and services
1988-1991
Does not include direct purchases abroad by resident households, except purchase of cars by Hungarian individuals for own use.

41/ (a) Household final consumption expenditure
1996
Includes NPISHs final consumption expenditure.

(b) Changes in inventories
1990-2002
Includes Acquisitions less disposal of valuables.

42/ Changes in inventories
1980-1994
Includes Acquisitions less disposal of valuables.

43/ (a) Changes in inventories
1970-2001
Includes a statistical discrepancy.

(b) Gross Domestic Product
2000-2001
Provisional data.

44/ Changes in inventories
1980-2002
Includes Acquisitions less disposal of valuables.

45/ (a) Changes in inventories
1994-2000
Includes Acquisitions less disposal of valuables.

(b) Gross Domestic Product
1999-2000
Data excludes Kosovo and Metohia effective January 1999.

46/ Changes in inventories
1990-1994, 1997-2000
Includes Acquisitions less disposal of valuables.

47/ (a) Exports of goods and services
1970-2002
Valued f.o.b.

(b) Imports of goods and services
1970-2002
Valued c.i.f. instead of f.o.b.

48/ General government final consumption expenditure
1970-1992
Includes Education and health.

49/ Household final consumption expenditure
1994-2002
Includes NPISHs final consumption expenditure.

Table 3. Gross Domestic Product by Kind of Economic Activity: Individual Countries or Areas

Major area, region and country	Year	Gross Domestic Product (at current prices) Million	Agriculture hunting forestry and fishing A-B	Mining Manufacturing and Utilities C-E	Of which: Manufacturing D	Construction F	Wholesale, retail trade, restaurants and hotels G-H	Transport storage and communication I	Other Activities J-P
			Percentage Distribution						
AFRICA									
Algeria	1970	25509	10	28	13	9	18	5	20
(Dinars)	1975	61574	8	36	9	11	10	5	17
	1980	162507	8	45	10	10	12	5	15
	1985	291597	8	37	11	13	14	5	14
	1990	554388	11	35	11	10	13	5	20
	1995	2004995	10	36	8	10	15	5	19
	1996	2570030	11	39	7	8	14	6	19
	1997	2780170	9	39	7	9	14	7	17
	1998	2810122	12	33	8	9	15	7	19
	1999	3238198	11	37	7	8	14	7	18
	2000	4098810	8	48	6	7	12	7	14
	2001	4241803	10	42	6	8	12	8	16
	2002	4479695	9	41	6	8	13	7	16
	2003	5044000	10	43	6	8	13	7	16
Angola [1]	1970	82 (u)	13	21	13	5	12	6	34
(Kwanzas)	1975	80 (u)	12	47	11	2	12	3	33
	1980	161 (u)	14	31	5	3	7	3	26
	1985	205 (u)	13	38	10	5	13	5	25
	1990	308 (u)	18	38	5	3	11	3	27
	1995	14	7	63	4	4	18	0	12
	2000	91666	6	69	3	3	14	0	7
	2002	426428	9	58	4	4	16	0	12
Benin [2]	1970	81809	33	13	...	2	12	5	27
(CFA Francs)	1975	132742	28	21	20	3	17	7	28
	1980	288239	32	12	12	3	17	7	22
	1985	469778	32	13	8	3	16	8	20
	1990	502300	35	9	9	4	20	10	24
	1995	1005882	34	10	9	5	19	8	18
	2000	1605500	37	10	9	4	18	8	16
	2003	2040300	35	11	9	4	18	8	16
Botswana	1970	70	32	18	6	10	15	3	19
(Pula)	1975	263	31	18	7	9	8	3	23
	1980	832	13	37	4	7	8	2	23
	1985	2146	6	48	5	5	7	3	24
	1990	6552	5	52	5	7	7	3	23
	1995	12262	4	41	5	6	10	4	31
	1996	14204	4	41	5	6	10	4	31
	1997	17740	3	46	5	6	10	3	28
	1998	20163	3	45	5	6	10	3	28
	1999	21524	3	38	5	6	11	4	33
	2000	25363	3	40	5	6	11	4	31
	2001	29353	3	41	5	5	11	4	30
	2002	32000	2	42	4	5	11	4	32
Burkina Faso	1970	109936	40	13	13	4	14	7	16
(CFA Francs)	1975	168467	45	14	13	3	9	5	19
	1980	360929	40	12	11	3	13	8	20
	1985	622711	47	13	11	1	10	7	20
	1990	778376	43	17	15	5	2	4	18
	1995	1106300	42	14	13	2	5	5	25
	2000	1560600	36	14	12	4	18	5	27
	2002	2003800	33	16	15	3	16	5	23
Burundi	1970	21476	63	7	6	2	7	1	14
(Francs)	1975	32671	60	7	7	3	9	1	14
	1980	85607	56	8	8	4	8	2	14
	1985	141347	55	13	12	4	11	2	13
	1990	196656	51	17	16	3	5	3	18
	1995	250448	49	11	11	5	5	3	18
	2000	512231	46	10	9	6	6	4	23
	2003	638392	49	9	8	5	6	4	21
Cameroon	1970	365638	21	17	15	4	21	4	26
(CFA Francs)	1975	747890	24	15	14	5	16	5	25
	1980	2044294	19	23	13	7	13	3	25
	1985	4672835	15	27	16	8	16	3	26
	1990	3896040	18	27	19	5	15	4	29

Table 3. Gross Domestic Product by Kind of Economic Activity: Individual Countries or Areas

Major area, region and country	Year	Gross Domestic Product (at current prices) Million	Agriculture hunting forestry and fishing A-B	Mining Manufacturing and Utilities C-E	Of which: Manufacturing D	Construction F	Wholesale, retail trade, restaurants and hotels G-H	Transport storage and communication I	Other Activities J-P
			Percentage Distribution						
	1995	4465080	23	26	20	2	19	4	20
	2000	6602500	22	26	20	2	19	5	19
	2003	7473689	23	27	20	2	19	6	20
Cape Verde (Escudos)	1970	1844	19	5	4	13	34	7	16
	1975	3009	18	6	5	10	32	9	20
	1980	5715	19	5	5	12	30	9	19
	1985	12625	13	7	6	11	28	15	21
	1990	21573	14	8	7	12	21	15	23
	1995	37705	14	8	7	9	17	17	27
	1996	41476	14	8	7	9	17	17	27
	1997	47158	14	7	6	9	18	18	28
	1998	52867	14	7	6	8	19	18	28
	1999	60400	14	7	6	9	18	18	28
	2000	64700	13	7	6	9	18	18	28
	2001	69000	14	7	6	9	18	18	28
	2002	73780	12	8	7	10	20	20	31
	2003	79889	12	8	7	10	20	20	31
Central African Republic [3] (CFA Francs)	1970	41341	34	14	8	2	26	5	18
	1975	86470	37	13	9	2	23	4	21
	1980	149718	39	12	8	2	22	4	18
	1985	337755	42	11	7	3	22	4	18
	1990	353000	43	11	7	3	23	5	16
	1995	531738	43	10	7	3	23	5	15
	2000	646020	55	15	10	5	14	3	9
	2003	730710	52	13	9	4	18	4	11
Chad [4] (CFA Francs)	1970	114202	46	14	13	2	26	3	8
	1975	187481	41	13	11	3	28	2	12
	1980	193869	64	10	9	1	16	4	12
	1985	412267	52	13	12	2	22	4	13
	1990	419083	39	18	17	2	21	4	18
	1995	720000	35	14	13	2	22	3	17
	2000	928000	38	12	11	2	21	3	18
	2002	1207343	38	14	13	2	22	3	16
Comoros (Comoro Francs)	1970	5424	41	5	5	13	20	3	14
	1975	12832	38	6	6	12	23	4	14
	1980	28628	45	4	4	8	16	4	22
	1985	51700	41	5	4	10	18	4	22
	1990	68074	41	5	4	3	25	4	23
	1995	80343	43	6	5	7	25	5	23
	2000	98694	41	6	5	6	22	4	21
	2002	117180	42	6	5	7	23	4	22
Congo (CFA Francs)	1970	72453	22	16	13	6	12	11	25
	1975	146458	15	29	10	4	12	9	24
	1980	360397	12	42	8	5	10	9	20
	1985	970850	7	48	6	6	11	7	18
	1990	762000	14	39	8	1	13	9	22
	1995	1056200	15	35	9	1	10	11	28
	2000	2292500	5	69	17	2	6	5	12
	2003	2271591	6	66	16	2	7	5	13
Cote d'Ivoire [5] (CFA Francs)	1970	414862	27	15	13	7	20	8	18
	1975	834545	29	15	13	7	18	9	18
	1980	2149886	29	13	11	7	18	7	21
	1985	3134800	27	16	12	6	18	7	24
	1990	3238000	30	22	20	2	17	7	22
	1995	5543000	24	19	17	2	19	5	13
	1996	6209810	25	19	17	2	18	5	12
	1997	6841856	23	24	22	2	18	5	11
	1998	7457508	24	23	20	2	19	6	10
	1999	7734000	22	24	21	3	21	5	11
	2000	7605000	24	23	22	3	18	5	13
	2001	7869500	24	23	21	3	19	6	13
	2002	8166900	25	23	21	3	17	6	13
Democratic Republic of the Congo [6] (Congo Francs)	1970	0.003 (u)	17	31	8	5	11	8	23
	1975	0.006 (u)	20	21	10	6	17	4	28
	1980	0.14 (u)	31	27	3	4	15	2	20
	1985	1.2 (u)	27	32	2	5	17	1	17

Table 3. Gross Domestic Product by Kind of Economic Activity: Individual Countries or Areas

Major area, region and country	Year	Gross Domestic Product (at current prices) Million	Agriculture hunting forestry and fishing A-B	Mining Manufacturing and Utilities C-E	Of which: Manufacturing D	Construction F	Wholesale, retail trade, restaurants and hotels G-H	Transport storage and communication I	Other Activities J-P
			Percentage Distribution						
	1990	22.4 (u)	31	25	1	6	18	1	19
	1995	396	52	14	6	3	18	3	8
	2000	297066	54	14	2	4	18	2	8
	2002	1915070	50	15	4	5	18	3	10
Djibouti [7]	1970	14155	3	16	12	12	33	9	23
(Djibouti Francs)	1975	27847	2	19	15	13	27	10	27
	1980	53527	4	11	8	5	19	9	38
	1985	62303	3	13	4	5	15	17	35
	1990	81203	3	9	3	10	16	15	34
	1995	90572	3	9	2	5	13	19	38
	1996	88233	3	8	2	5	14	19	38
	1997	87289	3	8	2	5	14	20	36
	1998	88461	3	7	2	6	14	23	35
	1999	95275	3	7	3	6	14	25	33
	2000	98267	3	8	3	6	14	24	33
	2001	101932	3	8	3	6	14	25	33
	2002	105274	3	8	3	6	14	25	32
	2003	110606	3	8	3	6	14	24	33
Egypt [8]	1970	2971	23	20	17	2	11	4	28
(Egyptian Pounds)	1975	5247	28	21	17	5	14	5	24
	1980	17149	20	30	13	4	13	9	22
	1985	40820	19	24	16	6	22	9	21
	1990	110143	16	27	16	5	20	10	16
	1995	229400	14	29	17	4	20	11	20
	1996	265900	16	24	16	5	17	9	23
	1997	287400	16	24	17	5	17	8	23
	1998	307600	16	24	18	5	16	8	23
	1999	340100	16	26	18	4	16	8	22
	2000	358700	15	26	18	4	16	8	23
	2001	381700	15	27	18	4	15	9	23
	2002	415000	16	30	20	4	14	10	26
Equatorial Guinea	1970	13780	73	1	1	5	4	1	12
(CFA Francs)	1975	12306	60	4	1	8	5	1	18
	1980	11908	60	3	1	7	7	2	19
	1985	38067	57	4	2	3	8	3	18
	1990	44349	52	5	1	4	7	2	27
	1995	81600	42	4	1	6	11	2	28
	2000	891900	42	4	1	6	11	2	28
	2003	1698890	35	4	1	6	11	2	37
Eritrea	1995	3726	11	16	14	7	26	13	27
(Nafka)	2000	6200	14	12	10	10	18	12	28
	2002	9031	10	12	10	11	19	12	26
Ethiopia	1995	33885	61	6	5	2	7	4	17
(Birr)	2000	49459	52	9	7	3	9	5	23
	2003	55346	45	8	7	3	11	6	28
Gabon [9]	1970	93100	17	39	4	6	13	5	19
(CFA Francs)	1975	462441	9	47	5	17	7	4	12
	1980	904500	7	51	5	7	7	4	19
	1985	1645800	6	53	5	6	7	5	18
	1990	1477400	8	44	6	4	12	6	25
	1995	2475200	9	47	5	4	13	6	21
	2000	3576883	6	50	4	3	14	6	21
	2003	3208524	8	47	4	3	15	6	22
Gambia	1970	97	50	3	2	2	26	4	14
(Dalasis)	1975	278	38	6	5	5	23	6	24
	1980	412	28	7	7	8	24	8	27
	1985	1073	26	6	6	4	34	10	22
	1990	2627	23	7	6	5	40	11	17
	1995	3508	26	7	5	6	25	16	22
	2000	5389	39	7	5	6	16	11	29
	2003	8790	41	8	6	7	15	10	19
Ghana [10]	1970	2259	47	14	11	4	12	4	20
(Cedis)	1975	5283	48	17	14	4	12	4	18
	1980	42854	58	9	8	2	17	3	12
	1985	343048	45	14	12	3	25	5	9

Table 3. Gross Domestic Product by Kind of Economic Activity: Individual Countries or Areas

Major area, region and country	Year	Gross Domestic Product (at current prices) Million	Agriculture hunting forestry and fishing A-B	Mining Manufacturing and Utilities C-E	Of which: Manufacturing D	Construction F	Wholesale, retail trade, restaurants and hotels G-H	Transport storage and communication I	Other Activities J-P
			Percentage Distribution						
	1990	2031700	48	16	10	7	3	2	16
	1995	7752600	39	17	9	8	6	4	18
	1996	11339200	39	16	9	8	6	4	17
	1997	14113400	36	16	9	8	6	4	17
	1998	17296000	36	16	8	8	6	4	17
	1999	20002100	36	17	8	8	7	4	18
	2000	27153000	35	17	9	8	7	5	18
	2001	38014000	35	17	9	8	7	5	18
	2002	48789123	35	17	9	8	9	6	25
	2003	64337885	35	17	9	8	9	6	25
Guinea... (French Francs)	1970	17742	20	21	4	9	27	6	13
	1975	25991	20	21	4	9	27	6	13
	1980	36837	20	21	4	9	27	6	13
	1985	61031	20	21	4	9	27	6	13
	1990	1860450	20	21	4	9	27	6	13
	1995	3696760	20	21	4	9	27	6	13
	2000	5351500	21	21	4	11	25	6	12
	2002	6350000	22	21	4	12	24	6	12
Guinea-Bissau.. (CFA Francs)	1970	41	59	11	11	2	15	2	10
	1975	65	51	14	14	3	19	3	11
	1980	123	46	17	17	5	18	3	11
	1985	608	44	16	16	6	19	3	12
	1990	7848	45	8	7	10	26	4	8
	1995	68045	43	8	7	8	24	4	8
	2000	159900	59	10	9	2	16	4	10
	2003	180746	58	10	9	2	16	4	10
Kenya [11].. (Kenyan Pounds)	1970	606	33	12	10	6	10	5	27
	1975	1194	30	13	11	5	10	5	27
	1980	2629	28	13	11	6	9	5	27
	1985	5042	29	12	10	5	10	6	29
	1990	9777	25	12	10	5	10	6	31
	1995	23264	26	10	8	4	14	7	28
	1996	26436	25	10	9	4	15	7	27
	1997	31168	24	10	9	3	18	7	28
	1998	34606	23	10	9	3	19	6	28
	1999	37107	20	12	11	4	19	6	28
	2000	39817	17	12	11	4	20	6	26
	2001	44136	16	12	11	4	26	7	26
	2002	48468	14	13	11	4	28	7	25
Lesotho [12]... (Loti)	1970	52	32	7	5	2	15	3	45
	1975	110	28	7	7	4	14	5	40
	1980	296	23	13	6	7	8	3	42
	1985	568	20	11	10	9	9	3	45
	1990	1600	19	13	11	14	8	4	33
	1995	3384	15	16	14	18	9	3	27
	1996	4054	16	18	14	17	9	3	26
	1997	4720	15	21	14	17	10	3	26
	1998	4921	16	20	16	14	9	3	28
	1999	5565	16	21	15	17	9	3	28
	2000	5986	17	21	15	16	10	3	28
	2001	6478	17	21	16	16	10	3	27
	2002	7323	16	21	15	16	9	3	27
Liberia... (Liberian Dollars)	1970	277	42	18	8	4	7	11	22
	1975	544	42	18	8	4	7	11	20
	1980	818	42	18	8	4	7	11	20
	1985	942	43	18	9	4	7	11	19
	1990	384	54	13	11	3	7	10	14
	1995	135	82	4	3	2	3	5	7
	2000	542	74	8	7	1	4	5	8
	2002	562	77	6	5	1	4	5	7
Libyan Arab Jamahiriya............................. (Lybian Dinars)	1970	1426	2	59	2	7	3	3	19
	1975	3780	2	55	2	12	6	5	18
	1980	10575	2	65	2	9	5	3	14
	1985	8277	3	46	4	11	7	5	25
	1990	8010	7	36	8	12	8	7	30

Table 3. Gross Domestic Product by Kind of Economic Activity: Individual Countries or Areas

Major area, region and country	Year	Gross Domestic Product (at current prices) Million	Agriculture hunting forestry and fishing A-B	Mining Manufacturing and Utilities C-E	Of which: Manufacturing D	Construction F	Wholesale, retail trade, restaurants and hotels G-H	Transport storage and communication I	Other Activities J-P
			Percentage Distribution						
	1995	10679	9	42	7	4	12	8	25
	2000	17395	8	47	6	6	10	7	22
	2002	24309	9	40	6	6	11	8	25
Madagascar (Malagasy Francs)	1970	249400	30	18	17	5	16	13	18
	1975	395200	41	18	16	5	13	10	14
	1980	689800	36	18	16	5	14	11	16
	1985	1553400	42	16	15	5	14	11	13
	1990	4601600	32	14	12	1	10	17	25
	1995	13458000	33	13	10	1	11	17	24
	2000	26242000	26	13	11	1	11	17	22
	2003	34270819	27	11	9	2	13	20	26
Malawi [13] (Kwacha)	1970	267	39	14	12	4	13	6	22
	1975	530	37	15	13	4	14	7	20
	1980	1005	33	17	16	6	9	4	20
	1985	1929	28	15	14	2	10	4	21
	1990	4782	33	20	19	2	15	4	25
	1995	21376	33	20	19	2	15	4	25
	2000	103799	33	20	19	2	15	4	25
	2002	154564	32	18	16	2	16	5	26
Mali [14] (CFA Francs)	1970	76300	69	7	4	4	9	2	9
	1975	129500	59	8	5	5	13	3	12
	1980	300600	61	7	4	4	14	3	11
	1985	520200	38	14	7	4	13	5	20
	1990	683300	46	13	8	4	14	5	14
	1995	1152970	50	11	8	4	14	5	11
	2000	1739500	45	12	9	5	16	6	14
	2003	2251625	43	14	11	6	17	6	14
Mauritania (Ouguiyas)	1970	11330	27	28	2	5	6	5	22
	1975	20595	25	22	1	5	11	5	25
	1980	38070	32	15	2	5	9	7	26
	1985	52665	20	20	9	6	13	6	23
	1990	82350	27	18	6	5	12	10	20
	1995	137340	24	28	10	7	13	7	24
	2000	215010	24	26	11	7	12	9	24
	2002	263017	23	24	10	6	13	9	26
Mauritius (Rupees)	1970	1067	21	16	14	4	9	10	35
	1975	3416	27	19	17	6	8	8	33
	1980	8805	11	21	19	6	13	10	31
	1985	16825	14	25	22	4	12	9	28
	1990	38462	11	25	23	6	15	9	25
	1995	70283	9	23	20	6	15	10	29
	1996	79086	9	23	21	6	16	9	29
	1997	88099	8	22	21	5	16	10	29
	1998	99564	8	22	21	5	16	10	29
	1999	107444	5	22	21	5	17	11	31
	2000	119529	6	22	21	5	16	11	32
	2001	131835	6	23	20	5	16	12	32
	2002	141408	6	22	20	5	16	12	32
	2003	156533	5	21	19	5	15	12	33
Morocco [15] (Dirhams)	1970	20020	20	23	16	4	20	4	25
	1975	36410	18	29	17	7	17	4	24
	1980	74090	18	25	17	6	14	5	25
	1985	129510	17	28	19	6	14	6	25
	1990	212850	18	27	18	5	13	6	26
	1995	282467	15	28	18	4	24	6	29
	1996	319390	19	27	17	4	24	6	17
	1997	318342	15	28	18	5	24	6	18
	1998	344005	17	27	17	4	24	6	18
	1999	345594	15	27	17	5	24	6	19
	2000	354208	14	27	18	5	25	7	19
	2001	383185	16	26	17	5	24	7	20
	2002	397782	16	25	17	5	24	7	20
	2003	428013	16	26	17	5	24	7	19
Mozambique (Meticais)	1970	79532	67	17	13	6	5	6	3
	1975	112329	67	18	13	6	4	6	2
	1980	142600	67	19	13	6	4	6	2

Table 3. Gross Domestic Product by Kind of Economic Activity: Individual Countries or Areas

Major area, region and country	Year	Gross Domestic Product (at current prices) Million	Agriculture hunting forestry and fishing A-B	Mining Manufacturing and Utilities C-E	Of which: Manufacturing D	Construction F	Wholesale, retail trade, restaurants and hotels G-H	Transport storage and communication I	Other Activities J-P
			Percentage Distribution						
	1985	268746	67	16	13	5	3	6	2
	1990	2515606	64	17	14	8	3	6	2
	1995	20678102	34	8	7	6	23	9	19
	2000	56917388	24	15	12	9	23	9	19
	2002	82747356	24	16	13	9	22	9	19
Namibia [16] (Namibia Dollars)	1970	362	14	38	5	5	9	5	27
	1975	696	14	39	5	5	9	5	27
	1980	1574	14	46	4	5	8	5	21
	1985	2735	12	38	5	3	8	5	33
	1990	6054	11	32	12	2	7	5	33
	1995	12706	11	22	11	3	10	7	37
	1996	15011	11	21	9	3	10	6	39
	1997	16754	10	22	10	3	11	6	39
	1998	18790	10	23	11	3	11	6	38
	1999	20681	10	22	10	2	11	6	38
	2000	23995	10	23	10	2	13	6	37
	2001	27231	9	25	10	3	13	5	36
	2002	30364	9	25	10	2	13	6	32
Niger (CFA Francs)	1970	111000	50	14	7	3	10	4	17
	1975	180300	49	14	8	3	10	4	18
	1980	536208	43	14	4	6	12	4	15
	1985	647100	37	18	7	4	16	4	19
	1990	682300	42	16	9	5	14	4	22
	1995	834600	43	16	6	2	17	5	18
	2000	1280400	34	16	7	2	19	5	17
	2003	1582752	40	15	7	2	20	5	18
Nigeria [17] (Naira)	1970	7381	47	15	8	6	15	4	16
	1975	22722	32	29	10	6	12	4	19
	1980	50346	27	37	9	5	13	5	12
	1985	72355	37	28	10	2	13	5	14
	1990	260637	32	40	6	2	14	2	10
	1995	1977737	32	46	6	1	14	2	5
	2000	4296276	40	18	6	2	9	3	29
	2002	5292589	35	32	11	5	7	2	20
Reunion (Euros)	1970	307	6	10	...	8	18	3	50
	1975	692	6	9	...	6	19	3	52
	1980	1288	6	11	...	5	17	4	54
	1985	2600	4	12	...	5	16	5	54
	1990	4326	4	13	...	6	20	4	50
	1995	5646	4	14	...	7	20	5	51
	2000	7070	4	14	...	7	20	5	51
	2002	8591	4	14	...	7	20	5	51
Rwanda [18] (Francs)	1970	23768	47	14	11	2	9	1	11
	1975	58174	45	13	11	4	13	1	12
	1980	119048	42	15	14	4	13	2	11
	1985	191487	38	13	12	8	11	4	13
	1990	212653	44	17	16	7	10	4	19
	1995	336489	44	11	10	5	14	4	22
	1996	426175	47	12	11	6	10	4	21
	1997	563416	46	12	12	6	10	4	21
	1998	627342	45	12	11	7	10	5	20
	1999	633299	41	12	11	8	11	7	22
	2000	681455	41	11	10	9	10	7	22
	2001	732276	41	11	10	9	10	7	21
	2002	784000	44	11	10	8	10	8	21
Sao Tome and Principe (Dobras)	1970	614	30	9	7	8	5	6	39
	1975	881	25	11	9	7	7	9	39
	1980	1629	26	10	7	8	6	7	44
	1985	2319	23	11	9	6	10	10	39
	1990	8250	28	9	5	7	11	5	40
	1995	64613	26	10	4	10	9	2	42
	2000	369500	20	5	3	12	20	3	39
	2002	491000	20	8	4	11	16	3	45
Senegal (CFA Francs)	1970	241668	24	0	...	2	54	...	13
	1975	409054	30	0	...	2	42	...	12
	1980	631400	19	13	11	3	23	10	33

Table 3. Gross Domestic Product by Kind of Economic Activity: Individual Countries or Areas

Major area, region and country	Year	Gross Domestic Product (at current prices) Million	Agriculture hunting forestry and fishing A-B	Mining Manufacturing and Utilities C-E	Of which: Manufacturing D	Construction F	Wholesale, retail trade, restaurants and hotels G-H	Transport storage and communication I	Other Activities J-P
			Percentage Distribution						
	1985	1158200	19	15	13	3	25	10	29
	1990	1551500	20	16	13	3	24	10	27
	1995	2234000	20	16	13	3	26	10	24
	1996	2380000	21	16	13	4	26	10	24
	1997	2554300	20	16	12	4	26	11	23
	1998	2746000	18	16	12	4	27	11	23
	1999	2925000	19	15	12	4	27	11	23
	2000	3114000	19	15	12	4	26	12	22
	2001	3379600	20	16	13	4	26	12	22
	2002	3511700	17	17	14	5	27	13	23
Seychelles [19] (Rupees)	1970	110	13	2	1	12	28	7	31
	1975	292	12	5	5	11	24	9	31
	1980	942	7	8	7	8	25	14	30
	1985	1205	6	12	10	6	25	14	29
	1990	1967	5	11	10	5	27	12	25
	1995	2420	4	15	13	8	9	30	27
	1996	2500	4	16	13	8	10	27	28
	1997	2830	3	17	14	8	10	29	27
	1998	3201	3	18	15	8	9	30	27
	1999	3330	3	17	15	10	8	31	26
	2000	3424	3	16	14	10	9	32	26
	2001	3419	3	16	14	9	9	32	27
	2002	3830	3	20	18	10	23	16	28
Sierra Leone (Leones)	1970	346	28	26	9	4	12	10	17
	1975	573	34	21	8	3	13	10	17
	1980	1156	32	19	7	4	13	14	17
	1985	4785	43	11	5	3	16	11	15
	1990	96133	37	14	7	2	25	11	11
	1995	657604	41	8	3	2	29	10	9
	2000	1330433	47	23	9	6	14	5	4
	2002	2068668	53	24	10	7	10	3	3
Somalia (Shillings)	1970	2436	53	7	6	5	9	6	12
	1975	4765	53	5	3	5	10	8	13
	1980	17341	64	5	4	3	9	4	10
	1985	87290	64	5	5	2	10	6	9
	1990	1738800	70	2	2	4	9	7	9
	1995	6424840	62	3	3	4	11	10	13
	2000	19641182	65	4	3	6	8	7	9
	2002	24414329	65	4	3	6	8	7	9
South Africa (Rand)	1970	13045	7	31	21	4	14	10	28
	1975	27868	7	34	21	5	13	10	26
	1980	64141	6	42	20	3	11	9	23
	1985	128773	5	37	20	3	10	9	29
	1990	289816	4	33	21	3	13	7	30
	1995	548100	4	29	19	3	13	8	35
	1996	617954	4	28	18	3	13	8	36
	1997	685730	4	27	18	3	13	8	37
	1998	738926	3	26	17	3	12	9	38
	1999	800769	3	25	17	3	12	9	39
	2000	888454	3	26	17	3	12	9	39
	2001	983450	3	26	17	3	12	9	38
	2002	1120895	4	27	18	2	12	9	37
	2003	1209495	3	26	17	2	12	9	38
Sudan [20] (Dinars)	1970	67	39	11	9	3	15	7	20
	1975	168	39	11	9	4	16	6	19
	1980	449	33	10	9	5	15	11	21
	1985	1703	34	11	8	4	18	10	17
	1990	15139	29	12	9	5	20	11	19
	1995	810318	50	9	8	3	15	9	11
	1996	1033070	29	13	10	4	19	11	17
	1997	1592931	30	13	10	4	20	12	18
	1998	1991613	39	12	10	4	19	11	13
	1999	2448876	41	11	9	4	19	11	13
	2000	2969452	38	11	10	4	17	10	12
	2001	3380555	40	11	9	4	17	10	12
	2002	3559000	31	17	9	4	17	14	11

Table 3. Gross Domestic Product by Kind of Economic Activity: Individual Countries or Areas

Major area, region and country	Year	Gross Domestic Product (at current prices) Million	Agriculture hunting forestry and fishing A-B	Mining Manufacturing and Utilities C-E	Of which: Manufacturing D	Construction F	Wholesale, retail trade, restaurants and hotels G-H	Transport storage and communication I	Other Activities J-P
			Percentage Distribution						
Swaziland [21]	1970	78	21	24	12	2	12	6	26
(Lilangeni)	1975	216	20	21	15	3	10	5	29
	1980	460	18	22	17	4	8	5	22
	1985	813	16	18	13	3	10	6	28
	1990	2253	11	33	29	2	8	5	23
	1995	4949	12	32	29	4	7	4	21
	1996	5686	14	30	28	4	7	4	21
	1997	6613	13	30	28	4	7	4	20
	1998	7449	13	30	28	4	7	4	19
	1999	8408	12	28	26	4	7	3	18
	2000	9639	11	26	25	5	6	4	17
	2001	10971	10	26	25	4	6	4	16
	2002	12287	12	28	26	4	7	4	18
Togo	1970	73171	25	21	9	3	20	7	17
(CFA Francs)	1975	128302	25	19	7	6	17	7	18
	1980	238872	27	18	7	5	19	6	24
	1985	338200	29	16	6	3	20	6	26
	1990	427600	29	20	7	4	22	6	24
	1995	652500	26	21	7	3	21	5	23
	2000	946100	35	18	6	3	15	4	18
	2002	1031100	39	18	6	3	16	4	19
Tunisia [22]	1970	756	17	16	8	5	20	6	23
(Dinars)	1975	1741	18	20	9	6	20	5	19
	1980	3541	14	25	12	6	18	5	19
	1985	7018	16	30	17	6	11	6	25
	1990	10816	16	26	17	4	14	7	25
	1995	17052	11	25	19	5	15	7	27
	1996	19066	14	24	18	4	15	7	26
	1997	20898	13	24	18	4	15	8	26
	1998	22561	13	24	18	5	15	8	26
	1999	24672	13	24	18	5	15	8	25
	2000	26651	12	24	18	5	15	8	26
	2001	28729	12	24	19	5	15	8	26
	2002	29879	10	24	19	5	15	9	27
	2003	32447	11	24	18	5	15	9	26
Uganda [23]	1970	135	43	5	4	3	30	2	21
(Shillings)	1975	321	60	4	3	2	18	1	20
	1980	1851	59	2	1	1	17	1	20
	1985	26961	52	5	5	3	13	3	16
	1990	1566257	49	7	6	5	13	4	16
	1995	5858367	43	9	7	6	12	4	18
	1996	6409571	38	10	8	7	13	4	19
	1997	7141605	37	10	9	6	11	4	21
	1998	7844329	36	10	9	7	12	4	21
	1999	8723138	35	11	9	8	12	4	21
	2000	9431690	34	11	9	8	12	5	22
	2001	10116389	31	11	9	9	12	5	23
	2002	10825290	29	11	9	9	12	6	24
United Republic Of Tanzania [24]	1970	9568	34	14	10	5	13	8	19
(Shillings)	1975	19829	34	13	11	5	13	8	20
	1980	42118	39	12	10	4	11	7	18
	1985	112000	46	8	7	2	13	6	15
	1990	736338	50	10	8	5	14	5	10
	1995	3020500	44	10	7	4	14	5	20
	2000	7277800	42	10	7	5	11	5	22
	2002	9374559	41	10	7	5	11	4	23
Zambia	1970	1185	7	41	10	8	9	9	23
(Kwacha)	1975	1837	9	33	14	8	11	9	26
	1980	3656	8	33	13	5	15	8	28
	1985	9351	9	45	19	4	9	6	21
	1990	123487	11	42	21	5	11	6	18
	1995	2999000	16	27	10	4	16	6	24
	1996	3951000	15	27	12	4	20	6	22
	1997	5141000	16	26	12	4	19	5	23
	1998	6028600	19	21	11	4	20	6	24
	1999	7479500	22	18	11	4	20	6	25
	2000	10074600	20	18	10	5	21	6	25

Table 3. Gross Domestic Product by Kind of Economic Activity: Individual Countries or Areas

Major area, region and country	Year	Gross Domestic Product (at current prices) Million	Agriculture hunting forestry and fishing A-B	Mining Manufacturing and Utilities C-E	Of which: Manufacturing D	Construction F	Wholesale, retail trade, restaurants and hotels G-H	Transport storage and communication I	Other Activities J-P
			Percentage Distribution						
	2001	13132693	20	17	10	6	20	6	25
	2002	16260430	20	17	10	7	21	6	24
	2003	20377051	21	17	11	7	21	5	24
Zimbabwe [25] (Zimbabwe Dollars)	1970	1079	14	29	19	5	14	8	25
	1975	1998	16	31	22	5	13	7	25
	1980	3441	13	34	23	3	13	6	28
	1985	9097	21	23	18	2	16	5	26
	1990	21494	15	27	20	3	15	6	27
	1995	61759	13	24	19	2	19	6	26
	1996	85551	19	21	17	2	18	5	25
	1997	102982	17	20	16	2	17	5	28
	1998	143364	19	18	14	3	16	5	27
	1999	210409	17	20	15	3	17	9	27
	2000	319998	18	22	17	3	18	8	31
	2001	498598	18	22	16	3	19	9	31
	2002	457042	17	21	16	3	19	8	32
NORTHERN AMERICA									
Bermuda (Bermudian Dollars)	1970	259	1	9	3	7	21	7	59
	1975	480	1	7	3	7	21	7	53
	1980	919	1	6	3	7	22	7	50
	1985	1433	1	6	3	8	20	6	56
	1990	1997	1	6	3	7	19	7	57
	1995	2544	1	5	3	5	18	7	62
	1996	2680	1	5	2	6	18	7	61
	1997	2889	1	5	2	6	18	7	63
	1998	3053	1	5	3	4	19	7	64
	1999	3272	1	5	2	6	17	7	64
	2000	3397	1	5	3	6	17	7	64
	2001	3599	1	5	3	7	16	7	64
	2002	3719	1	5	2	6	17	7	64
Canada (Canadian Dollars)	1970	88933	4	26	19	7	13	8	32
	1975	171163	5	26	18	8	13	7	33
	1980	310160	4	28	17	7	12	7	34
	1985	478829	3	28	17	6	13	8	38
	1990	669967	3	23	16	6	14	7	42
	1995	798300	3	24	17	5	13	7	43
	1996	824041	3	24	17	5	13	7	43
	1997	868979	2	24	17	5	13	7	43
	1998	900350	2	23	17	5	13	7	43
	1999	967511	2	24	18	5	13	7	42
	2000	1060058	2	24	18	5	13	7	42
	2001	1091424	2	24	18	5	13	7	41
	2002	1137511	2	24	18	5	13	7	42
United States (Dollars)	1970	1025500	3	29	24	5	19	7	39
	1975	1617800	3	27	22	5	19	7	40
	1980	2771500	2	28	21	5	18	7	41
	1985	4174900	2	26	19	4	18	7	43
	1990	5750800	2	23	18	4	17	6	47
	1995	7338400	2	22	18	4	18	7	48
	1996	7751100	2	21	17	4	18	7	48
	1997	8256500	2	21	17	4	18	7	49
	1998	8720200	1	20	16	4	18	7	50
	1999	9212800	1	19	16	5	18	7	50
	2000	9762100	1	19	16	5	18	7	51
	2001	10019700	1	18	14	5	18	7	52
	2002	10383100	1	17	14	5	19	7	54
LATIN AMERICA and the CARIBBEAN									
Anguilla (EC Dollars)	1970	6	5	4	1	15	30	13	25
	1975	12	5	4	1	15	30	13	25
	1980	24	5	4	1	15	30	13	25
	1985	52	5	3	1	14	32	13	25
	1990	147	5	3	1	17	33	10	25
	1995	202	3	3	1	11	35	12	25
	1996	214	3	4	1	12	32	12	28
	1997	240	3	4	1	12	33	13	26
	1998	255	3	5	1	12	33	13	26
	1999	280	3	5	1	14	32	12	27

Table 3. Gross Domestic Product by Kind of Economic Activity: Individual Countries or Areas

Major area, region and country	Year	Gross Domestic Product (at current prices) Million	Agriculture hunting forestry and fishing A-B	Mining Manufacturing and Utilities C-E	Of which: Manufacturing D	Construction F	Wholesale, retail trade, restaurants and hotels G-H	Transport storage and communication I	Other Activities J-P
			Percentage Distribution						
	2000	288	2	5	1	13	30	13	30
	2001	291	2	5	1	10	32	12	32
	2002	301	2	7	1	8	28	13	31
	2003	315	2	7	1	10	28	12	30
Antigua and Barbuda................................	1970	98	9	12	8	6	16	13	37
(EC Dollars)	1975	152	9	10	7	6	17	13	35
	1980	297	6	8	5	8	22	14	32
	1985	541	4	8	4	7	23	15	35
	1990	902	4	10	3	12	23	15	37
	1995	1176	4	9	2	10	22	15	38
	2000	1603	4	8	2	13	21	15	38
	2003	1781	4	9	2	14	19	15	39
Argentina...	1970	1.2 (u)	7	40	35	6	15	7	17
(Pesos)	1975	19.2 (u)	5	42	38	9	14	5	18
	1980	3800 (u)	5	34	29	8	16	5	32
	1985	5	8	34	30	6	16	5	32
	1990	68922	8	32	27	4	16	5	36
	1995	258032	5	20	16	5	16	7	39
	1996	272150	6	20	16	5	16	8	37
	1997	292859	5	20	16	5	17	8	36
	1998	298948	5	19	16	5	17	8	36
	1999	283522	4	19	15	5	16	8	39
	2000	284204	5	19	15	5	15	8	39
	2001	268697	5	19	14	4	15	9	42
	2002	312580	10	28	20	3	13	7	34
	2003	376232	10	29	22	3	13	8	30
Aruba [26]...	1970	685	1	5	1	9	28	6	43
(Aruban Florin)	1975	888	1	6	1	9	28	7	42
	1980	1151	1	6	1	8	28	7	42
	1985	1492	1	7	1	8	28	8	42
	1990	1934	1	8	1	7	27	8	42
	1995	2364	1	9	3	6	25	9	48
	1996	2470	0	8	3	7	25	8	49
	1997	2742	0	9	2	8	23	8	48
	1998	2981	0	9	3	8	24	8	47
	1999	3087	0	10	3	6	23	8	49
	2000	3326	0	9	3	6	24	9	49
	2001	3381	0	10	3	6	25	9	52
	2002	3403	0	9	3	7	24	8	48
Bahamas [27]..	1970	502	2	11	10	4	29	10	45
(Bahamian Dollars)	1975	723	2	9	8	4	29	10	43
	1980	1438	2	6	5	4	29	10	33
	1985	2171	2	5	3	4	29	10	31
	1990	3047	2	5	3	4	31	10	30
	1995	3069	3	7	3	2	23	10	41
	1996	3277	3	8	3	2	22	9	43
	1997	3451	4	8	3	2	20	9	45
	1998	3670	4	9	3	2	19	9	48
	1999	4005	5	11	3	2	20	10	56
	2000	4309	5	12	3	2	19	10	63
	2001	4307	6	14	3	1	20	11	72
	2002	4430	5	11	3	2	20	10	57
Barbados..	1970	370	11	9	8	7	19	6	37
(Barbados Dollars)	1975	812	12	10	9	6	24	6	29
	1980	1730	9	13	11	7	29	5	26
	1985	2410	6	14	10	5	28	8	30
	1990	3440	5	10	7	6	27	7	32
	1995	3742	5	9	6	4	26	9	32
	1996	3995	6	9	5	4	26	9	32
	1997	4413	4	8	5	5	24	8	32
	1998	4747	3	8	5	5	25	8	33
	1999	4965	4	8	5	5	24	9	33
	2000	5183	4	9	5	5	24	9	33
	2001	5093	4	8	5	5	22	9	35
	2002	5149	3	9	5	5	22	9	35

Table 3. Gross Domestic Product by Kind of Economic Activity: Individual Countries or Areas

Major area, region and country	Year	Gross Domestic Product (at current prices) Million	Agriculture hunting forestry and fishing A-B	Mining Manufacturing and Utilities C-E	Of which: Manufacturing D	Construction F	Wholesale, retail trade, restaurants and hotels G-H	Transport storage and communication I	Other Activities J-P
			Percentage Distribution						
Belize	1970	77	14	10	9	5	16	7	42
(Belize Dollars)	1975	189	28	13	12	6	14	6	30
	1980	389	24	22	21	5	15	4	26
	1985	418	18	17	15	5	13	8	38
	1990	811	18	16	13	7	16	9	28
	1995	1173	17	15	12	5	15	9	31
	1996	1207	18	15	11	5	15	9	32
	1997	1231	17	15	12	5	16	9	32
	1998	1258	16	14	11	5	16	9	32
	1999	1377	16	14	11	5	17	9	30
	2000	1514	15	15	11	6	19	9	30
	2001	1577	14	15	11	7	18	9	37
	2002	1640	13	15	12	7	19	9	39
Bolivia	1970	12 (t)	17	27	17	8	8	8	25
(Bolivianos)	1975	48 (t)	21	26	12	4	12	6	25
	1980	123 (t)	19	31	15	4	11	6	29
	1985	2867	29	25	12	4	11	11	22
	1990	15443	15	29	17	3	12	9	25
	1995	32235	15	26	17	3	11	10	25
	1996	37537	14	25	16	3	11	10	26
	1997	41644	15	24	15	3	11	11	27
	1998	46822	13	22	14	4	11	12	29
	1999	48156	13	22	14	3	11	12	32
	2000	51884	13	23	13	3	10	12	31
	2001	53010	13	22	13	3	10	12	31
	2002	55933	13	22	13	3	10	12	30
Brazil [28]	1970	0.1 (u)	10	28	26	6	16	3	13
(Reais)	1975	0.6 (u)	8	29	26	7	15	4	13
	1980	4.7 (u)	5	32	30	7	9	7	28
	1985	448 (u)	7	38	33	6	10	5	40
	1990	11	7	31	27	7	9	5	53
	1995	646192	8	24	21	8	8	4	41
	1996	778887	7	22	19	8	7	4	44
	1997	870743	7	23	19	9	7	5	44
	1998	914188	7	22	19	9	6	5	45
	1999	973846	7	23	18	8	6	5	43
	2000	1101255	7	25	20	8	7	5	37
	2001	1198736	7	26	20	8	7	5	37
	2002	1346028	8	27	21	7	7	5	37
British Virgin Islands [29]	1970	16	5	5	3	16	16	11	30
(US Dollars)	1975	21	7	5	3	8	25	11	37
	1980	44	5	4	3	5	32	10	37
	1985	72	4	6	3	7	27	10	42
	1990	240	3	7	3	6	26	12	38
	1995	385	2	6	4	8	29	12	45
	2000	691	1	6	4	8	28	11	47
	2002	870	1	6	4	9	27	11	47
Cayman Islands [30]	1970	16	4	7	2	12	32	4	40
(Dollars)	1975	45	2	6	2	12	28	5	41
	1980	110	1	6	2	13	26	9	48
	1985	264	0	5	2	9	20	12	48
	1990	590	0	5	2	9	24	11	49
	1995	849	0	5	2	9	22	10	46
	2000	1131	0	5	2	9	22	10	46
	2002	1270	0	5	2	9	22	10	46
Chile	1970	105	6	30	17	8	14	5	32
(Pesos)	1975	37891	5	28	13	9	14	6	39
	1980	1149700	6	26	14	8	14	5	43
	1985	2930460	6	29	14	7	12	5	39
	1990	10216526	7	31	17	7	12	6	30
	1995	28593362	6	29	18	9	11	6	32
	1996	31237289	5	27	18	9	11	6	34
	1997	34722636	5	26	17	10	11	6	35
	1998	36534873	6	24	17	9	11	7	36
	1999	37138542	6	26	17	8	11	7	37
	2000	40393464	6	27	17	7	10	7	36
	2001	43343584	5	28	18	7	10	7	37
	2002	45762505	5	28	18	7	10	7	36

Table 3. Gross Domestic Product by Kind of Economic Activity: Individual Countries or Areas

Major area, region and country	Year	Gross Domestic Product (at current prices) Million	Agriculture hunting forestry and fishing A-B	Mining Manufacturing and Utilities C-E	Of which: Manufacturing D	Construction F	Wholesale, retail trade, restaurants and hotels G-H	Transport storage and communication I	Other Activities J-P
			Percentage Distribution						
Colombia	1970	157666	27	20	18	4	10	7	33
(Pesos)	1975	480111	26	22	20	3	11	6	32
	1980	1871842	21	23	20	5	11	6	33
	1985	5886995	18	24	19	7	11	6	31
	1990	23979488	18	27	17	5	11	7	29
	1995	84439109	14	22	15	7	12	7	35
	1996	100711389	13	22	14	7	12	7	38
	1997	121707501	13	21	14	6	11	7	40
	1998	140483322	13	21	14	6	12	7	40
	1999	151565005	13	23	14	4	11	7	40
	2000	174896258	13	24	15	4	11	7	37
	2001	187935734	13	24	14	4	11	7	37
	2002	203141712	13	23	14	4	11	8	37
Costa Rica	1970	8291	16	20	19	6	19	6	26
(Colones)	1975	21352	15	23	22	7	17	7	25
	1980	52610	13	21	20	8	18	6	25
	1985	251474	13	26	23	5	18	7	23
	1990	664322	11	23	20	4	18	7	29
	1995	2105687	13	23	20	4	18	8	29
	1996	2459957	12	23	20	3	18	8	29
	1997	2984020	12	23	20	3	18	8	29
	1998	3625330	12	24	21	4	19	8	29
	1999	4512763	10	29	27	3	17	7	29
	2000	4914498	9	26	23	4	18	8	31
	2001	5391466	8	23	20	4	18	8	33
	2002	6051467	8	22	19	4	17	8	35
	2003	6969245	8	23	20	4	17	8	35
Cuba	1970	5192	8	43	40	7	33	7	7
(Cuban Pesos)	1975	9742	8	40	37	6	30	7	9
	1980	13075	7	33	30	6	31	7	17
	1985	19145	10	29	27	7	27	7	21
	1990	19645	11	27	24	7	25	6	24
	1995	21737	6	41	38	4	23	4	21
	1996	22815	7	40	37	5	21	4	21
	1997	22952	7	40	37	5	21	4	21
	1998	23901	6	41	37	5	21	4	21
	1999	25504	6	42	39	5	20	4	20
	2000	27635	7	41	37	6	21	5	20
	2001	28806	6	40	36	6	21	5	21
	2002	29239	6	31	27	4	22	7	29
Dominica	1970	55	32	7	4	5	10	6	30
(EC Dollars)	1975	73	26	7	4	7	12	6	32
	1980	160	28	7	4	12	9	7	32
	1985	266	23	8	5	6	9	11	30
	1990	452	21	9	6	6	11	13	28
	1995	592	16	11	6	8	13	15	30
	1996	638	17	11	6	8	12	15	30
	1997	662	16	11	6	7	12	15	29
	1998	701	16	12	7	7	12	15	30
	1999	723	16	12	7	7	12	15	30
	2000	732	15	13	7	7	12	14	30
	2001	713	14	12	7	7	12	14	32
	2002	685	15	12	7	6	12	12	34
	2003	696	16	11	6	6	13	12	33
Dominican Republic [31]	1970	1784	17	31	27	4	20	9	16
(Pesos)	1975	4323	15	34	31	6	21	7	17
	1980	7964	14	26	23	6	20	7	20
	1985	16782	12	30	26	5	21	10	18
	1990	77911	12	22	20	7	18	8	26
	1995	209646	9	21	18	7	16	8	31
	1996	232993	9	22	19	7	20	9	32
	1997	273559	10	21	18	7	22	11	22
	1998	308079	9	20	18	8	22	11	22
	1999	354744	9	20	17	9	22	12	21
	2000	411783	9	20	17	9	23	12	20
	2001	466243	9	19	16	8	22	14	19
	2002	511667	9	19	16	8	21	14	19
	2003	649274	9	18	15	8	21	15	19

Table 3. Gross Domestic Product by Kind of Economic Activity: Individual Countries or Areas

Major area, region and country	Year	Gross Domestic Product (at current prices) Million	Agriculture hunting forestry and fishing A-B	Mining Manufacturing and Utilities C-E	Of which: Manufacturing D	Construction F	Wholesale, retail trade, restaurants and hotels G-H	Transport storage and communication I	Other Activities J-P
			Percentage Distribution						
Ecuador [32]	1970	1762	36	17	10	2	11	6	36
(US Dollars)	1975	4536	27	24	8	3	12	5	33
	1980	12351	18	26	9	4	11	7	36
	1985	16797	20	29	10	2	12	8	27
	1990	11248	20	24	10	2	16	8	21
	1995	20196	17	21	11	3	15	9	29
	1996	21268	16	22	11	4	15	9	30
	1997	23636	16	20	11	4	15	8	31
	1998	23255	14	17	12	5	16	10	31
	1999	16674	12	23	10	5	15	11	26
	2000	15934	11	28	5	7	17	11	19
	2001	21024	9	22	8	7	16	16	23
	2002	24572	9	21	8	8	16	16	22
El Salvador [33]	1970	2571	28	21	19	3	23	5	21
(Colones)	1975	4478	23	20	19	5	26	4	22
	1980	8917	28	17	15	3	23	4	25
	1985	14331	18	19	16	3	27	4	28
	1990	36487	17	23	22	3	18	7	31
	1995	83130	13	23	21	4	20	7	27
	1996	90261	13	23	21	4	20	8	28
	1997	97428	13	23	21	4	20	8	29
	1998	105074	12	24	21	4	19	8	30
	1999	109066	10	25	23	4	19	8	30
	2000	114924	10	25	23	4	19	8	30
	2001	120783	9	25	23	5	19	9	30
	2002	124984	9	26	23	5	19	9	30
	2003	131219	8	26	24	5	19	9	30
French Guiana	1970	44	6	6	...	8	11	5	62
(Euros)	1975	88	6	6	...	8	11	5	62
	1980	186	6	3	...	8	13	5	65
	1985	484	6	4	...	11	13	12	54
	1990	995	10	8	...	13	13	8	47
	1995	1275	7	10	...	11	11	10	53
	2000	1429	7	10	...	11	11	9	54
	2002	1495	7	10	...	11	11	9	54
Grenada	1970	60	24	5	3	7	17	11	30
(EC Dollars)	1975	107	24	5	3	7	17	11	30
	1980	202	20	5	3	6	17	11	27
	1985	311	14	6	4	6	16	10	30
	1990	541	13	7	4	8	15	11	27
	1995	638	11	8	5	8	20	16	26
	1996	687	9	8	5	8	20	16	26
	1997	738	8	8	5	8	19	15	26
	1998	808	8	8	5	9	19	16	26
	1999	871	8	8	5	10	19	16	26
	2000	942	8	9	5	10	19	15	25
	2001	913	9	9	5	9	19	15	28
	2002	924	11	9	5	9	18	13	28
	2003	924	10	9	5	9	18	12	28
Guadeloupe	1970	203	11	7	...	4	17	3	54
(Euros)	1975	431	13	8	...	5	18	3	50
	1980	893	7	6	...	4	17	4	57
	1985	1494	10	4	...	5	17	6	56
	1990	2317	7	6	...	7	18	6	55
	1995	3378	7	8	...	7	17	7	55
	2000	4662	7	8	...	7	18	7	57
	2002	5329	7	8	...	7	18	7	59
Guatemala	1970	1904	27	17	16	2	29	5	20
(Quetzalas)	1975	3646	28	17	15	2	28	6	19
	1980	7879	25	19	17	3	27	7	19
	1985	11180	26	18	16	2	25	7	22
	1990	34317	26	18	15	2	24	8	22
	1995	85157	24	18	14	2	25	9	23
	1996	95479	24	18	14	2	25	9	23
	1997	107943	24	18	14	2	25	9	23
	1998	121548	23	18	14	2	25	9	23
	1999	132588	23	18	13	2	24	9	23

Table 3. Gross Domestic Product by Kind of Economic Activity: Individual Countries or Areas

Major area, region and country	Year	Gross Domestic Product (at current prices) Million	Agriculture hunting forestry and fishing A-B	Mining Manufacturing and Utilities C-E	Of which: Manufacturing D	Construction F	Wholesale, retail trade, restaurants and hotels G-H	Transport storage and communication I	Other Activities J-P
			Percentage Distribution						
	2000	146755	23	18	13	2	25	10	23
	2001	161581	22	18	13	2	25	10	23
	2002	178365	22	18	13	2	25	10	23
Guyana [34]	1970	536	17	28	11	7	10	5	20
(Dollars Guyana)	1975	1188	29	25	14	6	8	4	20
	1980	1508	21	25	11	6	8	5	24
	1985	1964	26	11	8	6	7	7	27
	1990	15665	38	13	5	4	6	7	20
	1995	88271	41	18	3	4	4	4	14
	1996	99038	38	19	3	4	4	5	15
	1997	106678	36	18	3	4	4	5	17
	1998	108002	34	16	3	5	4	6	19
	1999	123665	35	16	3	4	3	6	21
	2000	130013	30	16	3	4	4	6	23
	2001	133403	30	16	3	4	4	7	23
	2002	142019	33	16	3	4	4	6	21
Haiti	1970	1656	44	15	13	3	16	2	14
(Gourdes)	1975	3407	41	16	14	5	17	2	16
	1980	6919	32	20	18	5	19	2	17
	1985	10047	32	17	16	6	18	2	21
	1990	13068	35	16	15	6	17	2	22
	1995	35265	32	8	7	9	14	2	31
	1996	42744	31	8	7	10	13	2	31
	1997	51578	30	8	7	12	13	2	31
	1998	59055	30	8	7	12	13	2	31
	1999	66425	30	8	7	12	13	2	30
	2000	74411	29	8	7	13	14	2	30
	2001	81201	29	8	7	14	14	2	30
	2002	87712	28	8	7	14	14	2	31
Honduras [35]	1970	1382	28	16	13	5	13	6	24
(Lempiras)	1975	2248	25	18	14	5	14	6	24
	1980	5132	21	17	13	5	14	6	26
	1985	7279	19	16	13	5	12	6	31
	1990	12537	20	19	15	5	10	6	30
	1995	37507	19	22	16	5	10	4	27
	1996	47763	19	23	16	4	10	4	26
	1997	61322	20	22	16	4	10	4	27
	1998	70438	16	22	16	4	10	4	28
	1999	77095	14	23	17	5	11	4	29
	2000	87523	13	23	17	5	11	5	30
	2001	96981	11	23	18	5	11	5	32
	2002	105604	11	24	18	4	12	5	33
	2003	117929	13	23	17	5	11	5	31
Jamaica	1970	1174	6	29	16	13	21	5	26
(Jamaican Dollars)	1975	2618	7	27	17	10	22	6	31
	1980	4805	8	32	17	6	21	5	31
	1985	11278	6	28	20	9	24	8	28
	1990	30682	6	31	20	12	21	9	28
	1995	200027	9	24	15	11	21	8	28
	1996	237382	8	22	14	10	21	8	31
	1997	258026	8	21	14	10	21	9	30
	1998	273429	8	20	13	10	21	10	31
	1999	294076	7	21	13	9	20	10	33
	2000	329171	6	21	13	9	20	10	32
	2001	358036	6	21	13	10	20	11	31
	2002	392136	6	21	13	10	20	11	30
Martinique	1970	244	10	8	...	4	16	3	51
(Euros)	1975	512	10	9	...	5	18	3	51
	1980	930	6	7	...	4	17	4	60
	1985	1903	8	8	...	4	17	5	55
	1990	2945	6	10	...	5	18	6	53
	1995	3681	5	10	...	5	18	6	53
	2000	4464	5	10	...	5	19	6	53
	2003	5045	5	10	...	5	19	6	54
Mexico [36]	1970	495	11	21	18	5	26	5	29
(New Pesos)	1975	1226	10	20	18	5	26	6	27
	1980	4766	8	22	18	6	24	7	26

Table 3. Gross Domestic Product by Kind of Economic Activity: Individual Countries or Areas

Major area, region and country	Year	Gross Domestic Product (at current prices) Million	Agriculture hunting forestry and fishing A-B	Mining Manufacturing and Utilities C-E	Of which: Manufacturing D	Construction F	Wholesale, retail trade, restaurants and hotels G-H	Transport storage and communication I	Other Activities J-P
			Percentage Distribution						
	1985	50530	8	24	19	4	24	8	25
	1990	738898	7	22	19	4	23	8	28
	1995	1837019	5	22	19	4	19	9	37
	1996	2525575	6	22	20	4	20	9	33
	1997	3174275	5	22	19	4	19	10	32
	1998	3846350	5	22	19	4	18	10	33
	1999	4593685	4	22	19	5	18	10	34
	2000	5491373	4	21	18	5	19	10	33
	2001	5828591	4	20	18	5	19	10	35
	2002	6151219	4	20	17	4	19	10	36
	2003	6635793	4	19	17	5	19	10	35
Montserrat (EC Dollars)	1970	13	4	10	7	10	18	8	44
	1975	25	4	10	7	10	18	8	44
	1980	66	4	9	5	8	16	6	48
	1985	100	4	10	5	7	16	10	45
	1990	181	2	4	2	30	10	10	35
	1995	162	5	6	3	6	13	14	48
	1996	132	4	8	5	7	12	15	45
	1997	110	1	6	3	14	7	12	50
	1998	101	1	3	1	21	5	13	48
	1999	96	1	4	1	19	6	12	47
	2000	94	1	6	1	13	5	12	53
	2001	94	1	7	1	12	5	10	55
	2002	103	1	6	1	15	5	9	55
	2003	101	1	7	1	19	6	10	60
Netherlands Antilles [37] (Guilders)	1970	575	0	10	8	7	13	18	50
	1975	916	0	10	8	7	13	18	50
	1980	1734	1	10	9	8	13	18	41
	1985	2187	1	10	7	6	15	10	51
	1990	3619	1	9	7	5	18	10	58
	1995	4699	1	10	7	5	16	12	53
	2000	4956	1	8	4	4	16	9	57
	2002	5113	1	8	4	4	16	7	59
Nicaragua [38] (Gold Cordobas)	1970	2 (u)	13	24	20	5	15	10	39
	1975	4 (u)	13	25	22	8	15	10	36
	1980	7 (u)	13	30	25	5	13	10	32
	1985	38 (u)	13	31	27	8	12	8	30
	1990	507	18	20	17	5	18	7	27
	1995	24029	21	19	17	5	16	6	24
	1996	28009	22	19	16	5	16	5	24
	1997	31967	21	19	16	5	17	6	24
	1998	37805	20	19	15	5	16	6	25
	1999	44198	18	18	14	7	16	6	27
	2000	50145	19	18	14	7	16	4	29
	2001	53653	18	18	14	8	16	4	29
	2002	57051	18	19	14	6	16	5	29
	2003	61927	17	18	14	7	16	5	29
Panama (Balboas)	1970	1003	13	17	15	6	21	8	38
	1975	1820	11	17	15	7	23	10	42
	1980	3545	9	15	11	6	23	15	42
	1985	5006	9	17	13	4	17	17	49
	1990	5313	9	14	9	1	17	16	43
	1995	7906	8	13	9	5	21	14	40
	1996	8151	8	13	9	4	20	14	41
	1997	8658	7	13	9	4	21	14	42
	1998	9345	7	12	8	5	20	15	43
	1999	9637	7	12	8	5	18	16	44
	2000	10019	7	12	7	5	18	17	44
	2001	10079	8	13	8	4	19	16	43
	2002	10277	7	11	7	4	17	17	40
Paraguay [39] (Guaranies)	1970	74921	32	18	17	3	24	4	19
	1975	190439	37	17	16	4	23	4	15
	1980	560459	29	19	16	6	26	4	15
	1985	1393890	29	19	16	6	26	4	16
	1990	6474434	28	20	17	5	29	4	14
	1995	17699000	25	20	16	6	29	4	16
	2000	26920974	25	20	14	6	23	5	21
	2002	31976903	24	21	14	4	26	5	20

Table 3. Gross Domestic Product by Kind of Economic Activity: Individual Countries or Areas

Major area, region and country	Year	Gross Domestic Product (at current prices) Million	Agriculture hunting forestry and fishing A-B	Mining Manufacturing and Utilities C-E	Of which: Manufacturing D	Construction F	Wholesale, retail trade, restaurants and hotels G-H	Transport storage and communication I	Other Activities J-P
			Percentage Distribution						
Peru (New Soles)	1970	241 (u)	9	22	17	3	19	6	28
	1975	573 (u)	7	22	17	5	22	7	28
	1980	5143 (u)	6	24	16	4	20	7	29
	1985	170530 (u)	7	22	15	3	19	7	33
	1990	5851	8	22	15	4	19	8	30
	1995	120858	8	21	15	6	18	7	29
	1996	136929	8	21	15	6	18	7	29
	1997	157274	8	21	15	7	19	8	29
	1998	165949	8	20	14	7	18	8	29
	1999	173957	8	21	14	6	18	8	30
	2000	185281	8	22	15	5	18	8	30
	2001	188172	7	22	15	5	18	8	31
	2002	198437	7	22	14	5	18	8	31
Puerto Rico [40] (US Dollars)	1970	5647	3	27	24	8	19	5	33
	1975	8969	3	37	33	4	19	6	35
	1980	15956	2	39	36	3	16	5	31
	1985	21969	2	42	39	1	16	6	32
	1990	32287	1	42	39	2	16	5	34
	1995	45341	1	44	41	2	15	5	34
	1996	48187	1	43	40	3	15	5	35
	1997	54086	1	45	43	3	15	5	33
	1998	57841	1	43	40	3	15	5	33
	1999	61045	1	41	38	3	15	5	35
	2000	67897	1	42	40	3	14	5	35
	2001	69664	1	41	39	3	14	5	35
	2002	74993	1	41	39	3	13	4	35
Saint Kitts and Nevis (EC Dollars)	1970	34	16	12	11	9	9	9	31
	1975	74	16	12	11	8	9	9	32
	1980	129	13	13	12	8	14	8	28
	1985	211	8	11	10	7	18	10	35
	1990	430	5	12	11	12	18	13	28
	1995	623	5	11	9	10	19	13	32
	1996	663	4	11	9	10	20	14	32
	1997	742	5	11	9	9	20	13	32
	1998	775	4	10	8	10	21	12	33
	1999	823	3	11	9	11	20	12	34
	2000	888	2	11	9	14	17	12	36
	2001	929	2	11	9	15	15	12	35
	2002	963	3	11	8	14	15	12	35
	2003	1006	3	11	8	13	15	12	35
Saint Lucia (EC Dollars)	1970	79	16	10	7	10	19	7	38
	1975	129	16	10	7	10	19	7	38
	1980	305	12	13	9	12	25	12	31
	1985	441	15	13	8	7	23	10	38
	1990	1123	12	10	7	5	22	14	26
	1995	1496	8	10	6	7	22	16	30
	1996	1543	7	9	6	6	23	16	30
	1997	1562	7	9	5	6	24	16	31
	1998	1695	7	9	5	7	23	16	30
	1999	1786	8	9	5	7	23	16	29
	2000	1826	8	9	4	7	23	16	30
	2001	1747	7	9	4	7	22	17	32
	2002	1804	6	9	4	6	21	17	32
	2003	1857	6	9	4	6	20	17	30
Saint Vincent and the Grenadines (EC Dollars)	1970	37	15	10	8	9	12	14	25
	1975	71	15	10	8	9	12	14	25
	1980	160	12	12	9	12	13	15	26
	1985	305	16	13	10	6	11	15	25
	1990	535	18	12	7	8	12	17	23
	1995	713	12	12	7	10	15	17	24
	1996	752	11	12	7	9	15	18	25
	1997	793	8	12	7	11	15	18	25
	1998	857	9	11	6	12	16	18	24
	1999	892	9	10	5	11	16	17	25
	2000	906	9	11	5	9	17	17	26
	2001	935	8	12	6	10	17	16	26
	2002	975	9	11	5	10	17	16	26
	2003	1015	7	11	5	10	17	16	26

Table 3. Gross Domestic Product by Kind of Economic Activity: Individual Countries or Areas

Major area, region and country	Year	Gross Domestic Product (at current prices) Million	Agriculture hunting forestry and fishing A-B	Mining Manufacturing and Utilities C-E	Of which: Manufacturing D	Construction F	Wholesale, retail trade, restaurants and hotels G-H	Transport storage and communication I	Other Activities J-P
			Percentage Distribution						
Suriname (Guilders)	1970	532	7	44	19	3	17	5	23
	1975	931	6	29	16	4	15	5	23
	1980	1590	8	27	16	6	17	4	27
	1985	1746	8	21	12	6	15	7	38
	1990	3170	10	21	12	6	18	6	37
	1995	250571	17	32	15	3	17	7	16
	1996	289431	18	27	11	4	13	8	22
	1997	311191	14	29	11	3	15	8	28
	1998	377553	10	20	9	5	15	6	34
	1999	650353	10	22	9	4	16	7	32
	2000	1032979	12	23	9	3	16	8	32
	2001	1436483	12	19	7	4	14	8	32
	2002	1926645	10	16	5	3	13	11	37
Trinidad and Tobago [41] (Trinidad and Tobago Dollars)	1970	1644	5	34	24	7	19	14	21
	1975	5300	3	51	15	8	14	7	19
	1980	14966	2	49	9	13	10	10	21
	1985	18071	3	32	9	12	14	9	33
	1990	21539	3	36	13	9	15	8	26
	1995	31697	2	33	16	8	20	9	27
	1996	34587	2	33	16	8	20	9	26
	1997	35871	2	32	16	8	21	9	28
	1998	38065	1	29	15	9	21	9	29
	1999	42889	2	31	15	8	21	9	29
	2000	51485	1	37	17	7	20	9	26
	2001	56700	1	35	17	7	21	9	28
	2002	58200	1	38	18	7	23	10	30
Turks and Caicos Islands [42] (US Dollars)	1970	10	2	6	0	10	10	6	43
	1975	16	2	6	0	10	10	6	43
	1980	31	2	6	0	10	10	6	43
	1985	56	2	6	0	10	10	6	43
	1990	94	2	6	0	10	10	6	43
	1995	122	2	6	0	10	10	6	43
	1996	134	2	5	0	9	11	6	44
	1997	147	2	6	0	10	11	6	42
	1998	166	2	7	0	10	10	6	44
	1999	182	2	6	0	10	9	6	42
	2000	202	2	5	0	9	9	6	42
	2001	208	2	5	0	9	8	6	42
	2002	215	2	6	0	10	9	6	42
Uruguay [43] (Pesos)	1970	1	17	25	23	5	11	7	38
	1975	8	15	29	26	6	13	6	34
	1980	87	14	29	27	6	13	5	35
	1985	479	14	33	29	3	13	6	40
	1990	9784	11	29	26	3	13	7	43
	1995	122521	9	24	20	5	15	7	43
	1996	163546	8	23	19	5	15	8	44
	1997	204926	8	23	19	5	15	8	44
	1998	234267	7	23	18	6	14	8	45
	1999	237143	6	21	17	6	14	9	48
	2000	243027	6	21	17	6	13	9	49
	2001	247211	6	21	16	5	13	9	51
	2002	260967	9	23	17	4	12	9	49
	2003	315446	13	24	19	3	12	10	43
Venezuela (Bolivares)	1970	62884	5	33	18	8	15	5	27
	1975	142749	4	39	18	11	13	4	25
	1980	307262	4	38	18	12	11	5	27
	1985	464741	6	37	22	6	16	5	27
	1990	2279261	5	46	21	5	18	5	23
	1995	13685686	5	34	17	5	18	8	29
	1996	29437682	4	42	18	5	15	7	23
	1997	43343669	4	34	16	6	15	9	27
	1998	52482466	5	26	14	7	17	9	33
	1999	62577039	5	28	13	5	16	9	34
	2000	82450674	4	34	13	5	14	8	32
	2001	91324773	4	28	12	6	15	9	35
	2002	110782356	5	27	12	5	14	9	38

Table 3. Gross Domestic Product by Kind of Economic Activity: Individual Countries or Areas

Major area, region and country	Year	Gross Domestic Product (at current prices) Million	Agriculture hunting forestry and fishing A-B	Mining Manufacturing and Utilities C-E	Of which: Manufacturing D	Construction F	Wholesale, retail trade, restaurants and hotels G-H	Transport storage and communication I	Other Activities J-P
			Percentage Distribution						
ASIA									
Afghanistan	1970	62833	65	20	...	2	8	3	2
(Afghanis)	1975	109677	62	21	...	3	8	4	1
	1980	151642	62	21	...	4	7	4	1
	1985	191084	58	24	...	5	8	3	1
	1990	560976	52	26	...	7	9	4	2
	1995	2883410	64	14	...	6	11	2	2
	2000	6506380	64	14	...	6	11	2	2
	2002	9708009	59	14	...	6	13	2	3
Armenia	1990	50	16	32	32	18	4	7	16
(Drams)	1995	522256	41	24	24	7	10	4	14
	1996	661209	35	23	23	7	10	6	15
	1997	804336	29	22	22	8	10	8	17
	1998	955385	31	20	20	8	9	7	18
	1999	987444	27	21	21	8	10	8	20
	2000	1031338	23	22	22	10	10	7	20
	2001	1175877	26	20	20	10	11	7	19
	2002	1356983	24	20	20	13	11	7	17
Azerbaijan	1990	1466	27	22	18	8	3	8	23
(Azerbaijan Manats)	1995	10669000	25	27	12	4	6	17	15
	1996	13663200	25	26	10	9	6	10	15
	1997	15791400	20	25	8	12	6	10	19
	1998	17203100	18	22	8	13	6	12	25
	1999	18875400	18	28	6	11	7	11	21
	2000	23590500	16	36	5	7	7	12	17
	2001	26578000	15	38	7	6	8	10	17
	2002	30312300	14	34	6	11	8	10	15
	2003	35053400	13	36	6	10	8	9	15
Bahrain	1970	119	1	39	10	10	16	6	31
(Dinars)	1975	410	1	43	12	6	14	5	28
	1980	1241	1	46	12	7	13	6	35
	1985	1472	1	36	7	9	10	9	55
	1990	1614	1	34	12	6	11	7	51
	1995	2199	1	34	18	5	13	7	49
	1996	2294	1	34	15	4	13	7	51
	1997	2387	1	35	15	4	11	7	52
	1998	2325	1	28	13	4	12	8	57
	1999	2489	1	32	12	4	11	8	54
	2000	2997	1	41	11	4	10	7	49
	2001	2981	1	38	12	4	11	8	48
	2002	3165	1	38	12	4	11	8	47
Bangladesh	1970	75214	37	17	17	6	12	8	17
(Taka)	1975	145481	41	14	14	4	13	7	16
	1980	305196	34	16	16	6	13	10	18
	1985	614824	33	14	14	6	13	9	20
	1990	1100331	30	15	13	6	12	9	24
	1995	1663240	25	17	15	7	13	9	26
	1996	1807013	25	17	15	7	13	9	26
	1997	2001766	24	18	16	7	13	8	26
	1998	2196972	25	17	15	7	13	8	26
	1999	2370856	25	17	15	7	13	8	26
	2000	2535464	23	17	15	8	13	9	26
	2001	2714142	23	18	15	8	14	9	26
	2002	3004850	24	19	16	9	15	10	25
Bhutan	1970	346	53	5	4	11	11	4	16
(Ngultrum)	1975	870	53	5	4	11	11	4	16
	1980	1095	57	4	3	8	11	4	17
	1985	2392	52	6	5	12	8	4	17
	1990	4983	42	17	8	8	6	7	18
	1995	10064	39	23	11	9	7	7	12
	1996	11808	38	23	12	9	8	7	12
	1997	14314	38	25	11	10	7	7	15
	1998	16337	37	23	10	10	7	8	15
	1999	19123	35	23	9	11	7	9	15
	2000	21698	36	21	8	13	7	9	15
	2001	24317	35	20	8	15	7	9	15
	2002	27779	34	20	8	17	7	9	16

Table 3. Gross Domestic Product by Kind of Economic Activity: Individual Countries or Areas

Major area, region and country	Year	Gross Domestic Product (at current prices) Million	Agriculture hunting forestry and fishing A-B	Mining Manufacturing and Utilities C-E	Of which: Manufacturing D	Construction F	Wholesale, retail trade, restaurants and hotels G-H	Transport storage and communication I	Other Activities J-P
			Percentage Distribution						
Brunei Darussalam....................................	1970	546	1	89	9	1	2	1	6
(Brunei Darussalam Dollars)	1975	2770	1	88	12	2	3	1	7
	1980	10554	1	83	12	2	9	1	6
	1985	7752	1	70	10	2	11	2	16
	1990	6509	2	51	9	4	13	4	28
	1995	7394	3	38	...	5	11	5	40
	1996	7409	3	38	...	6	13	5	42
	1997	7628	3	38	...	7	13	5	43
	1998	6534	3	34	...	7	13	5	42
	1999	7145	3	40	...	6	10	5	39
	2000	7441	3	42	...	6	9	6	38
	2001	7436	3	38	...	4	9	5	40
	2002	7664	3	37	...	5	10	5	38
Cambodia [44]..	1970	10708	40	6	2	4	21	6	19
(Riels)	1975	8830	40	6	2	4	21	6	19
	1980	8395	40	6	2	4	21	6	19
	1985	16965	40	6	2	4	21	6	19
	1990	723653	51	10	7	2	14	7	18
	1995	8110680	49	8	7	5	15	6	14
	1996	8885580	46	9	8	5	15	6	14
	1997	9778060	46	11	10	4	15	6	14
	1998	11363640	46	12	12	4	14	6	14
	1999	12587090	43	12	12	5	14	6	14
	2000	12931530	38	16	15	5	14	7	15
	2001	13364930	37	16	16	6	14	7	14
	2002	14397172	35	18	17	6	14	7	14
China [45]..	1970	225270	35	37	...	4	6	4	12
(Yuan Renminbi)	1975	299730	32	41	...	4	5	5	11
	1980	451780	30	44	...	4	6	5	12
	1985	872944	29	40	...	5	10	5	15
	1990	1831950	27	37	...	5	8	6	18
	1995	5847810	21	42	...	7	8	5	17
	1996	6788460	20	43	...	7	8	5	17
	1997	7446260	19	43	...	7	8	6	17
	1998	7834520	19	43	...	7	8	5	17
	1999	8206750	18	43	...	7	8	5	18
	2000	8944220	16	44	...	7	8	5	18
	2001	9593330	16	44	...	7	9	6	19
	2002	10479060	15	44	...	7	9	6	19
Cyprus [46]..	1970	229	16	19	12	7	13	8	32
(Pounds)	1975	260	15	19	15	7	13	6	34
	1980	760	10	20	18	13	15	8	30
	1985	1481	7	18	16	10	19	9	32
	1990	2556	7	16	14	9	21	9	33
	1995	4007	5	14	12	8	21	8	37
	1996	4161	5	14	12	8	21	8	39
	1997	4371	4	14	11	8	21	8	40
	1998	4694	4	13	11	8	21	9	41
	1999	5019	4	13	10	7	21	9	42
	2000	5487	4	13	10	7	22	9	42
	2001	5865	4	12	10	7	22	10	42
	2002	6161	4	11	9	7	20	9	43
	2003	6655	4	11	9	7	19	9	44
Georgia [47]...	1990	15 (t)	30	24	24	9	6	7	19
(Laris)	1995	3694	42	10	10	2	26	8	6
	1996	3868	33	21	21	2	14	6	22
	1997	4555	28	19	19	4	13	8	24
	1998	5022	26	17	17	5	12	11	25
	1999	5669	25	17	17	4	14	12	23
	2000	6015	20	17	17	4	15	14	24
	2001	6647	21	17	17	4	16	14	23
	2002	7455	19	18	18	5	16	14	22
	2003	8466	20	18	18	5	16	14	22
Hong Kong SAR of China [48].....................	1970	23369	2	33	31	4	20	8	33
(Hong Kong Dollars)	1975	50012	1	29	27	6	21	7	36
	1980	143976	1	24	22	6	20	7	42
	1985	275832	0	23	20	5	21	8	40
	1990	591507	0	19	17	5	24	9	43

Table 3. Gross Domestic Product by Kind of Economic Activity: Individual Countries or Areas

Major area, region and country	Year	Gross Domestic Product (at current prices) Million	Agriculture hunting forestry and fishing A-B	Mining Manufacturing and Utilities C-E	Of which: Manufacturing D	Construction F	Wholesale, retail trade, restaurants and hotels G-H	Transport storage and communication I	Other Activities J-P
			Percentage Distribution						
	1995	1096263	0	10	8	5	25	10	52
	1996	1210925	0	9	7	5	26	9	53
	1997	1344546	0	9	6	5	24	9	54
	1998	1279850	0	9	6	6	24	9	55
	1999	1246134	0	8	5	5	24	9	55
	2000	1288338	0	9	6	5	25	10	54
	2001	1269975	0	8	5	5	26	10	55
	2002	1259771	0	8	4	4	26	10	55
	2003	1241561	0	8	5	5	25	10	55
India (Rupees)	1970	457435	42	15	13	4	8	3	21
	1975	834698	37	16	14	4	10	4	21
	1980	1441446	35	18	15	4	10	4	20
	1985	2779213	30	19	15	5	11	5	20
	1990	5675511	28	20	15	5	11	5	20
	1995	11880120	26	21	16	5	12	6	21
	1996	13682080	27	20	16	5	13	6	21
	1997	15225470	25	20	15	5	13	6	22
	1998	17409850	25	19	14	5	13	6	23
	1999	19369250	24	18	14	5	13	6	24
	2000	21042980	23	19	14	6	13	7	25
	2001	22960490	23	18	14	5	13	7	25
	2002	24695640	21	19	14	6	13	7	26
Indonesia [49] (Rupiahs)	1970	3238000	49	15	9	3	17	3	14
	1975	12643000	32	29	9	5	17	4	14
	1980	45446000	25	38	12	6	14	4	13
	1985	96997000	23	30	16	5	16	6	19
	1990	210866000	19	34	21	6	17	6	18
	1995	454513000	17	34	24	8	17	7	18
	1996	532567000	17	36	26	8	16	7	17
	1997	627695000	16	37	27	7	16	6	18
	1998	955754000	18	39	25	6	15	5	16
	1999	1099730000	20	37	26	6	16	5	16
	2000	1264919000	17	40	25	6	16	5	16
	2001	1449398000	17	40	25	6	16	5	16
	2002	1610012000	17	39	25	6	16	6	16
Iran (Islamic Republic of) [50] (Rials)	1970	754383	15	29	11	5	10	5	31
	1975	3282929	8	47	8	7	8	6	28
	1980	6447256	13	22	8	11	8	9	42
	1985	15335563	15	18	7	10	14	8	35
	1990	35623226	17	22	10	5	17	8	28
	1995	188969300	18	30	12	4	14	6	27
	1996	250411700	15	31	13	5	14	7	26
	1997	296604100	14	29	14	4	14	8	29
	1998	334740200	17	23	13	4	15	8	32
	1999	454232900	14	29	13	4	14	7	29
	2000	589894400	13	33	13	3	13	8	28
	2001	677792500	12	31	13	4	13	8	30
	2002	945231400	11	35	12	4	12	7	28
Iraq [51] (Dinars)	1970	1257	15	40	9	3	8	6	23
	1975	4090	8	57	7	9	5	5	17
	1980	15948	5	65	4	8	5	4	13
	1985	15494	14	33	10	9	12	5	27
	1990	23297	20	24	9	7	15	9	30
	1995	1940994	65	4	5	1	10	27	12
	1996	2379254	46	3	3	1	27	22	14
	1997	3269914	36	3	3	1	22	29	16
	1998	4570100	37	3	3	1	22	27	16
	1999	6809790	32	4	4	1	19	26	14
	2000	7398604	31	5	5	1	19	29	19
	2001	8878324	28	4	3	1	20	27	20
	2002	9903371	32	4	4	1	20	28	18
Israel (New Shekels)	1970	2	6	25	22	9	9	10	42
	1975	9	5	21	18	9	9	8	41
	1980	120	5	19	15	7	10	7	41
	1985	31596	4	21	19	3	10	8	44
	1990	115409	3	20	18	5	8	8	50
	1995	286428	2	17	15	7	9	8	47
	1996	333702	2	17	15	7	9	7	49

Table 3. Gross Domestic Product by Kind of Economic Activity: Individual Countries or Areas

Major area, region and country	Year	Gross Domestic Product (at current prices) Million	Agriculture hunting forestry and fishing A-B	Mining Manufacturing and Utilities C-E	Of which: Manufacturing D	Construction F	Wholesale, retail trade, restaurants and hotels G-H	Transport storage and communication I	Other Activities J-P
			Percentage Distribution						
	1997	373326	2	17	15	7	9	7	48
	1998	410914	2	17	16	6	9	7	48
	1999	449463	2	17	16	5	9	7	48
	2000	490721	1	17	16	5	9	7	49
	2001	495390	2	16	15	4	9	7	51
	2002	513558	2	16	15	4	8	7	52
Japan [52] (Yen)	1970	74450690	6	38	35	8	14	7	25
	1975	150563261	5	32	30	10	13	6	29
	1980	243796700	4	32	29	9	12	6	36
	1985	326815700	3	32	29	8	13	6	39
	1990	442072300	2	29	27	10	13	7	41
	1995	498872300	2	26	23	8	15	7	46
	1996	511946800	2	26	23	8	15	7	46
	1997	523051100	2	26	23	8	15	7	47
	1998	516579200	2	25	22	8	15	7	48
	1999	509115900	1	25	22	8	14	6	49
	2000	513376800	1	25	22	7	14	6	50
	2001	507455500	1	24	21	7	14	6	52
	2002	499986500	1	23	20	7	14	6	53
Jordan (Dinars)	1970	212	6	13	10	5	17	9	43
	1975	390	6	15	10	7	16	9	42
	1980	1196	5	15	10	12	15	10	35
	1985	2020	5	17	12	7	15	14	36
	1990	2668	7	25	16	4	8	14	36
	1995	4773	4	18	13	6	10	12	37
	1996	4982	3	17	11	5	10	13	38
	1997	5193	3	18	12	4	11	13	39
	1998	5646	3	18	13	3	11	13	39
	1999	5765	2	18	13	3	10	13	39
	2000	6012	2	18	13	3	10	13	40
	2001	6343	3	18	13	3	10	13	40
	2002	6625	2	19	13	3	11	13	40
Kazakhstan [53] (Tenge)	1990	96	34	21	21	12	8	10	15
	1995	1014190	12	24	24	6	17	11	26
	1996	1415750	12	21	21	4	17	11	29
	1997	1672142	11	25	11	4	16	12	28
	1998	1733264	9	24	12	5	16	14	27
	1999	2016456	10	28	14	5	14	12	26
	2000	2599902	8	33	33	5	13	11	24
	2001	3250593	9	31	16	5	13	11	26
	2002	3776277	8	29	29	6	13	12	26
Kuwait [54] (Dinars)	1970	1026	0	65	4	3	8	3	20
	1975	3485	0	77	6	2	6	2	12
	1980	7755	0	70	6	4	8	2	15
	1985	6450	1	53	6	4	9	4	30
	1990	5328	1	50	12	2	8	4	37
	1995	7925	0	50	11	3	8	5	35
	1996	9303	0	56	12	3	7	4	31
	1997	9060	0	54	13	3	7	4	34
	1998	7656	0	43	12	3	9	6	43
	1999	8886	0	48	11	3	8	5	39
	2000	10991	0	57	7	2	6	5	44
	2001	10057	0	51	7	2	7	5	53
	2002	10738	0	47	7	2	7	5	52
Kyrgyzstan [55] (Som)	1990	43	33	29	29	8	4	6	18
	1995	16145	41	13	13	6	11	5	19
	1996	23399	46	12	12	6	10	5	15
	1997	30686	41	17	17	5	10	4	16
	1998	34181	36	17	17	4	13	4	18
	1999	48744	35	22	22	3	13	5	15
	2000	65358	34	24	24	4	12	4	16
	2001	73883	35	23	18	4	13	4	15
	2002	75367	34	18	13	3	15	5	16
	2003	83421	35	18	14	3	16	5	14
Lao People's Democratic Republic (Kips)	1970	36	55	15	10	2	14	8	12
	1975	194	55	15	10	2	14	8	13
	1980	8481	55	15	10	2	14	8	12

Table 3. Gross Domestic Product by Kind of Economic Activity: Individual Countries or Areas

Major area, region and country	Year	Gross Domestic Product (at current prices) Million	Agriculture hunting forestry and fishing A-B	Mining Manufacturing and Utilities C-E	Of which: Manufacturing D	Construction F	Wholesale, retail trade, restaurants and hotels G-H	Transport storage and communication I	Other Activities J-P
			Percentage Distribution						
	1985	84374	54	16	10	2	14	9	10
	1990	612447	61	11	10	3	8	5	12
	1995	1430361	54	15	14	3	10	5	11
	2000	13672336	52	20	17	2	12	6	7
	2002	18390380	50	22	19	2	12	6	6
Lebanon..	1970	4866	8	26	12	4	28	7	27
(Lebanese Pounds)	1975	7500	10	17	15	3	34	6	31
	1980	14000	9	17	12	3	29	4	38
	1985	29988	9	18	13	3	28	4	40
	1990	1954275	9	18	13	3	28	4	38
	1995	17779000	13	24	18	9	30	3	28
	2000	24816000	11	18	9	4	24	2	45
	2002	26324000	11	18	9	4	25	2	46
Macao SAR of China................................	1970	1060	...	12	10	6	10	4	70
(Patacas)	1975	2361	...	12	9	6	10	3	69
	1980	5250	...	11	9	6	10	3	67
	1985	10950	...	12	10	7	10	4	71
	1990	26175	...	10	8	6	9	3	64
	1995	55333	...	9	7	5	9	3	63
	1996	55294	...	9	7	4	11	4	61
	1997	55894	...	9	7	4	9	6	62
	1998	51902	...	10	8	3	8	6	63
	1999	49021	...	11	8	3	8	6	61
	2000	49742	...	11	8	2	9	7	62
	2001	49802	...	9	7	2	10	6	62
	2002	54229	...	8	6	2	10	6	61
	2003	63289	...	10	7	2	9	6	62
Malaysia..	1970	10588	29	24	15	4	12	5	23
(Ringgit)	1975	22332	29	31	18	4	12	5	23
	1980	53308	21	38	21	6	10	5	20
	1985	77470	19	33	21	3	13	6	26
	1990	119081	15	38	24	4	14	6	25
	1995	222473	13	35	26	6	15	7	26
	1996	253732	12	37	28	7	15	7	26
	1997	281795	11	38	28	7	15	7	27
	1998	283243	13	39	29	5	15	7	27
	1999	300764	11	42	31	5	15	7	26
	2000	342157	9	47	33	4	14	7	24
	2001	334589	9	45	31	4	14	7	26
	2002	360960	10	44	31	4	14	7	25
	2003	392340	10	46	31	4	13	7	24
Maldives..	1970	74	41	7	5	1	12	18	18
(Rufiyaa)	1975	152	41	7	5	1	12	18	18
	1980	356	28	10	7	4	12	21	22
	1985	596	21	12	9	3	20	5	31
	1990	2060	17	12	9	3	20	11	31
	1995	4696	11	10	8	3	38	11	27
	2000	7348	8	11	8	2	34	14	26
	2002	8186	9	12	8	3	32	13	26
Mongolia..	1970	4980	16	25	11	3	32	17	13
(Tughriks)	1975	6530	16	25	11	3	32	17	13
	1980	8723	16	25	11	3	32	17	12
	1985	12102	15	25	11	3	32	18	12
	1990	13514	16	28	13	3	28	17	11
	1995	554249	38	26	12	2	18	6	12
	1996	659698	43	18	6	3	17	7	11
	1997	846344	35	24	6	2	22	8	10
	1998	833727	37	18	6	2	22	9	12
	1999	925801	37	18	6	2	22	9	13
	2000	1018886	29	20	6	2	25	11	15
	2001	1115640	25	20	8	2	28	13	15
	2002	1240787	21	20	6	2	29	15	16
Myanmar [56]...	1970	13504	41	11	10	2	26	5	13
(Kyats)	1975	23477	47	10	9	1	29	3	10
	1980	38609	47	11	10	2	26	4	11
	1985	55989	48	11	10	2	24	4	11
	1990	151941	57	9	8	2	23	3	7

Table 3. Gross Domestic Product by Kind of Economic Activity: Individual Countries or Areas

Major area, region and country	Year	Gross Domestic Product (at current prices) Million	Agriculture hunting forestry and fishing A-B	Mining Manufacturing and Utilities C-E	Of which: Manufacturing D	Construction F	Wholesale, retail trade, restaurants and hotels G-H	Transport storage and communication I	Other Activities J-P
			Percentage Distribution						
	1995	604729	60	8	7	2	23	3	4
	1996	791980	60	8	7	2	23	3	3
	1997	1109554	59	8	7	2	23	4	3
	1998	1559996	59	8	7	2	24	4	3
	1999	2120782	58	8	7	3	24	5	3
	2000	2663942	61	8	8	3	26	6	2
	2001	3669602	58	8	8	3	26	6	2
	2002	5688124	50	7	7	3	23	6	2
Nepal [57] (Rupees)	1970	9816	69	4	4	7	3	3	13
	1975	16571	69	4	4	4	3	4	12
	1980	23351	58	4	4	7	4	7	14
	1985	40507	49	6	5	8	10	6	17
	1990	103416	49	7	6	9	10	6	17
	1995	219175	39	11	9	11	11	6	18
	1996	248913	39	11	9	10	11	6	18
	1997	280513	39	11	9	10	11	7	18
	1998	300845	37	11	9	10	11	8	19
	1999	342036	39	11	9	10	11	7	19
	2000	379488	38	11	9	10	11	8	18
	2001	410287	37	11	9	10	11	8	20
	2002	421333	38	10	8	10	10	8	20
	2003	446177	38	10	8	10	10	8	20
Oman (Rials)	1970	113	16	55	0	4	7	2	15
	1975	767	3	55	0	9	9	3	18
	1980	2185	3	62	1	5	8	3	20
	1985	3591	2	53	2	6	11	4	24
	1990	4493	3	52	3	2	11	5	29
	1995	5307	3	44	5	3	14	6	32
	1996	5874	3	47	4	2	13	6	30
	1997	6090	3	45	4	3	14	7	30
	1998	5416	3	37	5	4	16	8	34
	1999	6041	3	45	4	2	14	7	31
	2000	7639	2	55	5	2	11	6	26
	2001	7670	2	52	8	2	12	7	27
	2002	7809	2	51	8	2	13	7	28
Pakistan [58] (Rupees)	1970	50938	34	16	14	4	13	7	18
	1975	130741	31	14	13	5	13	8	21
	1980	278196	27	16	13	4	13	9	19
	1985	514532	25	17	15	4	14	8	22
	1990	1020600	23	19	16	4	15	8	21
	1995	2120173	23	19	15	3	15	9	22
	1996	2428312	24	18	15	3	15	9	22
	1997	2677656	25	19	15	3	14	9	22
	1998	2938379	25	19	14	3	14	9	22
	1999	3147167	25	18	14	3	14	10	23
	2000	3416252	23	18	15	3	14	10	23
	2001	3726611	22	18	14	3	14	11	25
	2002	4018112	23	21	16	3	15	12	26
Philippines [59] (Pesos)	1970	39505	30	28	25	4	11	3	24
	1975	107953	30	28	26	7	11	4	20
	1980	243749	25	30	26	9	13	5	18
	1985	571883	25	30	25	5	16	6	19
	1990	1077237	22	28	25	6	16	5	23
	1995	1905951	22	26	23	6	15	5	26
	1996	2171922	21	26	23	6	15	5	27
	1997	2426743	19	26	22	6	15	5	29
	1998	2665060	17	26	22	6	15	5	31
	1999	2976904	17	25	22	5	16	5	31
	2000	3354727	16	26	22	6	16	6	30
	2001	3673687	15	26	23	6	16	7	30
	2002	4022694	15	27	23	6	16	7	30
	2003	4359045	14	27	23	5	16	7	30
Qatar (Riyals)	1970	1437	1	67	3	9	6	2	17
	1975	9707	1	72	3	8	4	2	15
	1980	28663	1	71	3	5	5	1	19
	1985	22398	1	52	8	6	5	2	36
	1990	26792	1	52	13	4	6	3	36
	1995	29622	1	47	8	7	8	4	36

Table 3. Gross Domestic Product by Kind of Economic Activity: Individual Countries or Areas

Major area, region and country	Year	Gross Domestic Product (at current prices) Million	Agriculture hunting forestry and fishing A-B	Mining Manufacturing and Utilities C-E	Of which: Manufacturing D	Construction F	Wholesale, retail trade, restaurants and hotels G-H	Transport storage and communication I	Other Activities J-P
			Percentage Distribution						
	1996	32976	1	48	8	7	8	4	36
	1997	41124	1	52	8	7	7	4	32
	1998	37330	1	44	8	7	8	5	37
	1999	45111	1	54	6	5	7	4	31
	2000	64646	0	67	5	4	6	3	22
	2001	64579	0	65	6	5	6	3	23
	2002	65088	0	65	6	4	6	3	23
Republic of Korea.. (Wons)	1970	2725185	27	24	21	5	17	7	19
	1975	10228062	25	29	26	5	18	6	17
	1980	37788497	15	32	28	8	13	8	23
	1985	81312283	13	33	29	8	14	7	24
	1990	178796762	9	32	29	11	13	7	28
	1995	377349800	6	32	29	11	13	7	32
	1996	418478988	6	31	29	12	12	7	33
	1997	453276389	5	31	29	12	11	7	34
	1998	444366540	5	34	31	10	10	7	35
	1999	482744175	5	34	31	9	11	7	35
	2000	521959212	5	34	31	8	12	7	34
	2001	551557522	4	34	30	8	12	7	35
	2002	596381162	4	32	29	8	12	7	38
Saudi Arabia.. (Riyals)	1970	22921	4	65	9	4	5	6	14
	1975	164526	1	72	5	10	4	2	11
	1980	490942	1	70	4	10	4	3	11
	1985	313941	4	37	8	12	10	8	30
	1990	391993	6	44	8	9	7	6	27
	1995	478652	7	44	9	9	7	6	27
	1996	590749	5	45	10	7	6	4	33
	1997	617902	5	43	10	6	6	4	34
	1998	546648	6	35	11	7	8	5	38
	1999	603589	6	40	10	7	8	5	35
	2000	706657	5	47	10	6	7	4	31
	2001	698403	5	45	10	6	7	4	32
	2002	705293	5	54	9	8	6	5	22
Singapore[60]... (Singapore Dollars)	1970	5805	2	23	20	7	27	11	30
	1975	13443	2	26	24	8	25	11	30
	1980	25091	1	32	29	6	22	14	29
	1985	38924	1	26	24	11	17	13	39
	1990	66884	0	28	26	5	17	13	37
	1995	118963	0	26	25	7	16	12	37
	1996	130035	0	25	24	8	16	11	39
	1997	141641	0	25	23	9	15	11	40
	1998	137085	0	25	23	9	14	11	41
	1999	137935	0	25	24	8	15	12	41
	2000	157700	0	28	27	6	15	11	38
	2001	152066	0	26	24	6	15	11	41
	2002	155727	0	28	26	5	15	12	40
Sri Lanka.. (Rupees)	1970	14259	36	15	14	6	14	9	14
	1975	26890	28	26	24	5	15	9	11
	1980	68809	26	20	17	9	14	10	11
	1985	158852	24	18	16	7	15	11	12
	1990	320098	23	20	17	7	15	10	13
	1995	666956	19	20	17	7	18	10	15
	1996	776739	18	20	17	7	18	10	15
	1997	897218	18	21	18	6	18	11	15
	1998	1018330	17	20	18	6	19	11	16
	1999	1108845	17	20	17	7	18	11	15
	2000	1253622	16	21	18	6	20	11	15
	2001	1396314	15	22	18	7	19	11	15
	2002	1570260	15	22	18	6	18	11	17
Syrian Arab Republic.................................. (Syrian Pounds)	1970	6848	20	23	19	3	20	11	23
	1975	20711	18	20	7	5	22	12	23
	1980	51270	20	16	4	7	25	7	25
	1985	83225	21	15	8	7	22	10	25
	1990	268328	28	20	5	4	23	10	15
	1995	570975	28	14	6	4	26	12	16
	1996	690857	28	22	8	4	22	11	14
	1997	745569	26	25	7	4	20	12	14
	1998	790444	29	23	8	4	19	11	14

Table 3. Gross Domestic Product by Kind of Economic Activity: Individual Countries or Areas

Major area, region and country	Year	Gross Domestic Product (at current prices) Million	Agriculture hunting forestry and fishing A-B	Mining Manufacturing and Utilities C-E	Of which: Manufacturing D	Construction F	Wholesale, retail trade, restaurants and hotels G-H	Transport storage and communication I	Other Activities J-P
			Percentage Distribution						
	1999	819092	24	27	6	3	19	13	14
	2000	903944	25	30	2	3	15	13	14
	2001	954051	26	28	6	3	16	13	15
	2002	999451	25	27	7	3	17	13	14
Tajikistan (Somani)	1990	73 (t)	30	34	34	11	8	7	19
	1995	70	37	34	34	3	8	4	16
	1996	308	36	26	26	3	15	4	9
	1997	518	32	22	22	3	21	3	10
	1998	1025	25	20	20	4	23	4	17
	1999	1345	25	22	22	5	20	7	13
	2000	1807	27	24	24	3	18	5	14
	2001	2529	26	23	23	4	19	4	15
	2002	3366	26	22	22	4	20	4	14
Thailand (Baht)	1970	148274	26	19	16	4	24	6	21
	1975	305149	27	21	19	3	25	5	20
	1980	662482	23	24	22	4	23	5	20
	1985	1056496	16	27	22	5	24	7	21
	1990	2184000	12	25	22	6	19	7	17
	1995	4186212	11	27	24	7	11	7	25
	1996	4611041	11	27	23	7	11	7	25
	1997	4732610	11	28	24	5	12	8	25
	1998	4626447	12	29	25	4	13	8	24
	1999	4637079	11	30	26	3	13	8	24
	2000	4916505	10	32	28	3	13	8	24
	2001	5123418	10	33	28	3	12	8	24
	2002	5441070	9	34	29	3	13	8	25
	2003	5925325	11	32	27	3	13	8	24
Timor-Leste[61] (Rupiah)	1990	181	33	4	3	13	8	8	34
	1995	315	33	4	3	13	8	8	34
	2000	321	26	4	3	14	8	7	40
	2002	378	27	4	3	15	9	8	36
Turkey (Liras)	1970	206000	37	17	15	6	12	8	18
	1975	674000	34	18	16	5	14	9	18
	1980	5231000	26	19	17	6	16	11	22
	1985	35095000	20	22	18	6	19	13	17
	1990	393060170	17	26	22	6	19	12	19
	1995	7762456069	16	26	23	5	20	13	19
	1996	14772110189	17	25	21	6	20	13	20
	1997	28835883135	15	25	22	6	21	14	21
	1998	52224945129	18	23	20	6	20	14	23
	1999	77415272308	16	23	20	6	20	13	26
	2000	124583458275	15	23	20	5	21	14	23
	2001	178412438500	13	26	22	5	22	15	23
	2002	276002987851	13	25	22	4	21	14	23
Turkmenistan (Manats)	1990	7600	11	76	76	5	2	4	6
	1995	652044	16	56	56	6	4	5	9
	1996	7751754	13	57	57	10	3	6	7
	1997	11108783	20	35	35	11	4	10	15
	1998	13994739	25	30	30	13	4	8	17
	1999	20056000	25	31	31	12	4	7	21
	2000	25648000	23	35	35	7	4	7	25
	2001	33863000	25	37	37	6	4	5	24
	2002	63800000	24	34	34	10	4	7	20
United Arab Emirates (Dirhams)	1970	3160	1	72	2	5	7	6	9
	1975	39460	1	69	1	11	8	3	10
	1980	109833	1	69	4	9	8	3	12
	1985	99416	1	57	9	9	9	4	23
	1990	124008	2	55	7	8	9	5	23
	1995	155210	3	49	9	8	8	6	27
	2000	195779	3	49	10	8	7	6	27
	2003	243391	3	51	10	8	7	6	27
Uzbekistan (Sums)	1990	32	34	24	24	11	5	6	22
	1995	302787	28	18	18	7	8	7	21
	1996	559072	22	19	19	8	9	7	22
	1997	976830	28	16	16	7	10	7	20
	1998	1416157	27	15	15	8	8	7	21

Table 3. Gross Domestic Product by Kind of Economic Activity: Individual Countries or Areas

Major area, region and country	Year	Gross Domestic Product (at current prices) Million	Agriculture hunting forestry and fishing A-B	Mining Manufacturing and Utilities C-E	Of which: Manufacturing D	Construction F	Wholesale, retail trade, restaurants and hotels G-H	Transport storage and communication I	Other Activities J-P
			Percentage Distribution						
	1999	2128660	29	14	14	7	9	6	21
	2000	3255600	30	14	14	6	9	8	19
	2001	4868400	27	16	16	7	9	7	21
	2002	7469300	27	16	16	7	9	7	21
Vietnam...... (Dong)	1970	3989	43	20	16	3	11	2	20
	1975	4071	43	20	16	3	11	2	20
	1980	14031	43	20	16	3	11	2	20
	1985	123000	44	21	17	3	10	2	20
	1990	41955000	39	19	12	4	17	3	18
	1995	228892000	27	22	15	7	20	4	20
	1996	272036000	28	23	15	7	19	4	19
	1997	313623000	26	26	16	7	19	4	19
	1998	361017000	26	27	17	6	19	4	19
	1999	399942000	25	29	18	5	18	4	18
	2000	444139000	24	31	19	6	18	4	17
	2001	485109000	25	30	18	5	18	4	18
	2002	540346284	25	30	19	6	18	4	18
Yemen...... (Rials)	1990	129960	25	22	8	3	9	14	25
	1995	511058	19	29	14	4	12	13	24
	1996	736385	16	38	11	4	10	11	19
	1997	888808	16	39	10	5	10	12	18
	1998	849321	19	28	10	5	11	14	22
	1999	1132619	16	38	8	5	9	12	21
	2000	1379812	15	42	7	4	9	10	19
	2001	1439834	15	39	7	4	8	10	19
	2002	1592168	16	37	9	5	9	12	20
EUROPE									
Albania [62]...... (Leks)	1970	6480	38	40	...	7	8	3	...
	1975	11462	38	40	...	7	8	3	...
	1980	15533	38	40	...	7	8	3	...
	1985	16857	39	40	...	7	8	3	...
	1990	16813	40	37	...	7	13	3	...
	1995	229793	55	12	...	10	20	4	...
	1996	315835	29	14	13	4	23	6	20
	1997	333071	29	13	12	4	19	7	24
	1998	425356	27	10	10	4	19	9	25
	1999	488610	26	10	10	4	21	10	23
	2000	551281	25	10	10	5	19	9	24
	2001	611622	25	13	12	10	22	10	26
	2002	677272	25	11	10	9	22	10	26
	2003	739048	25	10	9	9	22	10	26
Austria...... (Euros)	1970	28184	7	34	30	8	16	7	25
	1975	49196	5	29	26	9	15	6	27
	1980	74723	5	26	22	8	17	7	30
	1985	100772	4	25	21	6	16	7	35
	1990	133603	3	24	21	6	17	7	36
	1995	172287	2	22	19	7	16	7	40
	1996	178045	2	21	18	8	16	7	41
	1997	182486	2	22	19	8	16	7	40
	1998	190628	2	22	19	8	16	7	40
	1999	197064	2	22	19	8	16	7	40
	2000	206671	2	22	20	7	16	6	40
	2001	212511	2	22	19	7	16	7	41
	2002	218333	2	22	19	7	16	7	41
	2003	224270	2	21	19	7	16	7	41
Belarus [63]...... (Belarussian Roubles)	1990	4	25	40	40	8	5	7	19
	1995	121403	16	28	28	5	11	12	22
	1996	191839	15	29	29	5	9	11	21
	1997	366830	13	30	30	6	9	11	20
	1998	702161	12	29	29	6	11	10	21
	1999	3026064	13	28	28	6	11	11	20
	2000	9133776	12	27	27	6	11	11	20
	2001	17173230	10	26	26	6	11	12	24
	2002	26138302	10	25	25	6	11	10	25

Table 3. Gross Domestic Product by Kind of Economic Activity: Individual Countries or Areas

Major area, region and country	Year	Gross Domestic Product (at current prices) Million	Agriculture hunting forestry and fishing A-B	Mining Manufacturing and Utilities C-E	Of which: Manufacturing D	Construction F	Wholesale, retail trade, restaurants and hotels G-H	Transport storage and communication I	Other Activities J-P
			Percentage Distribution						
Belgium	1970	31788	4	32	31	7	11	6	30
(Euros)	1975	57501	3	28	26	7	12	6	32
	1980	88287	3	24	21	7	11	6	40
	1985	121935	3	24	21	5	11	6	46
	1990	163341	2	24	21	5	13	6	43
	1995	202174	2	22	19	5	13	7	47
	1996	206989	2	22	19	5	12	6	48
	1997	217173	2	22	19	5	12	6	47
	1998	225244	1	21	18	4	12	6	48
	1999	235713	1	20	18	5	12	6	48
	2000	247792	1	20	18	5	12	6	48
	2001	253800	1	20	17	5	12	6	48
	2002	260011	1	20	17	4	12	6	48
Bosnia and Herzegovina	1990	1	25	22	21	3	23	6	12
(Convertible Marka)	1995	2860	25	22	21	3	23	6	12
	1996	4125	20	22	21	4	23	6	23
	1997	6562	18	23	22	6	22	7	26
	1998	7439	12	24	23	6	19	9	29
	1999	8604	13	19	11	5	11	8	27
	2000	9433	11	19	10	5	10	9	30
	2001	10217	11	19	10	4	11	9	28
	2002	11264	10	18	10	4	12	10	28
Bulgaria	1970	13	20	43	34	5	4	3	24
(Leva)	1975	18	19	45	36	5	3	4	20
	1980	26	14	41	33	5	5	4	27
	1985	33	12	48	38	6	4	3	30
	1990	45	18	39	31	5	5	4	26
	1995	880	13	26	21	5	9	6	36
	1996	1761	14	25	20	4	11	7	33
	1997	17433	23	23	17	2	9	8	24
	1998	22421	17	25	17	4	7	8	29
	1999	23790	15	21	15	4	8	9	32
	2000	26753	12	23	16	4	8	10	31
	2001	29709	12	22	16	4	8	11	31
	2002	32324	11	21	15	4	8	12	31
	2003	34655	10	22	15	4	8	10	32
Croatia [64]	1990	280	10	26	...	5	16	8	27
(Kuna)	1995	98382	9	23	19	5	12	8	27
	1996	107981	8	22	18	6	13	7	28
	1997	123811	8	22	18	6	13	7	28
	1998	137604	8	21	18	6	13	7	30
	1999	141579	8	21	17	4	11	7	33
	2000	152519	7	21	18	4	11	8	32
	2001	165640	8	20	17	4	13	8	31
	2002	176429	7	20	...	4	13	10	31
Czech Republic [65]	1980	495654	7	37	27	9	7	7	25
(Koruny)	1985	565354	6	35	25	10	10	6	21
	1990	677090	7	33	24	10	11	4	27
	1995	1493310	4	30	24	8	13	9	29
	1996	1694342	4	32	25	7	12	8	28
	1997	1816477	4	31	25	7	13	9	29
	1998	1988582	4	29	24	7	14	9	30
	1999	2056925	3	28	24	7	14	9	31
	2000	2146174	4	29	24	6	15	9	30
	2001	2323091	3	29	24	6	15	9	30
	2002	2408433	3	28	24	6	15	10	30
	2003	2550798	3	28	24	6	14	11	31
Denmark	1970	122143	5	20	18	8	17	7	33
(Kroner)	1975	223381	5	19	18	7	16	6	39
	1980	385808	5	18	17	6	13	6	41
	1985	634018	5	19	17	4	14	6	40
	1990	825311	4	18	16	5	13	7	44
	1995	1009756	3	18	15	4	13	7	44
	1996	1060887	3	18	15	4	13	7	43
	1997	1116324	3	18	15	4	13	7	43
	1998	1155407	2	18	15	4	13	7	44
	1999	1207749	2	18	14	4	13	7	44

Table 3. Gross Domestic Product by Kind of Economic Activity: Individual Countries or Areas

Major area, region and country	Year	Gross Domestic Product (at current prices) Million	Agriculture hunting forestry and fishing A-B	Mining Manufacturing and Utilities C-E	Of which: Manufacturing D	Construction F	Wholesale, retail trade, restaurants and hotels G-H	Transport storage and communication I	Other Activities J-P
			Percentage Distribution						
	2000	1280784	2	19	15	4	13	8	43
	2001	1325272	2	19	15	4	13	8	44
	2002	1365214	2	19	15	4	13	8	44
Estonia (Krooni)	1990	798	14	41	37	7	8	6	36
	1995	40897	8	22	17	6	14	10	30
	1996	52423	7	21	16	6	15	10	29
	1997	64045	7	20	16	6	14	11	30
	1998	73538	6	20	16	6	15	13	30
	1999	76327	6	19	15	5	14	14	32
	2000	87379	5	20	16	5	14	15	30
	2001	97895	5	20	16	5	14	14	29
	2002	108024	5	20	17	6	14	14	30
Finland (Euros)	1970	7874	9	26	23	9	12	7	27
	1975	17770	9	27	24	9	12	7	28
	1980	32796	8	28	25	7	12	8	29
	1985	56663	7	25	22	6	12	8	32
	1990	88080	6	22	20	7	12	8	35
	1995	95262	4	25	23	4	10	9	38
	1996	98634	4	24	21	4	10	9	38
	1997	107030	4	24	22	4	11	9	37
	1998	116311	3	25	23	5	11	9	36
	1999	119985	3	24	22	5	11	9	37
	2000	130145	3	25	23	5	10	9	37
	2001	135228	3	24	22	5	10	9	38
	2002	139716	3	23	21	5	10	9	38
France (Euros)	1970	124467	7	28	26	7	11	6	33
	1975	230245	5	27	25	7	12	6	36
	1980	439384	4	26	23	6	11	6	39
	1985	727369	4	24	21	5	11	7	42
	1990	1009345	3	21	19	5	13	6	45
	1995	1181849	3	20	17	5	12	6	47
	1996	1212178	3	19	17	5	12	6	48
	1997	1251163	3	19	17	4	12	6	48
	1998	1305852	3	19	17	4	12	6	48
	1999	1355102	3	19	17	4	12	6	49
	2000	1420138	3	18	16	4	12	6	49
	2001	1475584	2	18	16	4	12	6	49
	2002	1526820	3	19	17	4	12	6	48
Germany (Euros)	1970	381209	3	36	33	8	12	6	27
	1975	580477	3	33	30	7	12	6	35
	1980	830212	2	31	28	7	11	6	36
	1985	1034570	2	31	28	6	11	5	40
	1990	1380690	2	29	27	6	11	5	41
	1995	1801300	1	24	21	6	11	5	46
	1996	1833700	1	23	21	6	11	5	47
	1997	1871600	1	23	21	6	11	5	47
	1998	1929400	1	24	21	5	11	5	47
	1999	1978600	1	23	21	5	11	5	48
	2000	2030000	1	23	21	5	11	5	48
	2001	2073700	1	23	21	4	11	6	48
	2002	2110400	1	23	21	4	11	6	48
Greece (Euros)	1970	993	14	22	19	10	19	8	36
	1975	2305	14	22	20	8	22	8	33
	1980	6106	13	21	19	9	19	7	32
	1985	16646	12	21	17	7	20	7	32
	1990	39111	10	18	15	7	18	7	35
	1995	79927	9	15	12	6	19	6	38
	1996	87851	8	15	12	6	20	6	38
	1997	97235	8	13	11	6	20	6	38
	1998	105773	7	13	11	6	19	6	39
	1999	112686	7	13	11	7	18	8	38
	2000	121668	7	13	11	7	18	8	38
	2001	131026	6	13	11	8	19	8	38
	2002	141354	6	13	11	7	18	8	38
	2003	152594	6	13	11	8	19	8	39

Table 3. Gross Domestic Product by Kind of Economic Activity: Individual Countries or Areas

Major area, region and country	Year	Gross Domestic Product (at current prices) Million	Agriculture hunting forestry and fishing A-B	Mining Manufacturing and Utilities C-E	Of which: Manufacturing D	Construction F	Wholesale, retail trade, restaurants and hotels G-H	Transport storage and communication I	Other Activities J-P
			Percentage Distribution						
Hungary [66] (Forints)	1970	372184	15	31	24	7	8	7	18
	1975	538863	15	31	24	7	8	7	18
	1980	804910	15	31	24	7	8	7	19
	1985	1153905	14	32	24	6	8	7	20
	1990	2282416	11	25	19	5	12	6	18
	1995	5614042	6	23	20	4	12	8	35
	1996	6893935	6	23	20	4	12	8	35
	1997	8540669	5	25	21	4	12	9	34
	1998	10087434	5	25	21	4	12	9	34
	1999	11393500	4	24	21	4	11	9	35
	2000	13172293	4	24	21	5	11	7	36
	2001	14849623	4	23	20	4	12	7	38
	2002	16743688	3	22	19	5	12	7	39
Iceland (Kroner)	1970	460	12	18	16	13	15	6	28
	1975	2148	10	17	14	11	9	9	32
	1980	16112	11	19	16	9	10	6	30
	1985	120373	10	20	15	8	11	7	32
	1990	362817	11	17	14	8	13	6	34
	1995	442256	10	17	14	7	13	7	36
	1996	474586	10	17	14	6	13	7	36
	1997	513749	9	17	14	7	12	7	36
	1998	568885	9	16	13	7	13	7	36
	1999	609413	8	14	11	7	13	7	38
	2000	662433	8	15	12	8	13	7	38
	2001	745188	7	18	15	8	14	10	35
	2002	778960	7	19	15	7	14	9	37
Ireland (Euros)	1970	2231	16	24	23	8	13	6	22
	1975	5222	17	24	23	8	12	6	23
	1980	12891	12	27	25	10	12	5	29
	1985	24500	10	27	25	6	13	5	30
	1990	36312	8	27	25	5	14	5	31
	1995	52641	7	29	27	5	11	5	33
	1996	58080	6	29	26	5	12	5	33
	1997	67123	5	30	27	5	12	5	33
	1998	77543	4	31	29	6	11	5	33
	1999	89614	4	32	30	6	11	5	32
	2000	102845	3	31	30	7	11	5	32
	2001	114743	3	31	30	7	11	5	32
	2002	129344	3	31	30	6	11	5	33
Italy (Euros)	1970	34765	8	29	27	9	14	6	28
	1975	71985	7	30	28	9	15	6	32
	1980	198524	6	31	29	7	16	7	31
	1985	420324	4	27	25	6	17	7	35
	1990	682153	3	25	22	6	16	7	39
	1995	923052	3	23	21	5	16	7	40
	1996	982443	3	23	20	5	16	7	41
	1997	1026285	3	22	20	5	16	7	41
	1998	1073019	3	22	20	4	16	7	41
	1999	1107994	3	22	19	4	15	7	41
	2000	1166548	3	21	19	4	15	7	42
	2001	1220147	3	21	19	5	16	7	43
	2002	1258349	2	21	18	5	15	7	43
	2003	1298780	2	20	18	5	15	7	44
Latvia (Lats)	1990	62	21	35	33	9	7	10	14
	1995	2329	9	25	20	4	11	14	24
	1996	2807	7	23	18	4	14	15	23
	1997	3270	5	24	19	4	15	15	24
	1998	3592	4	20	15	6	16	14	26
	1999	3890	4	17	13	6	17	13	30
	2000	4348	4	16	13	6	17	14	31
	2001	4813	4	17	13	5	18	14	31
	2002	5195	4	17	13	5	19	13	31
Lithuania [67] (Litas)	1990	134	27	21	21	10	9	8	27
	1995	24781	11	24	19	7	17	8	24
	1996	31529	12	23	18	7	17	9	25
	1997	38520	10	22	17	7	16	9	25
	1998	43555	9	21	17	8	16	9	26
	1999	42608	8	21	16	7	16	9	29

Table 3. Gross Domestic Product by Kind of Economic Activity: Individual Countries or Areas

Major area, region and country	Year	Gross Domestic Product (at current prices) Million	Agriculture hunting forestry and fishing A-B	Mining Manufacturing and Utilities C-E	Of which: Manufacturing D	Construction F	Wholesale, retail trade, restaurants and hotels G-H	Transport storage and communication I	Other Activities J-P
			Percentage Distribution						
	2000	44698	7	22	18	5	16	11	28
	2001	47498	6	23	18	5	17	11	27
	2002	50758	6	22	17	6	18	12	26
Luxembourg.. (Euros)	1970	1567	4	40	37	5	12	5	18
	1975	2469	3	28	25	7	16	5	39
	1980	3784	2	26	24	7	16	6	33
	1985	5842	2	27	25	5	16	7	56
	1990	9180	2	22	20	7	16	8	47
	1995	13214	1	16	14	7	14	9	61
	1996	13927	1	15	13	6	14	10	66
	1997	15490	1	14	13	6	13	10	63
	1998	17006	1	14	12	6	13	10	59
	1999	18739	1	13	11	6	12	10	63
	2000	21258	1	12	11	6	12	10	59
	2001	21987	1	12	11	6	12	10	62
	2002	22395	1	12	10	6	12	10	66
Malta [68].. (Maltese Lira)	1970	95	6	30	19	...	14	3	33
	1975	166	6	37	28	...	13	4	32
	1980	392	3	37	29	...	13	6	29
	1985	476	4	36	27	...	14	5	32
	1990	735	3	34	24	...	13	5	33
	1995	1146	2	29	21	...	12	6	37
	1996	1201	3	29	21	...	11	6	40
	1997	1288	3	28	20	...	10	5	40
	1998	1362	2	29	20	...	10	6	41
	1999	1456	2	29	20	...	10	6	40
	2000	1558	2	29	22	...	10	6	39
	2001	1632	2	27	20	...	9	6	40
	2002	1673	2	28	20	...	9	6	42
Netherlands.. (Euros)	1970	58136	6	27	23	7	14	7	32
	1975	105419	5	26	20	7	13	6	38
	1980	160721	4	25	17	7	13	6	40
	1985	199073	4	27	17	5	13	6	40
	1990	243561	4	23	18	6	15	6	41
	1995	302233	3	21	17	5	14	7	43
	1996	315059	3	21	16	5	14	7	44
	1997	333725	3	20	16	5	14	7	44
	1998	354194	3	19	15	5	14	7	44
	1999	374070	3	18	15	5	14	7	45
	2000	402291	3	19	15	5	14	7	45
	2001	429127	2	18	14	5	14	7	45
	2002	444649	2	17	13	5	14	7	47
Norway.. (Kroner)	1970	91100	5	22	19	6	15	14	27
	1975	169896	4	24	19	6	15	10	30
	1980	314363	4	31	14	5	12	9	30
	1985	547286	3	33	12	4	12	8	31
	1990	726799	3	27	12	4	12	10	37
	1995	937445	3	26	12	4	11	9	36
	1996	1026924	2	29	11	4	11	8	35
	1997	1111349	2	29	11	4	11	9	35
	1998	1132134	2	24	12	5	11	9	37
	1999	1233039	2	27	11	4	11	8	37
	2000	1469075	2	34	10	4	9	7	34
	2001	1526601	2	32	10	4	9	8	35
	2002	1520728	1	29	10	4	10	9	37
	2003	1568823	1	29	9	4	10	8	38
Poland.. (Zlotych)	1970	81	8	42	31	11	11	7	29
	1975	144	9	43	31	12	6	8	30
	1980	243	9	41	31	9	10	7	28
	1985	1005	9	41	31	11	11	7	28
	1990	58351	9	41	31	10	13	5	27
	1995	320882	6	27	20	6	18	6	25
	1996	403911	5	25	19	6	18	6	26
	1997	491941	5	25	19	7	19	6	27
	1998	576519	4	23	18	7	18	6	28
	1999	640627	3	23	18	7	18	6	29

Table 3. Gross Domestic Product by Kind of Economic Activity: Individual Countries or Areas

Major area, region and country	Year	Gross Domestic Product (at current prices) Million	Agriculture hunting forestry and fishing A-B	Mining Manufacturing and Utilities C-E	Of which: Manufacturing D	Construction F	Wholesale, retail trade, restaurants and hotels G-H	Transport storage and communication I	Other Activities J-P
			Percentage Distribution						
	2000	713391	3	22	17	7	19	6	30
	2001	750786	3	21	16	6	19	6	31
	2002	771113	3	21	15	6	20	7	31
Portugal (Euros)	1970	1056	25	32	30	4	12	6	20
	1975	2240	22	32	31	5	12	7	20
	1980	7458	16	22	19	6	20	6	28
	1985	20923	12	23	19	5	20	8	30
	1990	50817	8	22	19	6	17	6	34
	1995	80827	5	21	18	6	16	6	38
	1996	86230	5	21	18	6	16	6	38
	1997	93014	4	21	18	7	16	6	39
	1998	100962	4	20	17	7	16	6	39
	1999	108030	3	19	16	7	15	6	39
	2000	115548	3	19	16	7	15	6	40
	2001	123054	3	19	16	7	15	6	41
	2002	129280	3	19	16	7	15	6	41
	2003	130559	3	19	16	6	15	6	41
Republic of Moldova (Lei)	1990	13	35	29	...	7	5	7	14
	1995	6480	29	25	23	4	9	5	19
	1996	7798	27	23	21	4	10	6	23
	1997	8917	26	20	18	5	9	6	23
	1998	9122	26	17	14	3	11	7	25
	1999	12322	25	17	13	3	16	8	25
	2000	16020	25	16	14	3	13	10	23
	2001	19052	22	19	16	3	13	10	23
	2002	22556	21	17	15	3	12	10	26
Romania [69] (Lei)	1970	227348	19	42	38	10	4	6	13
	1975	384219	17	47	42	8	7	6	13
	1980	484684	14	50	44	7	6	7	13
	1985	623460	15	46	41	7	6	6	13
	1990	857851	22	41	37	5	6	6	15
	1995	72135548	20	33	26	7	10	8	18
	1996	108919636	19	33	29	6	12	9	16
	1997	252925736	18	31	26	5	11	9	18
	1998	373798214	14	26	21	5	13	10	21
	1999	545730127	13	25	19	5	14	10	23
	2000	803773100	11	27	22	5	13	10	24
	2001	1167242800	13	28	23	5	12	9	22
	2002	1512256600	12	29	24	5	12	10	23
Russian Federation [70] (Roubles)	1990	644200	15	37	37	9	5	9	18
	1995	1428522	7	26	26	8	20	12	21
	1996	2007825	7	27	27	8	18	12	19
	1997	2342514	6	27	27	8	17	11	22
	1998	2629623	5	27	27	7	19	10	23
	1999	4823234	7	28	28	6	21	9	20
	2000	7305646	6	28	28	6	21	8	20
	2001	8943600	6	25	25	7	20	8	23
	2002	10834200	5	24	24	7	21	9	25
San Marino (Italian Lire)	1970	22	8	29	27	9	14	6	28
	1975	46	7	30	28	9	15	6	32
	1980	128	6	31	29	7	16	7	31
	1985	271	4	27	25	6	17	7	35
	1990	439	3	25	22	6	16	7	39
	1995	595	3	23	21	5	16	7	40
	2000	843	3	21	19	4	15	7	42
	2003	939	2	20	18	5	15	7	44
Serbia and Montenegro [71] (New Dinars)	1990	34174	18	29	26	6	13	6	25
	1995	43984	16	26	22	5	10	6	22
	1996	79396	16	26	20	5	8	7	21
	1997	109352	18	30	20	5	8	8	23
	1998	148370	17	29	20	5	9	9	22
	1999	191099	19	28	20	4	10	9	23
	2000	381661	20	27	21	4	11	7	26
	2001	771800	18	28	20	4	9	8	23
	2002	1006900	18	28	20	4	9	8	24

Table 3. Gross Domestic Product by Kind of Economic Activity: Individual Countries or Areas

Major area, region and country	Year	Gross Domestic Product (at current prices) Million	Agriculture hunting forestry and fishing A-B	Mining Manufacturing and Utilities C-E	Of which: Manufacturing D	Construction F	Wholesale, retail trade, restaurants and hotels G-H	Transport storage and communication I	Other Activities J-P
			Percentage Distribution						
Slovakia..........	1980	206213	10	45	28	14	3	8	21
(Koruny)	1985	244360	7	42	27	15	3	9	21
	1990	292800	8	39	24	13	4	6	21
	1995	576502	5	30	25	5	13	10	29
	1996	638449	5	29	24	7	12	10	29
	1997	712679	5	25	21	7	14	10	31
	1998	781437	5	24	21	6	14	10	30
	1999	844108	4	26	21	5	14	10	31
	2000	934079	4	25	21	5	14	10	31
	2001	1009839	4	25	22	5	14	11	32
	2002	1096384	4	24	20	5	14	10	35
Slovenia..........	1990	196762	5	33	30	4	12	8	28
(Tolars)	1995	2342142	4	27	23	4	12	6	29
	1996	2698033	4	26	23	5	12	6	30
	1997	3065101	4	27	23	5	12	7	30
	1998	3422378	3	27	23	5	12	7	30
	1999	3839852	3	26	22	5	12	7	30
	2000	4222404	3	27	24	5	12	6	35
	2001	4740122	3	27	24	5	13	6	35
	2002	5275827	3	26	23	5	12	6	36
Spain..........	1970	16392	10	30	26	9	14	6	26
(Euros)	1975	37638	9	31	26	9	15	6	28
	1980	95334	7	29	24	8	17	7	31
	1985	175624	6	27	23	6	17	7	41
	1990	312424	5	24	20	8	17	7	43
	1995	437787	4	21	18	7	18	8	38
	1996	464251	5	21	18	7	18	8	38
	1997	494140	4	21	18	7	18	8	37
	1998	527975	4	21	18	7	18	8	37
	1999	565419	4	20	17	7	18	8	37
	2000	609734	3	19	17	8	18	8	37
	2001	653289	3	19	16	8	18	8	38
	2002	696208	3	18	16	9	18	8	38
	2003	743046	3	18	15	9	18	8	38
Sweden..........	1970	179928	5	27	24	7	11	9	33
(Kroner)	1975	314236	6	28	25	6	11	9	33
	1980	548581	4	23	20	6	11	9	36
	1985	899754	4	24	21	5	11	8	38
	1990	1421418	3	22	19	6	11	8	42
	1995	1770248	2	23	20	4	11	7	42
	1996	1815144	2	22	19	4	11	7	43
	1997	1888231	2	23	20	4	11	8	43
	1998	1971871	2	23	20	4	11	8	43
	1999	2076525	2	22	20	4	11	8	43
	2000	2194967	2	22	20	4	11	7	44
	2001	2266387	2	21	19	4	11	7	45
	2002	2342554	2	21	18	4	11	7	45
	2003	2435019	2	20	18	4	11	7	44
Switzerland..........	1970	95863	4	30	28	5	16	7	42
(Swiss Francs)	1975	148190	4	30	28	5	16	7	42
	1980	180095	4	30	28	6	16	7	39
	1985	237206	3	27	25	7	18	6	38
	1990	317304	3	26	24	8	19	6	40
	1995	363329	3	25	23	8	17	6	44
	1996	365833	3	25	23	8	17	6	44
	1997	371372	3	25	23	8	17	6	44
	1998	379989	3	25	23	8	17	6	44
	1999	388518	3	25	23	8	17	6	44
	2000	405772	3	25	23	8	17	6	43
	2001	413866	3	24	22	8	16	6	42
	2002	417297	3	25	23	8	17	6	43
TFYR Macedonia..........	1990	506	8	37	34	7	8	6	25
(Denars)	1995	169521	11	24	22	5	13	6	28
	1996	176444	11	24	22	5	13	6	28
	1997	186019	11	24	19	5	13	6	29
	1998	194979	11	23	18	6	13	7	28
	1999	209010	11	23	18	5	13	8	28

Table 3. Gross Domestic Product by Kind of Economic Activity: Individual Countries or Areas

Major area, region and country	Year	Gross Domestic Product (at current prices) Million	Agriculture hunting forestry and fishing A-B	Mining Manufacturing and Utilities C-E	Of which: Manufacturing D	Construction F	Wholesale, retail trade, restaurants and hotels G-H	Transport storage and communication I	Other Activities J-P
			Percentage Distribution						
	2000	236389	10	22	17	6	12	9	26
	2001	233841	10	22	17	5	13	9	27
	2002	238890	10	20	16	5	14	10	27
Ukraine [72]	1990	2	23	36	36	9	5	7	15
(Hryvnias)	1995	54516	14	34	34	6	7	12	20
	1996	81519	12	30	30	5	7	13	22
	1997	93365	12	27	27	5	9	13	22
	1998	102593	12	27	27	4	8	12	21
	1999	130442	12	30	30	4	7	12	19
	2000	170070	14	29	18	3	9	12	18
	2001	204190	14	27	17	4	12	12	21
	2002	220932	13	30	20	3	10	12	21
United Kingdom	1970	51515	3	34	30	6	13	8	31
(Pounds Sterling)	1975	105773	3	31	26	7	13	8	36
	1980	230695	2	33	24	6	12	7	36
	1985	354952	2	31	22	5	12	6	38
	1990	557300	2	25	21	6	13	7	40
	1995	719176	2	24	19	5	13	7	42
	1996	763290	2	24	19	5	13	7	42
	1997	810944	1	23	19	5	13	7	42
	1998	859436	1	22	18	5	14	7	44
	1999	903865	1	21	17	5	14	7	44
	2000	951265	1	20	16	5	14	7	45
	2001	994037	1	20	15	5	14	7	46
	2002	1043945	1	19	15	5	14	7	46
OCEANIA									
Australia	1970	38277	6	26	20	7	11	7	29
(Australian Dollars)	1975	79386	6	25	18	8	11	7	35
	1980	145643	6	26	17	7	10	7	37
	1985	248131	5	25	15	6	12	8	36
	1990	397881	4	21	13	6	13	8	41
	1995	502828	3	20	13	6	13	8	42
	1996	529886	3	19	12	6	13	8	42
	1997	561229	3	19	12	6	13	8	43
	1998	591917	3	18	12	6	13	8	44
	1999	628621	3	18	11	6	13	8	44
	2000	669307	3	18	11	5	12	8	45
	2001	712980	3	18	11	6	12	7	44
	2002	752760	4	16	10	5	12	7	43
Cook Islands	1970	10	9	6	6	3	33	8	45
(New Zealand Dollars)	1975	13	9	6	6	3	33	8	45
	1980	22	10	6	5	4	32	8	37
	1985	51	8	6	5	3	30	11	42
	1990	98	11	6	4	2	26	10	43
	1995	142	10	6	3	2	29	13	42
	2000	178	13	6	3	3	35	14	29
	2002	221	12	5	3	4	39	14	25
Fiji	1970	192	24	15	12	6	17	5	24
(Fiji Dollars)	1975	562	21	12	10	7	16	8	30
	1980	984	20	12	11	7	16	8	30
	1985	1316	16	13	8	5	16	9	34
	1990	1980	20	12	11	4	20	13	28
	1995	2799	19	12	11	4	20	14	25
	2000	3518	19	13	11	4	23	16	22
	2002	4072	18	13	11	4	23	16	21
French Polynesia [73]	1970	21468	7	8	6	6	24	8	47
(French Francs)	1975	45020	5	7	6	10	25	5	48
	1980	96832	5	8	7	10	23	6	48
	1985	226772	4	9	9	12	24	6	46
	1990	290064	5	9	7	6	23	7	48
	1995	373136	4	9	7	6	23	7	47
	2000	426800	4	9	7	6	23	7	47
	2003	462984	4	9	7	6	23	7	47

Table 3. Gross Domestic Product by Kind of Economic Activity: Individual Countries or Areas

Major area, region and country	Year	Gross Domestic Product (at current prices) Million	Agriculture hunting forestry and fishing A-B	Mining Manufacturing and Utilities C-E	Of which: Manufacturing D	Construction F	Wholesale, retail trade, restaurants and hotels G-H	Transport storage and communication I	Other Activities J-P
			Percentage Distribution						
Kiribati (Australian Dollars)	1970	13	34	3	1	4	15	14	30
	1975	42	34	3	1	4	15	14	30
	1980	25	34	3	1	4	15	14	30
	1985	30	35	3	1	4	14	12	31
	1990	36	19	4	1	4	20	16	37
	1995	62	21	3	1	2	16	15	43
	2000	83	17	2	1	7	16	12	45
	2002	98	14	2	1	9	14	12	49
Marshall Islands (U.S. Dollars)	1970	7	13	1	1	11	23	1	50
	1975	15	13	1	1	11	23	1	50
	1980	23	13	1	1	11	23	1	50
	1985	38	13	1	1	11	23	1	50
	1990	69	13	1	1	11	23	1	50
	1995	105	15	5	3	10	17	6	47
	1996	97	14	4	2	7	18	9	47
	1997	92	14	5	2	7	18	10	47
	1998	95	14	4	2	10	18	7	48
	1999	97	14	4	2	9	18	7	48
	2000	98	14	4	2	11	18	5	48
	2001	102	13	4	2	10	17	6	47
	2002	106	14	4	2	9	18	7	48
Micronesia (Federated States of) (U.S. Dollars)	1970	24	34	3	1	4	15	14	30
	1975	56	34	3	1	4	15	14	30
	1980	77	34	3	1	4	15	14	30
	1985	102	35	3	1	4	14	12	31
	1990	151	19	4	1	4	20	16	37
	1995	215	21	3	1	2	16	15	43
	2000	229	17	2	1	7	16	12	45
	2002	240	14	2	1	9	14	12	49
Nauru (Australian Dollars)	1970	12	34	3	1	4	15	14	30
	1975	19	34	3	1	4	15	14	30
	1980	32	34	3	1	4	15	14	30
	1985	52	35	3	1	4	14	12	31
	1990	66	19	4	1	4	20	16	37
	1995	55	21	3	1	2	16	15	43
	2000	57	18	2	1	3	16	13	48
	2002	65	19	2	1	4	15	14	46
New Caledonia [74] (CFP Francs)	1970	38204	27	13	0	4	17	17	23
	1975	63643	27	13	0	4	17	17	23
	1980	90847	27	13	0	4	17	17	23
	1985	139650	31	15	1	4	12	11	27
	1990	250427	16	20	1	3	17	14	31
	1995	329296	18	18	1	2	13	13	36
	2000	347303	19	18	1	2	14	13	34
	2002	393996	19	18	1	2	14	13	34
New Zealand (New Zealand Dollars)	1970	5846	10	27	24	6	21	8	29
	1975	11334	10	24	22	8	21	7	33
	1980	23464	10	26	22	5	19	8	32
	1985	46212	8	26	22	5	19	7	37
	1990	73113	6	22	17	4	16	8	41
	1995	92679	7	21	17	4	15	8	40
	1996	97239	7	20	17	4	14	8	42
	1997	100739	7	20	16	4	14	8	42
	1998	101959	6	19	16	4	15	7	44
	1999	107068	7	19	16	4	16	9	41
	2000	113778	7	19	16	4	16	10	41
	2001	122241	7	18	15	4	16	10	41
	2002	126195	7	19	16	4	16	10	42
Palau (U.S. Dollars)	1970	14	5	2	1	7	33	8	44
	1975	52	5	2	1	7	33	8	44
	1980	23	5	2	1	7	33	8	44
	1985	30	5	2	1	7	33	8	44
	1990	67	5	2	1	7	33	8	43
	1995	95	6	2	1	8	33	9	42
	2000	118	4	5	1	8	31	9	42
	2002	124	4	4	1	8	31	8	43

Table 3. Gross Domestic Product by Kind of Economic Activity: Individual Countries or Areas

Major area, region and country	Year	Gross Domestic Product (at current prices) Million	Agriculture hunting forestry and fishing A-B	Mining Manufacturing and Utilities C-E	Of which: Manufacturing D	Construction F	Wholesale, retail trade, restaurants and hotels G-H	Transport storage and communication I	Other Activities J-P
			Percentage Distribution						
Papua New Guinea [75]	1970	689	34	7	6	23	9	7	17
(Kina)	1975	1185	29	21	9	8	9	6	37
	1980	1894	33	23	10	5	10	5	21
	1985	2451	33	22	11	4	10	5	23
	1990	3138	28	25	9	5	9	6	22
	1995	5888	29	34	8	3	9	5	18
	2000	9515	27	38	8	4	9	4	15
	2002	10963	27	38	9	4	8	5	16
Samoa [76]	1970	43	17	23	20	7	14	10	29
(Tala)	1975	85	17	23	20	7	14	10	29
	1980	142	17	23	20	7	14	10	29
	1985	271	17	23	20	7	14	10	29
	1990	465	17	23	20	7	14	10	29
	1995	496	19	22	19	8	15	10	27
	2000	775	16	18	15	7	20	13	26
	2002	890	14	18	15	5	22	14	26
Solomon Islands	1970	29	59	5	3	2	8	2	26
(Solomon Islands Dollars)	1975	50	58	5	3	3	8	2	28
	1980	119	50	4	3	3	9	3	30
	1985	237	45	5	3	4	9	5	37
	1990	526	37	4	3	3	7	4	29
	1995	1242	40	4	3	3	8	4	32
	2000	1721	43	5	3	4	8	5	34
	2002	1848	40	4	3	3	7	4	32
Tonga [77]	1970	10	50	4	3	5	8	3	29
(Pa 'anga)	1975	25	43	6	4	3	11	3	42
	1980	47	34	8	6	5	15	7	41
	1985	86	32	6	5	7	12	6	28
	1990	147	30	7	5	5	12	8	30
	1995	198	25	6	4	6	13	7	30
	1996	209	25	6	4	6	12	7	30
	1997	208	24	6	4	5	12	7	32
	1998	219	26	6	4	5	12	7	32
	1999	238	26	7	5	5	11	8	33
	2000	252	23	7	5	6	13	7	33
	2001	274	23	7	4	5	13	7	34
	2002	296	24	7	5	6	11	7	33
Tuvalu	1970	1	8	2	1	9	27	-9	63
(Australian Dollars)	1975	2	8	2	1	9	27	-9	63
	1980	4	8	2	1	9	27	-9	63
	1985	5	9	4	2	10	11	1	64
	1990	12	24	5	3	8	18	1	36
	1995	16	23	8	4	5	14	6	37
	2000	25	19	9	3	10	15	7	35
	2002	36	19	9	3	10	15	7	35
Vanuatu	1970	3508	25	6	4	4	30	8	28
(Vatu)	1975	5084	25	6	4	4	30	8	28
	1980	7746	25	6	4	4	30	8	28
	1985	12534	29	5	4	3	32	7	28
	1990	17900	20	8	6	6	32	8	26
	1995	27255	25	7	5	6	32	7	24
	1996	28227	25	7	5	6	32	7	23
	1997	29477	25	7	5	5	32	7	23
	1998	29545	23	7	5	5	34	7	24
	1999	29523	22	7	5	5	35	7	24
	2000	30423	21	7	5	5	34	8	25
	2001	31153	20	6	4	5	33	8	27
	2002	28114	23	6	4	6	34	9	30

Notes for Table 3:

1/ Wholesale, retail trade, restaurants and hotels
Other activities
1985-1990
Restaurants and Hotels are included in "Other activities".

2/ Wholesale, retail trade, restaurants and hotels
Other activities
1970-1989
Restaurants and Hotels are included in "Other activities".

3/ (a) Manufacturing
1970, 1980-1985
Includes diamond cutting.

(b) Wholesale, retail trade, restaurants and hotels
Other activities
1980-1985
Restaurants and Hotels are included in "Other activities".

(c) Gross Domestic Product
1980-1988
Gross domestic production. This differs from domestic product, primarily in the exclusion of the product originating in general government agencies and in public establishments of administrative nature.

4/ Mining, manufacturing and utilities
1992-2001
Excludes gas.

5/ Wholesale, retail trade, restaurants and hotels
1970-1979
Includes the profit or loss of the Marketing Board.

6/ Wholesale, retail trade, restaurants and hotels
Other activities
1970-1977
Restaurants and Hotels are included in "Other activities".

7/ (a) Agriculture, hunting, forestry and fishing
1990-1998
Excludes hunting.

(b) Mining, manufacturing and utilities
1990-1998
Excludes gas.

8/ (a) Mining, manufacturing and utilities
1970-1991
Refers to oil and its products.

(b) Manufacturing
1996-2001
Includes non-petrolium mining activities.

(c) Wholesale, retail trade, restaurants and hotels
1986-1991
Includes finance and insurance.

(d) Other activities
1970-1991
Includes gas and water.

(e) Other activities
1996-2001
Includes Utilities, Government social and personal services only.

(f) Gross Domestic Product
1972-1979
For years 1972-1979 estimates relate to calendar year.

9/ Manufacturing
1972-1989
Includes repair services.

10/ Gross Domestic Product
1970-1979
Gross domestic product at purchaser's prices.

11/ Wholesale, retail trade, restaurants and hotels
Other activities
1970-1991
Restaurants and Hotels are included in "Other activities".

12/ Manufacturing
1970-1992
Includes handicrafts.

13/ Agriculture, hunting, forestry and fishing
1970-1979
Includes all non-monetary output.

14/ Manufacturing
1981-1992
Includes handicrafts.

15/ (a) Mining, manufacturing and utilities
1970-2002
Excludes gas.

(b) Wholesale, retail trade, restaurants and hotels
1998-1999
Includes Financial intermediation; real estate, renting and business actvities.

16/ Mining, manufacturing and utilities
1989-1992
Excludes gas.

17/ Wholesale, retail trade, restaurants and hotels
1970-1994
Includes import duties.

18/ Other activities
1970-1989
FISIM is netted out of Financial intermediation, real estate, renting and business activities.

19/ Manufacturing
1980-2001
Includes mining and handicrafts.

20/ Wholesale, retail trade, restaurants and hotels
1991-1994, 1996-1997
Includes Transport, storage and communications; Financial intermediation, real estate, renting and business activities; Education, health and social work; other community, social and personal services, and Private households with employ persons.

21/ Gross Domestic Product
1992-2001
Discrepancy between components and total.

22/ (a) Mining, manufacturing and utilities
1970-2002
Excludes gas.

(b) Other activities
1970-2002
Restaurants and Hotels are included in "Other activities".

23/ Other activities
1970-1976, 1981-1994
Includes only rented and owner-occupied dwellings.

24/ Manufacturing
1970-2002
Includes handicrafts.

25/ Mining, manufacturing and utilities
1970-1999
Excludes gas.

26/ Agriculture, hunting, forestry and fishing
1970-2002
Includes Mining and quarrying.

27/ (a) Agriculture, hunting, forestry and fishing
1989-1995
Does not include Hunting and Forestry.

(b) Mining, manufacturing and utilities
1989-1995
Excludes gas.

28/ Other activities
1992-2002
Restaurants and Hotels are included in "Other activities".

29/ Agriculture, hunting, forestry and fishing
1995-1999
Excludes hunting.

30/ Other activities
1972-1991
Excludes banks and insurance companies registered in Cayman Islands but with no physical presence in the Islands.

31/ (a) Manufacturing
1970-1991
Includes handicrafts and repair services.

(b) Wholesale, retail trade, restaurants and hotels
1970-1991
Restaurants and Hotels are included in "Other activities".

32/ (a) Mining, manufacturing and utilities
1970-1979
Excludes petroleum refining.

(b) Mining, manufacturing and utilities
1980-2001
Includes petroleum refining.

33/ (a) Other activities
1990-2003
Includes rents of owner-occupied dwellings.

(b) Other activities
1970-1989
Restaurants and Hotels are included in "Other activities".

34/ (a) Agriculture, hunting, forestry and fishing
1988-2001
Excludes hunting.

(b) Manufacturing
1970-2001
Includes Electricity, gas and water supply.

(c) Construction
1970-2001
Includes engineering and sewage services.

(d) Other activities
1970-2001
Restaurants and Hotels are included in "Other activities".

35/ Other activities
1970-1979
Restaurants and Hotels are included in "Other activities".

36/ Manufacturing
1988-2001
Basic petroleum manufacturing is included in Mining and quarrying.

37/ Agriculture, hunting, forestry and fishing
1970-2002
Includes Mining and quarrying.

38/ (a) Mining, manufacturing and utilities
1970-1978
Refers to metal ore mining only.

(b) Manufacturing
1970-1978
For 1972, excludes damages by earthquake amounting to 21.7 million cordobas at current prices, and 17.9 million cordobas at constant prices.

(c) Wholesale, retail trade, restaurants and hotels
1970-1978
Restaurants and Hotels are included in "Other activities".

39/ (a) Wholesale, retail trade, restaurants and hotels
1970-1995
Includes Financal intermediation, except insurance and pension funding.

(b) Other activities
1970-1995
Restaurants and Hotels are included in "Other activities".

40/ Construction
1970-2000
Refers to contract construction only.

41/ Other activities
1980-1992
Includes hotels and guest houses.

42/ Other activities
1996-2000
The data refers to the Tourism Sector as defined by Turks and Caicos.

43/ (a) Agriculture, hunting, forestry and fishing
1989-2001
Includes agricultural products and improvements and other non-agricultural products.

(b) Mining, manufacturing and utilities
1970-1986
Includes sewage services.

(c) Mining, manufacturing and utilities
1970-2001
Excludes gas.

(d) Manufacturing
1970-2001
Includes petroleum refining.

44/ Other activities
1987-2001
Refers to Other services.

45/ Gross Domestic Product
1992-1997
Discrepancy between production approach and expenditure approach.

46/ Gross Domestic Product
2000-2001
Provisional data.

47/ Manufacturing
1990-2003
Includes Mining and quarrying, and Electricity, gas and water supply.

48/ (a) Agriculture, hunting, forestry and fishing
1980-2002
Refers to Agriculture and fishing only.

(b) Wholesale, retail trade, restaurants and hotels
1980-2002
Refers to Wholesale, retail and import/export trades, restaurants and hotels only.

(c) Gross Domestic Product
1989-1991
Discrepancy between components and total.

49/ Other activities
1970-2002
Restaurants and Hotels are included in "Other activities".

50/ Mining, manufacturing and utilities
1970-1979, 1990-1992
Includes oil production.

51/ (a) Agriculture, hunting, forestry and fishing
Manufacturing
1970-2000
Agricultural services and related activities such as cotton ginning and pressing are included in Manufacturing.

(b) Wholesale, retail trade, restaurants and hotels
1970-2000
Distribution of gas and petroleum products are included in Wholesale and retail trade.

52/ Wholesale, retail trade, restaurants and hotels
1990-2001
Refers to Wholesale and retail trade only.

53/ Manufacturing
1990-2003
Includes Mining and quarrying, and Electricity, gas and water supply.

54/ Mining, manufacturing and utilities
1980-2001
Beginning 1980, the cost of fuel (natural gas, crude petroleum and gas-oil) consumed in the production of electricity and water has been taken into account as intermediate consumption in estimating the value added of Electricity, gas and water supply.

55/ Manufacturing
1990-2000
Includes Mining and quarrying, and Electricity, gas and water supply.

56/ (a) Mining, manufacturing and utilities
1970-1998
Gas and Water supply are included in "Other activities".

(b) Wholesale, retail trade, restaurants and hotels
1970-1998
Restaurants and Hotels are included in "Other activities".

(c) Gross Domestic Product
1970-1974
Estimates refer to year ending 30 September.

57/ Manufacturing
1970-2003
Includes cottage industries.

58/ Other activities
1970-2001
Restaurants and Hotels are included in "Other activities".

59/ (a) Wholesale, retail trade, restaurants and hotels
1980-1991
Refers to Wholesale and retail trade only.

(b) Other activities
1980-1991
Refers to finance, insurance, real estate and ownership of dwellings.

60/ Agriculture, hunting, forestry and fishing
1990-2002
Includes Quarrying.

61/ (a) Mining, manufacturing and utilities
1993-1998
Excludes gas. Refers to non-oil and gas mining only, excludes Quarrying.

(b) Other activities
1993-1998
Refers to household services, social & community, amusement & recreation, and other related personal services.

62/ Wholesale, retail trade, restaurants and hotels
1990-1995
Includes Financial intermediation, Education, Public administration, and Private households with employed persons.

63/ Manufacturing
1994-2002
Includes Mining and quarrying, and Electricity, gas and water supply.

64/ Mining, manufacturing and utilities
1990-1994
Excludes electricity and gas.

65/ Gross Domestic Product
1980-1990
Data derived from Material Product Balances (MPS) data.

66/ (a) Agriculture, hunting, forestry and fishing
1988-1991
Includes veterinary services and operation of irrigation systems.

(b) Mining, manufacturing and utilities
1980-1988
Excludes gas and operation of irrigation systems.

(c) Manufacturing
1988-1991
Includes Gas.

67/ Manufacturing
1990-1994
Includes Mining and quarrying, and Electricity, gas and water supply.

68/ (a) Mining, manufacturing and utilities
1970-2002
Construction included in "Mining, manufacturing and utilities".

(b) Other activities
1970-1997
Restaurants and Hotels are included in "Other activities".

69/ Other activities
1980-1988
Excludes personal services.

70/ Manufacturing
1990-2002
Includes Mining and quarrying, and Electricity, gas and water supply.

71/ Gross Domestic Product
1999-2003
Data excludes Kosovo and Metohia effective January 1999.

72/ Manufacturing
1990-1999
Includes Mining and quarrying, and Electricity, gas and water supply.

73/ Mining, manufacturing and utilities
Manufacturing
1970-1993
Includes manufacturing of energy-generating products.

74/ Other activities
1970-1996
Restaurants and Hotels are included in "Other activities".

75/ Other activities
1970-1976, 1978-1999
Restaurants and Hotels are included in "Other activities".

76/ Mining, manufacturing and utilities
1972
Includes forestry and fishing.

77/ Other activities
1994-2001
Includes Ownership of dwellings.

C. Growth Rates of Main National Accounting Aggregates at Constant Prices of 1990

Description of Analysis in Tables 4, 5 and 6

C. Economic development expressed in rates of growth in real terms of gross domestic product and its components.

Tables 4 to 6 reflect trends in economic development expressed as rates of real growth of GDP and its components for the world, developed, developing and transition economies, as well as for individual countries or areas during the period 1970-2003, with 1990 as the base year.

The figures shown in these tables are computed as geometric mean of annual rates of growth expressed in percentages for the years and periods of years indicated. The growth rates for the individual countries are based on the estimates of gross domestic product (GDP) at constant 1990 prices and their components by type of expenditure and by kind of economic activity. Table 4 presents growth rates of total GDP during the period 1970-2003, while Tables 5 and 6 show growth rates of its principal components by expenditure and by kind of economic activity, respectively, during the period 1970-2002.

The growth rates presented in the tables, however, may not be fully consistent between countries and regions. Their comparability could be affected by the wide variety of base years that are used by countries in the compilation of GDP at constant prices.

The first column of the three tables lists individual countries and their aggregation into world, regions and level of economic development totals. The next column in each table highlights the base year weights in 1990 of GDP, representing for individual countries' and sub-regions' weights of their GDP as a percentage of the region and those for the regions and economic development groupings, as a percentage of the world. In Tables 5 and 6, an additional third column presents, respectively, the shares of each expenditure and industry components as a percentage of GDP in 1990. The next three columns of the tables contain the growth rates of GDP during the average periods 1970-1979, 1980-1989 and 1990-1999. The remaining columns show the annual rates of growth over the preceding year starting from 1998 through 2003 for Table 4 and 1997 through 2002 for Tables 5 and 6.

Table 5 includes the rates of growth of each expenditure component of GDP as follows: (a) household final consumption expenditure; (b) general government final consumption expenditure; (c) gross fixed capital formation; (d) exports of goods and services; and (e) imports of goods and services.

In deriving the growth rates of the individual expenditure categories by regions and for the three economic groups of the developed, developing and transition economies, expenditures expressed in US dollars for the base year 1990 were used as weights. Global and regional growth rates for each of the expenditure categories were calculated by adding the expenditures of individual countries in US dollars that were derived by extrapolating the 1990 current price figures by the corresponding growth at constant prices. The expenditure totals of countries expressed in 1990 US dollars were first aggregated according to the economic development region that each belongs and then added up to arrive at the global level.

The country indicators utilized in the calculation were derived principally from official estimates, in national currency, of gross domestic product by type of expenditure at constant prices. For some countries, the indicator series were obtained by linking together separate series covering the full period.

Table 6 lists the average rates of growth of each economic activity component of GDP: (a) agriculture, (b) mining, manufacturing and utilities, (c) manufacturing, (d) construction, (e) wholesale and retail trade, restaurants and hotels , (f) transport, storage and communication and (g) other activities.

The calculation of the regional and world growth rates of the separate economic activity categories in table 6 was done in a similar manner as was described above in table 5 for the expenditure components. Value-added data at constant prices for each economic activity group were first compiled from appropriate series of indicators for all countries concerned and combined to form regional totals after conversion to 1990 United States dollars. These were then combined into separate totals for developed, developing and transition economies.

The country indicators utilized in the calculation were derived from estimates of gross domestic product at constant prices. The basic data were generally absolute figures of product expressed in national currency units; in a limited number of cases, indices computed by the countries themselves were used directly. For some countries, the indicators' series were obtained by linking together separate series covering the full period.

Various methods were utilized to obtain indicators for countries where constant price estimates of gross domestic product by kind of economic activity were not available. For example, the national indices of the quantum of production were employed for agriculture, total industrial activity (mining, manufacturing and utilities), manufacturing and, in some cases, for construction. In the absence of a national series for total industrial activity or manufacturing, use was made of indicators based on the world index of industrial production of the Statistics Division of the United Nations Secretariat. In other economic activities, such as agriculture and construction use was made of indices compiled by the World Bank, Asian Development Bank and other international and regional organizations. In the remaining cases, estimates from unofficial sources were utilized or estimated from indicator series prepared by the Statistics Division, generally by deflating related series at current prices with suitable price indices.

The country and regional weights used in the derivation of growth rates of expenditure and activity components of GDP are based on 1990 values expressed in US dollars of that year. In making the conversion and subsequent aggregation to calculate the growth rates, the same exchange rate for 1990 were used for the derivation of growth rates for total GDP (Table 4) as were used in the derivation of the growth rates of its expenditure and activity components shown in Tables 5 and 6.

Table 4. Annual Average Rate of Growth of Gross Domestic Product by Major Area, Region and Country

Major area, region and country	Base year weights as percentage of total for world or region in 1990	Average rates of growth			Annual rate of change (percentage)					
		1970-1979	1980-1989	1990-1999	1998	1999	2000	2001	2002	2003
WORLD	**100.0**	**4.0**	**2.9**	**2.4**	**2.4**	**3.2**	**4.1**	**1.5**	**2.1**	**2.8**
DEVELOPED ECONOMIES	**74.6**	**3.6**	**2.8**	**2.3**	**2.8**	**3.0**	**3.5**	**1.0**	**1.5**	**2.0**
DEVELOPING ECONOMIES	**17.3**	**5.7**	**3.5**	**4.7**	**2.0**	**3.7**	**5.4**	**2.6**	**3.4**	**4.6**
TRANSITION ECONOMIES	**8.2**	**5.4**	**3.0**	**-4.5**	**-1.3**	**4.0**	**7.5**	**5.4**	**4.6**	**6.5**
AFRICA	**2.3**	**4.3**	**2.7**	**2.4**	**3.9**	**3.3**	**3.5**	**3.6**	**3.1**	**4.0**
Eastern Africa	*11.0*	*3.1*	*2.9*	*3.2*	*3.5*	*4.4*	*2.2*	*3.4*	*0.8*	*1.0*
Burundi	0.2	3.2	3.8	-1.2	4.6	-1.0	-0.9	3.2	4.5	-0.5
Comoros	0.0	4.4	3.3	-0.1	-1.1	1.9	-1.1	1.9	2.5	2.5
Djibouti	0.1	1.6	1.8	1.6	-0.2	2.2	0.7	1.9	2.6	3.0
Eritrea	...	...	...	8.2	3.9	0.3	-12.0	8.7	-1.2	5.4
Ethiopia	...	...	...	5.8	-0.5	6.3	5.4	7.9	1.2	-3.8
Ethiopia (Former)	1.5	2.3	2.3	-2.0	...	...	...	...	...	...
Kenya	1.6	5.2	4.4	2.1	1.6	1.3	-0.2	1.1	1.0	1.3
Madagascar	0.6	1.0	0.5	1.6	3.9	4.7	4.8	6.0	-12.7	6.0
Malawi	0.3	7.4	3.2	4.0	1.5	3.1	3.3	-4.1	1.8	4.4
Mauritius	0.5	8.2	4.3	5.1	6.0	2.9	9.2	5.5	1.8	4.4
Mozambique	0.5	3.9	-0.3	4.6	12.6	7.5	1.5	13.0	8.3	7.0
Reunion	1.0	6.0	4.2	3.0	3.0	3.0	3.0	2.4	2.5	2.5
Rwanda	0.5	5.0	3.0	0.0	9.2	6.5	6.3	6.7	9.3	3.2
Seychelles	0.1	6.7	2.6	5.1	11.2	1.9	-0.1	-1.9	0.3	3.0
Somalia	0.2	3.3	1.4	-3.3	2.5	2.1	3.0	3.0	3.5	3.5
Uganda	0.7	0.0	2.9	7.1	9.3	6.6	4.7	6.5	5.1	5.0
United Republic Of Tanzania	0.7	3.7	2.3	5.5	5.0	19.3	5.1	6.2	7.2	4.7
Zambia	0.8	0.8	1.6	-0.4	-1.9	2.2	3.6	4.9	3.3	4.3
Zimbabwe	1.7	1.9	4.7	2.8	2.9	-0.7	-4.9	-8.4	-12.8	-13.2
Middle Africa	*8.6*	*1.7*	*2.8*	*0.0*	*3.9*	*1.1*	*3.0*	*5.1*	*6.2*	*4.4*
Angola	1.9	0.2	2.7	0.4	5.5	2.7	3.6	5.2	13.8	4.7
Cameroon	2.7	4.8	4.1	0.4	5.0	4.2	5.3	4.6	4.0	4.0
Central African Republic	0.2	1.9	0.9	1.1	4.8	3.6	1.8	-0.4	1.5	3.3
Chad	0.3	-1.7	5.0	3.0	5.3	-0.1	-0.4	8.7	8.5	13.1
Congo	0.5	4.6	6.2	0.5	3.8	-3.2	8.1	2.9	3.5	2.0
Democratic Republic of the Congo	1.8	0.2	1.8	-5.6	-1.7	-4.3	-6.9	-1.1	3.1	5.0
Equatorial Guinea	0.0	2.2	2.8	21.7	22.0	41.4	16.9	53.4	16.5	10.0
Gabon	1.0	1.1	0.4	2.4	2.1	-6.2	2.0	2.5	-0.2	0.7
Sao Tome and Principe	0.0	7.0	-1.4	1.2	2.5	2.5	3.0	3.0	3.0	5.0
Northern Africa	*44.1*	*6.0*	*3.0*	*2.8*	*5.4*	*3.9*	*3.9*	*3.9*	*3.4*	*5.5*
Algeria	11.7	6.4	2.8	1.5	5.1	3.2	2.4	2.1	4.1	6.7
Egypt	13.4	5.8	5.7	3.7	6.1	5.4	3.5	3.2	3.1	4.5
Libyan Arab Jamahiriya	5.3	8.1	-1.8	-0.4	0.4	0.1	3.2	3.3	-0.2	4.6
Morocco	4.9	5.4	3.9	2.5	7.7	-0.1	1.0	6.3	3.2	5.5
Sudan	6.4	3.6	2.9	4.9	6.0	6.0	8.3	6.4	5.5	5.8
Tunisia	2.3	7.3	3.6	5.0	4.8	6.1	4.7	4.9	1.7	5.8
Southern Africa	*22.6*	*3.1*	*2.4*	*1.6*	*1.1*	*2.2*	*3.6*	*2.9*	*3.5*	*2.0*
Botswana	0.7	16.3	12.0	5.1	8.1	4.1	6.6	8.4	2.3	3.7
Lesotho	0.1	8.6	3.6	3.9	-4.6	0.2	1.5	3.4	3.8	3.9
Namibia	0.4	2.2	1.7	4.2	3.3	4.3	3.9	0.6	3.0	4.5
South Africa	21.2	3.0	2.2	1.4	0.8	2.0	3.5	2.7	3.6	1.9
Swaziland	0.2	9.6	6.8	3.8	3.2	3.5	2.1	1.8	3.6	2.2
Western Africa	*13.9*	*4.7*	*1.9*	*3.3*	*3.9*	*3.3*	*3.6*	*3.0*	*1.9*	*4.4*
Benin	0.3	1.8	3.9	4.4	4.5	4.7	5.8	5.0	6.4	5.5
Burkina Faso	0.5	4.5	3.4	4.7	6.4	6.3	2.2	5.7	4.6	6.5
Cape Verde	0.1	0.3	5.7	5.2	7.4	8.6	6.8	3.0	4.6	5.0
Cote d'Ivoire	2.2	7.3	2.3	2.6	5.1	1.9	-2.7	0.1	-1.2	1.8
Gambia	0.1	4.7	3.9	3.8	9.9	6.4	5.6	5.7	-3.1	7.4
Ghana	1.2	0.7	1.9	4.3	4.7	4.4	3.7	4.2	4.5	4.7
Guinea	0.5	2.8	2.5	4.1	4.6	3.6	2.3	3.6	4.2	3.6

Table 4. Annual Average Rate of Growth of Gross Domestic Product by Major Area, Region and Country

Major area, region and country	Base year weights as percentage of total for world or region in 1990	Average rates of growth			Annual rate of change (percentage)					
		1970-1979	1980-1989	1990-1999	1998	1999	2000	2001	2002	2003
Guinea-Bissau	0.0	3.0	2.9	0.8	-28.0	7.6	7.5	7.8	-7.2	2.4
Liberia	0.1	3.1	-4.6	-6.8	29.7	22.9	22.3	4.9	3.3	2.8
Mali	0.5	3.6	2.2	4.7	5.9	6.8	3.7	1.4	9.7	-1.1
Mauritania	0.2	2.9	1.5	3.8	3.7	4.1	5.0	4.6	3.3	5.4
Niger	0.5	4.6	0.7	2.0	9.9	-1.6	-0.3	5.9	3.0	4.0
Nigeria	6.1	4.6	1.8	3.4	2.3	2.8	5.8	2.8	0.5	5.2
Senegal	1.1	12.1	2.4	3.2	5.7	5.0	5.6	5.6	2.4	6.3
Sierra Leone	0.1	2.0	1.4	-4.6	-0.8	-8.1	3.8	5.4	6.3	6.5
Togo	0.3	3.4	0.7	1.5	-2.2	2.9	-0.8	0.2	4.8	3.0
AMERICAS	**32.9**	**4.0**	**2.8**	**2.9**	**4.0**	**3.7**	**3.9**	**0.4**	**2.1**	**2.7**
NORTHERN AMERICA	**27.8**	**3.7**	**3.0**	**3.0**	**4.3**	**4.3**	**3.9**	**0.4**	**2.5**	**2.8**
Bermuda	0.0	3.7	1.1	1.9	3.4	3.6	2.0	-0.5	1.0	1.0
Canada	7.7	4.4	3.0	2.4	4.1	5.7	5.3	1.9	3.3	2.1
United States	76.8	3.7	3.0	3.0	4.3	4.1	3.8	0.3	2.4	2.9
LATIN AMERICA AND THE CARIBBEAN	**5.1**	**5.8**	**1.9**	**2.8**	**2.4**	**0.5**	**4.0**	**0.4**	**-0.4**	**1.6**
Caribbean	*1.2*	*4.3*	*3.1*	*2.4*	*4.6*	*4.0*	*5.5*	*1.3*	*2.8*	*2.5*
Anguilla	0.0	3.8	7.0	4.7	5.2	8.7	-0.1	2.2	-3.7	3.8
Antigua and Barbuda	0.0	1.0	6.5	3.3	4.9	4.9	0.8	2.3	2.9	2.5
Aruba	0.0	9.1	9.8	5.7	6.7	1.1	3.7	-0.7	-2.5	1.4
Bahamas	0.0	2.7	3.8	0.4	3.0	5.9	4.9	-2.0	0.7	0.9
Barbados	0.0	2.6	2.1	0.8	4.1	2.6	2.3	-2.1	-2.1	1.6
British Virgin Islands	0.0	3.2	6.7	7.9	11.4	9.1	10.1	10.1	10.1	10.1
Cayman Islands	0.0	9.4	9.3	1.8	1.5	1.5	1.2	1.2	1.2	1.2
Cuba	0.3	5.4	3.9	-2.2	1.2	6.2	5.6	3.0	1.1	2.6
Dominica	0.0	-1.6	5.3	2.4	3.2	0.8	1.3	-4.2	-3.9	-1.0
Dominican Republic	0.1	7.0	3.7	5.1	7.4	8.1	7.8	4.0	4.3	-0.4
Grenada	0.0	1.7	1.9	3.9	7.7	7.1	7.3	-4.9	0.1	0.0
Guadeloupe	0.0	5.7	2.0	1.8	4.1	0.6	4.6	4.6	4.6	3.7
Haiti	0.0	4.5	0.7	-1.1	3.1	2.3	0.9	-1.2	-0.9	0.0
Jamaica	0.1	-0.2	1.3	1.6	-0.3	-0.4	0.7	1.7	1.1	2.2
Martinique	0.0	4.2	4.9	1.3	4.1	0.6	2.1	2.1	2.1	2.1
Montserrat	0.0	3.8	4.6	-7.6	-10.8	-9.1	-3.6	-6.9	7.6	-4.7
Netherlands Antilles	0.0	2.9	0.6	1.7	0.7	-0.7	-2.1	0.6	0.2	0.5
Puerto Rico	0.4	4.0	3.6	4.1	5.4	2.4	5.6	-0.2	3.7	3.7
Saint Kitts and Nevis	0.0	3.2	5.8	4.2	1.2	3.5	3.4	2.2	1.8	1.2
Saint Lucia	0.0	5.3	6.3	2.2	4.6	1.7	-0.1	-5.8	2.3	0.5
Saint Vincent and the Grenadines	0.0	3.0	5.7	3.6	5.8	4.1	1.5	-0.2	1.5	2.6
Trinidad and Tobago	0.1	4.7	-1.6	3.8	7.7	10.6	11.3	2.6	2.7	3.8
Turks and Caicos Islands	0.0	1.0	6.5	4.4	10.9	8.7	6.3	5.5	2.9	2.5
Central America	*3.9*	*6.2*	*2.0*	*3.4*	*5.0*	*3.7*	*6.1*	*0.1*	*1.0*	*1.5*
Belize	0.0	3.6	4.6	4.6	2.4	6.1	7.5	5.3	3.6	4.5
Costa Rica	0.1	6.2	2.1	5.4	8.4	8.2	1.8	1.1	2.9	5.6
El Salvador	0.1	4.6	-1.2	4.7	3.8	3.4	2.2	1.7	2.1	2.0
Guatemala	0.1	5.9	0.9	4.0	4.8	3.8	3.6	2.3	2.2	2.1
Honduras	0.0	5.9	2.5	2.7	2.9	-1.9	5.0	2.6	2.5	2.0
Mexico	3.5	6.4	2.1	3.3	5.0	3.6	6.6	-0.2	0.9	1.3
Nicaragua	0.0	0.0	-0.9	3.0	3.7	7.0	4.2	3.0	1.0	2.3
Panama	0.1	4.5	3.1	5.0	4.4	3.2	2.5	0.3	0.8	1.5
South America	*10.3*	*5.8*	*1.8*	*2.7*	*1.2*	*-1.0*	*3.0*	*0.4*	*-1.4*	*1.6*
Argentina	1.9	2.7	-0.8	4.2	3.9	-3.4	-0.8	-4.4	-10.9	8.7
Bolivia	0.1	4.5	-0.4	4.0	5.0	0.4	2.3	1.5	2.8	2.9
Brazil	5.9	8.4	2.9	1.8	0.2	0.8	4.5	1.5	1.5	0.6
Chile	0.4	2.0	3.3	6.3	3.2	-0.8	4.2	3.1	2.1	3.3
Colombia	0.6	5.7	3.4	2.8	0.6	-4.2	2.9	1.4	2.5	2.0

Table 4. Annual Average Rate of Growth of Gross Domestic Product by Major Area, Region and Country

Major area, region and country	Base year weights as percentage of total for world or region in 1990	Average rates of growth			Annual rate of change (percentage)					
		1970-1979	1980-1989	1990-1999	1998	1999	2000	2001	2002	2003
Ecuador	0.2	9.4	2.3	2.2	2.1	-6.3	2.8	5.1	3.8	3.1
French Guiana	0.0	10.8	9.1	4.2	1.6	1.6	1.6	1.6	1.6	1.6
Guyana	0.0	1.7	-2.3	4.7	-1.7	3.8	-1.3	1.9	1.1	-0.2
Paraguay	0.1	8.5	3.9	2.3	-0.4	0.5	-0.4	2.7	-2.3	0.6
Peru	0.4	3.7	-0.2	3.1	-0.7	0.9	2.8	0.3	4.9	4.0
Suriname	0.0	3.9	0.4	-0.6	2.3	-1.4	0.0	4.9	1.4	5.6
Uruguay	0.1	2.7	1.0	3.3	4.2	-2.4	-1.4	-3.3	-11.2	2.8
Venezuela	0.6	4.8	-0.2	2.3	0.2	-6.1	3.2	2.8	-8.9	-16.7
ASIA	**24.1**	**5.2**	**4.2**	**3.8**	**0.3**	**2.7**	**4.7**	**2.1**	**2.9**	**4.5**
Eastern Asia	*72.0*	*5.0*	*4.7*	*3.3*	*0.1*	*2.5*	*4.6*	*1.8*	*2.5*	*4.1*
China	7.0	5.2	9.4	9.7	7.8	7.1	7.9	7.5	8.0	9.1
Democratic People's Rep. of Korea	0.3	11.9	8.1	-3.2	-1.1	6.2	1.3	3.7	0.8	0.8
Hong Kong SAR of China	1.4	8.8	7.2	3.8	-5.0	3.4	10.2	0.5	2.3	1.5
Japan	55.7	4.6	3.9	1.7	-1.1	0.1	2.8	0.4	0.1	2.7
Macao SAR of China	0.1	7.7	7.4	2.8	-4.6	-3.0	4.6	2.1	10.0	15.6
Mongolia	0.1	5.7	6.3	-0.4	3.5	3.2	1.1	1.0	4.0	5.0
Republic of Korea	4.6	8.5	7.5	6.1	-6.7	10.9	9.3	3.1	6.3	3.1
South Central Asia	*12.0*	*3.5*	*4.2*	*6.6*	*4.8*	*5.9*	*3.9*	*5.2*	*5.3*	*7.2*
Afghanistan	0.1	5.1	-1.6	-2.5	5.2	-12.4	-43.7	0.0	28.6	15.0
Bangladesh	0.6	0.5	3.8	4.7	4.9	5.9	5.3	4.8	5.3	5.5
Bhutan	0.0	6.4	8.4	6.1	6.4	7.4	5.7	7.1	6.7	6.5
India	5.9	2.6	5.9	5.6	6.0	7.1	3.9	5.5	4.3	7.8
Iran (Islamic Republic of)	1.6	6.0	-0.8	4.8	3.2	4.2	2.8	3.2	8.0	6.7
Kazakhstan	1.3	...	...	-5.0	-1.9	2.7	9.8	13.2	9.9	9.2
Kyrgyzstan	0.2	...	...	-5.0	2.1	3.7	5.4	5.3	0.0	6.7
Maldives	0.0	11.5	11.7	8.7	9.3	7.8	4.4	3.3	5.6	8.4
Nepal	0.1	2.6	4.0	4.9	2.9	4.5	6.1	4.8	-0.5	2.3
Pakistan	0.9	5.1	6.2	3.9	3.7	4.3	2.6	2.8	5.8	5.3
Sri Lanka	0.1	4.1	4.2	5.3	4.7	4.3	6.0	-1.4	4.0	5.5
Tajikistan	0.0	...	...	-11.6	5.3	3.7	8.3	10.2	8.9	10.2
Turkmenistan	0.2	...	...	-3.2	7.1	16.5	10.0	7.9	9.0	9.0
Uzbekistan	0.9	...	...	-0.6	4.4	4.4	4.0	4.5	4.2	4.4
South-Eastern Asia	*6.5*	*6.7*	*5.3*	*5.3*	*-7.7*	*4.0*	*6.6*	*2.3*	*4.2*	*4.6*
Brunei Darussalam	0.1	10.1	-2.6	1.4	-4.0	2.6	2.8	3.0	3.2	3.6
Cambodia	0.0	-7.3	-1.1	5.1	2.1	6.9	7.7	6.3	5.5	4.0
Indonesia	2.1	7.8	6.4	4.6	-13.1	0.8	4.9	3.4	3.7	4.1
Lao People's Democratic Republic	0.0	0.1	4.9	6.4	4.0	7.3	5.8	5.8	5.9	5.5
Malaysia	0.8	9.7	5.7	7.1	-7.4	6.1	8.3	0.4	4.1	5.2
Myanmar	0.3	3.9	1.7	6.0	5.0	10.9	13.7	10.5	5.5	5.1
Philippines	0.8	6.0	1.9	2.8	-0.6	3.4	6.0	3.0	4.4	4.5
Singapore	0.7	8.9	7.4	7.6	-0.9	6.4	9.4	-2.4	2.2	0.5
Thailand	1.6	7.0	7.2	5.1	-10.5	4.4	4.6	1.9	5.4	6.7
Timor-Leste	0.0	...	...	-3.5	1.0	-35.5	15.5	17.0	2.8	-2.0
Vietnam	0.1	-0.1	4.5	7.4	5.8	4.8	6.8	6.8	7.0	6.0
Western Asia	*9.6*	*7.4*	*0.5*	*3.7*	*3.1*	*-0.8*	*5.5*	*-0.5*	*1.2*	*3.7*
Armenia	0.3	...	...	-4.8	7.3	3.3	5.9	9.6	12.9	13.9
Azerbaijan	0.4	...	...	-6.8	10.0	7.4	11.1	9.9	10.6	11.2
Bahrain	0.1	12.8	-0.3	4.9	4.8	4.3	5.3	4.7	5.1	4.2
Cyprus	0.1	3.4	6.1	4.4	4.9	4.6	5.1	4.0	2.0	2.0
Georgia	0.4	...	...	-10.5	3.1	2.9	1.8	4.8	5.5	8.6
Iraq	0.7	11.8	-1.0	-8.4	15.0	8.0	11.0	15.0	-6.5	-21.8
Israel	1.0	5.6	3.1	5.4	3.2	2.8	8.1	-0.9	-1.1	0.5
Jordan	0.1	5.3	3.7	4.4	2.9	1.5	2.7	3.5	4.9	3.0
Kuwait	0.3	-0.1	-1.8	1.2	3.2	-4.9	-10.1	-1.1	0.4	1.9
Lebanon	0.1	-1.2	-6.7	6.6	3.0	4.0	2.0	1.4	2.0	3.0
Oman	0.2	4.8	8.1	4.9	2.7	-0.2	5.5	7.5	1.7	1.1
Qatar	0.1	4.2	2.5	5.5	8.4	3.2	7.3	6.3	3.0	4.0
Saudi Arabia	1.9	10.2	-4.1	2.8	2.8	-0.8	4.9	1.2	-9.5	4.7

Table 4. Annual Average Rate of Growth of Gross Domestic Product by Major Area, Region and Country

Major area, region and country	Base year weights as percentage of total for world or region in 1990	Average rates of growth			Annual rate of change (percentage)					
		1970-1979	1980-1989	1990-1999	1998	1999	2000	2001	2002	2003
Syrian Arab Republic	0.3	9.7	1.6	6.3	6.8	-3.6	0.6	3.4	3.2	1.0
Turkey	2.7	4.8	4.0	3.8	3.1	-4.7	7.4	-7.5	7.8	5.8
United Arab Emirates	0.6	35.6	1.0	3.5	-7.0	2.5	5.4	5.0	1.5	6.3
Yemen	0.2	...	...	4.1	4.9	3.7	5.1	3.9	3.2	4.2
Yemen Arab Republic (Former)	...	8.9	6.4	...	...	...	...	...	...	...
Yemen Democratic (Former)	...	1.9	4.2	...	...	...	...	...	...	...
EUROPE	**39.0**	**3.5**	**2.4**	**0.9**	**2.4**	**2.9**	**4.0**	**2.1**	**1.4**	**1.5**
Eastern Europe	*17.0*	*5.4*	*3.1*	*-6.2*	*-2.7*	*4.5*	*7.9*	*5.0*	*4.2*	*6.5*
Belarus	0.7	...	...	-2.0	8.4	3.4	5.8	4.7	5.0	6.8
Bulgaria	0.2	7.1	3.6	-3.4	4.0	2.3	5.4	4.1	4.8	4.8
Czech Republic	0.4	...	1.7	-0.3	-1.0	0.5	3.3	3.1	2.0	2.9
Czechoslovakia (Former)	...	4.7	...	...	...	...	...	...	...	...
Hungary	0.4	5.3	1.5	-0.1	4.9	4.2	5.2	3.8	3.5	2.9
Poland	0.7	6.7	0.3	2.0	4.8	4.1	4.0	1.0	1.4	2.4
Republic of Moldova	0.2	...	...	-11.4	-6.5	-3.4	2.1	6.1	7.8	6.3
Romania	0.4	10.0	1.5	-2.5	-4.8	-1.2	2.1	5.7	4.9	4.7
Russian Federation	10.9	...	...	-5.3	-5.3	6.4	10.0	5.1	4.7	7.3
Slovakia	0.2	...	1.0	0.5	4.2	1.5	2.0	3.8	4.4	4.2
Ukraine	2.9	...	...	-9.8	-1.9	-0.2	5.9	9.2	3.6	8.5
USSR (Former)	...	5.2	3.2	...	...	...	...	...	...	...
Northern Europe	*19.4*	*2.6*	*2.4*	*2.4*	*3.5*	*3.3*	*4.1*	*2.1*	*2.1*	*2.0*
Denmark	1.5	2.2	1.4	2.1	2.5	2.6	2.9	1.4	2.1	0.0
Estonia	0.1	...	...	-2.4	4.6	-0.6	7.3	6.5	6.0	4.5
Finland	1.5	3.7	3.6	1.3	5.0	3.4	5.1	1.2	2.2	1.9
Iceland	0.1	6.4	3.2	2.2	5.6	4.1	5.7	2.8	-0.6	4.0
Ireland	0.5	4.9	3.1	7.1	8.6	11.3	10.1	6.2	6.9	3.4
Latvia	0.2	...	...	-5.5	4.8	2.8	6.8	7.9	6.1	7.0
Lithuania	0.2	...	...	-4.1	7.3	-1.8	4.0	6.5	6.8	8.9
Norway	1.3	4.8	2.9	3.6	2.6	2.1	2.8	1.9	1.0	0.3
Sweden	2.7	2.0	2.3	1.7	3.6	4.6	4.3	0.9	1.9	1.6
United Kingdom	11.1	2.4	2.3	2.1	3.1	2.8	3.8	2.1	1.7	2.3
Southern Europe	*21.0*	*3.8*	*2.4*	*2.1*	*2.9*	*2.5*	*3.6*	*2.3*	*1.2*	*1.2*
Albania	0.0	6.2	2.9	-0.3	12.7	8.9	7.7	8.0	4.8	6.0
Andorra	0.0	8.7	7.2	4.9	4.0	4.1	4.9	4.4	4.3	5.2
Bosnia and Herzegovina	0.1	...	...	6.7	15.4	9.5	5.4	4.5	3.7	3.2
Croatia	0.3	...	...	-2.0	2.5	-0.9	2.9	3.8	5.2	4.7
Greece	0.9	5.0	0.8	1.9	3.4	3.4	4.4	4.0	3.8	4.3
Holy See	0.0	4.5	2.8	1.6	1.8	1.7	3.3	1.8	0.4	0.4
Italy	12.4	3.6	2.4	1.5	1.8	1.7	3.1	1.8	0.4	0.3
Malta	0.0	10.8	4.0	5.0	3.5	3.9	4.8	3.9	1.2	2.8
Portugal	0.8	4.8	3.3	2.8	4.6	3.8	3.7	1.6	0.4	-1.3
San Marino	0.0	3.6	2.4	2.8	7.5	9.0	3.1	1.8	0.4	0.3
Serbia and Montenegro	0.3	...	...	-9.1	2.5	-24.4	6.4	5.5	3.8	1.0
Slovenia	0.2	...	...	1.6	3.7	5.9	4.1	2.9	2.9	2.6
Spain	5.7	3.8	2.8	2.6	4.3	4.2	4.2	2.8	2.0	2.4
TFYR Macedonia	0.1	...	...	-1.5	3.4	4.3	4.5	-4.5	0.9	3.1
Yugoslavia (Former)	...	6.2	1.1	...	...	...	...	...	...	...
Western Europe	*42.6*	*3.0*	*2.1*	*2.1*	*2.7*	*2.7*	*3.3*	*1.3*	*0.6*	*0.1*
Austria	1.8	3.8	2.1	2.5	3.9	2.7	3.4	0.8	1.4	0.7
Belgium	2.2	3.2	2.1	2.1	2.0	3.2	3.8	0.6	0.7	1.1
France	13.7	3.5	2.4	1.7	3.4	3.2	3.8	2.1	1.2	0.5
Germany	18.8	2.9	1.9	2.2	2.0	2.0	2.9	0.8	0.2	-0.1
Liechtenstein	0.0	2.4	2.9	1.6	3.6	2.7	4.4	1.9	1.1	0.4
Luxembourg	0.1	2.8	4.5	5.1	6.9	7.8	9.1	1.2	1.3	1.2
Monaco	0.0	4.1	3.1	2.4	4.1	3.9	4.4	2.6	1.7	0.9
Netherlands	3.3	3.1	2.0	3.0	4.3	4.0	3.5	1.2	0.2	-0.8
Switzerland	2.6	0.9	2.1	0.9	2.4	1.5	3.2	0.9	0.2	-0.5

Table 4. Annual Average Rate of Growth of Gross Domestic Product by Major Area, Region and Country

Major area, region and country	Base year weights as percentage of total for world or region in 1990	Average rates of growth			Annual rate of change (percentage)					
		1970-1979	1980-1989	1990-1999	1998	1999	2000	2001	2002	2003
OCEANIA	**1.6**	**2.9**	**3.2**	**3.3**	**4.6**	**4.0**	**1.8**	**3.8**	**2.9**	3.4
Australia & New Zealand	*96.9*	*2.8*	*3.2*	*3.3*	*4.7*	*4.1*	*1.9*	*3.9*	*2.9*	*3.4*
Australia	85.0	3.0	3.4	3.4	5.3	4.0	1.8	3.9	2.7	3.5
New Zealand	11.9	1.9	2.0	2.6	0.4	5.0	2.7	3.5	4.3	2.7
Melanesia	*2.1*	*5.5*	*2.4*	*3.2*	*1.6*	*1.2*	*-0.9*	*-1.6*	*0.5*	*2.3*
Fiji	0.4	5.7	1.7	3.0	1.5	9.6	-2.8	3.8	4.4	5.2
New Caledonia	0.7	1.7	4.4	1.0	-3.2	0.9	2.1	-1.1	0.7	-0.1
Papua New Guinea	0.9	8.2	1.4	4.6	4.4	-0.8	-1.2	-3.4	-0.5	2.8
Solomon Islands	0.1	8.1	1.5	4.5	1.1	-1.3	-14.0	-5.0	-4.0	2.0
Vanuatu	0.0	7.7	3.2	3.1	2.1	-3.2	2.7	-1.8	-5.2	1.0
Micronesia	*0.1*	*4.7*	*1.1*	*1.2*	*0.1*	*0.2*	*1.0*	*2.1*	*1.4*	*2.3*
Kiribati	0.0	2.9	-4.9	4.9	5.0	13.4	1.6	1.8	0.9	2.5
Marshall Islands	0.0	6.6	6.1	-0.9	1.1	0.1	-0.9	1.7	4.0	3.0
Micronesia (Federated States of)	0.0	6.6	4.5	1.6	-2.1	0.9	2.1	1.5	0.8	2.4
Nauru	0.0	6.8	4.9	-5.4	-1.9	-1.9	-1.0	-0.8	0.9	2.5
Palau	0.0	2.9	-5.5	4.1	2.0	-5.4	0.3	4.5	1.1	1.5
Polynesia	*0.9*	*4.9*	*5.0*	*2.9*	*1.2*	*2.7*	*3.2*	*2.4*	*1.9*	*2.0*
Cook Islands	0.0	-3.4	2.0	2.3	-0.7	2.6	14.1	5.1	3.7	1.5
French Polynesia	0.8	5.6	5.6	3.1	1.1	2.7	2.7	2.1	1.9	1.9
Samoa	0.1	3.1	0.4	0.5	2.4	2.6	6.9	6.2	1.8	3.1
Tonga	0.0	2.6	5.1	2.1	2.4	2.8	6.3	1.7	1.6	2.1
Tuvalu	0.0	6.6	-1.5	6.1	14.9	3.0	3.0	3.0	-9.2	2.0

Table 5.A. Average Rates of Growth of Gross Domestic Product by Expenditure - Household Final Consumption Expenditure

Major area, region and country	Base year weights as percentage of total for world or region in 1990	Base year share as percentage of total GDP in 1990	Average rates of growth			Annual rate of change (percentage)					
			1970-1979	1980-1989	1990-1999	1997	1998	1999	2000	2001	2002
WORLD	**100.0**	**58.4**	**4.2**	**3.0**	**2.3**	**3.1**	**2.7**	**3.5**	**3.7**	**2.6**	**2.3**
DEVELOPED ECONOMIES	**75.2**	**58.9**	**3.8**	**2.8**	**2.4**	**2.6**	**3.3**	**3.6**	**3.3**	**2.2**	**2.1**
DEVELOPING ECONOMIES	**17.6**	**59.9**	**5.3**	**3.5**	**4.6**	**4.4**	**1.6**	**3.9**	**4.8**	**2.7**	**1.6**
TRANSITION ECONOMIES	**7.2**	**51.3**	**5.7**	**3.2**	**-2.3**	**4.8**	**-0.1**	**-0.4**	**5.7**	**8.4**	**8.4**
AFRICA	**2.6**	**64.1**	**4.6**	**3.4**	**3.4**	**3.9**	**2.9**	**4.4**	**-0.4**	**4.7**	**3.8**
Eastern Africa	*11.9*	*69.6*	*3.7*	*2.8*	*3.5*	*5.1*	*1.6*	*6.5*	*1.4*	*5.1*	*-0.8*
Burundi	0.3	83.0	2.9	3.4	-2.5	-2.0	3.5	7.2	-9.1	4.7	0.0
Comoros	0.1	79.7	-0.1	3.4	0.8	-1.2	-1.7	1.8	-5.7	-0.1	-1.4
Djibouti	0.1	67.2	2.6	-0.1	2.6	8.4	12.6	51.9	2.0	1.5	-5.9
Eritrea	...	...	...	...	-7.0	11.0	-10.5	-3.1	-11.7	15.7	-1.8
Ethiopia	...	...	...	...	4.3	-1.3	-1.2	19.9	5.6	11.5	-4.1
Ethiopia (Former)	1.7	72.9	2.7	1.0	3.3	...	...	...	...	...	...
Kenya	1.6	62.2	4.6	3.9	1.8	7.4	-0.6	-7.0	8.3	1.6	-13.7
Madagascar	0.8	86.0	0.4	0.5	1.8	4.2	3.8	-3.3	4.2	8.9	-8.3
Malawi	0.5	91.6	7.8	3.3	3.5	8.6	1.5	3.1	3.3	-7.2	-1.9
Mauritius	0.5	64.6	7.4	4.8	4.9	4.8	6.1	3.9	3.5	2.8	2.8
Mozambique	0.8	101.8	3.9	1.2	2.4	8.3	5.9	4.6	-1.8	2.3	17.6
Reunion	1.2	79.9	7.9	5.6	2.6	2.8	2.9	2.8	2.7	2.7	2.7
Rwanda	0.6	84.4	5.0	3.3	-2.5	21.2	5.1	2.1	1.3	6.0	11.6
Seychelles	0.1	52.0	7.5	4.9	1.9	10.3	12.1	-7.6	-13.3	12.8	0.3
Somalia	0.2	71.0	2.6	0.4	-3.1	-2.0	2.4	1.5	2.9	3.0	3.5
Uganda	0.9	82.0	3.1	4.1	7.4	3.6	9.6	7.4	4.7	5.3	4.6
United Republic Of Tanzania	0.8	72.7	2.9	1.6	5.6	1.6	7.3	26.9	-1.2	4.5	5.2
Zambia	0.2	14.1	3.2	3.3	-2.7	1.0	3.4	6.1	4.4	-14.2	14.8
Zimbabwe	1.6	62.5	3.9	3.3	1.0	14.1	-6.2	0.7	-13.5	3.7	-5.4
Middle Africa	*7.7*	*57.5*	*2.5*	*2.6*	*-1.1*	*5.0*	*1.3*	*-7.9*	*-5.1*	*5.2*	*5.3*
Angola	0.9	28.6	0.2	0.8	-5.6	6.9	-4.5	-32.6	-26.6	14.1	35.9
Cameroon	3.2	76.7	6.3	3.2	-0.7	8.1	5.0	-12.5	1.6	5.5	4.3
Central African Republic	0.3	88.1	3.7	1.3	1.2	5.0	4.9	6.0	5.1	0.4	-1.5
Chad	0.4	96.3	-1.9	5.9	3.2	-2.8	8.4	11.3	-1.6	2.6	8.4
Congo	0.4	50.9	4.3	5.9	-3.9	0.5	-0.9	-37.5	-17.7	18.9	-8.5
Democratic Republic of the Congo	1.5	55.1	-0.2	0.7	-4.2	-3.8	0.4	-10.5	-4.3	-4.4	-0.4
Equatorial Guinea	0.0	80.3	1.2	3.2	10.8	58.5	57.5	-40.7	-9.2	13.2	19.7
Gabon	0.8	49.7	1.6	4.2	1.7	5.2	-20.0	53.2	-17.5	10.1	2.8
Sao Tome and Principe	0.0	79.9	8.5	0.0	1.1	8.7	3.0	-2.7	-0.4	-5.6	19.2
Northern Africa	*43.8*	*63.8*	*6.2*	*3.5*	*4.4*	*2.3*	*4.7*	*7.3*	*0.2*	*4.7*	*4.7*
Algeria	10.3	56.6	8.7	3.1	-0.4	-1.9	2.2	2.9	2.4	3.0	2.6
Egypt	16.0	76.3	5.2	4.0	5.3	3.7	5.2	5.0	3.9	3.5	-1.4
Libyan Arab Jamahiriya	2.7	32.6	...	...	0.3	6.4	7.6	-0.7	-21.5	18.0	9.4
Morocco	4.9	64.6	3.4	3.6	1.5	-5.3	6.9	-2.7	3.4	4.3	3.0
Sudan	7.6	76.3	6.5	2.9	6.6	5.5	3.9	23.8	-5.1	5.6	18.0
Tunisia	2.3	63.6	7.8	4.5	4.4	4.5	5.6	5.8	5.5	5.8	3.9
Southern Africa	*21.8*	*62.0*	*3.5*	*3.4*	*2.3*	*3.3*	*1.4*	*1.6*	*3.3*	*3.0*	*3.0*
Botswana	0.3	30.0	10.5	4.0	6.1	2.9	7.9	6.1	4.1	-0.6	4.3
Lesotho	0.2	131.6	9.9	3.7	-0.4	0.3	-8.2	-13.8	-12.8	0.3	1.8
Namibia	0.3	47.2	2.7	3.1	2.3	7.6	2.4	1.0	2.0	-1.8	-4.0
South Africa	20.7	62.8	3.3	3.4	2.2	3.3	1.4	1.4	3.5	3.2	3.2
Swaziland	0.2	79.2	10.3	7.1	4.5	4.8	3.1	32.9	6.5	7.8	-6.9
Western Africa	*14.8*	*68.4*	*4.1*	*3.7*	*3.7*	*7.8*	*1.6*	*2.8*	*-6.7*	*6.1*	*5.8*
Benin	0.4	80.4	4.1	3.3	3.8	5.0	5.5	5.3	5.5	5.3	5.6
Burkina Faso	0.7	79.7	2.9	3.2	3.3	4.8	6.2	9.2	4.3	3.5	7.8
Cape Verde	0.1	88.9	-2.1	5.1	8.0	-2.3	4.6	16.1	-6.6	15.5	-11.0
Cote d'Ivoire	2.4	69.0	7.2	3.6	1.4	2.1	5.6	2.5	-0.9	10.8	-4.2
Gambia	0.1	82.1	5.3	-2.2	4.2	15.4	14.0	-26.7	6.8	8.7	-8.6
Ghana	1.6	85.5	-3.8	57.9	3.5	11.7	3.4	4.9	-0.2	2.8	2.4
Guinea	0.6	70.3	2.8	2.7	4.2	2.9	4.8	3.6	1.7	3.1	3.2

Table 5.A. Average Rates of Growth of Gross Domestic Product by Expenditure - Household Final Consumption Expenditure

Major area, region and country	Base year weights as percentage of total for world or region in 1990	Base year share as percentage of total GDP in 1990	Average rates of growth			Annual rate of change (percentage)					
			1970-1979	1980-1989	1990-1999	1997	1998	1999	2000	2001	2002
Guinea-Bissau	0.1	86.9	1.6	3.1	1.3	-10.1	-21.6	13.9	3.5	3.3	-1.0
Liberia	0.1	69.8	3.7	-3.5	-4.6	101.6	29.7	22.9	22.3	4.9	3.3
Mali	0.6	79.0	4.9	2.7	4.5	-3.7	-1.0	21.5	7.6	0.4	4.4
Mauritania	0.2	67.9	6.4	0.2	2.8	5.0	4.2	-1.1	-14.2	24.7	2.9
Niger	0.5	74.1	4.3	-0.3	3.0	-0.3	12.0	-4.0	6.9	1.5	8.1
Nigeria	5.7	59.6	1.9	2.9	5.4	12.8	-2.3	1.5	-18.0	5.0	12.7
Senegal	1.3	76.4	13.6	2.0	2.0	1.1	3.7	3.3	3.7	14.1	2.4
Sierra Leone	0.1	80.1	1.7	1.2	-4.6	-5.9	0.1	-11.6	13.1	4.6	6.3
Togo	0.3	69.8	1.2	3.8	1.0	12.2	7.2	-9.7	3.8	2.5	0.7
AMERICAS	**36.8**	**65.3**	**4.1**	**2.9**	**3.2**	**3.8**	**4.0**	**4.5**	**4.6**	**2.2**	**2.3**
NORTHERN AMERICA	**31.3**	**65.6**	**3.8**	**3.2**	**3.0**	**3.6**	**4.6**	**4.9**	**4.3**	**2.5**	**3.1**
Bermuda	0.0	68.3	3.5	3.0	1.5	3.8	2.8	5.0	5.7	2.5	1.0
Canada	6.5	55.1	4.6	2.7	2.1	4.7	2.7	3.9	4.0	2.6	3.3
United States [1]	78.4	66.6	3.7	3.2	3.1	3.6	4.8	4.9	4.3	2.5	3.1
LATIN AMERICA AND THE CARIBBEAN	**5.6**	**64.0**	**5.6**	**1.5**	**3.9**	**4.8**	**1.1**	**2.6**	**6.3**	**0.9**	**-2.3**
Caribbean	*1.2*	*63.2*	*4.2*	*2.4*	*2.4*	*4.4*	*5.2*	*3.3*	*4.1*	*0.8*	*2.9*
Anguilla	0.0	51.6	3.8	6.3	11.2	0.6	0.0	33.0	1.4	-6.5	4.3
Antigua and Barbuda	0.0	41.7	-4.3	9.1	0.4	-3.3	-5.6	-6.0	-12.4	-14.5	-6.8
Aruba	0.0	45.5	11.4	11.9	7.4	0.5	7.7	5.3	-1.2	5.0	1.8
Bahamas	0.0	66.5	2.3	5.0	-1.5	-3.3	8.4	3.0	1.5	-5.5	0.7
Barbados	0.0	63.6	1.2	0.8	1.2	13.7	3.9	6.6	5.2	-6.1	0.4
British Virgin Islands	0.0	49.0	0.9	4.7	6.5	0.6	5.8	8.2	14.4	6.3	7.0
Cayman Islands	0.0	62.5	8.3	8.8	1.7	0.5	1.5	0.7	0.7	0.7	0.8
Cuba	0.2	53.9	5.2	2.3	-3.1	0.6	1.8	4.1	4.6	3.4	1.0
Dominica	0.0	64.1	-0.4	2.5	0.7	3.5	-1.5	3.9	5.4	-0.4	2.1
Dominican Republic	0.1	79.4	5.6	3.7	4.6	7.6	8.7	3.7	8.8	4.0	7.4
Grenada	0.0	64.9	1.7	0.9	1.9	6.9	10.2	-14.8	12.3	8.3	0.5
Guadeloupe	0.1	92.8	5.3	2.3	2.1	9.2	4.1	5.9	5.9	5.9	4.2
Haiti	0.0	82.5	4.6	0.9	2.4	2.3	4.4	1.6	16.3	-5.3	-1.4
Jamaica	0.1	62.3	0.2	3.5	0.6	-3.4	-0.9	-4.0	1.3	2.6	-0.7
Martinique	0.1	83.6	4.4	4.3	1.5	1.6	4.1	2.5	2.5	2.5	2.6
Montserrat	0.0	61.6	4.0	-0.7	-13.4	160.6	10.5	-41.3	101.7	16.0	12.7
Netherlands Antilles	0.0	37.4	2.3	-1.3	2.1	-5.7	1.3	1.4	-2.5	-0.8	0.5
Puerto Rico	0.4	61.5	3.3	3.0	4.2	4.4	5.4	2.7	1.5	-1.4	2.5
Saint Kitts and Nevis	0.0	57.9	-0.7	3.0	6.9	-0.2	-6.1	33.1	-10.6	-15.8	23.0
Saint Lucia	0.0	69.8	5.2	4.6	1.5	30.7	5.7	10.6	-6.9	-15.8	8.4
Saint Vincent and the Grenadines	0.0	68.4	3.5	3.8	3.2	26.5	4.6	-7.8	-10.5	5.3	-5.1
Trinidad and Tobago	0.1	54.7	8.0	-4.0	3.7	17.1	8.8	10.8	7.2	4.8	2.7
Turks and Caicos Islands	0.0	63.5	1.0	6.6	4.6	22.4	11.6	4.4	-2.2	5.9	8.8
Central America	*4.2*	*70.1*	*5.6*	*1.8*	*3.1*	*6.3*	*5.4*	*3.9*	*7.6*	*2.6*	*1.4*
Belize	0.0	60.4	8.3	-1.4	3.6	-1.9	5.9	-7.4	12.4	-16.4	-2.0
Costa Rica	0.1	74.9	5.0	1.2	4.7	5.1	5.4	2.2	1.0	1.1	3.2
El Salvador	0.1	88.9	4.2	-1.3	4.9	3.0	2.4	3.7	3.9	3.3	1.3
Guatemala	0.1	83.6	5.4	1.3	4.0	4.0	4.2	3.6	3.5	3.8	3.6
Honduras	0.0	66.8	5.0	3.1	2.6	3.1	4.5	-1.0	3.8	4.4	2.5
Mexico [2]	3.7	69.6	5.9	1.9	3.0	6.5	5.4	4.3	8.2	2.7	1.2
Nicaragua	0.0	61.7	-0.1	-0.3	3.8	4.9	4.8	3.4	4.4	2.4	4.0
Panama	0.1	57.0	4.1	3.3	3.5	14.0	9.8	-4.0	3.6	-4.8	3.5
South America	*9.8*	*61.7*	*5.8*	*1.3*	*4.4*	*4.3*	*-0.7*	*2.0*	*6.0*	*0.2*	*-4.3*
Argentina	2.0	67.8	2.4	-0.4	4.8	9.0	3.5	-2.0	-0.7	-5.7	-14.4
Bolivia	0.1	76.9	3.4	0.9	3.6	5.4	5.3	2.8	2.7	1.7	1.5
Brazil	5.2	58.5	8.9	1.7	4.9	2.4	-3.4	6.1	9.9	1.3	-2.5
Chile	0.4	60.1	0.8	2.9	7.1	6.6	4.7	-1.0	3.7	2.7	1.7
Colombia [3]	0.6	63.8	5.7	2.8	1.9	2.4	-0.8	-5.4	2.0	2.2	1.1

Table 5.A. Average Rates of Growth of Gross Domestic Product by Expenditure - Household Final Consumption Expenditure

Major area, region and country	Base year weights as percentage of total for world or region in 1990	Base year share as percentage of total GDP in 1990	Average rates of growth 1970-1979	Average rates of growth 1980-1989	Average rates of growth 1990-1999	Annual rate of change (percentage) 1997	1998	1999	2000	2001	2002
Ecuador	0.2	67.0	7.2	2.6	1.8	4.2	4.5	-7.0	3.8	5.4	4.1
French Guiana	0.0	64.4	12.2	6.0	2.8	1.7	1.6	1.6	1.6	1.6	1.6
Guyana	0.0	60.9	0.2	-2.1	2.0	7.1	3.5	2.4	0.0	20.1	-12.5
Paraguay	0.1	77.2	6.4	4.1	4.3	8.6	-0.8	-4.5	-1.0	9.1	-4.6
Peru	0.5	71.7	2.0	0.3	2.9	4.5	-0.9	-0.4	3.5	1.4	4.5
Suriname	0.0	53.8	4.7	-3.0	-5.5	9.0	21.8	-69.8	-19.3	21.1	7.6
Uruguay [4]	0.1	69.1	1.0	1.4	4.7	5.5	7.0	-1.6	-1.6	-1.8	-17.1
Venezuela	0.6	60.9	9.6	1.8	1.1	5.2	-0.2	-4.3	3.8	4.7	-6.4
ASIA	**22.3**	**54.3**	**5.3**	**4.1**	**3.8**	**2.7**	**0.6**	**2.4**	**3.3**	**2.6**	**2.5**
Eastern Asia	*69.4*	*52.1*	*5.4*	*4.1*	*3.2*	*2.1*	*-0.1*	*2.2*	*2.8*	*2.5*	*2.3*
China	6.4	49.7	5.0	8.7	8.4	4.7	6.6	6.7	6.3	5.5	4.6
Democratic People's Rep. of Korea	0.4	72.7	11.9	8.9	-1.4	-6.3	-1.1	6.2	0.3	4.3	0.8
Hong Kong SAR of China	1.4	53.7	9.5	7.2	4.3	6.4	-7.9	0.7	6.6	1.5	-1.4
Japan	53.7	52.2	5.2	3.2	1.9	0.9	-0.4	0.0	1.2	1.7	1.3
Macao SAR of China	0.0	36.7	6.2	6.7	4.0	0.9	-1.5	0.1	1.9	2.5	5.4
Mongolia	0.1	63.3	5.7	6.3	-0.4	4.0	3.5	3.2	1.1	1.0	4.0
Republic of Korea	4.4	51.3	6.8	6.8	5.5	3.5	-11.9	11.2	8.1	4.8	6.8
South Central Asia	14.3	65.3	3.2	4.4	5.9	3.6	5.7	4.7	3.5	5.3	4.7
Bangladesh	0.9	83.3	-0.5	3.8	2.4	1.1	1.3	4.1	4.7	5.4	10.6
Bhutan	0.0	52.4	6.4	5.4	5.3	22.5	21.8	-0.9	4.9	10.1	5.5
India	7.3	67.2	2.8	5.1	4.8	3.0	6.5	6.1	2.8	5.8	3.9
Iran (Islamic Republic of)	1.7	55.1	5.9	1.9	5.5	4.4	6.9	2.5	7.4	4.5	7.9
Kazakhstan	1.5	63.4	...	...	-7.0	3.8	-0.5	0.1	2.6	7.4	11.1
Kyrgyzstan	0.3	68.0	...	...	-5.5	-8.1	19.1	-0.3	-5.3	2.1	4.8
Maldives	0.0	35.7	11.5	11.7	6.9	7.3	3.6	3.1	3.2	0.4	2.3
Nepal	0.1	83.5	2.2	3.9	4.8	5.4	4.2	2.7	3.9	4.0	3.2
Pakistan	1.1	68.3	6.0	4.5	4.4	1.6	7.5	0.4	2.1	3.3	-2.0
Sri Lanka	0.2	74.3	5.2	5.4	5.4	4.6	9.6	0.8	3.9	1.5	10.0
Tajikistan	0.0	63.0	...	...	-10.7	3.6	22.2	5.5	6.7	9.2	18.6
Turkmenistan	0.2	49.3	...	...	-2.7	23.0	-17.9	16.5	10.0	7.9	9.0
Uzbekistan	1.0	59.8	...	...	-0.4	15.9	2.2	8.7	3.7	4.1	3.4
South-Eastern Asia	*6.5*	*57.2*	*6.2*	*5.4*	*5.7*	*4.2*	*-6.0*	*4.1*	*5.9*	*4.1*	*4.3*
Brunei Darussalam	0.0	11.4	14.8	-2.0	1.1	3.0	2.0	-2.1	2.8	3.0	3.2
Cambodia	0.1	94.5	-7.3	-1.1	3.1	-0.8	2.3	3.8	2.4	1.9	2.3
Indonesia	2.2	56.8	8.0	6.1	7.7	7.1	-5.7	4.2	3.6	5.4	4.7
Lao People's Democratic Republic	0.0	92.8	0.1	6.1	2.8	8.8	-9.4	7.3	-0.4	1.2	-0.3
Malaysia	0.8	51.8	9.0	5.0	5.5	4.3	-10.2	2.9	12.5	2.8	4.4
Philippines	1.1	71.2	4.7	2.9	3.7	5.0	3.4	2.6	3.5	3.6	4.1
Singapore	0.6	46.0	7.2	5.9	5.6	5.5	-4.2	8.2	14.0	2.3	0.9
Thailand	1.6	56.5	6.3	5.5	4.6	-1.4	-11.5	4.3	4.9	3.7	4.7
Timor-Leste	0.0	92.9	...	...	-2.9	4.0	-11.8	-21.9	10.0	20.7	1.9
Vietnam	0.2	89.6	...	3.7	4.8	5.9	4.5	2.5	4.0	4.5	7.2
Western Asia	*9.8*	*55.0*	*6.8*	*3.2*	*4.1*	*5.0*	*4.4*	*-0.9*	*4.7*	*-1.4*	*-1.2*
Armenia	0.2	48.7	...	...	2.4	7.6	5.4	1.3	8.3	6.3	7.4
Azerbaijan	0.4	52.3	...	...	-2.7	11.9	13.9	12.2	12.2	10.4	6.6
Bahrain	0.1	56.0	7.7	0.9	14.4	8.5	4.3	5.3	3.2	1.4	0.9
Cyprus	0.1	59.1	4.1	6.0	5.2	4.0	8.4	3.1	8.7	5.0	2.5
Georgia	0.5	61.1	...	...	-7.8	4.9	-11.6	-1.3	9.1	-2.8	4.9
Iraq	0.7	50.5	5.0	6.4	-5.2	21.6	14.1	7.2	10.2	14.8	-5.8
Israel	1.0	54.3	7.2	5.0	6.4	2.9	4.3	4.1	7.7	3.1	0.0
Jordan	0.1	74.1	6.4	1.6	5.1	3.9	6.2	4.3	5.5	5.5	5.6
Kuwait	0.4	58.6	10.2	3.8	-1.0	0.8	5.3	0.2	37.9	1.8	9.7
Lebanon	0.1	90.0	-1.2	-6.1	7.9	3.1	-0.2	4.0	1.7	2.3	2.0
Oman	0.2	41.4	9.4	2.2	6.9	4.8	8.0	-2.7	0.8	-0.6	7.2
Qatar	0.1	27.8	13.1	2.0	-0.6	0.9	-1.3	-1.4	1.7	0.4	1.0
Saudi Arabia	1.4	39.8	9.6	1.5	1.6	-1.2	11.8	-9.9	-8.3	1.5	-21.9
Syrian Arab Republic	0.3	68.7	9.8	2.6	2.7	1.0	5.9	-4.5	-2.9	-5.1	2.0
Turkey	3.5	68.6	5.0	2.4	4.1	8.4	0.6	-2.6	6.2	-9.2	2.0

Table 5.A. Average Rates of Growth of Gross Domestic Product by Expenditure - Household Final Consumption Expenditure

Major area, region and country	Base year weights as percentage of total for world or region in 1990	Base year share as percentage of total GDP in 1990	Average rates of growth			Annual rate of change (percentage)					
			1970-1979	1980-1989	1990-1999	1997	1998	1999	2000	2001	2002
United Arab Emirates	0.4	38.6	36.3	8.7	6.0	0.5	3.5	5.9	1.8	2.5	-14.2
Yemen	0.3	72.1	...	...	3.0	5.9	10.6	3.9	-10.7	5.5	13.2
Yemen Arab Republic (Former)	...	...	9.1	3.9	...	...	...	...	...	...	...
Yemen Democratic (Former)	...	...	4.2	2.2	...	...	...	...	...	...	...
EUROPE	**36.7**	**54.8**	**3.9**	**2.5**	**0.5**	**2.4**	**2.7**	**3.0**	**3.3**	**2.9**	**2.1**
Eastern Europe	*15.3*	*49.3*	*5.7*	*3.2*	*-6.9*	*4.0*	*-0.9*	*-1.1*	*5.9*	*9.4*	*7.9*
Belarus	0.6	50.0	...	...	0.4	11.0	13.5	9.2	7.8	16.7	10.0
Bulgaria	0.3	66.8	7.1	3.2	-2.7	-11.0	2.4	9.8	4.2	5.2	4.2
Czech Republic	0.4	46.7	...	1.7	1.4	2.4	-1.8	1.9	2.3	3.8	3.9
Czechoslovakia (Former)	...	...	5.2	...	...	...	...	...	...	...	...
Hungary [5]	0.4	47.8	3.8	0.8	-0.5	1.8	4.5	5.6	5.5	5.7	10.5
Poland	0.6	46.0	6.1	0.1	2.7	7.0	5.0	5.5	2.6	2.0	3.3
Republic of Moldova	0.2	61.2	...	...	-8.5	9.9	4.8	-8.9	20.6	6.1	6.3
Romania	0.5	65.0	8.9	3.5	0.1	-3.3	0.9	-2.1	-1.0	6.2	3.1
Russian Federation	9.4	47.3	...	...	-1.8	5.0	-3.4	-3.0	7.3	10.6	9.1
Slovakia	0.2	53.7	...	2.5	0.1	5.8	6.0	2.7	-0.9	4.9	5.3
Ukraine	2.8	52.9	...	...	-7.0	-0.8	1.9	-1.6	2.5	9.0	5.2
USSR (Former)	...	...	5.7	3.4	...	...	...	...	...	...	...
Northern Europe	*19.7*	*55.6*	*2.6*	*2.8*	*2.3*	*3.7*	*3.8*	*4.3*	*4.1*	*2.6*	*3.1*
Denmark	1.3	48.3	1.6	0.7	2.0	2.9	2.3	0.7	-2.0	0.3	1.9
Estonia	0.2	64.4	...	...	-5.4	7.8	4.3	-2.9	6.5	4.8	9.3
Finland	1.4	48.2	3.3	3.8	0.8	3.4	4.2	3.4	3.1	1.9	1.5
Iceland	0.1	58.1	6.5	3.0	2.6	3.3	10.4	7.4	4.0	-3.1	-1.2
Ireland	0.5	56.4	4.5	1.8	4.7	7.3	8.1	9.8	8.7	5.3	2.2
Latvia [6]	0.2	52.7	...	...	-8.1	4.9	1.1	3.8	7.4	7.8	6.9
Lithuania	0.2	56.8	...	...	-1.9	5.3	4.7	3.2	6.4	4.0	6.2
Norway	1.1	46.5	3.9	1.8	3.1	3.4	2.8	3.3	4.0	2.6	3.7
Sweden	2.3	47.3	1.9	1.6	1.0	2.8	3.0	4.2	4.3	0.4	1.6
United Kingdom	12.3	60.6	2.6	3.4	2.3	3.7	3.8	4.6	4.5	3.1	3.6
Southern Europe	*22.6*	*58.9*	*4.0*	*2.7*	*2.2*	*3.4*	*3.8*	*3.1*	*3.1*	*1.8*	*2.0*
Albania	0.0	72.7	6.2	3.4	3.7	-0.2	0.2	7.1	4.5	9.5	10.9
Andorra	0.0	59.7	9.1	6.7	4.6	3.3	4.0	4.5	4.6	4.4	5.0
Bosnia and Herzegovina	0.2	69.3	...	...	5.2	30.0	20.0	14.1	5.6	1.6	55.3
Croatia	0.3	66.3	...	...	-3.3	13.0	-0.6	-2.9	4.2	4.6	6.6
Greece	1.2	71.2	5.8	1.9	2.2	2.7	3.5	2.4	2.0	2.9	2.8
Holy See	0.0	57.1	4.6	3.5	1.8	3.4	3.2	2.7	2.9	1.1	0.5
Italy	12.9	57.1	3.7	3.1	1.7	3.2	3.2	2.6	2.7	1.0	0.4
Malta	0.0	62.7	5.6	4.3	4.3	1.5	2.6	6.2	5.9	3.8	17.9
Portugal	0.9	61.5	4.3	2.6	3.4	3.4	5.1	5.2	2.5	1.1	0.5
San Marino	0.0	46.1	3.6	2.4	2.0	6.6	3.7	2.5	8.8	0.3	-0.4
Serbia and Montenegro	0.4	64.6	...	...	-8.5	0.4	6.5	-26.2	9.1	4.7	3.1
Slovenia	0.2	52.2	...	...	2.7	2.6	3.0	5.9	0.2	2.4	1.0
Spain	6.3	59.7	4.1	2.3	2.3	3.2	4.4	4.7	4.0	2.9	2.6
TFYR Macedonia	0.1	66.4	...	...	0.9	3.3	3.6	3.6	7.7	-8.5	1.0
Yugoslavia (Former)	...	...	6.1	0.2	...	...	...	...	...	...	...
Western Europe	*42.4*	*54.6*	*3.6*	*1.8*	*1.9*	*0.8*	*2.6*	*3.4*	*2.4*	*1.8*	*0.0*
Austria	1.8	53.7	4.2	2.4	2.6	2.1	2.7	2.5	3.4	1.4	0.7
Belgium	2.2	54.2	4.2	1.6	2.0	2.0	3.2	2.2	3.4	0.9	0.3
France	13.7	54.9	3.7	2.0	1.4	0.1	3.4	3.2	2.7	2.6	1.2
Germany	19.0	55.4	3.6	1.7	2.1	0.5	1.7	3.6	1.9	1.5	-1.1
Liechtenstein	0.0	55.0	3.4	2.4	1.7	2.5	3.5	3.4	2.4	3.0	1.2
Luxembourg	0.1	50.9	4.2	2.8	3.2	3.8	6.6	2.4	4.4	4.4	2.1
Monaco	0.0	54.9	4.3	2.7	2.1	0.8	4.1	3.9	3.2	3.2	1.7
Netherlands	3.0	49.1	3.6	0.8	2.8	3.0	4.9	4.8	3.2	1.4	0.8
Switzerland	2.6	55.0	1.9	1.7	1.0	1.4	2.3	2.2	1.3	2.0	0.3

Table 5.A. Average Rates of Growth of Gross Domestic Product by Expenditure - Household Final Consumption Expenditure

Major area, region and country	Base year weights as percentage of total for world or region in 1990	Base year share as percentage of total GDP in 1990	Average rates of growth			Annual rate of change (percentage)					
			1970-1979	1980-1989	1990-1999	1997	1998	1999	2000	2001	2002
OCEANIA	**1.6**	**59.2**	**3.3**	**3.1**	**3.1**	**4.4**	**4.5**	**4.0**	**2.8**	**3.7**	**3.7**
Australia & New Zealand	*96.4*	*58.9*	*3.3*	*3.1*	*3.1*	*4.4*	*4.5*	*4.1*	*2.8*	*3.7*	*3.9*
Australia	84.3	58.7	3.7	3.3	3.2	4.8	4.8	4.1	3.0	3.8	3.9
New Zealand	12.1	59.9	1.5	1.7	2.4	2.0	2.4	3.7	1.6	2.9	3.8
Melanesia	*2.5*	*71.3*	*4.8*	*4.5*	*2.4*	*6.4*	*3.8*	*1.6*	*2.0*	*2.0*	*-4.4*
Fiji	0.5	72.9	7.5	2.0	2.5	-1.1	9.3	-4.6	3.6	18.8	4.3
New Caledonia	1.1	97.6	1.0	11.0	0.6	2.0	-3.2	0.9	2.1	-1.1	0.7
Papua New Guinea	0.8	51.6	6.0	0.9	4.6	15.6	9.6	4.9	2.1	-0.5	-12.3
Solomon Islands	0.1	58.0	9.5	-0.1	-0.3	-2.8	1.7	-1.5	-14.0	-4.9	-4.0
Vanuatu	0.0	62.9	7.7	3.8	1.8	1.5	-2.9	-3.2	2.7	-1.6	-3.5
Micronesia	*0.1*	*54.5*	*4.6*	*2.9*	*0.3*	*-4.4*	*0.3*	*-2.3*	*0.7*	*2.0*	*1.3*
Kiribati	0.0	44.6	2.9	-4.9	4.5	5.7	5.0	9.3	1.6	1.8	0.9
Marshall Islands	0.0	97.6	5.8	13.3	-2.0	-10.3	1.6	0.0	-1.0	1.7	2.5
Micronesia (Federated States of)	0.0	44.6	6.6	4.5	1.2	-5.1	-2.1	-2.8	2.1	1.5	0.8
Nauru	0.0	44.6	6.8	4.9	-5.4	-7.3	-1.9	-1.9	-1.0	-0.8	0.9
Palau	0.0	44.6	2.9	-5.5	3.7	2.3	2.0	-8.8	0.3	4.5	1.1
Polynesia	*1.0*	*65.2*	*2.4*	*4.6*	*3.3*	*0.9*	*1.7*	*2.7*	*4.6*	*2.8*	*2.1*
Cook Islands	0.0	114.8	1.3	1.2	-0.5	7.1	-4.2	2.6	14.1	5.1	3.7
French Polynesia	0.8	61.9	2.1	5.6	3.8	1.1	1.1	2.7	2.7	2.1	1.9
Samoa	0.1	81.4	3.6	-1.0	1.2	1.6	4.7	11.5	23.1	6.3	4.8
Tonga	0.0	93.5	3.7	5.3	1.9	-5.8	10.8	-7.4	5.6	7.0	0.5
Tuvalu	0.0	102.9	5.8	5.2	5.0	3.5	14.9	3.0	3.0	3.0	-11.5

Notes for Table 5.A - Household final consumption expenditure

1/ 1970-2002
Includes NPISH's final consumption expenditure.

2/ 1980-2002
Includes NPISH's final consumption expenditure.

3/ (a) 1970-1992
Excludes direct purchases abroad by resident households and direct purchases in the domestic market by non-resident households.

(b) 1989-1992
Includes NPISH's final consumption expenditure.

4/ 1980-2002
Includes NPISH's final consumption expenditure.

5/ 1988-1991
Includes total final consumption expenditure of households purchased in the domestic market at market prices. Consumption from own-account production is evaluated at basic prices. The wage-like part of the business travel cost (i.e. per diem) is treated as household consumption expenditure.

6/ 1990-2002
Includes NPISH's final consumption expenditure.

Table 5.B. Average Rates of Growth of Gross Domestic Product by Expenditure - General Government Final Consumption Expenditure

Major area, region and country	Base year weights as percentage of total for world or region in 1990	Base year share as percentage of total GDP in 1990	Average rates of growth			Annual rate of change (percentage)					
			1970-1979	1980-1989	1990-1999	1997	1998	1999	2000	2001	2002
WORLD	**100.0**	**17.5**	**3.6**	**2.8**	**2.2**	**1.6**	**2.1**	**2.4**	**2.9**	**3.2**	**3.0**
DEVELOPED ECONOMIES	**76.6**	**18.0**	**3.0**	**2.6**	**1.5**	**1.1**	**1.7**	**2.8**	**2.7**	**2.9**	**3.4**
DEVELOPING ECONOMIES	**14.2**	**14.4**	**6.6**	**3.6**	**3.4**	**4.9**	**4.4**	**1.3**	**4.4**	**4.7**	**1.8**
TRANSITION ECONOMIES	**9.2**	**19.7**	**8.5**	**3.3**	**-2.7**	**-0.8**	**0.8**	**0.7**	**2.1**	**2.1**	**2.6**
AFRICA	**2.2**	**16.6**	**6.3**	**0.9**	**2.1**	**2.3**	**4.9**	**-3.1**	**5.4**	**7.1**	**0.1**
Eastern Africa	*13.0*	*19.6*	*6.0*	*2.3*	*4.6*	*1.1*	*7.0*	*7.1*	*10.0*	*-1.7*	*9.4*
Burundi	0.3	19.5	3.9	4.1	4.1	4.3	6.7	7.2	-9.1	4.7	0.7
Comoros	0.1	25.7	4.4	3.3	-3.5	0.3	-2.8	-22.9	-9.3	10.2	-6.2
Djibouti	0.2	33.6	2.9	3.2	-1.0	3.5	-14.8	-8.0	-3.6	-1.0	17.0
Eritrea	...	...	...	...	23.7	-16.9	78.1	8.2	-19.1	-19.5	18.0
Ethiopia	...	...	...	...	14.6	13.1	30.6	6.7	38.5	-18.1	13.0
Ethiopia (Former)	1.8	19.2	6.7	1.8	6.8	...	...	...	...	...	...
Kenya	1.8	18.7	9.2	1.8	7.9	4.2	3.4	4.3	4.3	4.4	4.3
Madagascar	0.3	8.0	2.3	-2.7	2.0	3.4	3.0	8.7	3.2	9.5	-15.1
Malawi	0.3	16.2	7.4	5.6	4.1	7.6	1.5	3.1	3.3	4.3	83.9
Mauritius	0.4	12.7	10.6	3.1	4.7	3.8	3.5	5.6	6.5	4.5	5.6
Mozambique	0.4	11.9	3.9	1.0	3.6	22.4	20.9	10.0	11.0	17.9	14.7
Reunion	1.7	28.2	6.2	4.9	2.9	2.8	3.0	2.9	2.9	2.9	2.9
Rwanda	0.3	10.2	5.0	4.0	-3.5	-3.4	4.9	7.1	-9.5	10.8	12.7
Seychelles	0.1	27.7	8.3	1.9	4.3	2.6	17.6	-9.3	-2.8	5.2	0.3
Somalia	0.1	10.3	4.0	-3.3	-5.0	-4.2	2.0	-10.7	2.0	3.0	3.5
Uganda	0.4	9.7	4.9	-0.6	7.3	10.3	9.3	5.2	8.4	8.1	8.1
United Republic Of Tanzania	0.4	9.8	3.6	2.4	15.7	1.9	-1.4	242.3	2.2	6.0	18.3
Zambia	2.5	54.7	4.1	-0.2	-2.3	0.0	-14.8	-19.4	-21.6	44.7	2.3
Zimbabwe	1.9	19.4	12.0	7.4	-1.8	-20.4	6.0	-6.1	57.0	-29.2	5.2
Middle Africa	*11.1*	*21.6*	*0.1*	*2.2*	*-0.3*	*7.4*	*1.6*	*-3.7*	*-2.0*	*22.3*	*4.8*
Angola	5.3	44.8	0.2	2.3	1.1	11.2	-10.5	31.4	1.5	35.1	2.9
Cameroon	1.9	11.4	1.3	4.1	-1.3	8.4	5.3	-18.8	6.3	3.2	0.6
Central African Republic	0.2	13.6	-1.7	0.3	-10.8	4.3	4.8	-69.8	-10.3	0.1	1.2
Chad	0.4	21.3	-3.9	9.5	3.7	-2.8	8.4	11.3	-1.6	2.6	20.4
Congo	0.6	18.6	6.8	5.3	-5.2	2.4	0.8	-51.7	-29.5	30.2	49.9
Democratic Republic of the Congo	1.9	17.9	-1.8	-2.6	-6.4	-0.6	3.3	-10.4	-4.3	-4.4	1.4
Equatorial Guinea	0.1	39.7	9.4	-2.5	18.2	-4.5	131.9	-30.8	-23.8	-3.9	29.2
Gabon	0.8	13.4	2.0	5.6	-1.5	7.2	14.7	-49.7	-22.9	14.3	-1.1
Sao Tome and Principe	0.0	38.2	15.3	9.7	3.5	0.8	2.3	18.4	5.3	-31.5	-12.3
Northern Africa	*39.8*	*15.0*	*9.0*	*0.1*	*2.4*	*2.1*	*7.5*	*-9.6*	*3.1*	*8.1*	*-6.1*
Algeria	11.5	16.2	11.2	0.6	4.2	2.3	3.1	2.5	2.5	1.9	2.5
Egypt	8.1	10.0	3.5	4.2	3.9	3.0	2.6	2.8	4.9	5.0	17.5
Libyan Arab Jamahiriya	8.4	26.0	11.2	-2.4	1.2	0.6	11.7	-12.6	-2.2	13.4	-26.7
Morocco	4.6	15.5	9.7	3.4	3.4	1.6	5.0	4.5	1.9	4.9	4.6
Sudan	4.9	12.8	3.3	1.1	-3.9	4.4	15.5	-60.2	39.6	21.1	-15.7
Tunisia	2.3	16.4	6.8	5.5	3.9	6.2	3.9	3.8	5.0	4.8	4.3
Southern Africa	*27.2*	*20.0*	*5.2*	*4.2*	*1.1*	*2.5*	*-1.3*	*0.9*	*3.1*	*3.4*	*4.0*
Botswana	1.0	23.8	13.5	15.4	7.1	8.1	7.8	5.6	8.2	9.5	13.4
Lesotho	0.1	14.0	16.4	5.0	5.3	6.0	18.0	-3.7	0.8	-3.6	14.8
Namibia	0.8	30.8	3.1	1.8	4.4	3.8	3.0	2.0	-0.3	0.9	-4.7
South Africa	25.1	19.7	5.1	4.1	0.6	2.1	-2.1	0.3	3.1	3.2	3.7
Swaziland	0.2	18.4	13.9	2.5	7.4	3.6	2.4	37.1	-5.8	-3.7	-1.4
Western Africa	*9.0*	*10.7*	*4.3*	*-4.1*	*2.1*	*-0.1*	*4.7*	*16.6*	*24.0*	*12.7*	*6.1*
Benin	0.3	13.2	2.3	-0.5	7.5	4.4	6.3	2.2	3.0	3.5	5.1
Burkina Faso	0.5	15.4	10.2	4.4	2.7	2.9	4.9	4.9	0.3	42.5	1.6
Cape Verde	0.1	18.9	0.8	8.7	4.8	4.6	-2.6	16.6	30.8	-18.6	18.4
Cote d'Ivoire	2.8	20.7	8.9	0.5	-0.8	2.6	-1.6	8.5	-2.0	29.6	11.6
Gambia	0.1	14.5	3.8	7.1	2.2	17.2	14.2	-39.1	14.1	5.2	-0.7
Ghana	0.8	10.9	1.0	-18.2	4.3	-12.0	11.4	-0.1	22.6	16.6	12.3

Table 5.B. Average Rates of Growth of Gross Domestic Product by Expenditure - General Government Final Consumption Expenditure

Major area, region and country	Base year weights as percentage of total for world or region in 1990	Base year share as percentage of total GDP in 1990	Average rates of growth			Annual rate of change (percentage)					
			1970-1979	1980-1989	1990-1999	1997	1998	1999	2000	2001	2002
Guinea	0.4	11.9	2.8	0.2	0.8	8.4	-7.3	3.3	3.6	5.2	2.6
Guinea-Bissau	0.0	10.3	0.3	2.0	1.0	-12.8	-8.0	45.0	27.6	-6.2	4.0
Liberia	0.1	13.0	6.4	-8.3	-6.0	101.5	29.7	22.9	22.3	4.9	3.3
Mali	0.4	15.2	3.9	4.5	4.2	-6.7	-4.4	79.2	17.1	2.6	9.0
Mauritania	0.2	18.8	10.4	-2.8	2.7	3.8	2.5	6.2	19.7	-3.4	2.0
Niger	0.5	17.2	1.4	3.1	0.9	25.3	4.9	13.4	-23.6	12.8	5.3
Nigeria	1.6	4.4	6.1	-3.7	5.9	-9.6	16.8	47.7	86.2	0.6	4.5
Senegal	1.0	14.7	12.0	3.1	1.2	6.9	4.9	9.9	14.9	23.7	-8.5
Sierra Leone	0.1	7.8	0.6	-0.7	-2.1	-1.4	1.1	3.8	-0.5	5.0	6.3
Togo	0.2	12.6	10.6	-3.0	0.2	-4.3	11.0	7.0	-3.5	-13.4	18.4
AMERICAS	**31.7**	**16.9**	**1.9**	**3.0**	**0.8**	**1.7**	**1.8**	**2.4**	**2.4**	**3.4**	**4.3**
NORTHERN AMERICA	**27.9**	**17.5**	**1.5**	**2.8**	**0.9**	**1.0**	**1.7**	**3.0**	**2.9**	**3.9**	**4.6**
Bermuda	0.0	12.5	3.9	2.7	2.3	1.3	11.8	5.0	5.7	2.5	1.0
Canada	10.2	22.5	3.8	2.4	0.9	-1.0	3.2	2.2	2.5	3.7	3.0
United States	77.5	17.0	1.2	2.9	0.9	1.3	1.5	3.1	2.9	3.9	4.9
LATIN AMERICA AND THE CARIBBEAN	**3.9**	**13.3**	**6.0**	**3.8**	**0.7**	**6.0**	**2.6**	**-2.1**	**-0.8**	**0.4**	**2.2**
Caribbean	*1.3*	*18.5*	*5.2*	*2.8*	*1.1*	*2.4*	*3.2*	*-0.1*	*2.6*	*3.7*	*3.9*
Anguilla	0.0	13.4	3.8	6.0	6.1	13.9	-20.2	18.8	30.0	4.7	-6.9
Antigua and Barbuda	0.0	19.0	1.1	7.3	4.8	1.3	11.7	7.7	0.1	17.5	25.5
Aruba	0.0	13.3	16.2	16.8	12.1	26.1	-0.7	2.9	-7.6	13.1	8.1
Bahamas	0.0	13.6	4.2	6.7	2.7	1.1	13.3	7.6	6.1	-1.2	5.3
Barbados	0.0	20.2	-0.3	3.6	2.3	5.3	2.4	2.6	3.5	3.8	0.4
British Virgin Islands	0.0	14.3	5.6	11.0	4.5	2.9	8.4	0.5	14.4	6.3	6.4
Cayman Islands	0.0	14.2	11.6	8.7	2.2	0.5	1.5	0.7	0.7	0.7	0.8
Cuba	0.5	31.0	5.2	1.6	-1.1	0.6	1.8	2.7	2.8	10.4	4.9
Dominica	0.0	20.3	1.8	0.2	3.1	9.9	4.0	1.7	1.2	-6.0	-4.5
Dominican Republic	0.0	2.7	2.1	5.2	6.5	0.7	6.3	3.6	-1.8	15.8	8.9
Grenada	0.0	20.5	2.9	0.7	2.1	3.3	7.9	-4.1	7.4	14.5	7.2
Guadeloupe	0.1	30.8	7.3	2.3	1.9	9.2	4.1	5.9	5.9	5.9	4.2
Haiti	0.0	6.8	2.9	-5.5	5.6	2.3	4.4	1.6	1.3	-5.3	3.9
Jamaica	0.0	14.0	8.0	0.3	3.5	11.7	9.1	-3.9	-2.2	2.4	3.4
Martinique	0.1	29.7	5.7	3.3	1.2	1.6	4.1	2.5	2.5	2.5	2.6
Montserrat	0.0	17.7	4.4	2.4	3.1	7.0	-10.7	-4.1	-15.0	-3.8	-6.8
Netherlands Antilles	0.1	39.5	2.3	0.7	1.9	-3.7	-4.3	1.6	-3.5	-1.7	-0.4
Puerto Rico	0.4	14.4	5.2	4.8	1.8	1.9	4.3	-5.7	4.6	-3.6	0.2
Saint Kitts and Nevis	0.0	18.0	2.7	4.1	6.2	3.4	0.4	14.8	3.0	-0.4	-6.7
Saint Lucia	0.0	15.2	3.6	7.7	3.8	7.0	3.1	-17.0	2.8	12.0	-0.4
Saint Vincent and the Grenadines	0.0	20.9	3.3	3.4	3.4	-3.6	2.4	6.8	5.2	1.9	5.5
Trinidad and Tobago	0.1	16.2	9.9	1.8	0.6	-0.2	-4.6	3.1	-3.3	5.7	20.2
Turks and Caicos Islands	0.0	25.1	1.0	6.5	4.9	-0.5	17.0	15.0	12.4	13.8	-7.9
Central America	*2.1*	*9.0*	*8.3*	*3.1*	*2.3*	*3.0*	*3.2*	*4.5*	*2.3*	*-0.2*	*-1.3*
Belize	0.0	14.4	6.6	3.7	5.5	5.6	5.4	8.2	-1.8	5.6	4.6
Costa Rica	0.1	15.0	7.4	0.6	1.8	4.6	2.2	1.8	1.4	3.6	2.1
El Salvador	0.0	9.9	6.8	2.0	2.5	2.8	2.5	0.4	1.0	4.0	-7.2
Guatemala	0.0	6.8	5.2	3.6	6.5	5.6	32.6	7.6	7.9	5.4	-2.1
Honduras	0.0	12.9	5.5	4.3	-0.3	-1.0	15.4	9.8	8.3	12.1	0.5
Mexico	1.7	8.4	8.7	3.3	2.4	2.9	2.3	4.7	2.0	-1.2	-1.3
Nicaragua	0.1	29.6	7.1	3.0	-1.6	-3.2	4.2	11.0	0.4	2.6	-13.0
Panama	0.1	18.1	6.5	2.0	2.0	7.0	4.3	-2.0	5.5	4.0	5.6
South America	*8.8*	*14.4*	*5.6*	*4.1*	*0.2*	*7.4*	*2.3*	*-4.0*	*-2.2*	*0.1*	*2.8*
Argentina	1.3	12.0	3.8	-0.7	4.4	3.2	3.4	2.6	0.6	-2.1	-5.1
Bolivia	0.0	11.8	8.7	-2.4	3.2	3.3	3.8	3.2	2.1	2.5	3.3
Brazil	5.9	16.9	6.6	6.3	-2.6	8.0	2.1	-9.3	-5.4	0.3	6.3
Chile	0.3	10.4	4.0	-0.6	3.7	5.8	2.2	2.7	2.9	3.1	2.4

Table 5.B. Average Rates of Growth of Gross Domestic Product by Expenditure - General Government Final Consumption Expenditure

Major area, region and country	Base year weights as percentage of total for world or region in 1990	Base year share as percentage of total GDP in 1990	Average rates of growth			Annual rate of change (percentage)					
			1970-1979	1980-1989	1990-1999	1997	1998	1999	2000	2001	2002
Colombia	0.4	11.4	6.5	5.1	9.9	15.8	2.1	3.6	-0.3	0.9	6.[illegible]
Ecuador	0.1	13.0	12.3	-0.3	-0.8	4.7	-2.2	-5.5	4.7	0.5	3.[illegible]
French Guiana	0.0	35.0	11.7	4.2	4.6	0.5	2.9	1.7	1.7	1.7	1.7
Guyana	0.0	13.6	7.9	1.3	7.8	12.8	1.7	8.6	-11.0	-32.9	2.[illegible]
Paraguay	0.0	6.2	4.3	5.6	6.7	2.3	0.7	3.7	14.1	-12.5	-9.7
Peru	0.2	8.9	3.4	0.5	3.2	7.6	2.5	3.5	3.1	0.1	1.[illegible]
Suriname	0.0	24.4	2.6	3.6	-14.0	28.4	8.8	-66.0	-19.3	21.1	7.[illegible]
Uruguay	0.1	13.9	3.9	1.5	2.2	2.9	2.9	1.8	-0.3	-4.2	-8.[illegible]
Venezuela	0.3	8.4	4.8	2.1	1.1	4.2	1.4	3.0	5.0	6.4	-2.[illegible]
ASIA	**19.2**	**13.9**	**6.1**	**4.1**	**3.7**	**2.8**	**3.3**	**4.1**	**5.3**	**4.1**	**2.[illegible]**
Eastern Asia	*67.6*	*13.1*	*5.6*	*4.3*	*3.8*	*2.2*	*2.9*	*4.2*	*5.4*	*3.9*	*2.7*
China	6.2	12.3	10.2	8.5	10.0	8.1	8.4	8.4	12.0	11.6	4.[illegible]
Democratic People's Rep. of Korea	0.2	10.2	11.9	7.9	2.6	-6.3	-1.1	6.2	0.3	4.3	0.[illegible]
Hong Kong SAR of China	0.7	7.3	7.9	6.6	4.5	2.5	0.3	3.0	2.2	6.1	2.[illegible]
Japan	53.3	13.3	5.3	3.7	2.9	1.0	2.1	4.4	4.7	2.6	2.[illegible]
Macao SAR of China	0.0	8.8	11.7	13.8	7.3	4.1	2.5	15.5	-9.8	1.6	2.[illegible]
Mongolia	0.1	26.6	5.7	6.3	-0.4	4.0	3.5	3.2	1.1	1.0	4.[illegible]
Republic of Korea	3.5	10.5	5.4	5.2	3.8	1.5	-0.4	1.3	0.1	1.3	2.[illegible]
South Central Asia	*11.2*	*13.2*	*5.2*	*3.7*	*6.9*	*5.8*	*6.9*	*8.6*	*1.9*	*7.4*	*0.6*
Bangladesh	0.2	4.4	19.2	3.9	4.3	13.2	0.6	0.9	4.5	4.5	24.[illegible]
Bhutan	0.0	15.7	6.4	6.2	7.2	29.5	-15.5	18.4	-3.5	12.3	9.[illegible]
India	5.0	11.8	4.3	7.3	6.2	11.1	12.9	13.2	0.6	7.2	-1.[illegible]
Iran (Islamic Republic of)	1.4	11.9	5.8	-5.3	3.2	-3.2	4.3	-6.3	11.3	2.5	4.[illegible]
Kazakhstan	1.2	12.4	...	...	-6.2	-9.4	-14.5	7.3	16.3	19.6	-4.[illegible]
Kyrgyzstan	0.4	25.0	...	...	-8.6	-4.2	4.8	3.6	5.8	-1.3	-0.[illegible]
Maldives	0.0	17.8	11.5	11.7	9.7	23.7	9.8	13.1	14.1	4.4	9.[illegible]
Nepal	0.0	8.7	2.9	5.8	3.6	1.2	2.9	3.7	6.4	14.5	2.[illegible]
Pakistan	0.9	14.3	5.9	10.1	0.7	6.8	-6.9	7.5	-5.3	18.2	-7.[illegible]
Sri Lanka	0.1	13.1	3.5	4.2	5.4	7.1	5.3	3.9	5.3	-1.7	-2.[illegible]
Tajikistan	0.0	6.8	...	...	-9.3	20.6	-22.9	14.5	2.6	11.5	19.[illegible]
Turkmenistan	0.3	23.0	...	...	-12.5	66.1	-24.9	16.5	10.0	7.9	9.[illegible]
Uzbekistan	1.6	25.4	...	...	-2.9	-2.5	4.6	4.9	-6.0	3.3	11.[illegible]
South-Eastern Asia	*6.4*	*13.7*	*6.0*	*3.7*	*3.9*	*2.0*	*-2.2*	*5.1*	*5.4*	*5.8*	*5.7*
Brunei Darussalam	0.1	11.7	-6.8	6.5	3.4	3.0	2.0	-2.6	2.8	3.0	3.[illegible]
Cambodia	0.0	6.9	-7.3	-1.1	4.7	-4.2	-12.6	5.6	15.5	13.1	7.[illegible]
Indonesia	1.3	8.8	11.9	5.7	0.6	0.1	-15.4	0.7	6.5	8.2	12.[illegible]
Lao People's Democratic Republic	0.0	11.6	0.1	9.6	-2.3	-2.1	-25.3	7.3	-8.3	-2.7	-7.[illegible]
Malaysia	0.8	13.8	9.7	5.9	5.7	5.7	-8.9	17.1	3.0	17.6	12.[illegible]
Myanmar	2.0	88.3	2.9	1.9	2.9	1.9	1.9	3.0	3.0	3.0	3.[illegible]
Philippines	0.6	10.1	7.3	1.0	3.5	4.6	-1.9	6.7	6.1	-5.3	2.[illegible]
Singapore	0.5	10.1	7.0	6.7	8.4	7.5	8.3	6.8	17.6	8.2	4.[illegible]
Thailand	1.0	9.4	9.6	4.5	5.3	-2.8	3.9	3.1	2.6	2.9	0.[illegible]
Timor-Leste	0.0	36.7	...	...	-12.6	4.0	-58.6	-35.5	307.5	12.8	-0.[illegible]
Vietnam	0.1	7.5	-0.3	6.2	6.6	4.0	3.2	-5.0	0.9	3.3	5.[illegible]
Western Asia	*14.8*	*21.5*	*8.9*	*3.4*	*1.0*	*4.7*	*5.8*	*-1.2*	*8.0*	*1.6*	*-0.9*
Armenia	0.3	16.9	...	...	-8.2	-2.1	-2.2	1.3	2.8	0.0	6.[illegible]
Azerbaijan	0.5	17.6	...	...	-5.3	2.2	-0.5	-1.6	2.4	5.1	1.[illegible]
Bahrain	0.1	23.8	11.6	4.9	-6.4	0.3	0.0	6.8	2.7	5.2	4.[illegible]
Cyprus	0.1	17.3	5.6	7.3	4.6	4.9	7.3	-7.7	-2.6	10.1	8.[illegible]
Georgia	0.5	16.8	...	...	-14.9	46.0	12.4	-1.3	-17.8	18.3	6.[illegible]
Iraq	1.3	26.4	6.7	6.0	-12.9	6.6	5.8	3.3	4.2	6.9	4.[illegible]
Israel	2.1	28.2	3.4	1.2	3.2	2.0	2.2	2.9	2.2	3.4	5.[illegible]
Jordan	0.1	24.9	4.3	1.2	3.7	7.8	-1.4	3.0	0.8	2.2	6.[illegible]
Kuwait	0.9	38.6	9.5	4.5	0.3	-2.5	-1.0	-0.4	39.2	-1.2	15.[illegible]
Lebanon	0.2	45.5	6.1	2.1	-9.2	4.2	-3.5	5.5	3.0	3.4	2.[illegible]
Oman	0.4	26.6	6.5	9.5	3.2	1.4	-1.3	3.2	8.7	9.2	4.[illegible]
Qatar	0.3	32.9	14.7	4.7	1.4	5.7	-1.6	-1.7	11.0	3.8	-44.[illegible]
Saudi Arabia	4.4	31.8	12.6	1.9	-0.9	9.6	11.5	-10.8	6.8	5.1	-13.[illegible]

Table 5.B. Average Rates of Growth of Gross Domestic Product by Expenditure - General Government Final Consumption Expenditure

Major area, region and country	Base year weights as percentage of total for world or region in 1990	Base year share as percentage of total GDP in 1990	Average rates of growth			Annual rate of change (percentage)					
			1970-1979	1980-1989	1990-1999	1997	1998	1999	2000	2001	2002
Syrian Arab Republic	0.3	14.3	13.8	-1.3	1.5	1.2	2.0	-1.6	19.1	2.3	0.1
Turkey	2.2	11.0	7.2	5.8	5.1	4.1	7.8	6.5	7.1	-8.5	5.4
United Arab Emirates	0.7	16.3	32.1	5.9	2.7	1.6	1.0	5.2	5.4	8.1	-2.8
Yemen	0.3	17.0	...	...	-2.1	7.4	17.0	-2.4	7.2	4.8	16.0
Yemen Arab Republic (Former)	...	...	10.9	10.0	...	...	...	...	...	...	...
Yemen Democratic (Former)	...	...	2.6	8.9	...	...	...	...	...	...	...
EUROPE	**45.1**	**20.2**	**3.9**	**2.3**	**2.4**	**0.7**	**1.5**	**1.8**	**1.9**	**2.3**	**2.7**
Eastern Europe	*16.9*	*20.1*	*8.7*	*4.9*	*8.6*	*-1.9*	*0.3*	*0.6*	*2.1*	*1.8*	*2.8*
Belarus	0.8	25.0	...	...	-6.7	6.8	6.1	5.5	5.8	2.2	-0.8
Bulgaria	0.1	7.2	7.1	5.3	-7.2	-3.0	11.1	5.1	11.6	1.4	4.0
Czech Republic [1]	0.5	25.4	...	2.8	-2.4	-4.4	-4.4	2.3	-1.0	5.3	5.7
Czechoslovakia (Former)	...	...	6.5	...	...	...	...	...	...	...	...
Hungary [2]	0.4	21.7	5.3	1.8	-0.5	3.1	1.8	1.5	1.9	4.3	5.2
Poland	0.7	21.3	7.0	0.3	2.8	3.2	1.6	1.2	1.1	0.6	0.6
Republic of Moldova	0.1	10.4	...	...	-7.1	17.9	-19.1	-38.7	-1.4	-6.3	30.9
Romania	0.3	13.3	10.5	-4.9	3.1	-8.1	2.1	-4.1	11.7	5.1	2.5
Russian Federation	11.2	20.8	...	...	-3.0	-2.3	0.9	3.0	2.1	-0.4	2.9
Slovakia	0.2	22.7	...	2.1	-0.5	-5.4	12.5	-7.1	1.6	4.6	4.7
Ukraine	2.5	17.6	...	...	-2.9	-3.5	-3.6	-7.6	1.0	9.8	2.4
USSR (Former)	...	...	10.0	6.3	...	...	...	...	...	...	...
Northern Europe	*20.4*	*21.3*	*3.2*	*1.3*	*1.7*	*0.4*	*2.3*	*2.7*	*1.3*	*2.0*	*2.9*
Denmark	1.9	25.6	3.9	1.2	2.0	0.8	3.1	2.0	1.1	2.1	2.1
Estonia	0.1	13.2	...	...	0.5	1.8	4.5	3.8	1.5	0.9	5.0
Finland	1.7	21.6	5.0	3.3	1.1	2.9	2.0	1.4	0.0	2.2	4.0
Iceland	0.1	20.1	7.5	4.9	2.6	2.5	3.4	4.6	4.3	3.1	4.0
Ireland	0.4	16.4	6.2	0.2	4.2	5.8	6.0	8.0	8.4	11.5	10.7
Latvia	0.1	8.5	...	...	1.2	0.3	6.1	0.0	-1.9	0.3	1.5
Lithuania	0.2	19.2	...	...	-4.9	6.3	6.0	-8.1	3.9	0.3	2.4
Norway	1.4	21.2	5.0	2.8	3.4	2.5	3.3	3.2	1.3	2.7	3.2
Sweden	3.7	27.4	3.3	1.7	1.1	-0.9	3.4	1.8	-1.2	0.9	3.2
United Kingdom	10.9	19.8	2.5	0.8	1.3	-0.2	1.4	3.2	1.9	1.7	2.4
Southern Europe	*19.6*	*18.9*	*4.3*	*3.2*	*1.7*	*1.7*	*1.8*	*2.2*	*2.8*	*3.2*	*2.5*
Albania	0.0	10.2	6.2	2.4	1.7	-1.5	4.3	20.3	-3.8	15.7	-3.2
Andorra	0.0	16.7	10.7	9.2	5.7	3.0	3.3	4.0	5.7	5.2	6.7
Bosnia and Herzegovina	0.1	19.7	...	...	10.9	30.0	20.0	14.1	5.6	1.6	-10.9
Croatia	0.3	23.6	...	...	-1.3	3.1	2.3	2.8	-1.5	-3.4	-1.8
Greece	0.7	15.1	6.9	1.3	1.1	3.0	1.7	2.1	2.2	-1.1	5.1
Holy See	0.0	20.2	4.5	3.2	0.5	0.4	0.3	1.4	1.8	3.6	1.8
Italy	12.4	20.2	3.6	2.9	0.4	0.2	0.2	1.3	1.6	3.6	1.7
Malta	0.0	17.6	6.2	4.9	4.8	-1.2	-3.6	-1.0	5.1	1.9	25.7
Portugal	0.6	16.2	8.4	5.3	3.3	2.2	4.1	5.6	4.0	3.4	2.9
San Marino	0.0	14.1	3.6	2.4	1.8	9.1	0.7	1.3	10.9	-0.5	-0.5
Serbia and Montenegro	0.4	21.2	...	...	-6.2	25.8	13.2	-25.3	7.4	-1.4	7.4
Slovenia	0.2	17.4	...	...	2.4	2.4	5.4	2.9	2.3	4.0	2.5
Spain	4.7	16.7	5.6	4.7	3.3	2.9	3.7	4.2	5.1	3.6	4.4
TFYR Macedonia	0.0	19.0	...	...	-0.7	-2.4	4.1	4.5	1.9	4.0	10.3
Yugoslavia (Former)	...	...	6.8	-0.9	...	...	...	...	...	...	...
Western Europe	*43.1*	*20.5*	*3.7*	*2.1*	*1.9*	*1.1*	*1.3*	*1.5*	*1.8*	*2.1*	*2.7*
Austria	1.7	18.9	3.5	1.6	2.2	-1.5	2.8	3.0	-0.1	-1.4	0.1
Belgium	2.2	20.3	4.3	1.3	1.4	0.2	1.0	3.6	2.7	2.7	1.9
France	15.1	22.3	3.5	2.7	2.0	2.1	-0.1	1.5	2.8	3.0	4.1
Germany	18.3	19.7	3.9	1.5	1.9	0.3	1.9	0.8	1.0	1.0	1.7
Liechtenstein	0.0	13.9	3.7	3.6	2.2	0.9	2.4	2.4	3.2	3.4	2.9
Luxembourg	0.1	18.3	3.0	4.0	4.2	3.0	1.3	7.3	4.8	7.0	4.2
Monaco	0.0	22.3	4.1	3.4	2.7	2.8	0.5	2.1	3.4	3.5	4.6
Netherlands	3.9	23.5	3.6	2.8	2.1	3.2	3.6	2.5	2.0	4.3	3.8
Switzerland	1.8	13.9	2.2	2.8	1.5	-0.2	1.2	1.2	2.1	2.4	1.9

Table 5.B. Average Rates of Growth of Gross Domestic Product by Expenditure - General Government Final Consumption Expenditure

Major area, region and country	Base year weights as percentage of total for world or region in 1990	Base year share as percentage of total GDP in 1990	Average rates of growth			Annual rate of change (percentage)					
			1970-1979	1980-1989	1990-1999	1997	1998	1999	2000	2001	2002
OCEANIA	**1.8**	**19.3**	**4.3**	**3.3**	**2.8**	**4.1**	**3.1**	**4.7**	**1.7**	**3.2**	**3**
Australia & New Zealand	*94.6*	*18.8*	*4.2*	*3.2*	*2.9*	*4.4*	*3.3*	*4.9*	*1.6*	*3.4*	*3.*
Australia	82.7	18.8	4.4	3.5	2.9	3.8	4.0	4.6	2.2	3.3	3
New Zealand	11.9	19.2	3.5	1.6	2.4	8.8	-2.2	7.3	-2.1	3.8	5
Melanesia	*3.5*	*32.9*	*4.8*	*4.1*	*1.7*	*-0.8*	*-1.2*	*0.7*	*2.2*	*-0.7*	*-2.*
Fiji	0.3	17.5	9.1	2.3	2.5	2.8	10.0	0.6	4.9	-4.2	-1
New Caledonia	1.8	50.2	2.9	9.8	1.0	2.0	-3.2	0.9	2.1	-1.1	0
Papua New Guinea	1.2	26.2	5.2	-0.7	2.3	-4.4	-1.8	0.9	3.1	1.0	-6
Solomon Islands	0.1	31.5	7.3	8.4	3.7	-6.1	4.2	-1.9	-14.4	-4.5	-4
Vanuatu	0.1	28.2	7.7	2.1	2.2	-5.0	2.1	-4.0	2.3	-1.5	-4
Micronesia	*0.1*	*27.5*	*4.8*	*2.8*	*0.7*	*-4.6*	*0.4*	*-2.2*	*0.6*	*2.0*	*1.*
Kiribati	0.0	22.3	2.9	-4.9	4.5	5.7	5.0	9.3	1.6	1.8	0
Marshall Islands	0.0	50.2	7.8	12.1	-0.7	-10.3	1.6	0.0	-1.0	1.7	2
Micronesia (Federated States of)	0.0	22.3	6.6	4.5	1.2	-5.1	-2.1	-2.8	2.1	1.5	0
Nauru	0.0	22.3	6.8	4.9	-5.4	-7.3	-1.9	-1.9	-1.0	-0.8	0
Palau	0.0	22.3	2.9	-5.5	3.7	2.3	2.0	-8.8	0.3	4.5	1
Polynesia	*1.8*	*38.2*	*5.7*	*3.6*	*3.4*	*1.2*	*1.2*	*3.0*	*3.5*	*2.5*	*1.*
Cook Islands	0.0	32.0	-3.4	2.0	2.3	-2.5	-0.7	2.6	14.1	5.1	3
French Polynesia	1.7	40.4	6.2	3.7	3.3	1.1	1.1	2.7	2.7	2.1	1
Samoa	0.1	18.8	3.3	-0.4	4.2	1.6	4.7	11.5	23.1	6.3	4
Tonga	0.0	19.0	1.0	6.7	4.7	8.0	-0.6	6.7	2.3	10.9	-3
Tuvalu	0.0	52.8	7.8	4.1	6.3	3.5	14.9	3.0	3.0	3.0	-11

Notes for Table 5.B - General government final consumption expenditure

1/ 1987-1990
Includes consumption expenditure of the private non-profit institutions serving households.

2/ 1988-1991
Includes health, social and cultural expenditure of enterprises and final consumption expenditure of non-profit institutions.

Table 5.C. Average Rates of Growth of Gross Domestic Product by Expenditure - Gross Fixed Capital Formation

Major area, region and country	Base year weights as percentage of total for world or region in 1990	Base year share as percentage of total GDP in 1990	Average rates of growth			Annual rate of change (percentage)					
			1970-1979	1980-1989	1990-1999	1997	1998	1999	2000	2001	2002
WORLD	**100.0**	**23.0**	**3.8**	**2.7**	**3.2**	**5.3**	**3.8**	**3.8**	**5.1**	**0.1**	**-0.3**
DEVELOPED ECONOMIES	**73.2**	**22.6**	**3.0**	**3.0**	**2.8**	**5.2**	**5.3**	**5.0**	**4.4**	**-0.7**	**-2.1**
DEVELOPING ECONOMIES	**17.3**	**23.1**	**7.8**	**2.0**	**5.8**	**5.7**	**-0.7**	**0.6**	**7.0**	**1.8**	**3.6**
TRANSITION ECONOMIES	**9.5**	**26.7**	**3.7**	**1.6**	**-9.4**	**5.1**	**3.9**	**2.2**	**7.1**	**7.8**	**10.1**
AFRICA	**2.0**	**20.0**	**5.8**	**-0.4**	**3.9**	**6.2**	**5.0**	**12.1**	**4.5**	**3.8**	**1.0**
Eastern Africa	*11.6*	*21.2*	*-4.1*	*0.7*	*4.7*	*5.7*	*2.5*	*1.4*	*4.5*	*-2.1*	*4.4*
Burundi	0.2	16.4	17.0	4.6	-2.6	-0.6	2.6	-26.6	21.0	-6.2	-4.7
Comoros	0.0	12.2	2.6	-1.1	1.7	0.6	-6.0	64.0	-13.4	11.2	13.9
Djibouti	0.1	27.2	-1.4	1.5	-6.6	26.0	9.0	-79.1	45.6	-17.6	52.4
Eritrea	...	...	...	...	-0.8	22.1	-0.3	16.3	-26.7	7.7	5.8
Ethiopia	...	...	...	...	18.4	5.9	-5.7	14.1	-30.8	41.5	2.6
Ethiopia (Former)	1.0	12.5	-0.8	8.2	-19.1	...	...	...	...	...	..
Kenya	1.7	20.7	3.1	-0.4	1.8	2.0	-0.1	-4.8	-2.3	0.9	-0.7
Madagascar	0.5	17.0	-3.8	0.5	1.8	2.7	2.2	50.4	5.8	8.1	-21.5
Malawi	0.3	17.1	3.5	0.0	1.0	40.4	1.5	3.1	3.3	-0.8	-28.4
Mauritius	0.8	30.9	9.6	4.4	6.4	10.8	-5.9	21.6	-7.9	1.4	1.9
Mozambique	0.5	19.7	3.9	2.8	6.6	16.3	0.0	15.9	156.7	-53.4	2.0
Reunion	1.4	29.1	1.5	5.3	2.6	2.5	2.4	2.4	2.1	2.1	2.1
Rwanda	0.3	13.9	5.0	1.4	2.9	17.6	12.6	18.9	7.3	7.4	8.5
Seychelles	0.1	23.0	1.6	6.9	8.0	-39.0	34.8	24.3	-14.0	-1.6	0.3
Somalia	0.2	23.0	7.2	4.3	-4.6	-4.0	3.0	5.5	3.7	3.0	3.5
Uganda	0.5	14.6	-7.4	1.4	15.1	5.4	10.9	6.0	3.5	3.4	9.8
United Republic Of Tanzania	1.4	38.3	4.3	3.5	3.3	3.3	5.0	-30.7	7.5	13.5	19.0
Zambia	1.2	30.7	-11.0	-8.9	0.5	13.6	7.7	6.1	12.8	14.3	18.0
Zimbabwe	1.5	18.2	-1.5	3.5	1.9	-2.8	7.7	-4.2	-20.5	-28.5	-11.4
Middle Africa	*7.0*	*16.4*	*2.2*	*-0.4*	*9.5*	*8.6*	*13.3*	*112.3*	*-1.0*	*10.5*	*7.0*
Angola	1.1	11.0	0.1	-3.3	25.8	21.6	9.7	450.0	3.7	5.2	13.1
Cameroon	2.1	15.3	4.7	4.6	1.1	2.2	4.7	42.8	-7.9	11.0	0.0
Central African Republic	0.1	11.1	-7.5	-0.7	1.2	6.7	6.7	-19.5	-16.5	-0.6	0.2
Chad	0.2	11.3	3.2	2.1	3.7	7.9	0.0	13.5	11.0	173.6	37.9
Congo	0.4	16.5	5.5	-0.7	-3.7	-1.4	-3.4	-20.1	-6.3	10.7	-11.5
Democratic Republic of the Congo	2.0	22.3	6.2	-0.6	-8.2	-3.8	1.6	-10.4	-4.3	-4.4	-1.1
Equatorial Guinea	0.0	17.4	-1.1	2.6	37.2	-1.0	70.1	-15.6	-19.8	61.1	-62.0
Gabon	1.1	21.4	0.2	-3.5	3.3	15.9	22.6	-15.5	-13.0	7.0	1.1
Sao Tome and Principe	0.0	36.2	-0.4	-1.0	5.8	-1.2	-4.3	27.9	6.6	-22.5	-9.2
Northern Africa	*50.4*	*22.9*	*10.7*	*0.0*	*3.2*	*7.4*	*4.5*	*10.7*	*6.6*	*2.3*	*-0.8*
Algeria	14.9	25.6	10.4	-0.8	-0.5	0.8	3.3	2.7	4.1	2.2	3.1
Egypt	15.0	22.4	11.1	1.4	2.8	16.4	1.8	-2.1	-2.2	0.6	4.2
Libyan Arab Jamahiriya	5.5	20.8	14.3	-3.8	-4.5	-10.4	-7.5	-0.8	24.6	-1.1	10.1
Morocco	5.8	24.0	15.9	7.1	6.3	8.3	13.7	5.0	1.3	-1.1	-27.3
Sudan	6.3	19.7	5.2	-0.4	10.8	9.6	7.7	56.2	17.4	6.4	4.1
Tunisia	2.8	24.4	10.8	-1.5	5.5	8.6	5.8	8.5	7.1	5.5	-1.5
Southern Africa	*22.3*	*19.8*	*3.6*	*0.5*	*1.6*	*5.2*	*5.4*	*-7.1*	*2.0*	*0.7*	*5.3*
Botswana	1.1	32.8	17.0	10.8	5.1	5.9	16.9	18.0	1.6	-6.0	6.1
Lesotho	0.3	53.1	23.0	6.3	3.8	3.6	-11.3	-7.1	6.9	-3.0	-13.4
Namibia	0.5	21.3	1.1	-1.7	8.9	-11.1	24.8	6.6	8.5	-19.2	-6.9
South Africa	20.2	19.1	3.5	0.2	1.2	5.7	4.6	-8.9	1.6	2.1	6.1
Swaziland	0.2	18.6	6.5	5.4	2.6	5.7	6.7	0.9	10.6	-3.7	-0.4
Western Africa	*8.7*	*12.6*	*8.5*	*-5.2*	*6.5*	*1.7*	*5.7*	*18.3*	*4.8*	*17.1*	*-6.5*
Benin	0.2	13.4	1.8	5.4	2.1	8.3	4.3	7.5	8.0	7.5	7.5
Burkina Faso	0.6	21.7	10.0	5.9	6.9	3.0	15.0	-9.5	-9.4	37.7	-4.8
Cape Verde	0.1	40.7	-0.2	5.9	0.0	23.6	34.1	2.5	58.4	-7.8	-36.4
Cote d'Ivoire	0.9	7.7	10.8	-9.0	5.7	2.9	6.4	8.2	-49.1	63.9	6.7
Gambia	0.1	17.9	20.4	1.8	4.2	23.4	14.2	-40.4	5.7	9.2	4.1
Ghana	0.7	12.2	-3.3	-1.0	15.7	14.8	-6.2	14.2	-18.2	5.3	-1.2

Table 5.C. Average Rates of Growth of Gross Domestic Product by Expenditure - Gross Fixed Capital Formation

Major area, region and country	Base year weights as percentage of total for world or region in 1990	Base year share as percentage of total GDP in 1990	Average rates of growth			Annual rate of change (percentage)					
			1970-1979	1980-1989	1990-1999	1997	1998	1999	2000	2001	2002
Guinea	0.5	17.5	2.8	6.8	2.5	7.5	2.7	4.5	5.6	6.0	5.3
Guinea-Bissau	0.1	29.9	-3.0	5.3	-4.4	4.6	-62.9	63.8	3.5	3.3	-8.0
Liberia	0.0	10.5	8.0	-17.2	-4.4	101.8	29.7	22.9	22.3	4.9	3.3
Mali	0.5	20.0	7.1	3.9	4.5	6.5	4.2	35.5	17.0	-0.4	10.2
Mauritania	0.2	18.3	2.0	0.4	2.8	-8.8	0.3	24.2	18.0	-4.4	8.1
Niger	0.3	11.7	21.1	-1.8	0.4	16.2	15.0	-9.9	2.4	18.2	-4.6
Nigeria	3.6	11.8	10.4	-9.1	6.4	-11.6	9.9	42.1	39.7	18.5	-19.0
Senegal	0.7	12.9	9.8	3.5	7.1	4.4	19.4	20.6	-2.7	12.6	19.9
Sierra Leone	0.1	9.1	2.0	2.2	-5.0	-0.7	1.3	7.6	-26.7	0.6	6.3
Togo	0.3	22.2	17.5	-3.6	-1.6	-0.4	-2.1	-6.8	9.8	-0.7	-2.9
AMERICAS	**25.8**	**18.0**	**5.3**	**1.9**	**5.0**	**10.2**	**9.0**	**5.6**	**5.4**	**-2.2**	**-2.5**
NORTHERN AMERICA	**21.5**	**17.8**	**4.8**	**2.6**	**5.2**	**10.0**	**9.7**	**7.9**	**5.5**	**-2.3**	**-1.8**
Bermuda	0.0	16.6	6.2	4.1	1.7	0.0	13.7	5.0	5.7	2.5	1.0
Canada	9.2	21.6	5.2	3.8	1.9	15.2	2.4	7.3	5.5	4.3	1.3
United States	74.0	17.4	4.8	2.5	5.6	9.5	10.4	7.9	5.5	-2.9	-2.1
LATIN AMERICA AND THE CARIBBEAN	**4.3**	**19.6**	**6.8**	**-0.9**	**3.5**	**11.3**	**5.5**	**-5.4**	**4.6**	**-2.1**	**-5.9**
Caribbean	*1.4*	*20.5*	*1.2*	*5.0*	*2.9*	*8.0*	*15.4*	*3.5*	*1.4*	*2.1*	*3.6*
Anguilla	0.0	40.8	3.8	7.0	5.0	-5.9	48.1	36.3	-0.5	-31.5	-35.0
Antigua and Barbuda	0.0	37.2	7.3	9.5	4.1	4.2	15.3	10.1	6.0	5.4	5.2
Aruba	0.0	31.4	7.2	7.9	3.9	16.0	8.0	-5.1	-6.7	-17.8	-0.2
Bahamas	0.0	21.5	17.6	12.4	0.7	0.1	12.2	6.6	5.2	-2.0	4.3
Barbados	0.0	18.9	1.3	0.5	0.8	20.3	6.3	6.1	-1.6	-10.9	-1.8
British Virgin Islands	0.0	25.5	-3.8	5.9	8.3	14.2	16.4	2.1	14.4	6.3	10.5
Cayman Islands	0.0	21.4	9.3	8.6	1.1	0.5	1.5	0.7	0.7	0.7	0.8
Cuba	0.4	24.5	5.0	13.8	-8.9	4.0	5.7	7.1	2.0	-2.8	-5.6
Dominica	0.0	39.7	-1.7	9.3	-1.0	11.6	-10.3	2.5	0.5	-12.4	-15.7
Dominican Republic	0.1	19.1	11.5	3.6	7.4	18.5	26.5	13.6	6.8	2.0	2.4
Grenada	0.0	38.9	34.9	5.6	6.4	8.6	8.7	18.2	13.0	-27.5	8.8
Guadeloupe	0.1	33.9	5.9	5.9	3.1	9.2	4.1	5.9	5.9	5.9	4.2
Haiti	0.0	14.3	13.0	-0.2	-0.2	-1.5	7.4	4.0	18.3	-6.8	1.3
Jamaica	0.1	27.3	-8.9	4.6	1.4	-2.5	-10.0	-1.4	2.3	4.0	-1.5
Martinique	0.1	26.7	1.3	7.6	2.2	1.6	4.1	2.5	2.5	2.5	2.6
Montserrat	0.0	71.7	5.6	8.4	-7.0	3.6	19.9	-13.0	-29.0	-15.2	30.1
Netherlands Antilles	0.0	26.6	4.3	4.0	1.1	-16.8	12.0	2.3	0.2	3.4	4.7
Puerto Rico	0.4	15.5	-4.6	4.4	7.4	3.8	26.5	1.6	-0.8	3.6	6.5
Saint Kitts and Nevis	0.0	55.4	13.7	11.5	-0.8	2.5	-1.2	-14.1	43.9	10.3	-9.8
Saint Lucia	0.0	24.6	5.5	5.2	1.9	-35.3	2.7	23.2	-4.2	-7.9	-10.3
Saint Vincent and the Grenadines	0.0	29.7	3.6	3.0	5.8	7.8	13.2	6.7	-14.7	8.5	2.8
Trinidad and Tobago	0.1	13.8	14.6	-9.1	6.2	71.6	-0.8	-12.2	-10.8	13.0	8.2
Turks and Caicos Islands	0.0	37.0	1.0	6.6	5.4	30.3	21.7	6.7	-12.6	10.7	10.1
Central America	*3.9*	*17.6*	*7.4*	*-1.0*	*6.1*	*19.8*	*10.8*	*7.9*	*9.2*	*-5.4*	*-0.9*
Belize	0.0	26.0	7.1	4.2	4.0	0.1	0.1	37.4	28.5	1.0	12.3
Costa Rica	0.1	20.2	10.6	-0.3	6.5	15.3	25.5	-4.1	-0.9	2.6	6.6
El Salvador	0.1	13.7	9.5	-2.2	5.7	8.1	9.6	-0.8	5.2	1.5	2.0
Guatemala	0.1	13.0	7.8	-2.6	6.6	19.9	11.9	5.8	-8.8	1.8	5.1
Honduras	0.0	20.2	7.2	0.1	7.4	15.8	10.3	6.3	-4.6	-8.1	-5.7
Mexico	3.5	17.9	7.6	-1.0	5.7	21.0	10.3	7.7	11.4	-5.8	-1.3
Nicaragua	0.1	18.9	-9.5	14.3	4.3	11.9	7.1	36.1	-8.0	-2.4	-1.6
Panama	0.0	8.5	1.5	-9.5	24.5	5.2	15.8	21.7	-7.7	-11.0	-4.1
South America	*11.6*	*20.3*	*7.1*	*-1.4*	*2.8*	*9.4*	*3.1*	*-10.5*	*3.2*	*-1.2*	*-8.9*
Argentina	1.5	14.0	3.1	-5.3	7.4	17.7	6.5	-12.6	-6.8	-15.7	-36.4
Bolivia	0.0	12.6	6.8	-4.0	9.7	26.8	29.2	-15.3	-8.9	-19.7	10.9
Brazil	7.4	22.9	9.4	-0.4	1.2	6.2	3.6	-5.6	8.2	2.0	-4.5
Chile	0.6	24.5	-1.0	6.1	7.0	10.5	1.9	-18.2	7.7	2.5	1.4

Table 5.C. Average Rates of Growth of Gross Domestic Product by Expenditure - Gross Fixed Capital Formation

Major area, region and country	Base year weights as percentage of total for world or region in 1990	Base year share as percentage of total GDP in 1990	Average rates of growth			Annual rate of change (percentage)					
			1970-1979	1980-1989	1990-1999	1997	1998	1999	2000	2001	2002
Colombia	0.7	20.4	4.3	3.2	-1.2	-2.0	-6.3	-34.6	-2.0	13.8	15.
Ecuador	0.1	17.6	10.4	-2.6	-1.3	2.7	3.9	-27.7	12.1	12.1	17.
French Guiana	0.0	47.8	15.4	10.3	0.9	-4.0	2.7	0.1	0.0	0.0	-0.
Guyana	0.0	42.3	-0.2	-3.9	0.4	6.9	-6.8	-12.5	-9.5	18.6	5.
Paraguay [1]	0.1	22.0	17.3	2.1	1.2	-1.4	-5.0	-4.3	-0.8	-19.3	-12.
Peru	0.4	19.0	5.8	-2.4	6.7	15.3	-1.4	-11.2	-4.9	-8.2	-0.
Suriname	0.0	18.4	6.0	-2.3	15.8	-12.1	-0.8	198.6	-10.0	4.0	17.
Uruguay	0.1	10.8	8.4	-5.9	7.5	9.5	8.7	-9.0	-13.1	-9.0	-33.
Venezuela	0.5	14.1	10.1	-7.1	1.9	23.9	-2.5	-16.4	1.1	13.6	-22.
ASIA	**30.9**	**29.5**	**5.6**	**4.5**	**3.6**	**2.6**	**-3.4**	**0.1**	**5.5**	**1.3**	**2.**
Eastern Asia	*76.4*	*31.3*	*4.8*	*5.0*	*3.0*	*2.1*	*-1.9*	*0.8*	*5.0*	*1.3*	*0.*
China	6.1	25.8	7.6	8.2	13.5	6.0	14.2	6.7	8.3	13.1	13.
Democratic People's Rep. of Korea	0.3	24.4	11.9	7.4	-10.6	-6.3	-1.1	6.2	0.3	4.3	0.
Hong Kong SAR of China	1.2	26.5	11.9	5.2	5.1	12.6	-7.3	-16.6	11.0	2.7	-4.
Japan	60.7	32.2	3.9	4.4	0.6	0.9	-3.9	-0.9	2.7	-0.9	-4.
Macao SAR of China	0.0	24.5	7.9	9.0	2.1	1.9	-12.4	-6.8	-28.4	-7.8	3.
Mongolia	0.1	40.8	5.7	6.3	-0.4	4.0	3.5	3.2	1.1	1.0	4.
Republic of Korea	5.8	37.3	15.9	8.2	4.8	-2.2	-21.2	3.7	11.4	-1.8	4.
South Central Asia	*10.0*	*24.8*	*4.6*	*3.4*	*7.7*	*2.9*	*4.9*	*7.3*	*3.8*	*6.2*	*12.*
Bangladesh	0.3	14.5	6.0	2.1	8.2	12.1	9.9	7.3	5.8	6.5	0.
Bhutan	0.0	36.7	6.4	6.5	7.9	-4.0	4.8	20.3	8.3	21.8	-8.
India	4.6	23.0	4.0	7.0	6.9	2.1	8.7	9.3	3.8	3.2	15.
Iran (Islamic Republic of)	1.3	23.3	4.8	-3.9	5.9	12.5	3.3	5.7	4.1	16.4	12.
Kazakhstan	1.7	39.0	...	...	-14.2	3.3	-7.2	0.5	16.1	25.2	10.
Kyrgyzstan	0.2	22.0	...	...	-8.8	-29.6	-1.6	28.1	26.9	-1.9	-7.
Maldives	0.0	31.6	11.5	11.7	10.5	25.6	3.1	14.4	-14.7	8.5	-4.
Nepal	0.0	16.4	14.4	6.4	5.6	-3.3	-4.7	1.6	7.4	3.1	0.
Pakistan	0.5	17.4	4.9	5.2	1.8	-3.7	-4.5	5.0	0.9	-3.1	12.
Sri Lanka	0.1	20.5	7.5	0.5	6.0	5.8	11.0	1.5	7.3	-13.1	5.
Tajikistan	0.0	6.8	...	...	-2.0	35.2	-20.0	32.8	25.3	14.2	-43.
Turkmenistan	0.3	37.9	...	...	-4.5	-12.1	-12.3	16.5	10.0	7.9	9.
Uzbekistan	0.9	30.7	...	...	-1.9	-3.4	-8.1	-4.5	-8.2	12.1	13.
South-Eastern Asia	*6.7*	*30.3*	*10.2*	*6.5*	*4.1*	*0.5*	*-30.2*	*-7.4*	*13.6*	*1.7*	*1.*
Brunei Darussalam	0.0	9.9	16.5	5.1	1.1	3.0	2.0	-1.8	2.8	3.0	3.
Cambodia	0.0	9.3	-7.3	-1.1	9.0	23.7	1.2	15.4	7.6	-0.6	29.
Indonesia	2.0	28.3	14.6	8.7	2.5	8.6	-33.0	-18.2	13.8	7.5	-0.
Lao People's Democratic Republic	0.0	16.9	0.1	14.7	11.1	1.4	-4.4	7.3	2.1	2.4	1.
Malaysia	0.9	33.0	15.2	6.6	6.2	9.2	-43.0	-6.5	25.7	-2.8	0.
Myanmar	0.2	14.7	7.4	-2.2	15.8	7.7	10.1	18.2	18.2	18.2	18.
Philippines	0.6	23.1	11.0	0.4	3.4	11.5	-11.2	-2.3	19.9	-3.7	2.
Singapore	0.7	32.3	9.7	6.4	8.8	10.1	-6.0	-4.9	7.9	-5.8	-9.
Thailand	2.1	40.4	6.7	8.5	-0.3	-20.5	-44.3	-3.2	5.3	0.9	6.
Timor-Leste	0.0	30.5	...	...	-7.4	4.0	16.0	-61.3	57.2	45.9	-7.
Vietnam	0.1	13.1	0.0	3.0	19.5	10.2	12.4	1.6	10.9	10.8	10.
Western Asia	*7.0*	*21.4*	*12.6*	*-0.9*	*4.9*	*10.8*	*6.8*	*-8.4*	*5.2*	*-6.3*	*3.*
Armenia	0.4	44.3	...	...	-14.6	2.1	12.0	0.6	16.2	4.0	25.
Azerbaijan	0.3	20.3	...	...	16.4	67.0	45.0	-2.0	2.6	20.6	64.
Bahrain	0.0	18.2	19.0	0.3	1.7	0.4	14.9	11.4	18.6	2.1	30.
Cyprus	0.1	24.6	3.1	3.8	0.3	-4.5	8.0	-1.4	4.6	1.4	10.
Georgia	0.3	23.7	...	...	-15.0	15.3	17.4	34.1	-4.3	0.5	7.
Iraq	0.6	26.7	17.9	1.3	-18.6	371.5	43.2	17.5	29.6	27.9	-23.
Israel	0.7	19.6	3.8	0.0	9.0	-1.0	-3.8	0.1	1.7	-4.8	-9.
Jordan	0.1	26.0	17.3	-0.3	2.4	-9.3	-15.5	-6.1	3.6	2.3	9.
Kuwait	0.2	15.6	13.8	-3.8	3.9	-7.3	14.9	-7.0	-7.8	1.9	-7.
Lebanon	0.1	39.0	10.0	-7.9	-0.2	-6.2	-7.2	-5.2	-3.9	4.3	2.
Oman	0.1	12.2	10.6	-1.0	4.1	33.4	22.7	-29.0	3.2	9.1	1.
Qatar	0.1	17.0	12.3	-1.0	7.9	29.5	-18.0	-29.4	54.5	19.8	-0.
Saudi Arabia	1.2	19.1	18.8	-6.5	2.8	4.2	20.2	-6.0	-6.6	5.1	-26.

Table 5.C. Average Rates of Growth of Gross Domestic Product by Expenditure - Gross Fixed Capital Formation

Major area, region and country	Base year weights as percentage of total for world or region in 1990	Base year share as percentage of total GDP in 1990	Average rates of growth			Annual rate of change (percentage)					
			1970-1979	1980-1989	1990-1999	1997	1998	1999	2000	2001	2002
Syrian Arab Republic	0.1	16.5	15.2	-2.7	6.0	-5.0	3.2	-2.6	-2.3	27.1	-0.9
Turkey	2.1	22.9	4.5	6.6	4.3	14.8	-3.9	-15.7	16.9	-31.5	-0.8
United Arab Emirates	0.4	19.4	44.0	-3.6	5.2	2.5	-2.2	1.0	1.6	1.4	-8.5
Yemen	0.1	12.4	...	...	5.2	8.6	53.4	-23.0	-18.2	7.5	-4.6
Yemen Arab Republic (Former)	...	...	21.6	-4.3	...	...	...	...	...	...	...
Yemen Democratic (Former)	...	...	4.4	-15.2	...	...	...	...	...	...	...
EUROPE	**39.7**	**23.4**	**1.9**	**2.3**	**1.2**	**3.4**	**6.3**	**4.9**	**5.1**	**0.8**	**-1.5**
Eastern Europe	*19.4*	*26.7*	*3.5*	*2.2*	*-6.7*	*1.2*	*0.4*	*3.1*	*8.9*	*5.5*	*2.5*
Belarus	0.7	25.0	...	...	-3.5	21.7	10.1	-4.0	2.3	-2.3	6.7
Bulgaria	0.2	21.3	7.1	4.3	-7.0	-20.9	35.2	20.8	15.4	23.3	9.3
Czech Republic	0.4	24.5	...	1.8	1.3	-2.9	0.7	-1.0	5.3	5.5	0.6
Czechoslovakia (Former)	...	...	4.7	...	...	...	...	...	...	...	...
Hungary	0.4	22.1	5.8	-0.9	2.2	9.2	13.3	5.9	7.7	3.5	7.2
Poland	0.6	20.2	10.0	-3.2	7.3	21.7	14.2	6.5	3.0	-8.8	-5.8
Republic of Moldova	0.2	23.0	...	...	-12.6	-5.3	9.2	-23.1	-8.7	17.3	5.7
Romania	0.4	19.8	13.8	0.6	-4.1	1.7	-5.7	-4.8	5.5	9.1	8.3
Russian Federation	13.4	28.7	...	...	-18.0	-9.6	-12.4	8.1	16.6	12.3	3.0
Slovakia	0.2	29.7	...	0.5	0.0	15.0	11.0	-19.6	-7.2	13.9	-0.9
Ukraine	2.9	23.5	...	...	-19.4	2.1	2.6	0.1	12.4	6.2	6.3
USSR (Former)	...	...	2.3	2.5	...	...	...	...	...	...	...
Northern Europe	*17.9*	*21.6*	*1.4*	*3.4*	*2.0*	*8.1*	*12.0*	*1.9*	*3.9*	*2.4*	*0.4*
Denmark	1.3	19.9	0.7	0.8	3.2	10.9	10.0	1.4	8.6	2.1	0.3
Estonia	0.1	23.8	...	...	0.4	17.6	11.3	-14.7	13.3	12.2	16.1
Finland	1.9	28.7	0.9	4.9	-2.3	13.8	8.4	2.5	4.1	4.3	-4.0
Iceland	0.1	19.9	6.4	1.8	4.2	11.0	32.8	-3.0	14.8	-7.0	-14.8
Ireland	0.4	18.7	7.1	-0.9	8.9	18.9	14.9	14.0	7.1	0.2	1.5
Latvia	0.2	23.1	...	...	-7.7	20.7	44.0	-4.0	20.0	17.0	10.4
Lithuania	0.3	27.6	...	...	-2.5	24.4	21.8	-6.1	-9.0	13.5	8.7
Norway	1.2	21.5	4.8	0.3	3.1	15.5	13.1	-5.6	-3.6	-4.2	-3.6
Sweden	2.7	23.1	0.2	4.2	-0.1	-0.3	7.8	8.2	5.7	-1.0	-3.0
United Kingdom	9.8	20.5	1.1	4.1	2.2	6.8	12.7	1.6	3.6	3.6	1.8
Southern Europe	*20.3*	*22.7*	*2.1*	*2.1*	*2.4*	*4.3*	*6.8*	*6.8*	*6.5*	*2.8*	*0.9*
Albania	0.0	34.6	6.2	3.1	-6.4	-8.8	16.0	19.4	13.7	11.9	-1.0
Andorra	0.0	25.9	6.5	9.2	5.2	5.0	9.6	8.7	6.3	4.9	3.3
Bosnia and Herzegovina	0.1	18.6	...	...	7.4	30.0	20.0	14.1	5.6	1.6	10.3
Croatia	0.2	13.4	...	...	4.2	23.3	2.5	-3.9	-3.8	9.7	10.1
Greece	0.9	23.1	4.9	-3.0	3.8	6.8	10.6	11.0	8.0	6.5	5.7
Holy See	0.0	21.5	2.5	2.2	1.3	2.2	4.0	5.1	7.3	2.7	0.6
Italy	11.4	21.5	1.6	1.8	1.2	2.1	4.0	5.0	7.1	2.6	0.5
Malta	0.0	31.7	1.4	6.0	4.5	-3.7	-3.9	4.0	17.5	-2.5	20.4
Portugal	0.9	26.2	3.2	3.0	5.5	13.9	11.5	6.4	4.4	0.1	-5.1
San Marino	0.0	38.4	3.6	2.4	3.5	0.6	3.5	22.1	-3.0	2.3	2.2
Serbia and Montenegro	0.2	12.7	...	...	-9.2	8.1	-0.7	-18.0	30.0	-13.0	5.1
Slovenia	0.2	18.8	...	...	7.7	13.8	10.2	22.6	2.6	-0.4	1.3
Spain	6.3	25.9	1.7	4.7	2.9	5.0	10.0	8.8	5.7	3.3	1.0
TFYR Macedonia	0.0	18.5	...	...	-3.5	-4.3	-2.6	-1.4	15.7	-8.0	6.7
Yugoslavia (Former)	...	...	8.6	-7.3	...	...	...	...	...	...	...
Western Europe	*42.3*	*23.2*	*1.5*	*2.1*	*1.9*	*1.4*	*4.4*	*5.5*	*4.5*	*-1.6*	*-4.3*
Austria	1.8	23.7	3.9	1.6	2.8	2.0	3.9	2.1	6.2	-2.3	-2.8
Belgium	2.1	22.5	1.9	2.6	2.2	7.1	3.3	4.4	4.4	0.3	-2.5
France	13.2	22.6	2.6	3.2	1.2	-0.1	7.0	8.3	7.8	1.9	-1.6
Germany	18.8	23.4	1.2	1.0	2.3	0.6	3.0	4.1	2.7	-4.2	-6.7
Liechtenstein	0.0	27.1	1.5	4.9	1.3	2.6	5.8	3.9	7.0	-2.4	-3.2
Luxembourg	0.1	23.5	1.5	4.8	6.1	12.7	11.8	14.6	-3.5	10.1	-1.4
Monaco	0.0	22.6	3.1	3.9	1.9	0.6	7.7	8.9	8.4	2.4	-1.1
Netherlands	3.2	22.5	0.3	1.9	3.1	6.6	4.2	7.8	1.4	-0.1	-4.5
Switzerland	3.0	27.1	0.0	4.1	0.6	1.5	4.5	2.7	5.8	-3.3	-4.1

Table 5.C. Average Rates of Growth of Gross Domestic Product by Expenditure - Gross Fixed Capital Formation

Major area, region and country	Base year weights as percentage of total for world or region in 1990	Base year share as percentage of total GDP in 1990	Average rates of growth			Annual rate of change (percentage)					
			1970-1979	1980-1989	1990-1999	1997	1998	1999	2000	2001	2002
OCEANIA	**1.6**	**22.8**	**2.0**	**4.5**	**4.0**	**8.0**	**5.5**	**8.4**	**-6.8**	**8.9**	**11.8**
Australia & New Zealand	*94.9*	*22.3*	*2.0*	*4.4*	*4.1*	*8.4*	*5.8*	*8.7*	*-7.0*	*9.1*	*12.1*
Australia	84.6	22.7	2.2	4.4	4.2	9.5	6.9	8.7	-7.7	9.6	12.5
New Zealand	10.3	19.7	0.6	4.5	3.0	-0.9	-4.1	8.6	-0.6	4.7	8.5
Melanesia	*4.1*	*45.6*	*2.0*	*8.5*	*0.2*	*-2.5*	*-1.8*	*-2.3*	*-0.6*	*0.5*	*1.2*
Fiji	0.3	16.6	7.3	-3.4	2.6	1.0	26.1	9.8	-24.0	23.5	13.2
New Caledonia	2.8	93.1	5.0	20.5	1.7	2.0	-3.2	0.9	2.1	-1.1	0.7
Papua New Guinea	0.9	22.9	-0.6	2.6	-4.6	-14.7	-5.2	-16.2	0.3	0.2	-1.7
Solomon Islands	0.0	17.4	8.1	5.3	0.1	-0.1	-1.1	-0.6	-13.8	-5.4	3.3
Vanuatu	0.1	40.5	7.7	3.6	2.4	-4.4	7.1	-2.6	2.9	-4.7	-3.3
Micronesia	*0.1*	*23.1*	*5.2*	*8.1*	*-0.5*	*-7.1*	*1.0*	*-1.4*	*0.0*	*2.0*	*2.0*
Kiribati	0.0	8.1	2.9	-4.9	4.5	5.7	5.0	9.3	1.6	1.8	0.9
Marshall Islands	0.1	88.4	10.0	22.4	-1.8	-11.2	2.0	0.0	-1.1	1.8	3.0
Micronesia (Federated States of)	0.0	8.1	6.6	4.5	1.2	-5.1	-2.1	-2.8	2.1	1.5	0.8
Nauru	0.0	8.1	6.8	4.9	-5.4	-7.3	-1.9	-1.9	-1.0	-0.8	0.9
Palau	0.0	8.1	2.9	-5.5	3.7	2.3	2.0	-8.8	0.3	4.5	1.1
Polynesia	*0.8*	*21.1*	*6.4*	*3.0*	*0.6*	*0.3*	*1.7*	*4.1*	*5.8*	*2.7*	*1.6*
Cook Islands	0.0	26.2	-3.4	2.0	2.3	-2.5	-0.7	2.6	14.1	5.1	3.7
French Polynesia	0.7	19.9	7.2	4.3	-0.1	1.1	1.1	2.7	2.7	2.1	1.9
Samoa	0.1	34.4	5.1	-5.1	6.0	1.6	4.7	11.5	23.1	6.3	1.6
Tonga	0.0	18.0	6.1	1.7	1.9	-19.2	5.3	14.0	11.1	-1.1	-2.7
Tuvalu	0.0	93.1	10.0	13.7	5.3	3.5	14.9	3.0	3.0	3.0	-11.5

Notes for Table 5.C - Gross fixed capital formation

1/ 1980-1996
Includes communications equipment.

Table 5.D. Average Rates of Growth of Gross Domestic Product by Expenditure - Exports of Goods and Services

Major area, region and country	Base year weights as percentage of total for world or region in 1990	Base year share as percentage of total GDP in 1990	Average rates of growth			Annual rate of change (percentage)					
			1970-1979	1980-1989	1990-1999	1997	1998	1999	2000	2001	2002
WORLD	**100.0**	**19.8**	**6.5**	**4.5**	**7.0**	**9.7**	**4.7**	**5.8**	**12.7**	**0.5**	**3.7**
DEVELOPED ECONOMIES	**67.4**	**17.9**	**6.1**	**4.6**	**6.0**	**10.4**	**4.8**	**5.0**	**11.2**	**0.1**	**1.2**
DEVELOPING ECONOMIES	**22.0**	**25.3**	**7.9**	**4.1**	**7.7**	**8.9**	**4.3**	**7.7**	**16.5**	**0.1**	**9.0**
TRANSITION ECONOMIES	**10.6**	**25.6**	**7.3**	**3.9**	**-0.4**	**5.5**	**5.6**	**6.7**	**14.0**	**7.3**	**7.9**
AFRICA	**3.3**	**27.7**	**5.1**	**1.9**	**3.3**	**3.8**	**3.7**	**6.9**	**10.1**	**0.3**	**4.0**
Eastern Africa	*7.5*	*18.9*	*2.5*	*2.0*	*7.1*	*6.8*	*0.7*	*17.0*	*-2.1*	*10.0*	*-2.2*
Burundi	0.1	8.0	3.7	2.1	5.8	4.7	7.3	26.7	54.8	9.4	18.5
Comoros	0.0	11.7	-0.7	1.1	2.6	-1.2	10.8	1.7	8.7	10.7	8.0
Djibouti	0.3	81.4	-0.5	-0.2	-2.4	9.5	2.5	10.0	-3.8	2.4	1.6
Eritrea	...	...	...	...	4.3	9.0	-48.7	-39.4	46.5	49.5	-14.1
Ethiopia	...	...	...	...	30.4	50.9	-9.4	87.0	-15.8	3.3	5.3
Ethiopia (Former)	0.4	7.7	3.1	-0.6	-22.5	...	...	...	...	...	...
Kenya	1.5	26.2	1.9	3.3	3.2	-13.5	-4.5	12.2	3.7	5.0	5.0
Madagascar	0.3	15.9	-1.2	1.4	7.4	4.0	5.6	15.6	31.5	-2.4	-51.1
Malawi	0.3	25.3	8.2	1.2	5.7	-5.8	1.5	3.1	3.3	5.4	-16.5
Mauritius	1.2	66.8	4.2	8.1	5.6	3.5	8.3	1.5	4.1	17.2	-7.0
Mozambique	0.1	6.1	3.9	-10.4	13.5	8.6	10.5	-1.5	33.2	50.1	12.3
Reunion	0.1	3.7	-0.4	-9.3	0.8	2.0	1.4	1.7	1.5	1.5	1.5
Rwanda	0.1	5.7	5.0	3.6	-1.9	22.9	-10.4	13.2	-29.1	45.3	3.3
Seychelles	0.2	62.5	9.1	6.8	10.6	48.0	11.2	1.9	-0.1	-1.9	0.3
Somalia	0.0	0.9	-2.0	-7.9	-10.3	-2.0	2.0	-73.8	6.3	3.0	3.5
Uganda	0.2	6.9	-15.6	5.6	10.5	-13.8	-1.5	8.5	0.3	17.0	8.2
United Republic Of Tanzania	0.4	14.4	3.7	1.1	9.8	-0.6	2.5	29.8	18.4	17.8	20.3
Zambia	1.0	34.3	1.6	-2.3	3.7	19.2	5.0	4.9	-14.4	28.3	-22.3
Zimbabwe	1.4	22.9	130.0	7.5	6.3	6.3	6.3	6.3	-16.6	-3.6	-1.9
Middle Africa	*11.3*	*36.6*	*3.6*	*3.5*	*4.8*	*3.2*	*5.6*	*27.3*	*15.3*	*-3.6*	*3.9*
Angola	2.7	39.0	0.2	8.0	5.6	0.0	13.3	4.5	8.3	-10.3	11.5
Cameroon	1.8	17.9	2.4	2.1	11.9	6.3	6.6	151.6	31.8	-6.6	-0.2
Central African Republic	0.2	17.3	4.3	4.4	-7.6	0.4	1.6	-33.8	19.0	-1.2	0.5
Chad	0.2	18.2	-2.6	4.7	2.8	24.2	13.0	-19.6	8.9	-7.7	-2.3
Congo	0.9	48.6	9.5	6.9	2.6	0.5	-1.0	42.8	17.1	-1.1	8.0
Democratic Republic of the Congo	3.8	59.4	3.2	4.5	-3.0	-3.9	0.0	-10.3	-4.3	-4.4	2.1
Equatorial Guinea	0.0	32.2	7.6	1.0	35.5	122.5	23.1	30.4	18.2	65.4	8.7
Gabon	1.7	46.0	7.4	-2.4	4.5	3.6	-2.7	4.4	11.0	-5.2	-1.5
Sao Tome and Principe	0.0	22.9	8.7	0.2	9.1	20.6	2.0	37.0	0.0	-1.0	9.9
Northern Africa	*43.5*	*27.3*	*8.4*	*1.4*	*2.1*	*2.1*	*2.3*	*7.3*	*16.5*	*-2.0*	*12.2*
Algeria	9.9	23.4	2.5	2.4	2.8	6.3	1.7	6.0	8.8	-2.2	3.6
Egypt	13.6	28.1	5.1	5.8	3.3	-3.6	9.1	3.8	3.3	-7.8	30.2
Libyan Arab Jamahiriya	9.7	50.4	24.4	-5.2	-8.1	-4.8	-27.4	28.7	53.8	-7.5	50.1
Morocco	4.3	24.6	5.0	4.1	5.0	6.8	1.3	6.7	4.8	7.8	8.4
Sudan	2.3	9.8	-0.4	2.4	5.6	5.5	3.8	20.3	114.8	-3.2	-20.5
Tunisia	3.7	43.6	10.8	4.8	4.5	10.1	4.4	4.7	5.3	11.5	-3.7
Southern Africa	*21.6*	*26.5*	*1.3*	*1.8*	*4.0*	*5.6*	*2.5*	*0.8*	*9.2*	*3.1*	*-2.1*
Botswana [1]	1.3	55.8	32.8	14.2	0.8	12.6	6.0	-19.6	39.8	6.0	-14.8
Lesotho	0.1	16.7	13.7	3.4	8.6	22.1	-12.5	15.1	25.1	32.6	22.3
Namibia	0.8	52.1	1.6	-1.3	4.5	-2.7	-0.3	8.7	-1.4	1.8	1.4
South Africa	18.9	24.7	0.9	1.3	4.2	5.6	2.5	1.4	8.4	2.5	-1.4
Swaziland	0.4	73.4	8.8	7.7	5.1	3.3	3.0	17.5	-8.6	16.6	-7.3
Western Africa	*16.2*	*32.4*	*6.4*	*2.7*	*1.9*	*3.5*	*9.8*	*-4.5*	*-1.8*	*-0.8*	*-4.1*
Benin	0.3	20.4	6.1	-3.8	6.2	9.5	11.1	13.8	7.2	3.0	4.0
Burkina Faso	0.2	11.2	8.4	-0.8	5.2	5.7	43.4	2.6	-7.7	20.9	-2.5
Cape Verde	0.0	17.1	-8.9	7.6	4.6	25.5	-6.0	3.7	0.9	3.9	25.2
Cote d'Ivoire	2.3	28.8	6.8	3.3	5.7	9.0	2.3	9.5	-2.0	-24.0	2.1
Gambia	0.1	43.2	-0.1	4.9	5.3	20.5	28.5	-62.3	13.3	5.6	6.2
Ghana	0.7	15.4	-4.6	0.6	9.5	-0.4	16.0	-4.5	-2.3	0.3	2.4

Table 5.D. Average Rates of Growth of Gross Domestic Product by Expenditure - Exports of Goods and Services

Major area, region and country	Base year weights as percentage of total for world or region in 1990	Base year share as percentage of total GDP in 1990	Average rates of growth			Annual rate of change (percentage)					
			1970-1979	1980-1989	1990-1999	1997	1998	1999	2000	2001	2002
Guinea	0.6	30.9	2.8	-1.3	4.1	3.5	12.8	3.2	3.0	3.3	5.2
Guinea-Bissau	0.0	9.9	9.1	15.3	6.3	21.1	-51.9	114.5	26.1	-5.7	-4.6
Liberia	0.1	34.2	0.6	-7.9	-9.4	172.4	29.7	22.9	22.3	4.9	3.3
Mali	0.3	17.3	-0.8	6.5	9.2	54.0	12.7	-10.4	19.3	24.1	-13.1
Mauritania	0.4	57.6	1.6	7.2	3.4	4.2	3.6	3.9	0.5	-1.0	1.2
Niger	0.3	16.8	10.5	2.3	1.6	-0.6	19.7	-10.7	-5.1	2.5	22.5
Nigeria	9.6	43.2	11.1	3.9	-1.6	-4.9	10.3	-12.4	-6.0	5.5	-12.2
Senegal	1.0	25.4	7.2	2.1	5.4	23.6	10.5	7.2	2.9	1.9	1.2
Sierra Leone	0.1	26.3	3.3	0.4	-4.2	-12.5	0.3	-5.6	-38.2	15.6	6.3
Togo	0.2	23.2	2.9	1.9	1.5	7.5	-0.3	20.6	1.0	0.3	3.4
AMERICAS	**20.4**	**12.3**	**6.0**	**5.3**	**7.2**	**10.7**	**4.3**	**5.5**	**9.9**	**-3.5**	**-0.1**
NORTHERN AMERICA	**15.7**	**11.2**	**6.0**	**5.5**	**7.2**	**11.4**	**3.6**	**5.0**	**9.5**	**-4.8**	**-1.2**
Bermuda	0.1	47.5	3.5	1.2	1.7	5.2	0.8	5.0	5.7	2.5	1.0
Canada	16.3	26.0	4.0	4.6	7.9	8.3	9.1	10.8	8.8	-3.1	-0.1
United States	60.7	9.7	6.7	5.7	6.9	12.2	2.1	3.4	9.7	-5.4	-1.6
LATIN AMERICA AND THE CARIBBEAN	**4.7**	**18.2**	**5.9**	**4.9**	**7.2**	**8.3**	**6.5**	**7.0**	**11.0**	**0.8**	**3.5**
Caribbean	*5.2*	*52.9*	*5.1*	*4.5*	*2.4*	*7.3*	*2.8*	*7.1*	*12.5*	*0.2*	*2.3*
Anguilla	0.0	75.6	3.8	9.8	2.5	11.4	21.7	-14.3	-5.9	8.1	-11.5
Antigua and Barbuda	0.0	82.7	3.5	5.2	2.3	7.5	2.6	0.9	-6.0	-4.2	-1.6
Aruba	0.1	80.1	9.2	10.0	5.9	2.7	2.9	2.7	-4.0	-4.3	-7.0
Bahamas	0.2	55.7	7.6	3.9	1.6	-0.8	11.3	5.8	4.3	-2.8	3.4
Barbados	0.1	49.1	6.1	-0.5	1.0	-1.3	0.1	-1.0	-0.6	0.1	-7.3
British Virgin Islands	0.0	94.5	15.8	11.9	8.8	14.0	11.2	10.9	14.4	6.3	11.3
Cayman Islands	0.0	64.1	11.8	8.4	2.2	0.5	1.5	0.7	0.7	0.7	0.8
Cuba	0.6	30.2	6.4	7.2	0.8	2.7	-8.2	22.8	0.6	-7.2	-10.7
Dominica	0.0	50.1	-4.6	9.4	6.1	11.4	7.6	1.0	-7.8	-17.6	-3.0
Dominican Republic	0.4	43.7	11.3	1.3	6.5	9.0	6.8	6.6	6.4	-7.2	-3.4
Grenada	0.0	44.4	-2.6	-2.3	8.1	3.3	17.4	30.8	7.6	-18.2	-9.0
Guadeloupe	0.0	4.9	0.5	-3.8	1.5	9.2	4.1	5.9	5.9	5.9	4.2
Haiti	0.1	18.1	8.9	0.1	4.5	5.8	21.8	3.5	6.3	-14.5	-2.9
Jamaica	0.2	51.7	0.6	4.1	0.7	-13.0	4.5	-1.2	1.3	1.7	-1.3
Martinique	0.0	8.4	4.0	2.2	1.0	1.6	4.1	2.5	2.5	2.5	2.6
Montserrat	0.0	28.6	2.5	4.9	-0.9	-63.3	-37.5	46.4	-22.8	-17.7	2.2
Netherlands Antilles	0.2	81.5	2.3	-2.3	1.4	-7.1	5.1	-0.5	-5.4	-2.4	-1.2
Puerto Rico	2.7	78.0	5.1	5.8	2.0	12.1	3.5	6.3	17.3	4.1	8.5
Saint Kitts and Nevis	0.0	51.7	9.9	5.1	2.5	4.8	3.4	-5.9	-0.6	4.1	1.6
Saint Lucia	0.0	68.5	5.4	6.7	0.8	-13.3	3.2	24.7	3.0	-11.9	2.6
Saint Vincent and the Grenadines	0.0	65.8	3.0	7.8	1.4	-4.0	5.3	11.3	1.9	-4.4	-2.5
Trinidad and Tobago	0.3	49.1	1.1	1.9	4.0	13.9	-0.7	3.6	45.0	-0.4	-11.5
Turks and Caicos Islands	0.0	70.0	1.0	6.5	5.0	4.6	6.4	22.7	19.5	4.9	-5.7
Central America	*6.5*	*20.3*	*7.7*	*6.3*	*11.4*	*11.0*	*11.6*	*11.5*	*15.2*	*-3.4*	*1.4*
Belize	0.0	60.3	-3.4	13.3	4.2	19.7	-0.5	13.5	5.5	15.3	10.5
Costa Rica	0.2	29.9	7.2	5.2	11.7	8.6	26.7	21.3	-0.3	-9.8	4.2
El Salvador	0.1	18.6	7.5	-6.5	14.7	30.2	6.3	7.1	16.8	-0.4	5.7
Guatemala	0.2	19.7	6.7	-2.2	6.7	10.2	8.5	4.6	3.8	-4.0	-6.7
Honduras	0.1	37.2	5.8	0.2	0.6	1.3	1.6	-11.2	8.0	5.1	2.1
Mexico	5.3	18.6	8.6	7.9	12.3	10.7	12.1	12.4	16.4	-3.6	1.4
Nicaragua	0.1	15.4	5.1	-3.5	2.4	14.4	5.8	12.3	12.5	8.7	-3.3
Panama	0.5	86.8	4.4	5.1	2.6	12.7	-2.4	-8.5	6.5	5.0	-1.8
South America	*11.2*	*13.3*	*5.5*	*4.3*	*6.1*	*6.6*	*3.6*	*3.0*	*6.7*	*5.2*	*5.8*
Argentina	1.6	10.3	5.9	2.9	8.0	12.2	10.6	-1.3	2.7	2.7	0.0
Bolivia	0.1	22.8	3.7	1.1	4.2	-2.1	6.5	-12.8	12.9	11.4	12.4
Brazil	3.8	7.9	8.6	9.8	4.7	1.8	0.2	12.0	11.0	10.1	18.9
Chile	1.2	33.1	9.8	6.7	9.6	11.2	5.2	7.3	5.4	6.1	1.3

Table 5.D. Average Rates of Growth of Gross Domestic Product by Expenditure - Exports of Goods and Services

Major area, region and country	Base year weights as percentage of total for world or region in 1990	Base year share as percentage of total GDP in 1990	Average rates of growth			Annual rate of change (percentage)					
			1970-1979	1980-1989	1990-1999	1997	1998	1999	2000	2001	2002
Colombia	1.0	18.6	6.4	4.9	6.6	3.2	7.4	5.9	6.1	2.7	-3.
Ecuador	0.4	31.4	15.9	3.9	6.9	7.8	-5.1	7.8	-1.0	-1.3	0.
French Guiana	0.1	67.3	22.9	37.8	2.9	1.8	0.8	1.4	1.4	1.4	1.
Guyana	0.0	68.1	-2.7	-1.7	7.6	3.2	-4.5	6.1	-3.1	0.0	2.
Paraguay	0.2	33.2	13.6	4.2	1.9	-11.8	-7.2	-27.0	-15.1	-0.4	14.
Peru	0.5	14.5	4.5	-1.3	5.7	13.1	5.6	7.6	7.9	7.1	6.
Suriname	0.0	27.4	4.8	-3.9	3.4	-6.6	-24.4	19.9	10.8	26.3	-33.
Uruguay	0.2	26.2	7.6	3.8	5.7	13.7	0.0	-7.3	6.4	-8.9	-10.
Venezuela	2.1	39.5	1.8	-0.6	5.1	9.4	4.2	-10.8	5.5	-0.9	-7.
ASIA	**22.3**	**18.3**	**9.3**	**5.0**	**7.7**	**9.9**	**2.4**	**6.7**	**17.3**	**-1.0**	**10.**
Eastern Asia	*63.7*	*16.2*	*10.5*	*8.9*	*7.3*	*12.6*	*2.0*	*7.5*	*17.9*	*-2.2*	*12.*
China	6.8	17.7	19.8	15.1	10.3	22.9	7.2	13.9	32.0	7.3	20.
Democratic People's Rep. of Korea	0.2	9.8	16.6	10.6	-3.3	-6.3	-1.1	6.2	0.3	4.3	0
Hong Kong SAR of China	9.9	130.7	8.2	13.5	8.4	5.3	-3.8	4.0	16.6	-1.8	9.
Japan	31.7	10.4	8.6	6.2	3.9	11.3	-2.3	1.5	12.4	-6.1	8.
Macao SAR of China	0.3	96.9	8.2	7.9	2.4	-1.7	-2.5	1.1	18.9	7.3	15.
Mongolia	0.1	18.9	5.7	6.3	-0.4	4.0	3.5	3.2	1.1	1.0	4.
Republic of Korea	7.3	29.1	21.8	11.3	14.0	21.4	14.1	15.8	20.5	0.7	14.
South Central Asia	*8.0*	*12.3*	*3.4*	*2.6*	*12.0*	*-5.7*	*11.0*	*11.9*	*15.9*	*4.8*	*16.*
Bangladesh	0.2	6.7	-3.1	9.6	11.3	12.3	6.0	4.8	22.8	16.8	-17.
Bhutan	0.0	28.3	6.4	15.2	6.5	6.4	0.6	1.8	5.3	-13.2	31.
India	2.3	7.2	2.6	5.5	11.7	-2.3	13.9	18.0	23.4	6.0	23.
Iran (Islamic Republic of)	1.3	14.8	5.3	-3.5	6.0	-4.8	10.5	2.1	1.7	0.3	8.
Kazakhstan	0.6	7.8	...	...	-4.6	1.2	-11.9	3.0	28.8	-1.8	21.
Kyrgyzstan	0.4	29.2	...	...	-9.3	21.1	-8.7	-10.4	10.5	-3.2	8.
Maldives	0.0	91.6	11.5	11.7	8.8	9.8	7.2	6.4	7.6	0.2	6.
Nepal	0.0	10.5	13.1	3.4	12.7	24.3	-10.1	4.0	8.1	0.7	-28.
Pakistan	0.8	16.9	1.6	7.7	4.5	-5.7	-2.9	16.0	11.8	5.4	39.
Sri Lanka	0.2	30.3	0.6	5.4	8.3	11.6	0.1	5.8	17.1	-8.0	2
Tajikistan	0.0	57.4	...	...	-9.9	13.8	-36.0	41.7	43.5	-11.2	-0.
Turkmenistan	0.7	57.5	...	...	3.0	-57.0	109.7	16.5	10.0	7.9	9.
Uzbekistan	1.4	28.8	...	...	-0.1	-8.3	1.7	8.6	2.9	4.1	4.
South-Eastern Asia	*11.0*	*31.0*	*9.9*	*6.7*	*9.1*	*7.4*	*4.7*	*-1.0*	*16.9*	*-2.9*	*5.*
Brunei Darussalam	0.4	105.6	10.8	-1.3	0.4	3.0	2.0	-7.3	2.8	3.0	3.
Cambodia	0.0	1.9	-7.3	-1.1	16.5	33.9	12.2	15.0	36.5	14.6	21.
Indonesia	2.9	25.3	9.1	1.7	4.4	7.8	11.2	-31.8	26.5	1.9	-1.
Lao People's Democratic Republic	0.0	18.3	0.2	23.9	14.2	13.9	61.4	7.3	35.0	18.3	30.
Malaysia	3.3	74.5	11.0	9.4	12.5	5.5	0.5	13.2	16.1	-7.5	4.
Myanmar	0.0	1.9	5.2	2.9	9.0	21.2	17.3	5.1	5.1	5.1	5.
Philippines	1.2	27.5	6.7	6.8	5.9	17.2	-21.0	3.6	17.0	-3.4	3.
Singapore [2]	0.3	9.0	-6.8	13.5	12.5	-6.4	70.3	5.4	-12.4	23.0	19.
Thailand	2.9	34.1	9.7	13.2	10.3	7.2	8.2	9.0	17.5	-4.1	10.
Timor-Leste	0.0	12.6	...	...	-0.2	4.0	14.9	-23.4	-47.2	36.6	67.
Vietnam [3]	-0.1	-9.2	-0.1	0.6	0.8	-12.0	15.6	-35.9	-14.1	-8.2	46.
Western Asia	*17.3*	*32.9*	*9.2*	*-3.5*	*6.1*	*8.5*	*-1.8*	*8.5*	*15.6*	*3.7*	*5.*
Armenia	0.5	35.0	...	...	-10.2	-6.5	-1.6	13.7	19.0	22.8	27.
Azerbaijan	1.0	43.9	...	...	7.4	45.0	13.9	50.0	15.4	34.1	13.
Bahrain	0.4	91.9	10.2	-0.2	4.5	0.7	1.5	3.8	8.3	4.1	5.
Cyprus	0.3	51.5	7.5	9.6	2.0	0.8	-2.4	6.3	9.1	4.1	-5.
Georgia	0.9	40.0	...	...	-17.5	29.5	8.7	19.1	23.4	11.4	23.
Iraq	0.7	18.5	19.0	-10.9	-12.5	143.1	26.7	25.6	20.2	26.0	-18.
Israel	1.8	30.8	9.2	4.9	7.8	8.6	6.4	12.0	24.0	-11.5	-3.
Jordan	0.2	61.9	24.1	8.5	1.9	-3.6	-6.0	2.9	6.1	4.3	7.
Kuwait	0.8	44.8	-0.9	-4.1	1.3	0.0	0.3	-8.1	-30.4	-4.8	-10.
Lebanon	0.0	16.3	-9.5	-10.7	5.7	-33.9	-1.2	-0.7	5.9	7.5	2.
Oman [4]	0.6	47.2	2.8	10.7	6.0	8.7	1.1	1.5	9.8	20.2	-3.
Qatar	0.4	53.5	3.8	-2.8	8.8	27.2	39.1	12.1	6.0	-5.5	4.
Saudi Arabia	4.9	46.8	10.3	-9.2	1.7	0.4	-22.1	15.8	31.4	-2.8	12.

Table 5.D. Average Rates of Growth of Gross Domestic Product by Expenditure - Exports of Goods and Services

Major area, region and country	Base year weights as percentage of total for world or region in 1990	Base year share as percentage of total GDP in 1990	Average rates of growth			Annual rate of change (percentage)					
			1970-1979	1980-1989	1990-1999	1997	1998	1999	2000	2001	2002
Syrian Arab Republic	0.4	28.3	2.2	4.9	10.7	15.1	0.5	9.6	0.5	13.0	11.8
Turkey	2.0	13.3	4.6	15.2	9.1	19.1	12.0	-7.0	19.2	7.4	11.0
United Arab Emirates	2.2	65.4	33.7	-1.4	7.1	4.1	-10.1	9.7	6.0	4.2	-1.1
Yemen	0.2	13.9	...	...	13.1	0.3	-19.2	36.4	46.2	2.0	-0.9
Yemen Arab Republic (Former)	...	...	30.3	15.5	...	...	...	...	...	...	...
Yemen Democratic (Former)	...	...	2.4	-5.3	...	...	...	...	...	...	...
EUROPE	**52.6**	**26.6**	**5.9**	**4.1**	**6.8**	**9.7**	**6.3**	**5.3**	**12.2**	**3.3**	**2.0**
Eastern Europe	*14.8*	*23.2*	*7.7*	*6.1*	*18.4*	*4.9*	*3.9*	*6.9*	*14.5*	*6.0*	*8.2*
Belarus	1.3	50.0	...	...	-6.9	33.9	-8.3	7.0	12.7	10.5	10.1
Bulgaria	0.3	33.1	7.1	3.6	2.4	12.8	-4.7	-5.0	16.6	10.0	6.2
Czech Republic	0.7	41.8	...	15.9	6.8	9.2	10.0	6.1	17.0	11.9	2.8
Hungary [5]	0.5	30.3	9.1	3.8	9.2	22.3	18.9	12.4	21.0	8.8	3.8
Poland	0.7	27.5	5.7	1.3	9.2	12.2	14.3	-2.6	23.2	3.1	4.8
Republic of Moldova	0.4	48.7	...	...	-9.1	1.7	-26.4	3.1	9.5	17.2	19.0
Romania	0.3	16.7	10.0	0.8	-0.2	11.4	-1.7	10.5	23.4	11.1	16.9
Russian Federation	7.4	18.2	...	...	-0.2	-0.5	1.9	11.2	9.5	4.2	9.9
Slovakia	0.2	25.7	...	-0.9	10.8	17.6	12.8	5.0	13.7	6.3	5.5
Ukraine	3.2	29.4	...	...	-8.8	-5.4	1.2	-2.2	21.5	3.5	9.1
Northern Europe	*20.6*	*28.4*	*5.1*	*3.7*	*6.8*	*10.2*	*5.7*	*6.1*	*11.7*	*2.9*	*1.5*
Denmark	2.0	35.8	4.5	5.0	4.4	4.1	4.3	12.3	13.0	3.0	5.8
Estonia	0.2	42.0	...	...	6.4	29.5	12.0	0.5	28.6	-0.2	6.0
Finland	1.3	22.7	5.6	3.2	7.5	13.7	9.2	6.5	19.3	-0.8	4.9
Iceland	0.1	34.4	6.2	2.8	2.7	5.8	2.0	4.0	5.0	7.7	3.7
Ireland	1.1	57.0	7.5	8.3	13.8	17.4	21.0	15.2	20.6	8.3	6.2
Latvia	0.4	47.7	...	...	-2.8	13.1	4.9	-6.4	12.0	6.9	6.3
Lithuania	0.4	52.1	...	...	-3.5	18.7	4.6	-16.8	9.8	21.2	19.5
Norway	2.0	40.4	6.0	4.9	5.7	7.7	0.6	2.8	4.0	4.1	-0.5
Sweden	3.0	29.7	4.3	4.0	6.8	13.8	8.6	7.4	11.5	0.2	0.2
United Kingdom	10.1	24.0	5.1	2.9	5.6	8.4	2.8	4.3	9.4	2.5	-0.9
Southern Europe	*16.4*	*20.9*	*7.8*	*3.7*	*6.9*	*9.8*	*5.6*	*3.1*	*11.0*	*2.1*	*-0.9*
Albania [6]	0.0	-7.4	6.2	-35.2	22.7	-34.6	57.1	12.1	2.0	23.7	6.2
Andorra	0.0	16.3	12.7	9.6	12.0	15.4	7.8	7.6	10.7	5.2	2.3
Bosnia and Herzegovina	0.3	48.0	...	...	4.9	30.0	20.0	14.1	5.6	1.6	-29.8
Croatia	0.8	77.7	...	...	-8.4	7.6	3.9	0.7	12.0	8.7	1.2
Greece	0.6	18.1	14.5	2.8	6.3	20.0	5.3	18.1	14.1	-1.1	-7.7
Holy See	0.0	19.7	8.9	3.2	5.6	6.5	3.5	0.2	11.9	1.1	-0.9
Italy	9.2	19.7	7.9	2.8	5.4	6.4	3.4	0.1	11.7	1.1	-1.0
Malta	0.1	85.3	13.0	2.9	6.1	4.1	7.9	8.4	6.0	2.5	24.2
Portugal	1.0	32.9	4.5	7.1	5.3	7.1	9.1	2.9	8.0	1.9	2.1
San Marino	0.1	216.9	3.6	2.4	1.8	13.2	-7.3	6.4	10.5	-1.9	0.6
Serbia and Montenegro	0.1	11.3	...	...	-9.2	23.9	31.4	-63.8	-14.7	82.3	3.4
Slovenia	0.7	90.8	...	...	-1.5	11.3	7.4	1.6	13.0	6.4	6.5
Spain	3.5	16.3	7.6	5.1	9.5	15.3	8.2	7.7	10.0	3.6	0.0
TFYR Macedonia	0.0	25.9	...	...	2.2	29.3	8.5	6.9	21.5	-12.0	2.3
Yugoslavia (Former)	...	...	4.8	6.2	...	...	...	...	...	...	...
Western Europe	*48.1*	*30.1*	*5.6*	*4.3*	*5.6*	*10.3*	*7.3*	*5.4*	*12.3*	*3.3*	*2.0*
Austria	2.7	39.6	7.0	4.5	5.5	12.4	8.1	8.5	13.4	7.5	3.7
Belgium	5.9	70.8	5.3	4.1	4.5	5.9	6.0	5.1	8.4	1.3	1.0
France	10.9	21.2	7.4	4.1	5.9	11.8	8.3	4.3	12.6	1.6	1.5
Germany	17.7	25.1	5.0	4.6	6.0	11.2	7.0	5.5	13.7	5.6	3.4
Liechtenstein	0.0	36.3	5.6	4.4	3.7	9.8	6.2	7.1	12.7	0.0	0.5
Luxembourg	0.5	104.1	3.6	5.3	8.3	14.8	14.1	14.8	16.8	2.6	-0.3
Monaco	0.0	21.2	8.0	4.9	6.6	12.6	9.0	5.0	13.2	2.2	2.0
Netherlands	6.8	54.5	5.5	4.1	6.2	8.8	7.4	5.1	11.3	1.7	0.1
Switzerland	3.5	36.3	4.1	3.6	2.9	8.6	5.0	5.8	11.5	-1.0	-0.4

Table 5.D. Average Rates of Growth of Gross Domestic Product by Expenditure - Exports of Goods and Services

Major area, region and country	Base year weights as percentage of total for world or region in 1990	Base year share as percentage of total GDP in 1990	Average rates of growth			Annual rate of change (percentage)					
			1970-1979	1980-1989	1990-1999	1997	1998	1999	2000	2001	2002
OCEANIA	**1.5**	**18.3**	**4.5**	**4.4**	**7.2**	**3.1**	**2.2**	**8.7**	**6.8**	**-1.4**	**0.6**
Australia & New Zealand	*95.1*	*17.9*	*4.3*	*4.7*	*7.4*	*3.7*	*2.2*	*9.0*	*7.1*	*-1.3*	*0.6*
Australia	77.5	16.7	4.4	5.0	7.7	3.7	2.0	9.3	7.3	-1.9	-0.7
New Zealand	17.7	27.0	3.8	3.6	5.7	3.8	2.9	7.3	6.2	2.0	7.1
Melanesia	*4.0*	*35.9*	*9.5*	*0.1*	*3.4*	*-10.9*	*3.4*	*0.5*	*0.2*	*-5.6*	*-1.3*
Fiji	1.2	62.3	4.9	3.4	4.2	-4.2	2.4	13.5	-3.0	-0.5	5.7
New Caledonia	0.4	11.0	5.5	-7.7	-1.5	2.0	-3.2	0.9	2.1	-1.1	0.7
Papua New Guinea	2.1	43.0	19.6	3.0	4.2	-16.4	5.6	-4.4	2.4	-8.9	-4.8
Solomon Islands	0.1	47.0	17.7	3.4	3.6	-2.9	0.6	-0.8	-14.1	-5.0	-3.9
Vanuatu	0.1	46.4	7.7	1.5	5.1	4.1	-3.8	-2.9	2.4	-1.7	-3.3
Micronesia	*0.3*	*49.8*	*5.0*	*-0.3*	*1.0*	*-2.5*	*-0.1*	*-2.9*	*1.2*	*2.1*	*1.0*
Kiribati	0.0	58.7	2.9	-4.9	4.5	5.7	5.0	9.3	1.6	1.8	0.9
Marshall Islands	0.0	11.0	10.5	-5.8	-4.7	-10.3	1.6	0.0	-1.0	1.7	2.5
Micronesia (Federated States of)	0.1	58.7	6.6	4.5	1.2	-5.1	-2.1	-2.8	2.1	1.5	0.8
Nauru	0.0	58.7	6.8	4.9	-5.4	-7.3	-1.9	-1.9	-1.0	-0.8	0.9
Palau	0.1	58.7	2.9	-5.5	3.7	2.3	2.0	-8.8	0.3	4.5	1.1
Polynesia	*0.6*	*11.5*	*-0.2*	*5.6*	*2.3*	*0.9*	*0.3*	*1.3*	*3.3*	*1.5*	*3.3*
Cook Islands	0.0	7.6	-6.6	-13.0	-0.4	-6.1	25.3	2.6	14.1	5.1	3.7
French Polynesia	0.4	9.4	-1.1	7.7	3.8	1.1	1.1	2.7	2.7	2.1	1.9
Samoa	0.1	30.6	4.5	3.1	-1.4	1.6	4.7	-0.2	-1.7	6.3	4.8
Tonga	0.1	34.0	-1.6	4.7	-4.1	-3.4	-20.4	-15.9	28.7	-20.2	25.6
Tuvalu	0.0	11.6	10.5	-12.6	2.0	3.5	14.9	3.0	3.0	3.0	-11.5

Notes for Table 5.D - Exports of goods and services

1/ 1974-1975
Exports of goods only.

2/ 1970-2002
Exports less imports.

3/ 1970-2002
Exports less imports.

4/ 1993-1998
Data for this year(s) have not been revised.

5/ 1988-1991
Does not include direct purchases in the domestic market by non-resident households.

6/ 1980-1990
Exports less imports.

Table 5.E. Average Rates of Growth of Gross Domestic Product by Expenditure - Imports of Goods and Services

Major area, region and country	Base year weights as percentage of total for world or region in 1990	Base year share as percentage of total GDP in 1990	Average rates of growth			Annual rate of change (percentage)					
			1970-1979	1980-1989	1990-1999	1997	1998	1999	2000	2001	2002
WORLD	**100.0**	**20.2**	**6.0**	**4.2**	**6.8**	**9.4**	**5.8**	**6.1**	**12.1**	**0.5**	**3.3**
DEVELOPED ECONOMIES	**67.9**	**18.3**	**5.3**	**4.5**	**6.2**	**9.8**	**8.5**	**8.0**	**10.9**	**0.2**	**1.7**
DEVELOPING ECONOMIES	**21.0**	**24.8**	**8.3**	**3.3**	**7.4**	**8.6**	**-0.5**	**3.5**	**14.1**	**-1.2**	**5.6**
TRANSITION ECONOMIES	**11.1**	**27.4**	**7.2**	**1.1**	**-2.8**	**8.0**	**2.2**	**-4.6**	**18.5**	**11.8**	**12.0**
AFRICA	**3.2**	**27.8**	**6.1**	**-1.2**	**4.1**	**6.3**	**3.5**	**7.1**	**2.0**	**5.1**	**6.0**
Eastern Africa	*11.7*	*29.7*	*0.9*	*2.3*	*5.4*	*11.5*	*-1.8*	*8.6*	*2.3*	*3.6*	*-4.9*
Burundi	0.2	26.2	8.7	-0.3	4.1	1.1	4.4	5.3	64.9	-13.9	9.6
Comoros	0.1	37.3	-3.9	1.4	0.5	0.3	2.3	-10.6	-11.3	6.1	-3.4
Djibouti	0.3	109.3	0.4	-0.2	-3.2	26.5	9.0	-10.3	3.6	-3.5	5.0
Eritrea	...	...	...	...	17.6	5.7	-4.3	2.1	-17.6	3.7	7.9
Ethiopia	...	...	...	...	20.2	1.8	11.7	123.9	25.3	9.6	-8.3
Ethiopia (Former)	0.7	12.2	7.1	1.7	-13.9	...	...	...	...	...	...
Kenya	1.8	31.4	0.7	0.3	5.2	2.6	-4.4	-6.1	17.7	5.8	-16.7
Madagascar	0.6	26.9	-1.8	-1.2	8.2	3.8	5.4	20.3	23.5	0.4	-38.5
Malawi	0.4	36.2	5.7	1.7	3.7	8.5	1.5	3.1	3.3	-0.4	9.5
Mauritius	1.3	74.3	7.5	6.7	5.5	9.9	7.5	4.5	-1.9	7.0	-4.4
Mozambique	0.7	38.3	3.9	0.7	5.3	0.4	8.4	40.4	-9.0	-14.9	16.6
Reunion	1.4	40.7	6.0	7.2	1.2	1.7	2.0	1.8	1.6	1.6	1.6
Rwanda	0.2	14.1	5.0	4.3	-6.3	36.4	-8.0	-0.1	-26.4	15.0	19.1
Seychelles	0.2	66.7	7.6	9.8	9.0	...	...	...	...	...	...
Somalia	0.0	5.7	2.8	-6.7	-14.9	0.0	1.5	-57.1	3.0	3.0	3.5
Uganda	0.4	17.7	-15.9	16.2	7.0	-10.0	13.0	1.6	1.0	13.5	10.5
United Republic Of Tanzania	1.0	38.9	3.2	2.3	5.0	-1.7	6.7	-4.6	0.1	8.1	6.1
Zambia	0.9	33.8	-6.7	-3.2	1.3	4.8	4.6	1.6	-20.1	1.2	1.8
Zimbabwe	1.4	22.8	-9.4	4.9	9.3	71.9	-23.3	-3.9	-21.6	-0.7	-12.4
Middle Africa	*9.8*	*32.0*	*5.1*	*-0.7*	*5.3*	*7.4*	*13.1*	*24.8*	*-12.6*	*15.0*	*-2.0*
Angola	1.7	23.7	-0.3	0.1	8.0	6.0	12.0	40.2	-27.4	7.5	9.7
Cameroon	2.1	21.1	5.9	-3.1	10.6	4.8	4.9	146.5	-7.9	11.0	-0.3
Central African Republic	0.3	30.1	0.7	3.5	-8.7	1.5	3.9	-59.3	12.4	1.1	-2.0
Chad [1]	0.5	45.9	-1.6	7.6	3.0	8.2	1.0	4.6	10.0	50.7	39.7
Congo	0.6	33.9	8.2	1.9	-5.6	-0.6	-2.8	-39.7	-16.3	17.8	5.2
Democratic Republic of the Congo	3.5	54.7	7.8	-0.5	-3.4	-2.8	3.6	-10.5	-4.3	-4.4	4.7
Equatorial Guinea	0.1	69.6	16.3	-3.1	37.5	31.7	71.6	-31.9	-18.4	58.0	-46.6
Gabon	1.1	30.9	7.4	-1.4	2.0	15.0	-7.5	15.3	-13.4	7.3	-1.6
Sao Tome and Principe	0.0	72.5	1.8	6.1	6.2	3.7	2.4	25.7	1.4	-25.8	2.4
Northern Africa	*48.9*	*30.8*	*9.3*	*-1.7*	*2.7*	*4.5*	*3.0*	*10.0*	*3.9*	*1.4*	*17.7*
Algeria	10.6	25.1	10.6	-0.9	-2.7	2.4	7.3	1.7	-2.5	3.9	2.6
Egypt	17.5	36.2	5.5	-0.9	2.2	8.0	2.9	-3.4	-1.1	-6.0	15.4
Libyan Arab Jamahiriya	5.7	29.8	23.7	-5.6	-2.8	-7.3	-4.0	-17.5	-7.2	33.4	82.4
Morocco	5.2	29.9	8.2	3.1	3.8	6.4	3.3	2.6	11.4	0.6	8.0
Sudan	5.6	24.5	8.0	-5.5	11.4	2.5	1.7	68.8	11.7	-1.5	22.3
Tunisia	4.2	50.6	11.5	2.1	3.6	8.8	5.7	3.0	8.9	13.6	-3.8
Southern Africa	*17.5*	*21.6*	*0.2*	*2.0*	*4.7*	*5.6*	*2.4*	*-5.4*	*4.7*	*0.7*	*2.4*
Botswana [2]	1.2	49.7	18.4	9.2	4.4	16.2	23.0	5.5	-4.0	-4.5	0.7
Lesotho	0.5	121.9	17.5	3.1	1.0	1.1	-11.3	-11.1	-6.1	7.1	14.3
Namibia	1.1	67.7	2.0	-1.3	4.5	3.4	7.7	0.1	-12.4	4.8	-8.5
South Africa	14.2	18.6	-0.6	1.8	4.8	5.4	1.5	-7.4	7.1	0.3	3.1
Swaziland	0.5	88.9	8.4	7.2	5.6	4.8	3.1	46.9	-5.8	11.5	-5.5
Western Africa	*12.1*	*24.2*	*8.0*	*-5.4*	*5.9*	*7.4*	*5.8*	*5.4*	*2.9*	*17.9*	*-7.4*
Benin	0.4	28.2	9.1	-1.8	3.7	11.4	9.9	16.6	5.3	4.5	3.0
Burkina Faso	0.6	28.8	10.5	-0.8	3.9	-1.0	32.1	-6.2	-9.9	46.5	-2.7
Cape Verde	0.1	68.6	-6.0	6.5	6.0	6.7	2.7	18.7	14.0	3.3	-22.2
Cote d'Ivoire	2.0	24.6	9.3	-3.3	5.7	8.6	5.6	-0.1	-17.0	10.9	7.0
Gambia	0.1	57.7	6.1	-4.3	5.3	26.8	25.0	-69.4	9.5	7.3	5.1
Ghana	1.0	24.0	-5.0	-1.2	7.6	14.7	4.1	1.0	-17.3	2.0	-2.6

Table 5.E. Average Rates of Growth of Gross Domestic Product by Expenditure - Imports of Goods and Services

Major area, region and country	Base year weights as percentage of total for world or region in 1990	Base year share as percentage of total GDP in 1990	Average rates of growth			Annual rate of change (percentage)					
			1970-1979	1980-1989	1990-1999	1997	1998	1999	2000	2001	2002
Guinea	0.6	30.6	2.8	2.0	2.0	0.2	8.6	3.6	3.5	4.0	4.0
Guinea-Bissau	0.1	37.0	1.2	7.6	0.3	-14.9	-37.4	49.0	34.1	-8.2	0.6
Liberia	0.1	27.8	4.4	-14.1	-5.5	199.7	29.7	22.9	22.3	4.9	3.3
Mali	0.6	33.7	5.2	4.0	7.8	8.3	-0.8	63.9	20.3	14.3	-16.0
Mauritania	0.4	60.1	12.0	2.1	1.3	6.5	5.5	-8.8	-6.3	21.2	1.1
Niger	0.4	20.9	10.3	-0.6	2.8	5.3	20.9	-15.4	6.4	4.4	12.6
Nigeria	4.2	19.1	11.2	-10.8	8.7	6.5	1.2	14.9	16.0	18.9	-15.9
Senegal	1.2	30.3	8.7	1.7	1.4	-1.6	13.9	-4.9	-3.3	68.5	-0.6
Sierra Leone	0.1	23.8	2.0	-1.0	-4.9	-5.4	-4.0	-2.5	-14.2	9.2	6.3
Togo	0.3	27.8	9.9	2.7	-2.5	16.7	2.1	1.0	13.2	1.0	-5.6
AMERICAS	**21.2**	**12.9**	**5.6**	**4.5**	**8.1**	**14.4**	**10.4**	**7.5**	**12.4**	**-2.6**	**1.8**
NORTHERN AMERICA	**17.0**	**12.3**	**5.3**	**5.5**	**8.0**	**13.8**	**10.6**	**10.4**	**12.4**	**-3.2**	**3.4**
Bermuda	0.1	43.7	3.9	4.2	1.4	2.2	7.3	5.0	5.7	2.5	1.0
Canada	15.4	26.0	6.3	4.7	6.2	14.3	5.1	7.8	8.0	-5.1	0.7
United States	64.9	10.9	5.1	5.8	8.3	13.7	11.8	10.9	13.2	-2.9	3.9
LATIN AMERICA AND THE CARIBBEAN	**4.2**	**16.4**	**6.4**	**1.1**	**8.9**	**16.5**	**10.0**	**-2.3**	**12.5**	**0.0**	**-4.1**
Caribbean	*5.2*	*56.3*	*3.9*	*3.3*	*2.1*	*6.7*	*8.1*	*3.3*	*5.7*	*0.0*	*2.0*
Anguilla	0.0	79.7	3.8	9.1	7.4	0.8	20.2	16.5	1.1	-13.1	-12.7
Antigua and Barbuda	0.0	82.6	2.5	8.4	1.8	0.4	4.2	-0.4	-8.0	-4.4	3.5
Aruba	0.1	69.2	11.5	12.3	8.1	4.8	3.4	2.0	-14.1	-2.4	0.8
Bahamas	0.2	53.0	41.6	13.6	2.6	0.5	12.7	7.1	5.7	-1.6	4.8
Barbados	0.1	51.7	2.8	-2.0	2.0	10.8	0.2	5.7	1.3	-6.6	-2.9
British Virgin Islands	0.0	84.2	3.7	9.6	7.6	8.0	5.8	9.5	14.4	6.3	8.8
Cayman Islands	0.0	58.5	10.6	8.6	0.2	0.5	1.5	0.7	0.7	0.7	0.8
Cuba	0.8	40.9	4.3	2.1	-4.8	10.5	-5.8	16.0	-8.0	-3.9	-15.0
Dominica	0.0	75.3	0.8	3.1	1.5	17.8	-3.2	2.3	1.5	-10.4	-9.5
Dominican Republic	0.4	47.2	8.1	0.9	6.3	12.8	18.3	4.0	6.9	-6.2	1.3
Grenada	0.0	71.8	1.7	-1.3	5.4	7.1	17.4	3.6	14.9	-13.7	-0.4
Guadeloupe	0.2	63.5	4.7	3.5	2.0	9.2	4.1	5.9	5.9	5.9	4.2
Haiti	0.1	21.7	12.3	-1.0	10.5	4.0	13.9	2.2	29.3	-11.1	-0.8
Jamaica	0.2	55.8	0.2	6.6	0.8	-8.6	-1.7	-3.7	1.8	3.5	-1.7
Martinique	0.2	50.3	4.4	3.8	1.5	1.6	4.1	2.5	2.5	2.5	2.6
Montserrat	0.0	81.4	4.3	1.3	-3.8	-27.3	-1.3	-5.3	-2.8	0.3	10.8
Netherlands Antilles	0.2	86.5	2.3	-2.5	1.4	-15.2	5.2	4.4	-4.5	-1.5	-0.3
Puerto Rico	2.4	71.4	1.8	4.9	2.6	5.7	10.7	2.6	8.1	2.3	5.8
Saint Kitts and Nevis	0.0	83.1	4.8	5.9	2.5	-3.2	-4.7	11.5	7.4	-6.1	5.0
Saint Lucia	0.0	78.1	5.4	4.4	0.7	-5.7	3.1	33.4	-4.1	-14.3	0.8
Saint Vincent and the Grenadines	0.0	76.8	3.8	3.8	2.4	20.2	6.2	-1.8	-15.5	5.6	-5.9
Trinidad and Tobago	0.2	33.5	14.0	-3.1	2.5	59.2	-1.8	-14.6	21.2	8.6	-9.2
Turks and Caicos Islands	0.0	95.6	1.0	6.6	5.4	21.6	14.0	15.7	4.5	9.0	-1.0
Central America	*6.7*	*21.9*	*7.7*	*2.1*	*12.1*	*21.5*	*15.9*	*11.9*	*18.8*	*-1.1*	*1.8*
Belize	0.0	61.3	4.0	5.9	3.4	15.5	5.2	12.3	15.8	-2.3	9.1
Costa Rica	0.3	39.0	7.3	2.4	9.3	14.7	25.2	0.4	-2.6	1.1	6.3
El Salvador	0.2	31.2	8.3	-4.3	10.0	16.8	9.2	2.7	14.5	4.4	0.5
Guatemala	0.2	23.7	5.7	-3.3	8.7	19.5	19.8	0.7	6.0	6.9	6.6
Honduras	0.1	39.9	5.2	-0.3	3.5	-1.4	7.5	4.3	3.7	4.0	2.1
Mexico	5.3	19.7	8.8	2.7	13.3	22.7	16.6	14.1	21.5	-1.5	1.6
Nicaragua	0.1	27.1	-0.4	7.7	5.1	22.1	7.2	20.7	-5.3	0.2	-0.5
Panama	0.4	78.7	3.3	1.6	5.2	17.2	4.5	-8.3	1.4	-3.0	0.4
South America	*7.7*	*9.7*	*7.0*	*-0.8*	*9.8*	*16.2*	*6.4*	*-14.6*	*8.8*	*1.1*	*-12.4*
Argentina	0.7	4.6	6.7	-4.1	17.8	26.9	8.4	-11.3	-0.2	-13.9	-50.1
Bolivia	0.1	23.9	3.9	-0.4	6.2	13.5	22.3	-17.1	6.4	-4.8	7.7
Brazil	2.8	6.1	9.6	-1.1	9.6	13.9	8.9	-14.8	13.8	1.2	-4.2
Chile	1.0	29.4	3.5	2.9	10.2	13.2	6.7	-9.5	10.8	3.2	0.5

Table 5.E. Average Rates of Growth of Gross Domestic Product by Expenditure - Imports of Goods and Services

Major area, region and country	Base year weights as percentage of total for world or region in 1990	Base year share as percentage of total GDP in 1990	Average rates of growth			Annual rate of change (percentage)					
			1970-1979	1980-1989	1990-1999	1997	1998	1999	2000	2001	2002
Colombia	0.8	16.0	5.3	2.2	8.0	6.2	-3.9	-24.7	6.0	11.6	0.1
Ecuador	0.3	28.6	10.4	-0.8	1.0	15.4	7.0	-29.5	15.8	17.2	17.2
French Guiana	0.1	114.3	15.9	11.6	1.5	-1.1	2.0	0.8	0.8	0.8	0.7
Guyana	0.0	92.3	-1.7	-2.5	5.7	5.5	-2.5	2.2	3.1	0.7	-1.7
Paraguay	0.2	39.5	13.1	3.5	8.5	-0.2	-7.0	-27.1	-6.7	-1.6	-6.3
Peru	0.4	13.0	1.5	-2.7	9.5	12.2	2.3	-15.2	3.7	2.6	2.4
Suriname	0.0	26.6	6.0	-6.8	7.9	-6.6	-12.2	3.0	-11.9	34.9	-17.7
Uruguay	0.2	20.1	4.9	-0.3	10.0	13.2	7.3	-5.8	-0.4	-6.5	-27.9
Venezuela	1.0	20.2	8.0	-2.3	6.4	33.9	9.4	-14.6	15.4	11.0	-26.7
ASIA	**21.6**	**18.2**	**9.5**	**5.2**	**6.8**	**5.1**	**-4.7**	**4.6**	**15.1**	**-1.1**	**8.3**
Eastern Asia	*58.4*	*14.6*	*9.2*	*7.0*	*6.5*	*5.1*	*-6.8*	*8.4*	*15.2*	*-1.7*	*8.6*
China	4.7	12.2	24.5	12.3	7.8	11.1	3.1	22.3	24.8	8.3	20.2
Democratic People's Rep. of Korea	0.3	17.2	17.6	14.3	-1.9	-6.3	-1.1	6.2	0.3	4.3	0.8
Hong Kong SAR of China	9.5	123.2	10.0	13.4	9.0	6.8	-6.3	-0.2	16.8	-1.5	7.1
Japan	29.1	9.4	7.0	4.1	3.3	1.2	-6.8	3.0	9.5	0.1	2.0
Macao SAR of China	0.2	67.4	9.1	9.3	3.3	-1.1	-1.0	11.1	7.9	8.8	12.9
Mongolia	0.1	39.9	5.7	6.3	-0.4	4.0	3.5	3.2	1.1	1.0	4.0
Republic of Korea	7.7	30.3	17.3	9.0	10.3	3.2	-22.1	28.8	20.0	-3.0	16.4
South Central Asia	*13.0*	*19.8*	*3.8*	*2.1*	*10.1*	*2.3*	*12.0*	*4.3*	*8.2*	*4.7*	*9.6*
Bangladesh	0.4	12.3	0.0	5.4	6.5	0.2	5.0	7.4	23.5	13.4	-7.3
Bhutan	0.0	32.3	6.4	4.6	8.4	6.2	16.9	9.4	1.7	4.8	8.3
India	2.8	8.6	2.6	6.0	12.9	13.2	20.8	7.0	6.5	3.5	8.6
Iran (Islamic Republic of)	2.5	27.4	2.6	-2.4	-1.1	-6.5	0.4	-5.3	8.3	17.3	27.8
Kazakhstan	2.2	30.5	...	...	-14.0	7.5	-7.2	0.6	28.5	0.2	2.1
Kyrgyzstan	0.6	49.5	...	...	-13.8	-20.2	1.5	-4.9	0.4	-13.8	13.1
Maldives	0.0	76.8	11.5	11.7	9.9	20.5	2.3	16.3	-5.1	1.4	0.6
Nepal	0.1	21.1	10.3	7.1	8.3	10.8	-6.9	-8.8	15.8	1.6	-8.8
Pakistan	0.9	18.5	7.4	2.0	2.1	-5.6	-5.4	-2.3	1.5	1.4	17.4
Sri Lanka	0.3	38.3	0.8	3.0	7.0	10.4	12.4	-2.6	14.8	-10.7	10.0
Tajikistan	0.0	39.6	...	...	-6.3	36.9	-29.1	19.8	55.4	-6.0	-12.3
Turkmenistan	0.8	70.0	...	...	1.0	-31.8	34.2	16.5	10.0	7.9	9.0
Uzbekistan	2.4	47.8	...	...	-5.6	-8.4	4.4	4.4	4.0	4.5	4.2
South-Eastern Asia	*11.3*	*35.9*	*10.4*	*6.8*	*7.7*	*3.9*	*-15.1*	*-6.4*	*21.6*	*-3.0*	*4.5*
Brunei Darussalam	0.1	38.6	7.6	7.9	-1.6	3.0	2.0	-11.4	2.8	3.0	3.2
Cambodia	0.0	8.1	-7.3	-1.1	11.7	6.8	7.5	17.6	17.5	12.6	16.9
Indonesia	2.7	23.7	17.8	3.7	4.9	14.7	-5.3	-40.7	21.1	8.1	-8.3
Lao People's Democratic Republic	0.0	39.6	0.3	25.5	6.5	8.8	22.5	7.3	15.5	8.9	13.6
Malaysia	3.2	72.4	12.0	9.2	11.6	5.8	-18.8	10.6	24.4	-8.6	6.3
Myanmar	0.1	3.6	0.0	-5.1	8.2	2.6	5.4	2.4	2.4	2.4	2.4
Philippines	1.5	33.3	7.2	5.0	6.8	13.5	-14.7	-2.8	4.3	3.5	4.7
Thailand	3.6	41.6	7.1	9.2	6.1	-11.3	-21.6	10.5	27.3	-5.5	11.3
Timor-Leste	0.0	72.6	...	...	-7.2	4.0	-36.8	-27.4	87.1	30.2	2.6
Western Asia	*17.2*	*32.4*	*13.2*	*0.8*	*5.7*	*8.4*	*4.7*	*-0.7*	*14.1*	*-0.6*	*9.1*
Armenia	0.7	46.3	...	...	-4.0	11.6	-4.9	-1.9	7.2	2.0	13.1
Azerbaijan	0.9	39.2	...	...	11.9	18.1	15.4	-0.4	17.3	48.0	48.3
Bahrain	0.4	90.3	11.8	0.1	1.8	1.4	2.5	-3.9	7.3	3.7	17.1
Cyprus	0.3	57.0	6.5	7.1	1.8	-0.5	7.8	-1.9	10.2	4.2	1.5
Georgia	1.0	45.7	...	...	-12.2	43.9	-9.2	5.6	6.5	2.6	11.2
Iraq	0.7	17.8	18.0	-4.1	-12.4	120.0	25.8	21.0	20.1	25.4	-17.9
Israel	2.0	34.7	5.6	3.3	9.2	4.1	1.7	16.1	11.4	-4.9	-1.7
Jordan	0.4	92.7	16.2	2.1	2.6	-5.3	-7.1	2.3	5.0	5.3	11.0
Kuwait	1.1	57.8	18.4	1.0	1.2	-2.0	17.3	-9.8	24.1	5.9	7.1
Lebanon	0.3	90.8	4.7	-3.6	-1.2	-8.9	-10.7	-1.3	-1.1	2.9	2.0
Oman	0.3	27.6	13.6	-1.2	7.4	12.9	13.6	-12.4	5.0	13.7	4.5
Qatar	0.2	32.1	14.0	-2.1	1.2	-0.9	-2.6	-24.2	51.2	-8.1	-0.2
Saudi Arabia	4.2	39.4	15.4	-1.7	-3.5	0.3	4.6	-13.3	12.1	-0.7	-7.7
Syrian Arab Republic	0.4	28.0	10.3	1.0	1.1	-1.6	-6.3	11.5	-2.4	10.4	7.7
Turkey	2.7	17.6	3.1	12.6	10.8	22.4	2.3	-3.7	25.4	-24.8	15.7

Table 5.E. Average Rates of Growth of Gross Domestic Product by Expenditure - Imports of Goods and Services

Major area, region and country	Base year weights as percentage of total for world or region in 1990	Base year share as percentage of total GDP in 1990	Average rates of growth			Annual rate of change (percentage)					
			1970-1979	1980-1989	1990-1999	1997	1998	1999	2000	2001	2002
United Arab Emirates	1.4	40.8	34.0	1.5	9.8	3.6	1.8	3.5	1.7	1.7	-12.3
Yemen	0.3	19.5	...	...	5.1	1.4	17.2	3.8	2.1	6.0	4.2
Yemen Arab Republic (Former)	...	...	20.3	-2.1	...	...	...	...	...	...	...
Yemen Democratic (Former)	...	...	6.1	2.5	...	...	...	...	...	...	...
EUROPE	**52.5**	**27.1**	**5.2**	**4.1**	**6.2**	**9.3**	**8.9**	**5.8**	**11.6**	**2.7**	**1.4**
Eastern Europe	*14.5*	*23.0*	*7.1*	*4.7*	*16.2*	*6.9*	*-0.8*	*-6.4*	*22.7*	*10.7*	*8.6*
Belarus	1.3	50.0	...	...	-8.7	26.5	-1.9	-0.2	13.4	12.4	9.1
Bulgaria	0.3	37.5	7.1	3.6	0.4	10.9	12.1	9.3	18.6	14.8	4.7
Czech Republic	0.6	39.4	...	0.8	9.2	8.1	6.6	5.4	17.0	13.6	4.3
Hungary [3]	0.4	25.7	6.5	1.4	11.4	23.1	25.2	13.3	19.4	6.1	6.1
Poland	0.5	20.7	6.7	0.2	13.2	21.4	18.5	1.0	15.6	-5.3	2.6
Republic of Moldova	0.4	51.0	...	...	-5.8	12.3	-10.4	-22.6	32.3	10.6	15.7
Romania	0.4	26.2	8.3	-0.5	3.7	7.5	11.3	-1.5	27.1	17.2	12.1
Russian Federation	7.2	17.9	...	...	-8.4	0.4	-17.4	-17.0	32.4	19.8	14.5
Slovakia	0.2	34.1	...	0.7	7.6	14.2	16.5	-6.7	10.5	11.0	5.2
Ukraine	3.1	29.4	...	...	-10.7	-4.6	2.0	-16.7	23.8	6.0	3.6
Northern Europe	*20.9*	*29.1*	*4.0*	*4.4*	*5.7*	*11.3*	*10.7*	*6.0*	*10.7*	*3.2*	*2.8*
Denmark	1.7	30.8	3.3	3.3	4.8	10.0	8.9	5.5	11.3	1.9	4.2
Estonia	0.2	49.9	...	...	2.9	29.1	12.9	-5.4	27.9	2.1	10.2
Finland	1.4	24.3	3.9	5.1	3.4	11.2	7.9	3.5	16.9	0.2	1.3
Iceland	0.1	33.1	6.9	2.3	5.0	8.5	23.4	4.2	8.0	-9.0	-2.3
Ireland	1.0	52.4	7.8	4.1	12.0	16.8	25.5	12.1	21.3	6.5	2.3
Latvia	0.4	49.0	...	...	-6.1	6.8	19.0	-5.2	4.9	12.6	4.5
Lithuania	0.5	60.6	...	...	-1.3	25.0	6.2	-12.4	4.7	17.7	17.6
Norway	1.6	33.9	3.0	2.5	4.8	12.4	8.5	-1.8	2.7	0.9	1.7
Sweden	2.9	29.1	2.6	3.7	4.5	12.5	11.3	4.9	11.3	-2.5	-2.5
United Kingdom	11.0	26.6	4.5	5.1	5.3	9.8	9.3	7.9	9.1	4.5	3.6
Southern Europe	*17.5*	*22.6*	*5.3*	*5.7*	*7.0*	*11.8*	*10.6*	*8.0*	*9.0*	*2.0*	*1.8*
Andorra	0.0	19.7	11.7	12.8	11.4	13.3	12.8	12.4	11.3	5.6	4.1
Bosnia and Herzegovina	0.3	56.3	...	...	6.2	30.0	20.0	14.1	5.6	1.6	20.3
Croatia	0.8	81.1	...	...	-6.9	25.1	-4.9	-3.5	3.7	9.3	8.8
Greece	1.0	27.9	7.8	5.1	7.1	14.2	9.2	15.0	8.9	-3.4	-4.7
Holy See	0.0	19.7	5.5	5.3	5.1	10.3	8.9	5.6	9.0	1.0	1.6
Italy	9.0	19.7	4.5	5.0	5.0	10.1	8.9	5.6	8.9	1.0	1.5
Malta	0.1	98.9	4.0	4.0	5.1	-1.5	2.5	10.1	10.5	0.3	44.4
Portugal	1.2	39.5	4.4	6.4	8.2	10.0	14.2	8.5	5.4	0.9	-0.5
San Marino	0.1	220.1	3.6	2.4	1.8	13.6	-8.1	7.0	10.4	-2.0	0.7
Serbia and Montenegro	0.2	13.5	...	...	-4.9	6.0	24.3	-53.2	-11.9	56.0	1.7
Slovenia	0.6	78.5	...	...	2.1	11.5	10.3	8.0	7.6	3.0	4.9
Spain	4.2	19.7	6.7	8.1	9.0	13.2	13.2	12.6	10.6	4.0	1.8
TFYR Macedonia	0.1	36.0	...	...	3.1	26.4	7.4	0.1	24.0	-16.0	11.7
Yugoslavia (Former)	...	...	7.8	2.5	...	...	...	...	...	...	...
Western Europe	*47.1*	*29.9*	*5.6*	*3.5*	*5.3*	*8.0*	*9.3*	*7.0*	*11.3*	*1.5*	*-0.6*
Austria	2.6	38.4	7.2	3.4	5.8	12.0	5.7	9.0	11.6	5.9	1.2
Belgium	5.7	68.9	6.0	3.3	4.2	5.1	7.3	4.2	8.5	1.1	1.2
France	11.2	22.2	6.0	3.9	4.8	6.9	11.6	6.2	14.6	1.3	0.6
Germany	17.5	25.2	5.7	3.2	6.0	8.3	9.1	8.4	10.5	0.9	-1.7
Liechtenstein	0.0	35.7	6.1	5.2	4.1	8.7	10.9	6.6	11.7	0.8	-4.1
Luxembourg	0.5	100.3	3.5	5.0	7.7	13.9	15.3	14.6	14.8	4.8	-1.6
Monaco	0.0	22.2	6.5	4.6	5.5	7.6	12.3	6.8	15.3	1.8	1.1
Netherlands	6.2	50.8	4.6	3.1	5.8	9.5	8.5	5.8	10.5	2.4	-0.2
Switzerland	3.4	35.7	4.5	4.4	3.4	7.6	9.6	5.3	10.5	-0.2	-5.0
OCEANIA	**1.6**	**19.6**	**3.8**	**6.1**	**6.1**	**7.9**	**4.0**	**11.7**	**-0.9**	**2.1**	**12.2**
Australia & New Zealand	*89.2*	*18.1*	*3.7*	*6.2*	*6.5*	*8.5*	*4.4*	*12.3*	*-1.1*	*2.3*	*13.2*
Australia	72.9	16.8	3.8	6.7	6.7	9.7	4.8	12.5	-1.3	2.3	13.8
New Zealand	16.3	26.8	3.1	4.2	5.5	2.6	2.0	11.4	-0.4	2.1	9.8

Table 5.E. Average Rates of Growth of Gross Domestic Product by Expenditure - Imports of Goods and Services

Major area, region and country	Base year weights as percentage of total for world or region in 1990	Base year share as percentage of total GDP in 1990	Average rates of growth			Annual rate of change (percentage)					
			1970-1979	1980-1989	1990-1999	1997	1998	1999	2000	2001	2002
Melanesia	*8.9*	*84.5*	*6.2*	*5.9*	*1.3*	*1.4*	*-0.7*	*2.9*	*0.7*	*-1.3*	*-2.3*
Fiji	1.3	67.2	7.7	4.3	3.5	-3.4	6.8	14.9	-1.6	-6.1	5.7
New Caledonia	5.2	147.2	6.5	12.4	0.9	2.0	-3.2	0.9	2.1	-1.1	0.7
Papua New Guinea	2.1	45.4	5.0	0.3	1.0	3.2	0.4	1.4	0.6	1.2	-11.6
Solomon Islands	0.2	56.8	17.1	3.9	-1.3	-4.1	1.7	-1.1	-14.3	-4.9	-4.1
Vanuatu	0.2	76.6	7.7	2.9	1.7	1.3	-0.2	-2.9	2.0	-2.2	-3.3
Micronesia	*0.3*	*54.5*	*5.4*	*4.4*	*0.0*	*-5.7*	*0.7*	*-1.9*	*0.4*	*2.0*	*1.5*
Kiribati	0.0	33.1	2.9	-4.9	4.5	5.7	5.0	9.3	1.6	1.8	0.9
Marshall Islands	0.1	147.2	11.6	14.2	-1.9	-11.2	2.0	0.0	-1.1	1.8	2.5
Micronesia (Federated States of)	0.1	33.1	6.6	4.5	1.2	-5.1	-2.1	-2.8	2.1	1.5	0.8
Nauru	0.0	33.1	6.8	4.9	-5.4	-7.3	-1.9	-1.9	-1.0	-0.8	0.9
Palau	0.0	33.1	2.9	-5.5	3.7	2.3	2.0	-8.8	0.3	4.5	1.1
Polynesia	*1.7*	*36.1*	*1.8*	*1.8*	*1.8*	*0.4*	*2.0*	*2.6*	*8.7*	*3.3*	*2.3*
Cook Islands	0.1	80.6	0.9	-1.1	-2.4	15.7	-5.4	2.6	14.1	5.1	3.7
French Polynesia	1.3	31.7	1.0	2.8	1.6	1.1	1.1	2.7	2.7	2.1	1.9
Samoa	0.2	65.1	5.2	-3.1	3.7	1.6	4.7	12.0	41.5	6.3	4.8
Tonga	0.1	65.3	3.5	4.0	0.6	-13.7	8.5	-15.3	9.8	7.5	1.7
Tuvalu	0.0	147.2	11.6	6.1	5.2	3.5	14.9	3.0	3.0	3.0	-11.5

Notes for Table 5.E - Imports of goods and services

1/ 1992-2001
Excludes Imports of goods.

2/ 1974-1975
Includes imports of goods plus net imports of services.

3/ 1988-1991
Does not include direct purchases abroad by resident households, except purchase of cars by Hungarian individuals for own use.

Table 6.A. Average Rates of Growth of Gross Domestic Product by Kind of Economic Activity - Agriculture, Hunting, Forestry and Fishing

Major area, region and country	Base year weights as percentage of total for world or region in 1990	Base year share as percentage of total GDP in 1990	Average rates of growth			Annual rate of change (percentage)					
			1970-1979	1980-1989	1990-1999	1997	1998	1999	2000	2001	2002
WORLD	**100.0**	**5.9**	**2.0**	**3.1**	**0.8**	**1.4**	**0.2**	**3.0**	**2.7**	**2.3**	**1.6**
DEVELOPED ECONOMIES	**32.2**	**2.6**	**1.5**	**0.9**	**1.0**	**1.5**	**0.8**	**2.4**	**2.6**	**-2.0**	**2.5**
DEVELOPING ECONOMIES	**42.5**	**14.6**	**2.4**	**3.3**	**3.0**	**1.2**	**3.8**	**1.9**	**1.6**	**3.1**	**1.1**
TRANSITION ECONOMIES	**25.3**	**18.3**	**2.3**	**6.1**	**-5.0**	**2.1**	**-12.3**	**8.4**	**6.9**	**8.9**	**1.1**
AFRICA	**6.8**	**17.4**	**1.9**	**2.6**	**3.8**	**2.2**	**5.2**	**3.4**	**0.2**	**4.9**	**-0.7**
Eastern Africa	*17.6*	*27.8*	*2.4*	*1.7*	*4.2*	*3.2*	*3.6*	*4.4*	*1.4*	*3.7*	*1.7*
Burundi	0.6	51.2	1.6	2.2	-1.4	-1.0	3.2	1.1	2.1	1.4	1.4
Comoros	0.1	41.4	2.2	3.6	0.0	-1.3	-1.3	-1.6	-3.0	3.5	-0.6
Djibouti [1]	0.0	2.6	-1.6	2.1	3.1	1.1	2.0	2.1	1.8	3.2	2.5
Eritrea	...	...	...	...	14.7	66.3	60.6	-7.4	-42.8	27.4	-37.4
Ethiopia	...	...	...	...	3.3	3.4	-3.6	4.2	2.9	5.4	2.2
Ethiopia (Former)	2.5	27.9	0.9	0.6	0.4	...	...	...	...	...	...
Kenya	2.3	25.0	4.1	3.7	1.2	1.2	1.6	1.2	-2.0	1.3	0.8
Madagascar	1.1	31.8	-0.2	-1.6	0.0	3.1	2.6	-11.3	0.6	2.4	-5.1
Malawi	0.6	32.8	6.1	0.7	4.5	0.1	10.3	10.1	5.4	-6.2	2.4
Mauritius	0.3	10.9	8.5	-1.3	-1.1	3.3	-1.9	-23.3	32.1	8.8	-14.1
Mozambique	1.9	64.5	3.9	-0.3	5.6	8.7	7.3	5.7	-9.1	12.6	6.7
Reunion	0.2	3.9	2.7	1.7	3.8	3.2	3.0	3.1	3.2	3.2	3.2
Rwanda	1.2	43.8	4.3	0.8	0.9	4.1	10.4	8.6	8.8	7.7	14.5
Seychelles	0.0	4.8	1.2	-1.4	-0.4	4.4	0.0	-0.6	0.3	13.8	-4.1
Somalia	0.8	70.5	1.4	4.0	-4.1	-4.2	0.3	12.0	3.0	3.0	3.5
Uganda	2.0	49.3	2.4	2.3	4.3	1.8	10.1	6.0	3.7	4.9	3.3
United Republic Of Tanzania	2.0	49.5	1.9	3.8	4.9	2.2	4.2	11.2	3.4	5.5	5.0
Zambia	0.5	11.5	-1.3	6.5	2.0	-5.1	1.2	10.1	1.6	-2.5	-1.7
Zimbabwe	1.4	14.8	2.5	2.6	4.0	3.2	5.1	4.3	9.9	-12.6	-14.0
Middle Africa	*10.2*	*20.7*	*1.4*	*1.8*	*1.3*	*5.4*	*2.5*	*5.2*	*1.4*	*7.9*	*6.0*
Angola	2.0	17.9	0.2	2.0	-0.5	5.6	6.3	1.3	9.1	18.2	12.1
Cameroon	2.8	17.7	4.9	1.3	5.7	8.1	-1.9	26.1	1.6	5.5	7.2
Central African Republic	0.6	42.9	2.0	2.4	3.6	4.5	5.4	18.3	3.3	0.1	-3.4
Chad	0.7	39.4	-1.2	2.7	4.8	7.3	10.8	-5.2	-2.7	7.7	3.9
Congo	0.4	14.3	2.2	3.7	-3.5	0.6	-3.2	-13.6	-31.6	21.4	6.8
Democratic Republic of the Congo	3.2	31.2	1.6	1.6	-5.8	-3.1	0.0	-15.9	1.9	-11.4	1.1
Equatorial Guinea	0.1	51.7	0.9	2.5	17.3	68.8	18.7	47.2	16.9	53.4	4.0
Gabon	0.5	8.0	-5.7	1.3	0.3	4.6	3.2	-32.6	-18.7	19.4	5.3
Sao Tome and Principe	0.0	28.2	8.4	-2.6	4.0	2.1	4.4	3.2	3.8	2.7	3.1
Northern Africa	*40.1*	*15.8*	*2.8*	*3.7*	*5.2*	*0.6*	*7.7*	*2.7*	*-3.3*	*6.4*	*-5.5*
Algeria	7.6	11.3	2.4	5.2	2.1	-13.5	11.4	0.6	-22.8	13.2	-0.6
Egypt	12.5	16.2	4.6	4.1	3.6	3.6	3.5	3.4	3.7	3.6	2.8
Libyan Arab Jamahiriya	2.2	7.2	4.0	3.8	12.1	6.6	0.6	-2.9	1.7	2.7	12.5
Morocco	5.0	17.7	1.0	4.9	-1.3	-26.5	27.9	-16.7	-15.7	27.6	5.6
Sudan	10.6	29.1	1.8	2.1	9.0	12.3	8.3	8.5	0.8	4.7	-18.8
Tunisia	2.1	15.7	5.3	1.0	6.1	3.0	-1.0	11.0	-1.0	-1.5	-11.0
Southern Africa	*5.8*	*4.5*	*3.5*	*3.2*	*-0.4*	*0.1*	*-5.3*	*4.8*	*6.8*	*-3.5*	*5.6*
Botswana	0.2	4.7	6.5	2.1	-0.2	-7.5	5.9	-7.6	-8.8	7.3	-2.5
Lesotho	0.1	19.5	5.3	-0.7	1.1	0.6	3.1	4.4	2.8	2.8	-3.2
Namibia	0.3	10.6	1.8	-1.5	4.7	-6.5	6.1	6.2	8.2	-10.4	0.7
South Africa	5.1	4.2	3.5	3.6	-0.8	0.8	-6.8	5.1	7.6	-3.3	6.5
Swaziland	0.1	10.6	2.3	3.0	0.4	-1.3	1.9	8.2	-4.1	-8.5	-0.6
Western Africa	*26.3*	*33.0*	*0.5*	*1.8*	*3.0*	*4.0*	*4.5*	*3.0*	*4.5*	*3.6*	*2.8*
Benin	0.7	34.9	3.6	5.8	5.4	5.7	6.5	4.1	6.4	3.1	7.1
Burkina Faso	1.3	43.4	4.4	2.7	3.0	-4.4	-4.2	13.6	1.8	15.0	-10.9
Cape Verde	0.0	14.4	1.2	4.0	2.4	-5.1	2.7	11.7	3.6	21.4	-11.5
Cote d'Ivoire	3.8	29.5	4.9	0.1	2.1	4.0	8.8	-8.9	6.0	2.9	-1.2
Gambia	0.1	22.5	2.3	2.8	7.3	3.2	1.2	95.8	9.0	7.7	-1.2
Ghana	3.3	48.2	1.1	1.0	2.9	3.8	2.6	6.9	2.1	4.0	4.4
Guinea	0.6	20.2	2.8	2.4	3.5	6.8	5.6	7.9	-0.3	6.3	5.1

Table 6.A. Average Rates of Growth of Gross Domestic Product by Kind of Economic Activity - Agriculture, Hunting, Forestry and Fishing

Major area, region and country	Base year weights as percentage of total for world or region in 1990	Base year share as percentage of total GDP in 1990	Average rates of growth			Annual rate of change (percentage)					
			1970-1979	1980-1989	1990-1999	1997	1998	1999	2000	2001	2002
Guinea-Bissau	0.1	44.6	0.3	2.3	2.8	14.9	-20.3	8.1	4.7	8.5	-10.0
Liberia	0.2	54.3	3.1	-5.4	1.0	69.7	31.3	19.8	21.5	5.9	4.6
Mali	1.3	45.8	-0.1	2.3	3.1	7.9	5.9	-7.4	6.9	-4.8	10.5
Mauritania	0.3	27.2	-3.0	0.5	4.4	5.0	6.4	9.1	1.5	5.6	-1.3
Niger	1.1	41.6	4.6	0.4	2.4	2.6	21.1	-5.0	-8.4	-6.7	23.3
Nigeria	11.4	32.4	-2.7	3.2	3.5	4.2	4.0	5.2	5.2	3.1	4.4
Senegal	1.2	19.9	11.4	-0.1	1.8	-1.7	-3.5	5.7	10.7	11.7	-13.4
Sierra Leone	0.3	36.9	2.6	3.6	-3.0	8.2	-7.4	-9.7	12.7	11.5	11.8
Togo	0.5	28.9	-0.9	-0.2	0.2	10.5	-2.2	2.9	-0.8	0.2	4.8
AMERICAS	**16.2**	**2.9**	**2.8**	**1.2**	**2.7**	**5.1**	**1.9**	**5.1**	**5.1**	**0.2**	**2.9**
NORTHERN AMERICA	**9.3**	**2.0**	**2.4**	**0.5**	**3.0**	**8.5**	**1.8**	**5.5**	**7.4**	**-2.0**	**3.8**
Bermuda	0.0	0.8	3.7	4.5	1.7	9.5	0.0	4.3	0.0	0.0	-0.3
Canada	7.1	2.7	0.2	2.5	1.1	-3.4	6.2	6.5	-1.0	-7.3	-5.2
United States	50.5	1.9	2.7	0.2	3.3	10.1	1.3	5.4	8.4	-1.4	4.7
LATIN AMERICA AND THE CARIBBEAN	**6.9**	**8.0**	**3.3**	**2.2**	**2.4**	**0.6**	**2.1**	**4.4**	**1.9**	**3.4**	**1.6**
Caribbean	*2.7*	*6.5*	*2.5*	*0.8*	*-1.2*	*-0.5*	*-3.2*	*10.3*	*3.1*	*-1.2*	*-2.7*
Anguilla	0.0	4.5	3.8	7.0	-0.3	5.1	7.2	-11.4	-7.7	-6.9	20.0
Antigua and Barbuda	0.0	4.1	-1.8	-1.1	1.8	4.8	4.2	3.3	3.3	0.9	1.0
Aruba	0.0	0.6	5.8	6.3	1.3	-2.9	-1.9	-2.3	12.3	0.7	-6.4
Bahamas [2]	0.0	2.4	3.0	3.0	4.7	15.3	6.9	10.1	8.8	1.5	8.4
Barbados	0.0	4.6	0.5	-2.6	-0.3	-1.6	-12.9	7.4	6.9	-9.7	-32.0
British Virgin Islands [3]	0.0	3.3	1.5	2.7	-2.8	0.0	0.0	0.0	0.0	0.0	0.0
Cayman Islands	0.0	0.3	-5.8	-10.8	7.6	-2.8	-0.3	0.1	0.1	0.1	-0.6
Cuba	1.0	11.4	3.4	0.0	-5.2	-0.2	-5.2	10.3	11.6	-7.3	-9.5
Dominica	0.0	21.5	-2.6	2.1	-0.8	-1.5	-2.0	-2.1	-1.1	-6.1	-1.3
Dominican Republic	0.5	12.3	3.3	1.7	1.9	3.3	1.1	8.8	5.6	8.1	2.5
Grenada	0.0	13.2	1.8	-0.8	-0.9	-0.9	-1.2	10.0	-2.2	-2.9	19.0
Guadeloupe	0.1	6.7	1.0	3.2	0.3	9.2	4.1	5.9	5.9	5.9	4.2
Haiti	0.4	35.1	1.6	1.2	-2.9	-1.9	2.1	2.5	-3.6	0.6	-3.7
Jamaica	0.1	6.4	1.5	-0.7	4.8	-13.7	-1.5	1.4	-10.9	5.2	-7.0
Martinique	0.1	5.6	1.5	2.1	0.6	1.6	4.1	2.5	2.5	2.5	2.6
Montserrat	0.0	2.2	6.8	-3.6	-16.0	-81.3	-33.3	7.6	46.5	-17.3	40.7
Netherlands Antilles	0.0	0.6	3.3	1.1	6.6	57.4	-24.3	34.5	-0.2	2.9	4.2
Puerto Rico	0.2	1.4	1.8	1.6	1.6	-6.5	-24.0	50.7	-9.6	-3.3	-1.3
Saint Kitts and Nevis	0.0	5.4	1.6	-2.3	-1.8	20.7	-11.7	-9.1	-8.5	11.1	13.3
Saint Lucia	0.0	12.4	6.0	5.0	-2.0	-17.9	3.9	14.8	14.0	-22.6	-1.0
Saint Vincent and the Grenadines	0.0	17.9	2.9	6.4	-1.8	-15.2	7.5	-4.2	7.2	-8.1	11.8
Trinidad and Tobago	0.1	2.5	-1.2	0.1	3.2	8.2	-15.1	16.5	-0.5	-56.1	-14.1
Turks and Caicos Islands	0.0	2.0	1.0	6.6	4.7	7.2	17.7	6.7	-3.6	0.0	8.7
Central America	*11.2*	*8.3*	*3.1*	*1.3*	*2.3*	*0.6*	*2.9*	*1.8*	*1.3*	*4.6*	*-2.4*
Belize	0.0	18.2	3.6	2.4	6.8	13.0	-1.8	11.7	4.4	12.3	7.8
Costa Rica	0.4	11.3	2.9	2.8	4.2	1.5	8.2	4.5	0.7	1.4	-2.5
El Salvador	0.4	17.1	3.9	-1.9	2.3	0.4	-0.7	7.7	-3.1	-2.6	0.2
Guatemala	0.9	25.9	5.0	1.0	2.9	2.8	3.2	2.1	2.6	1.2	1.8
Honduras	0.3	20.0	2.8	2.8	1.5	4.2	-1.9	-8.5	9.8	-0.5	4.8
Mexico	8.6	7.2	3.0	1.4	2.0	0.2	3.0	1.5	0.6	5.8	-3.4
Nicaragua	0.3	18.1	0.0	2.4	3.6	-0.6	-0.4	6.5	12.6	1.9	-0.4
Panama	0.2	9.5	2.0	2.3	2.2	0.0	6.3	2.1	1.6	0.8	-1.9
South America	*28.5*	*8.1*	*3.5*	*2.8*	*2.7*	*0.7*	*2.2*	*5.0*	*2.1*	*3.2*	*3.3*
Argentina	5.3	8.1	2.9	-0.1	3.8	0.5	8.7	2.5	-1.8	1.0	-2.3
Bolivia	0.3	15.4	4.5	1.4	3.1	4.5	-4.4	2.5	2.7	3.8	0.6
Brazil	13.4	6.7	4.2	3.8	2.3	-0.8	1.3	8.0	3.0	5.1	5.8
Chile	1.0	6.7	2.1	5.5	5.0	3.4	2.3	0.8	7.0	5.7	5.2
Colombia	3.8	17.6	4.6	2.6	1.5	0.7	0.0	0.0	3.8	0.7	0.6
Ecuador	1.0	20.1	2.8	4.1	4.8	10.0	-3.0	9.1	-0.1	0.7	7.2

Table 6.A. Average Rates of Growth of Gross Domestic Product by Kind of Economic Activity - Agriculture, Hunting, Forestry and Fishing

Major area, region and country	Base year weights as percentage of total for world or region in 1990	Base year share as percentage of total GDP in 1990	Average rates of growth 1970-1979	1980-1989	1990-1999	Annual rate of change (percentage) 1997	1998	1999	2000	2001	2002
French Guiana	0.1	10.0	8.0	17.5	-0.6	1.6	0.2	1.2	1.1	1.1	1.1
Guyana	0.1	38.1	0.9	-1.0	6.3	4.0	-6.6	15.8	-9.0	3.4	11.5
Paraguay	0.7	27.8	6.5	4.6	2.4	5.2	0.2	3.2	-4.4	10.5	-0.9
Peru	1.2	8.4	0.1	2.2	3.8	5.0	-0.3	11.0	6.8	-0.2	5.7
Suriname	0.1	9.9	17.8	0.6	-0.8	-2.6	-6.4	4.0	6.6	10.8	-2.7
Uruguay	0.4	11.3	-1.0	1.7	2.3	-6.1	6.5	-8.7	-3.0	-7.6	7.4
Venezuela	1.2	5.4	3.1	2.4	0.7	2.4	0.6	-2.1	2.4	2.6	-1.7
ASIA	**38.8**	**9.5**	**1.9**	**3.2**	**3.0**	**0.5**	**2.0**	**1.1**	**1.9**	**2.7**	**1.8**
Eastern Asia	*40.7*	*5.4*	*1.8*	*3.0*	*1.7*	*0.8*	*0.4*	*1.1*	*2.1*	*2.0*	*2.0*
China	20.1	27.4	2.4	5.3	4.4	3.5	3.5	2.8	2.4	2.8	2.9
Democratic People's Rep. of Korea	0.7	21.8	11.9	8.1	-3.2	-6.3	-1.1	6.2	1.3	3.7	0.8
Hong Kong SAR of China [4]	0.0	0.2	8.8	7.2	3.8	5.1	-5.0	3.4	10.2	4.1	4.1
Japan	14.4	2.5	0.5	0.7	-2.8	-6.2	-3.1	-5.6	1.6	0.4	2.5
Mongolia	0.1	15.6	5.7	15.4	1.5	4.3	6.4	4.2	-14.9	-18.5	-10.7
Republic of Korea	4.1	8.5	4.0	1.7	1.4	4.6	-6.6	5.4	2.0	1.9	-4.1
South Central Asia	*34.5*	*27.5*	*1.3*	*3.8*	*4.8*	*0.2*	*2.4*	*2.3*	*0.0*	*4.4*	*0.6*
Afghanistan	0.5	51.9	4.2	-2.6	-0.9	13.3	5.2	-12.4	-43.7	-6.6	25.6
Bangladesh	1.8	29.7	-0.3	2.4	3.1	3.2	4.7	7.4	3.1	2.8	4.6
Bhutan	0.0	42.0	6.4	6.7	3.4	4.1	2.8	5.4	5.1	1.5	2.5
India	17.5	28.2	0.3	4.4	2.8	-2.4	6.2	0.3	-0.4	5.7	-4.2
Iran (Islamic Republic of)	3.0	17.5	8.1	4.0	3.6	0.2	11.0	-7.4	3.7	-0.5	11.3
Kazakhstan	4.7	34.3	...	...	-7.2	-0.9	-19.3	21.4	-3.2	17.1	3.2
Kyrgyzstan	0.8	32.9	...	...	0.4	12.3	2.9	8.2	2.6	7.1	3.1
Maldives	0.0	16.6	6.8	6.9	0.8	1.3	6.4	3.3	-0.2	5.0	17.0
Nepal	0.3	48.8	0.8	3.5	2.5	4.4	0.9	2.8	4.9	5.5	2.2
Pakistan	2.1	22.8	2.9	4.0	4.4	4.5	1.9	6.1	-2.6	1.4	10.7
Sri Lanka	0.3	22.9	2.8	1.3	2.9	3.1	2.4	6.0	2.3	-3.8	2.2
Tajikistan	0.0	30.1	...	...	-17.1	-16.6	-17.4	-30.7	22.6	10.2	51.1
Turkmenistan	0.2	10.9	...	...	6.1	41.1	34.5	14.8	1.6	15.9	4.1
Uzbekistan	3.1	33.6	...	...	-2.2	5.8	-22.4	13.1	7.1	-4.6	4.2
South-Eastern Asia	*12.1*	*17.8*	*3.6*	*3.1*	*2.3*	*1.7*	*-1.2*	*3.2*	*3.5*	*2.6*	*0.6*
Brunei Darussalam	0.0	2.4	4.8	3.6	1.5	5.5	3.4	-6.2	1.8	18.2	9.0
Cambodia	0.2	50.9	-7.3	-0.3	3.4	5.5	3.0	0.0	-0.3	3.9	5.0
Indonesia	4.2	19.4	3.7	3.7	2.4	1.0	-1.3	2.2	1.9	1.0	1.7
Lao People's Democratic Republic	0.1	60.7	0.1	5.8	5.0	7.0	3.1	8.2	4.9	3.8	4.0
Malaysia	1.3	15.2	7.7	3.9	0.1	0.7	-2.8	0.5	2.0	1.8	3.0
Myanmar	1.9	57.3	4.3	2.1	4.1	3.7	2.8	4.4	4.4	4.4	4.4
Philippines	1.9	21.9	4.0	1.5	1.4	3.1	-6.4	6.5	4.3	3.7	3.3
Singapore [5]	0.0	0.3	1.9	-5.6	-2.4	0.9	-5.4	-4.2	-3.4	-6.1	-5.8
Thailand	2.0	12.5	4.2	4.3	1.6	-0.9	-1.5	2.2	6.4	2.7	-10.8
Timor-Leste	0.0	32.6	...	...	-0.4	0.0	0.0	-3.6	-12.4	15.2	0.7
Vietnam	0.5	38.7	-0.1	4.2	4.1	4.3	3.5	5.2	4.0	4.6	4.1
Western Asia	*12.7*	*12.7*	*1.7*	*2.8*	*3.9*	*-1.1*	*10.4*	*-3.9*	*4.7*	*0.7*	*5.5*
Armenia	0.5	15.9	...	...	-0.1	-4.5	12.8	1.4	-1.0	11.7	4.4
Azerbaijan	1.1	27.1	...	...	-6.1	-7.5	6.6	10.3	14.2	12.3	7.5
Bahrain	0.0	0.8	11.2	-1.0	4.0	-7.5	-0.7	2.7	6.0	-7.6	-4.5
Cyprus	0.1	6.9	-2.4	3.0	-0.3	-7.7	7.2	11.0	-9.1	7.4	5.4
Georgia	1.3	30.1	...	...	-10.7	3.9	-6.6	6.9	-12.0	8.2	-1.4
Iraq	1.5	19.8	1.7	3.7	4.9	-4.0	20.4	-7.3	8.2	2.7	6.7
Israel	0.3	2.7	4.0	-2.2	-1.8	0.2	9.5	-4.8	7.6	8.0	3.3
Jordan	0.1	7.1	4.1	9.0	1.5	-8.5	13.1	-5.2	5.8	4.5	6.5
Kuwait	0.0	0.9	0.0	16.4	-1.1	13.8	-4.3	8.9	-26.5	-2.8	-5.8
Lebanon	0.0	8.8	-1.6	-6.7	9.1	-0.5	2.1	-2.0	-1.3	-0.3	2.0
Oman	0.1	2.6	4.5	11.3	4.8	9.3	-0.6	6.8	-5.3	3.4	0.4
Qatar	0.0	0.8	12.4	1.9	0.8	-2.6	-14.0	16.2	-9.0	0.0	3.3
Saudi Arabia	1.3	6.4	-4.7	14.8	0.3	3.0	1.0	2.3	3.9	0.8	-1.0
Syrian Arab Republic	0.8	28.3	7.5	1.5	6.9	-2.9	22.3	-15.1	9.2	8.6	7.3
Turkey	5.0	17.5	1.7	0.6	1.5	-2.0	8.4	-5.0	3.9	-6.5	7.1
United Arab Emirates	0.1	1.6	27.5	10.7	8.7	8.8	5.6	-5.0	5.4	2.0	2.0

Table 6.A. Average Rates of Growth of Gross Domestic Product by Kind of Economic Activity - Agriculture, Hunting, Forestry and Fishing

Major area, region and country	Base year weights as percentage of total for world or region in 1990	Base year share as percentage of total GDP in 1990	Average rates of growth			Annual rate of change (percentage)					
			1970-1979	1980-1989	1990-1999	1997	1998	1999	2000	2001	2002
Yemen	0.6	24.9	...	...	4.6	8.8	13.7	0.2	3.7	7.7	5.0
Yemen Arab Republic (Former)	...	...	2.9	2.8	...	...	...	...	...	...	...
Yemen Democratic (Former)	...	...	-4.3	6.4	...	...	...	...	...	...	...
EUROPE	**37.0**	**5.6**	**1.8**	**3.9**	**-3.1**	**0.5**	**-4.9**	**4.1**	**3.2**	**2.4**	**0.6**
Eastern Europe	*51.2*	*16.9*	*2.3*	*6.3*	*-7.5*	*1.2*	*-12.9*	*7.9*	*8.6*	*10.0*	*0.3*
Belarus	3.0	25.0	...	...	-4.6	-5.6	-1.0	-7.6	9.2	1.4	3.0
Bulgaria	0.7	17.7	7.1	-1.1	2.7	35.3	1.2	5.5	-10.3	0.3	5.1
Czech Republic	0.5	6.8	...	0.1	5.0	-2.5	10.3	15.3	-1.4	-0.9	4.4
Czechoslovakia (Former)	...	...	-0.4	...	...	...	...	...	...	...	...
Hungary [6]	0.8	11.4	4.9	0.0	-10.3	-0.5	-1.5	0.9	-7.9	23.4	-10.0
Poland	1.1	8.6	-1.6	0.3	0.4	1.0	5.7	-1.6	-6.9	9.2	1.2
Republic of Moldova	1.3	34.6	...	...	-10.8	15.0	-6.2	-4.1	2.3	7.4	5.1
Romania	1.7	21.8	5.8	-0.5	1.2	-1.3	-10.4	3.3	-18.1	25.2	-3.9
Russian Federation	30.0	15.5	...	...	-5.2	1.6	-18.1	16.2	12.2	10.9	1.5
Slovakia	0.3	8.2	...	1.7	-6.6	10.0	5.4	0.3	1.9	4.9	-1.6
Ukraine	11.8	23.0	...	...	-6.7	-0.9	-11.2	-3.9	12.1	10.0	-3.9
USSR (Former)	...	...	2.2	6.9	...	...	...	...	...	...	...
Northern Europe	*11.4*	*3.3*	*1.3*	*0.7*	*-0.2*	*-3.4*	*-4.3*	*-2.0*	*1.0*	*-1.7*	*0.1*
Denmark	1.0	3.8	3.5	3.8	2.3	2.2	4.0	0.1	0.8	1.3	-4.5
Estonia	0.3	14.3	...	...	-4.9	5.8	0.0	-2.5	-1.0	-5.4	1.4
Finland	1.6	5.7	4.6	-0.7	-0.9	13.1	-7.9	0.8	13.0	-1.1	2.4
Iceland	0.1	10.5	5.7	2.6	-1.2	-1.7	-5.2	-0.8	1.2	-0.4	2.8
Ireland	0.8	8.2	4.0	-1.1	-3.2	-10.2	-5.2	-10.0	3.4	-1.5	-9.7
Latvia	0.8	21.1	...	...	-7.8	6.6	-3.5	-3.5	11.4	6.3	3.1
Lithuania	1.1	26.7	...	...	-15.2	7.4	-5.0	-14.3	6.5	-4.6	6.4
Norway	0.7	3.1	0.4	1.0	3.2	-1.3	2.4	-0.7	-2.0	-1.3	0.4
Sweden	1.5	3.2	-0.8	2.1	-1.1	1.6	-5.3	2.2	3.0	4.3	1.7
United Kingdom	3.4	1.7	-0.2	0.5	-3.2	-15.9	-7.7	-3.8	-8.4	-8.5	1.4
Southern Europe	*17.9*	*4.8*	*1.3*	*1.0*	*1.8*	*1.7*	*-0.4*	*2.0*	*-1.5*	*-1.8*	*-0.4*
Albania	0.2	40.2	8.3	1.2	2.8	1.0	5.0	3.7	4.5	4.1	0.2
Andorra	0.0	5.2	7.5	6.8	3.7	2.7	-1.0	-5.1	2.4	-1.8	3.3
Bosnia and Herzegovina	0.7	24.8	...	...	-0.5	14.7	-24.9	31.9	-12.8	1.7	0.1
Croatia	0.5	9.7	...	...	-1.8	2.3	5.6	-2.6	1.2	0.7	2.0
Greece	1.7	9.8	1.5	1.7	0.0	0.4	2.3	3.5	-4.2	-4.1	-1.3
Holy See	0.0	3.2	1.2	0.3	1.8	1.3	1.2	5.9	-2.8	-0.7	-2.5
Italy	7.2	3.2	0.3	0.0	1.7	1.1	1.2	5.8	-2.9	-0.7	-2.6
Malta	0.0	3.1	4.3	3.4	0.4	4.0	-3.3	-6.8	-3.8	5.5	-0.2
Portugal	1.1	7.6	2.3	0.7	0.4	-8.1	-3.4	7.2	-3.8	-1.1	5.3
San Marino	0.0	3.2	0.3	0.0	3.0	1.1	6.9	13.4	-2.9	-0.7	-2.6
Serbia and Montenegro	1.1	17.7	...	...	-8.3	18.7	-3.1	-13.9	10.8	-5.0	6.0
Slovenia	0.2	5.0	...	...	-1.0	-2.9	3.1	-2.1	-1.0	-2.5	1.1
Spain	5.4	5.2	2.6	2.4	1.5	2.6	-0.6	-5.0	1.7	-3.3	1.0
TFYR Macedonia	0.1	7.5	...	...	0.7	-0.4	3.0	0.7	-5.7	1.8	5.1
Yugoslavia (Former)	...	...	2.0	0.6	...	...	...	...	...	...	...
Western Europe	*19.5*	*2.6*	*1.4*	*1.5*	*2.0*	*0.1*	*3.3*	*3.4*	*0.7*	*-3.8*	*1.9*
Austria	1.1	3.3	1.6	1.5	3.5	-2.6	7.7	-3.2	24.4	-19.6	5.7
Belgium	0.9	2.3	0.5	2.6	2.5	2.9	3.4	5.1	1.0	-11.2	12.1
France	8.3	3.4	1.3	1.0	2.1	1.7	1.7	3.7	-2.2	-4.0	3.7
Germany	5.3	1.6	1.1	1.8	1.7	-0.3	2.3	3.4	0.1	1.3	-2.0
Liechtenstein	0.0	3.0	1.7	0.8	0.2	2.8	3.8	2.1	1.8	0.6	3.9
Luxembourg	0.0	1.5	0.5	-4.1	2.8	-7.7	9.3	7.3	-6.9	-10.5	-12.1
Monaco	0.0	3.4	1.9	1.7	2.8	2.4	2.4	4.4	-1.7	-3.5	4.2
Netherlands	2.4	4.1	4.1	4.0	3.1	-5.3	9.3	6.4	0.5	-2.5	-1.5
Switzerland	1.4	3.0	0.2	0.0	-0.5	1.7	2.6	0.9	0.7	-0.3	2.9
OCEANIA	**1.2**	**4.3**	**3.0**	**2.2**	**3.3**	**-0.4**	**4.9**	**7.1**	**0.7**	**1.7**	**13.9**
Australia & New Zealand	*87.5*	*3.9*	*2.8*	*2.2*	*3.6*	*-0.5*	*6.9*	*7.6*	*0.0*	*2.4*	*15.6*
Australia	69.6	3.5	3.0	1.9	3.6	-0.9	10.1	7.6	-0.5	2.3	19.3

Table 6.A. Average Rates of Growth of Gross Domestic Product by Kind of Economic Activity - Agriculture, Hunting, Forestry and Fishing

Major area, region and country	Base year weights as percentage of total for world or region in 1990	Base year share as percentage of total GDP in 1990	Average rates of growth			Annual rate of change (percentage)					
			1970-1979	1980-1989	1990-1999	1997	1998	1999	2000	2001	2002
New Zealand	18.0	6.5	1.7	3.6	3.8	0.7	-4.4	7.6	2.2	2.8	0.7
Melanesia	*10.8*	*22.6*	*4.9*	*2.1*	*1.8*	*1.2*	*-8.2*	*3.9*	*5.6*	*-3.7*	*2.3*
Fiji	1.7	19.6	3.2	2.5	1.5	-13.0	7.0	16.0	-0.1	1.7	0.5
New Caledonia	2.5	15.6	1.7	3.2	-1.2	7.1	-3.2	0.9	2.1	-1.1	0.7
Papua New Guinea	5.9	28.4	7.9	1.3	3.3	2.0	-14.0	4.3	9.1	-5.4	3.6
Solomon Islands	0.5	36.6	5.0	1.5	3.6	-1.0	-2.2	-7.5	-1.7	-14.6	-0.4
Vanuatu	0.2	20.0	7.7	0.8	5.0	4.6	7.0	-12.2	7.4	0.2	1.8
Micronesia	*0.4*	*15.2*	*5.4*	*1.2*	*-2.6*	*-20.3*	*10.5*	*-0.7*	*-8.3*	*-5.8*	*-2.5*
Kiribati	0.0	18.6	2.9	-6.7	-1.5	-14.6	6.0	19.9	-8.5	0.2	-4.5
Marshall Islands	0.1	13.5	6.6	6.1	-0.5	-9.0	-1.2	2.1	-4.3	2.2	4.9
Micronesia (Federated States of)	0.2	18.6	6.6	2.6	-2.1	-22.7	14.5	-5.7	-9.4	-11.0	-5.3
Nauru	0.1	18.6	6.8	3.1	-8.5	-24.5	14.8	-4.9	-12.2	-0.8	6.4
Palau	0.0	5.4	2.9	-5.1	1.1	-21.6	0.4	28.3	-0.4	3.6	-8.2
Polynesia	*1.3*	*6.4*	*1.6*	*3.3*	*1.7*	*0.1*	*2.5*	*1.0*	*3.2*	*0.1*	*0.5*
Cook Islands	0.0	11.5	1.0	0.3	6.7	0.0	37.5	9.1	0.0	-4.2	8.7
French Polynesia	0.8	4.5	1.7	4.8	1.9	1.1	1.1	2.7	2.7	2.1	1.9
Samoa	0.2	17.4	3.1	0.4	0.7	-6.5	3.4	-3.5	0.3	-4.6	-7.2
Tonga	0.2	30.0	-0.3	2.4	0.6	3.8	0.0	-3.6	9.4	-1.7	1.0
Tuvalu	0.0	23.7	6.6	9.5	4.1	2.3	1.2	24.3	3.0	3.0	-9.2

Notes for Table 6.A - Agriculture, hunting, forestry and fishing

1/ 1990-1998
Excludes hunting.

2/ 1989-1995
Excludes hunting and forestry.

3/ 1995-1999
Excludes hunting.

4/ 2000-2002
Refers to agriculture and fishing only.

5/ 1990-2002
Includes quarrying.

6/ 1988-1991
Includes veterinary services and operation of irrigation systems.

Table 6.B. Average Rates of Growth of Gross Domestic Product by Kind of Economic Activity - Mining, Manufacturing and Utilities

Major area, region and country	Base year weights as percentage of total for world or region in 1990	Base year share as percentage of total GDP in 1990	Average rates of growth			Annual rate of change (percentage)					
			1970-1979	1980-1989	1990-1999	1997	1998	1999	2000	2001	2002
WORLD	**100.0**	**26.5**	**3.9**	**2.3**	**3.0**	**4.2**	**1.1**	**3.3**	**5.7**	**-0.9**	**2.4**
DEVELOPED ECONOMIES	**70.1**	**24.9**	**3.2**	**2.1**	**1.8**	**3.4**	**1.0**	**2.5**	**4.5**	**-2.7**	**0.7**
DEVELOPING ECONOMIES	**19.0**	**29.2**	**6.7**	**3.0**	**5.9**	**6.6**	**1.9**	**4.8**	**7.7**	**2.2**	**5.9**
TRANSITION ECONOMIES	**10.8**	**35.1**	**6.6**	**1.6**	**-5.6**	**2.8**	**-2.6**	**7.4**	**11.3**	**5.9**	**5.0**
AFRICA	**2.5**	**28.4**	**4.7**	**1.9**	**1.5**	**3.7**	**2.2**	**4.8**	**7.9**	**2.7**	**5.6**
Eastern Africa	*6.5*	*16.7*	*2.7*	*2.5*	*2.0*	*4.3*	*2.7*	*3.8*	*2.4*	*3.4*	*1.2*
Burundi	0.1	17.2	5.8	6.5	-0.8	1.0	5.0	3.0	4.0	3.2	3.2
Comoros	0.0	5.1	4.7	6.9	1.7	0.6	0.4	3.7	-2.6	3.0	1.5
Djibouti [1]	0.0	9.4	3.5	-0.5	-1.5	-0.8	-12.0	4.8	4.8	6.9	4.0
Eritrea	...	...	...	...	2.4	-30.4	-6.4	2.0	3.8	3.4	3.6
Ethiopia	...	...	...	...	11.9	7.0	10.5	11.7	3.7	8.7	8.7
Ethiopia (Former)	0.5	8.7	3.4	4.1	-8.7	...	...	...	...	...	...
Kenya	0.7	11.6	9.9	4.2	2.6	2.0	1.7	1.2	-1.4	0.9	1.3
Madagascar	0.3	14.0	3.2	5.6	-0.3	3.6	3.0	-6.2	9.0	0.3	-19.7
Malawi	0.2	20.0	8.3	3.3	2.4	1.5	2.9	4.6	-0.2	-12.5	1.4
Mauritius	0.4	24.8	8.4	7.9	5.6	6.3	6.5	1.7	10.8	5.7	-2.4
Mozambique	0.3	17.1	3.9	-0.3	8.3	31.8	28.6	24.1	14.9	24.4	14.1
Reunion	0.5	13.4	3.9	5.0	4.3	3.8	3.6	3.7	3.8	3.8	3.8
Rwanda	0.3	17.0	4.9	2.4	-3.4	20.3	6.1	-3.7	-5.2	7.0	5.0
Seychelles	0.0	11.5	15.4	5.6	12.7	23.8	15.9	5.0	-1.3	-28.5	22.1
Somalia	0.0	2.5	3.6	-0.6	2.3	9.6	9.1	13.8	3.0	3.0	3.5
Uganda	0.2	6.9	-6.9	4.0	12.1	13.8	8.5	9.0	4.8	9.3	3.5
United Republic Of Tanzania	0.3	10.0	4.1	-1.3	7.1	1.7	2.9	42.1	6.5	6.3	8.7
Zambia	1.1	41.6	0.2	-1.2	-4.7	3.6	-11.2	-8.3	2.1	8.5	7.7
Zimbabwe [2]	1.6	26.9	2.3	3.8	0.7	-0.6	-1.8	-3.7	-7.0	-10.3	-15.2
Middle Africa	*9.4*	*31.2*	*1.8*	*5.4*	*1.3*	*2.6*	*3.6*	*7.1*	*7.5*	*2.8*	*8.4*
Angola	2.6	37.8	1.9	4.9	3.1	7.8	8.8	4.9	2.6	2.7	20.6
Cameroon	2.6	27.4	4.2	9.7	0.0	-3.7	-4.8	53.8	1.6	5.5	7.2
Central African Republic	0.1	10.6	2.7	1.1	3.1	6.7	7.3	-5.8	6.2	4.7	-14.1
Chad [3]	0.2	18.1	-2.7	6.4	0.6	10.8	8.8	-4.0	-1.7	12.0	5.1
Congo	0.7	39.1	10.1	9.7	6.0	-0.3	-0.4	50.4	24.8	-2.0	-0.8
Democratic Republic of the Congo	1.6	25.5	0.1	2.3	-5.8	-4.9	-1.8	-4.0	-10.7	15.3	-0.3
Equatorial Guinea	0.0	4.6	4.1	-0.3	22.9	71.7	23.0	40.9	16.9	53.4	18.4
Gabon	1.6	44.0	0.6	2.2	2.8	4.7	6.5	-34.3	26.8	-4.3	-1.3
Sao Tome and Principe	0.0	8.5	2.2	-2.0	-3.4	1.2	-2.2	-34.5	-1.5	3.4	3.6
Northern Africa	*43.7*	*28.1*	*5.6*	*2.2*	*1.7*	*4.1*	*4.8*	*8.2*	*12.6*	*3.1*	*7.8*
Algeria	14.6	35.5	5.0	3.0	-0.5	3.1	4.7	18.8	34.5	-0.1	0.6
Egypt [4]	12.8	27.1	4.7	8.6	4.8	3.2	7.4	6.1	3.3	3.8	2.8
Libyan Arab Jamahiriya [5]	6.8	35.8	6.9	-6.0	-2.5	1.4	0.1	-0.9	0.1	3.1	7.1
Morocco [6]	4.7	27.1	6.1	2.6	3.8	5.3	2.0	2.3	2.1	4.8	3.2
Sudan	2.7	11.8	1.5	7.8	1.6	16.8	3.6	5.9	13.7	11.4	82.7
Tunisia [7]	2.1	25.7	7.5	4.9	2.7	5.9	4.9	4.9	4.5	5.5	2.4
Southern Africa	*26.9*	*33.8*	*3.1*	*1.5*	*0.5*	*3.0*	*-0.7*	*-0.2*	*3.4*	*3.0*	*3.4*
Botswana	1.2	51.6	36.2	15.5	2.6	5.4	9.1	-1.1	11.0	14.5	-2.8
Lesotho	0.1	13.2	6.8	10.7	8.3	28.2	-11.9	7.9	2.3	6.1	5.5
Namibia [8]	0.5	32.1	1.5	-2.3	2.4	9.4	3.9	2.7	2.2	1.0	2.8
South Africa	25.0	33.4	3.0	1.2	0.3	2.6	-1.3	-0.2	3.0	2.3	3.9
Swaziland	0.2	32.7	8.9	13.1	4.1	5.9	2.6	0.7	0.2	0.8	1.2
Western Africa	*13.5*	*27.7*	*8.1*	*-0.4*	*2.2*	*4.4*	*-1.0*	*2.5*	*3.7*	*0.4*	*2.0*
Benin	0.1	9.4	6.5	0.3	3.2	2.9	-0.2	0.9	9.5	9.8	8.0
Burkina Faso	0.3	17.0	4.0	4.5	3.9	14.9	9.6	-9.9	-0.2	2.3	24.9
Cape Verde	0.0	8.2	1.8	7.6	3.5	-22.8	32.5	-19.9	33.1	11.8	17.5
Cote d'Ivoire	1.7	22.1	7.8	4.9	4.5	19.4	-1.8	14.5	-6.4	7.0	-1.2
Gambia	0.0	6.7	1.5	9.6	4.1	4.8	4.6	15.8	2.1	8.2	8.6
Ghana	0.7	15.9	-3.0	1.5	4.7	4.8	3.6	5.8	3.2	2.1	4.6
Guinea	0.4	20.9	2.8	2.5	4.1	2.6	3.9	5.5	2.6	3.8	3.5

Table 6.B. Average Rates of Growth of Gross Domestic Product by Kind of Economic Activity - Mining, Manufacturing and Utilities

Major area, region and country	Base year weights as percentage of total for world or region in 1990	Base year share as percentage of total GDP in 1990	Average rates of growth			Annual rate of change (percentage)					
			1970-1979	1980-1989	1990-1999	1997	1998	1999	2000	2001	2002
Guinea-Bissau	0.0	7.9	2.8	-1.2	-0.8	15.4	-34.8	2.0	5.1	5.4	10.5
Liberia	0.0	13.4	3.1	-4.4	-18.5	805.6	9.2	22.5	57.8	-2.3	-22.3
Mali	0.2	12.9	4.5	3.0	6.8	5.7	5.2	36.1	15.1	11.5	15.9
Mauritania	0.1	18.0	-2.2	4.5	6.4	3.2	0.6	0.4	5.8	3.5	0.0
Niger	0.3	16.3	4.6	0.2	1.3	3.2	2.9	1.8	1.5	1.7	2.3
Nigeria	8.7	40.4	10.6	-1.9	1.1	1.1	-2.9	-1.8	6.3	-3.7	-0.3
Senegal [9]	0.6	15.6	7.1	3.8	3.0	1.5	6.8	4.1	5.2	12.8	9.6
Sierra Leone	0.1	14.2	-4.0	-1.7	2.0	-19.8	18.0	11.6	7.6	5.9	11.0
Togo	0.2	19.8	0.9	0.7	3.3	5.2	-2.2	2.9	-0.8	0.2	4.8
AMERICAS	**29.6**	**23.8**	**3.5**	**1.9**	**2.6**	**4.7**	**2.7**	**3.5**	**3.9**	**-4.9**	**1.6**
NORTHERN AMERICA	**24.1**	**22.9**	**3.0**	**1.9**	**2.8**	**4.3**	**3.1**	**4.7**	**3.8**	**-5.6**	**1.9**
Bermuda	0.0	5.8	3.7	0.9	1.0	1.5	2.9	4.9	0.7	-2.0	-3.6
Canada	7.4	23.1	4.0	2.1	2.4	5.0	3.4	5.0	5.6	-3.3	1.9
United States	74.0	22.9	2.9	1.9	2.8	4.2	3.0	4.6	3.6	-5.9	1.9
LATIN AMERICA AND THE CARIBBEAN	**5.5**	**28.6**	**5.8**	**1.5**	**2.1**	**6.3**	**1.2**	**-1.3**	**4.3**	**-1.3**	**0.3**
Caribbean	*1.5*	*28.8*	*5.5*	*2.9*	*2.4*	*9.8*	*2.5*	*1.3*	*7.2*	*-0.2*	*3.2*
Anguilla	0.0	2.7	3.8	5.7	8.7	16.7	10.0	25.7	6.7	1.0	20.0
Antigua and Barbuda	0.0	9.9	-1.2	9.6	2.2	5.9	4.2	7.7	6.3	4.2	3.2
Aruba	0.0	8.0	11.8	12.3	8.0	14.5	9.8	8.1	-3.1	5.3	-7.4
Bahamas [10]	0.0	5.3	-2.4	0.6	3.2	13.2	5.2	8.7	7.8	0.9	8.1
Barbados	0.0	10.1	6.5	1.1	1.0	3.3	6.3	0.7	-0.7	-5.2	-22.1
British Virgin Islands	0.0	6.5	4.5	12.9	5.6	28.0	9.4	-5.7	10.0	10.1	10.2
Cayman Islands	0.0	4.9	7.3	9.0	-0.1	-2.8	-0.3	0.1	0.1	0.1	-0.6
Cuba	0.3	26.8	4.1	5.6	-0.5	7.9	3.0	6.3	5.1	-1.1	-0.9
Dominica	0.0	9.0	-2.7	8.5	3.3	4.2	12.4	-8.8	5.8	-6.8	-2.2
Dominican Republic	0.1	22.5	8.0	3.0	3.8	7.4	5.1	5.9	7.7	-0.3	4.1
Grenada	0.0	6.9	0.9	9.1	6.3	5.9	11.5	10.2	14.2	-4.5	-0.7
Guadeloupe	0.0	6.3	5.0	0.2	5.3	9.2	4.1	5.9	5.9	5.9	4.2
Haiti	0.0	16.3	7.0	-1.1	-7.6	0.5	1.6	1.6	-0.4	-4.7	0.5
Jamaica	0.1	31.4	-0.2	1.3	0.7	0.4	-0.4	0.1	0.6	1.6	1.4
Martinique	0.0	10.1	3.9	8.0	1.6	1.6	4.1	2.5	2.5	2.5	2.6
Montserrat	0.0	4.3	1.5	1.6	-14.9	-37.6	-73.6	25.8	3.6	3.5	-3.3
Netherlands Antilles	0.0	9.5	3.3	-0.2	1.2	-13.1	-4.9	-0.2	-3.9	-0.4	1.3
Puerto Rico	0.8	42.2	7.2	3.1	3.4	12.3	1.5	-1.7	8.8	-1.7	3.8
Saint Kitts and Nevis	0.0	12.2	6.6	3.0	1.4	11.2	0.3	6.7	16.8	5.3	-2.2
Saint Lucia	0.0	9.7	2.4	8.2	0.2	2.9	-0.9	-0.6	4.1	-1.8	2.7
Saint Vincent and the Grenadines	0.0	11.6	4.7	6.3	1.8	1.3	0.0	3.9	-2.5	7.7	0.0
Trinidad and Tobago	0.1	35.9	4.0	-2.5	2.7	7.1	7.3	10.2	6.0	12.2	8.8
Turks and Caicos Islands	0.0	6.0	1.0	6.6	3.6	24.0	27.2	-15.4	1.3	-2.7	16.2
Central America	*3.7*	*22.1*	*7.0*	*2.3*	*4.3*	*9.0*	*6.7*	*4.6*	*5.8*	*-2.9*	*0.0*
Belize	0.0	15.6	5.7	3.1	3.6	2.8	-1.5	0.9	21.5	1.9	4.9
Costa Rica	0.1	23.0	8.1	2.4	7.0	7.4	11.1	22.5	-2.0	-7.7	3.6
El Salvador	0.1	23.3	4.7	-1.2	4.9	7.9	6.6	3.6	3.8	4.2	3.1
Guatemala	0.1	17.8	6.7	0.7	4.0	5.4	5.0	4.1	4.8	0.1	3.0
Honduras	0.0	18.9	7.4	2.8	3.9	6.2	3.7	2.7	5.6	3.5	3.4
Mexico	3.3	22.4	7.3	2.5	4.2	9.2	6.7	4.1	6.3	-3.1	-0.3
Nicaragua [11]	0.0	20.0	2.2	-4.6	2.9	7.7	2.3	5.3	4.1	4.0	2.3
Panama	0.0	13.5	4.1	0.9	5.0	7.6	3.2	-1.7	-1.8	-4.7	-1.8
South America	*13.5*	*31.1*	*5.6*	*1.2*	*1.4*	*5.2*	*-0.5*	*-3.4*	*3.4*	*-0.9*	*0.0*
Argentina	2.5	31.6	2.5	-1.5	3.5	9.1	1.9	-6.7	-1.3	-5.5	-1.5
Bolivia	0.1	28.8	4.9	-1.4	4.0	3.6	3.5	0.5	3.4	0.6	2.6
Brazil	7.6	30.9	9.3	2.1	-0.2	3.5	-2.2	-2.1	5.5	0.0	2.2
Chile	0.6	31.5	1.5	3.3	5.2	6.7	1.1	2.1	4.1	2.2	2.0
Colombia	0.7	26.7	6.0	4.4	1.9	1.1	3.0	-2.1	4.5	-2.7	-0.2
Ecuador [12]	0.2	23.9	31.1	2.2	2.4	1.3	1.7	-6.1	-2.9	5.4	-2.6

Table 6.B. Average Rates of Growth of Gross Domestic Product by Kind of Economic Activity - Mining, Manufacturing and Utilities

Major area, region and country	Base year weights as percentage of total for world or region in 1990	Base year share as percentage of total GDP in 1990	Average rates of growth			Annual rate of change (percentage)					
			1970-1979	1980-1989	1990-1999	1997	1998	1999	2000	2001	2002
French Guiana	0.0	8.2	2.1	21.2	5.7	1.6	1.3	1.5	1.5	1.5	1.5
Guyana	0.0	13.4	-0.6	-6.9	6.0	8.3	-3.0	2.8	-4.5	3.4	5.0
Paraguay	0.1	20.1	8.6	3.9	3.1	0.7	1.2	4.2	3.2	0.7	-2.3
Peru	0.4	21.5	4.4	-1.0	3.2	6.7	-1.1	2.7	4.8	3.0	6.3
Suriname	0.0	20.6	10.6	-2.3	0.2	4.3	4.9	-4.0	-0.6	9.8	2.5
Uruguay [13]	0.1	28.7	3.4	-0.3	0.4	6.0	3.6	-6.5	-0.9	-4.5	-11.7
Venezuela [14]	1.2	45.7	-0.5	0.3	3.4	7.4	-0.8	-7.7	3.4	0.6	-11.0
ASIA	**26.8**	**29.4**	**5.8**	**4.4**	**4.3**	**5.2**	**-1.3**	**4.8**	**8.4**	**0.4**	**4.0**
Eastern Asia	*74.4*	*30.4*	*5.4*	*5.5*	*3.9*	*5.4*	*-1.0*	*5.2*	*8.4*	*0.2*	*3.3*
China	8.9	37.4	8.6	10.6	12.9	10.5	8.9	8.1	9.6	8.1	9.9
Democratic People's Rep. of Korea	0.4	37.6	11.9	8.1	-3.2	-6.3	-1.1	6.2	1.3	3.7	0.8
Hong Kong SAR of China	0.9	19.2	8.8	7.2	3.8	5.1	-5.0	3.4	10.2	-4.7	-5.0
Japan	55.6	29.3	4.5	4.4	0.7	3.0	-5.0	1.6	6.7	-4.0	-1.7
Macao SAR of China	0.0	10.3	7.1	7.1	2.7	2.6	7.4	0.3	4.7	-10.8	-3.8
Mongolia	0.1	27.8	5.7	4.3	-1.6	-3.3	4.2	1.1	2.7	16.5	4.7
Republic of Korea	5.0	31.7	16.6	10.0	7.6	6.8	-7.1	20.1	15.6	2.3	6.8
South Central Asia	*8.7*	*21.4*	*1.9*	*5.1*	*6.7*	*2.8*	*-0.1*	*3.6*	*6.9*	*4.3*	*7.5*
Afghanistan	0.1	26.5	6.2	-0.2	-8.3	13.3	5.2	-12.4	-43.7	14.6	16.5
Bangladesh	0.3	15.0	-3.3	3.5	6.7	7.9	3.3	5.2	6.9	5.3	11.6
Bhutan	0.0	16.6	6.4	22.3	7.5	1.5	3.8	7.0	-3.5	10.3	9.3
India	4.0	19.8	4.6	7.3	5.9	3.0	3.2	4.1	6.5	3.2	6.5
Iran (Islamic Republic of) [15]	1.3	22.3	-1.5	-0.3	4.9	4.1	-0.4	3.4	8.6	1.7	8.5
Kazakhstan	0.9	20.8	...	...	-7.0	4.1	-3.4	2.7	15.5	13.5	10.4
Kyrgyzstan	0.2	29.2	...	...	-9.9	37.1	5.1	-4.5	5.8	13.2	-10.6
Maldives	0.0	11.5	15.3	13.5	7.7	17.6	13.5	11.5	6.3	6.9	11.3
Nepal	0.0	6.7	2.4	7.5	9.8	6.4	2.4	5.3	7.9	4.5	-7.9
Pakistan	0.6	19.2	5.7	8.5	4.5	7.0	6.6	0.7	3.7	3.1	16.0
Sri Lanka	0.1	20.0	6.1	4.0	7.5	8.7	5.6	5.1	9.7	-3.4	3.1
Tajikistan	0.0	34.2	...	...	-15.7	-10.9	1.8	-3.9	10.4	8.6	8.0
Turkmenistan	0.5	75.9	...	...	-12.3	-45.1	-8.2	20.6	22.6	12.8	0.5
Uzbekistan	0.7	24.4	...	...	-6.3	2.1	-38.3	0.1	-1.7	20.2	4.2
South-Eastern Asia	*6.5*	*29.4*	*8.7*	*5.9*	*6.7*	*4.8*	*-7.0*	*6.8*	*8.9*	*0.2*	*6.1*
Brunei Darussalam	0.1	50.5	9.4	-6.0	0.4	1.6	-1.4	2.0	3.9	0.2	2.6
Cambodia	0.0	9.5	-7.3	-0.7	10.1	34.0	14.8	8.8	42.9	16.9	14.9
Indonesia	2.4	33.5	10.0	7.2	6.5	4.7	-8.7	2.6	5.9	3.2	3.7
Lao People's Democratic Republic	0.0	11.4	0.1	1.4	13.1	8.7	13.7	9.2	10.9	9.8	12.2
Malaysia	1.0	38.3	9.7	7.5	8.4	7.2	-9.0	10.1	15.5	-3.7	4.0
Myanmar [16]	0.1	8.7	3.5	1.7	6.7	8.5	6.7	7.9	8.0	8.2	8.3
Philippines	0.8	28.4	6.5	1.5	2.4	4.2	-0.5	1.4	5.6	2.3	5.2
Singapore	0.6	27.8	10.9	6.9	6.8	4.7	-0.4	12.4	14.6	-10.7	8.1
Thailand	1.3	25.1	10.9	9.1	7.9	2.5	-10.1	11.3	6.3	1.9	11.0
Timor-Leste [17]	0.0	4.4	...	...	-11.5	-6.0	-6.0	-45.0	8.3	9.0	2.5
Vietnam	0.1	18.8	-0.1	4.0	11.2	13.1	11.3	9.3	10.8	10.1	9.1
Western Asia	*10.4*	*31.9*	*8.5*	*-3.1*	*4.3*	*5.7*	*0.4*	*1.2*	*8.6*	*-0.7*	*4.8*
Armenia	0.3	31.8	...	...	-8.2	1.3	-2.2	5.4	6.6	3.9	14.2
Azerbaijan	0.3	22.0	...	...	12.6	17.1	-8.3	78.6	72.8	7.3	4.1
Bahrain	0.1	34.0	11.7	-5.7	6.0	2.5	7.7	8.7	7.4	3.4	3.6
Cyprus	0.1	16.4	4.7	5.2	1.2	0.5	2.8	1.4	3.9	-1.2	0.4
Georgia	0.3	24.1	...	...	-13.3	3.4	-2.0	3.2	3.4	-2.9	8.6
Iraq [18]	0.6	24.2	11.5	-3.2	-28.4	41.0	27.3	32.5	39.5	-13.1	-2.4
Israel	0.7	19.6	2.7	4.8	3.3	5.6	4.8	0.7	14.0	-6.1	-2.4
Jordan	0.1	25.1	5.2	6.8	3.8	9.9	6.9	1.6	2.5	3.4	4.8
Kuwait	0.6	50.3	-1.8	-3.7	1.4	0.0	2.2	-8.0	-33.8	-3.4	-7.3
Lebanon	0.0	17.9	0.1	-6.7	6.2	-2.6	5.2	0.9	0.8	2.0	2.0
Oman	0.4	51.8	1.7	11.9	4.0	3.2	0.5	0.7	9.5	4.0	-2.4
Qatar	0.2	52.4	5.2	-0.2	7.6	43.2	17.1	7.0	9.0	3.4	3.4
Saudi Arabia	2.9	44.2	10.6	-9.9	3.9	0.1	3.1	-5.3	6.5	-0.1	7.9
Syrian Arab Republic	0.2	20.4	7.2	9.8	10.9	17.4	4.2	-1.7	-27.7	0.2	-3.1
Turkey	2.4	25.5	6.8	5.9	4.5	10.4	2.0	-5.0	6.0	-7.5	9.4

Table 6.B. Average Rates of Growth of Gross Domestic Product by Kind of Economic Activity - Mining, Manufacturing and Utilities

Major area, region and country	Base year weights as percentage of total for world or region in 1990	Base year share as percentage of total GDP in 1990	Average rates of growth			Annual rate of change (percentage)					
			1970-1979	1980-1989	1990-1999	1997	1998	1999	2000	2001	2002
United Arab Emirates	1.2	55.3	36.1	-1.7	3.0	-1.3	-18.6	8.8	7.6	7.5	2.1
Yemen	0.2	22.3	...	...	9.0	5.0	2.9	5.4	6.8	0.7	1.1
Yemen Arab Republic (Former)	...	...	13.1	20.9	...	...	...	...	...	...	...
Yemen Democratic (Former)	...	...	-2.0	0.9	...	...	...	...	...	...	...
EUROPE	**39.9**	**27.0**	**3.1**	**1.3**	**2.3**	**2.9**	**1.7**	**1.7**	**4.8**	**1.2**	**1.4**
Eastern Europe	*23.2*	*36.8*	*6.7*	*3.5*	*13.6*	*2.2*	*-2.0*	*7.2*	*9.3*	*5.2*	*5.1*
Belarus	1.0	40.3	...	...	-0.3	17.7	10.6	8.8	8.6	7.2	6.1
Bulgaria	0.3	39.3	7.1	5.7	-5.9	-9.5	11.2	-12.3	13.1	4.1	3.5
Czech Republic	0.5	32.9	...	2.6	-2.1	-0.2	-8.7	-2.0	9.3	0.7	-0.4
Hungary [19]	0.4	25.4	5.5	0.7	-0.6	10.3	7.4	7.0	9.5	0.9	1.0
Poland	1.0	40.7	5.5	0.0	0.2	9.6	4.0	2.9	6.4	-0.3	0.0
Republic of Moldova	0.2	29.1	...	...	-8.7	-11.7	-15.7	-5.2	14.0	6.3	1.4
Romania	0.6	40.5	10.6	1.5	-3.1	-10.2	-5.1	-1.7	2.6	7.2	7.5
Russian Federation	14.9	37.0	...	...	-6.7	2.3	-4.8	10.2	11.1	4.9	3.7
Slovakia	0.3	39.1	...	-0.6	-3.8	-7.4	3.2	5.1	-1.5	3.8	-0.3
Ukraine	3.8	35.9	...	...	-11.5	-3.0	0.0	6.0	5.0	14.0	20.8
Northern Europe	*17.5*	*24.4*	*2.3*	*1.0*	*1.5*	*3.0*	*0.1*	*1.2*	*5.6*	*-0.7*	*0.5*
Denmark	1.0	18.3	2.7	1.5	1.4	7.1	0.1	-0.3	5.3	1.4	0.7
Estonia	0.2	40.9	...	...	-3.0	10.8	2.1	-3.6	13.9	8.5	8.6
Finland	1.3	22.3	4.0	4.1	3.5	8.7	6.7	5.3	11.0	0.3	2.2
Iceland	0.0	17.5	8.1	1.9	2.2	4.5	6.4	5.3	4.8	2.9	0.7
Ireland	0.5	27.0	6.0	3.3	8.8	15.8	14.1	12.9	8.9	6.2	7.3
Latvia	0.3	35.1	...	...	-9.4	12.4	3.5	-5.6	4.4	9.6	6.6
Lithuania	0.2	20.6	...	...	-1.4	4.2	11.8	-4.6	5.4	13.9	4.6
Norway	1.3	27.2	4.1	2.4	3.3	4.9	-2.1	-0.4	3.7	1.2	0.2
Sweden	2.2	21.9	1.7	2.4	3.9	6.7	6.7	8.0	9.6	-2.1	2.8
United Kingdom	10.5	25.4	1.9	0.2	-0.4	-0.4	-3.5	-1.9	3.4	-2.4	-1.6
Southern Europe	*19.1*	*24.6*	*4.9*	*1.4*	*1.5*	*3.7*	*3.0*	*1.1*	*3.1*	*1.6*	*0.3*
Albania	0.0	37.2	3.6	3.5	-10.3	-5.7	4.1	6.4	5.0	5.7	0.2
Andorra	0.0	24.1	10.1	6.4	4.4	5.5	4.3	3.8	4.6	3.9	2.9
Bosnia and Herzegovina	0.1	22.2	...	...	5.1	32.0	27.0	-8.4	3.8	3.0	-2.6
Croatia	0.3	26.5	...	...	-6.2	6.7	5.8	3.0	3.4	4.8	4.0
Greece	0.6	18.3	7.1	1.0	0.5	-2.8	5.8	2.4	5.2	2.7	3.2
Holy See	0.0	25.0	5.5	1.3	1.3	2.7	1.8	0.3	2.7	1.0	0.0
Italy	11.5	25.0	4.6	0.9	1.2	2.6	1.8	0.3	2.6	0.9	-0.1
Malta	0.0	34.3	14.0	3.2	2.8	3.7	7.8	2.5	6.1	-3.5	4.1
Portugal	0.7	22.5	5.1	3.4	2.4	5.4	2.8	1.2	2.7	2.0	0.1
San Marino	0.0	25.0	4.6	0.9	2.4	2.6	7.5	7.5	2.6	0.9	-0.1
Serbia and Montenegro	0.4	29.4	...	...	-9.6	23.0	-2.0	-26.1	0.8	10.8	5.1
Slovenia	0.2	33.4	...	...	-0.5	6.2	4.1	2.6	7.8	4.8	4.5
Spain	5.1	24.1	5.1	2.0	2.1	5.4	4.7	3.9	3.9	2.4	0.6
TFYR Macedonia	0.1	36.5	...	...	-5.6	3.5	2.8	-2.1	3.4	-11.8	-6.1
Yugoslavia (Former)	...	...	6.0	4.6	...	...	...	...	...	...	...
Western Europe	*40.2*	*25.5*	*2.6*	*1.2*	*1.0*	*2.7*	*3.0*	*0.5*	*3.9*	*0.6*	*1.1*
Austria	1.6	23.9	3.5	2.0	2.6	4.4	4.5	3.1	5.5	1.7	1.1
Belgium	1.9	23.5	4.4	2.7	1.7	6.6	0.7	1.2	5.0	0.1	0.4
France	10.7	21.2	3.3	0.8	2.0	3.2	5.2	3.0	4.2	2.9	3.3
Germany	20.5	29.5	1.9	1.1	0.2	2.3	2.0	-1.5	3.9	-0.7	-0.1
Liechtenstein	0.0	26.1	2.4	1.6	1.0	2.8	3.8	2.1	1.8	0.6	3.9
Luxembourg	0.1	22.1	1.5	0.8	2.8	6.0	0.7	1.9	7.0	1.4	2.0
Monaco	0.0	21.2	3.9	1.5	2.7	3.9	5.9	3.7	4.8	3.4	3.8
Netherlands	2.8	22.6	5.6	1.6	1.9	0.3	2.3	1.4	3.4	0.4	-1.1
Switzerland	2.5	26.1	0.9	0.8	0.3	1.7	2.6	0.9	0.7	-0.3	2.9
OCEANIA	**1.3**	**20.6**	**2.7**	**2.6**	**2.1**	**2.3**	**1.0**	**2.6**	**3.6**	**1.3**	**-0.8**
Australia & New Zealand	*97.6*	*20.7*	*2.6*	*2.6*	*2.0*	*2.8*	*0.8*	*2.4*	*3.8*	*1.4*	*-0.8*
Australia	84.9	20.6	2.7	2.8	2.0	3.3	1.3	2.3	4.0	1.6	-1.7
New Zealand	12.7	21.9	2.0	1.4	1.4	-0.6	-2.8	3.2	2.4	-0.1	5.9

Table 6.B. Average Rates of Growth of Gross Domestic Product by Kind of Economic Activity - Mining, Manufacturing and Utilities

Major area, region and country	Base year weights as percentage of total for world or region in 1990	Base year share as percentage of total GDP in 1990	Average rates of growth			Annual rate of change (percentage)					
			1970-1979	1980-1989	1990-1999	1997	1998	1999	2000	2001	2002
Melanesia	*2.0*	*19.9*	*14.0*	*0.5*	*6.6*	*-11.4*	*7.7*	*6.0*	*-3.4*	*-1.5*	*-3.9*
Fiji	0.2	12.0	4.0	0.7	4.1	-0.4	4.8	9.6	-5.8	10.7	1.8
New Caledonia	0.7	19.5	1.7	7.0	1.8	4.9	-3.2	0.9	2.1	-1.1	0.7
Papua New Guinea	1.1	24.9	26.5	-1.8	9.0	-17.0	11.8	7.2	-4.7	-2.9	-5.9
Solomon Islands	0.0	4.1	6.7	3.1	6.0	-1.0	-2.2	-7.5	-1.7	-14.6	-4.0
Vanuatu	0.0	7.8	7.7	7.8	2.1	1.4	-0.6	3.4	-0.9	-8.9	-10.8
Micronesia	*0.0*	*3.0*	*4.8*	*0.8*	*4.9*	*3.3*	*8.9*	*17.5*	*-3.8*	*3.6*	*-6.8*
Kiribati	0.0	4.0	2.9	-6.2	6.7	6.6	19.2	3.5	10.3	9.2	0.4
Marshall Islands	0.0	1.1	6.6	6.1	14.0	2.5	-20.1	10.0	-3.6	-0.7	8.5
Micronesia (Federated States of)	0.0	4.0	6.6	3.9	0.3	4.2	-23.2	24.9	-12.5	-0.3	-5.9
Nauru	0.0	4.0	6.8	4.4	-6.3	1.8	-23.0	26.0	-18.2	-0.8	7.7
Palau	0.0	1.7	2.9	-5.1	14.8	-1.7	261.8	20.5	2.3	7.6	-21.0
Polynesia	*0.4*	*9.8*	*3.7*	*5.0*	*3.0*	*0.2*	*0.0*	*2.7*	*3.2*	*3.4*	*1.6*
Cook Islands	0.0	6.3	-6.5	2.2	4.4	0.0	14.3	0.0	25.0	10.0	0.0
French Polynesia [20]	0.4	9.1	4.1	6.4	3.7	1.1	1.1	2.7	2.7	2.1	1.9
Samoa	0.1	22.6	3.1	0.4	-2.1	-4.7	-10.8	0.7	7.4	12.9	-0.5
Tonga	0.0	6.9	8.4	3.8	3.6	-9.1	5.0	14.3	-4.2	4.3	3.5
Tuvalu	0.0	5.0	6.6	13.8	7.0	3.3	19.1	-7.0	3.0	3.0	-9.2

Notes for Table 6.B - Mining, manufacturing and utilities

1/ 1990-1998
Excludes gas.

2/ 1970-1999
Excludes gas.

3/ 1992-2001
Excludes gas.

4/ 1970-1995
Refers to oil and its products.

5/ 1975-1985
Includes oil and gas production.

6/ 1970-2002
Excludes gas.

7/ 1970-2002
Excludes gas.

8/ 1989-1993
Excludes gas.

9/ 1970-1979
Includes Construction.

10/ 1989-1995
Excludes gas.

11/ 1970-1978
Refers to metal ore mining only.

12/ 1970-1979
Excludes petroleum refining.

13/ 1970-1986
Includes sewage services.

14/ 1970-2001
Excludes gas.

15/ 1970-1992
Includes oil production.

16/ 1970-1998
Gas and Water supply are included in "Other activities".

17/ 1993-1998
Excludes gas and quarrying. Refers to non-oil and gas mining only.

18/ 1970-1986
Gas distribution is included in "Wholesale and retail trade, restaurants and hotels".

19/ 1980-1988
Excludes gas and operation of irrigation systems.

20/ 1976-1982
Includes manufacturing of energy-generating products.

Table 6.C. Average Rates of Growth of Gross Domestic Product by Kind of Economic Activity - Manufacturing

Major area, region and country	Base year weights as percentage of total for world or region in 1990	Base year share as percentage of total GDP in 1990	Average rates of growth			Annual rate of change (percentage)					
			1970-1979	1980-1989	1990-1999	1997	1998	1999	2000	2001	2002
WORLD	**100.0**	**21.8**	**3.5**	**2.5**	**3.0**	**4.9**	**1.8**	**6.0**	**23.3**	**-2.2**	**2.1**
DEVELOPED ECONOMIES	**72.9**	**20.9**	**3.0**	**2.2**	**1.8**	**4.3**	**1.3**	**2.5**	**4.9**	**-3.0**	**0.8**
DEVELOPING ECONOMIES	**14.3**	**19.8**	**6.9**	**4.0**	**4.1**	**6.1**	**-1.2**	**4.4**	**7.8**	**-0.4**	**3.8**
TRANSITION ECONOMIES	**12.7**	**34.1**	**6.6**	**1.9**	**-0.1**	**8.5**	**15.1**	**43.1**	**174.1**	**-1.5**	**4.4**
AFRICA	**1.5**	**14.0**	**5.5**	**4.0**	**1.4**	**5.3**	**2.3**	**4.4**	**3.6**	**4.5**	**3.4**
Eastern Africa	***9.5***	***13.2***	***3.8***	***3.7***	***2.5***	***4.5***	***3.0***	***3.8***	***2.5***	***2.8***	***0.7***
Burundi	0.3	16.4	5.8	6.5	-1.0	1.0	5.0	3.0	4.0	3.2	3.2
Comoros	0.0	4.2	4.1	6.5	2.2	1.2	1.1	8.3	-2.5	3.4	2.6
Djibouti	0.0	3.1	6.0	0.3	-1.1	6.2	-1.9	14.8	5.4	7.7	2.5
Eritrea	...	...	...	...	2.2	-31.2	-7.0	1.7	4.9	4.0	3.3
Ethiopia	...	...	...	...	12.1	7.0	10.5	11.7	3.7	8.7	8.7
Ethiopia (Former)	0.8	7.5	3.5	3.9	-10.9	...	...	...	...	...	...
Kenya	1.2	10.1	10.6	4.8	2.6	1.8	1.5	1.0	-1.5	0.7	1.3
Madagascar	0.5	11.8	3.0	5.6	-0.8	3.1	2.4	-6.5	8.9	0.4	-19.7
Malawi	0.4	18.6	8.0	3.1	1.6	1.0	1.5	2.5	-3.0	-14.2	-0.1
Mauritius	0.8	23.4	8.3	8.0	5.3	6.0	6.1	0.9	9.4	5.0	-2.8
Mozambique	0.5	14.4	3.9	-0.3	6.1	31.8	14.4	14.7	20.3	27.2	13.0
Rwanda [1]	0.6	16.0	5.2	3.2	-3.3	19.4	4.1	-3.4	-5.3	7.2	5.0
Seychelles [2]	0.1	10.1	19.6	6.3	10.2	28.2	17.0	5.3	-4.1	-16.9	31.0
Somalia	0.0	2.0	3.0	-0.3	2.0	8.6	8.8	18.0	3.0	3.0	3.5
Uganda	0.3	5.9	-8.6	4.5	12.3	13.0	9.5	9.4	3.7	9.7	3.0
United Republic Of Tanzania [3]	0.4	8.1	4.5	-1.6	6.1	1.5	3.1	41.0	4.8	5.0	8.0
Zambia	1.1	20.7	1.8	3.3	1.6	5.1	1.8	2.8	3.6	4.0	5.7
Zimbabwe	2.4	20.5	3.5	4.2	0.8	-0.8	-3.4	-4.6	-6.6	-11.7	-14.5
Middle Africa	***5.8***	***9.4***	***3.6***	***3.8***	***1.2***	***2.3***	***0.7***	***23.9***	***5.6***	***5.2***	***5.8***
Angola	0.7	5.0	2.1	-2.7	-1.7	5.2	8.2	7.6	8.5	10.4	10.1
Cameroon	3.6	18.6	4.4	7.9	1.9	1.3	-0.6	35.1	1.6	5.5	7.2
Central African Republic	0.1	7.4	8.0	1.9	2.9	7.0	7.6	-9.0	6.0	4.8	-14.1
Chad	0.3	16.7	-2.8	6.2	0.6	11.3	9.3	-5.1	-1.8	11.8	4.8
Congo	0.3	8.4	0.8	7.5	5.4	-1.6	-2.1	52.4	24.8	-2.0	-0.8
Democratic Republic of the Congo	0.2	1.4	-1.2	-0.2	-12.8	-5.2	-2.2	-53.2	83.1	-6.0	-1.7
Equatorial Guinea	0.0	1.3	2.0	-4.6	18.4	69.3	20.0	47.9	16.9	53.4	18.4
Gabon	0.5	6.1	10.9	-3.7	-1.6	2.3	-6.9	-8.7	22.9	-2.7	-0.8
Sao Tome and Principe	0.0	4.9	3.1	-2.7	-4.5	1.1	-10.8	-34.6	-1.4	2.7	3.0
Northern Africa	***41.1***	***12.9***	***6.8***	***6.7***	***1.8***	***6.9***	***6.2***	***5.0***	***3.2***	***5.0***	***2.1***
Algeria	9.3	11.0	8.7	5.3	-9.4	-3.8	8.4	-5.3	-16.6	2.0	2.8
Egypt [4]	15.3	15.8	5.3	8.7	5.5	7.8	9.7	7.9	4.5	4.0	2.3
Libyan Arab Jamahiriya	3.0	7.9	13.5	9.9	3.5	8.2	-1.6	3.7	2.2	2.5	-15.8
Morocco	6.5	18.4	5.7	3.6	3.4	3.4	2.1	2.7	3.5	4.2	3.3
Sudan	4.1	9.0	2.8	8.1	1.9	19.4	3.6	6.0	11.5	12.0	9.9
Tunisia	2.8	16.9	12.0	7.2	4.3	7.5	4.3	5.6	6.6	6.9	2.0
Southern Africa	***33.8***	***20.8***	***4.9***	***1.5***	***0.2***	***2.9***	***-1.7***	***-0.3***	***5.0***	***3.5***	***5.2***
Botswana	0.2	5.0	14.1	13.3	4.3	3.6	5.4	5.7	3.5	-0.5	-4.3
Lesotho [5]	0.1	11.4	5.4	14.3	5.8	4.9	-3.4	-0.4	4.4	7.8	6.5
Namibia	0.4	12.5	2.6	9.5	3.2	18.0	8.9	-3.7	3.6	6.0	6.5
South Africa	32.7	21.5	4.9	1.3	0.0	2.7	-1.9	-0.3	5.1	3.6	5.3
Swaziland	0.3	28.7	10.2	15.3	4.3	5.6	1.6	1.2	1.5	0.9	1.3
Western Africa	***9.8***	***9.8***	***7.3***	***3.5***	***2.5***	***8.8***	***-0.9***	***8.2***	***1.2***	***6.7***	***5.0***
Benin	0.2	8.6	-7.7	-2.3	5.1	4.3	1.0	4.1	9.1	9.1	6.8
Burkina Faso	0.6	15.0	3.7	4.2	3.7	16.3	9.6	-10.2	-1.5	1.8	35.5
Cape Verde	0.0	7.5	1.1	7.5	2.9	-25.8	37.1	-24.1	37.7	14.5	17.7
Cote d'Ivoire	3.2	19.7	6.3	6.8	3.6	20.4	-4.5	15.6	-5.2	6.7	-1.2
Gambia	0.0	5.7	0.8	9.9	2.8	4.2	4.0	10.0	1.6	8.4	8.5
Ghana	0.8	9.6	-1.9	0.4	3.5	4.2	2.1	10.0	3.8	3.7	4.8
Guinea	0.1	3.8	2.8	3.3	3.7	-8.6	5.2	6.5	7.0	5.5	6.0
Guinea-Bissau	0.0	6.8	2.8	-1.3	-0.9	15.3	-34.8	2.0	5.1	5.4	10.5

Table 6.C. Average Rates of Growth of Gross Domestic Product by Kind of Economic Activity - Manufacturing

Major area, region and country	Base year weights as percentage of total for world or region in 1990	Base year share as percentage of total GDP in 1990	Average rates of growth			Annual rate of change (percentage)					
			1970-1979	1980-1989	1990-1999	1997	1998	1999	2000	2001	2002
Liberia	0.1	11.4	3.1	-4.2	-11.7	1023.1	5.5	21.4	62.6	1.0	-23.8
Mali [6]	0.3	7.8	4.2	6.1	6.1	8.4	6.2	24.9	15.2	11.5	15.9
Mauritania	0.1	6.1	3.8	4.5	8.1	6.5	5.3	12.2	0.2	6.4	-1.4
Niger	0.3	8.9	4.6	0.5	-0.6	4.6	3.7	4.5	3.2	3.8	-0.2
Nigeria	2.9	6.5	12.4	2.4	-0.4	0.9	-5.4	2.1	4.9	9.1	2.7
Senegal	1.0	13.1	...	4.2	3.0	0.5	7.2	4.3	5.2	6.1	11.0
Sierra Leone	0.1	7.0	3.3	-3.9	2.3	-44.0	18.0	11.6	7.6	5.9	11.0
Togo	0.1	6.9	0.1	0.9	1.9	5.6	-2.2	2.9	-0.8	0.2	4.8
AMERICAS	**28.7**	**18.7**	**3.4**	**1.7**	**2.8**	**5.7**	**3.5**	**3.7**	**4.7**	**-5.2**	**2.2**
NORTHERN AMERICA	**23.3**	**17.9**	**2.7**	**1.9**	**3.1**	**5.5**	**4.2**	**5.0**	**4.8**	**-5.9**	**2.5**
Bermuda	0.0	2.9	3.7	-0.3	0.1	1.6	1.5	7.6	0.0	-5.6	-6.5
Canada	6.6	16.0	4.5	2.2	2.6	6.6	4.9	7.0	5.4	-4.5	2.6
United States	74.4	18.1	2.6	1.9	3.1	5.4	4.1	4.8	4.7	-6.0	2.5
LATIN AMERICA AND THE CARIBBEAN	**5.5**	**23.1**	**6.4**	**1.2**	**1.5**	**6.4**	**0.5**	**-1.9**	**4.3**	**-2.0**	**0.5**
Caribbean	*1.5*	*25.7*	*6.2*	*3.2*	*2.4*	*10.5*	*2.3*	*1.6*	*8.9*	*-1.2*	*3.4*
Anguilla	0.0	0.6	3.8	4.6	11.1	3.1	9.7	59.9	3.4	-17.7	50.0
Antigua and Barbuda	0.0	3.3	-3.3	6.1	0.2	6.0	5.5	4.5	3.0	3.0	2.7
Aruba	0.0	1.3	11.9	12.4	14.7	6.5	19.8	4.7	-1.6	5.8	-9.0
Bahamas	0.0	2.6	-3.9	-2.8	-1.5	7.9	0.0	3.0	1.9	-4.9	1.5
Barbados	0.0	6.9	5.4	-0.3	-0.1	3.5	3.4	-2.2	-1.1	-8.0	-27.8
British Virgin Islands	0.0	2.8	5.7	11.5	11.3	35.3	13.0	-7.7	12.2	12.2	12.2
Cayman Islands	0.0	1.5	9.2	6.6	-2.5	-2.8	-0.3	0.1	0.1	0.1	-0.6
Cuba	0.3	23.6	4.1	5.3	-0.6	8.3	3.3	7.1	4.3	-1.2	-1.1
Dominica	0.0	5.9	-2.3	8.8	1.7	2.5	16.8	-17.3	8.5	-14.8	0.2
Dominican Republic [7]	0.1	20.0	7.0	3.3	3.9	7.5	5.7	6.0	7.5	-1.3	4.0
Grenada	0.0	4.2	1.2	11.2	6.2	5.3	14.1	12.1	13.8	-7.6	-4.0
Haiti	0.0	15.1	7.7	-0.8	-8.2	0.6	1.9	1.2	-0.2	0.2	0.3
Jamaica	0.1	19.6	-1.1	1.5	-1.5	-2.5	-4.4	-0.7	0.9	0.6	-0.8
Montserrat	0.0	2.1	1.6	0.7	-21.4	-45.2	-84.9	10.6	0.0	0.0	0.0
Netherlands Antilles	0.0	6.7	3.3	-1.7	-1.0	-24.8	-9.5	1.3	-9.5	-6.6	-5.4
Puerto Rico	0.9	39.2	8.4	3.2	3.4	12.5	1.3	-1.4	10.6	-1.3	4.2
Saint Kitts and Nevis	0.0	10.8	6.7	2.6	0.8	11.2	-0.9	8.0	17.0	6.6	-4.0
Saint Lucia	0.0	6.9	0.8	8.7	-1.7	-0.3	-2.1	-2.7	3.0	-4.9	5.0
Saint Vincent and the Grenadines	0.0	7.3	4.0	5.7	-0.9	0.0	-6.7	0.0	-9.5	5.3	-2.5
Trinidad and Tobago	0.0	13.4	1.7	-1.1	7.2	12.3	16.2	21.0	14.2	-1.4	12.2
Turks and Caicos Islands	0.0	0.4	1.0	6.6	3.8	28.6	-5.6	2.7	-16.7	0.0	23.6
Central America	*4.0*	*18.8*	*6.9*	*1.9*	*4.5*	*9.6*	*7.2*	*4.7*	*6.3*	*-3.5*	*-0.4*
Belize	0.0	13.1	5.4	2.7	3.5	2.5	-3.2	5.0	21.4	1.9	5.2
Costa Rica	0.1	20.4	8.2	2.0	7.2	7.7	11.4	24.7	-2.9	-9.1	3.4
El Salvador	0.1	21.7	4.6	-1.3	5.1	8.0	6.6	3.7	4.1	4.0	2.9
Guatemala	0.1	15.1	6.3	0.2	2.8	2.6	3.6	2.5	1.9	1.1	0.8
Honduras	0.0	14.5	7.6	2.4	3.5	6.1	3.4	2.6	4.9	5.2	2.8
Mexico [8]	3.6	19.0	7.1	2.2	4.4	9.9	7.4	4.2	6.9	-3.7	-0.6
Nicaragua	0.0	17.4	2.1	-4.1	2.3	7.6	-0.3	5.0	6.0	4.0	2.2
Panama	0.0	9.5	3.4	0.0	4.4	6.4	3.9	-7.5	-5.3	-5.7	-4.9
South America	*13.5*	*24.5*	*6.3*	*0.8*	*0.4*	*5.0*	*-1.8*	*-4.6*	*3.0*	*-1.4*	*0.4*
Argentina	2.7	26.8	2.2	-2.0	2.8	10.2	1.7	-8.6	-3.5	-7.9	-1.5
Bolivia	0.1	17.0	5.8	-1.7	4.1	2.0	2.5	2.9	1.8	1.8	2.2
Brazil	8.4	26.8	9.5	1.7	-0.7	3.2	-3.4	-2.6	5.4	0.6	1.9
Chile	0.4	17.0	0.6	3.1	4.1	4.7	-2.3	-0.5	4.0	0.5	2.8
Colombia	0.6	17.3	6.5	2.6	0.5	0.4	-0.3	-8.4	11.7	-1.2	0.4
Ecuador [9]	0.1	10.3	10.2	0.7	-0.1	8.5	8.3	-23.5	-32.4	20.8	-0.3
Guyana [10]	0.0	4.6	7.4	-4.9	4.4	2.3	-8.7	15.5	-13.9	2.5	7.1
Paraguay	0.1	17.3	7.8	3.2	0.9	-0.3	1.0	0.0	1.0	1.3	-3.2
Peru	0.3	15.3	3.0	-0.7	2.4	5.3	-3.5	-0.8	5.9	0.3	4.2

Table 6.C. Average Rates of Growth of Gross Domestic Product by Kind of Economic Activity - Manufacturing

Major area, region and country	Base year weights as percentage of total for world or region in 1990	Base year share as percentage of total GDP in 1990	Average rates of growth			Annual rate of change (percentage)					
			1970-1979	1980-1989	1990-1999	1997	1998	1999	2000	2001	2002
Suriname	0.0	11.7	13.4	-4.2	-3.5	0.4	2.2	-8.9	12.5	5.2	5.0
Uruguay	0.2	26.3	3.4	-0.6	-0.6	5.7	1.8	-7.9	-2.1	-6.7	-14.6
Venezuela [11]	0.7	20.5	5.5	1.5	1.3	5.1	-3.9	-6.4	2.1	-0.4	-11.0
ASIA	**25.1**	**24.0**	**5.3**	**5.2**	**4.1**	**5.5**	**-0.6**	**14.8**	**67.0**	**-3.2**	**2.5**
Eastern Asia	*78.1*	*26.8*	*5.2*	*5.1*	*1.4*	*3.9*	*-5.4*	*4.2*	*8.4*	*-4.0*	*-0.3*
Democratic People's Rep. of Korea	0.3	24.3	11.9	8.1	-3.2	-6.3	-1.1	6.2	1.3	3.7	0.8
Hong Kong SAR of China	1.0	16.7	8.8	7.2	3.8	5.1	-5.0	3.4	10.2	-8.6	-9.8
Japan	66.4	26.5	4.5	4.5	0.4	3.4	-5.9	1.7	7.2	-4.9	-2.0
Macao SAR of China	0.0	8.3	7.1	7.0	1.7	2.5	5.4	-0.3	9.1	-16.2	-4.3
Mongolia	0.0	12.8	5.7	4.3	-4.4	-15.0	3.2	-2.8	3.3	31.8	22.1
Republic of Korea	6.0	28.8	17.6	10.2	7.6	6.6	-7.4	21.0	15.9	2.1	6.3
South Central Asia	*9.2*	*17.2*	*4.2*	*6.4*	*7.5*	*2.7*	*-1.6*	*4.7*	*7.9*	*5.5*	*7.8*
Bangladesh	0.3	12.9	-3.4	2.6	6.5	8.5	3.2	4.8	6.7	5.0	11.2
Bhutan	0.0	8.0	6.4	12.2	9.1	0.3	2.1	3.7	-5.2	6.2	4.9
India	4.1	15.4	4.5	6.9	5.8	1.5	2.7	4.0	7.3	3.4	6.6
Iran (Islamic Republic of)	0.8	10.4	10.8	5.1	7.3	15.1	-3.8	12.2	9.6	9.5	10.8
Kazakhstan	1.2	20.8	...	...	-7.0	4.1	-3.4	2.7	15.5	13.5	10.4
Kyrgyzstan [12]	0.3	29.2	...	...	-9.9	37.1	5.1	-4.5	5.8	-17.3	-10.7
Maldives	0.0	8.6	14.8	14.8	6.9	16.0	12.0	11.0	4.5	5.4	13.1
Nepal [13]	0.0	5.8	2.0	7.3	10.2	7.1	3.4	5.3	7.2	3.8	-10.0
Pakistan	0.6	15.6	5.3	8.2	3.8	6.9	4.1	1.5	7.6	4.4	17.6
Sri Lanka	0.1	16.6	5.9	3.0	7.8	9.6	6.0	3.7	10.1	-3.3	1.6
Tajikistan	0.0	34.2	...	...	-15.7	-10.9	1.8	-3.9	10.4	8.6	8.0
Turkmenistan	0.7	75.9	...	...	-12.3	-45.1	-8.2	20.6	22.6	12.8	0.5
Uzbekistan	1.0	24.4	...	...	-6.3	2.1	-38.3	0.1	-1.7	20.2	4.2
South-Eastern Asia	*6.2*	*21.4*	*9.2*	*7.4*	*7.1*	*5.1*	*-8.9*	*8.2*	*9.6*	*-0.4*	*6.6*
Brunei Darussalam	0.0	9.0	11.5	-4.2	5.3	...	...	...	...	...	...
Cambodia	0.0	7.4	-7.3	2.2	10.3	36.3	15.4	9.0	44.6	17.3	15.1
Indonesia	1.9	20.7	13.8	13.2	7.4	5.3	-11.4	3.9	6.0	4.1	4.0
Lao People's Democratic Republic	0.0	9.9	0.0	3.7	12.9	9.3	9.6	7.1	7.2	12.1	13.0
Malaysia	0.9	24.2	12.7	8.7	9.7	10.1	-13.4	11.7	19.1	-6.2	4.0
Myanmar	0.1	7.8	3.1	1.4	5.4	5.0	6.7	6.5	6.5	6.5	6.5
Philippines	0.9	24.8	6.3	1.0	2.3	4.2	-1.1	1.6	5.6	2.9	3.5
Singapore	0.8	25.8	11.0	6.9	6.8	4.3	-0.7	13.0	15.1	-11.5	8.3
Thailand	1.5	21.5	10.9	8.6	7.9	1.6	-11.2	12.3	6.0	1.5	11.5
Timor-Leste	0.0	2.7	...	...	-13.2	-6.9	-6.9	-50.3	10.1	10.3	2.1
Vietnam	0.1	12.3	-0.1	3.2	9.4	12.8	10.2	8.0	13.2	10.6	11.6
Western Asia	*6.5*	*15.1*	*5.7*	*4.7*	*18.7*	*26.3*	*52.3*	*84.7*	*293.4*	*-3.7*	*3.8*
Armenia	0.4	31.8	...	...	-8.2	1.3	-2.2	5.4	6.6	3.9	14.2
Azerbaijan	0.3	17.6	...	...	59.4	148.8	207.3	173.8	399.4	-3.7	4.0
Bahrain	0.0	12.0	5.3	8.8	7.0	2.4	2.0	6.3	2.5	6.6	5.7
Cyprus	0.1	14.2	5.8	4.8	1.0	0.4	1.2	0.4	3.0	-2.6	-2.2
Georgia	0.4	24.1	...	...	-13.3	3.4	-2.0	3.2	3.4	-2.9	8.6
Iraq [14]	0.3	8.8	13.4	2.5	-16.7	37.0	23.7	29.8	42.6	-17.7	1.3
Israel	0.8	17.8	2.1	5.4	3.3	5.6	4.7	0.5	14.7	-6.7	-2.8
Jordan	0.1	16.1	3.7	4.5	5.3	10.8	8.7	1.3	1.8	2.5	4.5
Kuwait	0.2	11.6	9.5	1.2	0.9	0.7	4.2	0.5	129.5	-7.6	5.8
Lebanon	0.0	12.6	-2.0	-6.7	2.7	-8.4	-0.9	-0.3	0.7	0.5	2.0
Oman	0.0	2.9	2.0	28.8	5.7	1.8	-1.7	1.0	40.2	30.1	5.6
Qatar	0.1	12.9	17.5	7.4	2.2	35.4	8.0	1.6	-7.5	13.6	0.3
Saudi Arabia	0.7	8.1	3.8	0.7	5.3	4.6	2.3	4.3	4.8	3.5	-26.8
Syrian Arab Republic	0.1	5.5	4.0	5.5	10.9	26.2	1.6	9.4	-81.2	133.5	22.9
Turkey	2.7	22.0	6.7	5.9	4.7	11.4	2.0	-5.0	6.0	-7.5	9.4
United Arab Emirates	0.2	7.4	40.7	12.8	4.4	11.6	-1.9	-5.1	7.8	3.2	1.0
Yemen	0.1	8.0	...	...	2.6	1.1	3.8	0.7	6.1	0.7	0.7
Yemen Arab Republic (Former)	...	...	12.7	13.7	...	...	...	...	...	...	...
Yemen Democratic (Former)	...	...	-8.9	0.9	...	...	...	...	...	...	...

Table 6.C. Average Rates of Growth of Gross Domestic Product by Kind of Economic Activity - Manufacturing

Major area, region and country	Base year weights as percentage of total for world or region in 1990	Base year share as percentage of total GDP in 1990	Average rates of growth 1970-1979	1980-1989	1990-1999	Annual rate of change (percentage) 1997	1998	1999	2000	2001	2002
EUROPE	**43.7**	**24.1**	**2.8**	**1.5**	**2.4**	**3.9**	**2.1**	**1.6**	**5.0**	**1.3**	**1.6**
Eastern Europe	*25.1*	*35.7*	*6.6*	*3.4*	*16.0*	*3.3*	*-1.7*	*7.9*	*9.9*	*5.5*	*5.5*
Belarus [15]	1.1	40.3	...	...	-0.3	17.7	10.6	8.8	8.6	7.2	6.1
Bulgaria	0.3	31.4	7.1	5.7	-6.7	-16.8	3.2	-5.9	10.9	4.3	4.8
Czech Republic	0.4	23.8	...	2.6	-0.6	6.2	-8.5	-2.1	8.0	1.8	1.2
Hungary [16]	0.3	19.1	5.5	0.6	-0.5	13.4	10.3	8.3	11.0	2.5	2.8
Poland	0.9	31.2	5.5	0.0	2.3	14.4	7.5	4.0	7.3	-0.8	1.5
Romania	0.7	36.7	10.0	2.3	-4.3	-6.8	-5.9	-0.3	15.4	11.9	9.5
Russian Federation [17]	16.8	37.0	...	...	-6.7	2.3	-4.8	10.2	11.1	4.9	3.7
Slovakia	0.2	24.5	...	-0.6	-1.5	-4.4	5.2	2.9	0.7	11.3	-1.2
Ukraine [18]	4.3	35.9	...	...	-11.5	-3.0	0.0	6.0	5.0	14.0	20.8
Northern Europe	*16.0*	*19.8*	*1.0*	*1.4*	*1.5*	*4.4*	*1.9*	*1.1*	*4.2*	*-1.1*	*0.7*
Denmark	1.0	15.6	2.6	1.2	0.9	8.0	0.4	-0.5	6.7	2.6	-1.1
Estonia	0.2	37.0	...	...	-1.8	14.5	5.4	-2.3	16.7	10.5	10.0
Finland	1.3	20.1	4.0	4.1	3.5	9.4	7.8	5.4	12.4	-0.2	2.2
Iceland	0.0	14.0	8.0	1.1	2.0	4.2	6.1	4.5	4.8	3.2	0.8
Ireland	0.6	25.3	6.1	3.1	8.9	16.1	16.4	13.7	8.7	6.1	7.3
Latvia	0.3	33.2	...	...	-10.1	17.1	4.0	-5.9	6.8	10.2	7.2
Lithuania [19]	0.2	20.6	...	...	-4.1	7.6	14.1	-5.4	9.8	13.1	4.9
Norway	0.6	11.6	1.7	-0.3	1.0	3.5	-0.5	-0.1	-0.7	4.2	0.0
Sweden	2.1	18.7	1.3	2.1	4.5	7.4	8.0	9.0	10.8	-4.1	3.1
United Kingdom	9.7	20.9	0.3	1.1	-0.5	1.4	-2.0	-2.9	-0.6	-2.6	-1.6
Southern Europe	*18.6*	*21.6*	*5.1*	*1.5*	*1.3*	*4.1*	*3.0*	*0.3*	*3.4*	*1.3*	*-0.1*
Andorra	0.0	20.4	10.1	6.4	4.5	6.2	4.7	3.9	4.3	3.5	3.0
Bosnia and Herzegovina	0.1	21.4	...	...	-1.0	32.0	27.5	-46.1	0.6	3.3	4.7
Greece	0.6	14.9	6.8	0.5	0.0	-3.7	5.3	1.3	4.6	3.3	3.0
Holy See	0.0	22.5	5.9	1.4	1.3	3.3	1.8	-0.3	3.2	0.8	-0.7
Italy	11.7	22.5	5.0	1.0	1.2	3.2	1.8	-0.4	3.1	0.8	-0.7
Malta	0.0	23.9	17.0	1.6	2.8	-0.7	5.3	4.0	14.6	-7.0	3.8
Portugal	0.6	19.1	5.1	3.4	1.9	5.9	2.3	0.7	2.4	2.0	0.1
San Marino	0.0	22.5	5.0	1.0	2.4	3.2	7.5	6.8	3.1	0.8	-0.7
Serbia and Montenegro	0.4	26.1	...	...	-11.6	9.3	1.8	-24.5	9.2	3.3	4.1
Slovenia	0.2	29.9	...	...	-0.5	6.6	4.6	3.1	8.6	4.9	4.6
Spain	4.9	20.4	5.1	2.0	2.2	6.1	5.1	4.0	3.7	2.0	0.7
TFYR Macedonia	0.1	34.1	...	...	-6.1	3.2	3.3	-2.3	3.3	-23.6	-6.5
Yugoslavia (Former)	...	...	6.2	5.2	...	...	...	...	...	...	...
Western Europe	*40.3*	*22.6*	*2.4*	*1.4*	*1.0*	*3.7*	*3.0*	*0.3*	*4.4*	*0.8*	*1.3*
Austria	1.6	20.6	3.6	2.2	2.7	4.3	4.8	3.1	6.5	1.4	0.5
Belgium	1.9	20.8	3.7	2.7	1.5	6.5	1.5	0.0	4.8	0.4	1.0
France	10.7	18.8	3.5	1.4	2.0	4.4	4.5	3.0	4.6	2.8	4.1
Germany	20.8	26.5	1.9	1.1	0.1	3.4	2.1	-1.9	4.5	-0.2	-0.2
Liechtenstein	0.0	24.2	2.3	1.5	1.1	2.8	3.8	2.1	1.8	0.6	3.9
Luxembourg	0.1	20.3	1.4	1.0	2.5	7.0	-0.2	1.4	7.1	1.1	2.1
Monaco	0.0	18.8	4.1	2.1	2.7	5.1	5.2	3.7	5.2	3.4	4.6
Netherlands	2.5	17.8	3.8	2.2	2.2	2.5	3.0	2.4	4.4	-0.9	-1.6
Switzerland	2.6	24.2	0.8	0.8	0.4	1.7	2.6	0.9	0.7	-0.3	2.9
OCEANIA	**1.0**	**12.9**	**2.1**	**1.6**	**1.4**	**2.6**	**1.0**	**1.6**	**2.5**	**2.6**	**-0.4**
Australia & New Zealand	*98.4*	*13.1*	*2.0*	*1.6*	*1.4*	2.6	*1.0*	*1.6*	2.6	2.7	*-0.5*
Australia	82.4	12.5	2.0	1.7	1.4	3.3	2.0	1.0	2.7	3.0	-1.7
New Zealand	16.1	17.4	1.9	1.0	1.3	-0.7	-3.8	4.7	2.0	1.1	5.6
Melanesia	*1.0*	*6.3*	*10.5*	*1.8*	*3.5*	*2.8*	*2.9*	*3.2*	*-7.2*	*-3.3*	*5.0*
Fiji	0.3	10.6	4.8	0.6	3.9	-0.8	4.8	9.6	-6.2	11.5	1.5
New Caledonia	0.1	1.0	1.7	8.3	4.7	-12.1	-3.2	0.9	2.1	-1.1	0.7
Papua New Guinea	0.6	8.8	14.5	2.0	3.2	5.1	2.8	1.3	-8.1	-8.8	7.5
Solomon Islands	0.0	2.9	8.1	2.4	5.5	-1.0	-2.2	-7.5	-1.7	-14.6	-4.0
Vanuatu	0.0	5.9	7.7	8.5	2.1	0.7	-2.5	3.4	-3.2	-12.2	-14.4
Micronesia	*0.0*	*1.1*	*4.4*	*1.2*	*8.1*	*9.2*	*0.2*	*13.6*	*-16.7*	*4.9*	*-2.1*
Kiribati	0.0	1.2	2.9	-3.2	10.7	0.0	24.8	-9.9	5.9	18.6	-3.0

Table 6.C. Average Rates of Growth of Gross Domestic Product by Kind of Economic Activity - Manufacturing

Major area, region and country	Base year weights as percentage of total for world or region in 1990	Base year share as percentage of total GDP in 1990	Average rates of growth			Annual rate of change (percentage)					
			1970-1979	1980-1989	1990-1999	1997	1998	1999	2000	2001	2002
Marshall Islands	0.0	0.9	6.6	6.1	5.5	0.1	-5.9	11.0	0.1	-3.4	4.4
Micronesia (Federated States of)	0.0	1.2	6.6	6.0	10.1	4.7	-11.9	35.4	-35.1	4.7	-8.2
Nauru	0.0	1.2	6.8	6.5	2.9	2.3	-11.6	36.7	-38.8	-0.8	21.5
Palau	0.0	0.9	2.9	-5.6	8.3	37.6	19.4	-7.5	2.1	6.9	-3.6
Polynesia	*0.6*	*7.9*	*3.8*	*4.6*	*2.3*	*0.2*	*-0.2*	*2.6*	*3.2*	*3.3*	*1.1*
Cook Islands	0.0	4.0	-6.5	0.8	1.9	0.0	25.0	0.0	20.0	16.7	0.0
French Polynesia [20]	0.5	7.3	4.2	5.9	3.2	1.1	1.1	2.7	2.7	2.1	1.9
Samoa	0.1	19.9	3.1	0.4	-2.6	-6.1	-12.6	1.3	7.3	12.1	-4.6
Tonga	0.0	5.1	9.7	3.8	0.2	0.0	12.5	11.1	0.0	0.0	3.0
Tuvalu	0.0	2.8	6.6	14.5	0.4	25.4	20.6	-11.5	3.0	3.0	-9.2

Notes for Table 6.C - Manufacturing

1/ 1987-1988
Includes Electricity, gas and water supply.

2/ 1987-2000
Includes mining and handicrafts.

3/ 1970-2002
Includes handicrafts.

4/ 1996-2001
Includes non-petrolium mining activities.

5/ 1980-1992
Includes handicrafts.

6/ 1987-1992
Includes handicrafts.

7/ 1970, 1980-1991
Includes handicrafts and repair services.

8/ 1988-2001
Basic petroleum manufacturing is included in Mining and quarrying.

9/ 1970-1979
Excludes petroleum refining.

10/ 1970-2001
Includes Electricity, gas and water supply.

11/ 1970-1979, 1984-2001
Includes petroleum refining.

12/ 1990-2000
Includes Mining and quarrying, and Electricity, gas and water supply.

13/ 1985-2003
Includes cottage industries.

14/ 1970-1991
Includes agricultural services and related activities such as cotton ginning and pressing.

15/ 1994-2002
Includes Mining and quarrying, and Electricity, gas and water supply.

16/ 1988-1991
Includes Gas.

17/ 1990-2002
Includes Mining and quarrying, and Electricity, gas and water supply.

18/ 1991-2000
Includes Mining and quarrying, and Electricity, gas and water supply.

19/ (a) 1990-1991
Includes Mining and quarrying, and Electricity, gas and water supply.

(b) 1992-1994
Includes Mining and quarrying.

20/ 1976-1979
Includes manufacturing of energy-generating products.

Table 6.D. Average Rates of Growth of Gross Domestic Product by Kind of Economic Activity - Construction

Major area, region and country	Base year weights as percentage of total for world or region in 1990	Base year share as percentage of total GDP in 1990	Average rates of growth			Annual rate of change (percentage)					
			1970-1979	1980-1989	1990-1999	1997	1998	1999	2000	2001	2002
WORLD	**100.0**	**6.3**	**3.1**	**1.9**	**0.0**	**1.5**	**1.5**	**1.5**	**1.8**	**0.5**	**2.4**
DEVELOPED ECONOMIES	**72.9**	**6.1**	**1.9**	**1.6**	**0.1**	**0.4**	**2.4**	**2.6**	**1.2**	**-0.5**	**1.8**
DEVELOPING ECONOMIES	**15.7**	**5.7**	**7.4**	**2.1**	**4.6**	**4.6**	**-1.2**	**-1.8**	**3.0**	**2.4**	**2.8**
TRANSITION ECONOMIES	**11.4**	**8.7**	**5.9**	**4.1**	**-10.1**	**1.2**	**2.4**	**1.7**	**7.2**	**6.1**	**8.6**
AFRICA	**1.9**	**5.1**	**3.9**	**0.1**	**0.3**	**4.2**	**3.6**	**-0.1**	**2.8**	**4.3**	**4.6**
Eastern Africa	*9.2*	*4.3*	*1.5*	*1.8*	*4.8*	*9.2*	*9.7*	*4.9*	*6.2*	*6.4*	*7.9*
Burundi	0.1	3.4	11.3	2.8	1.3	3.1	7.1	5.1	6.1	5.3	5.3
Comoros	0.0	3.2	8.3	-4.0	5.7	-2.1	-1.6	136.0	-3.3	4.0	33.8
Djibouti	0.2	9.6	0.0	1.9	-5.9	26.9	8.5	-2.3	3.0	4.1	4.4
Eritrea	...	...	...	...	18.2	2.0	-2.6	4.3	-13.9	6.5	8.7
Ethiopia	...	...	...	...	11.0	7.0	10.5	11.7	3.7	8.7	8.7
Ethiopia (Former)	0.7	2.5	-0.1	2.8	-15.3	...	...	...	...	...	...
Kenya	1.5	4.8	3.6	2.0	0.4	2.0	0.5	1.0	-1.0	0.0	1.0
Madagascar	0.2	1.5	-0.2	6.9	2.6	3.5	2.7	37.1	4.8	31.9	-29.7
Malawi	0.1	2.2	11.3	-0.5	5.1	9.9	4.8	15.1	-1.9	-4.7	14.1
Mauritius	0.5	5.6	7.7	2.7	5.6	-0.9	6.0	8.5	7.5	1.5	7.6
Mozambique	0.8	7.7	3.9	-0.3	11.3	18.1	26.2	3.4	4.7	9.7	15.6
Reunion	1.1	5.7	6.8	3.7	3.8	3.4	3.3	3.4	3.4	3.4	3.4
Rwanda	0.6	6.8	9.3	8.9	1.9	16.0	17.4	23.8	16.1	7.6	15.2
Seychelles	0.1	4.8	5.0	-5.5	10.8	11.7	12.9	5.5	8.6	18.1	11.9
Somalia	0.1	3.6	0.0	1.2	0.8	6.9	3.8	16.8	3.0	3.0	3.5
Uganda	0.7	4.8	3.3	4.7	12.3	5.5	19.5	20.6	15.1	14.7	12.2
United Republic Of Tanzania	0.7	4.7	1.0	0.8	13.1	13.8	11.4	-17.1	8.4	8.7	11.0
Zambia	0.8	5.1	-3.8	-2.5	-4.7	29.0	-9.1	3.2	6.6	11.5	17.4
Zimbabwe	0.9	2.9	-2.6	1.0	1.3	16.6	6.0	-0.7	11.8	-11.6	-14.6
Middle Africa	*6.7*	*4.0*	*6.5*	*-2.2*	*-3.7*	*-6.5*	*2.1*	*2.6*	*2.6*	*20.0*	*7.4*
Angola	1.1	2.9	10.1	-4.3	0.4	4.4	8.5	5.9	7.4	6.9	10.0
Cameroon	2.4	4.6	10.0	-3.6	-9.3	-30.2	-0.6	6.0	1.6	5.5	7.2
Central African Republic	0.1	2.7	3.0	2.9	7.4	7.3	7.9	32.6	7.0	4.3	-14.2
Chad	0.1	1.8	-2.8	20.8	0.0	0.0	0.0	8.3	0.0	7.7	5.3
Congo	0.1	1.4	5.7	-4.9	2.8	0.9	-0.1	158.1	23.9	-1.7	-0.8
Democratic Republic of the Congo	1.9	5.6	-1.8	2.2	-4.2	-2.9	-0.8	4.5	-18.0	72.4	12.7
Equatorial Guinea	0.0	3.7	3.6	6.9	23.3	71.1	21.4	42.2	16.9	53.4	14.2
Gabon	0.7	3.7	10.3	-3.1	-3.9	3.4	-1.2	-40.4	24.6	-3.4	-1.0
Sao Tome and Principe	0.0	6.8	3.5	-2.8	6.2	4.8	-12.1	49.2	2.0	4.2	4.3
Northern Africa	*61.8*	*7.1*	*10.3*	*1.0*	*0.6*	*5.0*	*3.4*	*-0.2*	*1.6*	*3.8*	*3.6*
Algeria	23.8	10.3	8.1	2.1	-1.0	4.3	4.1	-7.5	-13.7	2.0	10.6
Egypt	12.5	4.7	16.5	3.2	4.5	11.2	4.0	2.0	2.1	2.1	-4.8
Libyan Arab Jamahiriya	12.9	12.2	14.3	-2.0	-4.0	-4.1	-5.9	9.0	33.2	9.0	-16.9
Morocco	5.1	5.3	8.5	0.0	1.4	7.0	4.1	4.9	7.2	5.9	-0.3
Sudan	5.7	4.5	5.1	1.2	2.8	0.4	10.0	2.4	3.3	3.5	48.0
Tunisia	1.9	4.1	4.8	1.8	5.5	6.8	7.1	5.5	10.1	3.2	10.3
Southern Africa	*14.0*	*3.1*	*2.0*	*-0.2*	*-0.5*	*3.4*	*2.6*	*-2.3*	*2.7*	*3.4*	*4.2*
Botswana	0.9	7.0	11.0	7.6	5.0	5.5	4.3	11.5	2.5	1.7	4.7
Lesotho	0.3	14.3	9.6	9.0	3.5	4.1	-11.9	-7.6	9.7	0.7	7.1
Namibia	0.2	2.3	1.2	-4.1	4.1	-11.8	15.3	-13.9	-5.5	51.5	-26.2
South Africa	12.4	3.0	1.9	-0.3	-0.5	3.4	2.6	-2.4	2.7	3.3	4.3
Swaziland	0.1	2.5	17.0	-5.3	11.9	10.0	13.6	12.0	9.5	15.2	12.6
Western Africa	*8.3*	*3.1*	*5.7*	*-1.1*	*5.6*	*8.6*	*8.8*	*15.4*	*5.8*	*6.9*	*7.2*
Benin	0.3	4.0	6.3	0.5	6.7	6.0	1.6	6.0	7.2	6.7	6.2
Burkina Faso	0.5	5.1	-0.9	18.8	0.3	1.0	7.6	5.8	2.2	1.0	2.3
Cape Verde	0.1	11.9	-1.9	7.5	3.2	-2.7	9.5	6.3	12.2	-26.7	16.3
Cote d'Ivoire	0.8	1.8	11.1	-2.6	8.0	6.1	-0.8	29.8	6.4	12.7	-1.2
Gambia	0.1	4.5	5.3	0.7	6.4	7.3	7.0	31.9	3.7	7.3	9.1
Ghana	1.5	6.7	-0.9	-1.2	6.1	7.8	5.1	2.0	5.1	4.8	5.0
Guinea	0.9	9.0	2.8	3.8	4.9	13.4	6.8	8.6	6.0	8.5	7.0

Table 6.D. Average Rates of Growth of Gross Domestic Product by Kind of Economic Activity - Construction

Major area, region and country	Base year weights as percentage of total for world or region in 1990	Base year share as percentage of total GDP in 1990	Average rates of growth			Annual rate of change (percentage)					
			1970-1979	1980-1989	1990-1999	1997	1998	1999	2000	2001	2002
Guinea-Bissau	0.1	10.0	2.8	-2.7	-1.3	47.7	-54.8	3.6	15.8	7.8	-39.9
Liberia	0.0	3.3	3.1	-2.5	-16.2	442.9	28.9	22.4	8.3	15.4	1.3
Mali	0.4	4.0	3.7	-3.8	10.5	0.5	1.9	151.9	14.9	11.7	15.8
Mauritania	0.2	5.2	1.4	6.1	0.7	4.9	-0.1	2.5	4.7	4.0	-0.3
Niger	0.4	4.6	4.6	0.5	-6.9	5.3	2.9	5.6	6.7	6.2	-2.9
Nigeria	2.0	1.7	9.9	-5.5	6.1	8.6	27.0	9.9	4.1	9.1	12.5
Senegal	0.7	3.1	...	3.6	9.0	15.2	12.7	15.8	4.5	-0.1	11.5
Sierra Leone	0.0	1.9	3.7	1.3	6.2	97.3	19.3	11.0	7.9	5.9	11.0
Togo	0.2	3.6	8.7	3.8	3.1	0.1	-2.2	2.9	-0.8	0.2	4.8
AMERICAS	**24.4**	**4.6**	**3.2**	**1.4**	**1.7**	**4.1**	**6.3**	**3.5**	**2.4**	**-1.4**	**1.6**
NORTHERN AMERICA	**20.0**	**4.5**	**2.5**	**1.3**	**1.9**	**2.9**	**7.0**	**5.4**	**2.9**	**-1.0**	**3.1**
Bermuda	0.0	7.4	3.7	3.5	-1.8	2.5	-20.4	37.2	-0.6	9.7	-18.6
Canada	10.6	6.4	3.3	2.8	-0.3	5.6	3.1	4.9	4.2	3.8	1.8
United States	71.5	4.3	2.4	1.1	2.2	2.6	7.5	5.4	2.7	-1.6	3.3
LATIN AMERICA AND THE CARIBBEAN	**4.4**	**5.4**	**6.9**	**1.9**	**1.0**	**9.3**	**3.4**	**-4.1**	**0.4**	**-3.0**	**-5.3**
Caribbean	*1.4*	*5.5*	*0.8*	*2.7*	*2.0*	*7.9*	*9.3*	*7.0*	*5.5*	*-1.0*	*3.2*
Anguilla	0.0	16.7	3.8	8.4	3.8	4.0	8.0	21.2	-6.4	-21.4	-13.6
Antigua and Barbuda	0.0	11.6	1.5	11.2	3.4	8.0	10.0	8.0	6.5	4.0	3.5
Aruba	0.0	7.0	7.7	8.2	3.8	35.2	8.1	-28.5	6.3	3.6	6.2
Bahamas	0.0	3.9	3.0	3.0	-7.1	1.4	-6.0	-3.2	-4.2	-10.7	-4.6
Barbados	0.0	5.6	0.3	2.4	0.6	14.6	16.4	10.9	0.0	-2.8	-19.3
British Virgin Islands	0.0	5.8	-8.0	9.6	7.5	11.5	34.5	7.7	17.3	17.3	17.3
Cayman Islands	0.0	9.5	10.1	6.4	0.0	-2.8	-0.3	0.1	0.1	0.1	-0.6
Cuba	0.4	7.3	10.1	7.5	-7.3	3.2	5.7	7.5	9.7	1.6	0.3
Dominica	0.0	6.2	0.3	4.4	3.4	-1.7	-4.1	3.8	2.0	1.3	-22.2
Dominican Republic	0.2	6.6	10.8	6.6	6.5	17.1	19.6	17.7	5.6	0.5	3.2
Grenada	0.0	8.2	2.4	7.3	5.5	8.2	16.9	9.4	17.0	-19.3	1.0
Guadeloupe	0.1	7.4	8.7	6.1	2.6	9.2	4.1	5.9	5.9	5.9	4.2
Haiti	0.0	5.8	13.7	1.4	6.2	11.3	8.1	4.6	8.0	0.9	0.9
Jamaica	0.1	11.7	-6.9	1.9	-1.4	-4.0	-5.8	-1.5	0.2	2.0	2.3
Martinique	0.0	4.8	1.4	9.2	2.7	1.6	4.1	2.5	2.5	2.5	2.6
Montserrat	0.0	30.3	3.1	13.9	-6.9	72.6	33.5	-13.5	-35.8	-7.7	39.4
Netherlands Antilles	0.0	5.0	3.3	-1.0	-2.3	-1.8	-1.7	-24.5	-5.8	-2.8	-1.5
Puerto Rico [1]	0.2	2.3	-10.5	2.8	7.1	15.3	10.1	8.7	8.0	4.1	9.2
Saint Kitts and Nevis	0.0	12.0	-0.8	11.5	3.8	6.0	7.0	12.6	29.2	4.2	-4.5
Saint Lucia	0.0	5.4	3.0	9.6	0.4	0.4	3.4	0.5	-1.0	-5.0	-4.8
Saint Vincent and the Grenadines	0.0	7.9	0.4	5.5	4.9	16.0	13.8	-4.5	-12.7	5.5	-1.7
Trinidad and Tobago	0.1	9.2	14.3	-7.5	4.0	-5.3	13.2	6.5	3.0	-23.5	-2.1
Turks and Caicos Islands	0.0	9.8	1.0	6.6	4.8	16.1	8.8	10.9	-3.6	-4.0	12.2
Central America	*3.0*	*3.5*	*6.4*	*-0.4*	*3.4*	*8.6*	*4.8*	*5.4*	*3.5*	*-4.1*	*0.6*
Belize	0.0	6.6	7.1	7.2	2.6	-5.7	-1.7	18.1	25.8	9.1	8.5
Costa Rica	0.1	4.3	11.5	-1.7	2.9	6.1	17.4	-1.6	4.4	14.4	-1.5
El Salvador	0.1	3.5	9.4	-2.1	3.8	6.1	8.5	-1.8	-3.4	9.6	4.6
Guatemala	0.0	2.0	14.3	-2.5	5.1	9.7	9.8	7.8	-18.3	12.2	-15.3
Honduras	0.0	4.6	5.4	3.1	0.9	-3.0	5.3	10.5	4.2	-5.2	-14.6
Mexico	2.7	3.6	6.4	-0.2	3.2	9.3	4.2	5.0	4.1	-5.3	1.7
Nicaragua	0.0	4.5	-9.9	9.4	1.4	-8.6	-1.5	39.1	0.3	4.1	-11.8
Panama	0.0	1.1	4.6	-13.6	21.5	5.5	6.7	16.0	2.5	-9.7	-10.0
South America	*13.5*	*6.1*	*7.7*	*2.2*	*0.4*	*9.5*	*2.6*	*-7.0*	*-0.8*	*-2.9*	*-7.6*
Argentina	1.8	4.4	2.8	-4.9	4.9	16.6	8.7	-7.9	-9.3	-11.6	-33.4
Bolivia	0.0	3.1	4.9	-6.8	5.9	4.9	35.9	-16.9	-6.8	-6.2	14.4
Brazil	9.0	7.1	13.2	6.2	-1.5	7.6	1.5	-3.8	3.0	-2.6	-2.5
Chile	0.7	7.4	-3.3	5.5	5.8	6.3	1.9	-9.9	-0.9	3.0	2.1
Colombia	0.7	4.7	4.2	5.0	-3.2	2.2	-7.2	-27.0	-3.9	13.8	8.6
Ecuador	0.1	2.0	6.3	-0.9	-3.9	2.7	-0.2	-24.9	18.3	4.0	14.7

Table 6.D. Average Rates of Growth of Gross Domestic Product by Kind of Economic Activity - Construction

Major area, region and country	Base year weights as percentage of total for world or region in 1990	Base year share as percentage of total GDP in 1990	Average rates of growth			Annual rate of change (percentage)					
			1970-1979	1980-1989	1990-1999	1997	1998	1999	2000	2001	2002
French Guiana	0.0	12.7	10.9	15.1	2.0	1.6	1.5	1.6	1.6	1.6	1.6
Guyana [2]	0.0	4.0	0.6	-0.9	5.8	13.1	4.7	-10.0	6.6	2.0	0.5
Paraguay	0.1	5.5	19.6	3.2	2.5	0.6	1.0	2.5	2.0	-22.7	-11.0
Peru	0.4	3.9	3.5	0.3	7.6	14.9	0.6	-10.5	-6.1	-6.7	7.9
Suriname	0.0	6.1	28.1	-4.2	-2.9	-20.6	16.4	-14.6	-11.9	4.5	0.6
Uruguay	0.1	3.4	9.0	-5.0	5.2	2.4	9.8	8.9	-11.1	-5.6	-22.2
Venezuela	0.6	4.5	11.8	-9.7	3.4	17.2	-0.3	-16.5	-2.7	13.5	-19.8
ASIA	**31.9**	**8.3**	**5.3**	**2.4**	**1.7**	**0.9**	**-2.8**	**-1.3**	**0.5**	**0.2**	**1.7**
Eastern Asia	*78.8*	*9.1*	*3.9*	*3.3*	*1.1*	*-0.2*	*-2.0*	*-1.6*	*-0.8*	*-0.7*	*-0.8*
China	3.9	4.7	4.4	11.2	9.9	2.6	9.0	4.3	9.6	12.1	8.3
Democratic People's Rep. of Korea	0.2	6.3	11.9	8.1	-3.2	-6.3	-1.1	6.2	1.3	3.7	0.8
Hong Kong SAR of China	0.9	5.1	8.8	7.2	3.8	5.1	-5.0	3.4	10.2	-4.3	-1.0
Japan	65.8	9.8	3.4	2.6	-0.5	-1.2	-2.5	-1.4	-2.4	-3.8	-3.6
Macao SAR of China	0.0	5.8	7.1	7.3	-4.1	-2.4	-21.1	-3.6	-27.3	-18.6	37.2
Mongolia	0.0	3.1	5.7	5.8	-9.9	-2.7	-1.1	1.6	-14.6	10.8	18.5
Republic of Korea	6.3	11.4	12.0	7.5	4.8	1.4	-8.6	-9.1	-3.1	5.6	3.2
South Central Asia	*9.1*	*6.3*	*4.0*	*1.8*	*6.5*	*5.3*	*5.6*	*7.3*	*4.9*	*6.7*	*9.8*
Afghanistan	0.1	6.5	15.8	-0.7	-2.2	13.3	5.2	-12.4	-43.7	5.2	27.0
Bangladesh	0.4	5.7	-7.5	7.9	7.8	9.5	8.9	8.5	8.6	7.9	12.9
Bhutan	0.0	8.0	6.4	3.0	11.2	9.9	20.6	22.0	18.8	12.9	16.4
India	3.6	5.0	2.0	5.0	5.6	10.2	6.2	8.0	6.9	3.7	6.3
Iran (Islamic Republic of)	1.1	5.3	9.1	-5.6	2.2	-9.7	-5.2	13.9	7.7	7.5	14.9
Kazakhstan	1.9	12.3	...	...	-15.3	8.0	22.3	8.0	14.0	27.4	19.5
Kyrgyzstan	0.2	7.7	...	...	-16.2	-17.0	-27.7	-2.0	29.7	14.0	1.4
Maldives	0.0	3.2	31.7	8.5	9.9	30.3	29.7	14.0	-13.8	11.9	-0.6
Nepal	0.1	8.6	2.0	9.3	5.3	6.6	2.2	6.8	9.6	0.9	1.7
Pakistan	0.4	3.7	7.4	4.6	2.5	1.3	-4.9	5.2	-0.4	0.9	15.3
Sri Lanka	0.1	6.6	2.7	4.7	5.7	6.5	6.9	6.7	6.9	2.3	-1.1
Tajikistan	0.0	11.0	...	...	-23.3	9.8	46.1	-17.6	19.5	4.4	29.2
Turkmenistan	0.1	4.8	...	...	7.5	-3.0	23.6	8.9	-39.0	-9.9	89.0
Uzbekistan	1.2	10.8	...	...	-5.7	2.6	14.3	-6.4	-7.7	25.0	4.2
South-Eastern Asia	*4.1*	*5.3*	*10.4*	*4.0*	*5.3*	*2.1*	*-24.4*	*-3.7*	*4.4*	*1.1*	*1.4*
Brunei Darussalam	0.0	4.3	11.1	4.1	2.6	8.9	2.0	-15.1	-3.5	-28.8	34.0
Cambodia	0.0	2.4	-7.3	-3.3	10.3	-5.2	-14.7	30.6	7.1	9.4	26.8
Indonesia	1.4	5.6	16.4	6.2	5.4	7.4	-36.4	-1.9	5.6	4.2	4.1
Lao People's Democratic Republic	0.0	2.9	-0.2	6.8	6.3	5.0	-14.1	-0.6	-9.2	13.0	-6.5
Malaysia	0.4	3.9	11.2	3.1	8.2	10.6	-24.0	-4.4	1.0	2.3	2.3
Myanmar	0.1	1.8	6.9	3.9	17.3	9.8	6.5	16.5	16.5	16.5	16.5
Philippines	0.6	6.0	14.4	-2.9	2.5	16.2	-9.6	-1.6	26.3	-5.0	-3.3
Singapore	0.4	5.4	5.4	4.4	11.6	16.6	2.4	-9.0	-1.8	-3.2	-10.8
Thailand	1.1	6.0	5.1	9.2	-1.3	-25.6	-38.3	-6.8	-9.5	-0.9	6.0
Timor-Leste	0.0	13.4	...	...	1.7	6.0	6.0	-27.3	33.4	18.5	-0.6
Vietnam	0.1	3.8	-0.1	3.7	9.9	11.3	-0.5	2.4	7.5	4.9	10.6
Western Asia	*7.9*	*6.9*	*16.1*	*-4.0*	*1.4*	*6.3*	*2.0*	*-6.6*	*4.8*	*-0.5*	*13.8*
Armenia	0.6	17.9	...	...	-22.3	3.9	10.6	7.7	28.9	4.8	47.0
Azerbaijan	0.4	8.1	...	...	5.2	66.1	52.1	4.7	2.6	5.9	105.0
Bahrain	0.1	5.8	23.2	-2.5	0.2	-6.2	1.0	16.9	1.4	9.7	11.0
Cyprus	0.1	9.5	3.0	-0.1	1.9	-3.9	-0.3	-0.7	-2.2	2.0	4.5
Georgia	0.4	8.7	...	...	-19.3	51.6	35.3	-21.5	4.0	10.4	43.1
Iraq	0.6	7.3	28.1	-4.4	-28.1	71.2	26.7	-13.6	107.6	28.3	-29.6
Israel	0.6	5.0	2.4	0.0	7.0	1.5	-6.1	-8.2	-3.0	-7.3	-5.0
Jordan	0.0	4.0	12.3	-1.4	2.4	-12.8	-19.1	-16.2	8.5	7.9	1.6
Kuwait	0.1	1.8	17.2	-8.0	2.8	-2.9	-1.8	0.6	43.3	-2.1	3.0
Lebanon	0.0	3.3	-4.5	-6.7	8.2	-8.1	-18.8	-11.5	-2.3	4.7	2.0
Oman	0.1	2.3	4.8	3.0	3.7	48.1	4.2	-28.0	3.6	12.2	4.6
Qatar	0.1	4.2	10.2	-0.3	8.6	45.4	-24.4	-12.7	3.9	23.8	4.2
Saudi Arabia	2.0	8.7	22.2	-4.7	-2.0	-0.1	2.0	-2.4	5.9	0.4	22.9
Syrian Arab Republic	0.1	3.8	17.1	-5.8	5.8	5.2	0.5	-5.1	1.9	6.1	7.0
Turkey	2.1	6.3	1.8	6.7	0.4	4.6	0.7	-12.5	4.4	-5.5	-4.9

Table 6.D. Average Rates of Growth of Gross Domestic Product by Kind of Economic Activity - Construction

Major area, region and country	Base year weights as percentage of total for world or region in 1990	Base year share as percentage of total GDP in 1990	Average rates of growth			Annual rate of change (percentage)					
			1970-1979	1980-1989	1990-1999	1997	1998	1999	2000	2001	2002
United Arab Emirates	0.6	7.9	48.6	-0.4	3.5	6.7	2.5	-3.7	3.3	2.5	1.2
Yemen	0.1	2.7	...	...	1.8	28.4	1.4	0.7	8.2	2.3	2.3
Yemen Arab Republic (Former)	...	...	16.5	-3.1	...	...	...	...	...	...	...
Yemen Democratic (Former)	...	...	31.6	3.8	...	...	...	...	...	...	...
EUROPE	**40.3**	**6.5**	**2.0**	**2.1**	**-2.5**	**-0.8**	**1.2**	**2.4**	**3.5**	**1.6**	**3.2**
Eastern Europe	*22.8*	*8.7*	*5.9*	*4.4*	*-13.4*	*-2.3*	*-2.5*	*3.3*	*10.0*	*4.5*	*1.7*
Belarus	0.8	8.0	...	...	-8.5	21.4	13.8	-2.4	-2.1	-5.2	10.8
Bulgaria	0.2	5.2	7.1	5.7	-4.1	-21.4	32.4	2.9	1.4	3.9	3.2
Czech Republic	0.7	9.9	...	0.6	-7.4	-8.3	-19.2	-2.0	-6.3	-12.5	-8.2
Czechoslovakia (Former)	...	...	4.7	...	...	...	...	...	...	...	...
Hungary	0.3	5.5	1.7	0.0	-2.8	8.2	5.8	4.3	6.9	4.5	16.7
Poland	1.0	9.5	3.4	-3.1	3.5	13.6	9.3	3.5	-0.7	-7.9	-8.6
Republic of Moldova	0.2	6.5	...	...	-7.5	-15.9	-14.8	4.1	-30.4	24.5	5.7
Romania	0.4	5.4	7.7	0.4	-0.1	-19.3	-4.5	-2.3	6.3	5.3	6.9
Russian Federation	14.9	8.9	...	...	-12.1	-5.4	-6.3	6.0	17.4	9.9	2.7
Slovakia	0.4	13.2	...	0.2	-9.3	-1.5	-15.6	-29.9	12.0	-11.0	9.3
USSR (Former)	...	...	6.3	5.0	...	...	...	...	...	...	...
Northern Europe	*18.2*	*6.1*	*2.0*	*2.7*	*-0.7*	*3.0*	*4.7*	*2.6*	*4.2*	*3.8*	*7.4*
Denmark	1.0	4.5	-2.3	1.3	-0.5	-4.1	10.1	-1.3	5.6	-3.8	1.3
Estonia	0.1	7.1	...	...	0.3	15.2	18.3	-8.2	13.8	4.3	13.9
Finland	1.8	7.4	1.4	3.2	-2.5	9.3	8.0	-1.8	-2.6	-2.7	2.7
Iceland	0.1	8.2	1.5	3.1	1.8	11.3	12.0	6.5	15.0	8.0	-15.0
Ireland	0.4	4.8	6.4	-3.8	10.1	12.4	22.2	18.7	22.1	6.5	3.1
Latvia	0.3	9.4	...	...	-17.1	8.2	17.0	8.1	8.2	6.1	10.8
Lithuania	0.3	9.8	...	...	-8.9	7.4	16.9	-12.3	-18.2	7.4	12.8
Norway	0.9	4.3	2.8	2.3	0.9	6.5	3.5	-7.1	-1.7	1.5	-0.1
Sweden	2.6	6.1	0.8	2.2	-1.4	-4.5	-0.1	3.2	1.3	5.2	2.3
United Kingdom	10.7	6.2	2.8	3.1	-1.4	3.7	3.2	3.8	4.6	5.0	10.9
Southern Europe	*21.3*	*6.6*	*0.5*	*1.4*	*1.0*	*0.8*	*3.5*	*3.7*	*4.1*	*5.0*	*2.2*
Albania	0.0	6.6	6.3	2.7	6.3	-6.4	21.0	15.0	18.0	16.5	0.9
Andorra	0.0	8.5	5.0	7.0	4.3	2.3	6.8	8.4	6.7	7.2	7.2
Bosnia and Herzegovina	0.1	3.1	...	...	13.2	79.9	25.1	-5.2	-2.3	-5.1	-1.4
Croatia	0.2	5.4	...	...	-2.4	13.0	0.5	-10.0	-7.1	2.3	13.9
Greece	1.1	7.4	3.2	-1.3	0.8	2.5	10.6	2.3	5.7	13.0	2.0
Holy See	0.0	5.8	0.9	1.4	0.1	-1.7	-0.1	1.2	2.9	4.1	0.6
Italy	11.2	5.8	0.1	1.0	0.0	-1.8	-0.2	1.2	2.8	4.1	0.5
Portugal	0.7	5.5	3.4	3.7	2.7	8.0	5.4	2.9	4.9	2.5	-3.9
San Marino	0.0	5.8	0.1	1.0	1.2	-1.8	5.5	8.4	2.8	4.1	0.5
Serbia and Montenegro	0.3	5.9	...	...	-13.2	9.9	5.8	-39.2	-0.6	25.5	2.6
Slovenia	0.1	4.3	...	...	2.4	7.7	4.6	15.8	2.8	-2.2	1.1
Spain	7.5	8.5	0.2	2.6	2.0	2.2	7.2	8.5	6.0	5.5	4.8
TFYR Macedonia	0.1	7.1	...	...	-9.5	0.2	2.9	12.2	-3.0	-5.0	-4.1
Yugoslavia (Former)	...	...	5.3	-3.7	...	...	...	...	...	...	...
Western Europe	*37.7*	*5.7*	*0.7*	*0.4*	*0.2*	*-2.9*	*-0.7*	*1.4*	*1.3*	*-2.3*	*2.1*
Austria	1.8	6.5	3.3	-0.3	3.9	0.0	3.9	1.4	0.8	-3.2	-0.5
Belgium	1.7	5.1	2.3	-0.7	1.3	4.3	-1.8	3.5	7.7	0.6	-0.9
France	11.3	5.4	0.4	0.7	-1.9	-10.4	-0.4	2.2	7.1	1.5	16.9
Germany	16.6	5.7	0.8	-0.3	0.5	-1.5	-2.7	0.1	-2.9	-6.1	-5.9
Liechtenstein	0.0	8.3	3.0	6.4	2.5	2.8	3.8	2.1	1.8	0.6	3.9
Luxembourg	0.1	6.9	2.1	3.4	3.3	4.7	7.1	3.6	5.4	6.3	4.1
Monaco	0.0	5.4	0.9	1.4	-1.2	-9.8	0.3	2.9	7.7	2.0	17.5
Netherlands	2.9	5.6	-1.3	0.6	0.3	3.3	3.2	5.4	4.2	2.1	-3.2
Switzerland	3.3	8.3	1.5	5.6	1.8	1.7	2.6	0.9	0.7	-0.3	2.9
OCEANIA	**1.5**	**5.8**	**1.4**	**2.9**	**2.7**	**9.1**	**7.4**	**6.2**	**-14.8**	**10.6**	**5.7**
Australia & New Zealand	*97.5*	*5.8*	*1.5*	*2.9*	*2.8*	*9.5*	*7.6*	*6.3*	*-15.2*	*10.9*	*5.8*
Australia	89.3	6.1	1.8	3.0	2.9	10.1	8.8	5.7	-15.6	11.7	5.3
New Zealand	8.2	3.9	-0.8	1.9	1.3	3.8	-6.1	13.8	-9.6	2.0	11.6

Table 6.D. Average Rates of Growth of Gross Domestic Product by Kind of Economic Activity - Construction

Major area, region and country	Base year weights as percentage of total for world or region in 1990	Base year share as percentage of total GDP in 1990	Average rates of growth			Annual rate of change (percentage)					
			1970-1979	1980-1989	1990-1999	1997	1998	1999	2000	2001	2002
Melanesia	*1.5*	*4.1*	*-5.2*	*1.7*	*1.4*	*-10.0*	*-0.4*	*-1.6*	*-5.2*	*-4.5*	*-0.1*
Fiji	0.3	4.0	7.5	-3.9	5.0	7.3	14.9	5.6	-11.5	-0.4	5.4
New Caledonia	0.4	3.0	1.7	3.5	-4.3	6.6	-3.2	0.9	2.1	-1.1	0.7
Papua New Guinea	0.8	4.9	-10.1	2.7	2.4	-17.3	-3.1	-4.7	-5.5	-6.6	-2.1
Solomon Islands	0.0	3.2	9.4	6.2	2.8	-1.0	-2.2	-7.5	-1.7	-14.6	-4.0
Vanuatu	0.0	5.8	7.7	7.3	1.2	0.8	-16.4	8.7	7.5	0.7	-1.2
Micronesia	*0.1*	*5.7*	*4.5*	*0.9*	*2.6*	*5.5*	*30.0*	*11.3*	*13.7*	*17.4*	*-4.1*
Kiribati	0.0	3.6	2.9	-4.7	10.0	34.7	50.3	107.6	1.3	28.4	-11.5
Marshall Islands	0.0	11.4	6.6	6.1	-2.5	-9.4	43.8	-0.6	9.2	-5.5	-1.9
Micronesia (Federated States of)	0.0	3.6	6.6	4.2	5.0	22.2	35.6	39.3	37.2	34.2	-7.7
Nauru	0.0	3.6	6.8	4.7	-1.8	19.4	35.9	40.6	-40.2	-0.8	13.5
Palau	0.0	7.1	2.9	-5.8	4.5	1.1	15.8	-22.3	4.0	4.9	4.4
Polynesia	*0.9*	*6.2*	*9.5*	*0.8*	*1.6*	*1.5*	*1.1*	*2.5*	*4.0*	*2.4*	*0.5*
Cook Islands	0.0	1.8	-1.5	-2.8	3.8	0.0	33.3	0.0	25.0	20.0	16.7
French Polynesia	0.9	6.2	10.6	0.8	1.7	1.1	1.1	2.7	2.7	2.1	1.9
Samoa	0.1	7.4	3.1	0.4	-0.5	6.8	-4.7	3.3	21.5	4.1	-17.9
Tuvalu	0.0	8.5	6.6	5.6	0.7	0.1	30.2	-21.0	3.0	3.0	-9.2

Notes for Table 6.D - Construction

1/ 1970-2000
Refers to contract construction only.

2/ 1970-2001
Includes engineering and sewage services.

Table 6.E. Average Rates of Growth of Gross Domestic Product by Kind of Economic Activity - Wholesale and Retail Trade, Restaurants and Hotels

Major area, region and country	Base year weights as percentage of total for world or region in 1990	Base year share as percentage of total GDP in 1990	Average rates of growth			Annual rate of change (percentage)					
			1970-1979	1980-1989	1990-1999	1997	1998	1999	2000	2001	2002
WORLD	**100.0**	**13.9**	**3.9**	**3.5**	**3.0**	**5.3**	**4.1**	**2.9**	**4.5**	**1.9**	**3.7**
DEVELOPED ECONOMIES	**79.1**	**14.8**	**3.2**	**3.5**	**3.5**	**5.2**	**5.0**	**3.0**	**4.1**	**1.7**	**3.7**
DEVELOPING ECONOMIES	**17.2**	**13.9**	**5.8**	**3.4**	**4.3**	**5.7**	**0.9**	**2.7**	**5.6**	**2.3**	**3.3**
TRANSITION ECONOMIES	**3.7**	**6.3**	**8.5**	**3.6**	**-1.2**	**6.1**	**-0.6**	**0.3**	**7.7**	**7.1**	**6.3**
AFRICA	**2.4**	**14.3**	**4.6**	**3.6**	**2.8**	**2.3**	**2.9**	**2.4**	**0.0**	**5.3**	**6.9**
Eastern Africa	*9.1*	*11.8*	*3.4*	*2.8*	*3.6*	*3.8*	*3.3*	*5.3*	*4.5*	*7.2*	*1.4*
Burundi	0.1	4.8	1.9	7.2	-1.8	1.0	5.3	3.1	4.2	3.4	3.4
Comoros	0.1	25.1	7.1	4.1	-1.5	-2.3	-2.5	-7.1	-1.3	-4.5	-3.8
Djibouti	0.1	15.6	-1.8	0.4	-0.5	4.9	4.0	-1.6	0.6	4.1	1.8
Eritrea	...	...	...	...	1.6	-13.3	-18.1	1.3	-8.8	4.5	3.8
Ethiopia	...	...	...	...	8.8	7.1	19.4	8.0	10.2	11.2	12.2
Ethiopia (Former)	0.7	6.5	1.8	2.9	-6.8	...	...	...	...	...	...
Kenya	1.1	9.7	1.9	4.1	3.6	3.9	2.9	1.4	1.1	29.1	1.4
Madagascar	0.4	10.2	2.2	0.6	2.2	3.8	3.4	5.6	4.8	31.9	-17.1
Malawi	0.4	15.4	7.4	0.6	4.3	17.2	-6.0	10.2	-0.2	1.1	1.6
Mauritius	0.5	15.0	8.3	5.7	6.1	6.5	5.0	4.8	6.2	2.5	3.2
Mozambique	0.1	2.9	3.9	-0.3	2.1	9.2	11.4	2.6	2.6	6.2	2.8
Reunion	1.4	19.9	8.8	2.6	3.5	3.1	3.0	3.0	3.0	3.0	3.0
Rwanda [1]	0.3	10.2	10.3	0.7	-2.9	24.6	6.6	-0.2	-3.2	5.0	5.0
Seychelles	0.1	27.0	7.5	3.8	-17.2	-14.9	-22.9	12.0	4.6	224.6	158.6
Somalia	0.1	9.2	5.7	-2.3	-4.8	7.1	3.6	-35.7	3.0	3.0	3.5
Uganda	0.6	12.8	-1.9	3.3	8.8	4.4	11.2	5.5	3.1	6.9	5.8
United Republic Of Tanzania	0.7	14.0	1.2	2.4	5.3	2.0	3.9	31.6	6.5	6.7	7.0
Zambia	0.6	10.6	5.2	5.5	1.1	4.7	3.5	3.4	3.2	7.2	5.0
Zimbabwe	1.8	15.2	1.9	2.8	4.0	2.3	0.9	2.0	10.5	-6.9	-11.1
Middle Africa	*8.7*	*14.6*	*0.3*	*1.7*	*1.3*	*2.6*	*2.9*	*8.9*	*-2.8*	*5.2*	*7.5*
Angola	1.4	10.7	0.6	1.1	0.0	5.6	6.1	4.1	4.0	5.3	11.6
Cameroon [2]	2.8	15.0	0.7	0.1	4.0	1.9	2.1	23.1	1.6	5.5	7.2
Central African Republic	0.4	23.5	-0.4	-0.1	-2.6	2.4	3.4	-23.8	-4.1	-4.1	37.8
Chad [3]	0.4	21.3	-0.1	5.1	2.6	4.9	2.9	1.7	1.7	10.4	5.5
Congo	0.5	13.4	4.4	5.8	-3.4	4.9	8.2	-48.1	-14.7	13.2	2.6
Democratic Republic of the Congo	2.2	17.8	0.7	2.0	-6.2	-3.8	0.1	-15.9	2.0	-3.2	6.0
Equatorial Guinea	0.0	7.4	4.1	2.3	24.1	71.8	21.4	41.1	16.9	53.4	14.2
Gabon	0.9	12.4	-4.2	5.5	6.8	4.3	0.3	48.1	-22.0	3.7	0.0
Sao Tome and Principe	0.0	10.8	8.4	-0.1	7.2	0.7	-27.1	156.5	-2.2	2.8	2.5
Northern Africa	*47.9*	*15.6*	*7.3*	*5.1*	*3.8*	*2.6*	*4.4*	*3.3*	*-1.8*	*2.7*	*10.5*
Algeria	10.5	12.9	6.7	3.6	2.2	2.6	4.4	-2.2	-15.2	2.3	5.8
Egypt [4]	18.5	19.7	8.4	6.8	3.4	3.7	6.6	10.0	0.7	1.5	1.9
Libyan Arab Jamahiriya	3.2	8.5	14.7	-1.6	10.3	3.8	0.9	-5.1	1.6	2.9	-1.8
Morocco [5]	4.5	13.1	5.2	4.1	8.1	0.1	4.9	1.7	3.1	4.4	2.8
Sudan	8.9	19.9	3.2	7.8	0.5	0.5	0.5	0.5	1.6	4.2	63.1
Tunisia	2.4	14.5	12.5	3.9	5.7	5.5	6.8	7.3	4.4	4.1	1.2
Southern Africa	*19.9*	*12.6*	*2.9*	*3.2*	*1.2*	*1.0*	*-0.8*	*0.6*	*4.6*	*3.5*	*3.1*
Botswana [6]	0.3	6.9	20.8	0.4	10.8	13.9	4.7	5.6	6.2	6.5	8.2
Lesotho	0.1	7.5	4.9	4.6	5.3	7.8	-5.1	-2.5	-2.0	1.2	4.4
Namibia	0.2	6.9	2.4	2.6	4.9	8.9	7.9	0.6	5.7	3.7	4.6
South Africa	19.2	13.0	2.7	3.2	0.9	0.4	-1.1	0.3	4.5	3.4	2.8
Swaziland	0.1	8.0	3.2	4.4	5.0	8.7	8.0	8.1	5.6	4.1	6.4
Western Africa	*14.4*	*14.9*	*5.2*	*1.7*	*1.8*	*2.0*	*2.0*	*-4.0*	*-0.6*	*16.4*	*2.6*
Benin	0.5	20.2	4.4	6.7	3.3	6.5	2.7	6.3	4.4	5.7	4.9
Burkina Faso	0.1	1.7	4.0	-14.2	31.1	-2.1	3.7	8.7	12.8	4.1	-8.2
Cape Verde	0.1	21.2	-2.0	4.3	3.0	10.0	7.6	8.7	5.9	-10.5	15.6
Cote d'Ivoire [7]	2.7	17.2	3.9	4.1	-0.3	-2.5	6.2	1.6	-4.5	1.0	-1.2
Gambia	0.2	39.8	13.4	2.3	-3.4	4.2	3.0	-44.6	-9.3	31.5	-27.5
Ghana	0.2	3.0	-1.0	3.7	7.8	9.4	7.0	5.6	4.0	5.1	5.6

Table 6.E. Average Rates of Growth of Gross Domestic Product by Kind of Economic Activity - Wholesale and Retail Trade, Restaurants and Hotels

Major area, region and country	Base year weights as percentage of total for world or region in 1990	Base year share as percentage of total GDP in 1990	Average rates of growth			Annual rate of change (percentage)					
			1970-1979	1980-1989	1990-1999	1997	1998	1999	2000	2001	2002
Guinea	1.0	26.7	2.8	2.8	3.7	-1.3	4.7	3.2	1.9	2.0	1.8
Guinea-Bissau	0.1	25.7	11.7	5.8	-2.7	7.8	-50.3	5.5	6.8	8.5	-0.1
Liberia	0.0	6.6	3.1	-0.9	-14.9	400.0	30.7	52.0	14.8	5.8	3.3
Mali	0.5	14.1	6.7	1.8	7.7	6.1	4.9	-0.6	6.2	4.6	9.1
Mauritania	0.2	12.5	7.7	4.4	3.9	3.5	2.5	4.8	3.6	4.6	12.0
Niger	0.5	14.1	4.6	0.8	4.7	2.1	5.8	5.1	6.4	5.7	7.8
Nigeria	6.0	14.0	2.9	3.6	-0.2	2.0	-2.1	-14.6	-5.3	32.1	2.5
Senegal [8]	1.8	24.0	13.8	-4.7	2.9	7.4	7.9	4.1	2.1	30.0	6.0
Sierra Leone	0.2	24.7	1.3	6.9	-6.6	-24.7	0.8	-9.8	-22.0	-7.9	-10.3
Togo	0.5	21.9	5.5	0.7	1.5	4.3	-2.2	2.9	-0.8	0.2	4.8
AMERICAS	**39.5**	**16.7**	**3.8**	**3.6**	**4.2**	**7.8**	**8.2**	**5.1**	**6.3**	**1.7**	**5.4**
NORTHERN AMERICA	**34.0**	**17.0**	**3.5**	**4.3**	**4.4**	**7.9**	**9.1**	**6.0**	**6.5**	**2.1**	**6.4**
Bermuda	0.0	19.0	3.7	-0.2	0.5	0.4	-0.2	-0.4	-3.9	-4.5	2.4
Canada	6.3	13.7	5.1	3.6	2.5	4.0	7.3	5.8	5.3	2.9	6.7
United States	79.8	17.4	3.4	4.4	4.6	8.1	9.2	6.0	6.5	2.0	6.4
LATIN AMERICA AND THE CARIBBEAN	**5.5**	**14.9**	**4.8**	**0.2**	**2.4**	**7.3**	**2.0**	**-0.9**	**5.1**	**-1.1**	**-2.1**
Caribbean	*1.4*	*19.4*	*4.8*	*2.4*	*2.3*	*5.6*	*7.1*	*4.4*	*5.1*	*2.6*	*3.7*
Anguilla	0.0	33.0	3.8	10.5	4.1	13.5	3.1	5.9	-4.6	7.5	-9.3
Antigua and Barbuda	0.0	22.8	2.3	6.9	3.0	5.0	0.4	3.4	1.3	-2.8	0.3
Aruba	0.0	27.2	9.0	9.5	4.1	1.1	11.8	-2.2	6.3	4.0	-8.3
Bahamas	0.1	30.8	3.0	3.0	2.4	12.5	4.3	7.4	6.2	-0.9	5.8
Barbados	0.0	27.0	7.2	2.4	0.4	2.7	5.9	1.8	5.7	-4.0	-24.5
British Virgin Islands	0.0	26.2	14.3	4.1	7.9	14.5	7.7	4.6	8.9	8.9	8.9
Cayman Islands	0.0	24.1	6.5	8.9	1.1	-2.8	-0.3	0.1	0.1	0.1	-0.6
Cuba	0.4	24.7	9.6	0.9	-4.2	-2.3	-2.7	9.1	5.4	4.1	3.1
Dominica	0.0	10.8	-4.7	8.6	4.6	2.4	1.4	2.8	2.7	-1.6	-5.8
Dominican Republic [9]	0.1	17.5	7.4	4.4	7.6	12.4	9.4	8.6	10.7	-0.1	3.6
Grenada	0.0	15.2	1.5	4.8	4.9	2.1	4.2	7.7	3.5	-2.6	1.6
Guadeloupe	0.0	18.1	6.3	1.8	1.8	9.2	4.1	5.9	5.9	5.9	4.2
Haiti	0.0	16.9	5.7	0.0	-3.4	0.8	3.0	2.2	4.7	0.6	0.0
Jamaica	0.1	20.9	-3.4	1.5	2.1	0.9	-1.6	-0.5	1.3	0.2	0.3
Martinique	0.1	18.5	5.2	5.6	1.1	1.6	4.1	2.5	2.5	2.5	2.6
Montserrat	0.0	10.2	2.3	2.3	-14.4	-48.5	-30.3	-3.0	-13.1	-0.8	0.3
Netherlands Antilles	0.0	17.7	3.3	3.4	1.0	-0.9	6.6	-0.1	-3.3	-0.2	1.1
Puerto Rico	0.4	16.0	2.2	3.8	4.6	5.8	12.6	1.5	2.3	0.7	4.5
Saint Kitts and Nevis	0.0	18.3	4.5	11.2	2.0	5.5	3.6	-1.5	-9.0	-7.8	0.6
Saint Lucia	0.0	22.1	5.8	4.6	2.9	6.7	3.4	7.7	8.0	-12.8	-1.9
Saint Vincent and the Grenadines	0.0	11.6	0.9	6.5	7.5	7.7	8.2	8.5	7.8	2.4	1.6
Trinidad and Tobago	0.1	15.4	3.5	-2.3	4.6	18.3	8.7	7.5	11.9	26.6	14.4
Turks and Caicos Islands	0.0	10.3	1.0	6.5	3.1	2.8	1.7	0.2	5.0	-6.5	14.6
Central America	*5.2*	*22.2*	*6.0*	*1.1*	*3.2*	*10.1*	*5.6*	*3.0*	*11.4*	*-1.7*	*-0.2*
Belize	0.0	15.7	2.6	3.4	4.4	8.1	6.6	3.0	18.8	-0.5	7.0
Costa Rica	0.1	17.8	5.5	0.9	5.2	6.1	8.5	2.4	1.5	1.9	1.3
El Salvador	0.1	18.1	3.3	-4.3	5.5	2.9	4.0	2.0	3.6	1.9	1.0
Guatemala	0.1	24.1	5.3	-0.3	4.0	3.8	4.5	3.2	4.1	2.7	2.8
Honduras	0.0	10.3	6.9	-0.9	2.9	3.5	3.1	0.7	4.0	3.0	2.8
Mexico	4.8	22.6	6.3	1.3	3.1	10.7	5.6	3.1	12.4	-2.0	-0.4
Nicaragua [10]	0.1	17.7	-2.7	4.9	1.1	5.6	7.2	10.4	4.0	3.8	3.1
Panama	0.1	16.7	4.6	-0.7	6.2	8.9	2.2	-2.9	1.6	-1.7	3.9
South America	*7.2*	*11.7*	*4.3*	*-0.6*	*1.8*	*5.9*	*-1.1*	*-4.5*	*0.6*	*-1.3*	*-4.9*
Argentina	1.8	15.6	2.6	-1.5	4.5	10.9	3.4	-6.9	-2.4	-7.8	-16.8
Bolivia	0.0	12.1	3.5	1.8	3.5	4.1	2.0	0.8	2.3	1.9	2.1
Brazil	3.1	8.8	4.9	-0.6	0.0	3.0	-4.7	-0.6	0.5	0.7	0.2
Chile	0.3	12.2	2.4	3.1	7.3	7.6	3.5	-4.4	3.8	2.5	2.0

Table 6.E. Average Rates of Growth of Gross Domestic Product by Kind of Economic Activity - Wholesale and Retail Trade, Restaurants and Hotels

Major area, region and country	Base year weights as percentage of total for world or region in 1990	Base year share as percentage of total GDP in 1990	Average rates of growth			Annual rate of change (percentage)					
			1970-1979	1980-1989	1990-1999	1997	1998	1999	2000	2001	2002
Colombia	0.4	11.4	6.1	2.4	0.1	1.8	-1.5	-15.7	7.5	2.2	2.4
Ecuador	0.1	16.0	8.8	1.5	1.6	4.4	1.1	-11.3	3.8	4.3	3.7
French Guiana	0.0	13.4	12.4	9.0	3.4	1.6	-0.1	1.1	1.1	1.1	0.9
Guyana	0.0	5.8	1.8	-3.3	3.8	5.6	5.3	-8.0	5.2	0.5	0.1
Paraguay [11]	0.1	29.0	8.8	3.5	0.3	0.1	-4.2	-9.2	-4.9	2.4	-3.5
Peru	0.5	18.9	4.2	-0.7	2.9	7.5	-2.7	-0.6	4.2	0.9	4.3
Suriname	0.0	18.1	23.1	-5.0	-0.5	11.4	2.1	-5.6	-4.2	-12.7	1.0
Uruguay	0.1	12.6	2.8	0.3	5.2	8.8	2.4	-3.4	-5.3	-3.1	-24.3
Venezuela	0.7	17.6	4.7	-2.0	-0.7	4.1	-3.0	-9.6	4.0	3.4	-10.9
ASIA	**22.4**	**12.9**	**3.7**	**5.3**	**4.6**	**4.2**	**-1.7**	**-0.3**	**2.7**	**2.0**	**3.1**
Eastern Asia	*72.1*	*12.9*	*2.5*	*5.7*	*4.3*	*3.7*	*-2.4*	*-1.4*	*1.4*	*1.3*	*2.3*
China	4.2	7.7	6.0	12.8	6.1	8.5	7.7	7.2	7.8	9.4	7.2
Democratic People's Rep. of Korea	0.2	9.1	13.9	7.6	-2.7	-6.3	-1.1	6.2	1.3	3.7	0.8
Hong Kong SAR of China [12]	2.6	24.2	8.8	7.2	3.8	5.1	-5.0	3.4	10.2	0.2	5.1
Japan [13]	56.9	13.2	1.7	4.8	3.8	2.9	-3.1	-4.4	-1.2	0.5	1.2
Macao SAR of China	0.0	9.3	7.1	7.2	1.3	-18.1	-8.5	-3.4	16.7	8.6	12.2
Mongolia	0.1	27.8	5.7	1.2	-2.0	16.4	-3.0	1.5	25.6	9.2	13.0
Republic of Korea	4.8	13.4	8.7	8.4	5.7	4.0	-10.9	14.1	9.8	4.0	5.6
South Central Asia	*10.4*	*11.2*	*6.2*	*4.7*	*6.9*	*6.2*	*5.3*	*5.4*	*4.8*	*7.9*	*6.6*
Afghanistan	0.1	9.1	3.4	-0.2	0.3	13.3	5.2	-12.4	-43.7	10.6	30.7
Bangladesh	0.6	12.5	6.4	3.1	5.4	6.0	6.5	7.3	6.5	5.7	12.0
Bhutan	0.0	6.5	6.4	2.4	5.6	7.4	3.2	3.1	5.6	3.5	4.5
India	5.1	11.1	4.1	6.1	7.6	7.6	7.6	7.2	4.1	8.8	4.2
Iran (Islamic Republic of)	2.2	17.5	11.0	1.7	3.4	3.7	5.2	0.9	6.2	8.5	9.7
Kazakhstan	0.8	8.0	...	...	-2.9	3.0	-2.6	1.9	5.2	13.5	9.2
Kyrgyzstan	0.1	4.0	...	...	-8.7	7.7	9.5	3.9	11.4	13.5	9.1
Maldives	0.0	20.4	11.5	17.4	14.2	7.4	5.4	6.4	5.3	0.0	3.2
Nepal	0.1	10.2	3.3	3.4	5.8	4.1	5.8	3.9	6.8	1.5	-10.4
Pakistan	1.0	14.9	5.5	7.1	3.3	-1.1	3.0	1.9	5.2	2.2	16.1
Sri Lanka	0.2	15.4	5.8	6.8	5.8	6.1	5.2	2.2	10.5	-4.1	1.0
Tajikistan	0.0	8.2	...	...	-5.9	46.4	13.6	-33.9	68.2	-4.7	13.3
Turkmenistan	0.0	2.1	...	...	4.0	4.1	8.1	31.2	-4.9	27.5	-0.7
Uzbekistan	0.3	4.9	...	...	6.3	16.9	-14.4	11.7	7.3	4.0	4.2
South-Eastern Asia	*8.6*	*17.2*	*6.4*	*5.5*	*5.0*	*3.7*	*-9.8*	*2.8*	*6.1*	*2.6*	*5.5*
Brunei Darussalam	0.1	12.6	26.0	1.3	-1.2	6.1	2.1	-14.8	-0.4	2.1	11.5
Cambodia	0.0	13.7	-7.3	-2.0	2.4	-0.1	-2.8	6.0	2.7	3.2	3.8
Indonesia	2.7	17.0	7.9	6.8	4.8	5.8	-18.2	-0.1	5.7	5.3	3.6
Lao People's Democratic Republic	0.0	7.6	68.5	39.8	10.3	10.6	9.5	9.5	7.0	6.9	7.5
Malaysia	0.8	13.6	10.7	5.1	9.3	8.0	-3.4	3.1	4.8	3.0	2.6
Myanmar [14]	0.5	22.7	3.1	0.3	4.6	5.0	5.2	5.6	5.6	5.6	5.6
Philippines [15]	1.0	15.8	6.4	3.3	3.6	4.0	2.5	4.9	4.9	5.3	5.6
Singapore	0.9	17.3	7.4	6.2	7.4	6.2	-6.1	6.0	13.8	-3.1	1.8
Thailand	2.3	19.4	6.2	7.5	3.0	-3.5	-12.5	3.6	3.8	-0.4	11.9
Timor-Leste	0.0	7.7	...	...	-6.0	3.7	3.7	-57.0	44.3	30.7	-3.0
Vietnam	0.2	17.2	-0.1	5.7	6.5	6.9	4.4	2.1	6.0	4.0	7.3
Western Asia	*8.8*	*11.9*	*8.6*	*3.5*	*3.9*	*6.9*	*4.5*	*-1.4*	*7.8*	*-1.9*	*1.9*
Armenia	0.1	4.0	...	...	-1.9	4.7	6.4	11.0	8.5	16.4	15.2
Azerbaijan	0.1	3.3	...	...	-0.7	14.1	9.4	26.2	9.8	9.9	9.9
Bahrain	0.1	11.2	13.1	1.7	6.3	3.4	7.4	-4.7	3.2	5.3	8.5
Cyprus	0.2	21.4	5.4	9.5	4.7	3.1	6.5	4.2	7.0	4.0	-2.4
Georgia	0.2	6.0	...	...	-8.7	5.8	2.4	4.7	10.3	12.7	4.6
Iraq [16]	0.8	14.8	15.8	2.1	-1.4	1.3	15.9	-4.0	9.9	20.4	-6.3
Israel	0.7	8.2	6.7	2.5	4.9	1.6	3.3	4.5	5.9	-3.8	-3.2
Jordan	0.0	8.5	3.6	-2.9	7.8	5.2	-11.7	-2.1	2.8	3.5	4.8
Kuwait	0.2	7.6	11.7	0.5	-2.4	0.0	5.9	2.0	32.7	1.0	5.9
Lebanon	0.1	28.4	-2.3	-6.7	4.3	-5.6	-3.3	-1.3	3.0	3.8	2.0
Oman	0.2	11.0	6.8	13.5	6.1	6.4	10.1	-8.1	6.3	11.2	3.2
Qatar	0.1	5.5	14.8	-1.1	4.5	5.6	11.6	3.4	10.5	3.0	2.7

Table 6.E. Average Rates of Growth of Gross Domestic Product by Kind of Economic Activity - Wholesale and Retail Trade, Restaurants and Hotels

Major area, region and country	Base year weights as percentage of total for world or region in 1990	Base year share as percentage of total GDP in 1990	Average rates of growth			Annual rate of change (percentage)					
			1970-1979	1980-1989	1990-1999	1997	1998	1999	2000	2001	2002
Saudi Arabia	1.0	7.0	10.0	1.8	1.8	7.2	11.3	8.5	4.8	3.9	-22.5
Syrian Arab Republic	0.4	22.7	9.9	1.4	3.1	-5.1	0.9	1.4	-7.9	0.3	4.6
Turkey	4.1	19.1	7.1	5.9	4.9	11.1	2.7	-4.9	9.5	-7.9	8.7
United Arab Emirates	0.4	9.0	41.3	2.1	5.5	4.8	4.9	-2.8	4.1	2.4	2.2
Yemen	0.2	8.9		...	1.6	6.3	7.7	-1.0	8.6	4.2	4.7
Yemen Arab Republic (Former)	...	...	10.5	4.7	...	...	...	...	...	...	...
Yemen Democratic (Former)	...	...	-2.1	1.8	...	...	...	...	...	...	...
EUROPE	**34.2**	**12.2**	**4.1**	**2.4**	**0.6**	**3.3**	**3.5**	**2.2**	**3.7**	**1.8**	**1.1**
Eastern Europe	*8.1*	*5.8*	*8.5*	*3.7*	*-10.5*	*4.9*	*1.3*	*1.7*	*7.8*	*6.8*	*5.6*
Belarus	0.3	5.0	...	...	-2.1	16.7	23.6	6.9	7.9	15.9	6.4
Bulgaria	0.1	4.9	7.1	5.7	-6.6	-25.2	-10.6	22.1	7.1	7.6	4.9
Czech Republic	0.4	10.9	...	1.1	3.5	4.2	9.9	0.2	1.2	6.9	8.4
Czechoslovakia (Former)	...	...	6.7		...	...	...	...	...	...	...
Hungary	0.4	11.7	5.3	-0.2	-0.1	6.5	5.4	0.5	2.0	5.9	8.8
Poland	0.7	13.0	5.6	1.2	5.5	8.1	5.4	7.9	3.7	3.6	5.2
Republic of Moldova	0.1	5.0	...	...	5.3	-12.5	16.6	43.5	-23.6	1.5	3.2
Romania	0.2	6.2	7.9	5.8	-1.6	-10.8	4.1	0.4	1.1	1.5	6.8
Russian Federation	4.7	5.2	...	...	-2.1	5.1	-6.7	-2.0	12.1	3.9	8.1
Slovakia	0.1	4.2	...	3.8	15.0	24.0	6.8	3.5	3.6	5.1	-2.4
Ukraine	1.2	5.0	...	...	-10.6	-1.6	-1.7	7.8	9.1	41.7	-11.6
USSR (Former)	...	...	8.9	3.9	...	...	...	...	...	...	...
Northern Europe	*19.4*	*12.2*	*2.1*	*2.6*	*3.2*	*5.5*	*5.8*	*4.1*	*3.7*	*1.7*	*2.9*
Denmark	1.6	12.7	1.8	0.0	3.0	-0.6	4.2	3.6	1.8	1.2	8.2
Estonia	0.1	8.0	...	...	-1.6	3.6	5.6	1.5	7.9	7.9	9.7
Finland	1.5	11.6	2.5	4.5	-0.2	5.4	7.9	4.0	3.7	3.2	1.6
Iceland	0.1	13.3	4.5	3.4	3.9	6.9	12.8	7.2	5.3	-1.4	2.2
Ireland	0.6	13.6	6.1	1.6	5.5	8.7	8.5	5.9	13.1	8.6	2.8
Latvia	0.1	6.6	...	...	1.5	12.8	18.8	10.2	9.2	10.8	11.9
Lithuania	0.2	9.2	...	...	3.2	10.8	8.3	-2.8	10.0	10.6	8.2
Norway	1.3	11.7	4.0	1.5	5.3	10.2	8.3	2.9	8.6	-2.6	2.9
Sweden	2.5	11.1	2.0	2.5	2.6	1.5	6.7	6.4	2.5	0.7	3.0
United Kingdom	11.6	12.7	1.7	2.9	3.1	6.3	5.1	3.9	2.8	1.9	2.1
Southern Europe	*28.3*	*16.5*	*4.5*	*1.9*	*2.0*	*3.2*	*3.2*	*0.7*	*4.3*	*1.9*	*0.4*
Albania [17]	0.0	12.7	12.0	2.7	3.6	-25.0	10.0	12.0	10.0	11.0	0.5
Andorra	0.0	17.2	9.6	6.3	4.5	3.6	3.2	4.8	2.5	2.8	3.5
Bosnia and Herzegovina	0.3	23.3	...	...	-2.1	21.8	5.9	-36.5	-2.9	18.1	15.2
Croatia	0.4	16.2	...	...	-2.6	14.6	-0.5	-8.9	6.7	9.5	11.5
Greece	1.4	17.9	5.7	2.0	1.5	8.1	3.6	-2.5	3.9	9.9	2.1
Holy See	0.0	16.1	5.2	2.5	1.7	2.2	2.9	-0.2	5.7	1.4	-0.5
Italy	16.4	16.1	4.3	2.1	1.6	2.1	2.9	-0.2	5.6	1.4	-0.6
Malta	0.0	12.8	10.6	2.9	2.1	-0.8	-1.4	0.0	3.5	2.8	1.6
Portugal	1.1	17.1	3.9	1.1	2.3	5.4	4.1	2.8	3.0	2.0	0.3
San Marino	0.0	16.1	4.3	2.1	2.9	2.1	8.7	6.9	5.6	1.4	-0.6
Serbia and Montenegro	0.4	12.8	...	...	-12.0	0.7	20.0	-20.6	23.4	-12.8	5.8
Slovenia	0.2	12.4	...	...	1.8	3.0	2.4	5.7	3.9	2.5	2.2
Spain	8.1	17.2	4.6	1.9	2.1	3.6	3.6	4.9	1.8	1.3	1.2
TFYR Macedonia	0.0	8.0	...	...	6.2	-2.0	3.4	7.1	27.9	-21.7	10.1
Yugoslavia (Former)	...	...	8.2	-4.6	...	...	...	...	...	...	...
Western Europe	*44.2*	*12.7*	*3.3*	*2.1*	*1.9*	*2.0*	*3.3*	*2.3*	*2.6*	*1.0*	*-0.1*
Austria	2.5	16.7	4.6	2.2	2.2	1.9	4.2	3.0	4.1	0.7	1.5
Belgium	2.4	13.1	2.2	0.2	1.1	1.2	1.3	0.8	1.2	1.4	0.5
France	14.3	12.7	4.2	2.5	1.4	3.7	4.4	2.9	3.4	2.1	-0.5
Germany	16.9	11.0	3.1	1.8	2.2	-0.4	1.6	1.1	1.7	0.9	-0.8
Liechtenstein	0.0	19.2	2.2	4.1	1.3	2.8	3.8	2.1	1.8	0.6	3.9
Luxembourg	0.2	15.6	6.0	2.7	4.5	7.8	14.7	6.3	6.5	3.6	0.6
Monaco	0.0	12.7	4.8	3.2	2.0	4.4	5.1	3.5	4.0	2.6	0.0
Netherlands	4.0	14.5	3.7	2.3	3.8	7.5	6.7	6.3	4.4	-0.8	0.1
Switzerland	4.0	19.2	0.7	3.3	0.6	1.7	2.6	0.9	0.7	-0.3	2.9

Table 6.E. Average Rates of Growth of Gross Domestic Product by Kind of Economic Activity - Wholesale and Retail Trade, Restaurants and Hotels

Major area, region and country	Base year weights as percentage of total for world or region in 1990	Base year share as percentage of total GDP in 1990	Average rates of growth			Annual rate of change (percentage)					
			1970-1979	1980-1989	1990-1999	1997	1998	1999	2000	2001	2002
OCEANIA	**1.5**	**13.1**	**2.0**	**2.4**	**3.2**	**4.3**	**4.5**	**5.1**	**1.3**	**4.2**	**6.7**
Australia & New Zealand	*96.1*	*13.0*	*1.9*	*2.4*	*3.3*	*4.2*	*4.6*	*5.1*	*1.3*	*4.4*	*6.9*
Australia	81.9	12.6	1.9	2.7	3.4	4.5	5.1	4.7	1.0	4.4	7.4
New Zealand	14.2	15.6	1.5	0.8	2.5	2.1	1.5	7.9	3.3	3.8	3.7
Melanesia	*2.2*	*14.2*	*5.6*	*2.6*	*2.8*	*11.8*	*-0.2*	*5.4*	*-3.3*	*-1.8*	*0.7*
Fiji	0.5	19.7	5.8	2.4	5.0	2.6	6.3	9.9	3.6	3.5	5.0
New Caledonia	0.9	16.8	1.7	3.5	0.0	28.9	-3.2	0.9	2.1	-1.1	0.7
Papua New Guinea	0.6	9.5	10.5	1.6	3.6	8.3	-2.3	7.8	-13.6	-5.9	-2.2
Solomon Islands	0.0	7.1	7.9	3.0	6.7	-1.0	-2.2	-7.5	-1.7	-14.6	-4.0
Vanuatu	0.1	32.2	7.7	3.6	4.1	2.7	2.8	-1.2	2.9	-4.9	-4.9
Micronesia	*0.2*	*22.9*	*4.2*	*0.7*	*0.1*	*1.2*	*-0.1*	*-3.0*	*6.2*	*-2.6*	*1.8*
Kiribati	0.0	20.1	2.9	-3.3	3.5	12.0	3.7	1.3	16.7	-7.8	2.8
Marshall Islands	0.0	22.6	6.6	6.1	-3.0	-12.9	4.4	0.1	-4.5	2.9	4.1
Micronesia (Federated States of)	0.1	20.1	6.6	6.2	-0.5	4.3	0.9	-0.3	16.5	-9.9	-1.4
Nauru	0.0	20.1	6.8	6.6	-7.0	1.9	1.1	0.6	4.4	-0.8	-3.4
Palau	0.0	32.8	2.9	-5.5	3.5	1.9	-3.4	-7.7	-1.0	4.1	4.3
Polynesia	*1.5*	*22.4*	*4.5*	*4.0*	*3.3*	*1.1*	*1.4*	*2.9*	*3.8*	*3.0*	*2.5*
Cook Islands	0.0	26.1	-4.2	0.1	6.0	0.0	4.8	13.6	26.0	23.8	11.5
French Polynesia	1.4	23.3	5.0	4.4	3.4	1.1	1.1	2.7	2.7	2.1	1.9
Samoa	0.1	13.5	3.1	0.4	1.7	7.1	6.6	7.3	8.8	8.8	9.9
Tonga	0.0	12.1	6.5	5.0	0.6	-7.7	4.2	-8.0	21.7	0.0	-2.0
Tuvalu	0.0	18.0	6.6	-13.0	13.4	-13.5	10.2	15.8	3.0	3.0	-9.2

Notes for Table 6.E - Wholesale, retail trade, restaurants and hotels

1/ 1987-1989
Includes "Transport, storage and communication" and "Other activities".

2/ 1980-1990
Includes "Transport, storage and communication" and "Other activities".

3/ 1980-1992
Includes "Transport, storage and communication" and "Other activities".

4/ 1986-1995
Includes finance and insurance.

5/ 1998-1999
Includes Financial intermediation; real estate, renting and business actvities.

6/ 1974-1975
Includes import duties.

7/ 1975-1979
Includes the profit or loss of the Marketing Board.

8/ 1970-1979
Includes "Transport, storage and communication" and "Other activities".

9/ 1970-1991
Restaurants and Hotels are included in "Other activities".

10/ 1970-1978
Restaurants and Hotels are included in "Other activities".

11/ 1970-1996
Includes Financal intermediation, except insurance and pension funding.

12/ 2000-2002
Refers to Wholesale, retail and import/export trades, restaurants and hotels only.

13/ 1990-2001
Refers to Wholesale and retail trade only.

14/ 1970-1998
Restaurants and Hotels are included in "Other activities".

15/ 1980-1991
Refers to Wholesale and retail trade only.

16/ 1970-1991
Distribution of petroleum products is included in "Wholesale and retail trade, restaurants and hotels".

17/ 1990-1991
Includes "Other activities".

Table 6.F. Average Rates of Growth of Gross Domestic Product by Kind of Economic Activity - Transport, Storage and Communication

Major area, region and country	Base year weights as percentage of total for world or region in 1990	Base year share as percentage of total GDP in 1990	Average rates of growth			Annual rate of change (percentage)					
			1970-1979	1980-1989	1990-1999	1997	1998	1999	2000	2001	2002
WORLD	**100.0**	**6.7**	**4.3**	**3.7**	**4.0**	**4.8**	**4.3**	**5.7**	**7.3**	**3.8**	**3.4**
DEVELOPED ECONOMIES	**72.8**	**6.5**	**3.5**	**3.6**	**3.8**	**4.0**	**4.4**	**5.5**	**6.8**	**3.3**	**2.4**
DEVELOPING ECONOMIES	**17.4**	**6.7**	**8.4**	**4.3**	**6.2**	**8.4**	**4.4**	**6.2**	**8.9**	**5.0**	**6.4**
TRANSITION ECONOMIES	**9.9**	**8.0**	**5.5**	**3.0**	**-6.2**	**1.3**	**3.3**	**6.3**	**6.9**	**5.4**	**5.9**
AFRICA	**2.3**	**6.7**	**6.9**	**3.3**	**3.9**	**6.9**	**6.9**	**1.3**	**3.6**	**5.0**	**13.4**
Eastern Africa	*9.9*	*6.0*	*2.2*	*4.2*	*4.3*	*4.9*	*6.1*	*6.6*	*1.8*	*9.1*	*-1.5*
Burundi	0.1	3.0	10.8	5.8	1.9	0.3	4.4	2.4	3.4	2.6	2.6
Comoros	0.0	4.2	1.7	6.4	0.4	-1.4	-1.4	0.2	-0.8	0.0	-0.5
Djibouti	0.2	14.8	0.7	2.6	7.3	2.2	12.2	12.8	0.0	3.1	3.1
Eritrea	...	...	...	...	2.1	-2.1	-8.7	1.3	2.4	4.5	3.8
Ethiopia	...	...	...	...	8.4	7.1	19.4	8.0	10.2	11.2	12.2
Ethiopia (Former)	1.1	4.9	4.5	5.8	-4.5	...	...	...	...	...	...
Kenya	1.5	6.1	4.2	5.5	2.5	1.7	1.3	1.3	1.9	3.5	2.4
Madagascar	1.5	17.2	2.4	3.9	1.5	3.5	3.1	10.0	4.2	32.3	-17.2
Malawi	0.2	4.2	7.2	0.4	3.0	9.5	1.1	10.8	-4.1	-0.6	14.5
Mauritius	0.7	9.1	8.1	5.0	7.2	9.0	11.7	7.4	11.4	9.5	6.7
Mozambique	0.4	5.6	3.9	-0.3	5.7	17.3	4.8	9.0	1.2	21.6	9.3
Reunion	0.6	3.9	6.5	5.6	3.1	3.1	3.2	3.1	2.9	2.9	2.9
Rwanda	0.3	4.3	10.8	18.1	0.0	26.7	27.3	30.1	11.9	8.1	8.1
Seychelles	0.1	12.0	11.4	1.1	19.4	20.7	31.3	-1.5	-0.9	-15.9	-48.7
Somalia	0.2	6.6	0.8	3.5	-2.1	-4.7	7.1	-34.1	3.0	3.0	3.5
Uganda	0.4	3.7	-8.6	2.6	9.0	11.8	5.2	8.7	8.5	11.0	12.7
United Republic Of Tanzania	0.6	5.4	3.6	1.3	5.3	4.4	5.6	20.0	6.1	6.3	6.4
Zambia	0.6	5.6	2.6	2.9	0.2	-0.2	8.6	5.7	2.4	2.8	1.8
Zimbabwe	1.4	5.5	-1.2	4.1	7.0	0.9	0.8	4.7	-13.3	4.9	-16.0
Middle Africa	*4.9*	*3.8*	*2.4*	*1.9*	*2.0*	*34.6*	*25.8*	*-45.1*	*-4.9*	*6.9*	*7.4*
Angola	0.9	3.2	-0.8	-1.1	1.6	6.1	8.6	5.3	2.5	4.9	11.6
Cameroon	1.6	4.0	4.7	1.0	4.4	62.6	40.5	-67.0	1.6	5.5	7.2
Central African Republic	0.2	4.7	0.4	0.2	-1.3	2.6	3.8	-15.1	-3.7	-4.3	37.7
Chad	0.2	4.0	-1.7	5.0	3.4	11.5	3.4	-3.3	0.0	17.2	5.6
Congo	0.7	9.4	3.9	4.2	-2.8	0.5	-3.3	3.0	-15.6	13.8	2.6
Democratic Republic of the Congo	0.2	0.8	-1.7	2.7	-5.7	-2.8	0.4	-17.6	4.0	3.9	14.6
Equatorial Guinea	0.0	2.1	4.0	-5.6	25.0	68.3	18.4	48.8	16.9	53.4	14.2
Gabon	1.0	6.5	5.9	5.2	2.0	3.1	-4.1	17.4	-22.7	4.2	0.2
Sao Tome and Principe	0.0	5.4	8.6	0.1	-3.5	-1.9	-71.5	175.6	-5.6	2.8	2.5
Northern Africa	*51.5*	*7.8*	*10.2*	*4.1*	*3.9*	*4.3*	*4.3*	*4.3*	*3.2*	*2.7*	*23.2*
Algeria	8.6	4.9	11.4	3.6	3.0	2.6	4.4	4.8	-8.4	2.3	-5.3
Egypt	19.8	9.8	17.5	10.7	3.5	3.4	5.3	4.3	7.1	1.2	4.9
Libyan Arab Jamahiriya	5.2	6.5	12.7	0.8	8.6	10.9	0.9	2.3	1.5	3.3	-12.0
Morocco	4.5	6.2	6.9	4.1	5.7	2.4	8.7	8.1	8.8	-0.2	4.6
Sudan	10.9	11.4	7.0	-1.6	-0.1	0.5	0.5	0.5	1.6	4.2	190.3
Tunisia	2.4	6.8	7.6	4.3	6.5	11.1	7.7	9.2	7.6	13.2	5.7
Southern Africa	*24.4*	*7.2*	*5.5*	*2.2*	*4.5*	*7.6*	*6.4*	*7.3*	*6.9*	*7.6*	*6.7*
Botswana	0.3	2.7	14.7	15.9	11.6	4.3	9.1	16.3	2.6	5.1	6.9
Lesotho	0.1	3.7	1.6	5.1	6.5	12.3	-4.4	5.3	4.3	3.5	2.4
Namibia	0.3	4.7	2.6	4.1	5.2	7.6	-10.4	12.3	5.8	6.2	6.1
South Africa	23.6	7.4	5.6	2.1	4.4	7.6	6.7	7.1	7.0	7.7	6.7
Swaziland	0.1	5.2	9.5	3.0	4.0	1.3	-1.3	5.1	7.3	3.4	3.6
Western Africa	*9.4*	*4.5*	*6.8*	*2.6*	*3.3*	*5.0*	*8.8*	*2.2*	*1.5*	*3.5*	*3.2*
Benin	0.5	9.7	6.4	-0.2	3.9	5.3	6.0	6.0	4.1	5.9	6.6
Burkina Faso	0.4	4.4	5.5	-2.0	3.6	8.2	4.1	8.7	14.2	2.8	-7.8
Cape Verde	0.1	15.1	2.4	7.2	9.7	10.0	7.6	8.7	5.9	15.8	15.6
Cote d'Ivoire	2.5	7.3	9.2	2.0	2.4	0.0	16.7	0.4	-1.8	3.6	-1.2
Gambia	0.1	10.7	7.4	9.9	6.8	8.3	8.0	-4.1	-10.8	34.5	-28.3
Ghana	0.3	1.9	3.4	5.7	6.6	7.9	5.5	5.3	6.0	5.5	5.7

Table 6.F. Average Rates of Growth of Gross Domestic Product by Kind of Economic Activity - Transport, Storage and Communication

Major area, region and country	Base year weights as percentage of total for world or region in 1990	Base year share as percentage of total GDP in 1990	Average rates of growth			Annual rate of change (percentage)					
			1970-1979	1980-1989	1990-1999	1997	1998	1999	2000	2001	2002
Guinea	0.5	6.0	2.8	2.6	5.6	-1.1	7.5	3.5	1.5	1.8	2.2
Guinea-Bissau	0.0	3.7	11.7	5.6	-0.6	-17.5	-22.0	7.6	3.4	7.8	42.8
Liberia	0.1	10.0	3.1	1.3	-16.7	379.2	29.6	26.8	4.8	5.0	25.0
Mali	0.3	4.7	6.6	7.1	6.1	0.5	2.2	57.7	5.9	4.8	9.0
Mauritania	0.3	9.5	5.9	-0.1	8.2	19.0	7.4	5.6	3.2	4.8	11.9
Niger	0.3	3.8	4.6	0.2	4.6	4.5	3.5	2.1	3.3	2.7	11.8
Nigeria	1.9	2.1	8.4	-1.6	1.9	6.8	8.2	-12.4	-6.5	-0.1	-2.7
Senegal [1]	1.6	10.1	...	-1.2	5.0	11.8	7.5	6.7	8.0	2.5	9.1
Sierra Leone	0.2	10.7	4.5	-1.8	-13.8	-46.1	1.5	-10.1	-21.9	-7.9	-10.3
Togo	0.3	5.6	1.0	1.9	3.8	-1.6	-2.2	2.9	-0.8	0.2	4.8
AMERICAS	**31.4**	**6.4**	**4.8**	**3.4**	**4.6**	**3.6**	**4.5**	**6.1**	**8.2**	**2.3**	**3.9**
NORTHERN AMERICA	**26.7**	**6.4**	**4.2**	**3.6**	**4.6**	**2.8**	**4.5**	**6.4**	**8.3**	**2.1**	**4.4**
Bermuda	0.0	6.5	3.7	0.5	2.5	2.6	1.0	-1.5	4.0	4.8	-3.0
Canada	8.2	6.7	5.7	3.4	3.5	6.0	2.7	8.1	8.0	3.1	1.3
United States	77.0	6.4	4.0	3.6	4.7	2.5	4.7	6.2	8.3	2.0	4.7
LATIN AMERICA AND THE CARIBBEAN	**4.7**	**6.1**	**8.5**	**2.2**	**4.5**	**7.6**	**4.7**	**4.6**	**7.9**	**3.8**	**1.1**
Caribbean	*1.2*	*6.6*	*4.7*	*4.3*	*4.0*	*6.2*	*4.9*	*3.9*	*9.4*	*3.3*	*4.5*
Anguilla	0.0	10.3	3.8	6.5	8.7	22.9	4.0	11.9	5.6	-3.7	3.0
Antigua and Barbuda	0.0	14.9	3.2	7.2	5.4	9.2	5.0	10.5	-1.1	1.7	-1.6
Aruba	0.0	8.3	10.6	11.1	6.0	10.9	0.2	6.7	6.7	3.5	-9.3
Bahamas	0.1	10.4	3.0	3.0	-0.5	9.0	1.1	4.1	3.0	-3.9	2.6
Barbados	0.0	7.1	1.3	3.6	1.4	2.8	2.7	3.9	1.3	1.2	30.8
British Virgin Islands	0.0	11.9	7.4	10.0	5.4	0.0	14.0	14.0	9.1	9.1	9.1
Cayman Islands	0.0	10.7	18.0	14.3	0.5	-2.8	-0.3	0.1	0.1	0.1	-0.6
Cuba	0.3	6.2	4.4	5.4	-3.9	3.9	1.2	6.6	9.1	14.8	2.6
Dominica	0.0	13.3	-0.1	12.4	6.5	6.0	7.3	7.3	-3.3	-5.5	-12.0
Dominican Republic	0.1	7.8	7.7	4.0	10.2	11.7	13.5	11.1	15.0	16.4	9.7
Grenada	0.0	11.1	1.2	6.4	8.1	3.2	15.0	11.4	13.7	-3.0	-9.9
Guadeloupe	0.0	5.8	9.3	5.4	4.2	9.2	4.1	5.9	5.9	5.9	4.2
Haiti	0.0	2.1	8.4	-1.2	-0.5	1.0	1.0	5.1	9.0	3.5	-0.2
Jamaica	0.1	8.5	1.9	3.7	6.6	5.7	5.6	8.6	8.0	6.3	6.3
Martinique	0.0	6.0	7.5	9.6	2.7	1.6	4.1	2.5	2.5	2.5	2.6
Montserrat	0.0	10.2	3.5	6.3	-4.2	-33.4	-14.9	-11.0	16.2	-18.3	2.0
Netherlands Antilles	0.0	9.6	3.3	-5.8	1.5	3.2	0.3	-5.4	-10.1	-7.2	-6.1
Puerto Rico	0.4	5.4	5.2	4.4	5.6	4.9	0.0	-1.1	11.0	-1.4	2.6
Saint Kitts and Nevis	0.0	12.6	-0.8	11.4	5.2	6.1	0.3	6.4	3.8	7.3	3.1
Saint Lucia	0.0	14.2	6.0	9.8	3.7	0.6	3.4	7.5	4.1	-1.4	3.2
Saint Vincent and the Grenadines	0.0	17.4	2.1	7.3	5.9	7.0	6.5	10.7	4.8	-5.3	-2.8
Trinidad and Tobago	0.1	8.1	3.7	5.5	4.7	6.6	18.4	-1.0	8.6	-26.3	0.0
Turks and Caicos Islands	0.0	6.2	1.0	6.5	4.3	7.2	14.5	5.0	3.2	6.8	0.4
Central America	*5.2*	*8.4*	*10.4*	*2.6*	*5.2*	*9.5*	*6.8*	*7.8*	*9.0*	*4.1*	*2.6*
Belize	0.0	9.1	7.8	11.7	6.2	-3.3	2.8	7.3	2.6	4.3	2.7
Costa Rica	0.1	7.3	11.2	4.5	7.7	9.9	8.1	6.9	10.2	8.9	11.8
El Salvador	0.1	7.3	5.6	-1.0	6.2	7.7	4.2	9.5	6.1	4.3	3.7
Guatemala	0.1	8.0	8.2	2.5	6.0	5.9	7.6	6.8	7.6	6.8	5.7
Honduras	0.0	5.6	4.1	5.0	3.2	4.4	2.7	1.7	5.0	5.3	3.2
Mexico	4.6	8.3	11.1	2.7	5.2	9.9	6.7	7.8	9.1	3.8	2.2
Nicaragua	0.1	7.1	-0.8	-3.1	3.1	3.8	6.5	9.2	2.0	2.2	6.2
Panama	0.2	15.9	10.9	4.4	4.9	5.7	10.9	10.5	10.0	4.6	3.3
South America	*8.4*	*5.2*	*8.0*	*1.8*	*4.2*	*6.8*	*3.5*	*2.9*	*7.1*	*3.6*	*-0.4*
Argentina	1.6	5.2	2.0	1.3	6.2	11.2	8.9	-1.3	1.7	-4.6	-7.9
Bolivia	0.1	9.3	11.3	3.4	5.5	9.2	7.1	-0.8	2.5	2.1	5.1
Brazil	4.3	4.7	12.4	1.7	3.0	4.3	0.9	6.3	10.5	6.4	1.5
Chile	0.4	6.1	3.1	4.6	8.7	10.9	6.6	0.8	9.2	7.7	2.3

Table 6.F. Average Rates of Growth of Gross Domestic Product by Kind of Economic Activity - Transport, Storage and Communication

Major area, region and country	Base year weights as percentage of total for world or region in 1990	Base year share as percentage of total GDP in 1990	Average rates of growth			Annual rate of change (percentage)					
			1970-1979	1980-1989	1990-1999	1997	1998	1999	2000	2001	2002
Colombia	0.7	6.6	7.8	2.7	3.6	5.8	2.5	-1.9	1.5	4.3	3.4
Ecuador	0.2	8.2	10.6	4.7	4.5	8.2	9.4	-0.3	7.7	1.7	1.3
French Guiana	0.0	7.6	13.8	23.8	7.3	1.7	-2.4	0.3	0.3	0.3	0.0
Guyana	0.0	6.7	3.2	1.0	4.7	8.9	-3.1	2.1	7.1	5.4	-14.7
Paraguay	0.0	3.9	9.6	4.4	3.4	4.2	3.0	2.6	10.9	8.6	1.1
Peru	0.5	7.7	6.2	0.8	3.3	5.6	-1.0	2.1	2.6	-0.4	3.7
Suriname	0.0	5.7	13.8	-0.8	5.9	6.6	5.8	1.8	25.5	26.6	5.0
Uruguay	0.1	6.5	2.7	2.2	8.4	7.1	3.3	4.8	1.5	0.1	-9.1
Venezuela	0.5	4.6	7.3	0.7	2.8	9.0	5.9	1.6	8.1	8.8	-3.8
ASIA	**24.6**	**6.8**	**4.2**	**5.3**	**5.2**	**6.9**	**3.6**	**3.2**	**6.8**	**4.1**	**3.4**
Eastern Asia	*70.0*	*6.6*	*2.8*	*5.6*	*4.7*	*6.4*	*3.4*	*2.4*	*5.3*	*4.2*	*1.4*
China	6.4	6.3	7.0	9.8	10.6	10.8	10.6	9.3	7.8	6.5	8.1
Democratic People's Rep. of Korea	0.3	7.0	13.1	10.2	-2.9	-6.3	-1.1	6.2	1.3	3.7	0.8
Hong Kong SAR of China	1.8	9.0	8.8	7.2	3.8	5.1	-5.0	3.4	10.2	2.1	4.0
Japan	54.0	6.6	1.7	4.8	3.1	4.7	2.4	-1.7	2.2	2.7	-2.0
Macao SAR of China	0.0	3.2	7.1	7.2	9.4	42.1	-1.5	3.4	12.0	-8.3	9.3
Mongolia	0.1	16.6	5.7	8.3	-7.3	5.8	7.4	6.1	25.2	14.9	16.2
Republic of Korea	4.5	6.7	14.4	7.4	8.9	13.4	-0.8	14.5	17.9	10.5	7.4
South Central Asia	*11.6*	*6.6*	*8.2*	*3.8*	*9.1*	*6.4*	*8.8*	*9.2*	*10.5*	*6.2*	*10.1*
Afghanistan	0.1	4.1	8.6	-1.2	-7.7	13.3	5.2	-12.4	-43.7	13.9	17.2
Bangladesh	0.8	9.2	3.3	4.9	4.7	5.7	5.9	6.1	7.9	6.0	12.3
Bhutan	0.0	7.0	6.4	13.1	10.7	14.0	13.3	12.0	2.0	4.7	11.8
India	4.7	5.4	6.1	7.1	7.7	8.2	8.1	11.1	12.2	8.5	11.8
Iran (Islamic Republic of)	1.8	7.6	14.4	-3.0	11.9	2.2	3.0	13.5	5.5	6.8	6.8
Kazakhstan	1.8	9.5	...	...	-8.9	3.3	-0.9	-0.5	18.8	9.5	9.9
Kyrgyzstan	0.2	5.6	...	...	-11.3	4.6	-1.8	3.1	5.7	-6.2	1.1
Maldives	0.0	11.0	13.8	15.6	11.2	17.0	21.4	3.5	7.6	1.6	6.8
Nepal	0.1	5.5	3.3	3.0	8.8	7.7	8.1	6.8	7.0	6.2	1.9
Pakistan	1.0	7.6	6.5	6.1	5.1	7.2	5.1	3.6	5.0	0.1	9.8
Sri Lanka	0.2	9.9	4.6	4.8	5.1	6.4	4.7	6.9	4.2	3.4	3.3
Tajikistan	0.0	6.8	...	...	-23.4	76.9	50.6	-53.1	113.0	-13.0	36.6
Turkmenistan	0.1	3.5	...	...	4.0	60.5	-19.1	-0.3	9.1	-12.4	49.2
Uzbekistan	0.8	5.9	...	...	0.0	2.5	201.1	-4.1	32.6	-9.8	4.2
South-Eastern Asia	*6.4*	*6.7*	*9.6*	*7.6*	*6.9*	*7.3*	*-4.9*	*4.3*	*8.6*	*6.2*	*5.8*
Brunei Darussalam	0.0	4.3	15.6	11.8	3.1	9.4	3.3	-7.9	0.9	-4.7	9.5
Cambodia	0.0	6.8	-7.3	-0.3	5.2	-12.6	-0.8	14.6	8.2	8.3	0.8
Indonesia	1.9	6.3	14.5	7.6	4.7	7.0	-15.1	-0.8	8.6	7.3	7.8
Lao People's Democratic Republic	0.0	5.2	0.3	1.9	5.1	10.3	6.5	5.8	9.0	8.6	8.4
Malaysia	0.7	5.9	12.6	8.7	9.2	11.8	-0.3	4.3	11.0	7.5	2.6
Myanmar	0.1	2.7	2.1	4.1	9.5	10.8	8.7	10.4	10.4	10.4	10.4
Philippines	0.6	4.9	7.4	4.5	4.4	8.2	6.5	5.3	10.4	8.8	8.9
Singapore	1.3	13.1	14.9	9.4	8.3	8.4	6.5	7.0	7.6	2.6	5.0
Thailand	1.6	7.1	6.6	8.2	7.7	4.7	-9.1	6.2	7.8	6.5	4.8
Timor-Leste	0.0	8.2	...	...	-6.5	3.2	3.2	-57.5	45.9	27.2	-2.7
Vietnam	0.1	3.5	-0.1	4.2	6.7	8.9	3.9	6.3	7.4	6.9	7.1
Western Asia	*12.0*	*8.5*	*8.0*	*3.9*	*3.8*	*10.9*	*5.7*	*0.1*	*10.3*	*-0.1*	*5.6*
Armenia	0.3	7.0	...	...	-17.3	9.2	1.4	1.7	0.4	15.8	6.0
Azerbaijan	0.5	8.1	...	...	-16.4	3.0	15.4	9.8	16.1	11.5	7.7
Bahrain	0.1	6.7	22.1	0.4	4.2	1.5	5.8	8.3	6.1	13.1	9.0
Cyprus	0.1	9.0	7.0	8.4	3.6	5.8	9.0	10.1	13.4	10.0	3.5
Georgia	0.4	7.4	...	...	1.2	34.4	48.8	5.7	12.8	1.4	8.1
Iraq	0.9	9.0	19.0	-0.7	6.2	68.3	7.2	5.1	20.5	9.3	-5.3
Israel	1.3	8.2	2.7	5.7	2.3	5.8	7.1	2.0	4.4	-0.3	2.6
Jordan	0.1	13.9	6.5	5.4	4.4	1.6	18.8	5.8	1.3	2.7	4.2
Kuwait	0.2	3.7	9.3	4.8	4.3	6.2	12.0	12.3	55.5	-1.1	0.6
Lebanon	0.0	3.8	-1.9	-13.2	0.5	1.2	-1.6	-3.3	5.0	10.8	2.0
Oman	0.1	4.5	16.9	21.7	10.5	13.4	16.1	4.6	3.0	18.9	10.1
Qatar	0.1	2.5	14.9	1.8	9.8	11.7	14.7	6.0	10.2	21.6	3.3

Table 6.F. Average Rates of Growth of Gross Domestic Product by Kind of Economic Activity - Transport, Storage and Communication

Major area, region and country	Base year weights as percentage of total for world or region in 1990	Base year share as percentage of total GDP in 1990	Average rates of growth 1970-1979	1980-1989	1990-1999	Annual rate of change (percentage) 1997	1998	1999	2000	2001	2002
Saudi Arabia	1.8	6.3	4.7	1.8	-2.0	5.3	4.0	2.6	4.0	8.3	9.8
Syrian Arab Republic	0.4	9.5	7.5	5.0	8.0	10.6	-0.5	8.6	5.4	5.2	5.6
Turkey	4.8	11.8	9.4	4.2	4.5	7.2	2.7	-4.9	9.5	-7.9	8.7
United Arab Emirates	0.4	4.7	30.2	3.6	5.5	2.8	4.9	-1.6	4.6	6.3	3.5
Yemen	0.5	13.9	...	...	-4.1	18.3	6.3	2.0	1.0	4.4	5.0
Yemen Arab Republic (Former)	...	...	9.6	8.4	...	...	...	...	...	...	...
Yemen Democratic (Former)	...	...	9.1	0.3	...	...	...	...	...	...	...
EUROPE	**39.8**	**6.8**	**3.9**	**3.2**	**2.7**	**4.2**	**4.5**	**7.5**	**7.1**	**4.8**	**2.2**
Eastern Europe	*20.5*	*8.2*	*5.4*	*3.2*	*-3.5*	*-1.1*	*-1.7*	*8.8*	*5.6*	*5.5*	*5.3*
Belarus	0.7	6.6	...	...	-6.7	6.7	2.7	2.2	2.2	2.3	2.4
Bulgaria	0.1	4.0	7.1	5.7	-2.5	15.6	-2.4	11.2	9.6	10.6	11.5
Czech Republic	0.3	4.2	...	-0.9	2.2	5.7	4.2	1.6	8.2	15.1	11.7
Czechoslovakia (Former)	...	...	4.7	...	...	...	...	...	...	...	...
Hungary	0.4	6.3	5.3	2.2	-1.4	9.3	3.3	5.5	2.3	3.6	3.5
Poland	0.5	5.2	5.9	2.4	-1.8	5.6	6.3	8.8	5.2	3.4	8.1
Republic of Moldova	0.2	6.6	...	...	-15.4	4.8	-8.3	-2.7	21.4	9.1	9.4
Romania	0.4	5.8	12.4	0.5	-1.1	-9.5	-10.0	42.4	4.6	2.0	5.6
Russian Federation	15.0	9.3	...	...	-7.1	-1.7	-2.7	10.1	6.1	5.2	5.6
Slovakia	0.2	5.8	...	-2.1	3.1	3.5	-3.8	9.4	2.3	14.4	-4.3
Ukraine	2.8	6.7	...	...	-13.6	-7.4	1.2	-7.3	2.8	5.1	0.7
USSR (Former)	...	...	5.2	3.2	...	...	...	...	...	...	...
Northern Europe	*21.9*	*7.7*	*2.1*	*3.3*	*2.9*	*5.4*	*4.4*	*4.1*	*4.2*	*1.6*	*2.2*
Denmark	1.5	6.9	1.3	2.4	3.6	2.5	-3.4	17.2	6.6	0.7	2.1
Estonia	0.1	6.4	...	...	-0.5	16.7	10.0	5.6	6.6	10.2	1.7
Finland	1.8	8.0	3.4	3.7	4.0	7.6	8.2	4.7	7.2	2.1	2.4
Iceland	0.1	6.5	5.8	3.1	5.4	5.8	7.8	9.8	14.9	6.2	-8.7
Ireland	0.4	5.1	4.8	2.0	6.5	7.7	13.8	5.6	0.9	17.0	1.6
Latvia	0.3	10.4	...	...	-2.2	7.4	-2.8	0.2	7.0	9.5	2.4
Lithuania	0.3	7.8	...	...	-3.5	5.8	1.7	-0.2	2.2	4.4	10.9
Norway	1.9	10.0	4.6	3.2	5.2	9.0	2.7	2.7	-1.4	7.9	1.7
Sweden	3.1	7.9	4.4	3.8	3.4	6.1	2.3	5.3	5.0	0.1	3.2
United Kingdom	12.3	7.5	1.2	3.3	1.6	4.4	5.5	2.2	4.3	-0.3	2.1
Southern Europe	*21.1*	*6.8*	*5.5*	*3.3*	*3.0*	*4.3*	*3.7*	*4.6*	*6.8*	*6.1*	*1.8*
Albania	0.0	3.3	5.7	4.1	-1.2	-20.6	20.0	14.9	15.0	14.9	10.0
Andorra	0.0	7.2	9.6	6.3	4.9	5.9	3.7	3.6	8.7	9.5	5.0
Bosnia and Herzegovina	0.1	6.1	...	...	10.4	32.3	63.8	5.1	8.5	11.4	9.6
Croatia	0.3	7.6	...	...	-4.0	3.5	4.3	-5.1	4.5	6.9	6.8
Greece	1.0	6.8	7.5	3.9	5.8	8.4	4.1	33.4	16.2	1.3	5.9
Holy See	0.0	6.7	6.9	4.2	2.8	3.0	2.2	3.4	5.7	5.7	0.6
Italy	12.2	6.7	5.9	3.8	2.7	2.9	2.2	3.3	5.5	5.7	0.6
Malta	0.0	5.1	16.0	5.4	6.5	-0.9	7.5	11.0	-1.6	8.8	5.7
Portugal	0.7	5.9	4.6	4.7	4.1	2.7	9.2	4.6	6.8	2.0	0.3
San Marino	0.0	6.7	5.9	3.8	4.0	2.9	7.9	10.8	5.5	5.7	0.6
Serbia and Montenegro	0.3	6.4	...	...	-6.1	27.6	18.5	-29.3	-17.9	24.2	6.8
Slovenia	0.2	7.8	...	...	0.1	4.2	5.2	3.2	4.7	5.9	2.4
Spain	6.1	7.2	4.6	1.9	2.6	5.8	4.1	3.7	8.0	7.8	2.7
TFYR Macedonia	0.0	6.4	...	...	-1.3	3.3	6.9	13.7	0.8	32.3	10.2
Yugoslavia (Former)	...	...	7.4	4.0	...	...	...	...	...	...	...
Western Europe	*36.5*	*5.8*	*3.5*	*3.0*	*4.5*	*4.8*	*6.3*	*10.7*	*9.0*	*5.6*	*1.8*
Austria	1.9	7.2	5.5	3.6	3.0	2.4	3.3	2.4	2.1	1.3	1.5
Belgium	2.1	6.5	1.7	2.1	1.9	-1.4	6.3	4.9	6.3	4.9	1.2
France	12.0	5.9	5.8	5.1	3.8	6.4	8.5	7.9	6.8	3.2	-1.0
Germany	14.9	5.4	3.1	1.8	5.9	4.3	4.7	16.3	12.0	8.5	3.4
Liechtenstein	0.0	5.8	2.4	2.2	1.4	2.8	3.8	2.1	1.8	0.6	3.9
Luxembourg	0.1	7.7	5.9	1.1	12.9	7.8	15.7	11.6	13.7	6.4	7.2
Monaco	0.0	5.9	6.4	5.8	4.5	7.1	9.3	8.6	7.4	3.7	-0.5
Netherlands	3.2	6.5	2.4	3.1	4.8	8.6	9.4	6.8	10.4	3.9	2.4
Switzerland	2.2	5.8	0.9	1.4	0.7	1.7	2.6	0.9	0.7	-0.3	2.9

Table 6.F. Average Rates of Growth of Gross Domestic Product by Kind of Economic Activity - Transport, Storage and Communication

Major area, region and country	Base year weights as percentage of total for world or region in 1990	Base year share as percentage of total GDP in 1990	Average rates of growth			Annual rate of change (percentage)					
			1970-1979	1980-1989	1990-1999	1997	1998	1999	2000	2001	2002
OCEANIA	**1.9**	**8.0**	**4.6**	**4.5**	**5.6**	**4.7**	**5.4**	**5.8**	**4.1**	**4.6**	**4.2**
Australia & New Zealand	*96.5*	*7.9*	*4.7*	*4.5*	*5.7*	*4.7*	*5.5*	*5.8*	*4.3*	*4.7*	*4.2*
Australia	84.6	7.9	5.1	4.6	5.5	4.8	5.6	5.1	3.5	4.4	4.1
New Zealand	12.0	8.0	2.1	3.8	6.9	3.6	5.0	10.4	9.4	6.5	5.0
Melanesia	*2.5*	*9.9*	*4.0*	*2.0*	*3.7*	*9.4*	*0.3*	*4.4*	*-6.9*	*2.0*	*2.4*
Fiji	0.6	12.9	10.6	6.5	6.5	4.6	5.8	15.8	-10.8	2.8	5.4
New Caledonia	1.2	13.8	1.7	1.4	1.5	15.8	-3.2	0.9	2.1	-1.1	0.7
Papua New Guinea	0.7	6.1	5.5	0.0	4.7	6.2	0.5	1.9	-15.5	6.0	2.0
Solomon Islands	0.0	3.9	12.8	7.1	4.3	-1.0	-2.2	-7.5	-1.7	-14.6	-4.0
Vanuatu	0.0	8.5	7.7	2.4	-4.7	1.5	1.0	-47.8	8.4	21.7	-0.5
Micronesia	*0.2*	*12.1*	*4.7*	*1.4*	*0.0*	*5.7*	*-2.4*	*0.9*	*-3.1*	*3.4*	*-4.4*
Kiribati	0.0	16.5	2.9	-4.5	4.5	10.9	10.7	0.8	3.1	1.4	1.7
Marshall Islands	0.0	1.3	6.6	6.1	15.6	-0.7	-30.1	8.1	-8.9	21.3	14.6
Micronesia (Federated States of)	0.1	16.5	6.6	4.9	0.8	1.8	-10.2	0.4	-7.4	5.3	-4.1
Nauru	0.0	16.5	6.8	5.3	-5.8	-0.6	-9.9	1.3	-5.9	-0.8	4.4
Palau	0.0	8.3	2.9	-5.4	4.7	17.5	3.6	4.8	3.0	7.9	-6.9
Polynesia	*0.8*	*6.8*	*2.8*	*5.3*	*3.1*	*1.3*	*1.9*	*3.6*	*4.3*	*3.4*	*2.5*
Cook Islands	0.0	10.1	-3.0	5.3	5.0	0.0	-5.6	17.6	25.0	12.0	3.6
French Polynesia	0.7	6.5	2.8	5.9	3.1	1.1	1.1	2.7	2.7	2.1	1.9
Samoa	0.1	10.5	3.1	0.4	2.1	4.0	11.5	6.3	10.9	12.2	6.8
Tonga	0.0	7.8	12.1	7.6	2.9	0.0	6.7	6.2	5.9	0.0	2.0
Tuvalu	0.0	0.9	6.6	1.3	6.2	19.8	-17.1	11.0	3.0	3.0	-9.2

Notes for Table 6.F - Transport, storage and communications

1/ 1980-1987
Includes "Other activities".

Table 6.G. Average Rates of Growth of Gross Domestic Product by Kind of Economic Activity - Other Activities

Major area, region and country	Base year weights as percentage of total for world or region in 1990	Base year share as percentage of total GDP in 1990	Average rates of growth			Annual rate of change (percentage)					
			1970-1979	1980-1989	1990-1999	1997	1998	1999	2000	2001	2002
WORLD	**100.0**	**38.4**	**4.4**	**3.3**	**3.3**	**3.4**	**3.5**	**3.0**	**3.7**	**2.6**	**2.5**
DEVELOPED ECONOMIES	**83.4**	**42.9**	**4.1**	**3.0**	**2.5**	**3.3**	**3.5**	**3.1**	**3.7**	**2.5**	**2.6**
DEVELOPING ECONOMIES	**12.7**	**28.2**	**6.2**	**5.0**	**4.3**	**5.0**	**2.7**	**3.8**	**3.8**	**2.9**	**2.2**
TRANSITION ECONOMIES	**3.9**	**18.3**	**9.5**	**1.6**	**0.5**	**-1.9**	**6.9**	**-1.7**	**4.0**	**4.3**	**1.9**
AFRICA	**1.4**	**22.7**	**4.6**	**3.7**	**2.9**	**2.3**	**5.4**	**3.8**	**1.4**	**2.5**	**1.3**
Eastern Africa	*11.4*	*23.7*	*5.5*	*4.4*	*3.2*	*3.9*	*4.3*	*4.3*	*8.0*	*3.3*	*0.9*
Burundi	0.2	18.1	5.5	5.5	2.4	2.0	5.9	3.9	4.9	4.2	4.2
Comoros	0.0	22.8	3.8	4.5	-1.2	-1.4	-1.4	-5.6	-0.8	1.1	0.1
Djibouti	0.1	34.3	5.4	1.9	0.7	-0.7	-3.1	-1.9	-0.3	1.4	2.1
Eritrea	...	...	...	...	8.0	-4.9	11.2	6.0	7.3	1.6	0.2
Ethiopia	...	...	...	...	8.4	7.1	19.4	8.0	10.2	11.2	12.2
Ethiopia (Former) [1]	1.2	17.5	6.0	4.0	2.5	...	...	...	...	...	...
Kenya [2]	2.2	31.2	7.1	5.9	2.7	3.1	2.2	1.6	0.9	1.1	1.2
Madagascar	0.6	25.3	1.3	3.4	0.6	3.7	3.3	-10.0	4.3	32.2	-17.2
Malawi	0.4	25.4	9.5	4.5	3.6	10.2	-0.1	1.2	2.2	1.5	3.0
Mauritius	0.5	24.9	8.1	3.7	6.0	5.7	5.9	6.7	7.8	6.3	5.3
Mozambique	0.1	2.3	3.9	-0.3	1.5	10.3	1.1	1.5	11.3	11.1	6.6
Reunion	2.2	49.9	6.2	4.1	3.1	3.0	3.1	3.0	2.9	2.9	2.9
Rwanda [3]	0.4	18.6	4.5	7.0	3.1	24.0	3.3	5.1	5.0	3.4	3.1
Seychelles	0.1	25.0	7.1	1.1	1.9	7.1	-17.3	15.4	0.2	39.2	3.8
Somalia	0.1	9.2	8.2	-0.4	-3.3	-4.5	2.7	-33.3	3.0	3.0	3.5
Uganda	0.5	15.8	5.6	2.6	6.8	6.8	6.3	6.6	7.4	6.2	5.9
United Republic Of Tanzania	0.3	9.8	8.2	2.4	12.2	0.9	3.4	165.0	4.2	3.4	4.5
Zambia	0.6	18.4	6.2	3.1	5.5	3.6	3.1	8.0	5.3	3.1	3.2
Zimbabwe	1.9	26.6	3.2	5.3	0.5	0.6	3.7	-14.5	32.2	-8.4	-10.4
Middle Africa	*9.3*	*24.8*	*1.9*	*2.1*	*-1.2*	*5.8*	*-0.4*	*-0.3*	*-4.5*	*8.7*	*3.6*
Angola [4]	2.3	26.9	-0.2	3.9	-1.0	5.3	6.4	-7.4	1.4	1.1	2.5
Cameroon	3.4	28.5	5.4	4.2	-3.7	4.8	0.5	-17.5	1.6	5.5	7.2
Central African Republic	0.2	16.2	1.3	-1.9	-2.9	1.0	2.5	-18.6	-4.4	-4.0	37.9
Chad	0.2	18.4	-0.6	7.8	0.4	-3.0	-3.3	12.3	2.1	5.2	5.5
Congo	0.5	22.4	3.0	7.0	-4.1	-1.3	1.8	-29.8	-15.5	13.7	2.6
Democratic Republic of the Congo [5]	1.5	19.4	0.0	-1.6	-5.4	10.1	-15.9	-11.9	-5.3	19.2	-18.4
Equatorial Guinea	0.0	27.0	3.7	1.6	27.9	71.1	21.9	41.7	16.9	53.4	23.9
Gabon	1.1	25.3	2.5	-1.9	4.7	2.3	-6.1	78.7	-22.8	4.3	0.2
Sao Tome and Principe	0.0	40.1	6.4	-1.8	0.3	2.5	9.3	-20.9	-0.2	2.8	2.5
Northern Africa	*40.4*	*20.8*	*5.7*	*3.9*	*3.2*	*0.9*	*5.9*	*2.3*	*-0.7*	*4.1*	*-0.9*
Algeria	10.3	20.0	7.6	2.7	1.9	3.6	9.9	-2.5	-15.7	2.3	9.0
Egypt [6]	9.6	16.2	4.7	7.0	5.3	4.4	4.2	5.6	4.4	4.6	3.1
Libyan Arab Jamahiriya	7.0	29.7	11.4	3.0	2.8	-2.8	2.1	3.7	4.6	2.6	-9.7
Morocco	5.5	25.5	8.4	5.8	-0.7	2.3	3.7	3.4	2.8	4.6	2.2
Sudan	5.4	19.2	-0.3	1.0	4.6	-8.9	9.0	0.2	1.7	7.1	-18.2
Tunisia [7]	2.6	25.0	2.0	4.5	5.1	5.4	5.1	5.4	6.7	4.1	3.5
Southern Africa	*29.4*	*29.6*	*3.7*	*3.5*	*2.4*	*2.5*	*2.7*	*3.7*	*2.6*	*2.3*	*2.4*
Botswana [8]	0.7	22.9	17.1	13.8	7.7	5.3	8.5	7.4	5.2	5.6	7.6
Lesotho	0.2	32.7	8.5	6.9	-0.2	3.4	4.3	3.0	5.6	2.3	3.8
Namibia [9]	0.6	32.6	3.2	3.8	4.2	2.3	2.8	3.2	2.6	2.4	-7.3
South Africa	27.8	29.8	3.6	3.3	2.2	2.4	2.5	3.6	2.5	2.1	2.5
Swaziland	0.2	23.3	7.1	7.1	4.2	2.4	1.8	3.5	4.2	2.1	2.9
Western Africa	*9.4*	*15.4*	*6.8*	*4.9*	*6.1*	*3.1*	*15.7*	*11.1*	*2.6*	*-5.7*	*5.6*
Benin [10]	0.4	23.6	0.3	2.7	2.9	4.6	5.0	3.7	3.7	5.1	5.2
Burkina Faso	0.4	17.8	6.2	6.4	6.7	1.9	0.9	16.6	11.7	3.3	-7.2
Cape Verde	0.1	22.6	1.7	7.3	6.2	10.0	7.6	8.7	5.9	13.9	15.6
Cote d'Ivoire	2.1	21.6	7.7	4.9	5.9	4.2	7.5	9.8	-1.7	5.7	-1.2
Gambia	0.0	17.4	3.5	3.4	-1.2	6.3	4.1	-34.7	77.5	-32.6	3.4
Ghana	0.8	15.9	4.8	4.7	4.5	7.3	4.6	3.8	5.7	4.9	4.1
Guinea	0.3	13.0	2.8	3.0	6.1	5.1	4.2	1.4	2.2	2.1	2.2

Table 6.G. Average Rates of Growth of Gross Domestic Product by Kind of Economic Activity - Other Activities

Major area, region and country	Base year weights as percentage of total for world or region in 1990	Base year share as percentage of total GDP in 1990	Average rates of growth			Annual rate of change (percentage)					
			1970-1979	1980-1989	1990-1999	1997	1998	1999	2000	2001	2002
Guinea-Bissau	0.0	7.8	11.7	4.9	-1.1	-2.0	10.8	-31.3	28.8	5.0	-18.7
Liberia	0.0	14.0	3.0	-7.8	-15.3	387.9	29.8	45.5	22.4	-1.1	-0.3
Mali	0.3	14.5	5.8	5.4	3.0	2.6	3.0	21.2	5.9	4.8	9.0
Mauritania	0.2	20.4	10.8	0.1	3.4	5.1	4.8	4.9	3.5	4.6	12.0
Niger	0.5	22.1	4.6	0.5	3.6	2.5	2.3	1.3	1.5	1.7	-22.3
Nigeria	2.6	9.5	13.7	6.7	10.7	0.1	45.9	20.3	2.6	-17.9	17.4
Senegal	1.3	27.3	12.1	11.8	3.0	5.6	7.2	3.4	3.6	-16.3	6.7
Sierra Leone	0.1	10.5	5.0	4.3	-8.8	-62.4	1.5	-10.1	-21.9	-7.9	-10.3
Togo	0.3	24.3	3.5	0.5	2.6	1.4	-2.2	2.9	-0.8	0.2	4.8
AMERICAS	**38.6**	**45.0**	**4.0**	**3.0**	**2.6**	**4.2**	**4.1**	**3.4**	**4.0**	**2.2**	**3.4**
NORTHERN AMERICA	**33.5**	**46.2**	**3.8**	**2.8**	**2.6**	**4.4**	**4.4**	**3.7**	**4.2**	**2.3**	**3.8**
Bermuda	0.0	56.6	3.7	2.0	3.3	4.5	6.9	2.0	3.7	1.9	-5.4
Canada	7.1	41.6	4.0	2.8	2.6	3.8	3.4	4.7	3.8	3.4	3.5
United States	79.6	46.6	3.8	2.8	2.6	4.4	4.5	3.6	4.3	2.3	3.9
LATIN AMERICA AND THE CARIBBEAN	**5.1**	**38.7**	**5.8**	**4.4**	**2.8**	**3.5**	**2.5**	**1.9**	**2.5**	**1.2**	**0.6**
Caribbean	*0.8*	*31.5*	*4.4*	*4.4*	*3.2*	*2.6*	*2.8*	*5.6*	*3.9*	*2.2*	*3.9*
Anguilla	0.0	25.1	3.8	8.3	5.7	-0.8	4.3	6.7	12.9	12.5	-1.4
Antigua and Barbuda	0.0	36.7	0.6	4.8	4.5	9.4	8.9	1.8	2.7	2.3	6.5
Aruba	0.0	42.2	9.0	9.9	7.3	6.7	5.3	4.4	3.9	5.3	-9.3
Bahamas	0.0	30.0	0.4	1.5	3.0	12.5	4.3	7.5	6.3	-0.8	5.9
Barbados	0.0	31.7	-1.3	1.9	0.3	1.9	2.2	2.5	1.1	0.7	38.7
British Virgin Islands	0.0	37.9	2.5	8.2	7.4	7.1	11.9	11.9	10.4	10.5	10.5
Cayman Islands [11]	0.0	49.0	10.8	9.3	0.8	-2.8	-0.3	0.1	0.1	0.1	-0.6
Cuba	0.1	23.6	5.8	7.5	0.2	0.8	3.3	2.9	3.7	4.7	3.7
Dominica	0.0	28.4	0.5	2.6	3.0	0.1	6.0	2.8	2.4	1.6	2.7
Dominican Republic	0.1	25.8	7.6	4.9	3.4	3.3	3.4	3.6	3.3	3.2	2.7
Grenada	0.0	26.7	1.6	4.3	1.6	2.2	5.8	6.0	5.5	4.9	-1.2
Guadeloupe	0.0	54.6	6.1	1.8	2.2	9.2	4.1	5.9	5.9	5.9	4.2
Haiti	0.0	21.6	6.5	3.2	2.5	0.5	2.3	0.8	1.1	-0.7	0.2
Jamaica	0.0	27.6	2.8	2.5	5.1	-6.8	-0.3	5.8	5.0	0.1	3.6
Martinique	0.1	52.5	5.6	4.0	1.6	1.6	4.1	2.5	2.5	2.5	2.6
Montserrat	0.0	34.9	3.9	3.6	-6.9	-16.4	-10.8	-13.1	10.4	-2.2	5.4
Netherlands Antilles	0.0	58.1	0.9	3.7	1.8	-0.8	-2.3	4.0	-2.0	1.2	2.6
Puerto Rico	0.3	33.5	3.9	5.2	4.8	4.0	2.6	8.4	4.6	0.6	4.2
Saint Kitts and Nevis	0.0	28.1	5.5	5.0	2.9	6.4	0.4	3.5	6.1	0.8	2.6
Saint Lucia	0.0	26.3	6.4	5.6	1.6	2.9	4.5	1.6	3.1	1.0	1.4
Saint Vincent and the Grenadines	0.0	23.4	5.3	2.6	3.6	4.5	3.0	3.0	3.4	0.0	3.3
Trinidad and Tobago [12]	0.0	26.2	7.4	-1.4	0.5	-5.1	2.6	-2.0	2.6	12.0	2.6
Turks and Caicos Islands [13]	0.0	42.8	1.0	6.5	4.2	4.3	14.7	3.9	6.6	1.7	2.9
Central America	*2.5*	*28.6*	*5.4*	*2.5*	*2.8*	*3.6*	*3.7*	*3.0*	*3.9*	*1.9*	*2.7*
Belize	0.0	28.3	3.5	3.3	1.3	-0.2	3.1	1.6	26.4	-25.0	8.6
Costa Rica	0.1	29.4	5.2	2.4	3.7	3.6	4.6	5.1	5.1	4.3	4.0
El Salvador [14]	0.0	30.5	6.5	1.2	3.7	4.0	2.7	2.1	2.2	-0.7	1.7
Guatemala	0.1	22.3	5.4	2.5	4.5	4.5	5.2	4.6	4.0	2.2	1.7
Honduras [15]	0.0	29.7	8.6	3.5	3.1	6.7	5.5	0.1	5.2	6.8	4.8
Mexico	2.2	28.4	5.5	2.6	2.7	3.5	3.6	2.8	4.0	1.8	2.7
Nicaragua	0.0	27.3	-1.8	-3.2	1.7	4.7	4.8	5.8	-0.1	1.3	2.7
Panama	0.1	43.2	6.4	2.6	4.7	3.1	5.2	6.3	1.8	2.3	0.6
South America	*10.0*	*43.4*	*6.1*	*4.9*	*2.8*	*3.5*	*2.2*	*1.3*	*2.0*	*0.9*	*-0.3*
Argentina	1.5	36.2	2.9	0.8	6.0	5.7	4.0	0.7	1.9	-2.4	-6.3
Bolivia	0.0	24.7	5.8	-1.6	5.0	8.4	7.8	8.0	0.8	1.4	0.9
Brazil	6.9	52.8	8.5	7.2	1.7	2.4	1.7	2.0	2.2	1.9	1.4
Chile	0.3	30.3	3.3	3.0	4.8	5.4	4.0	1.0	3.3	2.6	2.0
Colombia	0.4	28.9	5.9	3.7	5.7	6.1	0.3	-0.7	-0.1	0.6	1.8
Ecuador	0.1	20.6	8.2	2.6	1.1	2.5	-0.1	-10.7	4.3	7.2	2.4

Table 6.G. Average Rates of Growth of Gross Domestic Product by Kind of Economic Activity - Other Activities

Major area, region and country	Base year weights as percentage of total for world or region in 1990	Base year share as percentage of total GDP in 1990	Average rates of growth 1970-1979	1980-1989	1990-1999	Annual rate of change (percentage) 1997	1998	1999	2000	2001	2002
French Guiana	0.0	47.0	11.4	6.0	5.1	1.6	2.8	2.0	2.0	2.0	2.1
Guyana [16]	0.0	20.1	4.1	-0.3	2.0	3.9	1.7	0.8	4.3	-0.6	-8.6
Paraguay [17]	0.0	13.7	8.4	3.5	3.6	4.2	0.7	3.8	3.2	0.1	-2.2
Peru	0.3	30.0	4.0	1.0	1.6	5.2	0.5	1.7	0.8	-0.3	3.8
Suriname	0.0	37.4	17.6	2.7	-0.8	-0.8	2.3	-0.8	0.9	0.9	0.7
Uruguay	0.1	43.5	2.4	2.7	2.4	5.2	4.9	3.3	1.1	0.3	-1.8
Venezuela	0.3	22.6	7.9	1.9	1.4	1.1	1.2	-1.4	2.2	2.1	-2.2
ASIA	**21.0**	**33.5**	**5.8**	**3.9**	**4.7**	**3.9**	**2.6**	**3.1**	**3.4**	**3.2**	**2.3**
Eastern Asia	*81.1*	*37.7*	*5.6*	*3.9*	*4.4*	*3.5*	*2.2*	*2.8*	*3.1*	*3.0*	*2.6*
China	3.7	17.7	6.0	12.6	8.5	9.1	8.3	7.5	7.8	8.8	7.4
Democratic People's Rep. of Korea	0.2	18.2	10.8	7.6	-3.5	-6.3	-1.1	6.2	1.3	3.7	0.8
Hong Kong SAR of China	1.8	43.3	8.8	7.2	3.8	5.1	-5.0	3.4	10.2	2.1	1.1
Japan	68.9	41.4	5.4	3.1	3.9	2.7	2.2	2.1	2.5	2.5	1.7
Macao SAR of China	0.1	64.1	7.1	7.2	2.0	1.0	-3.9	-5.3	6.6	1.8	7.7
Mongolia	0.0	11.0	5.7	1.2	3.2	-1.3	0.2	5.3	4.1	2.8	5.6
Republic of Korea	3.8	27.9	5.3	7.6	6.0	4.7	-2.1	5.0	3.7	2.7	8.2
South Central Asia	*7.3*	*20.3*	*7.2*	*3.0*	*7.8*	*7.1*	*11.1*	*8.0*	*3.5*	*5.4*	*6.6*
Afghanistan	0.0	1.8	3.2	1.1	-0.8	13.3	5.2	-12.4	-43.7	-9.3	105.8
Bangladesh	0.4	24.3	3.6	5.6	4.2	4.2	4.2	4.3	4.2	4.3	8.8
Bhutan	0.0	18.4	6.4	9.9	6.9	15.1	4.7	4.1	12.3	10.2	7.2
India	3.5	20.0	4.1	6.5	7.6	11.7	8.9	11.4	4.5	5.1	7.1
Iran (Islamic Republic of)	1.4	27.6	12.6	-3.7	4.6	5.9	2.3	1.9	0.3	2.5	2.1
Kazakhstan	0.6	14.6	...	...	0.8	-5.3	2.8	-1.6	5.4	11.6	10.3
Kyrgyzstan	0.1	18.5	...	...	-3.5	-5.3	2.1	6.0	2.5	-13.4	0.7
Maldives	0.0	31.2	13.5	16.0	6.3	10.6	7.8	9.1	6.0	5.9	4.4
Nepal	0.0	16.6	2.9	4.6	6.1	4.2	6.7	5.8	4.5	7.2	2.5
Pakistan [18]	0.5	20.7	7.0	6.3	5.0	1.2	6.3	5.9	4.4	9.0	11.5
Sri Lanka	0.1	13.0	4.0	3.6	5.0	6.3	4.3	1.8	1.7	1.6	13.7
Tajikistan	0.0	19.2	...	...	-5.6	16.0	80.0	124.2	-9.0	28.5	-53.6
Turkmenistan	0.0	5.9	...	...	11.3	80.9	23.9	39.6	33.0	1.0	-5.7
Uzbekistan	0.6	21.6	...	...	-0.8	-49.5	584.4	4.8	-6.9	14.4	4.2
South-Eastern Asia	*4.0*	*20.7*	*6.3*	*6.4*	*5.6*	*6.3*	*-4.9*	*1.1*	*3.4*	*3.7*	*4.0*
Brunei Darussalam	0.1	28.1	11.6	11.0	4.5	6.6	4.4	-11.5	2.8	4.4	-0.1
Cambodia	0.0	18.3	-7.3	-0.9	3.9	-1.1	4.7	5.6	7.8	0.6	6.3
Indonesia [19]	1.1	18.1	8.7	7.5	3.0	4.8	-15.3	-2.0	3.3	2.6	3.5
Lao People's Democratic Republic	0.0	12.2	0.0	4.1	2.9	2.5	0.1	3.6	-0.7	1.6	-17.0
Malaysia	0.6	24.7	9.5	6.5	8.7	12.7	-0.1	5.2	3.4	6.4	4.8
Myanmar	0.1	6.8	5.3	2.4	7.0	7.3	8.0	9.3	9.7	10.3	10.9
Philippines	0.6	22.9	1.8	3.0	3.6	5.8	3.3	3.0	2.2	1.8	4.0
Singapore	0.8	37.4	8.7	9.1	8.1	11.2	-0.3	5.2	5.4	4.2	0.2
Thailand	0.8	16.5	7.8	6.1	5.0	-1.4	-8.0	-5.1	1.1	1.9	8.4
Timor-Leste [20]	0.0	33.8	...	...	-5.6	0.9	1.0	-44.2	26.6	14.1	7.9
Vietnam	0.1	17.9	-0.1	5.8	8.0	7.0	6.0	1.6	4.8	3.3	6.1
Western Asia	*7.7*	*26.8*	*7.7*	*4.3*	*4.5*	*3.7*	*3.3*	*2.8*	*6.3*	*2.3*	*-6.3*
Armenia	0.1	15.9	...	...	10.0	3.5	2.8	3.7	0.6	6.9	7.2
Azerbaijan	0.3	22.8	...	...	-3.3	6.2	-1.8	-3.9	6.0	4.6	2.7
Bahrain	0.1	50.7	13.8	8.0	3.2	4.7	0.7	2.5	7.3	-1.1	5.7
Cyprus	0.1	33.0	4.5	7.1	6.7	5.5	4.8	5.0	5.4	4.1	3.7
Georgia	0.2	19.4	...	...	-12.5	2.5	6.0	-2.1	3.1	3.0	2.1
Iraq	0.6	29.6	12.5	4.3	-13.7	45.9	13.4	-3.4	49.2	24.2	-19.9
Israel	1.6	50.2	7.4	4.8	6.5	-0.1	4.1	5.0	7.8	2.2	0.9
Jordan	0.1	35.9	6.0	4.5	4.4	4.3	4.2	3.8	3.2	4.1	5.4
Kuwait	0.4	36.5	7.4	3.4	6.3	4.4	4.3	0.6	25.1	1.5	4.5
Lebanon	0.1	37.7	-0.5	-5.0	7.4	19.0	10.5	12.6	2.9	3.3	2.0
Oman	0.2	29.1	12.6	15.4	4.6	5.8	-0.6	3.5	4.1	6.6	4.4
Qatar	0.1	36.3	16.1	7.3	2.6	5.8	5.6	0.2	4.2	6.9	1.4
Saudi Arabia	1.5	26.7	8.8	4.7	4.5	5.1	1.0	2.7	3.4	2.2	-33.4
Syrian Arab Republic	0.1	15.4	13.1	-0.8	3.9	3.9	2.5	4.2	13.6	1.9	4.4
Turkey	1.6	18.9	4.7	2.5	2.4	2.5	4.2	1.6	1.7	-1.8	0.8

Table 6.G. Average Rates of Growth of Gross Domestic Product by Kind of Economic Activity - Other Activities

Major area, region and country	Base year weights as percentage of total for world or region in 1990	Base year share as percentage of total GDP in 1990	Average rates of growth			Annual rate of change (percentage)					
			1970-1979	1980-1989	1990-1999	1997	1998	1999	2000	2001	2002
United Arab Emirates	0.4	23.1	40.5	8.6	4.5	4.2	4.3	-1.2	3.3	2.8	2.3
Yemen	0.2	24.6	...	...	10.6	6.9	4.3	6.4	4.9	3.2	2.1
Yemen Arab Republic (Former)	...	...	10.0	8.5	...	...	...	...	...	...	...
Yemen Democratic (Former)	...	...	3.9	4.9	...	...	...	...	...	...	...
EUROPE	**37.3**	**36.7**	**4.1**	**3.2**	**3.2**	**2.1**	**3.3**	**2.5**	**3.8**	**2.6**	**1.6**
Eastern Europe	*8.3*	*17.9*	*10.2*	*5.9*	*18.9*	*-2.9*	*4.4*	*-2.7*	*3.9*	*4.1*	*1.1*
Belarus	0.3	18.5	...	...	0.9	10.0	5.0	5.4	6.3	3.2	1.2
Bulgaria	0.2	26.3	7.1	5.7	-6.3	-19.7	3.0	2.5	5.3	1.9	2.9
Czech Republic	0.3	27.3	...	-1.2	2.5	-2.1	3.1	2.2	-1.5	3.8	-0.8
Czechoslovakia (Former)	...	...	5.2	...	...	...	...	...	...	...	...
Hungary	0.2	18.4	5.1	4.4	1.6	-0.8	3.1	3.5	5.1	3.9	2.4
Poland	0.5	26.8	14.2	1.5	-0.3	0.3	2.9	1.8	2.9	1.4	0.3
Republic of Moldova	0.1	13.6	...	...	-7.1	-2.4	-0.4	-3.0	-9.5	4.9	13.9
Romania [21]	0.2	14.5	6.9	2.9	3.0	-10.1	1.6	-0.7	9.7	-0.1	4.4
Russian Federation	5.2	17.6	...	...	-1.2	-3.2	3.4	-3.2	-0.2	1.8	-0.9
Slovakia	0.1	20.6	...	1.0	2.1	11.3	7.7	-1.5	2.7	3.3	22.1
Ukraine	1.2	15.3	...	...	5.4	-4.4	7.8	-6.3	14.1	10.7	3.6
Northern Europe	*20.6*	*39.0*	*4.0*	*2.8*	*3.1*	*3.8*	*5.2*	*3.8*	*5.0*	*3.6*	*2.2*
Denmark	1.8	43.9	3.8	1.7	1.7	3.1	2.9	2.1	2.9	1.8	1.1
Estonia	0.1	36.0	...	...	-2.8	7.8	3.1	0.9	4.0	5.4	3.6
Finland	1.5	34.8	4.1	3.8	1.3	3.8	2.6	3.9	3.8	1.7	1.8
Iceland	0.1	34.4	5.7	3.9	2.4	5.0	3.8	4.8	4.7	3.5	2.6
Ireland	0.4	31.0	7.1	4.6	7.5	9.8	9.2	9.5	9.6	8.2	8.2
Latvia	0.1	13.9	...	...	3.0	5.6	2.9	6.4	6.0	6.3	4.1
Lithuania	0.2	27.1	...	...	-4.2	6.9	7.4	7.9	4.8	1.7	5.0
Norway	1.3	36.6	3.5	2.8	2.8	3.6	3.2	5.2	2.8	3.0	0.7
Sweden	3.1	41.9	3.0	2.2	1.1	1.7	0.9	3.5	2.6	1.6	0.8
United Kingdom	12.0	39.6	4.2	3.0	3.6	4.0	6.8	3.7	5.9	4.2	2.5
Southern Europe	*22.2*	*38.9*	*4.2*	*3.4*	*2.1*	*2.6*	*2.5*	*2.3*	*4.1*	*2.9*	*1.8*
Andorra	0.0	43.0	9.5	8.4	4.5	2.9	3.0	2.8	5.4	6.1	3.8
Bosnia and Herzegovina	0.0	11.5	...	...	17.3	39.8	36.7	6.1	14.7	-1.0	4.1
Croatia	0.2	26.6	...	...	5.0	4.0	3.3	3.4	1.2	1.6	2.8
Greece	0.9	35.1	5.5	2.6	2.2	3.1	2.7	-0.8	3.3	3.6	4.8
Holy See	0.0	38.8	4.7	3.6	1.6	2.0	1.6	2.1	3.7	2.1	1.6
Italy	13.1	38.8	3.8	3.2	1.5	1.8	1.6	2.1	3.6	2.1	1.6
Malta	0.0	33.2	9.4	4.8	7.2	4.7	5.5	1.9	3.5	6.5	5.3
Portugal	0.7	34.1	7.6	4.2	4.3	4.8	5.8	6.2	4.8	4.4	1.6
San Marino	0.0	38.8	3.8	3.2	2.8	1.8	7.3	9.4	3.6	2.1	1.6
Serbia and Montenegro	0.2	24.7	...	...	-9.8	17.5	-2.2	-21.7	19.6	-5.6	5.5
Slovenia	0.1	27.5	...	...	3.5	3.8	3.3	4.7	4.2	3.9	3.6
Spain	6.7	43.0	4.5	4.0	2.2	2.8	3.4	2.9	4.7	4.5	1.5
TFYR Macedonia	0.0	24.6	...	...	2.0	1.4	1.6	1.3	2.5	-0.6	2.8
Yugoslavia (Former)	...	...	7.6	0.9	...	...	...	...	...	...	...
Western Europe	*48.8*	*42.1*	*4.0*	*3.2*	*2.6*	*2.1*	*2.7*	*2.8*	*3.1*	*1.8*	*1.4*
Austria	1.8	36.3	3.8	2.9	2.5	0.5	3.8	1.8	3.6	1.5	1.1
Belgium	2.6	43.0	5.0	4.1	2.6	3.1	2.2	3.2	2.4	1.1	-0.2
France	16.7	44.8	4.1	3.3	1.5	1.0	1.9	2.4	3.7	1.9	1.9
Germany	21.0	41.0	4.5	3.1	3.5	2.5	3.0	3.0	3.1	2.1	1.2
Liechtenstein	0.0	39.8	2.1	2.1	3.2	2.8	3.8	2.1	1.8	0.6	3.9
Luxembourg	0.2	47.0	8.9	7.6	5.4	7.5	5.2	6.1	7.6	1.1	-0.9
Monaco	0.0	44.8	4.6	4.1	2.2	1.7	2.6	3.1	4.3	2.5	2.4
Netherlands	3.7	40.8	3.2	4.1	2.8	4.1	3.3	3.7	2.2	2.2	1.1
Switzerland	2.8	39.8	0.5	1.4	2.4	1.7	2.6	0.9	0.7	-0.3	2.9
OCEANIA	**1.7**	**40.8**	**3.8**	**4.2**	**3.4**	**3.6**	**5.5**	**4.0**	**3.7**	**4.0**	**4.0**
Australia & New Zealand	*97.6*	*41.1*	*3.8*	*4.2*	*3.4*	*3.8*	*5.7*	*4.0*	*3.8*	*4.1*	*4.1*
Australia	85.7	41.1	4.1	4.4	3.5	4.0	6.2	4.2	3.9	4.0	4.2
New Zealand	11.9	40.6	2.2	2.4	2.3	2.3	2.2	2.3	2.9	4.9	3.5

Table 6.G. Average Rates of Growth of Gross Domestic Product by Kind of Economic Activity - Other Activities

Major area, region and country	Base year weights as percentage of total for world or region in 1990	Base year share as percentage of total GDP in 1990	Average rates of growth			Annual rate of change (percentage)					
			1970-1979	1980-1989	1990-1999	1997	1998	1999	2000	2001	2002
Melanesia	*1.3*	*26.3*	*6.2*	*3.8*	*2.5*	*-4.9*	*-6.3*	*6.9*	*0.8*	*-0.7*	*0.9*
Fiji	0.2	27.6	8.2	0.6	2.2	-3.4	0.5	3.6	-0.6	-0.9	0.8
New Caledonia	0.5	31.3	1.7	6.7	2.8	-13.3	-3.2	0.9	2.1	-1.1	0.7
Papua New Guinea [22]	0.5	21.7	9.0	3.3	2.4	4.4	-13.3	17.5	0.3	0.7	2.1
Solomon Islands	0.0	29.3	8.2	2.0	2.6	-1.0	-2.2	-7.5	-1.7	-14.6	-3.7
Vanuatu	0.0	25.7	7.7	2.9	1.2	0.5	1.2	-2.5	0.9	0.9	-11.6
Micronesia	*0.1*	*40.8*	*4.5*	*1.3*	*2.4*	*-2.6*	*-3.7*	*-4.8*	*5.0*	*3.0*	*4.8*
Kiribati	0.0	37.3	2.9	-3.6	6.8	6.9	2.6	10.1	1.4	1.9	3.8
Marshall Islands	0.0	50.1	6.6	6.1	-1.1	-10.1	5.5	0.0	-3.0	1.9	3.8
Micronesia (Federated States of)	0.0	37.3	6.6	5.4	3.9	-3.4	-7.7	-8.1	11.0	4.2	6.9
Nauru	0.0	37.3	6.8	5.8	-2.8	-5.6	-7.4	-7.2	10.2	-0.8	-1.9
Palau	0.0	43.5	2.9	-5.5	3.7	1.7	-3.2	-7.3	0.1	3.2	4.2
Polynesia	*1.0*	*45.7*	*5.4*	*5.6*	*3.2*	*1.2*	*1.2*	*2.6*	*2.7*	*2.3*	*2.0*
Cook Islands	0.0	42.5	-6.5	4.3	0.7	-8.1	-11.8	-10.0	3.7	1.8	-1.8
French Polynesia	0.9	47.5	6.2	6.1	3.3	1.1	1.1	2.7	2.7	2.1	1.9
Samoa	0.0	29.1	3.1	0.4	1.3	5.6	7.1	4.1	5.4	6.0	6.4
Tonga [23]	0.0	29.6	3.6	3.3	3.5	3.2	4.6	7.4	0.0	4.1	1.9
Tuvalu	0.0	36.4	6.6	-7.5	6.5	-0.1	29.5	0.2	3.0	3.0	-9.2

Notes for Table 6.G - Other activities

1/ 1970-1992
Restaurants and Hotels are included in "Other activities".

2/ 1970-1972, 1980-1991
Restaurants and Hotels are included in "Other activities".

3/ 1982-1986
FISIM is netted out of Financial intermediation, real estate, renting and business activities.

4/ 1985-1990
Restaurants and Hotels are included in "Other activities".

5/ 1970-1977
Restaurants and Hotels are included in "Other activities".

6/ (a) 1970-1995
Includes gas and water.

(b) 1996-2001
Includes Utilities, Government social and personal services only.

7/ 1970-2002
Restaurants and Hotels are included in "Other activities".

8/ 1989-1992
Includes Social and personal services, but excludes services provided by the general government like Education, Health etc.

9/ 1980-1991
FISIM is netted out of Financial intermediation, real estate, renting and business activities.

10/ (a) 1970-1989
Restaurants and Hotels are included in "Other activities".

(b) 1994-2003
Includes non-market Education; health and social work; other community, social and personal services.

11/ 1972, 1983-1991
Excludes banks and insurance companies registered in Cayman Islands but with no physical presence in the Islands.

12/ 1987-1992
Includes hotels and guest houses.

13/ 1996-2000
The data refers to the Tourism Sector as defined by Turks and Caicos.

14/ 1970-2003
Restaurants and Hotels are included in "Other activities".

15/ 1970-1979
Restaurants and Hotels are included in "Other activities".

16/ 1970-2001
Restaurants and Hotels are included in "Other activities".

17/ 1970-1996
Restaurants and Hotels are included in "Other activities".

18/ 1970-2001
Restaurants and Hotels are included in "Other activities".

19/ 1970-2002
Restaurants and Hotels are included in "Other activities".

20/ 1993-1998
Refers to household services, social & community, amusement & recreation, and other related personal services.

21/ 1980-1988
Excludes personal services.

22/ 1986-1999
Restaurants and Hotels are included in "Other activities".

23/ 1994-2000
Includes Ownership of dwellings.

D. Implicit Price Deflators of Gross Domestic Product: Individual Countries or Areas (Index Numbers 1990 = 100)

Description of Analysis In Table 7

D. Price development expressed in terms of indices of implicit price deflators of gross domestic product

In this final section of the publication, an attempt is made to present a disaggregation of economic development by analyzing the movements of prices and exchange rates in relation to overall economic growth. The period coverage includes the years 1970, 1975, 1980, 1985, and 1990 through 2003.

In Table 7, GDP indices based on current prices expressed in US dollars and national currencies are shown in columns 1 and 2. The annual changes of GDP in volume terms are reflected in column 3, where the indices are based on the movement of GDP at constant prices. Column 4 presents indices of price changes of GDP expressed in US dollars and column 5 includes indices of price changes of GDP in national currency. The price indices in columns 4 and 5 are obtained by dividing, respectively, the indices of GDP at current prices alternatively expressed in US dollars and national currencies shown in columns 1 and 2, by the volume indices presented in column 3. Column 6 provides an implied development in exchange rates derived either by dividing the GDP deflators in national currency (col. 5) by the GDP deflators converted in United States dollar listed in column 4, or by dividing the GDP indices expressed in national currencies by the United States dollar indices listed in column 2 and 1, respectively.

Although column 6 of the table reflects an implied movement of domestic exchange rates vis-à-vis the US dollar from the base year 1990, it does not illustrate the extent to which these changes have affected economic growth. For this effect, it is necessary to relate exchange rate movements in column 6 with price changes in columns 4 and 5 in order to determine whether adjustments in exchange rates have been sufficient to reflect inflationary pressures in the economy.

The data as presented in the table reflect situations in four groups of countries. In the first group, the movement of exchange rates as calculated in column 6 is exactly the same as the movement of domestic prices reflected in the price indices presented in column 5. For these countries, there is no movement over time of the price index in terms of US dollars that is presented in column 4. Thus, the price index in the latter column is always close to 100 for those countries. In this case the growth of GDP in US dollars is not affected by domestic price changes as all domestic price changes have been eliminated through the movement of the exchange rate .

A second group of countries are those having fixed exchange rates. There is no movement of the exchange rates in column 6 i.e., the index always remains 100. In this case all domestic inflation is reflected in the growth of GDP in US dollar terms.

In a third group of countries, the exchange rate index in column 6 is not fixed but lags behind the movement of domestic prices as reflected in the price indices presented in column 5. For this group of countries, the price index in terms of US dollars as presented in column 4 is higher than 100 and the countries' domestic inflation thus affects the growth of GDP in US dollars, though not to the extent that this was the case for countries with a fixed exchange rate. Only some of the domestic inflation is eliminated from the growth of GDP in US dollars through the movement of the exchange rates.

There is a fourth group of countries where the exchange rates overreact to the movements of prices in the domestic economy. For these countries, the index of exchange rates in column 6 is much higher than the price index in terms of national currency in column 5. This case implies that the price index in terms of US dollars as shown in column 4 is lower than 100 and this has the effect that the growth of GDP in terms of US dollars is lower when compared in terms of national currency.

Again, a note of caution is advised when using the price index information presented in the table. For one, the deflators shown may not be fully comparable between countries because a wide variety of methods had been applied to obtain the data on price movements. To cite an example, for some countries, explicit price indices were used directly in the calculations while for other countries implicit price indices were derived by dividing volume indices into indices of current price development of GDP. Likewise, even as the index numbers are shown for a common base year 1990 = 100, GDP data at constant prices used in the calculations actually have been compiled according to different original weight base periods.

Please be noted that the "-" symbol has been employed due to the very small magnitude of the data.

Table 7. Implicit Price Deflators of Gross Domestic Product in US Dollars and in National Currency

(Index numbers 1990 = 100)

Region, country or area and currency unit	Year	GDP in Current Prices: National Currency (1)	GDP in Current Prices: US Dollars (2)	GDP at Constant Prices (3)	GDP Implicit Price Deflators: National Currency (4)	GDP Implicit Price Deflators: US Dollars (5)	Exchange Rates (6)
AFRICA							
Algeria	1970	4.6	8.3	43.3	10.6	19.3	55.1
	1975	11.1	25.2	54.9	20.2	45.9	44.1
	1980	29.3	68.4	76.1	38.5	89.9	42.8
	1985	52.6	93.7	96.3	54.6	97.3	56.1
	1990	100.0	100.0	100.0	100.0	100.0	100.0
	1991	155.5	75.4	98.8	157.4	76.3	206.2
	1992	193.9	79.5	100.6	192.7	79.1	243.8
	1993	214.6	82.3	98.5	217.9	83.6	260.6
	1994	268.3	68.6	97.6	275.0	70.3	391.4
	1995	361.7	68.0	101.3	357.1	67.1	532.1
	1996	463.6	75.8	105.4	439.7	71.9	611.2
	1997	501.5	77.8	106.6	470.4	73.0	644.2
	1998	506.9	77.3	112.0	452.4	69.0	655.8
	1999	584.1	78.6	115.6	505.2	68.0	743.2
	2000	739.3	88.0	118.4	624.5	74.3	840.2
	2001	765.1	88.8	120.9	632.9	73.4	862.0
	2002	808.0	90.8	125.8	642.1	72.2	889.6
	2003	909.8	105.3	134.3	677.6	78.4	864.0
Angola	1970	26.6	27.8	75.2	35.4	37.0	95.7
	1975	26.0	30.4	84.6	30.7	36.0	85.4
	1980	52.3	52.3	78.6	66.5	66.5	100.0
	1985	66.6	66.6	85.8	77.5	77.5	100.0
	1990	100.0	100.0	100.0	100.0	100.0	100.0
	1991	217.9	118.3	100.3	217.2	117.9	184.2
	1992	471.8	56.1	94.5	499.4	59.4	840.4
	1993	4 565.3	51.3	71.1	6 418.9	72.2	8 891.5
	1994	78 443.5	39.4	72.9	107 637.4	54.1	198 927.1
	1995	4 499 955.8	49.0	80.7	5 577 609.6	60.7	9 192 558.3
	1996	271 263 636.4	63.4	89.8	301 922 289.9	70.6	427 933 574.0
	1997	568 831 168.8	74.3	96.7	588 019 995.6	76.8	765 559 473.7
	1998	829 870 129.9	63.2	102.1	813 059 111.3	61.9	1 313 000 593.3
	1999	5 575 000 000.0	59.8	104.8	5 319 753 079.5	57.0	9 327 850 012.3
	2000	29 761 688 311.7	88.7	108.6	27 412 758 075.3	81.7	33 560 211 801.1
	2001	63 997 077 922.1	86.8	114.2	56 027 342 529.2	76.0	73 727 728 012.1
	2002	138 450 649 350.6	95.2	130.0	106 510 546 692.5	73.2	145 498 384 473.1
	2003	239 180 419 285.7	95.9	136.1	175 742 402 042.6	70.5	249 369 278 806.5
Benin	1970	16.3	16.0	56.4	28.9	28.3	102.0
	1975	26.4	33.6	68.3	38.7	49.1	78.7
	1980	57.4	73.9	72.6	79.0	101.8	77.6
	1985	93.5	56.7	94.3	99.2	60.1	165.0
	1990	100.0	100.0	100.0	100.0	100.0	100.0
	1991	106.6	102.9	104.8	101.7	98.2	103.6
	1992	113.9	117.1	109.2	104.3	107.3	97.2
	1993	119.3	114.7	112.7	105.8	101.8	104.0
	1994	166.2	81.5	116.3	142.9	70.1	203.9
	1995	200.3	109.2	121.7	164.6	89.8	183.3
	1996	226.5	120.5	128.9	175.7	93.5	187.9
	1997	250.6	116.9	136.2	184.0	85.8	214.4
	1998	274.2	126.5	142.4	192.6	88.9	216.7
	1999	292.6	129.4	149.1	196.3	86.8	226.1
	2000	319.6	122.2	157.6	202.8	77.5	261.5
	2001	346.1	128.5	165.6	209.0	77.6	269.2
	2002	377.3	147.4	176.1	214.2	83.7	256.0
	2003	406.2	190.3	185.8	218.7	102.4	213.5
Botswana	1970	1.1	2.8	7.9	13.5	35.1	38.4
	1975	4.0	10.1	19.7	20.4	51.3	39.7
	1980	12.7	30.4	33.6	37.8	90.5	41.8
	1985	32.8	32.0	53.8	60.9	59.6	102.3
	1990	100.0	100.0	100.0	100.0	100.0	100.0
	1991	115.5	106.3	108.7	106.3	97.8	108.7
	1992	127.9	112.7	115.5	110.7	97.6	113.4
	1993	139.2	106.9	115.3	120.8	92.7	130.2
	1994	168.5	116.8	119.9	140.5	97.4	144.3
	1995	187.2	125.6	123.8	151.2	101.5	149.0
	1996	216.8	121.3	130.6	165.9	92.9	178.7

Table 7. Implicit Price Deflators of Gross Domestic Product in US Dollars and in National Currency

(Index numbers 1990 = 100)

Region, country or area and currency unit	Year	GDP in Current Prices: National Currency (1)	GDP in Current Prices: US Dollars (2)	GDP at Constant Prices (3)	GDP Implicit Price Deflators: National Currency (4)	GDP Implicit Price Deflators: US Dollars (5)	Exchange Rates (6)
	1997	270.8	138.0	138.0	196.3	100.0	196.2
	1998	307.7	135.5	149.1	206.4	90.9	227.1
	1999	328.5	132.2	155.3	211.6	85.1	248.6
	2000	387.1	141.2	165.5	233.9	85.3	274.2
	2001	448.0	142.7	179.5	249.7	79.5	314.0
	2002	488.4	143.6	183.7	265.9	78.2	340.1
	2003	537.2	201.9	190.5	282.1	106.0	266.1
Burkina Faso	1970	14.1	13.8	48.7	29.0	28.4	102.0
	1975	21.6	27.5	60.8	35.6	45.2	78.7
	1980	46.4	59.8	75.4	61.5	79.3	77.6
	1985	80.0	48.5	87.7	91.2	55.3	165.0
	1990	100.0	100.0	100.0	100.0	100.0	100.0
	1991	104.3	100.6	109.5	95.2	91.9	103.6
	1992	104.4	107.4	109.9	95.0	97.7	97.2
	1993	106.9	102.8	115.5	92.6	89.0	104.0
	1994	124.7	61.1	120.1	103.9	50.9	203.9
	1995	142.1	77.5	127.2	111.7	61.0	183.3
	1996	155.6	82.8	135.5	114.9	61.1	187.9
	1997	171.5	80.0	142.0	120.8	56.4	214.4
	1998	188.4	86.9	151.0	124.7	57.6	216.7
	1999	195.0	86.2	160.6	121.5	53.7	226.1
	2000	200.5	76.7	164.1	122.2	46.7	261.5
	2001	233.3	86.6	173.4	134.5	50.0	269.2
	2002	257.4	100.6	181.4	141.9	55.4	256.0
	2003	285.3	133.7	193.2	147.7	69.2	213.5
Burundi	1970	10.9	21.4	50.2	21.8	42.6	51.1
	1975	16.6	36.1	51.8	32.1	69.7	46.0
	1980	43.5	82.8	65.3	66.7	126.9	52.6
	1985	71.9	102.0	82.9	86.7	123.0	70.5
	1990	100.0	100.0	100.0	100.0	100.0	100.0
	1991	107.8	101.7	105.3	102.3	96.5	106.0
	1992	115.1	94.6	107.3	107.3	88.2	121.6
	1993	120.6	85.1	99.7	121.0	85.3	141.8
	1994	137.6	93.3	96.7	142.4	96.5	147.5
	1995	127.4	87.3	89.8	141.7	97.2	145.8
	1996	135.3	76.5	82.1	164.7	93.2	176.8
	1997	174.7	84.9	82.4	212.1	103.1	205.7
	1998	204.0	78.0	86.2	236.7	90.5	261.5
	1999	232.1	70.5	85.3	272.0	82.7	329.1
	2000	260.5	61.9	84.6	308.0	73.2	420.8
	2001	280.3	57.8	87.3	321.2	66.3	484.9
	2002	295.9	54.4	91.2	324.5	59.7	543.5
	2003	324.6	51.4	90.7	357.9	56.6	632.2
Cameroon	1970	9.4	9.2	46.6	20.1	19.7	102.0
	1975	19.2	24.4	55.2	34.8	44.2	78.7
	1980	52.5	67.6	83.6	62.8	80.9	77.6
	1985	119.9	72.7	119.1	100.7	61.0	165.0
	1990	100.0	100.0	100.0	100.0	100.0	100.0
	1991	95.7	92.3	96.2	99.4	95.9	103.6
	1992	94.5	97.2	93.3	101.2	104.1	97.2
	1993	89.2	85.7	91.9	97.0	93.3	104.0
	1994	96.4	47.3	88.9	108.4	53.1	203.9
	1995	114.6	62.5	91.7	125.0	68.2	183.3
	1996	123.0	65.5	96.3	127.8	68.0	187.9
	1997	137.8	64.3	101.2	136.3	63.6	214.4
	1998	147.4	68.0	106.2	138.8	64.1	216.7
	1999	154.2	68.2	110.7	139.3	61.6	226.1
	2000	169.5	64.8	116.5	145.4	55.6	261.5
	2001	168.8	62.7	121.9	138.5	51.4	269.2
	2002	180.5	70.5	126.8	142.4	55.6	256.0
	2003	191.8	89.9	131.9	145.5	68.2	213.5
Cape Verde	1970	8.5	20.8	55.7	15.3	37.4	41.1
	1975	13.9	38.2	51.9	26.9	73.7	36.5
	1980	26.5	46.2	60.0	44.2	77.0	57.4
	1985	58.5	44.7	82.6	70.8	54.1	130.8

Table 7. Implicit Price Deflators of Gross Domestic Product in US Dollars and in National Currency

(Index numbers 1990 = 100)

Region, country or area and currency unit	Year	GDP in Current Prices: National Currency (1)	GDP in Current Prices: US Dollars (2)	GDP at Constant Prices (3)	GDP Implicit Price Deflators: National Currency (4)	GDP Implicit Price Deflators: US Dollars (5)	Exchange Rates (6)
	1990	100.0	100.0	100.0	100.0	100.0	100.0
	1991	106.3	104.2	101.4	104.8	102.8	102.0
	1992	113.0	116.4	104.5	108.2	111.4	97.1
	1993	134.8	117.4	112.1	120.2	104.7	114.8
	1994	155.3	132.8	119.9	129.5	110.7	116.9
	1995	174.8	159.3	128.9	135.6	123.6	109.7
	1996	192.3	163.0	134.0	143.4	121.6	117.9
	1997	218.6	164.3	141.3	154.7	116.3	133.0
	1998	245.1	174.8	151.7	161.5	115.2	140.2
	1999	280.0	189.4	164.8	169.9	115.0	147.8
	2000	299.9	175.5	176.0	170.4	99.7	170.9
	2001	319.8	181.8	181.3	176.4	100.3	176.0
	2002	342.0	204.4	189.5	180.4	107.8	167.3
	2003	370.3	265.4	199.0	186.1	133.4	139.5
Central African Republic	1970	11.7	11.5	79.3	14.8	14.5	102.0
	1975	24.5	31.1	77.9	31.5	40.0	78.7
	1980	42.4	54.7	91.2	46.5	59.9	77.6
	1985	95.7	58.0	98.1	97.5	59.1	165.0
	1990	100.0	100.0	100.0	100.0	100.0	100.0
	1991	102.6	99.0	99.4	103.1	99.5	103.6
	1992	100.4	103.3	93.1	107.9	111.0	97.2
	1993	97.3	93.6	93.4	104.2	100.2	104.0
	1994	125.3	61.4	97.9	127.9	62.7	203.9
	1995	150.6	82.2	103.8	145.1	79.1	183.3
	1996	144.9	77.1	100.5	144.2	76.7	187.9
	1997	153.6	71.7	106.2	144.6	67.5	214.4
	1998	163.7	75.5	111.4	146.9	67.8	216.7
	1999	172.3	76.2	115.4	149.3	66.0	226.1
	2000	183.0	70.0	117.5	155.8	59.6	261.5
	2001	189.2	70.3	117.0	161.7	60.1	269.2
	2002	196.5	76.7	118.8	165.4	64.6	256.0
	2003	207.0	97.0	122.7	168.7	79.0	213.5
Chad	1970	27.3	26.7	74.6	36.5	35.8	102.0
	1975	44.7	56.8	89.8	49.8	63.3	78.7
	1980	46.3	59.6	60.1	76.9	99.1	77.6
	1985	98.4	59.6	92.0	106.9	64.8	165.0
	1990	100.0	100.0	100.0	100.0	100.0	100.0
	1991	111.9	108.0	108.5	103.1	99.5	103.6
	1992	105.2	108.2	117.2	89.8	92.3	97.2
	1993	98.3	94.5	115.2	85.4	82.1	104.0
	1994	156.3	76.6	121.7	128.5	63.0	203.9
	1995	171.8	93.7	123.2	139.4	76.1	183.3
	1996	194.0	103.3	125.3	154.9	82.4	187.9
	1997	214.5	100.1	132.8	161.5	75.4	214.4
	1998	239.6	110.6	139.8	171.4	79.1	216.7
	1999	218.3	96.5	139.6	156.4	69.1	226.1
	2000	221.4	84.7	139.1	159.2	60.9	261.5
	2001	259.6	96.4	151.3	171.6	63.7	269.2
	2002	288.1	112.5	164.2	175.5	68.5	256.0
	2003	346.0	162.1	185.8	186.2	87.2	213.5
Comoros	1970	8.0	7.8	48.7	16.4	16.0	102.0
	1975	18.8	23.9	61.1	30.8	39.2	78.7
	1980	42.1	54.2	77.2	54.5	70.2	77.6
	1985	75.9	46.0	94.6	80.3	48.7	165.0
	1990	100.0	100.0	100.0	100.0	100.0	100.0
	1991	102.3	98.7	101.8	100.5	97.0	103.6
	1992	103.5	106.5	100.0	103.5	106.5	97.2
	1993	109.6	105.4	101.8	107.7	103.6	104.0
	1994	113.6	74.3	99.5	114.2	74.7	152.9
	1995	118.0	85.8	97.3	121.3	88.3	137.5
	1996	120.2	85.3	98.9	121.6	86.3	140.9
	1997	124.4	77.4	97.8	127.2	79.1	160.8
	1998	128.2	78.9	96.7	132.5	81.5	162.5
	1999	138.2	81.5	98.6	140.3	82.7	169.6
	2000	145.0	73.9	97.4	148.8	75.9	196.1

Table 7. Implicit Price Deflators of Gross Domestic Product in US Dollars and in National Currency

(Index numbers 1990 = 100)

Region, country or area and currency unit	Year	GDP in Current Prices: National Currency (1)	GDP in Current Prices: US Dollars (2)	GDP at Constant Prices (3)	GDP Implicit Price Deflators: National Currency (4)	GDP Implicit Price Deflators: US Dollars (5)	Exchange Rates (6)
	2001	160.7	79.6	99.3	161.8	80.1	201.9
	2002	172.1	89.7	101.8	169.0	88.0	192.0
	2003	181.6	113.4	104.4	174.0	108.7	160.1
Congo	1970	9.5	9.3	36.2	26.3	25.8	102.0
	1975	19.2	24.4	47.4	40.5	51.5	78.7
	1980	47.3	60.9	61.2	77.3	99.6	77.6
	1985	127.4	77.2	102.6	124.2	75.3	165.0
	1990	100.0	100.0	100.0	100.0	100.0	100.0
	1991	100.9	97.4	102.4	98.5	95.1	103.6
	1992	101.9	104.8	104.1	97.9	100.7	97.2
	1993	99.8	95.9	103.1	96.8	93.0	104.0
	1994	128.9	63.2	97.5	132.2	64.8	203.9
	1995	138.6	75.6	99.6	139.2	75.9	183.3
	1996	170.6	90.8	103.9	164.2	87.4	187.9
	1997	177.9	83.0	103.4	172.1	80.3	214.4
	1998	150.9	69.7	107.3	140.7	64.9	216.7
	1999	190.2	84.1	103.8	183.3	81.0	226.1
	2000	300.9	115.0	112.2	268.3	102.6	261.5
	2001	268.2	99.6	115.4	232.4	86.3	269.2
	2002	275.7	107.7	119.4	230.8	90.2	256.0
	2003	298.1	139.6	121.8	244.7	114.7	213.5
Cote d'Ivoire	1970	12.8	12.6	42.8	30.0	29.4	102.0
	1975	25.8	32.7	58.3	44.2	56.1	78.7
	1980	66.4	85.6	71.6	92.7	119.4	77.6
	1985	96.8	58.7	86.9	111.4	67.5	165.0
	1990	100.0	100.0	100.0	100.0	100.0	100.0
	1991	100.5	97.0	100.1	100.4	96.9	103.6
	1992	98.4	101.2	99.4	98.9	101.8	97.2
	1993	97.5	93.8	99.0	98.5	94.7	104.0
	1994	142.6	69.9	101.2	140.9	69.1	203.9
	1995	171.2	93.4	108.3	158.1	86.2	183.3
	1996	191.8	102.1	115.6	165.9	88.3	187.9
	1997	211.3	98.6	122.2	173.0	80.7	214.4
	1998	230.3	106.3	128.4	179.3	82.8	216.7
	1999	238.9	105.6	130.9	182.4	80.7	226.1
	2000	234.9	89.8	127.4	184.3	70.5	261.5
	2001	243.0	90.3	127.6	190.5	70.8	269.2
	2002	252.2	98.5	126.0	200.1	78.2	256.0
	2003	264.6	124.0	128.3	206.2	96.6	213.5
Democratic Republic of the Congo	1970	-	20.0	87.9	-	22.8	0.1
	1975	-	41.0	98.9	-	41.4	0.1
	1980	0.6	157.4	91.7	0.7	171.7	0.4
	1985	5.3	77.0	100.4	5.3	76.7	6.9
	1990	100.0	100.0	100.0	100.0	100.0	100.0
	1991	2 108.4	97.2	91.6	2 301.8	106.1	2 169.2
	1992	78 829.8	87.7	82.0	96 155.1	107.0	89 836.7
	1993	1 201 429.2	114.4	70.9	1 694 195.7	161.4	1 049 971.2
	1994	309 696 293.0	62.1	68.1	454 441 519.0	91.1	498 640 775.8
	1995	1 768 646 717.3	60.3	68.6	2 577 232 608.8	87.9	2 933 281 785.4
	1996	12 935 685 573.9	61.7	67.9	19 059 244 632.3	90.9	20 956 238 616.6
	1997	34 898 615 453.3	63.6	64.2	54 354 223 358.0	99.1	54 846 999 232.3
	1998	44 618 133 095.1	66.5	63.1	70 694 068 137.2	105.4	67 090 969 893.1
	1999	231 460 473 425.6	57.0	60.4	383 209 686 922.0	94.4	406 107 437 824.2
	2000	1 326 777 579 276.5	53.1	56.2	2 359 435 365 023.1	94.4	2 500 417 613 389.7
	2001	6 539 370 254 577.9	52.5	55.6	11 758 437 000 811.5	94.4	12 461 033 439 868.7
	2002	8 553 238 052 702.1	59.1	57.3	14 917 139 917 931.4	103.1	14 468 534 967 835.9
	2003	10 263 510 495 757.0	60.6	60.2	17 047 536 758 649.5	100.7	16 926 206 929 190.2
Djibouti	1970	17.4	14.4	70.1	24.9	20.6	120.6
	1975	34.3	34.3	86.7	39.5	39.5	100.0
	1980	65.9	65.9	84.5	78.0	78.0	100.0
	1985	76.7	76.7	82.8	92.6	92.6	100.0
	1990	100.0	100.0	100.0	100.0	100.0	100.0
	1991	102.0	102.0	96.9	105.4	105.4	100.0
	1992	105.4	105.4	102.5	102.8	102.8	100.0
	1993	105.5	105.5	107.5	98.2	98.2	100.0

Table 7. Implicit Price Deflators of Gross Domestic Product in US Dollars and in National Currency

(Index numbers 1990 = 100)

Region, country or area and currency unit	Year	GDP in Current Prices		GDP at Constant Prices	GDP Implicit Price Deflators		Exchange Rates
		National Currency (1)	US Dollars (2)	(3)	National Currency (4)	US Dollars (5)	(6)
	1994	111.8	111.8	104.9	106.6	106.6	100.0
	1995	111.5	111.5	110.8	100.7	100.7	100.0
	1996	108.7	108.7	105.1	103.4	103.4	100.0
	1997	107.5	107.5	110.0	97.8	97.8	100.0
	1998	108.9	108.9	109.8	99.2	99.2	100.0
	1999	117.3	117.3	112.2	104.6	104.6	100.0
	2000	121.0	121.0	113.0	107.1	107.1	100.0
	2001	125.5	125.5	115.1	109.1	109.1	100.0
	2002	129.6	129.6	118.1	109.7	109.7	100.0
	2003	136.2	136.2	121.7	111.9	111.9	100.0
Egypt	1970	2.7	9.6	33.7	8.0	28.5	28.1
	1975	4.8	18.9	43.4	11.0	43.5	25.2
	1980	15.6	34.5	57.3	27.2	60.2	45.2
	1985	37.1	82.1	81.3	45.6	100.9	45.2
	1990	100.0	100.0	100.0	100.0	100.0	100.0
	1991	123.6	61.1	100.3	123.2	60.9	202.5
	1992	142.8	66.6	100.8	141.6	66.1	214.3
	1993	158.9	73.5	106.0	150.0	69.3	216.3
	1994	185.2	84.8	110.1	168.2	77.0	218.4
	1995	208.3	95.2	115.2	180.9	82.6	218.9
	1996	241.4	110.3	121.1	199.4	91.1	218.8
	1997	260.9	119.4	125.9	207.2	94.8	218.6
	1998	279.3	127.8	133.6	209.0	95.6	218.6
	1999	308.8	141.0	140.8	219.3	100.1	219.0
	2000	325.7	145.4	145.8	223.4	99.7	224.0
	2001	346.6	135.2	150.4	230.4	89.9	256.3
	2002	376.8	129.8	155.1	243.0	83.7	290.3
	2003	405.8	107.5	162.1	250.4	66.3	377.5
Equatorial Guinea	1970	31.1	120.9	60.1	51.7	201.2	25.7
	1975	27.7	35.3	75.5	36.8	46.7	78.7
	1980	26.9	34.6	76.8	34.9	45.0	77.6
	1985	85.8	52.0	89.9	95.5	57.9	165.0
	1990	100.0	100.0	100.0	100.0	100.0	100.0
	1991	104.7	101.0	98.9	105.9	102.2	103.6
	1992	95.6	98.3	109.4	87.4	89.9	97.2
	1993	103.3	99.3	119.9	86.2	82.8	104.0
	1994	147.7	72.4	138.0	107.1	52.5	203.9
	1995	184.0	100.4	160.2	114.8	62.6	183.3
	1996	320.6	170.7	232.8	137.7	73.3	187.9
	1997	727.6	339.4	398.6	182.6	85.2	214.4
	1998	597.1	275.6	486.3	122.8	56.7	216.7
	1999	1 053.0	465.6	687.6	153.1	67.7	226.1
	2000	2 011.1	769.1	803.8	250.2	95.7	261.5
	2001	2 849.8	1 058.5	1 233.0	231.1	85.8	269.2
	2002	3 374.6	1 318.2	1 436.4	234.9	91.8	256.0
	2003	3 830.7	1 794.5	1 580.1	242.4	113.6	213.5
Eritrea	1990	100.0	100.0	100.0	100.0	100.0	100.0
	1992	127.0	93.8	102.4	124.1	91.6	135.4
	1993	143.3	59.3	112.5	127.4	52.7	241.5
	1994	191.7	72.6	141.4	135.6	51.3	264.0
	1995	216.4	72.7	145.4	148.9	50.0	297.5
	1996	257.8	84.0	158.7	162.4	52.9	306.8
	1997	288.9	89.1	171.0	169.0	52.1	324.1
	1998	321.2	93.5	177.6	180.9	52.6	343.8
	1999	347.5	90.6	178.2	195.0	50.8	383.7
	2000	360.2	90.7	156.8	229.7	57.9	397.0
	2001	451.4	110.5	170.4	264.9	64.8	408.6
	2002	524.6	126.7	168.4	311.6	75.3	413.9
	2003	630.3	151.7	177.5	355.2	85.5	415.4
Ethiopia	1990	100.0	100.0	100.0	100.0	100.0	100.0
	1992	123.6	91.3	92.3	133.9	98.9	135.4
	1993	158.5	65.6	103.3	153.4	63.5	241.5
	1994	168.4	63.8	104.9	160.4	60.8	264.0
	1995	201.4	67.7	111.4	180.8	60.8	297.5
	1996	225.5	73.5	123.2	183.0	59.6	306.8

Table 7. Implicit Price Deflators of Gross Domestic Product in US Dollars and in National Currency

(Index numbers 1990 = 100)

Region, country or area and currency unit	Year	GDP in Current Prices		GDP at Constant Prices	GDP Implicit Price Deflators		Exchange Rates
		National Currency (1)	US Dollars (2)	(3)	National Currency (4)	US Dollars (5)	(6)
	1997	246.4	76.0	129.6	190.1	58.7	324.1
	1998	266.8	77.6	128.9	207.0	60.2	343.8
	1999	290.9	75.8	137.0	212.3	55.3	383.7
	2000	293.9	74.0	144.5	203.4	51.2	397.0
	2001	304.2	74.4	155.8	195.2	47.8	408.6
	2002	303.0	73.2	157.8	192.1	46.4	413.9
	2003	328.9	79.2	151.8	216.7	52.2	415.4
Gabon	1970	6.3	6.2	82.4	7.6	7.5	102.0
	1975	31.3	39.8	114.5	27.3	34.7	78.7
	1980	61.2	78.9	91.1	67.2	86.6	77.6
	1985	111.4	67.5	103.1	108.1	65.5	165.0
	1990	100.0	100.0	100.0	100.0	100.0	100.0
	1991	103.2	99.6	106.1	97.2	93.8	103.6
	1992	100.2	103.1	102.7	97.6	100.4	97.2
	1993	103.6	99.6	106.7	97.1	93.3	104.0
	1994	157.5	77.2	110.7	142.3	69.8	203.9
	1995	167.5	91.4	116.2	144.2	78.7	183.3
	1996	195.0	103.8	120.8	161.4	85.9	187.9
	1997	211.0	98.4	126.3	167.1	78.0	214.4
	1998	186.3	86.0	128.9	144.5	66.7	216.7
	1999	192.2	85.0	120.9	159.0	70.3	226.1
	2000	242.1	92.6	123.3	196.3	75.1	261.5
	2001	215.0	79.9	126.4	170.1	63.2	269.2
	2002	215.0	84.0	126.2	170.4	66.6	256.0
	2003	217.2	101.7	127.1	170.9	80.1	213.5
Gambia	1970	3.7	13.9	43.5	8.5	32.0	26.4
	1975	10.6	46.2	56.6	18.7	81.6	22.9
	1980	15.7	71.8	70.1	22.4	102.4	21.8
	1985	40.9	82.7	81.8	49.9	101.0	49.4
	1990	100.0	100.0	100.0	100.0	100.0	100.0
	1991	111.1	99.5	105.5	105.4	94.4	111.7
	1992	117.2	103.9	105.9	110.6	98.1	112.7
	1993	123.5	106.6	112.9	109.4	94.4	115.8
	1994	132.3	108.9	117.2	112.9	93.0	121.5
	1995	133.5	110.3	113.2	117.9	97.4	121.1
	1996	145.3	117.0	119.2	121.9	98.1	124.2
	1997	153.0	118.3	120.2	127.4	98.4	129.4
	1998	169.2	125.3	132.0	128.1	94.9	135.0
	1999	187.3	129.6	140.5	133.3	92.2	144.6
	2000	205.1	126.5	148.4	138.3	85.2	162.2
	2001	233.0	117.1	156.8	148.6	74.7	199.0
	2002	270.2	106.9	152.0	177.8	70.4	252.7
	2003	334.6	95.8	163.2	205.0	58.7	349.4
Ghana	1970	0.1	35.6	75.8	0.1	46.9	0.3
	1975	0.3	73.8	77.1	0.3	95.7	0.4
	1980	2.1	250.3	80.8	2.6	309.8	0.8
	1985	16.9	101.4	79.1	21.4	128.2	16.7
	1990	100.0	100.0	100.0	100.0	100.0	100.0
	1991	126.7	112.4	105.3	120.3	106.8	112.7
	1992	148.1	110.6	109.4	135.4	101.1	133.9
	1993	190.6	95.8	114.8	166.0	83.5	198.9
	1994	256.2	87.4	118.6	216.1	73.7	293.2
	1995	381.6	103.7	123.3	309.4	84.1	367.9
	1996	558.1	111.2	129.0	432.6	86.2	501.7
	1997	694.7	110.6	134.4	516.8	82.3	628.2
	1998	851.3	120.0	140.7	604.9	85.3	709.1
	1999	984.5	120.4	147.0	669.9	81.9	818.0
	2000	1 336.5	79.9	152.5	876.6	52.4	1 671.6
	2001	1 871.0	85.1	158.8	1 178.0	53.6	2 197.4
	2002	2 401.4	98.8	166.0	1 446.8	59.5	2 430.9
	2003	3 166.7	119.1	173.8	1 822.3	68.5	2 659.1
Guinea	1970	1.0	25.5	58.7	1.6	43.4	3.7
	1975	1.4	44.6	67.2	2.1	66.4	3.1
	1980	2.0	68.9	79.3	2.5	86.9	2.9
	1985	3.3	89.0	77.6	4.2	114.7	3.7

Table 7. Implicit Price Deflators of Gross Domestic Product in US Dollars and in National Currency

(Index numbers 1990 = 100)

Region, country or area and currency unit	Year	GDP in Current Prices: National Currency (1)	GDP in Current Prices: US Dollars (2)	GDP at Constant Prices (3)	GDP Implicit Price Deflators: National Currency (4)	GDP Implicit Price Deflators: US Dollars (5)	Exchange Rates (6)
	1990	100.0	100.0	100.0	100.0	100.0	100.0
	1991	121.1	106.0	102.6	118.0	103.3	114.2
	1992	143.4	104.9	105.7	135.7	99.3	136.6
	1993	165.3	114.2	110.7	149.4	103.2	144.7
	1994	180.3	121.9	115.1	156.7	105.9	147.9
	1995	198.7	132.3	120.2	165.4	110.1	150.2
	1996	213.7	140.5	125.7	170.0	111.8	152.1
	1997	222.7	134.2	131.7	169.1	101.9	165.9
	1998	238.6	127.3	137.8	173.1	92.4	187.4
	1999	258.1	122.8	142.8	180.8	86.0	210.2
	2000	287.6	108.7	146.1	196.9	74.4	264.6
	2001	313.0	105.9	151.3	206.9	70.0	295.5
	2002	341.3	114.0	157.7	216.5	72.3	299.3
	2003	375.7	127.7	163.3	230.0	78.2	294.2
Guinea-Bissau	1970	0.5	40.1	55.6	0.9	72.2	1.3
	1975	0.8	70.4	64.7	1.3	108.8	1.2
	1980	1.6	101.1	61.2	2.6	165.3	1.5
	1985	7.8	106.4	82.7	9.4	128.7	7.3
	1990	100.0	100.0	100.0	100.0	100.0	100.0
	1991	167.6	100.1	103.0	162.7	97.2	167.4
	1992	302.3	95.3	105.9	285.5	90.0	317.3
	1993	463.8	100.5	108.7	426.5	92.5	461.3
	1994	571.2	96.8	116.2	491.4	83.3	589.9
	1995	867.1	104.9	121.4	714.5	86.4	826.9
	1996	1 372.0	113.7	127.4	1 076.7	89.2	1 206.8
	1997	2 073.2	119.4	135.5	1 530.6	88.2	1 736.0
	1998	1 552.1	88.5	97.5	1 591.4	90.7	1 754.6
	1999	1 902.5	103.9	104.9	1 812.9	99.0	1 831.2
	2000	2 037.6	96.2	112.8	1 806.2	85.3	2 117.6
	2001	2 288.6	105.0	121.6	1 881.9	86.3	2 180.2
	2002	2 225.8	107.4	112.9	1 971.5	95.1	2 073.0
	2003	2 303.2	133.2	115.7	1 991.4	115.2	1 728.6
Kenya	1970	6.2	19.9	39.4	15.7	50.5	31.2
	1975	12.2	38.1	48.5	25.2	78.7	32.0
	1980	26.9	83.0	65.7	40.9	126.4	32.4
	1985	51.6	71.9	76.0	67.8	94.6	71.7
	1990	100.0	100.0	100.0	100.0	100.0	100.0
	1991	113.1	94.3	101.4	111.6	92.9	120.0
	1992	131.0	93.2	100.6	130.2	92.6	140.6
	1993	163.7	64.7	101.0	162.1	64.1	253.1
	1994	201.3	82.3	103.6	194.3	79.4	244.6
	1995	0.0	106.0	108.2	219.9	98.0	224.4
	1996	270.4	108.5	112.7	239.9	96.3	249.2
	1997	318.8	124.4	115.0	277.1	108.1	256.3
	1998	354.0	134.4	116.9	302.8	114.9	263.4
	1999	379.5	123.7	118.4	320.5	104.4	306.9
	2000	407.3	122.5	118.2	344.5	103.6	332.4
	2001	451.4	131.7	119.5	377.6	110.1	342.8
	2002	495.7	144.3	120.8	410.5	119.4	343.7
	2003	551.3	166.4	122.3	450.6	136.0	331.4
Lesotho	1970	3.3	11.8	31.6	10.3	37.3	27.6
	1975	6.9	24.1	40.2	17.1	59.9	28.6
	1980	18.5	61.4	64.3	28.7	95.4	30.1
	1985	35.5	41.2	69.1	51.4	59.7	86.1
	1990	100.0	100.0	100.0	100.0	100.0	100.0
	1991	118.4	110.9	103.8	114.0	106.8	106.7
	1992	146.5	132.9	108.8	134.6	122.1	110.2
	1993	166.5	131.9	112.6	147.9	117.1	126.3
	1994	185.4	135.1	116.5	159.2	116.0	137.2
	1995	211.5	150.9	121.6	174.0	124.1	140.2
	1996	253.4	152.5	133.7	189.6	114.1	166.2
	1997	295.1	165.7	144.5	204.1	114.6	178.1
	1998	307.6	144.0	137.8	223.2	104.5	213.7
	1999	347.9	147.3	138.1	251.8	106.6	236.1
	2000	374.2	139.5	140.2	267.0	99.5	268.2

Table 7. Implicit Price Deflators of Gross Domestic Product in US Dollars and in National Currency

(Index numbers 1990 = 100)

Region, country or area and currency unit	Year	GDP in Current Prices: National Currency (1)	GDP in Current Prices: US Dollars (2)	GDP at Constant Prices (3)	GDP Implicit Price Deflators: National Currency (4)	GDP Implicit Price Deflators: US Dollars (5)	Exchange Rates (6)
	2001	405.0	121.7	144.9	279.4	84.0	332.7
	2002	457.8	112.4	150.4	304.3	74.7	407.4
	2003	506.1	173.1	156.3	323.8	110.7	292.4
Liberia	1970	72.1	72.1	248.9	29.0	29.0	100.0
	1975	141.6	141.6	279.7	50.6	50.6	100.0
	1980	212.9	212.9	307.2	69.3	69.3	100.0
	1985	245.1	245.1	282.6	86.7	86.7	100.0
	1990	100.0	100.0	100.0	100.0	100.0	100.0
	1991	90.5	90.5	85.8	105.5	105.5	100.0
	1992	58.1	58.1	55.7	104.4	104.4	100.0
	1993	41.7	41.7	37.3	111.8	111.8	100.0
	1994	34.4	34.4	29.2	117.8	117.8	100.0
	1995	35.1	35.1	28.0	125.5	125.5	100.0
	1996	41.5	41.5	31.3	132.3	132.3	100.0
	1997	75.2	75.2	63.2	119.1	119.1	100.0
	1998	93.5	93.5	81.9	114.2	114.2	100.0
	1999	114.9	114.9	100.7	114.2	114.2	100.0
	2000	140.9	140.9	123.2	114.4	114.4	100.0
	2001	139.0	139.0	129.2	107.6	107.6	100.0
	2002	146.1	146.1	133.4	109.6	109.6	100.0
	2003	158.1	158.1	137.1	115.3	115.3	100.0
Libyan Arab Jamahiriya	1970	17.8	14.1	57.7	30.8	24.5	126.1
	1975	47.2	45.1	77.3	61.0	58.4	104.5
	1980	132.0	126.3	117.2	112.7	107.8	104.5
	1985	103.3	98.8	97.7	105.8	101.2	104.5
	1990	100.0	100.0	100.0	100.0	100.0	100.0
	1991	109.9	110.9	104.7	105.0	105.9	99.1
	1992	113.9	113.3	100.3	113.5	112.9	100.5
	1993	116.5	108.1	88.7	131.4	121.9	107.8
	1994	124.4	109.8	86.6	143.8	126.9	113.3
	1995	133.3	109.0	87.4	152.6	124.8	122.3
	1996	152.1	119.1	90.8	167.5	131.1	127.7
	1997	176.6	131.1	92.0	192.0	142.5	134.7
	1998	159.1	114.4	92.4	172.2	123.9	139.0
	1999	176.5	107.8	92.5	190.8	116.5	163.8
	2000	217.2	120.1	95.5	227.5	125.8	180.9
	2001	214.7	100.5	98.6	217.7	101.9	213.7
	2002	303.5	67.6	98.4	308.3	68.7	448.7
	2003	326.2	71.4	102.9	316.8	69.4	456.6
Madagascar	1970	5.4	29.2	84.6	6.4	34.5	18.6
	1975	8.6	59.9	87.4	9.8	68.5	14.3
	1980	15.0	106.0	93.4	16.0	113.5	14.1
	1985	33.8	76.1	87.3	38.7	87.2	44.3
	1990	100.0	100.0	100.0	100.0	100.0	100.0
	1991	106.6	86.8	93.7	113.8	92.6	122.8
	1992	121.4	97.3	94.8	128.0	102.6	124.8
	1993	140.0	109.3	96.8	144.6	112.9	128.1
	1994	198.1	96.5	96.7	204.8	99.8	205.3
	1995	292.5	102.4	98.4	297.3	104.1	285.5
	1996	351.9	129.5	100.5	350.1	128.8	271.8
	1997	392.3	115.1	104.2	376.4	110.5	340.7
	1998	442.4	121.5	108.3	408.5	112.2	364.2
	1999	508.1	120.8	113.4	448.0	106.5	420.6
	2000	570.3	125.9	118.8	479.9	105.9	452.9
	2001	654.1	148.3	126.0	519.3	117.8	441.0
	2002	658.8	144.1	110.0	599.1	131.0	457.2
	2003	744.8	179.7	116.6	638.9	154.2	414.4
Malawi	1970	5.6	18.3	36.6	15.2	49.9	30.5
	1975	11.1	35.0	56.2	19.7	62.2	31.7
	1980	21.0	70.6	76.3	27.6	92.6	29.8
	1985	40.3	64.0	86.4	46.7	74.1	63.0
	1990	100.0	100.0	100.0	100.0	100.0	100.0
	1991	118.7	115.5	107.2	110.7	107.8	102.7
	1992	137.0	103.8	97.6	140.3	106.3	132.0
	1993	184.1	114.1	107.1	171.9	106.6	161.3

Table 7. Implicit Price Deflators of Gross Domestic Product in US Dollars and in National Currency

(Index numbers 1990 = 100)

Region, country or area and currency unit	Year	GDP in Current Prices		GDP at Constant Prices	GDP Implicit Price Deflators		Exchange Rates
		National Currency (1)	US Dollars (2)	(3)	National Currency (4)	US Dollars (5)	(6)
	1994	214.9	67.1	123.9	173.5	54.2	320.1
	1995	447.0	79.8	129.6	345.0	61.6	560.1
	1996	739.4	131.8	126.4	585.0	104.3	561.0
	1997	891.6	148.0	134.9	661.1	109.7	602.6
	1998	1 135.7	99.7	136.9	829.7	72.9	1 138.7
	1999	1 653.3	102.3	141.1	1 171.5	72.5	1 615.6
	2000	2 170.7	99.5	145.8	1 489.0	68.2	2 182.0
	2001	2 583.2	97.6	139.8	1 847.2	69.8	2 645.7
	2002	3 232.3	115.0	142.3	2 271.4	80.8	2 810.2
	2003	3 862.0	109.1	148.6	2 598.3	73.4	3 539.9
Mali	1970	11.2	5.5	57.3	19.5	9.6	204.0
	1975	19.0	24.1	64.6	29.3	37.3	78.7
	1980	44.0	56.7	81.8	53.8	69.3	77.6
	1985	76.1	46.1	82.6	92.2	55.9	165.0
	1990	100.0	100.0	100.0	100.0	100.0	100.0
	1991	101.2	97.7	99.8	101.4	97.8	103.6
	1992	107.9	111.0	109.5	98.6	101.4	97.2
	1993	107.3	103.2	104.9	102.3	98.4	104.0
	1994	147.3	72.2	109.1	135.0	66.2	203.9
	1995	168.7	92.0	115.7	145.9	79.6	183.3
	1996	199.8	106.3	127.3	156.9	83.5	187.9
	1997	208.2	97.1	135.9	153.1	71.4	214.4
	1998	233.1	107.6	144.0	161.8	74.7	216.7
	1999	244.5	108.1	153.9	158.9	70.3	226.1
	2000	254.6	97.4	159.5	159.6	61.0	261.5
	2001	282.0	104.7	161.8	174.3	64.7	269.2
	2002	321.0	125.4	177.6	180.8	70.6	256.0
	2003	329.5	154.4	175.6	187.7	87.9	213.5
Mauritania	1970	13.8	20.0	67.1	20.5	29.7	68.9
	1975	25.0	46.8	80.3	31.2	58.3	53.5
	1980	46.2	81.2	87.4	52.9	92.8	57.0
	1985	64.0	66.9	87.0	73.5	76.8	95.6
	1990	100.0	100.0	100.0	100.0	100.0	100.0
	1991	109.0	107.2	102.9	105.9	104.2	101.7
	1992	117.3	108.6	105.2	111.5	103.3	108.0
	1993	139.1	92.8	114.3	121.7	81.2	149.9
	1994	150.8	98.3	119.8	125.9	82.1	153.3
	1995	166.8	103.6	126.6	131.7	81.8	161.0
	1996	180.1	105.8	130.0	138.5	81.3	170.2
	1997	197.5	104.8	136.6	144.6	76.8	188.4
	1998	225.0	96.2	141.6	158.9	68.0	233.8
	1999	245.3	94.4	147.4	166.4	64.0	259.9
	2000	261.1	88.1	154.8	168.7	56.9	296.4
	2001	298.3	94.1	161.9	184.3	58.1	317.1
	2002	319.4	94.7	167.3	190.9	56.6	337.1
	2003	351.9	107.8	176.3	199.6	61.2	326.3
Mauritius	1970	2.8	7.4	30.2	9.2	24.5	37.4
	1975	8.9	21.9	49.9	17.8	43.9	40.5
	1980	22.9	44.3	55.1	41.6	80.4	51.7
	1985	43.7	42.1	69.1	63.3	60.9	103.9
	1990	100.0	100.0	100.0	100.0	100.0	100.0
	1991	112.8	107.1	104.1	108.3	102.9	105.3
	1992	130.6	124.8	110.6	118.1	112.8	104.7
	1993	149.9	126.2	116.2	129.0	108.7	118.7
	1994	166.5	137.8	121.1	137.5	113.8	120.8
	1995	182.7	156.2	126.4	144.5	123.6	117.0
	1996	205.6	170.3	133.5	154.1	127.6	120.8
	1997	229.1	161.7	141.1	162.3	114.5	141.7
	1998	258.9	160.4	149.6	173.0	107.2	161.4
	1999	279.3	164.9	154.0	181.4	107.1	169.4
	2000	310.8	176.0	168.1	184.9	104.7	176.6
	2001	342.8	174.9	177.3	193.4	98.7	196.0
	2002	367.7	182.4	180.5	203.7	101.0	201.6
	2003	407.0	216.8	188.4	216.0	115.1	187.7

Table 7. Implicit Price Deflators of Gross Domestic Product in US Dollars and in National Currency

(Index numbers 1990 = 100)

Region, country or area and currency unit	Year	GDP in Current Prices: National Currency (1)	GDP in Current Prices: US Dollars (2)	GDP at Constant Prices (3)	GDP Implicit Price Deflators: National Currency (4)	GDP Implicit Price Deflators: US Dollars (5)	Exchange Rates (6)
Morocco	1970	9.4	15.3	41.1	22.9	37.3	61.4
	1975	17.1	34.8	52.2	32.7	66.6	49.2
	1980	34.8	72.9	68.6	50.8	106.3	47.8
	1985	60.8	49.8	80.6	75.5	61.8	122.1
	1990	100.0	100.0	100.0	100.0	100.0	100.0
	1991	113.9	107.8	106.9	106.5	100.8	105.6
	1992	114.1	110.2	102.6	111.2	107.3	103.6
	1993	117.1	103.8	101.6	115.2	102.2	112.8
	1994	131.4	117.6	112.5	116.7	104.6	111.7
	1995	132.7	128.1	105.1	126.2	121.8	103.6
	1996	150.1	141.9	117.5	127.7	120.7	105.7
	1997	149.6	129.4	114.9	130.1	112.6	115.6
	1998	161.6	138.7	123.7	130.6	112.1	116.5
	1999	162.4	136.5	123.6	131.3	110.4	119.0
	2000	166.4	129.1	124.8	133.3	103.4	128.9
	2001	180.0	131.3	132.7	135.7	98.9	137.1
	2002	186.9	139.8	136.9	136.5	102.1	133.7
	2003	201.1	173.1	144.5	139.2	119.8	116.2
Mozambique	1970	3.2	104.2	73.9	4.3	140.9	3.0
	1975	4.5	162.4	94.6	4.7	171.7	2.8
	1980	5.7	162.5	108.7	5.2	149.5	3.5
	1985	10.7	229.9	86.4	12.4	265.9	4.6
	1990	100.0	100.0	100.0	100.0	100.0	100.0
	1991	143.0	92.6	101.9	140.3	90.9	154.4
	1992	200.9	74.2	93.2	215.6	79.6	270.9
	1993	318.5	76.4	99.5	320.1	76.8	417.0
	1994	529.5	81.5	106.4	497.4	76.5	649.9
	1995	822.0	84.6	110.0	747.5	77.0	971.3
	1996	1 300.6	107.0	117.4	1 107.9	91.1	1 215.6
	1997	1 582.9	127.4	130.4	1 214.0	97.7	1 242.5
	1998	1 864.8	145.9	146.9	1 269.7	99.3	1 278.1
	1999	2 063.6	150.1	157.9	1 306.6	95.0	1 375.0
	2000	2 262.6	138.8	160.3	1 411.1	86.6	1 630.3
	2001	2 827.7	129.4	181.1	1 561.1	71.4	2 185.0
	2002	3 289.4	131.6	196.2	1 676.9	67.1	2 498.9
	2003	3 966.6	158.0	209.9	1 889.9	75.3	2 509.9
Namibia	1970	6.0	21.6	68.1	8.8	31.7	27.7
	1975	11.5	40.2	75.5	15.2	53.3	28.6
	1980	26.0	86.4	82.7	31.4	104.4	30.1
	1985	45.2	52.4	80.4	56.2	65.2	86.1
	1990	100.0	100.0	100.0	100.0	100.0	100.0
	1991	113.3	106.1	108.2	104.7	98.1	106.7
	1992	133.0	120.6	115.9	114.7	104.1	110.2
	1993	153.7	121.7	113.9	134.9	106.8	126.3
	1994	190.8	139.0	122.3	156.0	113.7	137.2
	1995	209.9	149.7	127.3	164.9	117.6	140.2
	1996	248.0	149.2	131.4	188.7	113.6	166.2
	1997	276.7	155.4	137.3	201.6	113.2	178.1
	1998	310.4	145.3	141.9	218.7	102.4	213.7
	1999	341.6	144.7	148.0	230.8	97.8	236.1
	2000	396.3	147.8	153.7	257.8	96.1	268.2
	2001	449.8	135.2	154.7	290.8	87.4	332.7
	2002	501.6	123.1	159.3	314.8	77.3	407.4
	2003	572.9	196.0	166.5	344.1	117.7	292.4
Niger	1970	16.3	15.9	63.0	25.8	25.3	102.0
	1975	26.4	33.6	64.2	41.2	52.3	78.7
	1980	78.6	101.3	98.9	79.5	102.4	77.6
	1985	94.8	57.5	86.9	109.2	66.2	165.0
	1990	100.0	100.0	100.0	100.0	100.0	100.0
	1991	98.6	95.2	101.4	97.2	93.8	103.6
	1992	96.6	99.3	102.2	94.5	97.3	97.2
	1993	94.9	91.2	103.2	91.9	88.4	104.0
	1994	115.4	56.6	105.8	109.0	53.5	203.9
	1995	122.3	66.7	107.9	113.4	61.9	183.3
	1996	151.4	80.6	112.1	135.1	71.9	187.9
	1997	158.7	74.0	114.8	138.3	64.5	214.4

Table 7. Implicit Price Deflators of Gross Domestic Product in US Dollars and in National Currency

(Index numbers 1990 = 100)

Region, country or area and currency unit	Year	GDP in Current Prices: National Currency (1)	GDP in Current Prices: US Dollars (2)	GDP at Constant Prices (3)	GDP Implicit Price Deflators: National Currency (4)	GDP Implicit Price Deflators: US Dollars (5)	Exchange Rates (6)
	1998	179.5	82.9	126.1	142.4	65.7	216.7
	1999	182.1	80.5	124.1	146.8	64.9	226.1
	2000	187.7	71.8	123.7	151.7	58.0	261.5
	2001	205.1	76.2	131.1	156.5	58.1	269.2
	2002	217.5	85.0	135.0	161.1	62.9	256.0
	2003	232.0	108.7	140.4	165.2	77.4	213.5
Nigeria	1970	2.8	31.9	51.5	5.5	61.9	8.9
	1975	8.7	113.9	70.4	12.4	161.8	7.7
	1980	19.3	284.0	80.0	24.2	355.1	6.8
	1985	27.8	249.7	77.1	36.0	324.0	11.1
	1990	100.0	100.0	100.0	100.0	100.0	100.0
	1991	124.3	100.8	104.8	118.7	96.3	123.3
	1992	210.9	98.0	107.8	195.7	90.9	215.2
	1993	269.1	98.0	110.6	243.4	88.7	274.5
	1994	350.8	128.2	111.7	314.1	114.8	273.6
	1995	758.8	278.6	114.6	662.1	243.1	272.4
	1996	1 083.5	211.2	119.1	909.9	177.3	513.1
	1997	1 127.9	217.9	122.9	917.8	177.3	517.6
	1998	1 088.5	222.9	125.7	865.8	177.3	488.3
	1999	1 273.8	110.9	129.2	985.7	85.8	1 148.7
	2000	1 648.4	130.3	136.8	1 205.2	95.3	1 265.2
	2001	1 824.3	131.8	140.6	1 297.7	93.8	1 383.8
	2002	2 030.6	135.4	141.3	1 436.8	95.8	1 500.0
	2003	2 400.7	149.3	148.7	1 614.9	100.5	1 607.6
Reunion	1970	7.1	7.0	37.6	18.9	18.5	102.0
	1975	16.0	20.3	48.1	33.3	42.3	78.7
	1980	29.8	38.4	66.5	44.8	57.7	77.6
	1985	60.1	36.4	81.6	73.6	44.6	165.0
	1990	100.0	100.0	100.0	100.0	100.0	100.0
	1991	110.4	106.6	101.6	108.7	105.0	103.6
	1992	119.1	122.5	105.1	113.3	116.6	97.2
	1993	118.8	114.2	109.6	108.4	104.2	104.0
	1994	124.3	121.9	112.1	110.9	108.8	102.0
	1995	130.5	142.4	115.1	113.4	123.7	91.7
	1996	136.4	145.2	118.4	115.2	122.6	93.9
	1997	142.5	133.0	122.1	116.8	108.9	107.2
	1998	149.1	137.6	125.8	118.6	109.4	108.3
	1999	155.9	137.9	129.5	120.3	106.4	113.1
	2000	163.5	125.0	133.4	122.5	93.7	130.8
	2001	174.2	129.4	136.6	127.5	94.7	134.6
	2002	198.6	155.2	140.0	141.8	110.8	128.0
	2003	226.4	212.1	143.5	157.7	147.8	106.7
Rwanda	1970	11.2	9.2	47.0	23.8	19.6	121.1
	1975	27.4	24.3	49.0	55.9	49.7	112.4
	1980	56.0	49.8	79.4	70.5	62.7	112.4
	1985	90.0	73.4	90.3	99.7	81.3	122.6
	1990	100.0	100.0	100.0	100.0	100.0	100.0
	1991	111.3	73.5	96.3	115.5	76.3	151.5
	1992	125.8	77.9	102.8	122.5	75.8	161.4
	1993	131.2	75.1	93.9	139.8	80.0	174.7
	1994	78.8	29.6	48.1	164.0	61.6	266.4
	1995	158.2	49.8	64.2	246.6	77.7	317.4
	1996	200.4	54.0	73.7	271.9	73.2	371.5
	1997	264.9	72.6	84.3	314.3	86.1	365.1
	1998	295.0	78.0	92.0	320.5	84.8	378.1
	1999	297.8	72.8	98.0	303.9	74.3	409.0
	2000	320.5	67.3	104.1	307.7	64.6	476.3
	2001	344.4	64.2	111.1	310.0	57.8	536.1
	2002	368.7	63.9	121.5	303.6	52.6	576.7
	2003	391.5	60.1	125.3	312.4	48.0	650.9
Sao Tome and Principe	1970	7.4	37.1	64.3	11.6	57.7	20.1
	1975	10.7	59.9	78.4	13.6	76.4	17.8
	1980	19.7	81.4	116.4	17.0	69.9	24.3
	1985	28.1	90.3	106.3	26.5	85.0	31.1
	1990	100.0	100.0	100.0	100.0	100.0	100.0

Table 7. Implicit Price Deflators of Gross Domestic Product in US Dollars and in National Currency

(Index numbers 1990 = 100)

Region, country or area and currency unit	Year	GDP in Current Prices		GDP at Constant Prices	GDP Implicit Price Deflators		Exchange Rates
		National Currency (1)	US Dollars (2)	(3)	National Currency (4)	US Dollars (5)	(6)
	1991	139.2	98.8	101.2	137.5	97.7	140.8
	1992	176.5	78.7	101.9	173.2	77.3	224.2
	1993	248.1	82.7	103.0	240.8	80.3	299.9
	1994	439.9	86.1	105.3	417.8	81.7	511.1
	1995	783.2	79.0	107.4	729.2	73.6	991.0
	1996	1 198.8	78.0	109.0	1 099.7	71.5	1 537.1
	1997	2 424.3	76.3	110.1	2 201.9	69.3	3 176.2
	1998	3 406.1	70.9	112.9	3 018.2	62.8	4 802.3
	1999	4 049.9	81.5	115.7	3 501.1	70.5	4 966.8
	2000	4 478.8	80.5	119.1	3 759.2	67.5	5 566.3
	2001	5 115.2	82.9	122.7	4 168.2	67.6	6 169.0
	2002	5 951.6	93.9	126.4	4 708.5	74.3	6 340.8
	2003	6 624.1	101.6	132.7	4 991.0	76.5	6 521.7
Senegal	1970	15.6	15.3	27.3	57.1	56.0	102.0
	1975	26.4	33.5	30.7	86.0	109.2	78.7
	1980	40.7	52.4	73.7	55.3	71.2	77.6
	1985	74.7	45.2	85.5	87.4	52.9	165.0
	1990	100.0	100.0	100.0	100.0	100.0	100.0
	1991	100.0	96.5	99.6	100.4	96.9	103.6
	1992	102.8	105.8	101.8	101.0	103.9	97.2
	1993	99.1	95.3	99.5	99.6	95.7	104.0
	1994	130.3	63.9	102.4	127.3	62.4	203.9
	1995	144.0	78.5	107.2	134.3	73.2	183.3
	1996	153.4	81.6	112.8	135.9	72.4	187.9
	1997	164.6	76.8	119.0	138.4	64.5	214.4
	1998	177.0	81.7	125.8	140.7	64.9	216.7
	1999	188.5	83.4	132.1	142.8	63.1	226.1
	2000	200.7	76.8	139.4	144.0	55.1	261.5
	2001	217.8	80.9	147.2	148.0	55.0	269.2
	2002	226.3	88.4	150.7	150.2	58.7	256.0
	2003	242.6	113.6	160.2	151.4	70.9	213.5
Seychelles	1970	5.6	5.4	40.3	13.8	13.3	104.1
	1975	14.8	13.1	48.9	30.3	26.9	112.9
	1980	47.9	40.0	70.4	68.0	56.8	119.8
	1985	61.3	45.8	75.8	80.8	60.4	133.7
	1990	100.0	100.0	100.0	100.0	100.0	100.0
	1991	100.7	101.6	102.7	98.0	98.9	99.1
	1992	112.9	117.7	110.2	102.5	106.8	96.0
	1993	123.6	127.3	117.0	105.7	108.8	97.1
	1994	124.1	131.0	116.0	106.9	112.9	94.7
	1995	123.0	137.9	115.3	106.7	119.6	89.2
	1996	127.1	136.5	117.5	108.2	116.2	93.1
	1997	143.8	152.7	135.2	106.4	113.0	94.2
	1998	162.7	165.1	150.4	108.2	109.8	98.6
	1999	169.3	169.1	153.3	110.5	110.3	100.1
	2000	174.1	162.6	153.1	113.7	106.2	107.1
	2001	173.8	158.4	150.2	115.7	105.4	109.8
	2002	194.7	189.6	150.6	129.3	125.9	102.7
	2003	196.0	193.7	155.1	126.4	124.9	101.2
Sierra Leone	1970	0.4	65.4	72.0	0.5	90.7	0.6
	1975	0.6	99.9	81.2	0.7	122.9	0.6
	1980	1.2	173.5	88.7	1.4	195.5	0.7
	1985	5.0	148.0	102.8	4.8	143.9	3.4
	1990	100.0	100.0	100.0	100.0	100.0	100.0
	1991	239.6	122.9	97.2	246.6	126.5	195.0
	1992	353.3	107.1	83.9	420.9	127.6	329.8
	1993	453.9	121.1	78.8	576.2	153.8	374.7
	1994	556.5	143.7	78.9	705.5	182.1	387.4
	1995	684.1	137.2	77.6	881.7	176.8	498.7
	1996	902.0	148.4	82.3	1 095.8	180.2	608.0
	1997	868.1	133.9	67.8	1 279.8	197.5	648.1
	1998	1 093.6	105.9	67.3	1 626.0	157.5	1 032.5
	1999	1 258.2	105.6	61.8	2 036.0	170.9	1 191.3
	2000	1 384.0	100.2	64.2	2 157.3	156.2	1 381.4

Table 7. Implicit Price Deflators of Gross Domestic Product in US Dollars and in National Currency

(Index numbers 1990 = 100)

Region, country or area and currency unit	Year	GDP in Current Prices: National Currency (1)	GDP in Current Prices: US Dollars (2)	GDP at Constant Prices (3)	GDP Implicit Price Deflators: National Currency (4)	GDP Implicit Price Deflators: US Dollars (5)	Exchange Rates (6)
	2001	2 006.0	153.0	67.6	2 966.8	226.2	1 311.5
	2002	2 151.9	155.3	71.9	2 993.9	216.0	1 386.0
	2003	2 390.8	154.2	76.5	3 123.3	201.5	1 550.4
Somalia	1970	0.1	34.3	66.3	0.2	51.7	0.4
	1975	0.3	76.2	79.0	0.3	96.4	0.4
	1980	1.0	277.1	90.2	1.1	307.2	0.4
	1985	5.0	222.4	98.5	5.1	225.7	2.3
	1990	100.0	100.0	100.0	100.0	100.0	100.0
	1991	134.2	61.8	99.0	135.5	62.4	217.2
	1992	147.6	58.7	87.1	169.4	67.3	251.5
	1993	228.3	100.2	87.1	262.0	115.1	227.7
	1994	281.0	113.3	68.8	408.3	164.6	248.0
	1995	369.5	112.9	68.8	536.9	164.0	327.3
	1996	498.8	126.8	71.5	697.6	177.3	393.5
	1997	648.5	149.1	69.6	932.0	214.3	435.0
	1998	810.6	193.7	71.3	1 136.7	271.7	418.4
	1999	1 013.2	202.9	72.8	1 391.6	278.6	499.5
	2000	1 129.6	206.4	75.0	1 506.2	275.3	547.2
	2001	1 259.4	131.8	77.2	1 630.4	170.6	955.4
	2002	1 404.1	122.6	79.9	1 756.2	153.4	1 144.8
	2003	1 565.4	154.6	82.7	1 891.8	186.9	1 012.3
South Africa	1970	4.5	16.3	61.8	7.3	26.4	27.6
	1975	9.6	33.6	73.9	13.0	45.5	28.6
	1980	22.1	73.5	86.1	25.7	85.4	30.1
	1985	44.4	51.6	92.1	48.3	56.0	86.1
	1990	100.0	100.0	100.0	100.0	100.0	100.0
	1991	114.5	107.3	99.0	115.7	108.4	106.7
	1992	128.4	116.5	96.9	132.6	120.3	110.2
	1993	147.0	116.4	98.1	149.9	118.7	126.3
	1994	166.4	121.2	101.2	164.3	119.7	137.2
	1995	189.1	134.9	104.4	181.2	129.2	140.2
	1996	213.2	128.3	108.9	195.8	117.8	166.2
	1997	236.6	132.9	111.8	211.7	118.9	178.1
	1998	255.0	119.3	112.6	226.4	106.0	213.7
	1999	276.3	117.0	114.9	240.5	101.8	236.1
	2000	306.6	114.3	118.9	257.8	96.1	268.2
	2001	339.3	102.0	122.1	277.9	83.5	332.7
	2002	386.8	94.9	126.5	305.8	75.1	407.4
	2003	417.3	142.7	128.8	324.0	110.8	292.4
Sudan	1970	0.4	5.7	52.6	0.8	10.9	7.7
	1975	1.1	14.3	61.5	1.8	23.3	7.7
	1980	3.0	26.7	74.9	4.0	35.7	11.1
	1985	11.2	22.0	81.1	13.9	27.1	51.2
	1990	100.0	100.0	100.0	100.0	100.0	100.0
	1991	204.6	132.4	106.0	192.9	124.8	154.6
	1992	454.2	21.0	110.7	410.2	18.9	2 165.1
	1993	934.6	26.4	113.8	821.3	23.2	3 540.3
	1994	2 445.4	38.0	119.9	2 039.4	31.7	6 435.8
	1995	5 352.7	41.5	126.3	4 239.2	32.8	12 908.3
	1996	6 824.1	24.6	130.0	5 248.6	18.9	27 795.4
	1997	10 522.3	30.0	137.9	7 627.8	21.8	35 016.5
	1998	13 155.9	29.5	146.2	8 997.0	20.2	44 622.6
	1999	16 176.4	28.8	155.0	10 436.5	18.6	56 122.3
	2000	19 615.1	34.3	167.9	11 685.2	20.5	57 138.3
	2001	22 330.7	38.8	178.6	12 502.8	21.7	57 489.4
	2002	23 509.4	40.2	188.4	12 476.5	21.3	58 512.4
	2003	26 614.1	45.9	199.4	13 349.9	23.0	57 996.3
Swaziland	1970	3.5	12.5	21.0	16.5	59.6	27.6
	1975	9.6	33.6	37.1	25.9	90.6	28.6
	1980	20.4	67.8	49.2	41.5	137.8	30.1
	1985	36.1	42.0	61.5	58.7	68.4	85.9
	1990	100.0	100.0	100.0	100.0	100.0	100.0
	1991	108.0	101.2	102.6	105.2	98.6	106.7
	1992	124.2	112.7	104.1	119.3	108.3	110.2
	1993	149.0	118.0	107.8	138.2	109.4	126.3

Table 7. Implicit Price Deflators of Gross Domestic Product in US Dollars and in National Currency

(Index numbers 1990 = 100)

Region, country or area and currency unit	Year	GDP in Current Prices: National Currency (1)	GDP in Current Prices: US Dollars (2)	GDP at Constant Prices (3)	GDP Implicit Price Deflators: National Currency (4)	GDP Implicit Price Deflators: US Dollars (5)	Exchange Rates (6)
	1994	180.5	131.6	111.4	162.1	118.1	137.2
	1995	219.6	156.7	115.6	190.0	135.5	140.2
	1996	252.4	151.9	120.2	210.0	126.4	166.2
	1997	293.5	164.8	124.8	235.2	132.1	178.1
	1998	330.6	154.7	128.8	256.8	120.2	213.7
	1999	373.2	158.0	133.3	280.0	118.6	236.1
	2000	427.8	159.5	136.1	314.4	117.2	268.2
	2001	486.9	146.3	138.4	351.7	105.7	332.7
	2002	545.3	133.9	143.4	380.2	93.3	407.4
	2003	598.0	204.5	146.6	408.0	139.5	292.4
Togo	1970	17.1	16.8	68.9	24.9	24.4	102.0
	1975	30.0	38.1	75.8	39.6	50.3	78.7
	1980	55.9	72.0	88.7	63.0	81.1	77.6
	1985	79.1	47.9	83.0	95.2	57.7	165.0
	1990	100.0	100.0	100.0	100.0	100.0	100.0
	1991	96.9	93.6	100.9	96.1	92.7	103.6
	1992	103.7	106.7	97.2	106.7	109.8	97.2
	1993	82.4	79.2	83.9	98.3	94.5	104.0
	1994	127.5	62.5	97.5	130.7	64.1	203.9
	1995	152.6	83.2	106.1	143.8	78.4	183.3
	1996	173.5	92.4	110.3	157.3	83.7	187.9
	1997	204.4	95.3	115.1	177.6	82.8	214.4
	1998	195.3	90.1	112.6	173.5	80.1	216.7
	1999	203.5	90.0	115.8	175.7	77.7	226.1
	2000	221.3	84.6	114.9	192.6	73.6	261.5
	2001	227.8	84.6	115.1	197.9	73.5	269.2
	2002	241.1	94.2	120.7	199.9	78.1	256.0
	2003	251.4	117.8	124.3	202.3	94.8	213.5
Tunisia	1970	7.0	11.7	34.7	20.1	33.6	59.8
	1975	16.1	35.2	51.8	31.1	67.9	45.8
	1980	32.7	71.0	70.4	46.5	100.9	46.1
	1985	64.9	68.3	86.4	75.1	79.0	95.0
	1990	100.0	100.0	100.0	100.0	100.0	100.0
	1991	111.2	105.6	103.9	107.0	101.7	105.3
	1992	126.7	125.8	112.0	113.1	112.4	100.7
	1993	135.6	118.6	114.5	118.4	103.6	114.3
	1994	146.2	127.0	118.1	123.8	107.5	115.2
	1995	157.7	146.4	120.9	130.4	121.1	107.7
	1996	176.3	159.1	129.5	136.1	122.8	110.8
	1997	193.2	153.5	136.6	141.5	112.4	125.9
	1998	208.6	160.9	143.1	145.8	112.4	129.6
	1999	228.1	168.9	151.8	150.3	111.3	135.1
	2000	246.4	157.9	158.9	155.1	99.4	156.1
	2001	265.6	162.2	166.6	159.4	97.3	163.8
	2002	276.3	170.7	169.4	163.1	100.7	161.9
	2003	300.0	204.5	179.2	167.4	114.1	146.7
Uganda	1970	-	51.7	70.3	-	73.5	-
	1975	-	118.4	71.1	-	166.6	-
	1980	0.1	683.1	68.2	0.2	1 001.6	-
	1985	1.7	109.9	75.7	2.3	145.2	1.6
	1990	100.0	100.0	100.0	100.0	100.0	100.0
	1991	138.7	81.1	105.5	131.5	76.8	171.2
	1992	230.2	87.1	110.4	208.5	78.9	264.4
	1993	250.7	90.0	118.2	212.2	76.1	278.7
	1994	323.2	141.5	130.9	246.8	108.1	228.4
	1995	374.0	165.6	143.2	261.1	115.6	225.9
	1996	409.2	167.8	152.2	268.9	110.3	243.9
	1997	456.0	180.6	160.2	284.6	112.7	252.5
	1998	500.8	173.2	175.2	285.9	98.9	289.2
	1999	556.9	164.2	186.7	298.2	87.9	339.2
	2000	602.2	157.0	195.5	308.0	80.3	383.5
	2001	645.9	157.8	208.3	310.1	75.8	409.4
	2002	691.2	164.9	219.0	315.6	75.3	419.2
	2003	783.5	171.1	229.9	340.8	74.4	457.9

Table 7. Implicit Price Deflators of Gross Domestic Product in US Dollars and in National Currency

(Index numbers 1990 = 100)

Region, country or area and currency unit	Year	GDP in Current Prices: National Currency (1)	GDP in Current Prices: US Dollars (2)	GDP at Constant Prices (3)	GDP Implicit Price Deflators: National Currency (4)	GDP Implicit Price Deflators: US Dollars (5)	Exchange Rates (6)
United Republic Of Tanzania	1970	1.3	35.5	54.7	2.4	64.8	3.7
	1975	2.7	71.3	68.1	4.0	104.8	3.8
	1980	5.7	136.1	78.3	7.3	173.8	4.2
	1985	15.2	169.8	82.7	18.4	205.2	9.0
	1990	100.0	100.0	100.0	100.0	100.0	100.0
	1991	127.0	113.0	105.7	120.1	106.9	112.4
	1992	153.5	100.6	109.4	140.3	91.9	152.6
	1993	190.7	91.8	114.0	167.3	80.5	207.8
	1994	247.5	94.7	117.4	210.7	80.7	261.3
	1995	410.2	139.2	121.6	337.3	114.5	294.7
	1996	511.7	172.1	126.7	403.7	135.8	297.3
	1997	638.8	203.5	130.9	487.8	155.4	313.8
	1998	756.7	222.1	137.5	550.4	161.5	340.8
	1999	873.6	228.8	164.0	532.6	139.5	381.8
	2000	988.4	240.9	172.4	573.3	139.7	410.3
	2001	1 125.1	250.4	183.2	614.3	136.7	449.3
	2002	1 273.1	256.9	196.4	648.2	130.8	495.5
	2003	1 413.7	265.5	205.7	687.2	129.1	532.4
Zambia	1970	1.0	40.7	82.0	1.2	49.6	2.4
	1975	1.5	70.0	93.1	1.6	75.2	2.1
	1980	3.0	113.7	91.7	3.2	124.0	2.6
	1985	7.6	73.1	95.4	7.9	76.6	10.4
	1990	100.0	100.0	100.0	100.0	100.0	100.0
	1991	189.9	89.0	99.4	191.0	89.5	213.4
	1992	461.3	81.1	101.5	454.5	79.9	568.6
	1993	1 200.2	80.3	101.3	1 185.0	79.3	1 494.8
	1994	1 814.5	82.1	92.6	1 960.1	88.7	2 209.9
	1995	2 428.6	85.1	90.3	2 690.5	94.3	2 852.9
	1996	3 199.5	80.2	96.2	3 325.4	83.4	3 987.9
	1997	4 163.2	95.9	99.4	4 188.9	96.5	4 339.8
	1998	4 882.0	79.4	97.5	5 005.3	81.4	6 147.7
	1999	6 056.9	76.8	99.7	6 074.8	77.1	7 884.1
	2000	8 158.4	79.4	103.2	7 901.8	76.9	10 270.5
	2001	10 634.9	89.2	108.3	9 819.9	82.4	11 921.6
	2002	13 167.7	90.7	111.9	11 769.9	81.0	14 522.0
	2003	16 501.4	105.6	116.7	14 140.1	90.5	15 627.0
Zimbabwe	1970	5.0	17.2	49.5	10.1	34.8	29.1
	1975	9.3	40.0	62.2	14.9	64.3	23.3
	1980	16.0	61.1	65.0	24.6	94.0	26.2
	1985	42.3	64.3	80.0	52.9	80.4	65.8
	1990	100.0	100.0	100.0	100.0	100.0	100.0
	1991	137.8	93.3	105.5	130.6	88.4	147.7
	1992	160.0	76.9	98.1	163.1	78.4	208.0
	1993	197.6	74.7	100.2	197.3	74.6	264.4
	1994	261.3	78.6	106.0	246.5	74.1	332.5
	1995	287.3	81.3	106.2	270.7	76.6	353.4
	1996	398.0	97.6	117.2	339.7	83.3	408.0
	1997	479.1	97.0	120.3	398.3	80.6	494.0
	1998	667.0	69.1	123.8	538.9	55.8	965.8
	1999	978.9	62.7	122.9	796.6	51.0	1 562.2
	2000	1 488.8	82.2	116.9	1 273.6	70.3	1 811.7
	2001	2 319.7	103.3	107.1	2 166.9	96.5	2 245.4
	2002	2 126.4	94.7	93.4	2 277.8	101.5	2 244.8
	2003	7 967.8	28.0	81.0	9 833.4	34.6	28 446.2
NORTHERN AMERICA							
Bermuda	1970	13.0	13.0	67.1	19.3	19.3	100.0
	1975	24.0	24.0	78.3	30.7	30.7	100.0
	1980	46.0	46.0	95.2	48.3	48.3	100.0
	1985	71.8	71.8	95.6	75.1	75.1	100.0
	1990	100.0	100.0	100.0	100.0	100.0	100.0
	1991	104.3	104.3	101.6	102.7	102.7	100.0
	1992	105.2	105.2	97.4	108.0	108.0	100.0
	1993	114.0	114.0	102.0	111.8	111.8	100.0
	1994	117.1	117.1	102.5	114.2	114.2	100.0
	1995	127.4	127.4	109.7	116.1	116.1	100.0

Table 7. Implicit Price Deflators of Gross Domestic Product in US Dollars and in National Currency

(Index numbers 1990 = 100)

Region, country or area and currency unit	Year	GDP in Current Prices		GDP at Constant Prices	GDP Implicit Price Deflators		Exchange Rates
		National Currency (1)	US Dollars (2)	(3)	National Currency (4)	US Dollars (5)	(6)
	1996	134.2	134.2	112.9	118.9	118.9	100.0
	1997	144.7	144.7	116.6	124.0	124.0	100.0
	1998	152.9	152.9	120.6	126.7	126.7	100.0
	1999	163.8	163.8	124.9	131.2	131.2	100.0
	2000	170.1	170.1	127.4	133.6	133.6	100.0
	2001	180.2	180.2	126.8	142.2	142.2	100.0
	2002	186.2	186.2	128.0	145.4	145.4	100.0
	2003	212.4	212.4	129.3	164.3	164.3	100.0
Canada	1970	13.3	14.8	50.7	26.2	29.2	89.6
	1975	25.5	29.3	63.7	40.1	46.0	87.2
	1980	46.3	46.2	76.2	60.7	60.6	100.2
	1985	71.5	61.1	86.9	82.2	70.3	117.0
	1990	100.0	100.0	100.0	100.0	100.0	100.0
	1991	100.7	102.5	97.9	102.9	104.8	98.2
	1992	102.9	99.3	98.7	104.2	100.6	103.6
	1993	106.8	96.6	101.0	105.7	95.6	110.6
	1994	113.3	96.8	105.9	107.0	91.4	117.0
	1995	119.2	101.3	108.8	109.5	93.1	117.6
	1996	123.0	105.3	110.6	111.2	95.2	116.9
	1997	129.7	109.3	115.3	112.5	94.8	118.7
	1998	134.4	105.7	120.0	112.0	88.1	127.1
	1999	144.4	113.4	126.9	113.8	89.4	127.3
	2000	158.2	124.3	133.6	118.5	93.1	127.3
	2001	162.9	122.7	136.1	119.7	90.2	132.7
	2002	169.8	126.2	140.5	120.8	89.8	134.5
	2003	178.6	148.7	143.5	124.5	103.7	120.1
United States	1970	17.8	17.8	53.1	33.6	33.6	100.0
	1975	28.1	28.1	60.9	46.2	46.2	100.0
	1980	48.2	48.2	73.2	65.9	65.9	100.0
	1985	72.6	72.6	85.3	85.1	85.1	100.0
	1990	100.0	100.0	100.0	100.0	100.0	100.0
	1991	103.1	103.1	99.5	103.6	103.6	100.0
	1992	108.9	108.9	102.6	106.2	106.2	100.0
	1993	114.5	114.5	105.3	108.7	108.7	100.0
	1994	121.6	121.6	109.6	111.0	111.0	100.0
	1995	127.6	127.6	112.5	113.4	113.4	100.0
	1996	134.8	134.8	116.6	115.6	115.6	100.0
	1997	143.6	143.6	121.8	117.9	117.9	100.0
	1998	151.6	151.6	127.1	119.3	119.3	100.0
	1999	160.2	160.2	132.3	121.1	121.1	100.0
	2000	169.8	169.8	137.3	123.6	123.6	100.0
	2001	174.2	174.2	137.7	126.5	126.5	100.0
	2002	180.6	180.6	141.0	128.0	128.0	100.0
	2003	188.8	188.8	145.1	130.1	130.1	100.0
LATIN AMERICA AND THE CARIBBEAN							
Anguilla	1970	3.8	5.2	29.0	13.2	17.8	74.1
	1975	7.8	9.8	33.9	23.1	28.8	80.4
	1980	16.0	16.0	42.6	37.7	37.7	100.0
	1985	35.6	35.6	50.7	70.2	70.2	100.0
	1990	100.0	100.0	100.0	100.0	100.0	100.0
	1991	102.8	102.8	81.8	125.6	125.6	100.0
	1992	111.7	111.7	88.4	126.4	126.4	100.0
	1993	121.8	121.8	95.0	128.2	128.2	100.0
	1994	136.2	136.2	101.8	133.8	133.8	100.0
	1995	137.7	137.7	97.5	141.2	141.2	100.0
	1996	145.4	145.4	100.9	144.1	144.1	100.0
	1997	163.0	163.0	110.2	147.9	147.9	100.0
	1998	173.4	173.4	115.9	149.6	149.6	100.0
	1999	190.4	190.4	126.0	151.2	151.2	100.0
	2000	195.9	195.9	125.8	155.7	155.7	100.0
	2001	197.9	197.9	128.5	154.0	154.0	100.0
	2002	204.7	204.7	123.8	165.4	165.4	100.0
	2003	214.3	214.3	128.5	166.8	166.8	100.0

Table 7. Implicit Price Deflators of Gross Domestic Product in US Dollars and in National Currency

(Index numbers 1990 = 100)

Region, country or area and currency unit	Year	GDP in Current Prices: National Currency (1)	GDP in Current Prices: US Dollars (2)	GDP at Constant Prices (3)	GDP Implicit Price Deflators: National Currency (4)	GDP Implicit Price Deflators: US Dollars (5)	Exchange Rates (6)
Antigua and Barbuda	1970	10.8	14.6	47.4	22.8	30.8	74.1
	1975	16.8	21.0	46.3	36.3	45.2	80.4
	1980	33.0	33.0	55.4	59.5	59.5	100.0
	1985	60.0	60.0	72.2	83.1	83.1	100.0
	1990	100.0	100.0	100.0	100.0	100.0	100.0
	1991	107.9	107.9	102.7	105.0	105.0	100.0
	1992	112.0	112.0	103.6	108.1	108.1	100.0
	1993	120.6	120.6	108.9	110.8	110.8	100.0
	1994	132.1	132.1	115.6	114.3	114.3	100.0
	1995	130.4	130.4	126.1	103.5	103.5	100.0
	1996	142.8	142.8	116.5	122.5	122.5	100.0
	1997	153.5	153.5	123.0	124.8	124.8	100.0
	1998	163.8	163.8	129.1	126.9	126.9	100.0
	1999	172.1	172.1	135.4	127.0	127.0	100.0
	2000	177.8	177.8	136.5	130.2	130.2	100.0
	2001	183.0	183.0	139.6	131.1	131.1	100.0
	2002	189.1	189.1	143.7	131.6	131.6	100.0
	2003	197.5	197.5	147.3	134.1	134.1	100.0
Argentina	1970	-	22.0	86.9	-	25.3	-
	1975	-	37.1	100.0	-	37.1	-
	1980	-	146.3	111.8	-	130.9	-
	1985	-	62.4	101.2	-	61.6	-
	1990	100.0	100.0	100.0	100.0	100.0	100.0
	1991	262.5	134.2	110.5	237.5	121.5	195.6
	1992	328.8	161.8	121.9	269.8	132.8	203.2
	1993	343.1	167.5	129.5	265.0	129.3	204.9
	1994	373.5	182.3	137.1	272.5	133.0	204.9
	1995	374.4	182.6	133.2	281.2	137.1	205.0
	1996	394.9	192.6	140.5	281.0	137.1	205.0
	1997	424.9	207.3	151.9	279.7	136.4	205.0
	1998	433.7	211.6	157.8	274.9	134.1	205.0
	1999	411.4	200.7	152.4	269.9	131.7	205.0
	2000	412.4	201.2	151.2	272.7	133.0	205.0
	2001	389.9	190.2	144.6	269.7	131.6	205.0
	2002	453.5	72.2	128.8	352.1	56.0	628.2
	2003	545.9	91.8	140.0	389.8	65.5	594.9
Aruba	1970	35.4	35.4	16.0	221.8	221.8	100.0
	1975	45.9	45.9	24.7	186.1	186.1	100.0
	1980	59.5	59.5	38.1	156.2	156.2	100.0
	1985	77.1	77.1	58.8	131.1	131.1	100.0
	1990	100.0	100.0	100.0	100.0	100.0	100.0
	1991	105.3	105.3	104.0	101.3	101.3	100.0
	1992	110.9	110.9	108.2	102.6	102.6	100.0
	1993	116.9	116.9	112.5	103.9	103.9	100.0
	1994	123.1	123.1	119.2	103.2	103.2	100.0
	1995	122.2	122.2	132.6	92.1	92.1	100.0
	1996	127.7	127.7	134.3	95.1	95.1	100.0
	1997	141.8	141.8	144.8	97.9	97.9	100.0
	1998	154.1	154.1	154.4	99.8	99.8	100.0
	1999	159.6	159.6	156.1	102.2	102.2	100.0
	2000	171.9	171.9	162.0	106.1	106.1	100.0
	2001	174.8	174.8	160.8	108.7	108.7	100.0
	2002	175.9	175.9	156.7	112.3	112.3	100.0
	2003	185.1	185.1	159.0	116.4	116.4	100.0
Bahamas	1970	16.5	16.4	55.8	29.5	29.5	100.2
	1975	23.7	23.7	41.8	56.8	56.8	100.0
	1980	47.2	47.2	77.4	60.9	60.9	100.0
	1985	71.3	71.3	91.2	78.1	78.1	100.0
	1990	100.0	100.0	100.0	100.0	100.0	100.0
	1991	94.8	94.8	96.8	97.9	97.9	100.0
	1992	93.8	93.8	91.2	102.8	102.8	100.0
	1993	93.7	93.7	89.3	104.8	104.8	100.0
	1994	100.2	100.2	91.1	110.0	110.0	100.0
	1995	100.7	100.7	92.1	109.4	109.4	100.0
	1996	107.6	107.6	95.9	112.1	112.1	100.0

Table 7. Implicit Price Deflators of Gross Domestic Product in US Dollars and in National Currency

(Index numbers 1990 = 100)

Region, country or area and currency unit	Year	GDP in Current Prices: National Currency (1)	GDP in Current Prices: US Dollars (2)	GDP at Constant Prices (3)	GDP Implicit Price Deflators: National Currency (4)	GDP Implicit Price Deflators: US Dollars (5)	Exchange Rates (6)
	1997	113.3	113.3	99.1	114.3	114.3	100.0
	1998	120.4	120.4	102.1	118.0	118.0	100.0
	1999	131.5	131.5	108.1	121.6	121.6	100.0
	2000	141.4	141.4	113.4	124.7	124.7	100.0
	2001	141.3	141.3	111.1	127.2	127.2	100.0
	2002	145.4	145.4	111.9	130.0	130.0	100.0
	2003	149.0	149.0	112.9	131.9	131.9	100.0
Barbados	1970	10.8	10.8	67.4	16.0	16.0	100.0
	1975	23.6	23.4	71.3	33.1	32.8	100.9
	1980	50.3	50.3	89.0	56.5	56.5	100.0
	1985	70.1	70.1	85.1	82.3	82.3	100.0
	1990	100.0	100.0	100.0	100.0	100.0	100.0
	1991	98.7	98.7	97.1	101.6	101.6	100.0
	1992	92.3	92.3	92.3	100.1	100.1	100.0
	1993	96.2	96.2	93.2	103.2	103.2	100.0
	1994	101.3	101.3	96.9	104.6	104.6	100.0
	1995	108.8	108.8	98.3	110.7	110.7	100.0
	1996	116.1	116.1	100.1	116.0	116.0	100.0
	1997	128.3	128.3	106.5	120.4	120.4	100.0
	1998	138.0	138.0	110.9	124.4	124.4	100.0
	1999	144.3	144.3	113.8	126.9	126.9	100.0
	2000	150.7	150.7	116.4	129.4	129.4	100.0
	2001	148.0	148.0	114.0	129.9	129.9	100.0
	2002	149.7	149.7	111.7	134.0	134.0	100.0
	2003	155.1	155.1	113.4	136.7	136.7	100.0
Belize	1970	9.5	11.4	41.5	22.8	27.4	83.3
	1975	23.3	25.8	50.7	45.9	50.8	90.4
	1980	48.0	48.0	61.3	78.3	78.3	100.0
	1985	51.6	51.6	62.5	82.6	82.6	100.0
	1990	100.0	100.0	100.0	100.0	100.0	100.0
	1991	106.7	106.7	102.6	104.0	104.0	100.0
	1992	115.4	115.4	108.8	106.1	106.1	100.0
	1993	130.8	130.8	115.7	113.0	113.0	100.0
	1994	136.2	136.2	118.6	114.8	114.8	100.0
	1995	144.7	144.7	123.5	117.1	117.1	100.0
	1996	148.9	148.9	125.5	118.6	118.6	100.0
	1997	151.8	151.8	129.8	117.0	117.0	100.0
	1998	155.2	155.2	132.9	116.7	116.7	100.0
	1999	169.9	169.9	141.0	120.5	120.5	100.0
	2000	186.7	186.7	151.6	123.2	123.2	100.0
	2001	194.4	194.4	159.6	121.9	121.9	100.0
	2002	202.3	202.3	165.3	122.4	122.4	100.0
	2003	212.3	212.3	172.8	122.9	122.9	100.0
Bolivia	1970	-	20.8	67.2	-	30.9	-
	1975	-	49.3	89.0	-	55.4	-
	1980	-	103.1	98.5	-	104.7	-
	1985	18.6	133.8	89.4	20.8	149.7	13.9
	1990	100.0	100.0	100.0	100.0	100.0	100.0
	1991	123.9	109.8	105.3	117.7	104.3	112.9
	1992	142.5	115.9	107.0	133.2	108.4	122.9
	1993	158.4	117.8	111.6	142.0	105.6	134.4
	1994	179.0	122.9	116.8	153.2	105.2	145.6
	1995	208.7	138.0	122.2	170.8	112.9	151.3
	1996	243.1	152.0	127.6	190.5	119.1	159.9
	1997	269.7	162.8	133.9	201.4	121.6	165.6
	1998	303.2	174.6	140.6	215.6	124.1	173.7
	1999	311.8	170.2	141.2	220.8	120.5	183.2
	2000	336.0	172.4	144.4	232.6	119.3	194.9
	2001	343.3	164.8	146.6	234.1	112.4	208.2
	2002	362.2	160.3	150.7	240.4	106.4	226.0
	2003	383.8	159.0	155.0	247.5	102.5	241.4
Brazil	1970	-	15.3	38.1	-	40.2	-
	1975	-	46.7	62.1	-	75.2	-
	1980	-	56.1	85.8	-	65.4	-
	1985	-	45.3	90.5	-	50.1	-

Table 7. Implicit Price Deflators of Gross Domestic Product in US Dollars and in National Currency

(Index numbers 1990 = 100)

Region, country or area and currency unit	Year	GDP in Current Prices: National Currency (1)	GDP in Current Prices: US Dollars (2)	GDP at Constant Prices (3)	GDP Implicit Price Deflators: National Currency (4)	GDP Implicit Price Deflators: US Dollars (5)	Exchange Rates (6)
	1990	100.0	100.0	100.0	100.0	100.0	100.0
	1991	553.9	93.0	101.3	546.8	91.8	595.3
	1992	5 889.0	89.1	100.8	5 842.6	88.4	6 607.6
	1993	129 512.1	100.0	105.7	122 490.5	94.6	129 499.8
	1994	3 208 220.0	124.6	112.0	2 865 234.5	111.3	2 574 043.8
	1995	5 936 702.2	160.7	116.7	5 087 333.6	137.7	3 694 844.6
	1996	7 155 799.2	176.8	119.8	5 973 128.2	147.6	4 046 881.6
	1997	7 999 699.6	184.3	123.7	6 466 111.6	149.0	4 340 368.7
	1998	8 398 838.0	179.7	124.0	6 773 830.5	145.0	4 672 643.0
	1999	8 946 928.6	122.4	125.0	7 159 317.9	98.0	7 306 746.5
	2000	10 117 462.0	137.3	130.6	7 747 346.2	105.1	7 368 785.8
	2001	11 013 040.5	116.0	132.6	8 308 399.7	87.5	9 492 952.3
	2002	12 366 243.2	105.2	134.5	9 191 404.7	78.2	11 760 256.0
	2003	13 622 282.5	110.0	135.3	10 064 588.1	81.2	12 389 419.7
British Virgin Islands	1970	6.6	6.6	32.3	20.5	20.5	100.0
	1975	8.9	8.9	35.3	25.2	25.2	100.0
	1980	18.1	18.1	49.1	36.9	36.9	100.0
	1985	30.0	30.0	57.2	52.5	52.5	100.0
	1990	100.0	100.0	100.0	100.0	100.0	100.0
	1991	105.4	105.4	102.0	103.3	103.3	100.0
	1992	115.2	115.2	104.6	110.1	110.1	100.0
	1993	121.7	121.7	108.3	112.4	112.4	100.0
	1994	144.1	144.1	114.5	125.9	125.9	100.0
	1995	160.1	160.1	120.2	133.2	133.2	100.0
	1996	183.8	183.8	131.7	139.5	139.5	100.0
	1997	212.9	212.9	144.5	147.3	147.3	100.0
	1998	246.6	246.6	161.1	153.1	153.1	100.0
	1999	275.3	275.3	175.7	156.6	156.6	100.0
	2000	287.4	287.4	193.5	148.6	148.6	100.0
	2001	323.1	323.1	213.0	151.7	151.7	100.0
	2002	361.7	361.7	234.5	154.3	154.3	100.0
	2003	404.9	404.9	258.1	156.9	156.9	100.0
Cayman Islands	1970	2.6	2.7	16.2	16.3	16.4	99.3
	1975	7.7	7.7	24.8	31.1	31.1	100.0
	1980	18.6	18.6	39.7	46.9	46.9	100.0
	1985	44.7	44.7	60.3	74.2	74.2	100.0
	1990	100.0	100.0	100.0	100.0	100.0	100.0
	1991	104.4	104.4	101.3	103.0	103.0	100.0
	1992	116.6	116.6	100.7	115.8	115.8	100.0
	1993	126.3	126.3	101.6	124.3	124.3	100.0
	1994	137.1	137.1	102.1	134.3	134.3	100.0
	1995	144.0	144.0	101.6	141.6	141.6	100.0
	1996	151.9	151.9	101.8	149.2	149.2	100.0
	1997	165.6	165.6	102.3	161.9	161.9	100.0
	1998	174.7	174.7	103.9	168.1	168.1	100.0
	1999	180.8	180.8	105.4	171.5	171.5	100.0
	2000	191.6	191.6	106.7	179.7	179.7	100.0
	2001	203.1	203.1	107.9	188.2	188.2	100.0
	2002	215.3	215.3	109.2	197.2	197.2	100.0
	2003	228.1	228.1	110.5	206.6	206.6	100.0
Chile	1970	-	27.7	58.3	-	47.5	-
	1975	0.4	23.0	52.1	0.7	44.2	1.6
	1980	11.3	88.0	75.0	15.0	117.3	12.8
	1985	28.7	54.4	72.2	39.7	75.3	52.8
	1990	100.0	100.0	100.0	100.0	100.0	100.0
	1991	130.9	114.3	108.0	121.2	105.8	114.5
	1992	164.2	138.1	121.2	135.5	113.9	118.9
	1993	194.4	146.7	129.7	149.9	113.1	132.6
	1994	231.4	167.9	137.1	168.8	122.5	137.8
	1995	279.9	215.1	151.7	184.5	141.8	130.1
	1996	305.8	226.1	162.9	187.7	138.8	135.2
	1997	339.9	247.1	173.7	195.7	142.3	137.5
	1998	357.6	236.9	179.3	199.5	132.1	151.0
	1999	363.5	217.8	177.9	204.3	122.4	166.9
	2000	395.4	223.4	185.3	213.3	120.5	177.0

Table 7. Implicit Price Deflators of Gross Domestic Product in US Dollars and in National Currency

(Index numbers 1990 = 100)

Region, country or area and currency unit	Year	GDP in Current Prices		GDP at Constant Prices	GDP Implicit Price Deflators		Exchange Rates
		National Currency (1)	US Dollars (2)	(3)	National Currency (4)	US Dollars (5)	(6)
	2001	424.2	203.7	191.0	222.1	106.7	208.2
	2002	447.9	198.2	195.1	229.6	101.6	226.0
	2003	483.9	213.4	201.6	240.0	105.8	226.8
Colombia	1970	0.7	17.9	41.8	1.6	42.8	3.7
	1975	2.0	32.5	55.1	3.6	59.0	6.2
	1980	7.8	82.9	71.5	10.9	116.0	9.4
	1985	24.6	86.6	79.9	30.7	108.4	28.3
	1990	100.0	100.0	100.0	100.0	100.0	100.0
	1991	129.1	102.4	102.0	126.5	100.4	126.0
	1992	165.7	109.6	106.1	156.1	103.3	151.2
	1993	218.0	126.9	112.2	194.3	113.1	171.8
	1994	281.6	167.4	118.0	238.7	141.9	168.2
	1995	352.1	193.8	124.1	283.7	156.1	181.7
	1996	420.0	203.5	126.7	331.6	160.7	206.4
	1997	507.5	223.4	131.0	387.5	170.6	227.2
	1998	585.8	206.3	131.7	444.7	156.6	283.9
	1999	632.1	180.8	126.2	500.8	143.2	349.7
	2000	729.4	175.5	129.9	561.5	135.1	415.7
	2001	783.7	171.2	131.7	595.1	130.0	457.9
	2002	847.1	169.9	135.0	627.6	125.9	498.6
	2003	925.4	161.5	137.7	672.1	117.3	572.9
Costa Rica	1970	1.2	17.3	45.5	2.7	37.9	7.2
	1975	3.2	34.3	61.0	5.3	56.3	9.4
	1980	7.9	84.6	78.8	10.1	107.4	9.4
	1985	37.9	68.7	79.9	47.4	86.0	55.1
	1990	100.0	100.0	100.0	100.0	100.0	100.0
	1991	132.0	98.7	102.3	129.1	96.6	133.7
	1992	173.6	118.2	111.6	155.5	105.9	146.9
	1993	206.3	132.9	119.9	172.0	110.8	155.2
	1994	249.6	145.5	125.6	198.8	115.9	171.5
	1995	317.0	161.5	130.5	242.9	123.8	196.3
	1996	370.3	163.3	131.6	281.3	124.0	226.8
	1997	449.2	176.9	139.0	323.2	127.2	254.0
	1998	545.7	194.3	150.7	362.2	129.0	280.9
	1999	679.3	217.8	163.1	416.6	133.6	312.0
	2000	739.8	219.8	166.0	445.7	132.4	336.5
	2001	811.6	226.0	167.7	483.9	134.7	359.1
	2002	910.9	231.8	172.6	527.7	134.3	392.9
	2003	1 049.1	241.0	182.3	575.4	132.2	435.3
Cuba	1970	26.4	26.4	43.8	60.3	60.3	100.0
	1975	49.6	49.6	57.1	86.9	86.9	100.0
	1980	66.6	66.6	67.0	99.3	99.3	100.0
	1985	97.5	97.5	101.0	96.5	96.5	100.0
	1990	100.0	100.0	100.0	100.0	100.0	100.0
	1991	82.7	82.7	89.3	92.6	92.6	100.0
	1992	75.9	75.9	79.0	96.1	96.1	100.0
	1993	76.8	76.8	67.2	114.3	114.3	100.0
	1994	97.7	97.7	67.7	144.4	144.4	100.0
	1995	110.7	110.7	69.4	159.5	159.5	100.0
	1996	116.1	116.1	74.8	155.3	155.3	100.0
	1997	116.8	116.8	76.7	152.4	152.4	100.0
	1998	121.7	121.7	77.6	156.7	156.7	100.0
	1999	129.8	129.8	82.5	157.4	157.4	100.0
	2000	140.7	140.7	87.1	161.5	161.5	100.0
	2001	146.6	146.6	89.7	163.5	163.5	100.0
	2002	148.8	148.8	90.7	164.1	164.1	100.0
	2003	158.9	158.9	93.0	170.8	170.8	100.0
Dominica	1970	12.3	16.6	64.8	19.0	25.6	74.1
	1975	16.1	20.0	54.6	29.5	36.7	80.4
	1980	35.3	35.3	65.1	54.3	54.3	100.0
	1985	58.9	58.9	77.6	76.0	76.0	100.0
	1990	100.0	100.0	100.0	100.0	100.0	100.0
	1991	106.0	106.0	102.1	103.8	103.8	100.0
	1992	114.7	114.7	104.7	109.6	109.6	100.0
	1993	119.8	119.8	104.4	114.8	114.8	100.0

Table 7. Implicit Price Deflators of Gross Domestic Product in US Dollars and in National Currency

(Index numbers 1990 = 100)

Region, country or area and currency unit	Year	GDP in Current Prices: National Currency (1)	GDP in Current Prices: US Dollars (2)	GDP at Constant Prices (3)	GDP Implicit Price Deflators: National Currency (4)	GDP Implicit Price Deflators: US Dollars (5)	Exchange Rates (6)
	1994	128.8	128.8	105.9	121.7	121.7	100.0
	1995	131.0	131.0	108.0	121.4	121.4	100.0
	1996	141.3	141.3	111.8	126.4	126.4	100.0
	1997	146.5	146.5	114.6	127.9	127.9	100.0
	1998	155.1	155.1	118.2	131.3	131.3	100.0
	1999	160.1	160.1	119.1	134.4	134.4	100.0
	2000	162.1	162.1	120.7	134.3	134.3	100.0
	2001	157.9	157.9	115.6	136.6	136.6	100.0
	2002	151.7	151.7	111.1	136.5	136.5	100.0
	2003	154.1	154.1	110.0	140.1	140.1	100.0
Dominican Republic	1970	2.3	19.5	39.6	5.8	49.3	11.7
	1975	5.5	47.3	61.0	9.1	77.6	11.7
	1980	10.2	87.1	78./	13.0	110.7	11.7
	1985	21.5	59.0	86.6	24.9	68.1	36.5
	1990	100.0	100.0	100.0	100.0	100.0	100.0
	1991	154.3	103.6	100.8	153.1	102.8	148.9
	1992	183.5	122.4	111.0	165.2	110.3	149.8
	1993	206.3	138.7	117.3	175.9	118.3	148.7
	1994	229.9	148.9	121.9	188.6	122.2	154.4
	1995	269.1	168.7	127.5	211.1	132.4	159.5
	1996	299.1	185.1	138.0	216.7	134.1	161.6
	1997	351.1	209.8	149.3	235.2	140.6	167.3
	1998	395.4	220.8	160.4	246.6	137.7	179.1
	1999	455.3	242.1	173.4	262.5	139.6	188.1
	2000	528.5	274.5	186.9	282.8	146.9	192.5
	2001	598.4	301.0	194.3	307.9	154.9	198.8
	2002	656.7	300.9	202.7	324.0	148.4	218.3
	2003	833.4	230.4	201.8	413.0	114.2	361.6
Ecuador	1970	15.7	15.7	34.7	45.2	45.2	100.0
	1975	40.3	40.3	59.4	68.0	68.0	100.0
	1980	109.8	109.8	81.3	135.0	135.0	100.0
	1985	149.3	149.3	90.4	165.2	165.2	100.0
	1990	100.0	100.0	100.0	100.0	100.0	100.0
	1991	110.0	110.0	105.0	104.7	104.7	100.0
	1992	118.4	118.4	108.8	108.9	108.9	100.0
	1993	133.9	133.9	111.0	120.6	120.6	100.0
	1994	165.1	165.1	116.2	142.1	142.1	100.0
	1995	179.5	179.5	118.2	151.9	151.9	100.0
	1996	189.1	189.1	121.1	156.2	156.2	100.0
	1997	210.1	210.1	126.0	166.8	166.8	100.0
	1998	206.7	206.7	128.6	160.7	160.7	100.0
	1999	148.2	148.2	120.5	123.0	123.0	100.0
	2000	141.7	141.7	123.9	114.3	114.3	100.0
	2001	186.9	186.9	130.2	143.5	143.5	100.0
	2002	218.5	218.5	135.2	161.6	161.6	100.0
	2003	243.7	243.7	139.4	174.8	174.8	100.0
El Salvador	1970	7.0	19.3	72.8	9.7	26.5	36.5
	1975	12.3	33.6	95.1	12.9	35.4	36.5
	1980	24.4	66.9	100.1	24.4	66.9	36.5
	1985	39.3	107.6	91.1	43.1	118.1	36.5
	1990	100.0	100.0	100.0	100.0	100.0	100.0
	1991	116.7	99.7	103.6	112.7	96.3	117.1
	1992	136.6	111.9	111.4	122.6	100.4	122.1
	1993	165.4	130.2	119.6	138.3	108.9	127.1
	1994	193.9	152.1	126.8	152.9	119.9	127.5
	1995	227.8	178.2	134.9	168.8	132.1	127.8
	1996	247.4	193.5	137.2	180.2	141.0	127.8
	1997	267.0	208.8	143.1	186.6	146.0	127.9
	1998	288.0	225.3	148.4	194.0	151.8	127.8
	1999	298.9	233.8	153.6	194.7	152.3	127.8
	2000	315.0	246.4	156.9	200.8	157.1	127.8
	2001	331.0	259.1	159.5	207.5	162.4	127.8
	2002	342.5	268.1	162.9	210.3	164.6	127.8
	2003	359.6	281.5	166.1	216.5	169.5	127.8

Table 7. Implicit Price Deflators of Gross Domestic Product in US Dollars and in National Currency

(Index numbers 1990 = 100)

Region, country or area and currency unit	Year	GDP in Current Prices		GDP at Constant Prices	GDP Implicit Price Deflators		Exchange Rates
		National Currency (1)	US Dollars (2)	(3)	National Currency (4)	US Dollars (5)	(6)
French Guiana	1970	4.4	4.3	14.7	29.9	29.3	102.0
	1975	8.8	11.2	31.0	28.4	36.1	78.7
	1980	18.7	24.1	40.5	46.1	59.4	77.6
	1985	48.6	29.5	61.7	78.8	47.7	165.0
	1990	100.0	100.0	100.0	100.0	100.0	100.0
	1991	113.5	109.5	111.9	101.4	97.9	103.6
	1992	122.2	125.7	120.9	101.1	104.0	97.2
	1993	122.4	117.7	117.3	104.3	100.3	104.0
	1994	126.1	123.7	124.5	101.3	99.3	102.0
	1995	128.1	139.8	126.5	101.3	110.5	91.7
	1996	131.1	139.5	128.5	102.0	108.6	93.9
	1997	134.1	125.1	130.6	102.7	95.8	107.2
	1998	137.2	126.6	132.7	103.4	95.4	108.3
	1999	140.4	124.1	134.8	104.1	92.1	113.1
	2000	143.6	109.8	137.0	104.8	80.2	130.8
	2001	146.9	109.1	139.2	105.6	78.4	134.6
	2002	150.3	117.4	141.4	106.3	83.0	128.0
	2003	153.8	144.1	143.7	107.0	100.3	106.7
Grenada	1970	11.0	14.9	68.1	16.2	21.9	74.1
	1975	19.7	24.5	73.9	26.6	33.1	80.4
	1980	37.3	37.3	76.4	48.8	48.8	100.0
	1985	57.5	57.5	96.6	59.5	59.5	100.0
	1990	100.0	100.0	100.0	100.0	100.0	100.0
	1991	104.8	104.8	102.9	101.8	101.8	100.0
	1992	106.8	106.8	104.0	102.7	102.7	100.0
	1993	106.4	106.4	102.7	103.6	103.6	100.0
	1994	112.0	112.0	106.3	105.4	105.4	100.0
	1995	118.0	118.0	109.1	108.2	108.2	100.0
	1996	126.9	126.9	114.5	110.9	110.9	100.0
	1997	136.4	136.4	120.5	113.3	113.3	100.0
	1998	149.3	149.3	129.7	115.1	115.1	100.0
	1999	160.9	160.9	138.9	115.8	115.8	100.0
	2000	174.1	174.1	149.1	116.7	116.7	100.0
	2001	168.7	168.7	141.8	119.0	119.0	100.0
	2002	170.8	170.8	142.0	120.3	120.3	100.0
	2003	170.8	170.8	142.0	120.3	120.3	100.0
Guadeloupe	1970	8.7	8.6	48.3	18.1	17.8	102.0
	1975	18.6	23.6	61.7	30.1	38.3	78.7
	1980	38.6	49.7	76.2	50.6	65.2	77.6
	1985	64.5	39.1	77.5	83.2	50.4	165.0
	1990	100.0	100.0	100.0	100.0	100.0	100.0
	1991	108.0	104.2	82.1	131.5	126.9	103.6
	1992	118.2	121.6	88.1	134.1	138.0	97.2
	1993	128.9	124.0	94.5	136.4	131.1	104.0
	1994	144.1	141.4	101.5	141.9	139.2	102.0
	1995	145.8	159.0	97.1	150.1	163.7	91.7
	1996	154.0	163.9	101.3	152.0	161.8	93.9
	1997	171.0	159.5	110.7	154.5	144.2	107.2
	1998	182.3	168.2	115.2	158.2	146.0	108.3
	1999	188.2	166.4	116.0	162.2	143.5	113.1
	2000	201.2	153.9	121.3	165.8	126.8	130.8
	2001	215.1	159.8	126.9	169.5	125.9	134.6
	2002	230.0	179.7	132.8	173.2	135.3	128.0
	2003	244.0	228.6	137.7	177.2	166.0	106.7
Guatemala	1970	5.5	24.9	52.9	10.5	47.1	22.3
	1975	10.6	47.7	69.4	15.3	68.7	22.3
	1980	23.0	103.0	91.7	25.0	112.4	22.3
	1985	32.6	146.1	86.6	37.6	168.7	22.3
	1990	100.0	100.0	100.0	100.0	100.0	100.0
	1991	137.8	123.0	103.7	133.0	118.6	112.1
	1992	157.3	136.5	108.7	144.8	125.6	115.3
	1993	187.2	149.0	112.9	165.8	131.9	125.6
	1994	217.6	169.7	117.5	185.2	144.4	128.2
	1995	248.1	191.6	123.3	201.2	155.4	129.5
	1996	278.2	206.3	126.9	219.2	162.5	134.9
	1997	314.5	232.6	132.4	237.6	175.7	135.2

Table 7. Implicit Price Deflators of Gross Domestic Product in US Dollars and in National Currency

(Index numbers 1990 = 100)

Region, country or area and currency unit	Year	GDP in Current Prices: National Currency (1)	GDP in Current Prices: US Dollars (2)	GDP at Constant Prices (3)	GDP Implicit Price Deflators: National Currency (4)	GDP Implicit Price Deflators: US Dollars (5)	Exchange Rates (6)
	1998	354.2	248.5	138.7	255.3	179.1	142.6
	1999	386.4	234.7	144.1	268.2	162.9	164.6
	2000	427.6	247.1	149.3	286.5	165.6	173.1
	2001	470.8	268.8	152.7	308.3	176.0	175.2
	2002	519.8	298.1	156.2	332.8	190.9	174.4
	2003	560.9	316.8	159.5	351.7	198.7	177.0
Guyana	1970	3.4	67.6	111.5	3.1	60.6	5.1
	1975	7.6	127.3	135.0	5.6	94.3	6.0
	1980	9.6	149.3	132.0	7.3	113.0	6.5
	1985	12.5	116.6	110.1	11.4	105.9	10.8
	1990	100.0	100.0	100.0	100.0	100.0	100.0
	1991	248.7	87.9	106.0	234.6	83.0	282.8
	1992	298.3	94.4	114.3	261.1	82.6	316.2
	1993	377.4	117.7	123.7	305.2	95.2	320.6
	1994	481.4	137.6	134.1	359.1	102.6	349.8
	1995	563.5	156.9	140.9	400.0	111.4	359.2
	1996	632.2	178.1	150.8	419.3	118.1	355.1
	1997	681.0	189.1	160.2	425.1	118.0	360.2
	1998	689.4	181.1	157.5	437.9	115.0	380.7
	1999	789.4	175.3	163.5	482.9	107.3	450.2
	2000	830.0	179.9	161.3	514.6	111.5	461.5
	2001	851.6	179.7	164.4	518.0	109.3	473.8
	2002	906.6	188.0	166.2	545.5	113.1	482.3
	2003	957.3	195.2	165.9	577.1	117.7	490.4
Haiti	1970	12.7	12.7	63.1	20.1	20.1	100.0
	1975	26.1	26.1	76.1	34.3	34.3	100.0
	1980	52.9	52.9	100.4	52.7	52.7	100.0
	1985	76.9	76.9	95.7	80.3	80.3	100.0
	1990	100.0	100.0	100.0	100.0	100.0	100.0
	1991	108.6	90.0	100.3	108.3	89.7	120.7
	1992	114.9	58.6	87.0	132.0	67.4	196.0
	1993	152.2	59.4	84.9	179.2	69.9	256.4
	1994	236.7	78.7	77.9	303.9	101.0	300.8
	1995	269.9	89.3	81.3	331.7	109.8	302.2
	1996	327.1	104.2	83.5	391.5	124.7	314.0
	1997	394.7	118.5	84.7	466.0	139.9	333.1
	1998	451.9	134.8	87.3	517.6	154.4	335.3
	1999	508.3	150.0	89.3	569.3	168.1	338.8
	2000	569.4	134.5	90.1	632.3	149.3	423.4
	2001	621.4	127.2	89.0	698.3	142.9	488.6
	2002	671.2	114.7	88.2	761.2	130.1	585.0
	2003	810.2	95.6	88.2	918.7	108.4	847.3
Honduras	1970	11.0	22.7	46.5	23.7	48.7	48.6
	1975	17.9	36.9	55.7	32.2	66.2	48.6
	1980	40.9	84.2	78.7	52.0	106.9	48.6
	1985	58.1	119.4	85.7	67.7	139.3	48.6
	1990	100.0	100.0	100.0	100.0	100.0	100.0
	1991	130.1	100.6	103.3	126.0	97.5	129.3
	1992	150.0	112.2	109.1	137.5	102.8	133.7
	1993	181.0	115.0	115.9	156.2	99.3	157.4
	1994	230.2	112.6	114.3	201.3	98.5	204.5
	1995	299.2	129.9	119.0	251.4	109.1	230.3
	1996	381.0	133.8	123.3	309.1	108.6	284.7
	1997	489.1	154.7	129.4	377.9	119.5	316.2
	1998	561.8	172.6	133.2	421.9	129.6	325.5
	1999	614.9	177.9	130.7	470.6	136.2	345.7
	2000	698.1	193.5	137.2	509.0	141.0	360.9
	2001	773.6	205.6	140.8	549.6	146.0	376.3
	2002	842.3	210.8	144.3	583.6	146.0	399.6
	2003	940.6	223.0	147.2	638.9	151.5	421.8
Jamaica	1970	3.8	33.0	84.6	4.5	39.0	11.6
	1975	8.5	67.4	92.3	9.2	73.0	12.7
	1980	15.7	63.2	78.4	20.0	80.5	24.8
	1985	36.8	47.5	78.8	46.7	60.3	77.4
	1990	100.0	100.0	100.0	100.0	100.0	100.0

Table 7. Implicit Price Deflators of Gross Domestic Product in US Dollars and in National Currency

(Index numbers 1990 = 100)

Region, country or area and currency unit	Year	GDP in Current Prices: National Currency (1)	GDP in Current Prices: US Dollars (2)	GDP at Constant Prices (3)	GDP Implicit Price Deflators: National Currency (4)	GDP Implicit Price Deflators: US Dollars (5)	Exchange Rates (6)
	1991	148.4	88.0	100.9	147.1	87.2	168.7
	1992	276.8	86.6	111.3	248.7	77.8	319.6
	1993	385.7	111.1	113.5	339.9	97.9	347.3
	1994	516.2	112.1	114.5	450.8	97.9	460.5
	1995	651.9	133.3	115.7	563.6	115.2	489.2
	1996	773.7	149.7	114.5	676.0	130.8	516.7
	1997	841.0	170.6	112.5	747.6	151.7	492.8
	1998	891.2	175.2	112.1	794.9	156.2	508.8
	1999	958.5	176.4	111.6	858.8	158.0	543.5
	2000	1 072.9	180.5	112.4	954.9	160.6	594.4
	2001	1 166.9	182.3	114.3	1 021.0	159.5	640.3
	2002	1 278.1	189.6	115.6	1 106.0	164.1	673.9
	2003	1 397.6	173.9	118.1	1 183.5	147.2	803.7
Martinique	1970	8.3	8.1	41.5	20.0	19.6	102.0
	1975	17.4	22.1	52.5	33.1	42.0	78.7
	1980	31.6	40.7	61.9	51.0	65.7	77.6
	1985	64.6	39.2	77.1	83.8	50.8	165.0
	1990	100.0	100.0	100.0	100.0	100.0	100.0
	1991	107.6	103.8	96.0	112.0	108.1	103.6
	1992	114.4	117.6	97.6	117.2	120.5	97.2
	1993	118.8	114.3	99.2	119.8	115.2	104.0
	1994	122.8	120.4	100.8	121.8	119.5	102.0
	1995	125.0	136.4	102.5	122.0	133.1	91.7
	1996	128.8	137.1	104.1	123.6	131.6	93.9
	1997	132.2	123.4	105.8	124.9	116.6	107.2
	1998	141.0	130.1	110.2	127.9	118.1	108.3
	1999	145.5	128.7	110.9	131.2	116.0	113.1
	2000	151.6	115.9	113.3	133.8	102.3	130.8
	2001	157.9	117.3	115.7	136.5	101.4	134.6
	2002	164.4	128.5	118.1	139.2	108.7	128.0
	2003	171.3	160.5	120.7	142.0	133.0	106.7
Mexico	1970	0.1	15.1	44.1	0.2	34.2	0.4
	1975	0.2	37.3	60.6	0.3	61.6	0.4
	1980	0.6	79.0	83.6	0.8	94.5	0.8
	1985	6.8	74.9	92.0	7.4	81.4	9.1
	1990	100.0	100.0	100.0	100.0	100.0	100.0
	1991	128.5	119.7	104.2	123.3	114.8	107.3
	1992	152.3	138.4	108.0	141.0	128.1	110.0
	1993	170.0	153.5	110.1	154.4	139.4	110.8
	1994	192.2	160.2	115.0	167.2	139.3	120.0
	1995	248.6	108.9	107.9	230.5	101.0	228.2
	1996	341.8	126.5	113.4	301.3	111.5	270.2
	1997	429.6	152.6	121.1	354.7	126.0	281.5
	1998	520.6	160.3	127.2	409.2	126.0	324.8
	1999	621.7	182.9	131.8	471.6	138.7	339.9
	2000	743.2	221.1	140.5	529.1	157.4	336.2
	2001	788.8	237.5	140.2	562.5	169.4	332.2
	2002	832.5	242.5	141.5	588.3	171.4	343.3
	2003	898.1	234.1	143.3	626.6	163.3	383.6
Montserrat	1970	7.3	9.8	39.7	18.3	24.8	74.1
	1975	14.0	17.4	48.6	28.9	35.9	80.4
	1980	36.6	36.6	61.4	59.6	59.6	100.0
	1985	55.0	55.0	69.0	79.6	79.6	100.0
	1990	100.0	100.0	100.0	100.0	100.0	100.0
	1991	84.1	84.1	79.1	106.3	106.3	100.0
	1992	85.8	85.8	81.2	105.7	105.7	100.0
	1993	85.8	85.8	83.3	103.0	103.0	100.0
	1994	94.7	94.7	84.9	111.5	111.5	100.0
	1995	89.4	89.4	78.4	114.0	114.0	100.0
	1996	73.0	73.0	61.9	117.9	117.9	100.0
	1997	61.0	61.0	48.8	124.8	124.8	100.0
	1998	55.9	55.9	43.6	128.4	128.4	100.0
	1999	52.8	52.8	39.6	133.2	133.2	100.0
	2000	51.8	51.8	38.2	135.6	135.6	100.0

Table 7. Implicit Price Deflators of Gross Domestic Product in US Dollars and in National Currency

(Index numbers 1990 = 100)

Region, country or area and currency unit	Year	GDP in Current Prices		GDP at Constant Prices	GDP Implicit Price Deflators		Exchange Rates
		National Currency (1)	US Dollars (2)	(3)	National Currency (4)	US Dollars (5)	(6)
	2001	51.7	51.7	35.6	145.3	145.3	100.0
	2002	56.6	56.6	38.3	147.9	147.9	100.0
	2003	55.8	55.8	36.5	153.0	153.0	100.0
Netherlands Antilles	1970	15.9	15.1	71.5	22.2	21.1	105.4
	1975	25.3	25.2	76.7	33.0	32.8	100.6
	1980	47.9	47.6	99.2	48.3	48.0	100.6
	1985	60.4	60.1	94.2	64.2	63.8	100.6
	1990	100.0	100.0	100.0	100.0	100.0	100.0
	1991	104.9	104.9	101.8	103.0	103.0	100.0
	1992	109.9	109.9	105.1	104.6	104.6	100.0
	1993	117.1	117.1	109.9	106.6	106.6	100.0
	1994	125.9	125.9	115.9	108.6	108.6	100.0
	1995	129.8	129.8	116.3	111.7	111.7	100.0
	1996	135.9	135.9	117.7	115.5	115.5	100.0
	1997	138.8	138.8	117.1	118.5	118.5	100.0
	1998	136.3	136.3	118.0	115.6	115.6	100.0
	1999	133.2	133.2	117.2	113.6	113.6	100.0
	2000	137.0	137.0	114.8	119.3	119.3	100.0
	2001	140.3	140.3	115.5	121.5	121.5	100.0
	2002	141.3	141.3	115.7	122.1	122.1	100.0
	2003	144.8	144.8	116.3	124.5	124.5	100.0
Nicaragua	1970	-	23.8	109.7	-	21.7	-
	1975	-	48.8	143.8	-	33.9	-
	1980	-	67.1	114.6	-	58.5	-
	1985	-	134.1	118.3	-	113.3	-
	1990	100.0	100.0	100.0	100.0	100.0	100.0
	1991	2 379.7	78.5	99.8	2 384.2	78.7	3 030.6
	1992	2 954.2	83.3	100.2	2 948.5	83.1	3 548.1
	1993	3 542.5	88.8	99.8	3 549.5	89.0	3 988.3
	1994	3 945.6	82.7	103.1	3 825.7	80.2	4 770.6
	1995	4 738.5	88.5	109.2	4 338.1	81.0	5 354.4
	1996	5 523.4	92.3	116.2	4 754.8	79.4	5 985.9
	1997	6 303.9	94.0	120.8	5 219.6	77.9	6 704.5
	1998	7 455.1	99.3	125.3	5 952.1	79.3	7 509.0
	1999	8 715.8	104.0	134.1	6 501.1	77.6	8 380.0
	2000	9 888.6	109.9	139.7	7 080.3	78.7	9 001.0
	2001	10 580.3	111.5	143.8	7 357.5	77.5	9 488.9
	2002	11 250.4	111.2	145.3	7 744.7	76.6	10 112.9
	2003	12 212.0	113.9	148.5	8 221.0	76.7	10 718.4
Panama	1970	18.9	18.9	46.1	40.9	40.9	100.0
	1975	34.3	34.3	58.0	59.1	59.1	100.0
	1980	66.7	66.7	78.8	84.7	84.7	100.0
	1985	94.2	94.2	94.2	100.0	100.0	100.0
	1990	100.0	100.0	100.0	100.0	100.0	100.0
	1991	110.0	110.0	109.4	100.5	100.5	100.0
	1992	125.0	125.0	118.4	105.6	105.6	100.0
	1993	136.5	136.5	124.9	109.3	109.3	100.0
	1994	145.6	145.6	128.4	113.4	113.4	100.0
	1995	148.8	148.8	130.7	113.9	113.9	100.0
	1996	153.4	153.4	134.3	114.2	114.2	100.0
	1997	162.9	162.9	140.3	116.1	116.1	100.0
	1998	175.9	175.9	146.5	120.1	120.1	100.0
	1999	181.4	181.4	151.2	120.0	120.0	100.0
	2000	188.6	188.6	154.9	121.8	121.8	100.0
	2001	189.7	189.7	155.3	122.2	122.2	100.0
	2002	193.4	193.4	156.4	123.6	123.6	100.0
	2003	199.7	199.7	158.8	125.7	125.7	100.0
Paraguay	1970	1.2	11.3	31.8	3.6	35.5	10.2
	1975	2.9	28.7	44.9	6.5	63.9	10.2
	1980	8.7	84.5	73.8	11.7	114.4	10.2
	1985	21.5	86.3	82.6	26.1	104.5	24.9
	1990	100.0	100.0	100.0	100.0	100.0	100.0
	1991	127.9	118.7	102.5	124.8	115.8	107.8
	1992	149.4	122.4	104.3	143.2	117.4	122.0
	1993	185.2	130.6	108.6	170.5	120.2	141.8

Table 7. Implicit Price Deflators of Gross Domestic Product in US Dollars and in National Currency

(Index numbers 1990 = 100)

Region, country or area and currency unit	Year	GDP in Current Prices		GDP at Constant Prices	GDP Implicit Price Deflators		Exchange Rates
		National Currency (1)	US Dollars (2)	(3)	National Currency (4)	US Dollars (5)	(6)
	1994	231.1	149.2	112.0	206.3	133.2	154.9
	1995	273.4	171.3	117.2	233.2	146.1	159.6
	1996	305.9	182.9	118.7	257.6	154.0	167.2
	1997	323.3	182.6	121.8	265.4	149.9	177.1
	1998	362.0	163.3	121.3	298.4	134.6	221.7
	1999	372.9	147.0	121.9	305.9	120.6	253.6
	2000	415.8	146.7	121.5	342.3	120.7	283.5
	2001	434.3	130.1	124.8	348.1	104.3	333.9
	2002	493.9	106.3	121.9	405.2	87.2	464.8
	2003	584.1	111.8	122.6	476.4	91.2	522.4
Peru	1970	-	20.0	77.7	-	25.8	-
	1975	-	45.6	99.0	-	46.0	-
	1980	-	57.2	112.4	-	50.9	-
	1985	-	49.9	110.2	-	45.3	-
	1990	100.0	100.0	100.0	100.0	100.0	100.0
	1991	485.1	118.0	102.8	472.0	114.8	411.2
	1992	768.3	115.9	101.3	758.3	114.4	663.1
	1993	1 183.8	111.9	106.2	1 115.2	105.4	1 058.3
	1994	1 684.8	144.2	119.8	1 406.8	120.4	1 168.3
	1995	2 065.7	172.2	130.0	1 588.4	132.4	1 199.3
	1996	2 340.3	179.2	133.3	1 755.9	134.5	1 305.8
	1997	2 688.1	189.6	142.4	1 887.6	133.1	1 418.0
	1998	2 836.3	181.9	141.5	2 004.8	128.6	1 559.5
	1999	2 973.2	165.1	142.8	2 082.6	115.7	1 800.7
	2000	3 166.7	170.5	146.8	2 157.3	116.1	1 857.5
	2001	3 216.2	172.3	147.2	2 185.4	117.1	1 866.5
	2002	3 391.6	181.2	154.3	2 198.0	117.4	1 871.6
	2003	3 614.4	195.2	160.4	2 253.0	121.7	1 851.4
Puerto Rico	1970	17.5	17.5	48.2	36.3	36.3	100.0
	1975	27.8	27.8	56.3	49.3	49.3	100.0
	1980	49.4	49.4	69.6	71.0	71.0	100.0
	1985	68.0	68.0	80.3	84.7	84.7	100.0
	1990	100.0	100.0	100.0	100.0	100.0	100.0
	1991	107.3	107.3	104.6	102.6	102.6	100.0
	1992	114.4	114.4	109.4	104.5	104.5	100.0
	1993	122.9	122.9	114.0	107.8	107.8	100.0
	1994	132.1	132.1	119.2	110.8	110.8	100.0
	1995	140.4	140.4	121.9	115.2	115.2	100.0
	1996	149.2	149.2	127.9	116.7	116.7	100.0
	1997	167.5	167.5	135.0	124.1	124.1	100.0
	1998	179.1	179.1	142.2	125.9	125.9	100.0
	1999	189.1	189.1	145.7	129.8	129.8	100.0
	2000	210.3	210.3	153.8	136.7	136.7	100.0
	2001	215.8	215.8	153.5	140.6	140.6	100.0
	2002	232.3	232.3	159.2	145.9	145.9	100.0
	2003	250.0	250.0	165.1	151.4	151.4	100.0
Saint Kitts and Nevis	1970	7.9	10.6	41.4	19.0	25.7	74.1
	1975	17.2	21.5	48.4	35.6	44.3	80.4
	1980	30.1	30.1	57.2	52.6	52.6	100.0
	1985	49.0	49.0	72.7	67.4	67.4	100.0
	1990	100.0	100.0	100.0	100.0	100.0	100.0
	1991	103.4	103.4	102.3	101.1	101.1	100.0
	1992	114.2	114.2	105.4	108.3	108.3	100.0
	1993	124.6	124.6	112.3	111.0	111.0	100.0
	1994	139.3	139.3	118.2	117.9	117.9	100.0
	1995	144.9	144.9	122.4	118.3	118.3	100.0
	1996	154.4	154.4	130.5	118.3	118.3	100.0
	1997	172.7	172.7	139.2	124.0	124.0	100.0
	1998	180.4	180.4	140.9	128.0	128.0	100.0
	1999	191.4	191.4	145.8	131.2	131.2	100.0
	2000	206.7	206.7	150.8	137.0	137.0	100.0
	2001	216.2	216.2	154.1	140.3	140.3	100.0
	2002	224.0	224.0	156.9	142.8	142.8	100.0
	2003	234.1	234.1	158.8	147.5	147.5	100.0

Table 7. Implicit Price Deflators of Gross Domestic Product in US Dollars and in National Currency

(Index numbers 1990 = 100)

Region, country or area and currency unit	Year	GDP in Current Prices		GDP at Constant Prices	GDP Implicit Price Deflators		Exchange Rates
		National Currency (1)	US Dollars (2)	(3)	National Currency (4)	US Dollars (5)	(6)
Saint Lucia	1970	7.0	9.4	32.9	21.2	28.7	74.1
	1975	11.5	14.3	41.5	27.6	34.4	80.4
	1980	27.2	27.2	51.6	52.6	52.6	100.0
	1985	39.3	39.3	67.5	58.1	58.1	100.0
	1990	100.0	100.0	100.0	100.0	100.0	100.0
	1991	107.6	107.6	100.6	107.0	107.0	100.0
	1992	119.5	119.5	107.9	110.8	110.8	100.0
	1993	119.6	119.6	108.2	110.5	110.5	100.0
	1994	124.6	124.6	109.7	113.6	113.6	100.0
	1995	133.1	133.1	110.8	120.1	120.1	100.0
	1996	137.3	137.3	114.0	120.4	120.4	100.0
	1997	139.0	139.0	113.1	122.9	122.9	100.0
	1998	150.8	150.8	118.4	127.4	127.4	100.0
	1999	159.0	159.0	120.4	132.0	132.0	100.0
	2000	162.5	162.5	120.3	135.1	135.1	100.0
	2001	155.5	155.5	113.3	137.2	137.2	100.0
	2002	160.6	160.6	116.0	138.5	138.5	100.0
	2003	165.3	165.3	116.5	141.9	141.9	100.0
Saint Vincent and the Grenadines	1970	6.9	9.3	41.5	16.6	22.5	74.1
	1975	13.3	16.6	40.2	33.1	41.2	80.4
	1980	29.9	29.9	55.6	53.7	53.7	100.0
	1985	56.9	56.9	73.2	77.8	77.8	100.0
	1990	100.0	100.0	100.0	100.0	100.0	100.0
	1991	107.1	107.1	100.2	106.9	106.9	100.0
	1992	117.8	117.8	108.1	108.9	108.9	100.0
	1993	120.4	120.4	110.1	109.3	109.3	100.0
	1994	122.8	122.8	106.8	115.0	115.0	100.0
	1995	133.3	133.3	115.9	115.0	115.0	100.0
	1996	140.6	140.6	117.2	120.0	120.0	100.0
	1997	148.2	148.2	120.7	122.8	122.8	100.0
	1998	160.2	160.2	127.8	125.4	125.4	100.0
	1999	166.7	166.7	133.0	125.3	125.3	100.0
	2000	169.3	169.3	135.0	125.4	125.4	100.0
	2001	174.8	174.8	134.8	129.6	129.6	100.0
	2002	182.2	182.2	136.8	133.2	133.2	100.0
	2003	189.7	189.7	140.3	135.2	135.2	100.0
Suriname	1970	16.8	24.6	70.7	23.7	34.7	68.3
	1975	29.4	45.4	83.6	35.1	54.3	64.7
	1980	50.1	77.5	91.3	54.9	84.9	64.7
	1985	55.1	85.2	100.6	54.8	84.7	64.7
	1990	100.0	100.0	100.0	100.0	100.0	100.0
	1991	118.3	103.4	103.4	114.4	100.0	114.4
	1992	161.2	100.7	100.7	160.1	100.0	160.1
	1993	347.0	93.4	93.4	371.6	100.0	371.6
	1994	2 120.6	43.6	90.7	2 336.8	48.1	4 859.3
	1995	7 904.4	49.3	90.6	8 727.5	54.5	16 022.8
	1996	9 130.3	62.8	91.9	9 934.1	68.3	14 538.4
	1997	9 816.8	67.6	96.9	10 126.7	69.7	14 529.0
	1998	11 910.2	82.0	99.2	12 007.6	82.6	14 529.0
	1999	20 515.9	65.9	97.8	20 972.2	67.4	31 139.1
	2000	32 586.1	68.0	97.8	33 311.0	69.5	47 915.6
	2001	45 314.9	57.4	102.6	44 166.0	56.0	78 931.4
	2002	60 777.4	71.5	104.0	58 416.2	68.7	85 027.4
	2003	80 043.9	84.9	109.9	72 854.2	77.3	94 251.5
Trinidad and Tobago	1970	7.6	16.2	76.2	10.0	21.3	47.1
	1975	24.6	48.2	87.1	28.2	55.3	51.1
	1980	69.5	123.0	127.3	54.6	96.7	56.5
	1985	83.9	145.5	112.0	74.9	129.9	57.6
	1990	100.0	100.0	100.0	100.0	100.0	100.0
	1991	104.7	104.7	102.7	102.0	102.0	100.0
	1992	107.3	107.3	101.0	106.3	106.3	100.0
	1993	113.7	90.3	99.5	114.2	90.7	125.9
	1994	136.1	97.6	103.1	132.0	94.7	139.4
	1995	147.2	105.2	107.2	137.3	98.1	139.9
	1996	160.6	113.6	112.7	142.5	100.9	141.3
	1997	166.5	113.2	120.4	138.3	94.0	147.1

Table 7. Implicit Price Deflators of Gross Domestic Product in US Dollars and in National Currency

(Index numbers 1990 = 100)

Region, country or area and currency unit	Year	GDP in Current Prices: National Currency (1)	GDP in Current Prices: US Dollars (2)	GDP at Constant Prices (3)	GDP Implicit Price Deflators: National Currency (4)	GDP Implicit Price Deflators: US Dollars (5)	Exchange Rates (6)
	1998	176.7	119.3	129.7	136.3	92.0	148.2
	1999	199.1	134.4	143.5	138.8	93.7	148.2
	2000	239.0	161.3	159.6	149.7	101.0	148.2
	2001	263.2	179.5	163.8	160.7	109.6	146.7
	2002	270.2	183.8	168.2	160.6	109.3	147.0
	2003	289.6	195.5	174.6	165.9	112.0	148.1
Turks and Caicos Islands	1970	10.8	10.8	47.4	22.8	22.8	100.0
	1975	16.8	16.8	46.3	36.3	36.3	100.0
	1980	33.0	33.0	55.4	59.5	59.5	100.0
	1985	60.0	60.0	72.2	83.1	83.1	100.0
	1990	100.0	100.0	100.0	100.0	100.0	100.0
	1991	107.9	107.9	102.7	105.0	105.0	100.0
	1992	112.0	112.0	103.6	108.1	108.1	100.0
	1993	120.6	120.6	108.9	110.8	110.8	100.0
	1994	132.1	132.1	115.6	114.3	114.3	100.0
	1995	130.4	130.4	126.1	103.5	103.5	100.0
	1996	142.8	142.8	116.5	122.5	122.5	100.0
	1997	157.0	157.0	125.2	125.4	125.4	100.0
	1998	176.9	176.9	138.8	127.4	127.4	100.0
	1999	194.4	194.4	151.0	128.8	128.8	100.0
	2000	216.0	216.0	160.5	134.6	134.6	100.0
	2001	222.3	222.3	169.4	131.3	131.3	100.0
	2002	229.7	229.7	174.3	131.8	131.8	100.0
	2003	239.9	239.9	178.7	134.3	134.3	100.0
Uruguay	1970	-	27.5	70.9	-	38.7	-
	1975	0.1	41.4	76.6	0.1	54.0	0.2
	1980	0.9	115.2	95.5	0.9	120.7	0.8
	1985	4.9	56.6	83.3	5.9	67.9	8.6
	1990	100.0	100.0	100.0	100.0	100.0	100.0
	1991	207.2	120.1	103.2	200.8	116.4	172.5
	1992	398.1	153.9	112.6	353.7	136.7	258.6
	1993	604.3	179.3	115.5	523.2	155.2	337.0
	1994	900.9	208.9	123.9	726.9	168.5	431.3
	1995	1 252.3	230.7	122.1	1 025.4	188.9	542.9
	1996	1 671.6	245.2	128.9	1 296.6	190.2	681.7
	1997	2 094.5	259.4	135.3	1 548.3	191.8	807.4
	1998	2 394.4	267.4	141.0	1 698.7	189.7	895.4
	1999	2 423.8	250.0	137.5	1 762.2	181.7	969.6
	2000	2 483.9	240.1	135.6	1 832.3	177.1	1 034.6
	2001	2 526.7	221.9	131.0	1 928.5	169.3	1 138.9
	2002	2 667.3	146.7	116.4	2 292.3	126.1	1 817.6
	2003	3 224.1	133.7	119.7	2 694.2	111.7	2 412.1
Venezuela	1970	2.8	29.1	62.7	4.4	46.4	9.5
	1975	6.3	68.5	79.8	7.8	85.9	9.1
	1980	13.5	147.3	94.0	14.3	156.7	9.2
	1985	20.4	127.5	88.0	23.2	144.9	16.0
	1990	100.0	100.0	100.0	100.0	100.0	100.0
	1991	133.3	110.0	109.7	121.4	100.3	121.1
	1992	181.3	124.3	116.4	155.8	106.8	145.8
	1993	239.3	123.6	116.7	205.0	105.9	193.7
	1994	380.6	120.2	114.0	334.0	105.5	316.6
	1995	600.4	159.2	118.5	506.9	134.4	377.1
	1996	1 291.5	145.1	118.2	1 092.4	122.8	889.8
	1997	1 901.7	182.5	125.8	1 512.1	145.1	1 041.9
	1998	2 302.6	197.2	126.0	1 827.8	156.6	1 167.5
	1999	2 745.5	212.6	118.3	2 320.6	179.7	1 291.5
	2000	3 617.4	249.5	122.1	2 961.8	204.3	1 449.8
	2001	4 006.8	259.7	125.5	3 191.6	206.8	1 543.0
	2002	4 860.5	196.4	114.4	4 248.8	171.6	2 475.4
	2003	5 425.3	158.3	95.3	5 693.4	166.2	3 426.3
ASIA	...	...	...	...	...	...	...
Afghanistan	1970	11.2	25.8	78.0	14.4	33.1	43.4
	1975	19.6	45.1	116.3	16.8	38.8	43.4
	1980	27.0	63.5	117.3	23.0	54.2	42.5
	1985	34.1	69.8	131.0	26.0	53.3	48.8

Table 7. Implicit Price Deflators of Gross Domestic Product in US Dollars and in National Currency

(Index numbers 1990 = 100)

Region, country or area and currency unit	Year	GDP in Current Prices		GDP at Constant Prices	GDP Implicit Price Deflators		Exchange Rates
		National Currency (1)	US Dollars (2)	(3)	National Currency (4)	US Dollars (5)	(6)
	1990	100.0	100.0	100.0	100.0	100.0	100.0
	1991	142.9	98.8	99.4	143.8	99.4	144.6
	1992	197.8	88.7	86.9	227.5	102.0	223.1
	1993	236.3	76.5	77.5	304.8	98.7	308.8
	1994	275.1	67.1	75.2	365.8	89.3	409.8
	1995	514.0	64.0	71.7	717.1	89.3	803.4
	1996	1 533.5	68.2	76.4	2 007.9	89.3	2 249.4
	1997	2 233.0	77.2	86.5	2 581.6	89.3	2 892.1
	1998	2 350.0	81.3	91.0	2 581.6	89.3	2 892.1
	1999	2 059.6	71.2	79.8	2 581.6	89.3	2 892.1
	2000	1 159.8	40.1	44.9	2 581.6	89.3	2 892.1
	2001	1 119.3	38.7	44.9	2 491.3	86.1	2 892.1
	2002	1 730.6	59.8	57.8	2 995.2	103.6	2 892.1
	2003	2 134.4	73.8	66.4	3 212.4	111.1	2 892.1
Armenia	1990	100.0	100.0	100.0	100.0	100.0	100.0
	1991	158.8	60.5	88.3	180.0	68.5	262.8
	1992	621.7	2.1	51.4	1 210.1	4.2	29 009.0
	1993	8 479.7	3.1	46.9	18 098.3	6.6	273 423.4
	1994	371 898.0	4.3	49.4	753 083.2	8.7	8 668 193.2
	1995	1 038 282.9	8.5	52.8	1 966 948.0	16.1	12 189 439.4
	1996	1 314 530.8	10.6	55.9	2 352 307.0	18.9	12 433 678.7
	1997	1 599 076.7	10.8	57.7	2 769 515.3	18.8	14 740 143.7
	1998	1 899 373.4	12.5	62.0	3 064 657.4	20.2	15 162 612.6
	1999	1 963 108.7	12.2	64.0	3 067 634.5	19.1	16 067 922.9
	2000	2 050 374.4	12.7	67.8	3 025 618.0	18.7	16 201 977.0
	2001	2 337 727.2	14.0	74.2	3 148 734.6	18.9	16 669 016.8
	2002	2 697 779.5	15.7	83.8	3 219 615.2	18.7	17 217 817.8
	2003	3 185 672.0	18.3	95.4	3 337 910.9	19.2	17 380 268.9
Azerbaijan	1990	100.0	100.0	100.0	100.0	100.0	100.0
	1991	182.3	69.4	99.3	183.6	69.9	262.8
	1992	1 644.0	2.0	76.9	2 139.0	2.6	81 381.4
	1993	10 715.0	7.1	59.1	18 129.9	12.1	150 112.6
	1994	127 789.0	5.4	47.5	269 114.3	11.4	2 357 695.2
	1995	727 762.6	11.0	41.9	1 737 978.7	26.2	6 626 940.7
	1996	932 005.5	14.4	42.4	2 198 145.9	34.0	6 458 354.6
	1997	1 077 176.0	18.0	44.9	2 401 187.1	40.1	5 984 046.5
	1998	1 173 472.0	20.2	49.3	2 378 772.6	40.9	5 809 307.0
	1999	1 287 544.3	20.8	53.0	2 431 168.8	39.3	6 186 436.4
	2000	1 609 174.6	24.0	58.8	2 734 599.8	40.7	6 717 948.6
	2001	1 812 960.4	25.9	64.6	2 804 550.0	40.1	6 991 866.9
	2002	2 067 687.6	28.3	71.5	2 893 328.7	39.6	7 298 529.8
	2003	2 391 091.4	32.4	79.5	3 008 875.7	40.8	7 373 468.5
Bahrain	1970	7.4	5.8	33.1	22.3	17.6	126.6
	1975	25.4	24.1	61.9	41.0	39.0	105.2
	1980	76.9	76.7	100.7	76.4	76.2	100.3
	1985	91.2	91.2	83.0	109.8	109.8	100.0
	1990	100.0	100.0	100.0	100.0	100.0	100.0
	1991	105.9	105.9	104.6	101.3	101.3	100.0
	1992	110.7	110.7	112.7	98.2	98.2	100.0
	1993	121.1	121.1	127.2	95.2	95.2	100.0
	1994	129.7	129.7	126.9	102.2	102.2	100.0
	1995	136.3	136.3	131.9	103.3	103.3	100.0
	1996	142.1	142.1	137.3	103.5	103.5	100.0
	1997	147.9	147.9	141.6	104.5	104.5	100.0
	1998	144.0	144.0	148.3	97.1	97.1	100.0
	1999	154.2	154.2	154.7	99.7	99.7	100.0
	2000	185.7	185.7	162.9	114.0	114.0	100.0
	2001	184.7	184.7	170.5	108.3	108.3	100.0
	2002	196.1	196.1	179.2	109.4	109.4	100.0
	2003	211.6	211.6	186.7	113.4	113.4	100.0
Bangladesh	1970	6.8	32.5	63.2	10.8	51.3	21.1
	1975	13.2	38.0	57.1	23.1	66.6	34.8
	1980	27.7	62.0	68.6	40.4	90.4	44.7
	1985	55.9	69.0	82.5	67.7	83.6	81.0
	1990	100.0	100.0	100.0	100.0	100.0	100.0

Table 7. Implicit Price Deflators of Gross Domestic Product in US Dollars and in National Currency

(Index numbers 1990 = 100)

Region, country or area and currency unit	Year	GDP in Current Prices: National Currency (1)	GDP in Current Prices: US Dollars (2)	GDP at Constant Prices (3)	GDP Implicit Price Deflators: National Currency (4)	GDP Implicit Price Deflators: US Dollars (5)	Exchange Rates (6)
	1991	108.6	102.6	104.2	104.2	98.5	105.9
	1992	113.9	101.1	109.0	104.5	92.8	112.7
	1993	123.1	107.5	113.4	108.5	94.8	114.5
	1994	138.6	119.2	119.0	116.4	100.1	116.3
	1995	151.2	129.7	124.5	121.4	104.2	116.5
	1996	164.2	135.8	131.2	125.1	103.5	120.9
	1997	181.9	143.3	138.1	131.7	103.7	127.0
	1998	199.7	147.2	144.8	137.9	101.6	135.7
	1999	215.5	151.7	153.4	140.4	98.9	142.0
	2000	230.4	152.8	161.5	142.7	94.6	150.8
	2001	246.7	152.8	169.3	145.7	90.3	161.4
	2002	273.1	163.1	178.2	153.2	91.5	167.5
	2003	298.5	177.4	187.9	158.8	94.4	168.2
Bhutan	1970	6.9	16.2	23.9	29.0	67.7	42.8
	1975	17.5	36.5	30.7	56.8	118.7	47.8
	1980	22.0	48.9	49.2	44.7	99.4	44.9
	1985	48.0	67.9	68.3	70.3	99.5	70.7
	1990	100.0	100.0	100.0	100.0	100.0	100.0
	1991	110.4	85.0	103.5	106.7	82.1	129.9
	1992	127.5	86.1	108.2	117.9	79.6	148.1
	1993	144.3	82.9	114.7	125.8	72.2	174.2
	1994	172.3	96.2	122.1	141.2	78.8	179.2
	1995	202.0	109.0	131.1	154.0	83.1	185.2
	1996	237.0	117.1	138.0	171.7	84.8	202.4
	1997	287.3	138.5	148.4	193.6	93.3	207.4
	1998	327.9	139.1	157.9	207.6	88.1	235.7
	1999	383.8	156.0	169.6	226.3	92.0	246.0
	2000	435.4	169.6	179.3	242.9	94.6	256.7
	2001	488.0	181.0	192.0	254.2	94.3	269.6
	2002	557.5	200.8	204.9	272.1	98.0	277.7
	2003	639.9	240.5	218.2	293.3	110.2	266.1
Brunei Darussalam	1970	8.4	5.0	53.3	15.7	9.3	168.9
	1975	42.6	32.5	72.8	58.4	44.7	130.8
	1980	162.1	137.3	118.1	137.3	116.2	118.1
	1985	119.1	98.1	98.1	121.5	100.1	121.4
	1990	100.0	100.0	100.0	100.0	100.0	100.0
	1991	101.7	106.7	104.0	97.8	102.6	95.3
	1992	100.9	112.2	102.9	98.0	109.1	89.9
	1993	101.2	113.5	103.4	97.8	109.8	89.1
	1994	102.7	121.9	105.3	97.6	115.8	84.3
	1995	113.6	145.3	108.5	104.7	133.9	78.2
	1996	113.8	146.3	109.6	103.8	133.5	77.8
	1997	117.2	143.1	113.6	103.2	126.0	81.9
	1998	100.4	108.7	109.0	92.1	99.7	92.3
	1999	109.8	117.4	111.8	98.2	105.0	93.5
	2000	114.3	120.2	115.0	99.4	104.5	95.1
	2001	114.2	115.6	118.4	96.5	97.6	98.9
	2002	117.7	119.2	122.2	96.3	97.5	98.8
	2003	123.8	128.8	126.6	97.8	101.7	96.1
Cambodia	1970	1.5	154.7	219.0	0.7	70.7	1.0
	1975	1.2	127.6	149.1	0.8	85.6	1.0
	1980	1.2	121.3	104.4	1.1	116.2	1.0
	1985	2.3	140.1	91.2	2.6	153.6	1.7
	1990	100.0	100.0	100.0	100.0	100.0	100.0
	1991	223.2	132.8	107.6	207.4	123.4	168.1
	1992	419.0	138.4	115.1	363.8	120.2	302.8
	1993	904.4	140.7	119.9	754.5	117.4	642.8
	1994	941.3	154.7	129.1	729.3	119.9	608.5
	1995	1 120.8	191.3	136.7	819.9	139.9	585.9
	1996	1 227.9	195.7	143.0	858.7	136.9	627.3
	1997	1 351.2	191.8	149.1	906.0	128.6	704.3
	1998	1 570.3	175.4	152.3	1 030.8	115.1	895.2
	1999	1 739.4	191.1	162.8	1 068.4	117.4	910.3
	2000	1 787.0	194.6	175.3	1 019.6	111.0	918.2

Table 7. Implicit Price Deflators of Gross Domestic Product in US Dollars and in National Currency

(Index numbers 1990 = 100)

Region, country or area and currency unit	Year	GDP in Current Prices: National Currency (1)	GDP in Current Prices: US Dollars (2)	GDP at Constant Prices (3)	GDP Implicit Price Deflators: National Currency (4)	GDP Implicit Price Deflators: US Dollars (5)	Exchange Rates (6)
	2001	1 846.9	197.3	186.4	991.0	105.8	936.2
	2002	1 989.5	212.7	196.6	1 012.0	108.2	935.2
	2003	2 156.0	227.0	204.4	1 054.5	111.0	949.9
China	1970	12.3	23.9	25.1	49.1	95.3	51.5
	1975	16.4	42.1	32.3	50.7	130.4	38.9
	1980	24.7	78.7	42.0	58.7	187.4	31.3
	1985	47.7	77.6	70.0	68.1	110.8	61.4
	1990	100.0	100.0	100.0	100.0	100.0	100.0
	1991	116.2	104.4	110.6	105.1	94.4	111.3
	1992	145.4	126.1	126.3	115.1	99.8	115.3
	1993	189.1	156.9	143.4	131.8	109.4	120.5
	1994	255.2	141.6	161.8	157.7	87.5	180.2
	1995	319.2	182.8	178.9	178.5	102.2	174.6
	1996	370.6	213.2	196.0	189.1	108.8	173.8
	1997	406.5	234.5	213.3	190.5	109.9	173.3
	1998	427.7	247.1	230.0	186.0	107.4	173.1
	1999	448.0	258.8	246.2	182.0	105.1	173.1
	2000	488.2	282.1	265.7	183.7	106.1	173.1
	2001	523.7	302.6	285.7	183.3	105.9	173.1
	2002	572.0	330.6	308.5	185.4	107.1	173.0
	2003	637.0	368.1	336.6	189.2	109.4	173.1
Cyprus	1970	9.0	9.8	38.2	23.4	25.8	91.0
	1975	10.2	12.6	31.8	31.9	39.6	80.5
	1980	29.7	38.6	54.5	54.6	70.9	77.1
	1985	57.9	43.3	71.6	80.9	60.5	133.7
	1990	100.0	100.0	100.0	100.0	100.0	100.0
	1991	104.7	103.2	100.7	103.9	102.5	101.4
	1992	121.4	123.7	110.1	110.2	112.3	98.1
	1993	128.1	118.0	110.9	115.5	106.4	108.6
	1994	142.8	132.9	117.3	121.7	113.2	107.4
	1995	156.8	158.7	124.5	125.9	127.5	98.8
	1996	162.8	159.9	126.9	128.3	126.1	101.8
	1997	171.0	152.4	130.0	131.5	117.2	112.2
	1998	183.6	162.4	136.4	134.7	119.1	113.0
	1999	196.3	165.7	142.6	137.7	116.1	118.5
	2000	214.7	158.0	149.9	143.2	105.4	135.9
	2001	229.5	163.4	155.9	147.2	104.8	140.4
	2002	241.0	180.8	159.0	151.6	113.7	133.3
	2003	260.4	230.5	162.2	160.5	142.1	113.0
Democratic People's Rep. of Korea	1970	17.3	17.0	17.3	99.8	98.4	101.4
	1975	30.4	29.9	30.4	99.8	98.4	101.4
	1980	52.3	51.6	52.4	99.8	98.4	101.4
	1985	83.7	82.6	83.9	99.8	98.4	101.4
	1990	100.0	100.0	100.0	100.0	100.0	100.0
	1991	92.2	93.1	94.9	97.2	98.1	99.1
	1992	80.2	82.9	87.6	91.5	94.6	96.8
	1993	68.0	69.9	84.5	80.4	82.7	97.2
	1994	54.6	55.9	82.8	65.9	67.5	97.7
	1995	30.6	31.2	79.4	38.6	39.3	98.2
	1996	62.4	63.0	76.5	81.6	82.4	99.1
	1997	60.9	61.4	71.7	84.9	85.7	99.1
	1998	60.6	61.1	70.9	85.5	86.3	99.1
	1999	60.6	61.2	75.3	80.5	81.3	99.1
	2000	62.6	63.1	76.3	82.0	82.8	99.1
	2001	65.0	65.6	79.1	82.2	82.9	99.1
	2002	65.5	66.2	79.7	82.2	83.0	99.1
	2003	66.1	66.7	80.3	82.3	83.1	99.1
Georgia	1990	100.0	100.0	100.0	100.0	100.0	100.0
	1991	127.9	48.7	78.9	162.2	61.7	262.8
	1992	924.1	3.2	43.5	2 126.4	7.3	29 009.0
	1993	184 356.8	10.0	30.7	599 891.0	32.5	1 843 903.9
	1994	12 072 388.9	7.3	27.5	43 835 258.9	26.5	165 510 510.5
	1995	24 680 922.2	12.6	28.3	87 365 147.8	44.8	195 195 195.2
	1996	25 850 317.4	13.6	31.4	82 288 269.0	43.4	189 609 609.6
	1997	30 437 019.7	15.6	34.7	87 667 782.3	45.0	194 819 819.8

Table 7. Implicit Price Deflators of Gross Domestic Product in US Dollars and in National Currency

(Index numbers 1990 = 100)

Region, country or area and currency unit	Year	GDP in Current Prices		GDP at Constant Prices	GDP Implicit Price Deflators		Exchange Rates
		National Currency (1)	US Dollars (2)	(3)	National Currency (4)	US Dollars (5)	(6)
	1998	33 558 970.9	16.1	35.8	93 747 629.9	44.9	208 681 181.2
	1999	37 879 719.3	12.5	36.8	102 854 221.2	33.8	303 981 481.5
	2000	40 196 458.4	13.5	37.5	107 182 205.6	36.1	296 721 721.7
	2001	44 417 641.2	14.3	39.3	113 053 339.3	36.3	311 263 763.8
	2002	49 816 906.1	15.1	41.5	120 185 370.8	36.5	329 680 930.9
	2003	56 569 328.4	17.6	45.0	125 668 989.8	39.0	322 169 669.7
Hong Kong SAR of China	1970	4.0	5.1	22.6	17.5	22.5	77.8
	1975	8.5	13.3	30.8	27.5	43.3	63.4
	1980	24.3	38.1	53.3	45.7	71.5	63.9
	1985	46.6	46.6	69.8	66.8	66.8	100.0
	1990	100.0	100.0	100.0	100.0	100.0	100.0
	1991	114.8	115.0	105.1	109.2	109.5	99.8
	1992	133.8	134.6	111.6	119.8	120.6	99.4
	1993	154.3	155.4	118.7	130.0	130.9	99.3
	1994	174.1	175.5	125.2	139.0	140.1	99.2
	1995	185.3	186.6	130.1	142.5	143.4	99.3
	1996	204.7	206.2	135.7	150.9	152.0	99.3
	1997	227.3	228.7	142.6	159.4	160.4	99.4
	1998	216.4	217.6	135.5	159.7	160.6	99.4
	1999	210.7	211.6	140.1	150.3	151.0	99.6
	2000	217.8	217.8	154.4	141.1	141.1	100.0
	2001	214.7	214.5	155.1	138.4	138.3	100.1
	2002	213.0	212.7	158.6	134.3	134.1	100.1
	2003	209.9	210.0	161.0	130.3	130.4	100.0
India	1970	8.1	18.8	42.2	19.1	44.6	42.8
	1975	14.7	30.7	48.6	30.3	63.3	47.9
	1980	25.4	56.5	56.6	44.9	99.9	44.9
	1985	49.0	69.3	73.5	66.6	94.2	70.7
	1990	100.0	100.0	100.0	100.0	100.0	100.0
	1991	115.2	88.6	100.4	114.7	88.3	129.9
	1992	131.8	89.0	105.9	124.5	84.1	148.1
	1993	151.4	86.9	111.1	136.3	78.2	174.2
	1994	178.4	99.6	119.4	149.4	83.4	179.2
	1995	209.3	113.0	128.5	162.9	87.9	185.3
	1996	241.1	119.1	138.0	174.6	86.3	202.4
	1997	268.3	129.3	144.2	186.0	89.7	207.5
	1998	306.8	130.1	152.9	200.7	85.1	235.7
	1999	341.3	138.7	163.8	208.4	84.7	246.0
	2000	370.8	144.4	170.2	217.8	84.8	256.8
	2001	404.6	150.1	179.5	225.4	83.6	269.6
	2002	435.1	156.7	187.2	232.4	83.7	277.7
	2003	485.4	182.4	201.7	240.6	90.4	266.1
Indonesia	1970	1.5	7.8	25.2	6.1	30.9	19.7
	1975	6.0	26.6	37.2	16.1	71.6	22.5
	1980	21.6	63.3	54.4	39.6	116.4	34.0
	1985	46.0	76.3	71.6	64.3	106.7	60.3
	1990	100.0	100.0	100.0	100.0	100.0	100.0
	1991	118.5	112.0	108.9	108.8	102.8	105.8
	1992	133.9	121.6	116.8	114.7	104.1	110.2
	1993	156.4	138.1	125.3	124.8	110.2	113.3
	1994	181.3	154.6	134.7	134.6	114.8	117.3
	1995	215.5	176.6	145.8	147.9	121.2	122.0
	1996	252.6	198.7	157.2	160.7	126.4	127.1
	1997	297.7	188.5	164.6	180.9	114.6	157.9
	1998	453.3	83.4	143.0	317.0	58.3	543.4
	1999	521.5	122.4	144.1	361.9	84.9	426.3
	2000	599.9	131.3	151.2	396.8	86.8	457.0
	2001	687.4	123.4	156.4	439.5	78.9	556.8
	2002	763.5	151.1	162.1	471.0	93.2	505.3
	2003	844.1	181.4	168.7	500.3	107.5	465.4
Iran (Islamic Republic of)	1970	2.1	11.0	57.3	3.7	19.2	19.2
	1975	9.2	53.7	86.3	10.7	62.2	17.2
	1980	18.1	101.0	87.4	20.7	115.6	17.9
	1985	43.0	81.9	110.4	39.0	74.1	52.6
	1990	100.0	100.0	100.0	100.0	100.0	100.0

Table 7. Implicit Price Deflators of Gross Domestic Product in US Dollars and in National Currency

(Index numbers 1990 = 100)

Region, country or area and currency unit	Year	GDP in Current Prices: National Currency (1)	GDP in Current Prices: US Dollars (2)	GDP at Constant Prices (3)	GDP Implicit Price Deflators: National Currency (4)	GDP Implicit Price Deflators: US Dollars (5)	Exchange Rates (6)
	1991	136.7	105.3	111.5	122.7	94.5	129.8
	1992	181.4	109.1	117.8	153.9	92.6	166.2
	1993	270.9	120.0	115.4	234.8	104.0	225.8
	1994	371.8	120.0	117.4	316.8	102.2	309.9
	1995	530.5	121.2	120.8	439.2	100.3	437.8
	1996	702.9	126.3	128.2	548.3	98.5	556.6
	1997	832.6	118.1	133.2	624.9	88.6	705.1
	1998	939.7	115.5	137.6	683.1	84.0	813.3
	1999	1 275.1	120.5	143.3	890.0	84.1	1 058.3
	2000	1 655.9	113.9	147.3	1 124.3	77.3	1 453.8
	2001	1 902.7	121.7	152.0	1 251.9	80.1	1 563.4
	2002	2 653.4	151.4	164.2	1 616.4	92.3	1 752.1
	2003	3 295.5	158.5	175.2	1 881.5	90.5	2 078.6
Iraq	1970	5.4	9.2	40.5	13.3	22.7	58.8
	1975	17.6	36.1	61.2	28.7	59.0	48.6
	1980	68.5	110.7	110.7	61.9	100.0	61.9
	1985	66.5	82.5	82.5	80.6	100.0	80.6
	1990	100.0	100.0	100.0	100.0	100.0	100.0
	1991	85.6	33.9	33.9	252.6	100.0	252.6
	1992	212.3	38.9	38.9	545.9	100.0	545.9
	1993	534.3	27.2	27.2	1 963.6	100.0	1 963.6
	1994	2 645.0	27.4	27.4	9 635.9	100.0	9 635.9
	1995	8 331.6	26.4	26.4	31 618.8	100.0	31 618.8
	1996	10 212.8	26.9	26.9	37 961.6	100.0	37 961.6
	1997	14 035.9	33.6	33.6	41 737.9	100.0	41 737.9
	1998	19 616.9	38.7	38.7	50 725.0	100.0	50 725.0
	1999	29 230.6	41.8	41.8	69 985.2	100.0	69 985.2
	2000	31 758.0	46.4	46.4	68 501.4	100.0	68 501.4
	2001	38 109.6	53.3	53.3	71 479.7	100.0	71 479.7
	2002	42 509.6	49.8	49.8	85 275.3	100.0	85 275.3
	2003	42 982.5	39.0	39.0	110 261.0	100.0	110 261.0
Israel	1970	-	10.5	42.3	-	24.8	-
	1975	-	25.1	61.1	-	41.1	-
	1980	0.1	41.1	69.7	0.1	58.9	0.3
	1985	27.4	46.8	80.9	33.9	57.9	58.5
	1990	100.0	100.0	100.0	100.0	100.0	100.0
	1991	128.7	113.8	107.3	119.9	106.1	113.0
	1992	154.6	126.8	115.3	134.1	109.9	122.0
	1993	178.4	127.1	119.7	149.1	106.2	140.4
	1994	214.0	143.3	128.4	166.7	111.6	149.3
	1995	248.2	166.2	137.2	180.9	121.1	149.4
	1996	289.1	182.7	144.8	199.7	126.2	158.3
	1997	323.5	189.1	148.7	217.5	127.1	171.1
	1998	356.0	188.9	153.5	232.0	123.1	188.5
	1999	389.5	189.7	157.7	246.9	120.3	205.3
	2000	425.2	210.3	170.4	249.5	123.4	202.2
	2001	429.2	205.8	168.8	254.2	121.9	208.6
	2002	445.0	189.4	167.0	266.4	113.4	235.0
	2003	459.5	203.4	167.9	273.8	121.2	225.9
Japan	1970	16.8	6.8	43.3	38.9	15.7	248.6
	1975	34.1	16.6	54.0	63.0	30.8	205.0
	1980	55.1	35.2	67.0	82.4	52.6	156.6
	1985	73.9	44.9	78.9	93.7	56.9	164.7
	1990	100.0	100.0	100.0	100.0	100.0	100.0
	1991	106.3	114.3	103.3	102.9	110.7	93.0
	1992	109.1	124.7	104.3	104.6	119.6	87.5
	1993	110.0	143.3	104.6	105.2	137.0	76.8
	1994	111.3	157.6	105.7	105.3	149.2	70.6
	1995	112.8	173.7	107.7	104.8	161.3	65.0
	1996	115.8	154.1	111.4	104.0	138.4	75.1
	1997	118.3	141.6	113.4	104.3	124.8	83.6
	1998	116.9	129.3	112.2	104.2	115.2	90.4
	1999	115.2	146.4	112.3	102.6	130.4	78.7
	2000	116.1	156.0	115.4	100.6	135.2	74.4

Table 7. Implicit Price Deflators of Gross Domestic Product in US Dollars and in National Currency

(Index numbers 1990 = 100)

Region, country or area and currency unit	Year	GDP in Current Prices		GDP at Constant Prices	GDP Implicit Price Deflators		Exchange Rates
		National Currency (1)	US Dollars (2)	(3)	National Currency (4)	US Dollars (5)	(6)
	2001	114.8	136.8	115.9	99.1	118.0	83.9
	2002	113.1	130.6	116.1	97.5	112.5	86.6
	2003	113.2	141.4	119.2	95.0	118.6	80.1
Jordan	1970	7.9	14.8	43.5	18.2	33.9	53.8
	1975	14.6	30.4	43.0	34.0	70.6	48.2
	1980	44.8	99.8	82.1	54.5	121.5	44.9
	1985	75.7	127.3	105.9	71.5	120.3	59.5
	1990	100.0	100.0	100.0	100.0	100.0	100.0
	1991	107.0	104.3	101.8	105.1	102.4	102.6
	1992	136.7	133.5	118.2	115.7	112.9	102.4
	1993	147.1	140.9	123.7	118.9	113.9	104.4
	1994	164.9	156.6	129.8	127.0	120.7	105.3
	1995	178.9	169.5	138.1	129.5	122.7	105.5
	1996	186.7	174.8	141.0	132.4	123.9	106.8
	1997	194.6	182.2	145.3	133.9	125.3	106.8
	1998	211.6	198.1	149.6	141.4	132.4	106.8
	1999	216.0	202.2	151.9	142.3	133.2	106.8
	2000	225.3	210.9	156.0	144.5	135.2	106.8
	2001	237.7	222.5	161.4	147.3	137.9	106.8
	2002	248.3	232.4	169.3	146.6	137.3	106.8
	2003	262.1	245.4	174.4	150.3	140.7	106.8
Kazakhstan	1990	100.0	100.0	100.0	100.0	100.0	100.0
	1991	179.4	68.3	88.7	202.2	77.0	262.8
	1992	2 543.7	8.8	84.0	3 028.8	10.4	29 009.0
	1993	30 732.0	16.3	76.2	40 317.1	21.4	188 438.4
	1994	442 306.6	16.6	66.6	663 680.5	24.9	2 668 043.0
	1995	1 059 305.8	23.2	61.2	1 732 290.6	37.9	4 575 825.8
	1996	1 478 728.8	29.3	61.4	2 406 987.5	47.6	5 052 802.8
	1997	1 746 527.1	30.8	62.5	2 794 414.0	49.3	5 663 476.0
	1998	1 810 367.0	30.8	61.3	2 952 155.2	50.2	5 878 628.6
	1999	2 106 157.6	23.5	63.0	3 344 487.6	37.3	8 973 223.2
	2000	2 715 557.2	25.4	69.2	3 925 935.2	36.8	10 670 670.7
	2001	3 395 194.6	30.8	78.3	4 335 588.0	39.4	11 016 203.7
	2002	3 944 263.5	34.3	86.0	4 584 774.5	39.8	11 507 444.9
	2003	4 304 769.1	38.3	93.9	4 584 354.4	40.8	11 229 416.9
Kuwait	1970	19.3	15.6	173.0	11.1	9.0	123.8
	1975	65.4	65.1	137.2	47.7	47.4	100.5
	1980	145.6	155.3	138.6	105.0	112.1	93.7
	1985	121.1	116.1	107.8	112.3	107.7	104.3
	1990	100.0	100.0	100.0	100.0	100.0	100.0
	1991	58.8	59.6	61.1	96.1	97.6	98.5
	1992	109.3	107.6	114.1	95.9	94.3	101.7
	1993	135.7	129.7	152.5	89.0	85.0	104.6
	1994	138.5	134.6	165.7	83.6	81.2	102.9
	1995	148.7	143.8	168.0	88.5	85.6	103.5
	1996	174.6	168.2	163.5	106.8	102.9	103.8
	1997	170.0	161.7	165.4	102.8	97.8	105.2
	1998	143.7	136.0	170.6	84.2	79.7	105.7
	1999	166.8	158.0	162.2	102.8	97.4	105.5
	2000	206.3	194.0	145.9	141.4	133.0	106.3
	2001	188.8	177.5	144.2	130.9	123.1	106.3
	2002	201.5	191.3	144.9	139.1	132.0	105.4
	2003	192.4	186.2	147.6	130.3	126.1	103.3
Kyrgyzstan	1990	100.0	100.0	100.0	100.0	100.0	100.0
	1991	216.1	82.2	92.1	234.8	89.3	262.8
	1992	1 732.0	6.0	79.3	2 183.6	7.5	29 009.0
	1993	12 511.0	7.7	67.1	18 657.6	11.5	161 861.9
	1994	28 082.2	8.6	53.6	52 404.6	16.1	325 576.1
	1995	37 722.2	11.6	50.7	74 430.9	22.9	324 981.5
	1996	54 670.6	14.2	54.3	100 735.6	26.2	384 671.4
	1997	71 695.6	13.8	59.7	120 187.2	23.1	521 396.1
	1998	79 863.1	12.8	60.9	131 097.2	21.0	625 752.8
	1999	113 887.9	9.7	63.1	180 356.2	15.4	1 171 403.4
	2000	152 705.4	10.7	66.6	229 344.8	16.0	1 432 547.5

Table 7. Implicit Price Deflators of Gross Domestic Product in US Dollars and in National Currency

(Index numbers 1990 = 100)

Region, country or area and currency unit	Year	GDP in Current Prices		GDP at Constant Prices	GDP Implicit Price Deflators		Exchange Rates
		National Currency (1)	US Dollars (2)	(3)	National Currency (4)	US Dollars (5)	(6)
	2001	172 624.5	11.9	70.1	246 161.2	16.9	1 452 791.5
	2002	176 090.4	12.5	70.1	251 147.0	17.8	1 409 521.5
	2003	194 908.4	14.9	74.8	260 593.5	19.9	1 310 762.0
Lao People's Democratic Republic	1970	-	34.7	57.8	-	60.0	-
	1975	-	62.3	63.1	0.1	98.8	0.1
	1980	1.4	98.0	59.3	2.3	165.2	1.4
	1985	13.8	177.3	81.2	17.0	218.4	7.8
	1990	100.0	100.0	100.0	100.0	100.0	100.0
	1991	117.8	118.8	104.0	113.3	114.2	99.2
	1992	137.9	136.3	111.3	123.8	122.4	101.2
	1993	155.7	153.8	117.9	132.1	130.5	101.2
	1994	180.9	178.4	127.0	142.4	140.5	101.4
	1995	233.5	205.4	136.5	171.2	150.5	113.7
	1996	281.8	216.5	145.9	193.2	148.5	130.1
	1997	359.3	201.8	155.9	230.4	129.4	178.0
	1998	692.2	148.5	162.2	426.9	91.6	466.0
	1999	1 686.6	168.1	174.0	969.5	96.6	1 003.5
	2000	2 232.4	200.3	184.1	1 212.8	108.8	1 114.5
	2001	2 564.3	202.7	194.7	1 317.2	104.1	1 265.2
	2002	3 002.8	211.3	206.2	1 456.3	102.5	1 420.9
	2003	3 525.9	236.1	217.5	1 620.9	108.5	1 493.3
Lebanon	1970	0.2	52.9	243.0	0.1	21.8	0.5
	1975	0.4	115.9	260.2	0.1	44.5	0.3
	1980	0.7	144.9	225.1	0.3	64.4	0.5
	1985	1.5	65.0	136.0	1.1	47.8	2.4
	1990	100.0	100.0	100.0	100.0	100.0	100.0
	1991	197.2	147.6	138.3	142.6	106.8	133.5
	1992	478.9	194.4	144.5	331.4	134.5	246.4
	1993	671.6	268.1	154.6	434.3	173.4	250.5
	1994	767.1	317.4	167.0	459.3	190.0	241.7
	1995	909.7	390.0	177.9	511.5	219.3	233.3
	1996	1 030.8	455.9	185.0	557.2	246.5	226.1
	1997	1 125.6	508.2	191.5	587.9	265.5	221.5
	1998	1 254.1	575.0	197.2	636.0	291.6	218.1
	1999	1 269.8	585.4	205.1	619.2	285.4	216.9
	2000	1 269.8	585.5	209.2	607.0	279.9	216.9
	2001	1 295.2	597.2	212.1	610.6	281.5	216.9
	2002	1 347.0	621.1	216.4	622.6	287.1	216.9
	2003	1 415.2	652.5	222.9	635.0	292.8	216.9
Macao SAR of China	1970	4.0	5.4	23.3	17.4	23.0	75.4
	1975	9.0	14.1	33.6	26.8	42.0	63.9
	1980	20.1	31.6	48.4	41.5	65.2	63.6
	1985	41.8	42.0	67.1	62.4	62.6	99.7
	1990	100.0	100.0	100.0	100.0	100.0	100.0
	1991	115.9	116.1	103.7	111.8	112.0	99.8
	1992	151.0	151.9	117.4	128.6	129.4	99.4
	1993	172.7	173.9	123.5	139.8	140.7	99.3
	1994	191.5	193.0	128.8	148.7	149.8	99.2
	1995	211.4	212.9	133.0	158.9	160.0	99.3
	1996	211.2	212.7	132.5	159.5	160.6	99.3
	1997	213.5	214.8	132.1	161.6	162.6	99.4
	1998	198.3	199.4	126.1	157.3	158.2	99.4
	1999	187.3	188.0	122.2	153.2	153.8	99.6
	2000	190.0	190.0	127.9	148.6	148.5	100.0
	2001	190.3	190.0	130.6	145.7	145.5	100.1
	2002	207.2	206.9	143.7	144.2	144.0	100.1
	2003	241.8	241.8	166.2	145.5	145.5	100.0
Malaysia	1970	8.9	7.9	22.9	38.9	34.4	113.2
	1975	18.8	21.2	37.5	50.0	56.5	88.5
	1980	44.8	55.6	56.5	79.3	98.5	80.5
	1985	65.1	70.9	72.5	89.8	97.8	91.8
	1990	100.0	100.0	100.0	100.0	100.0	100.0
	1991	113.5	111.6	109.5	103.6	101.9	101.7
	1992	126.5	134.4	119.3	106.1	112.6	94.2
	1993	144.6	151.9	131.1	110.3	115.9	95.2

Table 7. Implicit Price Deflators of Gross Domestic Product in US Dollars and in National Currency

(Index numbers 1990 = 100)

Region, country or area and currency unit	Year	GDP in Current Prices		GDP at Constant Prices	GDP Implicit Price Deflators		Exchange Rates
		National Currency (1)	US Dollars (2)	(3)	National Currency (4)	US Dollars (5)	(6)
	1994	164.1	169.2	143.2	114.7	118.2	97.0
	1995	186.8	201.8	157.2	118.8	128.3	92.6
	1996	213.1	229.1	173.0	123.2	132.4	93.0
	1997	236.6	227.5	185.6	127.5	122.6	104.0
	1998	237.9	163.9	172.0	138.3	95.3	145.1
	1999	252.6	179.8	182.5	138.4	98.5	140.5
	2000	287.3	204.5	197.7	145.3	103.4	140.5
	2001	281.0	200.0	198.6	141.5	100.7	140.5
	2002	303.1	215.8	206.8	146.6	104.3	140.5
	2003	329.5	234.5	217.5	151.5	107.8	140.5
Maldives	1970	3.6	7.2	10.7	33.7	67.8	49.7
	1975	7.4	12.2	18.1	40.7	67.4	60.4
	1980	17.3	21.8	33.6	51.3	64.9	79.0
	1985	28.9	38.9	60.8	47.6	64.0	74.3
	1990	100.0	100.0	100.0	100.0	100.0	100.0
	1991	121.0	112.8	107.7	112.4	104.7	107.3
	1992	145.6	131.6	114.0	127.8	115.5	110.7
	1993	170.8	148.9	121.0	141.2	123.1	114.7
	1994	200.2	165.1	129.0	155.2	128.0	121.3
	1995	228.0	185.0	138.1	165.0	133.9	123.2
	1996	257.3	208.8	150.3	171.2	138.9	123.2
	1997	290.4	235.7	167.6	173.2	140.6	123.2
	1998	308.6	250.4	183.2	168.4	136.7	123.2
	1999	336.7	273.2	197.5	170.5	138.3	123.2
	2000	356.7	289.5	206.2	173.0	140.4	123.2
	2001	371.4	289.8	212.9	174.5	136.1	128.2
	2002	397.4	296.5	224.8	176.7	131.9	134.0
	2003	446.9	333.5	243.7	183.4	136.8	134.0
Mongolia	1970	36.9	39.7	34.0	108.5	116.9	92.8
	1975	48.3	65.1	44.5	108.5	146.2	74.2
	1980	64.5	95.9	59.5	108.5	161.2	67.3
	1985	89.6	102.7	82.8	108.2	124.0	87.2
	1990	100.0	100.0	100.0	100.0	100.0	100.0
	1991	180.7	81.8	90.8	199.1	90.2	220.8
	1992	452.0	45.8	82.1	550.3	55.7	987.4
	1993	1 588.3	25.3	79.7	1 993.7	31.8	6 276.8
	1994	2 706.8	28.3	81.5	3 321.2	34.7	9 575.9
	1995	4 101.4	39.4	87.3	4 699.5	45.1	10 408.6
	1996	4 881.7	38.4	88.7	5 504.7	43.3	12 724.0
	1997	6 262.8	34.2	92.2	6 790.5	37.0	18 329.3
	1998	6 169.5	31.6	95.5	6 461.1	33.1	19 508.8
	1999	6 850.8	28.9	98.6	6 951.1	29.3	23 709.2
	2000	7 539.6	30.2	99.6	7 570.0	30.3	24 980.7
	2001	8 255.6	32.4	100.6	8 204.7	32.2	25 468.6
	2002	9 181.6	35.6	104.7	8 770.2	34.0	25 761.3
	2003	10 157.8	38.2	109.9	9 242.1	34.7	26 601.9
Myanmar	1970	8.9	16.6	58.0	15.3	28.6	53.6
	1975	15.5	21.6	66.2	23.3	32.6	71.6
	1980	25.4	34.2	88.3	28.8	38.8	74.2
	1985	36.8	38.6	111.4	33.1	34.7	95.4
	1990	100.0	100.0	100.0	100.0	100.0	100.0
	1991	122.9	100.4	99.3	123.7	101.0	122.5
	1992	164.1	109.3	108.9	150.7	100.3	150.1
	1993	237.1	118.7	115.5	205.3	102.7	199.9
	1994	311.2	124.8	124.2	250.6	100.5	249.4
	1995	398.0	132.9	132.8	299.7	100.1	299.5
	1996	521.2	142.3	141.3	368.8	100.7	366.3
	1997	730.3	152.6	149.3	489.0	102.2	478.5
	1998	1 026.7	160.5	156.7	655.1	102.4	639.5
	1999	1 395.8	208.2	173.8	802.9	119.8	670.4
	2000	1 753.3	243.8	197.7	887.0	123.3	719.2
	2001	2 415.1	294.7	218.4	1 105.9	134.9	819.6
	2002	3 743.6	326.1	230.4	1 624.6	141.5	1 148.0
	2003	5 505.9	339.7	242.1	2 274.5	140.3	1 620.8

Table 7. Implicit Price Deflators of Gross Domestic Product in US Dollars and in National Currency

(Index numbers 1990 = 100)

Region, country or area and currency unit	Year	GDP in Current Prices		GDP at Constant Prices	GDP Implicit Price Deflators		Exchange Rates
		National Currency (1)	US Dollars (2)	(3)	National Currency (4)	US Dollars (5)	(6)
Nepal	1970	9.5	27.5	51.3	18.5	53.7	34.5
	1975	16.0	42.8	56.1	28.6	76.3	37.5
	1980	22.6	55.3	63.0	35.9	87.7	40.9
	1985	45.0	72.5	80.0	56.3	90.7	62.1
	1990	100.0	100.0	100.0	100.0	100.0	100.0
	1991	116.4	91.8	106.4	109.4	86.3	126.9
	1992	144.5	99.4	110.7	130.5	89.7	145.5
	1993	165.8	100.2	115.0	144.2	87.1	165.5
	1994	192.7	114.6	124.4	154.8	92.1	168.2
	1995	211.9	120.0	128.8	164.6	93.2	176.7
	1996	240.7	124.7	135.6	177.5	91.9	193.0
	1997	271.2	137.3	142.8	190.0	96.2	197.5
	1998	290.9	129.5	147.0	197.9	88.1	224.6
	1999	330.7	142.3	153.6	215.4	92.7	232.4
	2000	367.0	151.6	163.0	225.2	93.0	242.1
	2001	396.7	155.5	170.7	232.4	91.1	255.2
	2002	407.4	153.6	169.9	239.8	90.4	265.2
	2003	431.4	166.4	173.8	248.3	95.8	259.3
Oman	1970	2.5	2.3	27.8	9.0	8.4	108.4
	1975	17.1	19.0	36.6	46.6	51.9	89.8
	1980	48.6	54.1	45.0	108.1	120.3	89.8
	1985	79.9	89.0	86.8	92.1	102.5	89.8
	1990	100.0	100.0	100.0	100.0	100.0	100.0
	1991	97.1	97.1	106.0	91.5	91.5	100.0
	1992	106.6	106.6	115.0	92.6	92.6	100.0
	1993	106.9	106.9	122.1	87.6	87.6	100.0
	1994	110.6	110.6	126.8	87.2	87.2	100.0
	1995	118.1	118.1	132.9	88.9	88.9	100.0
	1996	130.7	130.7	136.8	95.6	95.6	100.0
	1997	135.5	135.5	145.2	93.3	93.3	100.0
	1998	120.5	120.5	149.2	80.8	80.8	100.0
	1999	134.4	134.4	148.8	90.3	90.3	100.0
	2000	170.0	170.0	157.0	108.3	108.3	100.0
	2001	170.7	170.7	168.8	101.2	101.2	100.0
	2002	173.8	173.8	171.6	101.3	101.3	100.0
	2003	180.3	180.3	173.5	103.9	103.9	100.0
Pakistan	1970	5.0	22.6	33.1	15.1	68.3	22.0
	1975	12.8	28.1	40.7	31.4	68.9	45.6
	1980	27.3	59.8	55.6	49.0	107.4	45.6
	1985	50.4	68.7	75.5	66.8	91.0	73.4
	1990	100.0	100.0	100.0	100.0	100.0	100.0
	1991	118.7	108.3	107.8	110.1	100.4	109.6
	1992	130.6	113.0	109.2	119.6	103.5	115.5
	1993	153.0	118.1	113.3	135.0	104.3	129.5
	1994	182.8	129.8	118.9	153.8	109.2	140.8
	1995	207.7	142.5	124.7	166.6	114.3	145.8
	1996	237.9	143.2	125.9	189.0	113.7	166.2
	1997	262.4	138.5	129.1	203.2	107.3	189.4
	1998	287.9	138.4	133.9	215.1	103.4	208.0
	1999	308.4	134.6	139.6	221.0	96.4	229.1
	2000	334.7	134.8	143.1	233.9	94.2	248.3
	2001	365.1	127.4	147.2	248.1	86.5	286.6
	2002	393.7	142.4	155.8	252.8	91.4	276.4
	2003	433.1	162.0	164.0	264.1	98.8	267.3
Philippines	1970	3.7	15.1	47.6	7.7	31.7	24.3
	1975	10.0	33.6	63.0	15.9	53.3	29.8
	1980	22.6	73.2	84.6	26.7	86.6	30.9
	1985	53.1	69.4	79.4	66.9	87.4	76.5
	1990	100.0	100.0	100.0	100.0	100.0	100.0
	1991	115.9	102.5	99.4	116.5	103.1	113.0
	1992	125.5	119.6	99.8	125.8	119.8	104.9
	1993	136.9	122.7	101.9	134.4	120.4	111.6
	1994	157.2	144.6	106.3	147.8	136.0	108.7
	1995	176.9	167.3	111.3	158.9	150.3	105.8
	1996	201.6	187.0	117.8	171.1	158.7	107.8
	1997	225.3	185.8	123.9	181.8	149.9	121.2

Table 7. Implicit Price Deflators of Gross Domestic Product in US Dollars and in National Currency

(Index numbers 1990 = 100)

Region, country or area and currency unit	Year	GDP in Current Prices: National Currency (1)	GDP in Current Prices: US Dollars (2)	GDP at Constant Prices (3)	GDP Implicit Price Deflators: National Currency (4)	GDP Implicit Price Deflators: US Dollars (5)	Exchange Rates (6)
	1998	247.4	147.1	123.2	200.8	119.4	168.2
	1999	276.3	171.9	127.4	216.9	134.9	160.8
	2000	311.4	171.3	135.0	230.7	126.9	181.8
	2001	341.0	162.6	139.0	245.4	117.0	209.8
	2002	373.4	175.9	145.2	257.3	121.2	212.3
	2003	404.7	181.5	151.7	266.7	119.6	223.0
Qatar	1970	5.4	4.1	52.6	10.2	7.8	130.8
	1975	36.2	33.6	64.9	55.9	51.7	108.0
	1980	107.0	106.5	81.6	131.1	130.5	100.5
	1985	83.6	83.6	84.5	98.9	98.9	100.0
	1990	100.0	100.0	100.0	100.0	100.0	100.0
	1991	93.5	93.5	99.2	94.3	94.3	100.0
	1992	103.9	103.9	108.8	95.5	95.5	100.0
	1993	97.2	97.2	108.2	89.9	89.9	100.0
	1994	100.2	100.2	110.7	90.5	90.5	100.0
	1995	110.6	110.6	114.0	97.0	97.0	100.0
	1996	123.1	123.1	119.5	103.0	103.0	100.0
	1997	153.5	153.5	148.2	103.6	103.6	100.0
	1998	139.3	139.3	160.7	86.7	86.7	100.0
	1999	168.4	168.4	165.8	101.5	101.5	100.0
	2000	241.3	241.3	177.9	135.6	135.6	100.0
	2001	241.0	241.0	189.2	127.4	127.4	100.0
	2002	242.9	242.9	194.8	124.7	124.7	100.0
	2003	287.5	287.5	202.6	141.9	141.9	100.0
Republic of Korea	1970	1.5	3.5	21.3	7.1	16.3	43.9
	1975	5.7	8.4	31.2	18.3	26.8	68.4
	1980	21.1	24.6	43.6	48.4	56.4	85.8
	1985	45.5	37.0	63.6	71.5	58.2	122.9
	1990	100.0	100.0	100.0	100.0	100.0	100.0
	1991	121.1	116.9	109.2	110.9	107.0	103.6
	1992	137.4	124.6	115.2	119.3	108.2	110.3
	1993	155.2	136.9	121.5	127.7	112.6	113.4
	1994	180.9	159.3	131.5	137.5	121.2	113.5
	1995	211.0	193.7	143.2	147.3	135.2	109.0
	1996	234.1	205.9	152.9	153.1	134.7	113.7
	1997	253.5	188.6	160.6	157.9	117.5	134.4
	1998	248.5	125.5	149.8	165.9	83.8	198.0
	1999	270.0	160.7	166.2	162.5	96.7	168.0
	2000	291.9	182.7	181.7	160.7	100.6	159.8
	2001	308.5	169.1	187.3	164.7	90.3	182.4
	2002	333.6	188.7	199.2	167.5	94.7	176.8
	2003	351.6	208.8	205.4	171.2	101.7	168.4
Saudi Arabia	1970	5.8	4.9	58.0	10.1	8.4	120.2
	1975	42.0	44.7	100.5	41.8	44.5	93.9
	1980	125.2	141.0	147.7	84.8	95.5	88.8
	1985	80.1	82.8	89.1	89.9	93.0	96.7
	1990	100.0	100.0	100.0	100.0	100.0	100.0
	1991	112.8	112.8	109.8	102.7	102.7	100.0
	1992	117.7	117.7	112.8	104.3	104.3	100.0
	1993	113.2	113.2	112.1	101.0	101.0	100.0
	1994	114.8	114.8	112.7	101.9	101.9	100.0
	1995	122.1	122.1	113.2	107.8	107.8	100.0
	1996	150.7	150.7	114.8	131.3	131.3	100.0
	1997	157.6	157.6	117.8	133.8	133.8	100.0
	1998	139.5	139.5	121.1	115.1	115.1	100.0
	1999	154.0	154.0	120.1	128.2	128.2	100.0
	2000	180.3	180.3	126.0	143.1	143.1	100.0
	2001	178.2	178.2	127.5	139.8	139.8	100.0
	2002	179.9	179.9	115.3	156.0	156.0	100.0
	2003	198.1	198.1	120.7	164.1	164.1	100.0
Singapore	1970	8.7	5.1	20.9	41.5	24.6	168.9
	1975	20.1	15.4	32.9	61.1	46.7	130.8
	1980	37.5	31.8	49.5	75.8	64.2	118.1
	1985	58.2	47.9	66.8	87.1	71.8	121.4
	1990	100.0	100.0	100.0	100.0	100.0	100.0

Table 7. Implicit Price Deflators of Gross Domestic Product in US Dollars and in National Currency

(Index numbers 1990 = 100)

Region, country or area and currency unit	Year	GDP in Current Prices		GDP at Constant Prices	GDP Implicit Price Deflators		Exchange Rates
		National Currency (1)	US Dollars (2)	(3)	National Currency (4)	US Dollars (5)	(6)
	1991	111.6	117.0	106.8	104.5	109.6	95.3
	1992	121.4	135.1	113.9	106.6	118.6	89.9
	1993	141.0	158.1	127.9	110.3	123.7	89.1
	1994	161.2	191.3	142.4	113.2	134.3	84.3
	1995	177.9	227.5	153.9	115.6	147.8	78.2
	1996	194.4	249.9	166.4	116.8	150.2	77.8
	1997	211.8	258.5	180.6	117.3	143.1	81.9
	1998	205.0	222.0	179.0	114.5	124.0	92.3
	1999	206.2	220.5	190.5	108.2	115.7	93.5
	2000	235.8	247.9	208.5	113.1	118.9	95.1
	2001	227.4	230.0	203.5	111.7	113.0	98.9
	2002	232.8	235.7	208.1	111.9	113.3	98.8
	2003	234.8	244.3	209.1	112.3	116.8	96.1
Sri Lanka	1970	4.5	30.0	43.3	10.3	69.2	14.9
	1975	8.4	48.0	50.0	16.8	96.1	17.5
	1980	21.5	52.1	66.1	32.5	78.8	41.3
	1985	49.6	73.2	84.8	58.6	86.4	67.8
	1990	100.0	100.0	100.0	100.0	100.0	100.0
	1991	116.3	112.6	104.8	111.0	107.4	103.3
	1992	132.7	121.3	109.4	121.3	110.8	109.4
	1993	157.2	130.3	117.0	134.4	111.4	120.6
	1994	182.2	147.7	123.6	147.4	119.5	123.3
	1995	208.4	162.9	130.4	159.8	124.9	127.9
	1996	242.7	175.9	135.3	179.3	130.0	138.0
	1997	280.3	190.3	144.0	194.6	132.1	147.3
	1998	318.1	197.8	150.9	210.8	131.1	160.9
	1999	346.4	196.5	157.4	220.0	124.8	176.3
	2000	391.6	203.8	166.8	234.8	122.1	192.2
	2001	436.2	195.5	164.4	265.3	118.9	223.1
	2002	490.6	205.4	171.0	286.9	120.2	238.8
	2003	524.7	217.8	180.4	290.9	120.7	240.9
Syrian Arab Republic	1970	2.6	12.8	35.3	7.2	36.3	19.9
	1975	7.7	40.0	65.8	11.7	60.8	19.3
	1980	19.1	93.3	91.0	21.0	102.6	20.5
	1985	31.0	105.0	105.0	29.5	100.0	29.5
	1990	100.0	100.0	100.0	100.0	100.0	100.0
	1991	116.1	107.9	107.9	107.6	100.0	107.6
	1992	138.5	122.4	122.4	113.1	100.0	113.1
	1993	154.2	128.8	128.8	119.7	100.0	119.7
	1994	188.6	138.1	138.1	136.6	100.0	136.6
	1995	212.8	147.8	147.8	144.0	100.0	144.0
	1996	257.5	162.3	162.3	158.7	100.0	158.7
	1997	277.9	170.4	170.4	163.0	100.0	163.0
	1998	294.6	182.0	182.0	161.9	100.0	161.9
	1999	305.3	175.5	175.5	173.9	100.0	173.9
	2000	336.9	176.6	176.6	190.8	100.0	190.8
	2001	355.6	182.5	182.5	194.8	100.0	194.8
	2002	372.5	188.4	188.4	197.7	100.0	197.7
	2003	398.4	190.4	190.4	209.3	100.0	209.3
Tajikistan	1990	100.0	100.0	100.0	100.0	100.0	100.0
	1991	183.6	69.9	91.5	200.6	76.3	262.8
	1992	883.6	238.4	62.0	1 426.1	384.8	370.6
	1993	9 686.3	622.8	51.9	18 678.7	1 201.1	1 555.2
	1994	24 472.6	665.4	40.8	59 963.7	1 630.4	3 677.8
	1995	95 616.4	518.3	35.8	267 443.2	1 449.8	18 447.3
	1996	422 602.7	952.5	29.8	1 419 043.2	3 198.2	44 369.4
	1997	710 137.0	841.1	30.3	2 344 640.4	2 776.9	84 434.4
	1998	1 404 383.6	1 204.3	31.9	4 403 401.8	3 776.2	116 610.4
	1999	1 842 465.8	991.3	33.1	5 570 973.0	2 997.5	185 854.6
	2000	2 475 068.5	793.9	35.8	6 910 161.8	2 216.6	311 749.2
	2001	3 464 109.6	972.6	39.5	8 776 289.3	2 464.0	356 184.9
	2002	4 610 274.0	1 110.8	43.0	10 726 609.7	2 584.5	415 035.0
	2003	6 517 534.2	1 417.9	47.4	13 760 093.5	2 993.5	459 664.7

Table 7. Implicit Price Deflators of Gross Domestic Product in US Dollars and in National Currency

(Index numbers 1990 = 100)

Region, country or area and currency unit	Year	GDP in Current Prices: National Currency (1)	GDP in Current Prices: US Dollars (2)	GDP at Constant Prices (3)	GDP Implicit Price Deflators: National Currency (4)	GDP Implicit Price Deflators: US Dollars (5)	Exchange Rates (6)
Thailand	1970	6.8	8.4	24.4	27.8	34.2	81.3
	1975	14.0	17.5	32.1	43.6	54.7	79.7
	1980	30.3	37.9	47.0	64.6	80.7	80.0
	1985	48.4	45.6	61.2	79.0	74.4	106.1
	1990	100.0	100.0	100.0	100.0	100.0	100.0
	1991	114.8	115.1	108.6	105.7	106.0	99.7
	1992	129.6	130.6	117.4	110.5	111.3	99.3
	1993	144.9	146.4	127.0	114.1	115.3	99.0
	1994	166.2	169.1	138.5	120.0	122.1	98.3
	1995	191.7	196.8	151.2	126.7	130.1	97.4
	1996	211.1	213.2	160.2	131.8	133.1	99.1
	1997	216.7	176.8	158.0	137.2	111.9	122.6
	1998	211.8	131.0	141.4	149.8	92.7	161.7
	1999	212.3	143.7	147.7	143.8	97.3	147.8
	2000	225.1	143.6	154.5	145.7	92.9	156.8
	2001	234.6	135.1	157.5	148.9	85.8	173.7
	2002	249.1	148.4	166.0	150.1	89.4	167.9
	2003	271.3	167.3	177.1	153.2	94.5	162.1
Timor-Leste	1990	100.0	100.0	100.0	100.0	100.0	100.0
	1991	112.0	112.0	101.1	110.8	110.8	100.0
	1992	121.6	121.6	102.2	118.9	118.9	100.0
	1993	138.1	138.1	103.4	133.6	133.6	100.0
	1994	154.6	154.6	104.6	147.9	147.9	100.0
	1995	174.4	174.4	105.7	165.0	165.0	100.0
	1996	203.6	203.6	106.9	190.5	190.5	100.0
	1997	212.3	212.3	111.1	191.0	191.0	100.0
	1998	216.1	216.1	112.3	192.5	192.5	100.0
	1999	149.5	149.5	72.5	206.3	206.3	100.0
	2000	177.8	177.8	83.7	212.5	212.5	100.0
	2001	213.2	213.2	97.9	217.8	217.8	100.0
	2002	209.2	209.2	100.7	207.8	207.8	100.0
	2003	187.1	187.1	98.7	189.6	189.6	100.0
Turkey	1970	0.1	11.9	40.4	0.1	29.4	0.4
	1975	0.2	31.0	53.5	0.3	57.9	0.6
	1980	1.3	45.7	60.2	2.2	75.9	2.9
	1985	8.9	44.6	76.3	11.7	58.5	20.0
	1990	100.0	100.0	100.0	100.0	100.0	100.0
	1991	160.3	100.2	100.9	158.8	99.3	159.9
	1992	278.2	105.6	107.0	260.1	98.7	263.4
	1993	504.2	119.7	115.6	436.3	103.6	421.1
	1994	984.2	86.7	109.3	900.7	79.4	1 135.0
	1995	1 974.9	112.4	117.1	1 686.2	95.9	1 757.4
	1996	3 758.2	120.4	125.3	2 998.8	96.1	3 120.6
	1997	7 336.3	126.0	134.8	5 443.9	93.5	5 821.6
	1998	13 286.8	132.9	138.9	9 563.8	95.7	9 994.6
	1999	19 695.5	122.7	132.4	14 877.4	92.7	16 053.7
	2000	31 695.8	132.2	142.1	22 300.7	93.0	23 967.2
	2001	45 390.6	96.6	131.5	34 524.0	73.5	46 981.8
	2002	70 219.0	121.5	141.7	49 551.0	85.8	57 778.2
	2003	93 087.5	161.8	149.9	62 087.4	107.9	57 535.1
Turkmenistan	1990	100.0	100.0	100.0	100.0	100.0	100.0
	1991	193.4	73.6	95.3	203.0	77.2	262.8
	1992	10.5	36.3	81.0	13.0	44.8	29.0
	1993	131.8	50.2	82.2	160.3	61.0	262.8
	1994	1 146.5	39.8	68.0	1 686.2	58.5	2 882.6
	1995	8 579.5	51.5	63.1	13 596.6	81.6	16 654.2
	1996	101 996.8	20.9	67.3	151 492.1	31.0	489 139.1
	1997	146 168.2	23.5	59.7	245 032.0	39.4	622 134.6
	1998	184 141.3	25.1	63.9	288 225.1	39.3	734 259.3
	1999	263 894.7	33.8	74.4	354 556.4	45.4	780 780.8
	2000	337 473.7	43.2	81.9	412 194.2	52.8	780 780.8
	2001	445 565.8	57.1	88.3	504 452.9	64.6	780 780.8
	2002	839 473.7	107.5	96.3	871 945.5	111.7	780 780.8
	2003	1 024 828.9	131.3	104.9	976 578.5	125.1	780 780.8

Table 7. Implicit Price Deflators of Gross Domestic Product in US Dollars and in National Currency

(Index numbers 1990 = 100)

Region, country or area and currency unit	Year	GDP in Current Prices		GDP at Constant Prices	GDP Implicit Price Deflators		Exchange Rates
		National Currency (1)	US Dollars (2)	(3)	National Currency (4)	US Dollars (5)	(6)
United Arab Emirates	1970	2.5	2.0	5.0	51.3	39.6	129.7
	1975	31.8	29.5	46.8	68.0	63.0	107.9
	1980	88.6	87.7	97.5	90.8	89.9	101.0
	1985	80.2	80.2	89.0	90.1	90.1	100.0
	1990	100.0	100.0	100.0	100.0	100.0	100.0
	1991	100.4	100.4	100.2	100.2	100.2	100.0
	1992	103.5	103.5	103.0	100.5	100.5	100.0
	1993	104.5	104.5	102.1	102.3	102.3	100.0
	1994	111.9	111.9	104.4	107.2	107.2	100.0
	1995	125.2	125.2	111.8	112.0	112.0	100.0
	1996	140.3	140.3	123.4	113.7	113.7	100.0
	1997	144.3	144.3	125.8	114.7	114.7	100.0
	1998	135.9	135.9	117.0	116.2	116.2	100.0
	1999	147.4	147.3	119.9	122.9	122.9	100.0
	2000	157.9	157.8	126.4	124.9	124.9	100.0
	2001	168.9	168.9	132.7	127.3	127.3	100.0
	2002	172.3	172.2	134.7	127.9	127.8	100.0
	2003	196.3	196.2	143.2	137.1	137.0	100.0
Uzbekistan	1990	100.0	100.0	100.0	100.0	100.0	100.0
	1991	189.8	72.2	99.5	190.7	72.6	262.8
	1992	1 368.7	4.7	88.5	1 547.4	5.3	29 009.0
	1993	15 764.5	11.3	86.4	18 241.1	13.1	139 639.6
	1994	200 051.8	13.4	81.9	244 174.6	16.3	1 495 495.5
	1995	933 652.7	20.9	81.2	1 149 925.7	25.7	4 470 720.7
	1996	1 723 912.1	28.7	82.6	2 087 750.4	34.7	6 016 016.0
	1997	3 012 081.3	31.9	86.9	3 467 659.6	36.7	9 446 946.9
	1998	4 366 758.7	30.8	90.7	4 815 209.0	33.9	14 187 937.9
	1999	6 563 778.7	35.1	94.7	6 932 811.5	37.0	18 712 462.5
	2000	10 038 729.1	28.3	98.5	10 195 319.7	28.7	35 526 776.8
	2001	15 011 840.7	14.5	102.9	14 589 478.7	14.1	103 716 216.2
	2002	23 031 785.0	20.3	107.2	21 481 554.4	19.0	113 259 759.8
	2003	26 333 316.9	18.1	111.9	23 525 733.5	16.2	145 464 084.1
Vietnam	1970	-	61.6	61.9	-	99.6	-
	1975	-	62.9	56.0	-	112.3	-
	1980	-	65.7	58.4	0.1	112.6	0.1
	1985	0.3	90.5	80.8	0.4	112.0	0.3
	1990	100.0	100.0	100.0	100.0	100.0	100.0
	1991	182.8	118.1	106.0	172.5	111.4	154.8
	1992	263.5	152.5	115.1	228.8	132.4	172.8
	1993	334.3	203.7	124.4	268.7	163.7	164.1
	1994	425.5	251.6	135.4	314.3	185.8	169.2
	1995	545.6	320.4	148.3	367.8	216.0	170.3
	1996	648.4	381.0	162.2	399.8	234.9	170.2
	1997	747.5	426.6	175.4	426.2	243.2	175.2
	1998	860.5	424.3	185.5	463.8	228.7	202.8
	1999	953.3	443.2	194.4	490.4	228.0	215.1
	2000	1 058.6	484.4	207.5	510.2	233.4	218.5
	2001	1 156.3	509.0	221.7	521.5	229.6	227.1
	2002	1 287.9	546.4	237.3	542.7	230.3	235.7
	2003	1 415.9	591.8	251.5	562.9	235.3	239.2
Yemen	1990	100.0	100.0	100.0	100.0	100.0	100.0
	1991	118.2	96.4	100.3	117.8	96.1	122.6
	1992	147.8	120.6	105.2	140.4	114.6	122.6
	1993	183.4	149.6	109.5	167.5	136.7	122.6
	1994	235.8	192.4	111.9	210.7	172.0	122.6
	1995	393.2	94.4	124.0	317.1	76.1	416.7
	1996	566.6	59.0	131.3	431.5	44.9	960.8
	1997	683.9	51.8	141.9	481.8	36.5	1 319.2
	1998	653.5	47.1	148.9	438.9	31.7	1 386.5
	1999	871.5	54.8	154.4	564.4	35.5	1 589.0
	2000	1 061.7	64.3	162.3	654.1	39.6	1 650.2
	2001	1 107.9	64.4	168.7	656.8	38.2	1 721.1
	2002	1 225.1	68.4	174.2	703.5	39.3	1 792.1
	2003	1 367.2	73.0	181.5	753.4	40.2	1 871.9

Table 7. Implicit Price Deflators of Gross Domestic Product in US Dollars and in National Currency

(Index numbers 1990 = 100)

Region, country or area and currency unit	Year	GDP in Current Prices: National Currency (1)	GDP in Current Prices: US Dollars (2)	GDP at Constant Prices (3)	GDP Implicit Price Deflators: National Currency (4)	GDP Implicit Price Deflators: US Dollars (5)	Exchange Rates (6)
EUROPE							
Albania	1970	38.5	59.7	48.3	79.8	123.7	64.6
	1975	68.2	105.6	64.8	105.2	163.0	64.6
	1980	92.4	102.2	88.5	104.4	115.5	90.4
	1985	100.3	110.9	97.9	102.4	113.3	90.4
	1990	100.0	100.0	100.0	100.0	100.0	100.0
	1991	97.6	46.5	72.0	135.5	64.6	209.7
	1992	301.5	31.1	66.8	451.2	46.6	968.7
	1993	745.5	56.6	73.2	1 018.2	77.3	1 317.6
	1994	1 096.7	89.8	79.3	1 383.2	113.2	1 221.6
	1995	1 366.8	114.2	89.9	1 521.1	127.1	1 196.7
	1996	1 878.5	139.2	98.0	1 916.2	142.0	1 349.1
	1997	1 981.0	103.0	87.9	2 252.9	117.2	1 922.7
	1998	2 529.9	130.1	99.1	2 552.9	131.3	1 944.7
	1999	2 906.1	163.5	107.9	2 692.8	151.5	1 777.6
	2000	3 278.9	176.7	116.2	2 821.0	152.0	1 855.3
	2001	3 637.8	196.4	125.5	2 897.9	156.4	1 852.4
	2002	4 028.3	222.6	131.5	3 062.3	169.2	1 809.4
	2003	4 395.7	279.4	139.4	3 152.5	200.4	1 573.3
Andorra	1970	2.2	3.2	21.9	10.0	14.6	68.7
	1975	6.5	11.5	36.6	17.7	31.5	56.3
	1980	20.2	28.8	49.7	40.7	57.9	70.3
	1985	47.6	28.5	67.9	70.0	42.0	166.8
	1990	100.0	100.0	100.0	100.0	100.0	100.0
	1991	114.2	112.0	106.8	106.9	104.9	101.9
	1992	128.4	127.9	112.6	114.1	113.6	100.4
	1993	138.5	110.9	116.1	119.3	95.5	124.8
	1994	152.3	115.9	122.9	123.9	94.3	131.4
	1995	167.9	137.3	129.1	130.0	106.3	122.3
	1996	179.9	144.8	133.6	134.6	108.3	124.3
	1997	191.6	133.4	139.1	137.7	95.9	143.6
	1998	204.0	139.2	144.7	141.0	96.2	146.6
	1999	218.2	142.4	150.6	144.9	94.6	153.2
	2000	236.9	133.7	158.0	150.0	84.6	177.2
	2001	257.7	141.3	165.0	156.2	85.6	182.4
	2002	280.8	161.9	172.1	163.2	94.1	173.4
	2003	307.9	212.9	181.1	170.0	117.6	144.6
Austria	1970	21.1	9.2	55.4	38.1	16.6	228.7
	1975	36.8	24.0	67.2	54.8	35.8	153.2
	1980	55.9	49.1	79.0	70.8	62.2	113.8
	1985	75.4	41.5	85.3	88.4	48.6	182.0
	1990	100.0	100.0	100.0	100.0	100.0	100.0
	1991	107.2	104.4	103.3	103.8	101.0	102.7
	1992	113.6	117.6	105.7	107.5	111.2	96.7
	1993	117.5	114.8	106.1	110.7	108.2	102.3
	1994	123.8	123.2	108.9	113.7	113.2	100.5
	1995	129.0	145.4	110.7	116.5	131.4	88.7
	1996	133.3	143.1	112.9	118.0	126.8	93.1
	1997	136.6	127.2	114.7	119.1	110.9	107.3
	1998	142.7	131.1	119.2	119.7	110.0	108.9
	1999	147.5	129.8	122.4	120.5	106.1	113.6
	2000	154.7	117.8	126.5	122.2	93.1	131.4
	2001	159.1	117.6	127.5	124.8	92.2	135.2
	2002	163.4	127.1	129.2	126.5	98.3	128.6
	2003	167.9	156.5	130.2	128.9	120.2	107.2
Belarus	1990	100.0	100.0	100.0	100.0	100.0	100.0
	1991	225.0	85.6	100.0	225.0	85.6	262.8
	1992	2 300.0	7.9	88.9	2 587.5	8.9	29 009.0
	1993	246 250.0	11.2	82.1	299 845.6	13.6	2 201 801.8
	1994	444 825.0	9.8	72.5	613 235.9	13.6	4 516 771.8
	1995	3 035 075.0	17.5	65.0	4 672 315.9	27.0	17 298 673.7
	1996	4 795 975.0	24.1	66.8	7 183 704.8	36.2	19 864 739.7
	1997	9 170 750.0	23.5	74.4	12 328 413.8	31.6	39 068 943.9
	1998	17 554 025.0	25.3	80.7	21 760 631.0	31.4	69 260 135.1
	1999	75 651 600.0	20.3	83.5	90 654 237.2	24.3	373 565 940.9
	2000	228 344 400.0	17.3	88.3	258 659 300.2	19.6	1 316 441 441.4

Table 7. Implicit Price Deflators of Gross Domestic Product in US Dollars and in National Currency

(Index numbers 1990 = 100)

Region, country or area and currency unit	Year	GDP in Current Prices: National Currency (1)	GDP in Current Prices: US Dollars (2)	GDP at Constant Prices (3)	GDP Implicit Price Deflators: National Currency (4)	GDP Implicit Price Deflators: US Dollars (5)	Exchange Rates (6)
	2001	429 330 750.0	20.6	92.5	464 382 466.5	22.3	2 087 087 087.1
	2002	653 457 550.0	24.3	97.1	673 096 343.3	25.0	2 689 064 064.1
	2003	898 255 000.0	29.1	103.7	866 339 736.0	28.1	3 083 458 458.5
Belgium	1970	19.5	13.0	58.8	33.1	22.1	149.6
	1975	35.2	32.0	70.1	50.2	45.6	110.1
	1980	54.1	61.8	82.0	66.0	75.4	87.5
	1985	74.7	42.0	85.9	86.9	48.9	177.7
	1990	100.0	100.0	100.0	100.0	100.0	100.0
	1991	104.8	102.5	101.8	102.9	100.7	102.2
	1992	110.0	114.3	103.4	106.4	110.6	96.2
	1993	113.3	109.4	102.4	110.6	106.9	103.5
	1994	119.4	119.3	105.7	113.0	112.8	100.1
	1995	123.8	140.3	108.2	114.4	129.7	88.2
	1996	126.7	136.8	109.5	115.7	124.9	92.6
	1997	133.0	124.2	113.3	117.4	109.7	107.1
	1998	137.9	127.0	115.6	119.3	109.9	108.6
	1999	144.3	127.4	119.3	121.0	106.8	113.3
	2000	151.7	115.8	123.8	122.5	93.5	131.0
	2001	155.4	115.2	124.6	124.7	92.4	134.9
	2002	159.2	124.1	125.5	126.8	98.9	128.3
	2003	163.8	153.1	126.9	129.1	120.7	107.0
Bosnia and Herzegovina	1990	100.0	100.0	100.0	100.0	100.0	100.0
	1991	191.7	110.5	87.9	218.1	125.7	173.5
	1992	324.2	10.6	65.0	499.1	16.3	3 063.5
	1993	28 060.7	9.4	47.4	59 175.6	19.8	298 751.4
	1994	57 333.8	8.4	50.5	113 528.6	16.6	685 854.4
	1995	192 823.2	15.6	67.1	287 168.6	23.2	1 236 967.7
	1996	278 083.4	21.0	103.5	268 578.0	20.3	1 325 322.5
	1997	442 387.7	28.9	141.5	312 692.1	20.4	1 532 122.2
	1998	501 562.8	32.3	163.2	307 240.5	19.8	1 554 751.4
	1999	580 081.0	35.8	178.8	324 411.4	20.0	1 622 014.0
	2000	635 972.7	33.9	188.5	337 447.3	18.0	1 875 649.0
	2001	688 817.1	35.7	196.9	349 747.2	18.1	1 931 135.9
	2002	759 399.8	41.4	204.3	371 674.2	20.2	1 836 164.0
	2003	784 460.1	51.2	210.9	372 045.1	24.3	1 531 129.4
Bulgaria	1970	28.9	54.0	41.5	69.5	130.0	53.4
	1975	39.2	71.5	60.6	64.7	118.1	54.8
	1980	56.8	96.5	81.6	69.6	118.2	58.9
	1985	71.8	152.7	97.9	73.3	155.9	47.0
	1990	100.0	100.0	100.0	100.0	100.0	100.0
	1991	299.0	36.8	89.6	333.5	41.1	812.2
	1992	442.5	41.5	83.1	532.1	49.9	1 065.8
	1993	658.6	52.3	81.9	804.0	63.8	1 260.0
	1994	1 157.9	46.8	83.4	1 388.2	56.2	2 471.9
	1995	1 939.5	63.2	85.8	2 260.7	73.7	3 067.2
	1996	3 880.1	47.8	77.7	4 991.9	61.5	8 122.8
	1997	38 406.3	50.0	73.4	52 328.7	68.1	76 798.1
	1998	49 396.9	61.5	76.3	64 710.4	80.5	80 381.7
	1999	52 413.5	62.5	78.1	67 117.5	80.0	83 853.1
	2000	58 940.1	60.8	82.3	71 613.8	73.9	96 953.2
	2001	65 453.5	65.6	85.6	76 420.1	76.6	99 758.4
	2002	71 213.6	75.1	89.7	79 368.1	83.7	94 839.0
	2003	76 349.1	96.5	94.0	81 193.5	102.6	79 118.8
Croatia	1990	100.0	100.0	100.0	100.0	100.0	100.0
	1991	157.3	90.7	78.9	199.3	114.9	173.5
	1992	964.9	41.3	69.7	1 385.0	59.3	2 334.7
	1993	13 904.9	44.0	64.1	21 700.3	68.7	31 601.6
	1994	31 173.3	58.9	67.8	45 952.2	86.8	52 967.5
	1995	35 073.8	75.9	72.5	48 394.6	104.8	46 199.6
	1996	38 495.8	80.2	76.7	50 160.5	104.5	48 000.2
	1997	44 139.3	81.9	82.0	53 852.1	99.9	53 891.4
	1998	49 056.6	87.3	84.0	58 377.9	103.9	56 202.1
	1999	50 473.8	80.3	83.3	60 586.1	96.4	62 828.7
	2000	54 373.9	74.4	85.7	63 454.8	86.8	73 112.1

Table 7. Implicit Price Deflators of Gross Domestic Product in US Dollars and in National Currency

(Index numbers 1990 = 100)

Region, country or area and currency unit	Year	GDP in Current Prices: National Currency (1)	GDP in Current Prices: US Dollars (2)	GDP at Constant Prices (3)	GDP Implicit Price Deflators: National Currency (4)	GDP Implicit Price Deflators: US Dollars (5)	Exchange Rates (6)
	2001	59 051.5	80.2	88.9	66 409.9	90.1	73 672.2
	2002	62 898.0	90.5	93.6	67 221.9	96.7	69 508.7
	2003	67 703.4	114.3	98.0	69 109.5	116.7	59 216.6
Czech Republic	1980	73.2	92.1	87.0	84.2	105.9	79.5
	1985	83.5	87.4	92.4	90.3	94.6	95.5
	1990	100.0	100.0	100.0	100.0	100.0	100.0
	1991	120.4	73.3	88.4	136.2	82.9	164.2
	1992	134.6	85.5	87.9	153.0	97.2	157.4
	1993	162.9	100.3	88.0	185.2	114.0	162.4
	1994	188.9	117.8	89.9	210.0	131.0	160.4
	1995	220.5	149.2	95.3	231.5	156.5	147.9
	1996	250.2	165.5	99.4	251.8	166.5	151.2
	1997	268.3	151.9	98.6	272.0	154.0	176.6
	1998	293.7	163.3	97.6	301.0	167.3	179.8
	1999	303.8	157.7	98.0	309.8	160.9	192.6
	2000	317.0	147.4	101.2	313.1	145.6	215.0
	2001	343.1	161.9	104.4	328.8	155.1	211.9
	2002	355.7	195.0	106.4	334.3	183.3	182.4
	2003	376.7	239.7	109.5	344.0	218.9	157.2
Denmark	1970	14.8	12.2	70.7	20.9	17.3	121.2
	1975	27.1	29.2	76.1	35.5	38.3	92.9
	1980	46.7	51.3	85.6	54.6	60.0	91.1
	1985	76.8	44.9	93.9	81.8	47.8	171.2
	1990	100.0	100.0	100.0	100.0	100.0	100.0
	1991	103.9	100.5	101.1	102.8	99.4	103.4
	1992	107.6	110.3	101.7	105.7	108.4	97.5
	1993	109.1	104.1	101.7	107.2	102.3	104.8
	1994	117.0	113.8	107.3	109.1	106.1	102.8
	1995	122.3	135.2	110.2	111.0	122.6	90.5
	1996	128.5	137.2	113.0	113.7	121.4	93.7
	1997	135.3	126.7	116.4	116.2	108.9	106.7
	1998	140.0	129.3	119.3	117.4	108.4	108.3
	1999	146.3	129.8	122.4	119.6	106.1	112.7
	2000	155.2	118.8	125.9	123.2	94.3	130.6
	2001	160.6	119.4	127.7	125.7	93.5	134.5
	2002	165.4	129.7	130.4	126.9	99.5	127.6
	2003	169.1	158.9	130.4	129.7	121.8	106.4
Estonia	1990	100.0	100.0	100.0	100.0	100.0	100.0
	1991	207.6	79.0	92.0	225.7	85.9	262.8
	1992	1 615.7	9.2	72.5	2 227.9	12.7	17 597.6
	1993	2 736.2	13.8	66.3	4 124.0	20.8	19 854.0
	1994	3 744.1	19.2	65.0	5 757.9	29.5	19 506.4
	1995	5 126.9	29.8	67.8	7 561.8	43.9	17 214.3
	1996	6 571.8	36.4	70.5	9 326.8	51.6	18 068.7
	1997	8 028.7	38.5	77.4	10 378.5	49.8	20 843.5
	1998	9 218.8	43.6	80.9	11 392.5	53.9	21 133.1
	1999	9 568.4	43.4	80.4	11 899.8	54.0	22 038.4
	2000	10 953.9	43.0	86.3	12 695.5	49.8	25 478.4
	2001	12 272.2	46.8	91.9	13 360.7	50.9	26 243.4
	2002	13 541.9	54.3	97.3	13 910.7	55.8	24 942.6
	2003	14 324.1	68.8	101.7	14 080.5	67.7	20 805.4
Finland	1970	8.9	8.1	50.8	17.6	16.0	109.8
	1975	20.2	21.0	64.0	31.5	32.8	96.2
	1980	37.2	38.2	74.1	50.3	51.5	97.6
	1985	64.3	39.7	85.7	75.1	46.3	162.1
	1990	100.0	100.0	100.0	100.0	100.0	100.0
	1991	95.4	90.2	93.6	101.9	96.4	105.8
	1992	93.1	79.5	90.0	103.4	88.3	117.2
	1993	94.3	63.1	88.9	106.1	71.0	149.4
	1994	99.8	73.0	92.4	108.0	79.0	136.6
	1995	108.2	94.7	95.6	113.1	99.0	114.2
	1996	112.0	93.2	99.3	112.7	93.8	120.1
	1997	121.5	89.5	105.5	115.1	84.8	135.8
	1998	132.1	94.5	110.8	119.2	85.3	139.8
	1999	136.2	93.3	114.6	118.9	81.5	146.0

Table 7. Implicit Price Deflators of Gross Domestic Product in US Dollars and in National Currency

(Index numbers 1990 = 100)

Region, country or area and currency unit	Year	GDP in Current Prices: National Currency (1)	GDP in Current Prices: US Dollars (2)	GDP at Constant Prices (3)	GDP Implicit Price Deflators: National Currency (4)	GDP Implicit Price Deflators: US Dollars (5)	Exchange Rates (6)
	2000	147.8	87.5	120.4	122.7	72.7	168.8
	2001	153.5	88.3	121.9	126.0	72.5	173.8
	2002	158.6	96.0	124.5	127.4	77.1	165.2
	2003	162.7	118.1	126.9	128.3	93.1	137.8
France	1970	12.3	12.1	56.6	21.8	21.4	102.0
	1975	22.8	29.0	67.1	34.0	43.2	78.7
	1980	43.5	56.1	78.3	55.6	71.6	77.6
	1985	72.1	43.7	85.2	84.6	51.3	165.0
	1990	100.0	100.0	100.0	100.0	100.0	100.0
	1991	104.0	100.3	101.0	103.0	99.4	103.6
	1992	107.6	110.7	102.5	105.0	108.0	97.2
	1993	109.1	104.9	101.6	107.4	103.3	104.0
	1994	113.3	111.1	103.7	109.2	107.1	102.0
	1995	117.1	127.7	105.4	111.1	121.2	91.7
	1996	120.1	127.8	106.6	112.7	119.9	93.9
	1997	124.0	115.6	108.6	114.1	106.5	107.2
	1998	129.4	119.4	112.3	115.2	106.3	108.3
	1999	134.3	118.7	115.9	115.8	102.4	113.1
	2000	140.7	107.6	120.3	116.9	89.4	130.8
	2001	146.2	108.6	122.8	119.0	88.4	134.6
	2002	151.3	118.2	124.3	121.7	95.1	128.0
	2003	154.3	144.5	124.9	123.5	115.7	106.7
Germany	1970	27.6	12.2	60.6	45.5	20.1	226.5
	1975	42.0	27.6	67.8	62.0	40.7	152.3
	1980	60.1	53.5	79.7	75.5	67.1	112.5
	1985	74.9	41.1	84.4	88.7	48.7	182.2
	1990	100.0	100.0	100.0	100.0	100.0	100.0
	1991	108.8	105.9	105.1	103.5	100.8	102.7
	1992	116.8	120.9	107.4	108.7	112.5	96.7
	1993	119.8	117.1	106.3	112.7	110.2	102.3
	1994	125.7	125.2	108.8	115.6	115.1	100.4
	1995	130.5	147.1	110.7	117.9	132.9	88.7
	1996	132.8	142.6	111.5	119.1	127.9	93.1
	1997	135.6	126.3	113.1	119.9	111.7	107.3
	1998	139.7	128.3	115.3	121.2	111.3	108.9
	1999	143.3	126.1	117.6	121.8	107.2	113.6
	2000	147.0	111.9	121.0	121.5	92.5	131.4
	2001	150.2	111.0	122.0	123.1	91.0	135.3
	2002	152.9	118.8	122.2	125.1	97.2	128.6
	2003	154.2	143.8	122.1	126.3	117.8	107.3
Greece	1970	2.5	13.4	59.6	4.3	22.5	18.9
	1975	5.9	29.2	76.1	7.7	38.3	20.2
	1980	15.6	58.1	93.4	16.7	62.2	26.9
	1985	42.6	48.8	94.0	45.3	51.9	87.1
	1990	100.0	100.0	100.0	100.0	100.0	100.0
	1991	123.5	107.4	103.1	119.8	104.2	115.0
	1992	142.8	118.7	103.8	137.5	114.4	120.3
	1993	160.8	111.2	102.2	157.4	108.8	144.6
	1994	182.3	119.1	104.2	175.0	114.3	153.0
	1995	204.4	139.8	106.4	192.1	131.4	146.1
	1996	224.6	147.9	108.9	206.3	135.8	151.9
	1997	248.6	144.3	112.9	220.3	127.9	172.3
	1998	270.4	145.1	116.7	231.8	124.3	186.4
	1999	288.1	149.4	120.6	238.8	123.9	192.8
	2000	311.1	135.0	126.0	246.9	107.1	230.5
	2001	335.0	139.5	131.1	255.5	106.4	240.2
	2002	361.4	158.2	136.0	265.7	116.3	228.4
	2003	390.2	204.8	141.9	275.0	144.4	190.5
Holy See	1970	4.5	8.6	49.6	9.1	17.4	52.2
	1975	10.2	18.7	62.4	16.3	29.9	54.5
	1980	27.8	38.9	76.4	36.4	50.9	71.5
	1985	59.4	37.3	83.8	70.9	44.5	159.4
	1990	100.0	100.0	100.0	100.0	100.0	100.0
	1991	109.5	105.7	101.8	107.6	103.9	103.5
	1992	115.4	112.2	102.6	112.5	109.3	102.9

Table 7. Implicit Price Deflators of Gross Domestic Product in US Dollars and in National Currency

(Index numbers 1990 = 100)

Region, country or area and currency unit	Year	GDP in Current Prices: National Currency (1)	GDP in Current Prices: US Dollars (2)	GDP at Constant Prices (3)	GDP Implicit Price Deflators: National Currency (4)	GDP Implicit Price Deflators: US Dollars (5)	Exchange Rates (6)
	1993	118.9	90.5	101.7	116.9	89.0	131.3
	1994	125.6	93.3	103.8	121.0	89.9	134.6
	1995	135.7	99.8	106.8	127.0	93.4	136.0
	1996	144.4	112.1	107.9	133.7	103.9	128.8
	1997	151.0	106.2	110.3	136.9	96.3	142.1
	1998	158.0	109.0	112.3	140.7	97.1	144.9
	1999	163.3	107.6	114.3	142.9	94.2	151.7
	2000	172.1	98.1	118.0	145.8	83.1	175.4
	2001	180.0	99.7	120.2	149.8	83.0	180.6
	2002	185.8	108.2	120.7	153.9	89.6	171.7
	2003	192.0	134.1	121.1	158.5	110.7	143.2
Hungary	1970	16.3	17.2	56.2	29.0	30.6	94.9
	1975	23.6	33.9	76.1	31.0	44.6	69.6
	1980	35.3	68.5	89.3	39.5	76.7	51.5
	1985	50.6	63.8	97.4	51.9	65.4	79.3
	1990	100.0	100.0	100.0	100.0	100.0	100.0
	1991	110.5	93.4	88.1	125.4	106.1	118.2
	1992	130.1	104.1	85.4	152.4	121.9	125.0
	1993	156.9	107.9	84.9	184.8	127.0	145.5
	1994	193.0	116.0	87.4	220.8	132.7	166.4
	1995	246.0	123.7	88.7	277.2	139.4	198.8
	1996	302.0	125.1	89.9	335.9	139.1	241.5
	1997	374.2	126.6	94.0	398.0	134.7	295.5
	1998	442.0	130.3	98.6	448.3	132.2	339.2
	1999	499.2	133.0	102.7	486.1	129.5	375.2
	2000	577.1	129.3	108.0	534.2	119.7	446.4
	2001	650.6	143.5	112.2	579.9	127.9	453.3
	2002	733.6	179.8	116.1	632.0	154.9	408.0
	2003	813.8	229.3	119.4	681.3	192.0	354.9
Iceland	1970	0.1	8.4	41.3	0.3	20.4	1.5
	1975	0.6	22.4	56.3	1.1	39.9	2.6
	1980	4.4	53.9	76.3	5.8	70.7	8.2
	1985	33.2	46.6	85.5	38.8	54.5	71.2
	1990	100.0	100.0	100.0	100.0	100.0	100.0
	1991	108.2	106.9	100.1	108.1	106.8	101.2
	1992	108.1	109.5	96.8	111.7	113.2	98.7
	1993	111.4	96.1	97.7	114.1	98.4	116.0
	1994	118.4	98.6	101.7	116.4	97.0	120.0
	1995	121.9	109.8	101.8	119.7	107.9	111.0
	1996	130.8	114.6	107.0	122.2	107.1	114.1
	1997	141.6	116.4	112.2	126.2	103.7	121.7
	1998	156.8	128.8	118.4	132.4	108.7	121.7
	1999	168.0	135.3	123.3	136.2	109.7	124.1
	2000	182.6	135.4	130.3	140.1	103.9	134.9
	2001	205.4	122.9	134.0	153.3	91.7	167.2
	2002	214.7	136.5	133.2	161.2	102.5	157.3
	2003	222.4	169.0	138.5	160.6	122.0	131.6
Ireland	1970	6.1	8.9	44.1	13.9	20.2	68.9
	1975	14.4	19.2	56.1	25.6	34.3	74.8
	1980	35.5	44.1	70.1	50.7	63.0	80.5
	1985	67.5	43.1	79.5	84.9	54.3	156.4
	1990	100.0	100.0	100.0	100.0	100.0	100.0
	1991	103.8	101.0	101.9	101.8	99.1	102.8
	1992	110.3	113.4	105.3	104.7	107.7	97.2
	1993	119.1	106.3	108.2	110.1	98.3	112.0
	1994	128.1	115.8	114.4	111.9	101.2	110.6
	1995	145.0	140.5	125.7	115.3	111.8	103.2
	1996	159.9	154.7	135.8	117.8	113.9	103.4
	1997	184.9	169.4	150.9	122.5	112.3	109.1
	1998	213.5	183.8	163.9	130.3	112.1	116.2
	1999	246.8	201.8	182.4	135.3	110.6	122.3
	2000	283.2	200.3	200.8	141.0	99.7	141.4
	2001	316.0	217.1	213.3	148.2	101.8	145.6
	2002	356.2	257.4	228.0	156.2	112.9	138.4
	2003	375.1	325.0	235.8	159.1	137.8	115.4

Table 7. Implicit Price Deflators of Gross Domestic Product in US Dollars and in National Currency

(Index numbers 1990 = 100)

Region, country or area and currency unit	Year	GDP in Current Prices		GDP at Constant Prices	GDP Implicit Price Deflators		Exchange Rates
		National Currency (1)	US Dollars (2)	(3)	National Currency (4)	US Dollars (5)	(6)
Italy	1970	5.1	9.8	56.1	9.1	17.4	52.2
	1975	10.6	19.4	64.8	16.3	29.9	54.5
	1980	29.1	40.7	79.9	36.4	50.9	71.5
	1985	61.6	38.7	86.9	70.9	44.5	159.4
	1990	100.0	100.0	100.0	100.0	100.0	100.0
	1991	109.1	105.3	101.4	107.6	103.9	103.5
	1992	114.9	111.7	102.2	112.5	109.3	102.9
	1993	118.4	90.1	101.3	116.9	89.0	131.3
	1994	125.2	93.0	103.5	121.0	89.9	134.6
	1995	135.3	99.5	106.5	127.0	93.4	136.0
	1996	144.0	111.8	107.7	133.7	103.9	128.8
	1997	150.4	105.8	109.9	136.9	96.3	142.1
	1998	157.3	108.5	111.8	140.7	97.1	144.9
	1999	162.4	107.1	113.7	142.9	94.2	151.7
	2000	171.0	97.5	117.3	145.8	83.1	175.4
	2001	178.9	99.0	119.4	149.8	83.0	180.6
	2002	184.5	107.4	119.8	153.9	89.6	171.7
	2003	190.4	133.0	120.1	158.5	110.7	143.2
Latvia	1990	100.0	100.0	100.0	100.0	100.0	100.0
	1991	229.5	87.4	89.6	256.2	97.5	262.8
	1992	1 608.9	7.3	58.4	2 756.9	12.5	22 116.1
	1993	2 349.5	11.6	49.7	4 729.1	23.3	20 280.3
	1994	3 271.3	19.5	50.0	6 542.3	38.9	16 809.3
	1995	3 730.6	23.5	49.6	7 521.9	47.5	15 843.3
	1996	4 496.0	27.2	51.4	8 743.4	52.9	16 539.0
	1997	5 236.2	30.0	55.7	9 395.8	53.9	17 444.9
	1998	5 753.0	32.5	58.4	9 854.2	55.6	17 712.7
	1999	6 229.5	35.5	60.0	10 375.9	59.0	17 572.6
	2000	6 964.0	38.2	64.1	10 856.3	59.6	18 213.2
	2001	7 707.6	40.9	69.2	11 132.0	59.0	18 856.4
	2002	8 319.5	44.8	73.4	11 328.7	61.0	18 564.3
	2003	9 404.5	54.8	78.6	11 968.3	69.7	17 161.4
Liechtenstein	1970	24.4	7.8	58.3	41.9	13.3	314.8
	1975	40.2	21.6	64.6	62.2	33.5	185.8
	1980	53.3	44.2	76.6	69.5	57.6	120.6
	1985	72.8	41.2	85.3	85.4	48.3	176.9
	1990	100.0	100.0	100.0	100.0	100.0	100.0
	1991	105.5	102.2	99.6	106.0	102.7	103.2
	1992	108.6	107.3	99.7	108.9	107.6	101.2
	1993	111.4	104.7	99.6	111.8	105.1	106.4
	1994	114.3	116.1	100.6	113.7	115.4	98.5
	1995	117.0	137.4	101.8	114.9	135.0	85.1
	1996	118.8	133.6	103.0	115.4	129.7	89.0
	1997	121.9	116.7	105.9	115.1	110.2	104.5
	1998	126.2	121.0	109.7	115.1	110.3	104.4
	1999	130.6	120.8	112.7	115.9	107.2	108.1
	2000	137.9	113.4	117.6	117.3	96.5	121.6
	2001	142.0	116.9	119.8	118.6	97.6	121.5
	2002	144.5	128.8	121.1	119.3	106.3	112.2
	2003	146.6	151.3	121.6	120.6	124.4	96.9
Lithuania	1990	100.0	100.0	100.0	100.0	100.0	100.0
	1991	309.2	117.7	94.3	327.9	124.8	262.8
	1992	2 539.7	9.5	74.3	3 419.5	12.8	26 617.9
	1993	8 642.5	13.3	62.2	13 890.3	21.3	65 226.2
	1994	12 605.7	21.1	56.1	22 452.7	37.6	59 726.0
	1995	18 479.5	30.8	58.0	31 866.5	53.1	60 060.1
	1996	23 511.6	39.1	60.7	38 732.1	64.5	60 060.1
	1997	28 724.8	47.8	65.0	44 221.5	73.6	60 060.1
	1998	32 479.5	54.1	69.7	46 595.3	77.6	60 060.1
	1999	31 773.3	52.9	68.4	46 428.3	77.3	60 060.1
	2000	33 331.8	55.5	71.2	46 842.4	78.0	60 060.1
	2001	35 419.8	59.0	75.8	46 731.2	77.8	60 060.1
	2002	37 850.9	68.6	80.9	46 759.5	84.7	55 209.6
	2003	40 899.3	89.0	88.2	46 396.2	101.0	45 959.0

Table 7. Implicit Price Deflators of Gross Domestic Product in US Dollars and in National Currency

(Index numbers 1990 = 100)

Region, country or area and currency unit	Year	GDP in Current Prices		GDP at Constant Prices	GDP Implicit Price Deflators		Exchange Rates
		National Currency (1)	US Dollars (2)	(3)	National Currency (4)	US Dollars (5)	(6)
Luxembourg	1970	17.1	11.4	47.8	35.7	23.9	149.6
	1975	26.9	24.4	55.1	48.8	44.3	110.1
	1980	41.2	47.1	61.7	66.8	76.4	87.5
	1985	63.6	35.8	69.7	91.3	51.4	177.7
	1990	100.0	100.0	100.0	100.0	100.0	100.0
	1991	110.6	108.3	108.6	101.8	99.6	102.2
	1992	116.8	121.4	110.6	105.6	109.8	96.2
	1993	129.0	124.6	115.3	111.9	108.1	103.5
	1994	138.7	138.5	119.7	115.9	115.8	100.1
	1995	143.9	163.2	121.4	118.6	134.4	88.2
	1996	151.7	163.8	125.4	121.0	130.5	92.6
	1997	168.7	157.6	135.9	124.2	116.0	107.1
	1998	185.3	170.6	145.2	127.6	117.4	108.6
	1999	204.1	180.2	156.6	130.4	115.1	113.3
	2000	231.6	176.8	170.9	135.5	103.4	131.0
	2001	239.5	177.6	173.0	138.4	102.6	134.9
	2002	244.0	190.2	175.2	139.2	108.5	128.3
	2003	251.0	234.6	177.3	141.5	132.3	107.0
Malta	1970	12.9	9.8	25.2	51.1	39.0	131.1
	1975	22.6	18.6	39.5	57.1	47.2	121.1
	1980	53.3	49.1	68.2	78.2	72.0	108.7
	1985	64.8	43.9	74.2	87.3	59.2	147.6
	1990	100.0	100.0	100.0	100.0	100.0	100.0
	1991	109.8	108.0	106.3	103.4	101.6	101.7
	1992	119.1	118.6	111.2	107.0	106.6	100.4
	1993	127.9	106.4	116.2	110.1	91.5	120.3
	1994	140.0	117.7	122.8	114.0	95.9	118.9
	1995	155.9	140.3	130.6	119.4	107.5	111.1
	1996	163.5	144.1	135.5	120.6	106.4	113.4
	1997	175.3	144.4	142.0	123.5	101.7	121.5
	1998	185.4	151.7	146.9	126.2	103.2	122.2
	1999	198.2	157.9	152.6	129.9	103.5	125.5
	2000	212.0	153.8	159.9	132.6	96.2	137.9
	2001	222.1	156.8	166.1	133.7	94.4	141.6
	2002	227.7	166.8	168.1	135.4	99.3	136.5
	2003	238.7	201.1	172.8	138.1	116.4	118.7
Monaco	1970	10.9	10.7	50.0	21.8	21.4	102.0
	1975	20.6	26.2	60.6	34.0	43.2	78.7
	1980	40.7	52.4	73.2	55.6	71.6	77.6
	1985	69.6	42.2	82.2	84.6	51.3	165.0
	1990	100.0	100.0	100.0	100.0	100.0	100.0
	1991	104.7	101.0	101.7	103.0	99.4	103.6
	1992	109.1	112.2	103.9	105.0	108.0	97.2
	1993	111.4	107.1	103.7	107.4	103.3	104.0
	1994	116.4	114.2	106.5	109.2	107.1	102.0
	1995	121.1	132.1	109.1	111.1	121.2	91.7
	1996	125.1	133.2	111.0	112.7	119.9	93.9
	1997	130.0	121.3	113.9	114.1	106.5	107.2
	1998	136.6	126.1	118.6	115.2	106.3	108.3
	1999	142.6	126.1	123.2	115.8	102.4	113.1
	2000	150.3	115.0	128.6	116.9	89.4	130.8
	2001	157.0	116.6	131.9	119.0	88.4	134.6
	2002	163.2	127.5	134.1	121.7	95.1	128.0
	2003	167.2	156.6	135.4	123.5	115.7	106.7
Netherlands	1970	23.9	12.0	60.1	39.7	20.0	198.8
	1975	43.3	31.2	70.5	61.4	44.2	138.9
	1980	66.0	60.4	80.1	82.3	75.4	109.2
	1985	81.7	44.8	84.8	96.4	52.9	182.4
	1990	100.0	100.0	100.0	100.0	100.0	100.0
	1991	105.3	102.6	102.4	102.9	100.2	102.7
	1992	109.4	113.3	103.9	105.3	109.0	96.6
	1993	112.2	110.0	104.6	107.2	105.1	102.0
	1994	118.0	118.1	107.6	109.7	109.8	99.9
	1995	124.1	140.7	110.9	111.9	126.9	88.2
	1996	129.4	139.7	114.2	113.2	122.3	92.6
	1997	137.0	127.9	118.6	115.5	107.8	107.2

Table 7. Implicit Price Deflators of Gross Domestic Product in US Dollars and in National Currency

(Index numbers 1990 = 100)

Region, country or area and currency unit	Year	GDP in Current Prices: National Currency (1)	GDP in Current Prices: US Dollars (2)	GDP at Constant Prices (3)	GDP Implicit Price Deflators: National Currency (4)	GDP Implicit Price Deflators: US Dollars (5)	Exchange Rates (6)
	1998	145.4	133.5	123.8	117.5	107.8	108.9
	1999	153.6	135.2	128.7	119.3	105.0	113.6
	2000	165.2	125.7	133.2	124.0	94.4	131.4
	2001	176.2	130.3	134.8	130.7	96.6	135.2
	2002	182.6	142.0	135.1	135.1	105.1	128.6
	2003	186.6	174.0	134.1	139.2	129.8	107.2
Norway	1970	12.5	11.0	48.4	25.9	22.7	114.1
	1975	23.4	28.0	61.6	38.0	45.5	83.5
	1980	43.3	54.8	77.3	56.0	70.9	78.9
	1985	75.3	54.8	91.5	82.3	60.0	137.3
	1990	100.0	100.0	100.0	100.0	100.0	100.0
	1991	105.9	102.3	103.6	102.2	98.7	103.6
	1992	108.7	109.5	107.0	101.6	102.3	99.3
	1993	114.3	100.8	110.0	103.9	91.7	113.3
	1994	120.2	106.6	115.7	103.8	92.1	112.7
	1995	129.0	127.4	120.8	106.8	105.5	101.2
	1996	141.3	137.1	127.1	111.1	107.9	103.0
	1997	152.9	135.3	133.7	114.4	101.2	113.0
	1998	155.8	129.2	137.2	113.5	94.2	120.5
	1999	169.7	136.2	140.2	121.0	97.2	124.6
	2000	202.1	143.8	144.1	140.2	99.7	140.6
	2001	210.0	146.2	146.9	143.0	99.5	143.6
	2002	209.2	164.1	148.3	141.1	110.6	127.5
	2003	215.9	190.8	148.8	145.1	128.3	113.1
Poland	1970	0.1	32.9	60.8	0.2	54.0	0.4
	1975	0.2	70.5	97.0	0.3	72.6	0.3
	1980	0.4	89.6	102.9	0.4	87.0	0.5
	1985	1.7	111.1	102.0	1.7	109.0	1.5
	1990	100.0	100.0	100.0	100.0	100.0	100.0
	1991	144.4	129.7	93.0	155.3	139.5	111.3
	1992	205.2	143.0	95.3	215.2	150.0	143.4
	1993	278.0	145.8	98.9	281.2	147.5	190.7
	1994	401.8	168.0	104.1	385.9	161.3	239.2
	1995	549.9	215.4	111.4	493.8	193.5	255.3
	1996	692.2	243.9	118.1	586.3	206.6	283.8
	1997	843.1	244.2	126.1	668.4	193.6	345.2
	1998	988.0	270.1	132.2	747.1	204.2	365.8
	1999	1 097.9	262.9	137.6	797.9	191.1	417.6
	2000	1 222.6	267.2	143.1	854.5	186.8	457.5
	2001	1 286.7	298.6	144.5	890.5	206.6	430.9
	2002	1 321.5	307.7	146.5	902.1	210.0	429.5
	2003	1 377.1	336.4	150.0	918.0	224.2	409.4
Portugal	1970	2.1	10.3	45.7	4.5	22.5	20.2
	1975	4.4	24.6	56.6	7.8	43.4	17.9
	1980	14.7	41.8	72.6	20.2	57.5	35.1
	1985	41.2	34.4	75.9	54.2	45.4	119.5
	1990	100.0	100.0	100.0	100.0	100.0	100.0
	1991	114.9	113.4	104.4	110.1	108.6	101.4
	1992	129.4	136.7	105.5	122.7	129.6	94.7
	1993	136.1	120.7	103.3	131.7	116.8	112.8
	1994	147.5	126.6	104.3	141.3	121.4	116.4
	1995	159.1	150.1	108.8	146.2	137.9	106.0
	1996	169.7	156.8	112.7	150.6	139.2	108.2
	1997	183.0	148.8	117.1	156.3	127.1	123.0
	1998	198.7	157.3	122.5	162.2	128.4	126.3
	1999	212.6	161.0	127.2	167.2	126.7	132.0
	2000	227.4	149.0	131.8	172.5	113.0	152.6
	2001	242.2	154.1	134.0	180.7	115.0	157.2
	2002	254.4	170.2	134.6	189.0	126.5	149.4
	2003	256.9	206.2	132.8	193.4	155.2	124.6
Republic of Moldova	1990	100.0	100.0	100.0	100.0	100.0	100.0
	1991	204.2	77.7	97.6	209.2	79.6	262.8
	1992	1 513.8	2.4	80.5	1 880.0	3.0	62 222.2
	1993	14 362.0	2.6	57.2	25 121.9	4.6	546 546.5
	1994	37 356.5	5.8	39.5	94 592.5	14.8	641 141.1

Table 7. Implicit Price Deflators of Gross Domestic Product in US Dollars and in National Currency

(Index numbers 1990 = 100)

Region, country or area and currency unit	Year	GDP in Current Prices		GDP at Constant Prices	GDP Implicit Price Deflators		Exchange Rates
		National Currency (1)	US Dollars (2)	(3)	National Currency (4)	US Dollars (5)	(6)
	1995	51 101.7	7.6	38.9	131 203.7	19.4	675 045.0
	1996	61 495.3	8.9	36.7	167 750.0	24.3	691 363.9
	1997	70 322.6	10.1	37.3	188 722.0	27.2	694 231.7
	1998	71 940.9	8.9	34.8	206 578.3	25.6	806 411.4
	1999	97 173.5	6.2	33.7	288 758.2	18.3	1 578 950.2
	2000	126 337.5	6.8	34.4	367 674.9	19.7	1 866 999.5
	2001	150 248.4	7.8	36.5	411 962.2	21.3	1 931 702.9
	2002	177 885.6	8.7	39.3	452 407.5	22.2	2 037 612.2
	2003	215 275.2	10.3	41.8	515 106.7	24.6	2 093 826.3
Romania	1970	26.5	37.5	38.8	68.2	96.5	70.7
	1975	44.8	50.2	66.4	67.4	75.6	89.2
	1980	56.5	70.4	95.2	59.4	74.0	80.2
	1985	72.7	95.1	110.6	65.7	86.0	76.4
	1990	100.0	100.0	100.0	100.0	100.0	100.0
	1991	256.9	75.4	87.1	295.0	86.6	340.5
	1992	702.8	51.2	79.4	884.6	64.4	1 372.8
	1993	2 335.6	68.9	80.7	2 895.5	85.5	3 388.2
	1994	5 802.1	78.6	83.8	6 921.0	93.8	7 378.2
	1995	8 408.9	92.8	89.8	9 362.2	103.3	9 064.1
	1996	12 696.8	92.3	93.4	13 599.3	98.9	13 749.1
	1997	29 483.6	92.3	87.7	33 614.1	105.2	31 954.0
	1998	43 573.8	110.1	83.5	52 192.5	131.9	39 566.4
	1999	63 616.0	93.1	82.5	77 085.4	112.8	68 352.3
	2000	93 696.1	96.8	84.3	111 145.9	114.8	96 775.3
	2001	136 065.9	105.0	89.1	152 652.5	117.8	129 550.1
	2002	176 284.3	119.6	93.5	188 622.0	128.0	147 357.8
	2003	220 408.7	148.9	97.9	225 144.3	152.1	148 002.6
Russian Federation	1990	100.0	100.0	100.0	100.0	100.0	100.0
	1991	217.1	82.6	95.0	228.5	87.0	262.8
	1992	2 950.2	8.8	81.2	3 632.2	10.9	33 348.3
	1993	26.6	17.9	74.2	35.9	24.1	148.9
	1994	94.8	28.8	64.7	146.4	44.5	328.9
	1995	221.8	32.4	62.1	357.2	52.2	684.6
	1996	311.7	40.5	59.8	520.8	67.7	768.9
	1997	363.6	41.9	60.7	599.3	69.0	868.6
	1998	408.2	28.0	57.4	710.8	48.8	1 457.2
	1999	748.7	20.3	61.1	1 225.9	33.2	3 696.7
	2000	1 134.1	26.9	67.2	1 687.3	39.9	4 223.6
	2001	1 388.3	31.7	70.6	1 965.5	44.9	4 379.7
	2002	1 681.8	35.7	73.9	2 274.9	48.3	4 707.0
	2003	2 065.3	44.8	79.3	2 603.0	56.5	4 608.4
San Marino	1970	5.1	9.8	56.1	9.1	17.4	52.2
	1975	10.6	19.4	64.8	16.3	29.9	54.5
	1980	29.1	40.7	79.9	36.4	50.9	71.5
	1985	61.6	38.7	86.9	70.9	44.5	159.4
	1990	100.0	100.0	100.0	100.0	100.0	100.0
	1991	109.1	105.3	101.4	107.6	103.9	103.5
	1992	114.9	111.7	102.2	112.5	109.3	102.9
	1993	118.4	90.1	101.3	116.9	89.0	131.3
	1994	125.2	93.0	103.5	121.0	89.9	134.6
	1995	135.3	99.5	106.5	127.0	93.4	136.0
	1996	144.0	111.8	107.7	133.7	103.9	128.8
	1997	150.4	105.8	109.9	136.9	96.3	142.1
	1998	164.7	113.6	118.1	139.4	96.2	144.9
	1999	182.3	120.2	128.8	141.6	93.3	151.7
	2000	192.0	109.4	132.8	144.5	82.4	175.4
	2001	200.8	111.2	135.2	148.5	82.2	180.6
	2002	207.1	120.6	135.7	152.6	88.9	171.7
	2003	213.7	149.3	136.1	157.1	109.7	143.2
Serbia and Montenegro	1990	100.0	100.0	100.0	100.0	100.0	100.0
	1991	157.4	90.7	88.4	178.1	102.6	173.5
	1992	131.0	128.9	63.7	205.6	202.3	101.6
	1993	70.1	44.7	44.1	158.9	101.2	156.9
	1994	69.9	43.7	45.2	154.5	96.6	159.9
	1995	128.7	85.3	48.0	268.1	177.8	150.8

Table 7. Implicit Price Deflators of Gross Domestic Product in US Dollars and in National Currency

(Index numbers 1990 = 100)

Region, country or area and currency unit	Year	GDP in Current Prices: National Currency (1)	GDP in Current Prices: US Dollars (2)	GDP at Constant Prices (3)	GDP Implicit Price Deflators: National Currency (4)	GDP Implicit Price Deflators: US Dollars (5)	Exchange Rates (6)
	1996	232.3	53.2	50.8	457.1	104.7	436.7
	1997	320.0	63.9	54.6	586.2	117.2	500.4
	1998	434.2	51.6	55.9	776.0	92.2	841.7
	1999	559.2	59.1	42.3	1 322.8	139.8	946.4
	2000	1 116.8	36.5	45.0	2 483.0	81.1	3 062.7
	2001	2 258.4	38.7	47.5	4 759.3	81.6	5 830.0
	2002	2 946.4	51.6	49.3	5 981.8	104.7	5 713.2
	2003	3 273.4	64.2	49.7	6 580.0	129.1	5 095.8
Slovakia	1980	70.4	88.6	93.8	75.1	94.4	79.5
	1985	83.5	87.4	93.3	89.4	93.6	95.5
	1990	100.0	100.0	100.0	100.0	100.0	100.0
	1991	115.0	70.0	85.5	134.6	81.9	164.2
	1992	119.5	75.9	79.8	149.7	95.1	157.4
	1993	140.5	82.0	81.3	172.7	100.8	171.4
	1994	169.3	94.8	86.4	195.9	109.8	178.5
	1995	196.9	118.9	91.4	215.3	130.1	165.5
	1996	218.0	127.7	97.1	224.7	131.6	170.8
	1997	243.4	130.0	101.5	239.7	128.0	187.3
	1998	266.9	136.0	105.8	252.2	128.5	196.3
	1999	288.3	125.1	107.4	268.5	116.5	230.4
	2000	319.0	124.4	109.6	291.2	113.5	256.5
	2001	344.9	128.0	113.7	303.3	112.6	269.4
	2002	374.4	148.3	118.7	315.5	124.9	252.5
	2003	408.4	199.4	123.7	330.2	161.2	204.9
Slovenia	1990	100.0	100.0	100.0	100.0	100.0	100.0
	1991	177.6	72.9	91.1	194.9	80.0	243.6
	1992	517.4	72.0	86.1	600.7	83.7	718.1
	1993	729.4	72.9	88.6	823.5	82.3	1 000.4
	1994	941.7	82.8	93.3	1 009.5	88.7	1 137.9
	1995	1 190.3	113.7	97.1	1 225.6	117.1	1 047.0
	1996	1 371.2	114.7	100.8	1 359.8	113.7	1 195.8
	1997	1 557.8	110.4	105.3	1 479.0	104.8	1 410.7
	1998	1 739.3	118.5	109.2	1 592.1	108.5	1 467.6
	1999	1 951.5	121.5	115.7	1 686.8	105.0	1 605.7
	2000	2 145.9	109.1	120.4	1 782.1	90.6	1 966.9
	2001	2 409.1	112.3	123.9	1 945.0	90.7	2 144.4
	2002	2 681.3	126.3	127.5	2 102.8	99.1	2 122.3
	2003	2 888.7	157.9	130.8	2 208.1	120.7	1 829.6
Spain	1970	5.2	7.6	52.4	10.0	14.6	68.7
	1975	12.0	21.4	67.9	17.7	31.5	56.3
	1980	30.5	43.4	74.9	40.7	57.9	70.3
	1985	56.2	33.7	80.3	70.0	42.0	166.8
	1990	100.0	100.0	100.0	100.0	100.0	100.0
	1991	109.7	107.6	102.5	106.9	104.9	101.9
	1992	118.1	117.6	103.5	114.1	113.6	100.4
	1993	122.2	97.9	102.4	119.3	95.5	124.8
	1994	130.0	98.9	104.9	123.9	94.3	131.4
	1995	140.1	114.6	107.8	130.0	106.3	122.3
	1996	148.6	119.6	110.4	134.6	108.3	124.3
	1997	158.2	110.1	114.8	137.7	95.9	143.6
	1998	169.0	115.3	119.8	141.0	96.2	146.6
	1999	181.0	118.1	124.9	144.9	94.6	153.2
	2000	195.2	110.2	130.1	150.0	84.6	177.2
	2001	209.1	114.6	133.8	156.2	85.6	182.4
	2002	222.8	128.5	136.6	163.2	94.1	173.4
	2003	237.8	164.4	139.9	170.0	117.6	144.6
Sweden	1970	12.7	14.5	66.3	19.1	21.8	87.4
	1975	22.1	31.5	75.3	29.3	41.8	70.2
	1980	38.6	54.0	80.5	48.0	67.1	71.5
	1985	63.3	43.5	88.3	71.7	49.3	145.4
	1990	100.0	100.0	100.0	100.0	100.0	100.0
	1991	107.8	105.5	98.9	109.0	106.7	102.2
	1992	107.6	109.3	97.6	110.2	112.0	98.4
	1993	108.6	82.6	95.7	113.5	86.3	131.5
	1994	115.8	88.8	99.7	116.1	89.1	130.4

Table 7. Implicit Price Deflators of Gross Domestic Product in US Dollars and in National Currency

(Index numbers 1990 = 100)

Region, country or area and currency unit	Year	GDP in Current Prices: National Currency (1)	GDP in Current Prices: US Dollars (2)	GDP at Constant Prices (3)	GDP Implicit Price Deflators: National Currency (4)	GDP Implicit Price Deflators: US Dollars (5)	Exchange Rates (6)
	1995	124.5	103.3	103.7	120.1	99.6	120.5
	1996	127.7	112.7	105.1	121.5	107.3	113.3
	1997	132.8	103.0	107.6	123.4	95.7	129.0
	1998	138.7	103.3	111.6	124.4	92.6	134.3
	1999	146.1	104.7	116.7	125.2	89.7	139.6
	2000	154.4	99.8	121.7	126.9	82.0	154.8
	2001	159.4	91.4	122.8	129.8	74.4	174.5
	2002	164.8	100.2	125.2	131.6	80.0	164.5
	2003	171.3	125.4	127.2	134.7	98.6	136.6
Switzerland	1970	30.2	9.6	72.1	41.9	13.3	314.8
	1975	46.7	25.1	75.1	62.2	33.5	185.8
	1980	56.8	47.1	81.6	69.5	57.6	120.6
	1985	74.8	42.3	87.5	85.4	48.3	176.9
	1990	100.0	100.0	100.0	100.0	100.0	100.0
	1991	105.2	101.9	99.2	106.0	102.7	103.2
	1992	107.9	106.6	99.1	108.9	107.6	101.2
	1993	110.2	103.6	98.6	111.8	105.1	106.4
	1994	112.7	114.4	99.1	113.7	115.4	98.5
	1995	114.5	134.5	99.6	114.9	135.0	85.1
	1996	115.3	129.6	99.9	115.4	129.7	89.0
	1997	117.0	112.0	101.7	115.1	110.2	104.5
	1998	119.8	114.7	104.1	115.1	110.3	104.4
	1999	122.4	113.2	105.6	115.9	107.2	108.1
	2000	127.9	105.2	109.1	117.3	96.5	121.6
	2001	130.4	107.4	110.0	118.6	97.6	121.5
	2002	131.5	117.2	110.2	119.3	106.3	112.2
	2003	132.3	136.5	109.7	120.6	124.4	96.9
TFYR Macedonia	1990	100.0	100.0	100.0	100.0	100.0	100.0
	1991	181.8	104.8	93.8	193.8	111.7	173.5
	1992	2 330.8	51.8	87.7	2 658.7	59.1	4 497.3
	1993	11 692.7	56.9	81.1	14 413.9	70.1	20 551.3
	1994	28 934.6	75.7	79.7	36 306.8	95.0	38 225.1
	1995	33 502.2	100.1	78.8	42 511.9	127.0	33 470.4
	1996	34 870.4	98.7	79.7	43 729.9	123.8	35 325.2
	1997	36 762.6	83.2	80.9	45 448.9	102.9	44 180.6
	1998	38 533.4	80.1	83.6	46 071.6	95.7	48 119.6
	1999	41 306.3	82.2	87.2	47 350.9	94.2	50 275.5
	2000	46 717.2	80.2	91.2	51 247.5	88.0	58 229.3
	2001	46 213.6	76.9	87.1	53 083.9	88.3	60 114.1
	2002	47 211.5	83.0	87.8	53 746.3	94.5	56 856.2
	2003	49 114.1	102.3	90.6	54 231.1	113.0	47 996.3
Ukraine	1990	100.0	100.0	100.0	100.0	100.0	100.0
	1991	176.5	67.2	88.2	200.0	76.1	262.8
	1992	2 958.8	8.2	79.4	3 725.9	10.3	36 036.0
	1993	87 217.6	12.8	68.2	127 880.3	18.8	680 555.6
	1994	708 100.0	14.4	52.6	1 347 147.2	27.4	4 917 630.1
	1995	3 206 847.1	14.5	46.2	6 944 833.5	31.4	22 118 243.2
	1996	4 795 235.3	17.5	41.5	11 544 134.2	42.0	27 469 497.9
	1997	5 492 058.8	19.6	40.3	13 628 947.9	48.8	27 952 827.8
	1998	6 034 882.4	16.4	39.5	15 272 907.2	41.5	36 779 904.9
	1999	7 673 058.8	12.4	39.5	19 450 038.6	31.4	62 018 643.6
	2000	10 004 117.6	12.2	41.8	23 948 192.7	29.3	81 685 185.2
	2001	12 011 176.5	14.9	45.6	26 322 347.6	32.6	80 663 038.0
	2002	12 996 000.0	16.2	47.3	27 478 283.2	34.4	79 979 354.4
	2003	14 833 882.4	18.5	51.3	28 907 130.6	36.1	80 070 395.4
United Kingdom	1970	9.2	12.5	63.5	14.6	19.7	74.0
	1975	19.0	23.6	70.5	26.9	33.5	80.3
	1980	41.4	54.2	77.1	53.7	70.3	76.4
	1985	63.7	46.0	85.1	74.8	54.1	138.4
	1990	100.0	100.0	100.0	100.0	100.0	100.0
	1991	105.2	104.5	98.6	106.6	105.9	100.7
	1992	109.6	108.3	98.8	110.9	109.6	101.2
	1993	115.3	97.4	101.1	114.0	96.3	118.4
	1994	122.3	105.4	105.6	115.8	99.8	116.0
	1995	129.0	114.7	108.6	118.8	105.6	112.5

Table 7. Implicit Price Deflators of Gross Domestic Product in US Dollars and in National Currency

(Index numbers 1990 = 100)

Region, country or area and currency unit	Year	GDP in Current Prices: National Currency (1)	GDP in Current Prices: US Dollars (2)	GDP at Constant Prices (3)	GDP Implicit Price Deflators: National Currency (4)	GDP Implicit Price Deflators: US Dollars (5)	Exchange Rates (6)
	1996	137.0	120.3	111.5	122.8	107.9	113.8
	1997	145.5	134.2	115.2	126.3	116.5	108.5
	1998	154.2	143.8	118.8	129.8	121.1	107.2
	1999	162.2	147.8	122.1	132.8	121.0	109.7
	2000	170.7	145.4	126.7	134.7	114.8	117.4
	2001	178.4	144.6	129.4	137.8	111.7	123.3
	2002	187.3	158.1	131.7	142.3	120.1	118.5
	2003	197.7	181.8	134.7	146.7	134.9	108.8
OCEANIA							
Australia	1970	9.6	13.8	55.1	17.5	25.1	69.7
	1975	20.0	33.5	63.9	31.2	52.3	59.6
	1980	36.6	53.4	74.1	49.4	72.1	68.6
	1985	62.4	55.8	85.9	72.6	65.0	111.8
	1990	100.0	100.0	100.0	100.0	100.0	100.0
	1991	102.2	102.0	100.3	101.9	101.7	100.2
	1992	107.1	100.8	103.9	103.1	97.0	106.3
	1993	112.4	97.9	108.0	104.0	90.6	114.8
	1994	118.5	111.0	112.6	105.3	98.6	106.8
	1995	126.4	120.0	117.3	107.7	102.3	105.3
	1996	133.2	133.5	121.7	109.4	109.7	99.8
	1997	141.1	134.1	127.2	110.9	105.5	105.2
	1998	148.8	119.7	133.9	111.1	89.4	124.3
	1999	158.0	130.6	139.3	113.4	93.8	121.0
	2000	168.2	124.9	141.7	118.7	88.2	134.6
	2001	179.2	118.7	147.3	121.7	80.6	150.9
	2002	189.2	131.7	151.3	125.0	87.0	143.7
	2003	202.8	168.5	156.6	129.5	107.6	120.4
Cook Islands	1970	9.9	18.5	103.7	9.5	17.9	53.3
	1975	13.1	26.3	76.0	17.2	34.6	49.7
	1980	22.6	36.8	73.8	30.6	49.9	61.3
	1985	52.3	43.3	85.0	61.5	51.0	120.7
	1990	100.0	100.0	100.0	100.0	100.0	100.0
	1991	112.8	109.0	107.1	105.3	101.8	103.4
	1992	125.2	112.7	113.5	110.2	99.3	111.1
	1993	139.1	126.0	118.0	117.9	106.8	110.4
	1994	150.5	149.6	122.6	122.8	122.0	100.6
	1995	144.8	159.2	117.2	123.5	135.8	90.9
	1996	139.7	160.9	117.2	119.2	137.3	86.8
	1997	132.5	146.9	114.2	116.0	128.6	90.2
	1998	143.7	129.0	113.5	126.7	113.6	111.5
	1999	156.0	138.4	116.5	133.9	118.8	112.7
	2000	181.5	138.2	132.9	136.5	104.0	131.3
	2001	206.9	145.8	139.6	148.2	104.5	141.9
	2002	225.3	174.7	144.8	155.6	120.6	129.0
	2003	236.4	230.0	147.0	160.8	156.5	102.8
Fiji	1970	9.7	16.5	49.3	19.7	33.4	58.8
	1975	28.4	51.1	66.3	42.8	77.2	55.5
	1980	49.7	90.0	79.7	62.3	112.8	55.2
	1985	66.5	85.3	83.8	79.3	101.8	77.9
	1990	100.0	100.0	100.0	100.0	100.0	100.0
	1991	103.1	103.5	97.3	106.0	106.4	99.6
	1992	116.4	114.7	103.3	112.7	111.0	101.5
	1993	127.5	122.4	106.0	120.3	115.6	104.1
	1994	135.0	136.5	111.3	121.2	122.6	98.9
	1995	141.4	148.9	114.1	123.9	130.5	95.0
	1996	149.8	158.1	117.6	127.3	134.4	94.8
	1997	154.5	158.5	116.6	132.5	135.9	97.5
	1998	159.3	118.7	118.3	134.6	100.3	134.2
	1999	185.1	139.2	129.7	142.7	107.3	133.0
	2000	177.7	123.6	126.1	140.9	98.1	143.7
	2001	192.4	125.1	130.9	147.0	95.6	153.7
	2002	205.6	139.3	136.6	150.5	101.9	147.7
	2003	221.7	173.2	143.7	154.3	120.5	128.0

Table 7. Implicit Price Deflators of Gross Domestic Product in US Dollars and in National Currency

(Index numbers 1990 = 100)

Region, country or area and currency unit	Year	GDP in Current Prices		GDP at Constant Prices	GDP Implicit Price Deflators		Exchange Rates
		National Currency (1)	US Dollars (2)	(3)	National Currency (4)	US Dollars (5)	(6)
French Polynesia	1970	7.4	7.3	34.2	21.6	21.2	102.0
	1975	15.5	19.7	44.2	35.1	44.6	78.7
	1980	33.4	43.0	56.0	59.6	76.8	77.6
	1985	78.2	47.4	78.5	99.6	60.3	165.0
	1990	100.0	100.0	100.0	100.0	100.0	100.0
	1991	105.2	101.6	103.9	101.3	97.7	103.6
	1992	108.3	111.4	107.9	100.5	103.3	97.2
	1993	113.5	118.7	111.4	101.9	106.6	95.6
	1994	130.2	127.7	125.7	103.6	101.6	102.0
	1995	128.6	140.3	122.8	104.8	114.3	91.7
	1996	132.2	140.7	124.8	105.9	112.8	93.9
	1997	135.5	126.4	126.2	107.3	100.1	107.2
	1998	138.8	128.1	127.6	108.8	100.4	108.3
	1999	142.9	126.4	130.9	109.1	96.5	113.1
	2000	147.1	112.5	134.4	109.5	83.7	130.7
	2001	151.3	112.3	137.3	110.2	81.8	134.7
	2002	155.4	121.3	139.9	111.1	86.7	128.1
	2003	159.6	149.5	142.6	111.9	104.8	106.8
Kiribati	1970	35.2	50.5	124.3	28.3	40.6	69.7
	1975	115.6	193.9	252.2	45.8	76.9	59.6
	1980	67.4	98.3	87.4	77.1	112.5	68.6
	1985	83.8	74.9	92.0	91.1	81.5	111.8
	1990	100.0	100.0	100.0	100.0	100.0	100.0
	1991	119.4	119.1	106.9	111.7	111.4	100.2
	1992	126.8	119.3	105.2	120.5	113.4	106.3
	1993	133.5	116.3	107.0	124.8	108.7	114.8
	1994	149.3	139.9	115.9	128.8	120.7	106.8
	1995	170.5	161.9	122.2	139.5	132.5	105.3
	1996	174.9	175.3	125.8	139.0	139.3	99.8
	1997	182.1	173.1	133.0	136.9	130.2	105.2
	1998	201.2	161.9	139.6	144.1	116.0	124.3
	1999	228.9	189.2	158.3	144.6	119.5	121.0
	2000	228.7	169.8	160.8	142.2	105.6	134.6
	2001	250.9	166.2	163.7	153.2	101.5	150.9
	2002	269.8	187.8	165.2	163.3	113.7	143.7
	2003	290.4	241.3	169.4	171.5	142.5	120.4
Marshall Islands	1970	10.7	10.7	29.1	36.8	36.8	100.0
	1975	21.3	21.3	46.5	45.7	45.7	100.0
	1980	34.0	34.0	47.9	71.1	71.1	100.0
	1985	55.9	55.9	61.1	91.5	91.5	100.0
	1990	100.0	100.0	100.0	100.0	100.0	100.0
	1991	105.1	105.1	101.1	104.0	104.0	100.0
	1992	116.0	116.0	101.2	114.7	114.7	100.0
	1993	126.7	126.7	105.3	120.4	120.4	100.0
	1994	137.7	137.7	101.2	136.0	136.0	100.0
	1995	153.2	153.2	111.2	137.8	137.8	100.0
	1996	141.3	141.3	93.6	151.0	151.0	100.0
	1997	134.2	134.2	84.8	158.3	158.3	100.0
	1998	138.6	138.6	85.7	161.7	161.7	100.0
	1999	141.0	141.0	85.8	164.4	164.4	100.0
	2000	142.0	142.0	85.0	167.1	167.1	100.0
	2001	148.1	148.1	86.4	171.4	171.4	100.0
	2002	154.0	154.0	89.9	171.4	171.4	100.0
	2003	162.6	162.6	92.6	175.6	175.6	100.0
Micronesia (Federated States of)	1970	15.8	15.8	35.2	44.9	44.9	100.0
	1975	36.7	36.7	56.3	65.2	65.2	100.0
	1980	51.1	51.1	57.9	88.1	88.1	100.0
	1985	67.4	67.4	83.7	80.6	80.6	100.0
	1990	100.0	100.0	100.0	100.0	100.0	100.0
	1991	112.0	112.0	108.3	103.4	103.4	100.0
	1992	118.6	118.6	111.5	106.4	106.4	100.0
	1993	133.5	133.5	122.1	109.3	109.3	100.0
	1994	134.6	134.6	119.6	112.5	112.5	100.0
	1995	142.2	142.2	123.2	115.4	115.4	100.0
	1996	143.8	143.8	121.0	118.9	118.9	100.0
	1997	139.3	139.3	114.7	121.4	121.4	100.0

Table 7. Implicit Price Deflators of Gross Domestic Product in US Dollars and in National Currency

(Index numbers 1990 = 100)

Region, country or area and currency unit	Year	GDP in Current Prices: National Currency (1)	GDP in Current Prices: US Dollars (2)	GDP at Constant Prices (3)	GDP Implicit Price Deflators: National Currency (4)	GDP Implicit Price Deflators: US Dollars (5)	Exchange Rates (6)
	1998	138.4	138.4	112.3	123.2	123.2	100.0
	1999	143.4	143.4	113.3	126.5	126.5	100.0
	2000	151.1	151.1	115.8	130.6	130.6	100.0
	2001	157.3	157.3	117.5	133.9	133.9	100.0
	2002	158.5	158.5	118.4	133.9	133.9	100.0
	2003	164.8	164.8	121.3	135.9	135.9	100.0
Nauru	1970	17.7	25.5	34.8	51.0	73.2	69.7
	1975	29.2	49.0	48.4	60.4	101.3	59.6
	1980	48.1	70.2	67.4	71.4	104.2	68.6
	1985	79.2	70.9	93.8	84.5	75.6	111.8
	1990	100.0	100.0	100.0	100.0	100.0	100.0
	1991	99.5	99.3	96.3	103.4	103.2	100.2
	1992	95.3	89.7	89.2	106.8	100.5	106.3
	1993	91.2	79.5	82.7	110.4	96.1	114.8
	1994	87.3	81.8	76.6	114.0	106.8	106.8
	1995	83.6	79.4	71.0	117.8	111.9	105.3
	1996	80.1	80.3	65.8	121.7	122.0	99.8
	1997	76.6	72.9	61.0	125.7	119.5	105.2
	1998	78.2	63.0	59.8	130.7	105.2	124.3
	1999	79.9	66.0	58.7	136.0	112.4	121.0
	2000	86.6	64.3	58.1	148.9	110.6	134.6
	2001	92.1	61.0	57.7	159.6	105.7	150.9
	2002	99.0	68.9	58.2	170.1	118.4	143.7
	2003	106.6	88.5	59.7	178.6	148.4	120.4
New Caledonia	1970	15.3	15.0	58.0	26.3	25.8	102.0
	1975	25.4	32.3	68.4	37.1	47.2	78.7
	1980	36.3	46.7	67.4	53.8	69.3	77.6
	1985	55.8	33.8	66.8	83.4	50.6	165.0
	1990	100.0	100.0	100.0	100.0	100.0	100.0
	1991	108.7	104.9	104.9	103.6	100.0	103.6
	1992	112.4	115.6	105.4	106.6	109.6	97.2
	1993	116.0	121.4	106.0	109.5	114.5	95.6
	1994	122.5	120.1	108.7	112.6	110.5	102.0
	1995	131.5	143.4	115.2	114.1	124.5	91.7
	1996	134.0	142.6	115.7	115.8	123.2	93.9
	1997	139.5	130.1	118.1	118.1	110.2	107.2
	1998	135.3	124.9	114.3	118.4	109.3	108.3
	1999	136.6	120.8	115.3	118.5	104.7	113.1
	2000	138.7	106.0	117.7	117.8	90.0	130.8
	2001	135.1	100.3	116.5	116.0	86.2	134.7
	2002	157.3	122.8	117.3	134.1	104.7	128.1
	2003	161.5	151.3	117.2	137.9	129.1	106.8
New Zealand	1970	8.0	15.0	69.8	11.5	21.5	53.3
	1975	15.5	31.2	85.5	18.1	36.5	49.7
	1980	32.1	52.4	83.0	38.7	63.1	61.3
	1985	63.2	52.4	97.1	65.1	53.9	120.7
	1990	100.0	100.0	100.0	100.0	100.0	100.0
	1991	99.7	96.4	98.7	101.1	97.7	103.4
	1992	103.0	92.7	99.8	103.2	92.9	111.1
	1993	111.5	101.0	106.2	105.0	95.1	110.4
	1994	119.4	118.7	111.8	106.8	106.2	100.6
	1995	126.8	139.4	116.4	108.9	119.7	90.9
	1996	133.0	153.2	120.5	110.4	127.1	86.8
	1997	137.8	152.7	122.3	112.7	124.9	90.2
	1998	139.5	125.1	122.8	113.6	101.9	111.5
	1999	146.4	129.9	128.9	113.6	100.8	112.7
	2000	155.6	118.5	132.3	117.6	89.6	131.3
	2001	167.2	117.8	136.9	122.1	86.0	141.9
	2002	172.6	133.8	142.9	120.8	93.6	129.0
	2003	176.7	171.9	146.7	120.4	117.2	102.8
Palau	1970	20.4	20.4	126.5	16.1	16.1	100.0
	1975	78.4	78.4	256.6	30.6	30.6	100.0
	1980	33.9	33.9	88.9	38.1	38.1	100.0
	1985	44.7	44.7	75.6	59.2	59.2	100.0
	1990	100.0	100.0	100.0	100.0	100.0	100.0

Table 7. Implicit Price Deflators of Gross Domestic Product in US Dollars and in National Currency

(Index numbers 1990 = 100)

Region, country or area and currency unit	Year	GDP In Current Prices: National Currency (1)	GDP In Current Prices: US Dollars (2)	GDP at Constant Prices (3)	GDP Implicit Price Deflators: National Currency (4)	GDP Implicit Price Deflators: US Dollars (5)	Exchange Rates (6)
	1991	111.4	111.4	103.9	107.2	107.2	100.0
	1992	118.4	118.4	105.5	112.2	112.2	100.0
	1993	117.8	117.8	107.6	109.5	109.5	100.0
	1994	129.2	129.2	115.5	111.9	111.9	100.0
	1995	142.3	142.3	128.1	111.1	111.1	100.0
	1996	161.7	161.7	141.4	114.3	114.3	100.0
	1997	169.2	169.2	144.7	116.9	116.9	100.0
	1998	175.3	175.3	147.6	118.8	118.8	100.0
	1999	169.6	169.6	139.6	121.5	121.5	100.0
	2000	176.6	176.6	140.0	126.1	126.1	100.0
	2001	183.0	183.0	146.3	125.1	125.1	100.0
	2002	185.7	185.7	147.9	125.6	125.6	100.0
	2003	189.1	189.1	150.1	125.9	125.9	100.0
Papua New Guinea..............................	1970	22.0	23.5	44.3	49.6	53.0	93.5
	1975	37.8	47.2	50.7	74.5	93.1	80.0
	1980	60.4	85.9	87.8	68.8	97.9	70.3
	1985	78.1	74.6	93.6	83.4	79.7	104.7
	1990	100.0	100.0	100.0	100.0	100.0	100.0
	1991	117.2	117.6	109.5	107.0	107.4	99.7
	1992	134.6	133.2	124.7	107.9	106.8	101.0
	1993	155.1	151.4	147.4	105.2	102.7	102.4
	1994	171.5	161.9	156.2	109.8	103.7	105.9
	1995	187.6	140.0	151.0	124.3	92.7	134.0
	1996	219.3	158.8	162.7	134.8	97.6	138.1
	1997	225.1	149.5	156.3	144.0	95.6	150.6
	1998	250.6	115.4	163.2	153.6	70.7	217.1
	1999	279.8	104.0	161.8	173.0	64.3	269.2
	2000	303.2	104.1	159.8	189.8	65.1	291.3
	2001	313.0	88.2	154.4	202.7	57.1	354.8
	2002	349.4	85.7	153.6	227.5	55.8	407.9
	2003	374.2	100.3	157.9	237.0	63.5	373.1
Samoa..	1970	9.1	29.3	79.2	11.5	37.0	31.2
	1975	18.4	67.1	92.1	20.0	72.8	27.4
	1980	30.6	76.9	107.3	28.5	71.6	39.8
	1985	58.4	60.1	105.1	55.6	57.2	97.2
	1990	100.0	100.0	100.0	100.0	100.0	100.0
	1991	103.3	99.4	97.6	105.8	101.9	103.9
	1992	87.6	82.1	95.3	91.9	86.1	106.8
	1993	92.5	83.2	97.6	94.7	85.2	111.2
	1994	107.5	97.9	94.2	114.1	104.0	109.7
	1995	106.7	99.6	100.4	106.3	99.2	107.1
	1996	119.6	112.2	107.7	111.0	104.2	106.6
	1997	134.6	121.4	108.5	124.0	111.9	110.8
	1998	141.8	111.1	111.1	127.6	100.0	127.6
	1999	150.4	115.3	114.0	131.9	101.1	130.4
	2000	166.7	117.2	121.9	136.8	96.1	142.3
	2001	182.9	121.4	129.4	141.3	93.8	150.6
	2002	191.6	131.1	131.8	145.4	99.5	146.2
	2003	205.9	159.9	135.9	151.5	117.7	128.7
Solomon Islands....................................	1970	5.4	15.4	40.2	13.5	38.2	35.3
	1975	9.4	31.1	47.8	19.7	65.1	30.2
	1980	22.6	69.0	75.9	29.8	90.9	32.8
	1985	45.0	76.9	81.9	54.9	93.8	58.6
	1990	100.0	100.0	100.0	100.0	100.0	100.0
	1991	113.7	105.9	106.0	107.2	99.9	107.4
	1992	145.0	125.2	119.5	121.4	104.8	115.8
	1993	171.2	135.8	124.2	137.9	109.4	126.1
	1994	199.9	153.6	135.6	147.4	113.3	130.2
	1995	236.0	175.2	144.7	163.0	121.1	134.7
	1996	273.2	193.7	149.8	182.4	129.3	141.0
	1997	288.5	196.3	146.4	197.1	134.1	147.0
	1998	327.9	172.2	148.0	221.6	116.4	190.4
	1999	349.5	182.7	146.0	239.3	125.1	191.3
	2000	327.0	162.5	125.6	260.4	129.4	201.2

Table 7. Implicit Price Deflators of Gross Domestic Product in US Dollars and in National Currency

(Index numbers 1990 = 100)

Region, country or area and currency unit	Year	GDP in Current Prices		GDP at Constant Prices	GDP Implicit Price Deflators		Exchange Rates
		National Currency (1)	US Dollars (2)	(3)	National Currency (4)	US Dollars (5)	(6)
	2001	335.5	160.7	119.3	281.2	134.7	208.7
	2002	351.1	131.5	114.5	306.5	114.8	266.9
	2003	386.7	130.3	116.8	331.0	111.5	296.8
Tonga	1970	7.1	10.2	49.5	14.3	20.6	69.8
	1975	16.9	28.3	57.4	29.4	49.3	59.7
	1980	31.8	46.3	65.7	48.4	70.5	68.6
	1985	58.4	52.3	98.5	59.3	53.0	111.8
	1990	100.0	100.0	100.0	100.0	100.0	100.0
	1991	116.5	115.0	106.4	109.5	108.1	101.3
	1992	125.5	119.2	106.7	117.6	111.8	105.2
	1993	130.2	120.5	110.7	117.7	108.8	108.1
	1994	133.3	129.2	116.2	114.7	111.2	103.1
	1995	134.6	135.6	119.6	112.6	113.4	99.3
	1996	142.1	147.6	119.0	119.4	124.0	96.3
	1997	141.4	143.3	119.6	118.3	119.8	98.7
	1998	148.9	127.7	122.4	121.6	104.3	116.6
	1999	161.8	129.5	125.8	128.6	102.9	124.9
	2000	171.3	124.7	133.8	128.0	93.2	137.4
	2001	186.3	112.3	136.1	136.9	82.5	165.9
	2002	201.6	117.5	138.3	145.8	85.0	171.5
	2003	230.1	146.6	141.2	163.0	103.9	157.0
Tuvalu	1970	7.9	11.3	56.8	13.8	19.9	69.7
	1975	13.6	22.8	90.7	15.0	25.1	59.6
	1980	32.7	47.6	93.4	35.0	51.0	68.6
	1985	41.2	36.9	73.2	56.3	50.4	111.8
	1990	100.0	100.0	100.0	100.0	100.0	100.0
	1991	106.6	106.4	103.6	102.9	102.7	100.2
	1992	119.3	112.3	106.5	112.1	105.4	106.3
	1993	115.3	100.4	110.9	104.0	90.6	114.8
	1994	127.9	119.8	122.3	104.6	98.0	106.8
	1995	129.9	123.3	116.1	111.8	106.2	105.3
	1996	139.1	139.5	128.1	108.6	108.9	99.8
	1997	152.8	145.3	132.5	115.3	109.6	105.2
	1998	180.4	145.2	152.3	118.4	95.3	124.3
	1999	187.7	155.1	156.9	119.6	98.9	121.0
	2000	203.0	150.8	161.6	125.6	93.3	134.6
	2001	225.3	149.3	166.5	135.4	89.7	150.9
	2002	290.9	202.5	151.1	192.5	134.0	143.7
	2003	305.6	253.9	154.1	198.3	164.7	120.4
Vanuatu	1970	19.6	22.7	35.7	54.9	63.6	86.3
	1975	28.4	48.0	56.6	50.2	84.9	59.2
	1980	43.3	74.2	61.7	70.1	120.1	58.3
	1985	70.0	77.3	93.3	75.1	82.9	90.6
	1990	100.0	100.0	100.0	100.0	100.0	100.0
	1991	113.6	119.1	112.1	101.3	106.2	95.4
	1992	120.3	124.2	111.3	108.1	111.6	96.9
	1993	132.8	127.9	116.3	114.2	110.0	103.9
	1994	139.4	140.2	119.3	116.9	117.6	99.4
	1995	152.3	159.0	124.9	121.9	127.3	95.8
	1996	157.7	165.2	128.1	123.1	129.0	95.4
	1997	164.7	166.4	131.1	125.6	126.9	99.0
	1998	165.1	151.5	133.9	123.3	113.2	108.9
	1999	164.9	149.6	129.6	127.2	115.4	110.3
	2000	170.0	144.5	133.1	127.7	108.6	117.6
	2001	174.0	140.2	130.7	133.1	107.3	124.1
	2002	157.1	132.1	123.9	126.8	106.6	118.9
	2003	165.0	158.1	125.1	131.9	126.3	104.4